PHILOSOPHY OF LAW

A Five-Volume Anthology of Scholarly Articles

Series Editor
JULES L. COLEMAN
Yale Law School

A GARLAND SERIES

SERIES CONTENTS

VOLUME

1

JURISPRUDENCE

Edited with introductions by

JULES L. COLEMAN

and ANTHONY SEBOK

GARLAND PUBLISHING, INC.
New York & London
1994

Library of Congress Cataloging-in-Publication Data

Jurisprudence / edited with introductions by Jules L. Coleman
and Anthony Sebok.
p. cm. — (Philosophy of law ; v. 1)
ISBN 0–8153–1397–7 (alk. paper)
1. Jurisprudence. 2. Law—Philosophy. 3. Law—United States.
I. Coleman, Jules L. II. Sebok, Anthony James, 1963–
III. Series.
K235.J84 1994
340'.1—dc20 93–32672
CIP

Printed on acid-free, 250-year-life paper
Manufactured in the United States of America

CONTENTS

Series Introduction

When Robert Nozick asked me to edit five volumes of essays in legal philosophy, I had little idea what I was getting myself into. I was excited by the prospect, but that was before I began thinking concretely about what to include. Knowing that the task was highly challenging, I sought the advice of many colleagues, friends and peers. My first concern was to settle on a way of dividing the subject matter of legal philosophy into five books of roughly fifteen essays each. Some advised a chronological ordering: others favored groupings by authors. The great majority suggested groupings by subject matter. Among those, however, there was a vast difference of opinion regarding which subjects to include. I settled on grouping by subject matter, and eventually chose to devote one volume each to the following topics: Jurisprudence, Rights, Constitutional Law and Its Interpretation, Private Law Theory, and Criminal Law Theory. Any number of other divisions would have been equally plausible, some arguably better.

However, the task of dividing the subject matter of legal philosophy was easy compared with trying to settle on what should be included in each volume. Again I sought advice from others and was impressed by my respondents' knowledge of the field and by their frequent willingness to recommend their own work. It was then that I realized that this daunting project might make me more enemies than friends, and that, with the exception of some obvious classics, the majority of the essays I chose would be controversial selections, likely to puzzle some, and disappoint or even anger others.

I needed a working-decision procedure. First, I determined not to include too many essays by any single author. That decision led to obvious omissions in each volume. The *Jurisprudence* volume, for example, could have been made up almost entirely of essays by H.L.A. Hart. Second, I favored some diversity of approach and representativeness of schools of thought. As a result, some of the essays are included not because they are among the very best essays in absolute terms, but because they are among the best representations of a particular theory or point of view. Third, though each volume strives for diversity and representation — even including several essays by lawyer-economists in the Private Law and Rights volumes — I have not included essays representing what I regard as philosophical fads. Thus there are no essays by so-called Postmodernists, and although both Feminism and Critical Race Theory are important, I believe that there are as yet few philosophically substantial essays representative of either "tradition." These volumes are a collection of the important contributions to several areas of legal theory. They do not represent my view of the seventy-five or so best essays in legal philosophy.

Putting these volumes together has been extremely educational for me. In addition to numerous colleagues and friends, I am especially grateful to three of my former students who have worked diligently on this project; Sherry Ingram, Stephen Hetcher and especially Tony Sebok. Tony also co-edited the volumes on Constitutional Law and Its Interpretation and Jurisprudence, whose introductory essays he authored.

Introduction

To most lawyers, the expression "jurisprudence" refers to the body of rules and theories that make up a certain field of law. Thus we all know what is meant when "First Amendment jurisprudence" or the "jurisprudence of contract law" is mentioned. This refers to all the accepted decisions and commentaries that would help a judge or a lawyer decide a First Amendment case or a contract dispute. When philosophers or legal theorists speak of jurisprudence, however, they do not usually use the word in this professional, lawyerly way. Rather than describing the doctrinal debate within a certain field of law, they are referring to abstract debates over the meaning of "law" itself. To the philosopher, the central questions of jurisprudence are "What is law?" and "Is there a unique form of legal reasoning?" The philosopher of law believes that correct answers to these questions are important from both a philosophical and practical perspective; and that such answers may assist lawyers with the doctrinal questions that are more often the traditional focus of lawsuits and legal articles.

The practical importance of jurisprudence is evident in the kinds of dispute that erupt around the law. Bear in mind, for example, that there are those who believe in the existence of international law; if they are to make their case, they will at some point have to address the issue of whether laws can exist that are not enforced by a sovereign. Or consider the task facing a common law court, which must constantly issue new interpretations of settled legal principles: At some point, the court must come to terms with the objection that no one should be held legally liable for violating a rule that did not exist when the accused act was performed. Finally, consider the dilemma of the conscientious citizen who is convinced that the courts and the police are applying the law immorally: To what extent should one's moral commitments inform one's interpretation of the law? In each of these situations, the answers to these central questions of jurisprudence will affect the practical outcomes chosen.

The essays selected for this collection represent the leading mainstream approaches to jurisprudence and it is not by accident that the collection begins in the nineteenth century. The history of jurisprudence has been a dialogue across the ages, with each generation of scholars responding to both the theories that dominated their education and to the political and legal concerns of their day. In each emerging period, scholars return over and over again to their immediate predecessors' solutions to the problems of defining law and legal reasoning. Careful analysis of these essays will reveal that often a theorist's definition of law suggests his or her characterization of legal reasoning, and vice versa. This introduction will briefly review the general patterns into which various definitions of law and legal reasoning have fallen.

The collection begins with the nineteenth-century Englishman John Austin, who was concerned primarily with the definition of law. For Austin, a law was a command issued by a sovereign that was backed by a sanction. Neither the specific content of the command nor the nature of the sovereign was of much importance to him: he did not require any type of moral evaluation in order to determine whether a given command was a law or not. What was important about Austin's method was that it broke the law down into a set of analytic parts, each of which could be identified without reference to nonlegal criteria such as morality or history. In addition, since Austin's theory could include so many different types of legal systems, it did not suggest a very demanding theory of legal reasoning: as long as the sovereign could be identified, the kind of reasoning the sovereign required of the legal system was up to the sovereign. Austin's theory is regarded as an important and early form of "legal positivism"; the expression is based on the idea that laws are "posited" by an authority.

Austin's ideas were adopted in America in a slightly modified form. English positivism was adopted in the United States by a group of scholars who were as interested in the autonomous nature of Austin's analytical method as his command theory of law. Scholars such as Christopher Columbus Langdell and Joseph Beale developed an approach to legal reasoning (now known as American formalism) which defined law as an autonomous discipline characterized by careful, deductive reasoning from analytically true legal premises.[1] The formalists were not self-consciously trying to frame a new jurisprudence and they did not leave behind any careful theoretical defenses of their approach to legal reasoning.[2] Nonetheless, formalism provoked a reaction among American scholars that generated a lasting jurisprudential tradition.

Oliver Wendell Holmes, a contemporary of Langdell and Beale at Harvard Law School, issued many broadsides against formalism in the years prior to his ascent to the Supreme Court of Massachusetts and the United States Supreme Court. Holmes rejected the formalist idea that legal reasoning obliged the lawyer to view the law as free of contingent human concerns. Law is an instrument for social control, said Holmes, and if one wants to understand the reach of the law, one must analyze it from the point of view of the "bad man," who wants to know only about what he can get away with. In his attack on formalism, Holmes was in some ways returning to formalism's purely positivist roots; like Austin, Holmes emphasized that there was no necessary relationship between law and morality.[3]

Holmes' attack on formalism was furthered by two subsequent branches of theory, sociological jurisprudence and its more famous sibling, legal realism. Both developed Holmes' idea that the path of legal change and growth could not be fully explained by rational deduction from legal premise to legal conclusion. Roscoe Pound's sociological jurisprudence emphasized the emerging role of law to address social needs. Like Holmes, Pound recognized that many issues that had been once left to the private sector were being raised either in court or in the legislature, and he felt that legal theory should explicitly embrace this development and prepare lawyers to act like social engineers. Thus Pound embraced an expanded notion of the definition of law, while further promoting Holmes' idea that legal reasoning had to involve considerations of social welfare.

The legal realists are a difficult group to summarize, since they dominated American jurisprudence for so long and were so diverse.[4] The essay by Felix Cohen sets out the mainstream realist position; its title, "Transcendental Nonsense and the Functional Approach," indicates the general direction of the realist argument. Cohen attacked what he perceived to be the continuing influence of formalism's conception of law and legal reasoning among American lawyers. Like Pound, Cohen rejected the "mechanical jurisprudence" of formalism's deductive methodology. Unlike Pound, however, who viewed law as an autonomous discipline that could be used to further social ends, Cohen challenged the traditional conception (first encountered in Austin) that through the proper definition of law one could distinguish "legal" commands from crude political power.[5] Different realists had different explanations for why law was not an autonomous social institution. Some, like Jerome Frank, based their explanation on a more general diagnosis of the failure of modern society to establish and maintain any rational structures of government.[6] Karl Llewellyn, whom we have also chosen to make the realist's case, based his explanation on a rejection of the idea of the rule of law. Llewellyn was a rule-skeptic: he doubted that any authority, whether a legislature or a court, could promulgate a rule that could usefully constrain the choices of the rule-applier. Llewellyn's jurisprudence tried to salvage a role for judges out of the wreck of the rule of law; he hoped to encourage courts to recognize their unavoidable freedom of action, and to take their role as policymakers as seriously as legislators took theirs.

It is commonly assumed that realism was rapidly transformed from a rebellion among a younger generation of scholars into the reigning orthodoxy in American jurisprudence.[7] Nonetheless, it is worth noting that realism generated its own set of critics. The ease with which fascism rose in Europe and the collapse (and collaboration) of independent judiciaries in Germany and Italy made post-war scholars wonder to what extent the argument that law was not an autonomous discipline weakened a free society's resistance to usurpation by arguably illegal yet politically powerful forces.[8] A number of scholars turned away from realism and attempted to explain how the autonomy of law could be proved and what the definition of law would be if such a proof were forthcoming.

Hans Kelsen, a refugee from Hitler's Germany, offered a solution that, in retrospect, seems quite inconsistent with the general direction of American jurisprudence. In fact, Kelsen's highly abstract and formal arguments graphically illustrate how little the concerns of realism had touched continental theorists in the early and middle parts of the twentieth century. Kelsen called his theory the "pure theory" of law because it aimed to be pure or uncontaminated by elements of politics or morality, and as such he was trying to distinguish himself from two jurisprudential traditions. First, he was rejecting natural law theory, which urged a merger between law and morality so that law was defined as a subset of morality. Second, he was rejecting the realist claim that legal reasoning was nothing more than a set of measurable psychological or sociological processes. Kelsen argued that legal authority was unique in that it employed normative concepts, the ultimate authority of which (what he called the "basic norm") was itself not a matter of either moral or social fact. It is important to note that Kelsen was reviving—with rigor and precision—some of the elements of both Austin and the formalists. We will see that, despite its flaws, Kelsen's project had an important effect on the modern revival of positivism.

If Kelsen's language and methods seemed unusual and foreign, Lon Fuller confronted realism in a typically American voice. Fuller's response to the collapse of the autonomy of law in the mid-century was to argue that there was a minimum set of features that every legal system shared. He called this minimum content "the morality of law," and included within it such features as the requirement of publicity (i.e., no secret laws) and the prohibition of ex post facto laws. Fuller argued that were a lawmaker or a judge to violate the morality of law, one could determine at what point society's commands ceased being legal and began to be nothing but the product of political power. Like Pound, Fuller was concerned that the realists' rejection of the rule of law and the autonomy of law minimized law's potential as an instrument for social progress in a free society. Unlike Pound, however, Fuller believed that the introduction of a small dose of natural law theory was necessary to rebut the realist critique.

The final theorist who responded to the realist challenge was H.L.A. Hart. Hart was acutely aware that some (such as Fuller) had argued that Austin's command theory of law was consistent with the legal systems that arose under fascism. Hart, who taught jurisprudence at Oxford, set out to redefine English positivism to meet these criticisms. Following Kelsen, Hart continued to insist on the separation of law and morality but, unlike Kelsen, he tried to use sociology to improve positivism. Hart thought it was important to distinguish between society's primary legal rules, which existed regardless of their moral or political content, and society's secondary rules, which determined who the sovereign was and how the sovereign determined the content of the primary rules. The secondary rules—of which the most important is the "rule of recognition"—cannot be identified without assuming the point of view of those who consider themselves part of the legal system. Hart insisted, therefore, that the analysis of the rule of recognition involve an inquiry into what citizens believed to be justified authority in their society. Thus Hart's positivism avoided the crude reductionism of Austin's command theory without collapsing into Kelsen's unverifiable and possibly empty basic norm.

The advent of Kelsen, Fuller and Hart meant that American jurisprudence would have to reconsider the realist claim that there was no useful answer to the question, "What is law?" The definition each theorist provided, however, seemed to leave open the question of the character of legal reasoning. Although each set out the minimum conditions for a legal system, none could give a defense of various controversial judicial choices—something which, for all their flaws, the realists could. In the midst of the Warren Court's embattled tenure, Ronald Dworkin developed a theory of law that was designed to provide both a robust definition of law and a defense of the kind of legal reasoning used by activist judges during the civil rights era.

Dworkin's starting point was Hart's positivism. Dworkin argued that Hart's definition of law—as a set of primary rules identified by a secondary rule—misrepresented legal reasoning in that it suggested that in applying the law, a judge either mechanically applied an existing rule or, if there was no rule in existence, exercised "strong" discretion by creating a new rule. Dworkin believed that any theory which maintained that a judge created new legal rights in difficult cases misdescribed what people believed about the minimum content of a legal system. Dworkin, building on Fuller, believed that a legal system not only conformed to the morality of law, but also contained within itself the "right" answers to any legal dispute that arose under it. Positivism had to resort to a theory of strong discretion because its definition of law was too cramped; instead of just the "model of rules," argued Dworkin, the law was also filled with principles. Principles cannot be applied in an all-or-nothing fashion, and they come into existence through interpretation, not promulgation; yet according to Dworkin they are as binding upon judges as a tax code. Thus, said Dworkin, when a judge cannot find an existing rule to settle a dispute over a lawsuit, he does not have license to exercise discretion and create a legal right; the judge must instead turn to the panoply of principles embedded in the law to discover the right answer. Dworkin's theory seemed especially appropriate when applied to American constitutional law, where the text is silent on many issues (such as reapportionment or birth control) but where, arguably, various principles have been developed over the years (such as one man, one vote or privacy).

Dworkin's influence has been immense. His theory, which has continued to evolve over time, has clearly refocused attention on the problem of adjudication. It is an open question whether, despite his protests to the contrary, he has not simply adopted and improved Fuller's natural law theory.[9] Nor have legal positivists let Dworkin's criticisms go unanswered. Joseph Raz, a student of Hart's and a colleague of Dworkin's, has developed the next generation of positivism in response to Dworkin's criticisms. Raz argues that Dworkin misrepresents the positivist's definition of law by characterizing it as simply the "model of rules." Raz notes that nothing in Hart's theory prevents the rule of recognition from identifying principles as well as rules as part of the legal system. Positivists, says Raz, do not deny that sometimes a judge must use the sort of legal reasoning Dworkin describes; what the positivist rejects is that reasoning from principle is a *necessary* element of the definition of law. Thus, according to the positivist, the Warren Court's use of moral principle was proper because it did so under the authority of the American legal system's rule of recognition, and not because reasoning from moral principle is an intrinsic part of legal reasoning.

While many scholars have been concerned with developing one or the other side of the debate between Dworkin and the positivists, the most important recent development in jurisprudence is the radical rejection of the postwar focus on the definition of law and legal reasoning. To many younger scholars, the debate over the best justification of the Warren Court's adjudicatory process seems sterile, since it is not obvious to them that a defense of the liberal-centrist status quo is worth the effort. Two different movements have emerged with independent yet largely consistent critiques of mainstream jurisprudence: critical legal studies (CLS) and feminism.

Like realism, CLS begins with the assumption that law is a product of the power relations in society. But as Duncan Kennedy's essay reveals, CLS is not as optimistic as realism that existing legal institutions can be used to achieve desirable social ends. Unlike the realists, many of whom served in the highest levels of the government, most CLS scholars are suspicious of the conventional structures of power in today's society.[10] As Kennedy points out, because of resistance from powerful economic and political forces, modern liberal society cannot easily do away with the myth of law as an autonomous institution, and the radical lawyer or judge who tries self-consciously to work within the existing power structure will probably be co-opted. Given its rather pessimistic view of the power of the status quo to perpetuate itself, CLS has served much more effectively as an analysis of how law succeeds in protecting dominant social interests than as a theory of how law can be used to promote social ends.

Feminist legal scholars share CLS's view that law reflects existing power structures in society; however, they see the salient power dynamic through the lens of gender. It must be conceded that some feminists focus on the extent to which legal institutions have been used instrumentally to achieve power over women in society, and these critiques are consistent in form, if not their focus, with realism or positivism. On the other hand, a more interesting feminist critique, which Catherine MacKinnon has effectively articulated, raises the question of whether the definition of law as society now knows it is inherently "gendered". The issue MacKinnon raises goes beyond whether courts should use a "reasonable woman" standard in some cases instead of the "reasonable man" standard. She asks us to consider whether certain fundamental features of modern liberal legal systems (such as the idea of a right, or the concept of liberty) are really contingent features that have survived because they support men's position in society. It is clear that MacKinnon believes that law would look very different were these vestiges of male domination removed from our legal culture, and that the resulting concept of law would not have much in common with the concerns of Dworkin or the positivists.

The essays in this volume reveal a consistent set of concerns and a wide range of responses to those concerns. For those theorists attracted to positivism, the problem of the analysis of law as a social practice is the only sensible place to begin. Theorists attracted to natural law or formalism choose instead to define the character of legal reasoning. Theorists who are skeptical about law as an autonomous institution, or who perceive law to be in service of other social forces, begin by rejecting the usefulness of either of the foregoing positions. The history of critique, response, and countercritique illustrated by these essays describes a phenomenon as profound as the claims of any one of the theorists themselves. It is a process that will continue to evolve, determined as much by the past upon which it builds as the new problems it confronts.

Anthony Sebok

Notes

[1] *See* C. C. Langdell, "Address to Harvard Law School Association, 1886," in A. Sutherland, *The Law at Harvard* (1967) and J. Beale, *Treatise on the Conflict of Laws* 112 (1916); *see also* T. Grey, "Langdell's Orthodoxy," 45 Univ. Pitt. L. Rev. 1 (1983).

[2] In selecting Kennedy's essay, we have tried to provide a theorist who discusses, albeit from a critical perspective, an important aspect of the formalist argument.

[3] By the mid-twentieth century Holmes was considered a prominent American legal positivist. *See*, e.g., L. Fuller, *The Law in Quest of Itself* 47 (1940).

[4] For a detailed account of American legal realism, *see* L. Kalman, *Legal Realism at Yale, 1920-1970* (1986).

[5] Pound was acutely aware of where he and the realists parted company. His anxiety over realism was given full expression in a sharp attack he wrote in 1931. *See* Pound, "The Call for a Realistic Jurisprudence," 44 *Harv. L. Rev.* 697 (1931); but *see* Llewellyn, "Some Realism about Realism: A Response to Dean Pound," 44 *Harv. L. Rev.* 1222 (1931).

[6] *See*, e.g., J. Frank, *Law and the Modern Mind* (6th ed., 1948).

[7] An interesting illustration of the tendency to turn realism into America's native jurisprudence is the assumption by many that Wesley Hohfeld, whose essay on legal concepts is reproduced in this volume, was a realist. But as the reader will see, Hohfeld's visionary essay—which was written before realism gained prominence—is no less compatible with positivism's attempt to categorize legal rights and duties under a sovereign as with Cohen's "functional approach."

[8] *See*, e.g., Purcell, "American Jurisprudence Between the Wars: Legal Realism and the Crisis of Democratic Theory," 75 *Am. Hist. Rev.* 424 (1971).

[9] *See*, e.g., Dworkin, "'Natural' Law Revisited," 34 *U. Fla. L. Rev.*, 165 (1982).

[10] *See*, e.g., Tushnet, "Critical Legal Studies: An Introduction to Its Origins and Underpinnings," 36 *J. Legal Educ.* 505 (1986).

THE PROVINCE OF JURISPRUDENCE DETERMINED

LECTURE I

The *purpose* of the following attempt to determine the province of

THE matter of jurisprudence is positive law: law, simply and strictly so called: or law set by political superiors to political inferiors. But positive law (or law, simply and strictly so called) is often confounded with objects to which it is related by *resemblance*, and with

jurisprudence, stated or suggested.

objects to which it is related in the way of *analogy*: with objects which are *also* signified, *properly* and *improperly*, by the large and vague expression *law*. To obviate the difficulties springing from that confusion, I begin my projected Course with determining the province of jurisprudence, or with distinguishing the matter of jurisprudence from those various related objects: trying to define the subject of which I intend to treat, before I endeavour to analyse its numerous and complicated parts.

Law: what, in most comprehensive literal sense.

A law, in the most general and comprehensive acceptation in which the term, in its literal meaning, is employed, may be said to be a rule laid down for the guidance of an intelligent being by an intelligent being having power over him. Under this definition are concluded, and without impropriety, several species. It is necessary to define accurately the line of demarcation which separates these species from one another, as much mistiness and intricacy has been infused into the science of jurisprudence by their being confounded or not clearly distinguished. In the comprehensive sense above indicated, or in the largest meaning which it has, without extension by metaphor or analogy, the term *law* embraces the following objects:—Laws set by God to his human creatures, and laws set by men to men.

Law of God.

The whole or a portion of the laws set by God to men is frequently styled the law of nature, or natural law: being, in truth, the only natural law of which it is possible to speak without a metaphor, or without a blending of objects which ought to be distinguished broadly. But, rejecting the appellation Law of Nature as ambiguous and misleading, I name those laws or rules, as considered collectively or in a mass, the *Divine law*, or the *law of God*.

Human laws. Two classes.

Laws set by men to men are of two leading or principal classes: classes which are often blended, although they differ extremely; and which, for that reason, should be severed precisely, and opposed distinctly and conspicuously.

Of the laws or rules set by men to men, some are established by *political* superiors, sovereign and subject: by persons exercising supreme and subordinate *government*, in independent nations, or independent political societies. The aggregate of the rules thus established, or some aggregate forming a portion of that aggregate, is the appropriate matter of jurisprudence, general or particular. To the aggregate of the rules thus established, or to some aggregate forming a portion of that aggregate, the term *law*, as used simply and strictly, is exclusively applied. But, as contradistinguished to *natural* law, or to the law of *nature* (meaning, by those expressions, the law of God), the aggregate of the rules, established by political superiors, is frequently styled *positive* law, or law existing *by position*. As contradistinguished to the rules which I style *positive morality*, and on which I shall touch immediately, the aggregate of the rules, established by political superiors, may also be marked commodiously with the name of *positive law*. For the sake, then, of getting a name brief and distinctive at once, and agreeably to frequent usage, I style that aggregate of rules, or any portion of that aggregate, *positive law*: though rules, which are *not* established by political superiors, are also *positive*, or exist *by position*, if they be rules or laws, in the proper signification of the term.

1st class. Laws set by *political superiors.*

Though *some* of the laws or rules, which are set by men to men, are established by political superiors, *others* are *not* established by political superiors, or are *not* established by political superiors, in that capacity or character.

2nd class. Laws set by men not political superiors.

Closely analogous to human laws of this second class, are a set of objects frequently but *improperly* termed

Objects *improperly* but by *close*

analogy termed *laws.*

laws, being rules set and enforced by *mere opinion*, that is, by the opinions or sentiments held or felt by an indeterminate body of men in regard to human conduct. Instances of such a use of the term *law* are the expressions—'The law of honour;' 'The law set by fashion;' and rules of this species constitute much of what is usually termed 'International law.'

The two last placed in one class under the name *positive morality.*

The aggregate of human laws properly so called belonging to the second of the classes above mentioned, with the aggregate of objects *improperly* but by *close analogy* termed laws, I place together in a common class, and denote them by the term *positive morality.* The name *morality* severs them from *positive law*, while the epithet *positive* disjoins them from the *law of God.* And to the end of obviating confusion, it is necessary or expedient that they *should* be disjoined from the latter by that distinguishing epithet. For the name *morality* (or *morals*), when standing unqualified or alone, denotes indifferently either of the following objects: namely, positive morality *as it is*, or without regard to its merits; and positive morality *as it would be*, if it conformed to the law of God, and were, therefore, deserving of *approbation.*

Objects metaphorically termed laws.

Besides the various sorts of rules which are included in the literal acceptation of the term law, and those which are by a close and striking analogy, though improperly, termed laws, there are numerous applications of the term law, which rest upon a slender analogy and are merely metaphorical or figurative. Such is the case when we talk of *laws* observed by the lower animals; of *laws* regulating the growth or decay of vegetables; of *laws* determining the movements of inanimate bodies or masses. For where *intelligence* is not, or where it is too bounded to take the name of *reason*, and, therefore, is too bounded to conceive the purpose of a law, there is not the *will* which law can work on, or which duty can incite or restrain. Yet through these misapplications of a *name*, flagrant as the metaphor is, has the field of jurisprudence and morals been deluged with muddy speculation.

Having suggested the *purpose* of my attempt to determine the province of jurisprudence: to distinguish positive law, the appropriate matter of jurisprudence, from the various objects to which it is related by resemblance, and to which it is related, nearly or remotely, by a strong or slender analogy: I shall now state the essentials of *a law* or *rule* (taken with the largest signification which can be given to the term *properly*).

Laws or rules *properly* so called, are a species of commands.

Every *law* or *rule* (taken with the largest signification which can be given to the term *properly*) is a *command*. Or, rather, laws or rules, properly so called, are a *species* of commands.

Now, since the term *command* comprises the term *law*, the first is the simpler as well as the larger of the two. But, simple as it is, it admits of explanation. And, since it is the *key* to the sciences of jurisprudence and morals, its meaning should be analysed with precision.

Accordingly, I shall endeavour, in the first instance, to analyse the meaning of '*command*:' an analysis which I fear, will task the patience of my hearers, but which they will bear with cheerfulness, or, at least, with resignation, if they consider the difficulty of performing it. The elements of a science are precisely the parts of it which are explained least easily. Terms that are the largest, and, therefore, the simplest of a series, are without equivalent expressions into which we can resolve them *concisely*. And when we endeavour to *define* them, or to translate them into terms which we suppose are better understood, we are forced upon awkward and tedious circumlocutions.

The meaning of the

If you express or intimate a wish that I shall do or forbear from some act, and if you will visit me with an term *command.* evil in case I comply not with your wish, the *expression* or *intimation* of your wish is a *command.* A command is distinguished from other significations of desire, not by the style in which the desire is signified, but by the power and the purpose of the party commanding to inflict an evil or pain in case the desire be disregarded. If you cannot or will not harm me in case I comply not with your wish, the expression of your wish is not a command, although you utter your wish in imperative phrase. If you are able and willing to harm me in case I comply not with your wish, the expression of your wish amounts to a command, although you are prompted by a spirit of courtesy to utter it in the shape of a request. '*Preces* erant, sed *quibus contradici non posset.*' Such is the language of Tacitus, when speaking of a petition by the soldiery to a son and lieutenant of Vespasian.

A command, then, is a signification of desire. But a command is distinguished from other significations of desire by this peculiarity: that the party to whom it is directed is liable to evil from the other, in case he comply not with the desire.

The meaning of the term *duty.*

Being liable to evil from you if I comply not with a wish which you signify, I am *bound* or *obliged* by your command, or I lie under a *duty* to obey it. If, in spite of that evil in prospect, I comply not with the wish which you signify, I am said to disobey your command, or to violate the duty which it imposes.

The terms *command* and *duty* are correlative.

Command and duty are, therefore, correlative terms: the meaning denoted by each being implied or supposed by the other. Or (changing the expression) wherever a duty lies, a command has been signified; and whenever a command is signified, a duty is imposed.

Concisely expressed, the meaning of the correlative expressions is this. He who will inflict an evil in case his desire be disregarded, utters a command by expressing or intimating his desire: He who is liable to the evil in case he disregard the desire, is bound or obliged by the command.

The meaning of the term *sanction.*

The evil which will probably be incurred in case a command be disobeyed or (to use an equivalent expression) in case a duty be broken, is frequently called a *sanction*, or an *enforcement of obedience.* Or (varying the phrase) the command or the duty is said to be *sanctioned* or *enforced* by the chance of incurring the evil.

Considered as thus abstracted from the command and the duty which it enforces, the evil to be incurred by disobedience is frequently styled a *punishment.* But, as punishments, strictly so called, are only a *class* of sanctions, the term is too narrow to express the meaning adequately.

To the existence of a command, a duty, and a sanction, a *violent*, motive to compliance is not requisite.

I observe that Dr. Paley, in his analysis of the term *obligation*, lays much stress upon the *violence* of the motive to compliance. In so far as I can gather a meaning from his loose and inconsistent statement, his meaning appears to be this: that unless the motive to compliance be *violent* or *intense*, the expression or intimation of a wish is not a *command*, nor does the party to whom it is directed lie under a *duty* to regard it.

If he means, by a *violent* motive, a motive operating with certainty, his proposition is manifestly false. The greater the evil to be incurred in case the wish be disregarded, and the greater the chance of incurring it on that same event, the greater, no doubt, is the *chance* that the wish will *not* be disregarded. But no conceivable motive will *certainly* determine to compliance, or no conceivable motive will render obedience inevitable. If Paley's proposition be true, in the sense which I have now ascribed to it, commands and duties are simply impossible. Or, reducing his proposition to absurdity by a consequence as manifestly false, commands and duties are possible, but are never disobeyed or broken.

If he means by a *violent* motive, an evil which inspires fear, his meaning is simply this: that the party bound by a command is bound by the prospect of an evil. For that which is not feared is not apprehended as an evil: or (changing the shape of the expression) is not an evil in prospect.

The truth is, that the magnitude of the eventual evil, and the magnitude of the chance of incurring it, are foreign to the matter in question. The greater the eventual evil, and the greater the chance of incurring it, the greater is the efficacy of the command, and the greater is the strength of the obligation: Or (substituting expressions exactly equivalent), the greater is the *chance* that the command will be obeyed, and that the duty will not be broken. But where there is the smallest chance of incurring the smallest evil, the expression of a wish amounts to a command, and, therefore, imposes a duty. The sanction, if you will, is feeble or insufficient; but still there *is* a sanction, and, therefore, a duty and a command.

Rewards are not *sanctions.*

By some celebrated writers (by Locke, Bentham, and, I think, Paley), the term *sanction*, or *enforcement of obedience*, is applied to conditional good as well as to conditional evil: to reward as well as to punishment. But, with all my habitual veneration for the names of Locke and Bentham, I think that this extension of the term is pregnant with confusion and perplexity.

Rewards are, indisputably, *motives* to comply with the wishes of others. But to talk of commands and duties as *sanctioned* or *enforced* by rewards, or to talk of rewards as *obliging* or *constraining* to obedience, is surely a wide departure from the established meaning of the terms.

If *you* expressed a desire that *I* should render a service, and if you proffered a reward as the motive or inducement to render it, *you* would scarcely be said to *command* the service, nor should *I*, in ordinary language, be *obliged* to render it. In ordinary language, *you* would *promise* me a reward, on condition of my rendering the service, whilst *I* might be *incited* or *persuaded* to render it by the hope of obtaining the reward.

Again: If a law hold out a *reward* as an inducement to do some act, an eventual *right* is conferred, and not an *obligation* imposed, upon those who shall act accordingly: The *imperative* part of the law being addressed or directed to the party whom it requires to *render* the reward.

In short, I am determined or inclined to comply with the wish of another, by the fear of disadvantage or evil. I am also determined or inclined to comply with the wish of another, by the hope of advantage or good. But it is only by the chance of incurring *evil*, that I am *bound* or *obliged* to compliance. It is only by conditional *evil*, that duties are *sanctioned* or *enforced*. It is the 'power and the purpose of inflicting eventual *evil*, and *not* the power and the purpose of imparting eventual *good*, which gives to the expression of a wish the name of a *command*.

If we put *reward* into the import of the term *sanction*, we must engage in a toilsome struggle with the current of ordinary speech; and shall often slide unconsciously, notwithstanding our efforts to the contrary, into the narrower and customary meaning.

The meaning of the term *command*, briefly restated.

It appears, then, from what has been premised, that the ideas or notions comprehended by the term *command* are the following. 1. A wish or desire conceived by a rational being, that another rational being shall do or forbear. 2. An evil to proceed from the former, and to be incurred by the latter, in case the latter comply not with the wish. 3. An expression or intimation of the wish by words or other signs.

The inseparable

It also appears from what has been premised, that *command*, *duty*, and *sanction* are inseparably connected

connexion of the three terms, *command*, *duty*, and *sanction*.

terms: that each embraces the same ideas as the others, though each denotes those ideas in a peculiar order or series.

'A wish conceived by one, and expressed or intimated to another, with an evil to be inflicted and incurred in case the wish be disregarded,' are signified directly and indirectly by each of the three expressions. Each is the name of the same complex notion.

The manner of that connexion.

But when I am talking *directly* of the expression or intimation of the wish, I employ the term *command*: The expression or intimation of the wish being presented *prominently* to my hearer; whilst the evil to be incurred, with the chance of incurring it, are kept (if I may so express myself) in the background of my picture.

When I am talking *directly* of the chance of incurring the evil, or (changing the expression) of the liability or obnoxiousness to the evil, I employ the term *duty*, or the term *obligation*: The liability or obnoxiousness to the evil being put foremost, and the rest of the complex notion being signified implicitly.

When I am talking *immediately* of the evil itself, I employ the term *sanction*, or a term of the like import: The evil to be incurred being signified directly; whilst the obnoxiousness to that evil, with the expression or intimation of the wish, are indicated indirectly or obliquely.

To those who are familiar with the language of logicians (language unrivalled for brevity, distinctness, and precision), I can express my meaning accurately in a breath:—Each of the three terms *signifies* the same notion; but each *denotes* a different part of that notion, and *connotes* the residue.

Laws or *rules* distinguished

Commands are of two species. Some are *laws* or *rules*. The others have not acquired an appropriate name, nor does language afford an expression which will mark them briefly and precisely. I must, therefore, note them as well as I can by the ambiguous and inexpressive name of '*occasional* or *particular* commands.'

from commands which are *occasional* or *particular.*

The term *laws* or *rules* being not unfrequently applied to occasional or particular commands, it is hardly possible to describe a line of separation which shall consist in every respect with established forms of speech. But the distinction between laws and particular commands may, I think, be stated in the following manner.

By every command, the party to whom it is directed is obliged to do or to forbear.

Now where it obliges *generally* to acts or forbearances of a *class*, a command is a law or rule. But where it obliges to a *specific* act or forbearance, or to acts or forbearances which it determines *specifically* or *individually*, a command is occasional or particular. In other words, a class or description of acts is determined by a law or rule, and acts of that class or description are enjoined or forbidden generally. But where a command is occasional or particular, the act or acts, which the command enjoins or forbids, are assigned or determined by their specific or individual natures as well as by the class or description to which they belong.

The statement which I have given in abstract expressions I will now endeavour to illustrate by apt examples.

If you command your servant to go on a given errand, or *not* to leave your house on a given evening, or to rise at such an hour on such a morning, or to rise at that hour during the next week or month, the command is occasional or particular. For the act or acts enjoined or forbidden are specially determined or assigned.

But if you command him *simply* to rise at that hour, or to rise at that hour *always*, or to rise at that hour *till further orders*, it may be said, with propriety, that you lay down a *rule* for the guidance of your servant's conduct. For no specific act is assigned by the command, but the command obliges him generally to acts of a determined class.

If a regiment be ordered to attack or defend a post, or to quell a riot, or to march from their present quarters, the command is occasional or particular. But an order to exercise daily till further orders shall be given would be called a *general* order, and *might* be called a *rule*.

If Parliament prohibited simply the exportation of corn, either for a given period or indefinitely, it would establish a law or rule: a *kind* or *sort* of acts being determined by the command, and acts of that kind or sort being *generally* forbidden. But an order issued by Parliament to meet an impending scarcity, and stopping the exportation of corn *then shipped and in port*, would not be a law or rule, though issued by the sovereign legislature. The order regarding exclusively a specified quantity of corn, the negative acts or forbearances, enjoined by the command, would be determined specifically or individually by the determinate nature of their subject.

As issued by a sovereign legislature, and as wearing the form of a law, the order which I have now imagined would probably be *called* a law. And hence the difficulty of drawing a distinct boundary between laws and occasional commands.

Again: An act which is not an offence, according to the existing law, moves the sovereign to displeasure: and, though the authors of the act are legally innocent or unoffending, the sovereign commands that they shall be punished. As enjoining a specific punishment in that specific case, and as not enjoining generally acts or forbearances of a class, the order uttered by the sovereign is not a law or rule.

Whether such an order would be *called* a law, seems to depend upon circumstances which are purely immaterial: immaterial, that is, with reference to the present purpose, though material with reference to others. If made by a sovereign assembly deliberately, and with the forms of legislation, it would probably be called a law. If uttered by an absolute monarch, without deliberation or ceremony, it would scarcely be confounded with acts of legislation, and would be styled an arbitrary command. Yet, on either of these suppositions, its nature would be the same. It would not be a law or rule, but an occasional or particular command of the sovereign One or Number.

To conclude with an example which best illustrates the distinction, and which shows the importance of the distinction most conspicuously, *judicial commands* are commonly occasional or particular, although the commands which they are calculated to enforce are commonly laws or rules.

For instance, the lawgiver commands that thieves shall be hanged. A specific theft and a specified thief being given, the judge commands that the thief shall be hanged, agreeably to the command of the lawgiver.

Now the lawgiver determines a class or description of acts; prohibits acts of the class generally and indefinitely; and commands, with the like generality, that punishment shall follow transgression. The command of the lawgiver is, therefore, a law or rule. But the command of the judge is occasional or particular. For he orders a specific punishment, as the consequence of a specific offence.

According to the line of separation which I have now attempted to describe, a law and a particular command are distinguished thus:—Acts or forbearances of a *class* are enjoined *generally* by the former. Acts *determined specifically*, are enjoined or forbidden by the latter.

A different line of separation has been drawn by

Blackstone and others. According to Blackstone and others, a law and a particular command are distinguished in the following manner:—A law obliges *generally* the members of the given community, or a law obliges *generally* persons of a given class. A particular command obliges a *single* person, or persons whom it determines *individually*.

That laws and particular commands are not to be distinguished thus, will appear on a moment's reflection.

For, *first*, commands which oblige generally the members of the given community, or commands which oblige generally persons of given classes, are not always laws or rules.

Thus, in the case already supposed; that in which the sovereign commands that all corn actually shipped for exportation be stopped and detained; the command is obligatory upon the whole community, but as it obliges them only to a set of acts individually assigned, it is not a law. Again, suppose the sovereign to issue an order, enforced by penalties, for a general mourning, on occasion of a public calamity. Now, though it is addressed to the community at large, the order is scarcely a rule, in the usual acceptation of the term. For, though it obliges generally the members of the entire community, it obliges to acts which it assigns specifically, instead of obliging generally to acts or forbearances of a class. If the sovereign commanded that *black* should be the dress of his subjects, his command would amount to a law. But if he commanded them to wear it on a specified occasion, his command would be merely particular.

And, *secondly*, a command which obliges exclusively persons individually determined, may amount, notwithstanding, to a law or a rule.

For example, A father may set a *rule* to his child or children: a guardian, to his ward: a master, to his slave or servant. And certain of God's *laws* were as binding on the first man, as they are binding at this hour on the millions who have sprung from his loins.

Most, indeed, of the laws which are established by political superiors, or most of the laws which are simply and strictly so called, oblige generally the members of the political community, or oblige generally persons of a class. To frame a system of duties for every individual of the community, were simply impossible: and if it were possible, it were utterly useless. Most of the laws established by political superiors are, therefore, *general* in a twofold manner: as enjoining or forbidding generally acts of kinds or sorts; and as binding the whole community, or, at least, whole classes of its members.

But if we suppose that Parliament creates and grants an office, and that Parliament binds the grantee to services of a given description, we suppose a law established by political superiors, and yet exclusively binding a specified or determinate person.

Laws established by political superiors, and exclusively binding specified or determinate persons, are styled, in the language of the Roman jurists, *privilegia*. Though that, indeed, is a name which will hardly denote them distinctly: for, like most of the leading terms in actual systems of law, it is not the name of a definite class of objects, but of a heap of heterogeneous objects.[1]

[1] Where a *privilegium* merely imposes a duty, it exclusively obliges a determinate person or persons. But where a *privilegium* confers a right, and the right conferred *avails against the world at large*, the law is *privilegium* as viewed from a certain aspect, but is also *a general law* as viewed from another aspect. In respect of the right conferred, the law exclusively regards a determinate person, and, therefore, is *privilegium*. In respect of the duty imposed, and corresponding to the right conferred, the law regards generally the members of the entire community.

This I shall explain particularly at a subsequent point of my Course, when I consider the peculiar nature of so-called *privilegia*, or of so-called *private laws*.

The definition of a law or rule, *properly* so called.

It appears, from what has been premised, that a law, properly so called, may be defined in the following manner.

A law is a command which obliges a person or persons.

But, as contradistinguished or opposed to an occasional or particular command, a law is a command which obliges a person or persons, and obliges *generally* to acts or forbearances of a *class*.

In language more popular but less distinct and precise, a law is a command which obliges a person or persons to a *course* of conduct.

The meaning of the correlative terms *superior* and *inferior*.

Laws and other commands are said to proceed from *superiors*, and to bind or oblige *inferiors*. I will, therefore, analyse the meaning of those correlative expressions; and will try to strip them of a certain mystery, by which that simple meaning appears to be obscured.

Superiority is often synonymous with *precedence* or *excellence*. We talk of superiors in rank; of superiors in wealth; of superiors in virtue: comparing certain persons with certain other persons; and meaning that the former precede or excel the latter in rank, in wealth, or in virtue.

But, taken with the meaning wherein I here understand it, the term *superiority* signifies *might*: the power of affecting others with evil or pain, and of forcing them, through fear of that evil, to fashion their conduct to one's wishes.

For example, God is emphatically the *superior* of Man. For his power of affecting us with pain, and of forcing us to comply with his will, is unbounded and resistless.

To a limited extent, the sovereign One or Number is the superior of the subject or citizen: the master, of the slave or servant: the father, of the child.

In short, whoever can *oblige* another to comply with

his wishes, is the *superior* of that other, so far as the ability reaches: The party who is obnoxious to the impending evil, being, to that same extent, the *inferior*.

The might or superiority of God, is simple or absolute. But in all or most cases of human superiority, the relation of superior and inferior, and the relation of inferior and superior, are reciprocal. Or (changing the expression) the party who is the superior as viewed from one aspect, is the inferior as viewed from another.

For example, To an indefinite, though limited extent, the monarch is the superior of the governed: his power being commonly sufficient to enforce compliance with his will. But the governed, collectively or in mass, are also the superior of the monarch: who is checked in the abuse of his might by his fear of exciting their anger; and of rousing to active resistance the might which slumbers in the multitude.

A member of a sovereign assembly is the superior of the judge: the judge being bound by the law which proceeds from that sovereign body. But, in his character of citizen or subject, he is the inferior of the judge: the judge being the minister of the law, and armed with the power of enforcing it.

It appears, then, that the term *superiority* (like the terms *duty* and *sanction*) is implied by the term *command*. For superiority is the power of enforcing compliance with a wish: and the expression or intimation of a wish, with the power and the purpose of enforcing it, are the constituent elements of a command.

'That *laws* emanate from *superiors*' is, therefore, an identical proposition. For the meaning which it affects to impart is contained in its subject.

If I mark the peculiar source of a given law, or if I mark the peculiar source of laws of a given class, it is possible that I am saying something which may instruct the hearer. But to affirm of laws universally 'that

C*

they flow from *superiors*,' or to affirm of laws universally 'that *inferiors* are bound to obey them,' is the merest tautology and trifling.

Laws (*improperly* so called) which are not commands.

Like most of the leading terms in the sciences of jurisprudence and morals, the term *laws* is extremely ambiguous. Taken with the largest signification which can be given to the term properly, *laws* are a species of *commands*. But the term is improperly applied to various objects which have nothing of the imperative character: to objects which are *not* commands; and which, therefore, are *not* laws, properly so called.

Accordingly, the proposition 'that laws are commands' must be taken with limitations. Or, rather, we must distinguish the various meanings of the term *laws*; and must restrict the proposition to that class of objects which is embraced by the largest signification that can be given to the term properly.

I have already indicated, and shall hereafter more fully describe, the objects improperly termed laws, which are *not* within the province of jurisprudence (being either rules enforced by opinion and closely analogous to laws properly so called, or being laws so called by a metaphorical application of the term merely). There are other objects improperly termed laws (not being commands) which yet may properly be included within the province of jurisprudence. These I shall endeavour to particularise:—

1. Acts on the part of legislatures to *explain* positive law, can scarcely be called laws, in the proper signification of the term. Working no change in the actual duties of the governed, but simply declaring what those duties *are*, they properly are acts of *interpretation* by legislative authority. Or, to borrow an expression from the writers on the Roman Law, they are acts of *authentic* interpretation.

But, this notwithstanding, they are frequently styled

laws; *declaratory* laws, or declaratory statutes. They must, therefore, be noted as forming an exception to the proposition 'that laws are a species of commands.'

It often, indeed, happens (as I shall show in the proper place), that laws declaratory in name are imperative in effect: Legislative, like judicial interpretation, being frequently deceptive; and establishing new law, under guise of expounding the old.

2. Laws to repeal laws, and to release from existing duties, must also be excepted from the proposition 'that laws are a species of commands.' In so far as they release from duties imposed by existing laws, they are not commands, but revocations of commands. They authorize or permit the parties, to whom the repeal extends, to do or to forbear from acts which they were commanded to forbear from or to do. And, considered with regard to *this*, their immediate or direct purpose, they are often named *permissive laws*, or, more briefly and more properly, *permissions*.

Remotely and indirectly, indeed, permissive laws are often or always imperative. For the parties released from duties are restored to liberties or rights: and duties answering those rights are, therefore, created or revived.

But this is a matter which I shall examine with exactness, when I analyse the expressions 'legal right,' 'permission by the sovereign or state,' and 'civil or political liberty.'

3. Imperfect laws, or laws of imperfect obligation, must also be excepted from the proposition 'that laws are a species of commands.'

An imperfect law (with the sense wherein the term is used by the Roman jurists) is a law which wants a sanction, and which, therefore, is not binding. A law declaring that certain acts are crimes, but annexing no punishment to the commission of acts of the class, is the simplest and most obvious example.

Though the author of an imperfect law signifies a desire, he manifests no purpose of enforcing compliance with the desire. But where there is not a purpose of enforcing compliance with the desire, the expression of a desire is not a command. Consequently, an imperfect law is not so properly a law, as counsel, or exhortation, addressed by a superior to inferiors.

Examples of imperfect laws are cited by the Roman jurists. But with us in England, laws professedly imperative are always (I believe) perfect or obligatory. Where the English legislature affects to command, the English tribunals not unreasonably presume that the legislature exacts obedience. And, if no specific sanction be annexed to a given law, a sanction is supplied by the courts of justice, agreeably to a general maxim which obtains in cases of the kind.

The imperfect laws, of which I am now speaking, are laws which are imperfect, in the sense of *the Roman jurists*: that is to say, laws which speak the desires of political superiors, but which their authors (by oversight or design) have not provided with sanctions. Many of the writers on *morals*, and on the so called *law of nature*, have annexed a different meaning to the term *imperfect*. Speaking of imperfect obligations, they commonly mean duties which are *not legal*: duties imposed by commands of God, or duties imposed by positive morality, as contradistinguished to duties imposed by positive law. An imperfect obligation, in the sense of the Roman jurists, is exactly equivalent to no obligation at all. For the term *imperfect* denotes simply, that the law wants the sanction appropriate to laws of the kind. An imperfect obligation, in the other meaning of the expression, is a religious or a moral obligation. The term *imperfect* does not denote that the law imposing the duty wants the appropriate sanction. It denotes that the law imposing the duty is *not* a law established by a political superior: that it wants that *perfect*, or that surer or more cogent sanction, which is imparted by the sovereign or state.

Laws (*properly* so called) which may *seem* not imperative.

I believe that I have now reviewed all the classes of objects, to which the term *laws* is improperly applied. The laws (improperly so called) which I have here lastly enumerated, are (I think) the only laws which are not commands, and which yet may be properly included within the province of jurisprudence. But though these, with the so called laws set by opinion and the objects metaphorically termed laws, are the only laws which *really* are not commands, there are certain laws (properly so called) which may *seem* not imperative. Accordingly, I will subjoin a few remarks upon laws of this dubious character.

1. There are laws, it may be said, which *merely* create *rights*: And, seeing that every command imposes a *duty*, laws of this nature are not imperative.

But, as I have intimated already, and shall show completely hereafter, there are no laws *merely* creating *rights*. There are laws, it is true, which *merely* create *duties*: duties not correlating with correlating rights, and which, therefore may be styled *absolute*. But every law, really conferring a right, imposes expressly or tacitly a *relative* duty, or a duty correlating with the right. If it specify the remedy to be given, in case the right shall be infringed, it imposes the relative duty expressly. If the remedy to be given be not specified, it refers tacitly to pre-existing law, and clothes the right which it purports to create with a remedy provided by that law. Every law, really conferring a right, is, therefore, imperative: as imperative, as if its only purpose were the creation of a duty, or as if the relative duty, which it inevitably imposes, were merely absolute.

The meanings of the term *right*, are various and perplexed; taken with its proper meaning, it comprises ideas which are numerous and complicated; and the searching and extensive analysis, which the term, therefore, requires, would occupy more room than could be given to it in the present lecture. It is not, however, necessary, that the analysis should be performed here. I purpose, in my earlier lectures, to determine the province of jurisprudence; or to distinguish the laws established by political superiors, from the various laws, proper and improper, with which they are frequently confounded. And this I may accomplish exactly enough, without a nice inquiry into the import of the term *right*.

2. According to an opinion which I must notice *incidentally* here, though the subject to which it relates will be treated *directly* hereafter, *customary laws* must be excepted from the proposition 'that laws are a species of commands.'

By many of the admirers of customary laws (and, especially, of their German admirers), they are thought to oblige legally (independently of the sovereign or state), *because* the citizens or subjects have observed or kept them. Agreeably to this opinion, they are not the *creatures* of the sovereign or state, although the sovereign or state may abolish them at pleasure. Agreeably to this opinion, they are positive law (or law, strictly so called), inasmuch as they are enforced by the courts of justice: But, that notwithstanding, they exist *as positive law* by the spontaneous adoption of the governed, and not by position or establishment on the part of political superiors. Consequently, customary laws, considered as positive law, are not commands. And, consequently, customary laws, considered as positive law, are not laws or rules properly so called.

An opinion less mysterious, but somewhat allied to this, is not uncommonly held by the adverse party: by the party which is strongly opposed to customary law; and to all law made judicially, or in the way of judicial legislation. According to the latter opinion, all judge-made law, or all judge-made law established by *subject* judges, is purely the creature of the judges by whom it is established immediately. To impute it to the sovereign legislature, or to suppose that it speaks the will of the sovereign legislature, is one of the foolish or knavish *fictions* with which lawyers, in every age and nation, have perplexed and darkened the simplest and clearest truths.

I think it will appear, on a moment's reflection, that each of these opinions is groundless: that customary law is *imperative*, in the proper signification of the term; and that all judge-made law is the creature of the sovereign or state.

At its origin, a custom is a rule of conduct which the governed observe spontaneously, or not in pursuance of a law set by a political superior. The custom is transmuted into positive law, when it is adopted as such by the courts of justice, and when the judicial decisions fashioned upon it are enforced by the power of the state. But before it is adopted by the courts, and clothed with the legal sanction, it is merely a rule of positive morality: a rule generally observed by the citizens or subjects; but deriving the only force, which it can be said to possess, from the general disapprobation falling on those who transgress it.

Now when judges transmute a custom into a legal rule (or make a legal rule not suggested by a custom), the legal rule which they establish is established by the sovereign legislature. A subordinate or subject judge is merely a minister. The portion of the sovereign power which lies at his disposition is merely delegated. The rules which he makes derive their legal force from authority given by the state: an authority which the state may confer expressly, but which it commonly imparts in the way of acquiescence. For, since the state may reverse the rules which he makes, and yet permits him to enforce them by the power of the political community, its sovereign will 'that his rules shall obtain as law' is clearly evinced by its conduct, though not by its express declaration.

The admirers of customary law love to trick out their idol with mysterious and imposing attributes. But to those who can see the difference between positive law and morality, there is nothing of mystery about it. Considered as rules of positive morality, customary laws arise from the consent of the governed, and not from the position or establishment of political superiors. But, considered as moral rules turned into positive laws, customary laws are established by the state: established by the state directly, when the customs are promulged in its statutes; established by the state circuitously, when the customs are adopted by its tribunals.

The opinion of the party which abhors judge-made laws, springs from their inadequate conception of the nature of commands.

Like other significations of desire, a command is express or tacit. If the desire be signified by *words* (written or spoken), the command is express. If the desire be signified by conduct (or by any signs of desire which are *not* words), the command is tacit.

Now when customs are turned into legal rules by decisions of subject judges, the legal rules which emerge from the customs are *tacit* commands of the sovereign legislature. The state, which is able to abolish, permits its ministers to enforce them: and it, therefore, signifies its pleasure, by that its voluntary acquiescence, 'that they shall serve as a law to the governed.'

My present purpose is merely this: to prove that the positive law styled *customary* (and all positive law made judicially) is established by the state directly or circuitously, and, therefore, is *imperative*. I am far from disputing, that law made judicially (or in the way of improper legislation) and law made by statute (or in the properly legislative manner) are distinguished by weighty differences. I shall inquire, in future lectures, what those differences are; and why subject judges, who are properly ministers of the law, have commonly shared with the sovereign in the business of making it.

Laws which are not commands, enumerated.

I assume, then, that the only laws which are not imperative, and which belong to the subject-matter of jurisprudence, are the following:—1. Declaratory laws, or laws explaining the import of existing positive law. 2. Laws abrogating or repealing existing positive law. 3. Imperfect laws, or laws of imperfect obligation (with the sense wherein the expression is used by the Roman jurists).

But the space occupied in the science by these improper laws is comparatively narrow and insignificant. Accordingly, although I shall take them into account so often as I refer to them directly, I shall throw them out of account on other occasions. Or (changing the expression) I shall limit the term *law* to laws which are imperative, unless I extend it expressly to laws which are not.

LECTURE V

Laws proper or properly so called, and laws improper or improperly so called.

THE term *law*, or the term *laws*, is applied to the following objects:—to laws proper or properly so called, and to laws improper or improperly so called: to objects which have all the essentials of an imperative law or rule, and to objects which are wanting in some of those

[6] But here I would briefly remark, that, though the hypothesis of Hartley is no necessary ingredient in the theory of general utility, it is a necessary ingredient (if it be not unfounded) in every sound system of education or training. For the sake of our own happiness, and the happiness of our fellow-creatures, the affection of benevolence or sympathy should be strong and steady as possible: for though, like other motives, it may lead us to pernicious conduct, it is less likely than most of the others to seduce us from the right road. Now if benevolence or sympathy be engendered by the principle of association, the affection may be planted and nurtured by education or training. The truth or falsehood of the hypothesis, together with the process by which the affection is generated, are therefore objects of great practical moment, and well deserving of close and minute examination.

essentials, but to which the term is unduly extended either by reason of *analogy* or in the way of *metaphor.*

Strictly speaking, *all* improper laws are *analogous* to laws proper: and the term *law*, as applied to *any* of them, is a *metaphorical* or *figurative* expression.

For every metaphor springs from an analogy: and every analogical extension given to a term is a metaphor or figure of speech. The term is extended from the objects which it properly signifies to objects of another nature; to objects not of the class wherein the former are contained, although they are allied to the former by that more distant resemblance which is usually styled *analogy*. But, taking the expressions with the meanings which custom or usage has established, there is a difference between an employment of a term analogically and a metaphor.

Analogy and metaphor as used in common parlance, defined.

Analogy is a species of *resemblance.* The word resemblance is here taken in that large sense, in which all subjects which have any property in common, are said to resemble. But besides this more extended acceptation according to which resemblance is a genus, and analogy one of the species included therein, there is another and a narrower sense, in which resemblance is opposed to analogy. Two resembling subjects are said to *resemble* in the narrower meaning of the term, when they both belong to some determinate genus or species expressly or tacitly referred to; when they both have every property, which belongs to all the subjects included in the class. Two resembling subjects are said on the contrary to be *analogous*, when *one* of them belongs to some class expressly or tacitly referred to, and the *other* does *not*: when one possesses all the properties common to the class and the other only some of them. I choose, for instance, on account of a particular convenience, to range together in one class all animals having feet. When I am speaking with reference to this class, the foot of a lion and the foot of a man would be said to resemble in the narrower as well as in the wider sense of the word. But the foot of a table, though it resembles the foot of a lion and of a man in the more enlarged sense, does not resemble these in the narrower sense, but is only analogous to them. For *these* possess the whole of the qualities belonging universally to the class, while *it* possesses only a part of the same qualities. If I were not tacitly referring to a genus, I might say that all the three objects resemble, but if the genus be referred to, the foot of the lion and the foot of the man resemble, the foot of the table is only analogous to them.

Resemblance is hence an ambiguous term. When two things resemble in the narrower sense, that is, when they both possess all the properties which belong universally to the class, the common name (such as *foot* in the instance above given) is applied to both of them strictly and properly. When they are analogous, that is when the one possesses all, the other only some of the properties which belong universally to the class, the name denotes the one properly, the other improperly or analogically.

It is extremely important to fix our conception with respect to this ambiguity, as the words analogy and analogous often recur in the science of jurisprudence, and by the laxity with which they are employed involve it in a scarcely penetrable mist. The nature of unwritten law, and the principles of interpretation or construction, are among the most obscure of all the questions which arise in jurisprudence. This obscurity springs, as is usually the case, from nonsense or jargon; which jargon, on these questions, arises from hence, that men talk profusely of analogy and things analogous, without ascertaining the precise meaning of those terms, or taking pains to employ them with any precise meaning. Professor Thibaut of Berlin, in his treatise on the interpretation of the Roman Law, is, as far as I know, the only writer who has seen this perplexity; and notwithstanding my warm respect for that learned and discerning jurist, it seems to me that even he has scarcely solved the difficulty, though he has pointed out the path by which we may arrive at a solution.

A metaphor is the transference of a term from its primitive signification to subjects to which it is applied not in that, but in a secondary sense. An analogy real or supposed, is always the ground of the transference; hence every metaphor is an analogical application of a term, and every analogical application of a term is a metaphor. But a metaphorical or figurative application is scarcely, in common parlance, synonymous with an analogical application. By a metaphorical or figurative application, we usually mean one in which the analogy is faint, the alliance between the primitive and the derivative signification remote. When the analogy is clear, strong, and close; when the subjects to which the term is deflected lie on the confines of the class properly denoted by it, and have many of the properties common to the class, we hardly say that the name is employed figuratively or metaphorically.

In the language of logic, objects which have all the qualities composing the essence of the class, and all the qualities which are the necessary consequences of those composing the essence, *resemble*. When an object does not possess all the essence of the class, but possesses many of the qualities which compose the essence, or many of those which necessarily result from the essence, the application of the name to that object will be said to be analogical and not a metaphor. The difference between metaphor and analogy is hence a difference of degree, and not to be settled precisely by drawing a strict line between them.

Now a broad distinction obtains between laws

F*

Laws improper are of two kinds:—1. Laws closely analogous to laws proper. 2. Laws metaphorical or figurative.

improperly so called. Some are *closely*, others are *remotely* analogous to laws proper. The term *law* is extended to some by a decision of the reason or understanding. The term *law* is extended to others by a turn or caprice of the fancy.

In order that I may mark this distinction briefly and commodiously, I avail myself of the difference, established by custom or usage, between the meanings of the expressions *analogical* and *figurative*.—I style laws of the first kind *laws closely analogous to laws proper*. I say that they are called *laws* by an *analogical* extension of the term.—I style laws of the second kind *laws metaphorical* or *figurative*. I say that they are called *laws* by a *metaphor* or *figure of speech*.

Division of laws proper, and of such improper laws as are closely analogous to the proper.

Now laws proper, with such improper laws as are closely analogous to the proper, are divisible thus.

Of laws properly so called, some are set by God to his human creatures, others are set by men to men.

Of the laws properly so called which are set by men to men, some are set by men as political superiors, or by men, as private persons, in pursuance of legal rights. Others may be described in the following negative manner: They are not set by men as political superiors, nor are they set by men, as private persons, in pursuance of legal rights.

The laws improperly so called which are closely analogous to the proper, are merely opinions or sentiments held or felt by men in regard to human conduct. As I shall show hereafter, these opinions and sentiments are styled *laws*, because they are *analogous* to laws properly so called: because they resemble laws properly so called in *some* of their properties or *some* of their effects or consequences.

Distribution of laws proper, and of such

Accordingly, I distribute laws proper, with such improper laws as are closely analogous to the proper, under three capital classes.

The first comprises the laws (properly so called) which are set by God to his human creatures.

The second comprises the laws (properly so called) which are set by men as political superiors, or by men, as private persons, in pursuance of legal rights.

The third comprises laws of the two following species: 1. The laws (properly so called) which are set by men to men, but not by men as political superiors, nor by men, as private persons, in pursuance of legal rights: 2. The laws which are closely analogous to laws proper, but are merely opinions or sentiments held or felt by men in regard to human conduct.——I put laws of these species into a common class, and I mark them with the common name to which I shall advert immediately, for the following reason. No law of either species is a direct or circuitous command of a monarch or sovereign number in the character of political superior. In other words, no law of either species is a direct or circuitous command of a monarch or sovereign number to a person or persons in a state of subjection to its author. Consequently, laws of both species may be aptly opposed to laws of the second capital class. For every law of that second capital class is a direct or circuitous command of a monarch or sovereign number in the character of political superior: that is to say, a direct or circuitous command of a monarch or sovereign number to a person or persons in a state of subjection to its author.

improper laws as are closely analogous to the proper, under three capital classes:— 1. The law of God, or the laws of God. 2. Positive law, or positive laws. 3. Positive morality, rules of positive morality, or positive moral rules.

Laws comprised by these three capital classes I mark with the following names.

I name laws of the first class *the law* or *laws of God*, or *the Divine law* or *laws.*

For various reasons which I shall produce immediately, I name laws of the second class *positive law*, or *positive laws.*

For the same reasons, I name laws of the third class

positive morality, *rules of positive morality*, or *positive moral rules*.

Digression to explain the expressions *positive law* and *positive morality*.

My reasons for using the two expressions '*positive* law' and '*positive* morality,' are the following.

There are two capital classes of human laws. The first comprises the laws (properly so called) which are set by men as political superiors, or by men, as private persons, in pursuance of legal rights. The second comprises the laws (proper and improper) which belong to the two species mentioned on the preceding page.

As merely distinguished from the second, the first of those capital classes might be named simply *law*. As merely distinguished from the first, the second of those capital classes might be named simply *morality*. But both must be distinguished from the law of God: and, for the purpose of distinguishing both from the law of God, we must qualify the names *law* and *morality*. Accordingly, I style the first of those capital classes '*positive* law:' and I style the second of those capital classes '*positive* morality.' By the common epithet *positive*, I denote that both classes flow from human sources. By the distinctive names *law* and *morality*, I denote the difference between the human sources from which the two classes respectively emanate.

Strictly speaking, every law properly so called is a *positive* law. For it is *put* or set by its individual or collective author, or it exists by the *position* or institution of its individual or collective author.

But, as opposed to the law of nature (meaning the law of God), human law of the first of those capital classes is styled by writers on jurisprudence '*positive* law.' This application of the expression '*positive* law' was manifestly made for the purpose of obviating confusion; confusion of human law of the first of those capital classes with that Divine law which is the measure or test of human.

And, in order to obviate similar confusion, I apply the expression '*positive* morality' to human law of the second capital class. For the name *morality*, when standing unqualified or alone, may signify the law set by God, or human law of that second capital class. If you say that an act or omission violates *morality*, you speak ambiguously. You may mean that it violates the law which I style '*positive* morality,' or that it violates the Divine law which is the measure or test of the former.

Again: The human laws or rules which I style '*positive* morality,' I mark with that expression for the following additional reason.

I have said that the name *morality*, when standing unqualified or alone, may signify positive morality, or may signify the law of God. But the name *morality*, when standing unqualified or alone, is perplexed with a further ambiguity. It may import indifferently either of the two following senses:—1. The name *morality*, when standing unqualified or alone, may signify positive morality which is good or worthy of approbation, or positive morality as it would be if it were good or worthy of approbation. In other words, the name *morality*, when standing unqualified or alone, may signify positive morality which agrees with its measure or test, or positive morality as it would be if it agreed with its measure or test. 2. The name *morality*, when standing unqualified or alone, may signify the human laws, which I style positive morality, as considered without regard to their goodness or badness. For example, Such laws of the class as are peculiar to a given age, or such laws of the class as are peculiar to a given nation, we style the *morality* of that given age or nation, whether we think them good or deem them bad. Or, in case we mean to intimate that we approve or disapprove of them, we name them the *morality* of that given age or nation, and we qualify that name with the epithet *good* or *bad*.

Now, by the name '*positive* morality,' I mean the human laws which I mark with that expression, as considered without regard to their goodness or badness. Whether human laws be worthy of praise or blame, or whether they accord or not with their measure or test, they are 'rules of *positive* morality,' in the sense which I give to the expression, if they belong to either of the two species lastly mentioned on p. 123. But, in consequence of that ambiguity which I have now attempted to explain, I could hardly express my meaning with passable distinctness by the unqualified name *morality*.

Explanation of the following expressions: viz. *science of jurisprudence* and *science of positive morality*; *science of ethics or deontology*, *science of legislation*, and *science of morals*.

From the expression *positive law* and the expression *positive morality*, I pass to certain expressions with which they are closely connected.

The *science of jurisprudence* (or, simply and briefly, *jurisprudence*) is concerned with positive laws, or with laws strictly so called, as considered without regard to their goodness or badness.

Positive morality, as considered without regard to its goodness or badness, *might* be the subject of a science closely analogous to jurisprudence. I say '*might* be:' since it is only in one of its branches (namely, the law of nations or international law), that positive morality, as considered without regard to its goodness or badness, has been treated by writers in a scientific or systematic manner.—For the science of positive morality, as considered without regard to its goodness or badness, current or established language will hardly afford us a name. The name *morals*, or *science of morals*, would denote it ambiguously: the name *morals*, or *science of morals*, being commonly applied (as I shall show immediately) to a department of ethics or deontology. But, since the science of jurisprudence is not unfrequently styled 'the science of *positive* law,' the science in question might be styled analogically 'the science of *positive* morality.' The department of the science in question which relates to international law, has actually been styled by Von Martens, a recent writer of celebrity, '*positives* oder *practisches* Völkerrecht:' that is to say, '*positive* international law,' or '*practical* international law.' Had he named that department of the science '*positive* international *morality*,' the name would have hit its import with perfect precision.

The science of ethics (or, in the language of Mr. Bentham, *the science of deontology*) may be defined in the following manner:—It affects to determine the test of positive law and morality, or it affects to determine the principles whereon they must be fashioned in order that they may merit approbation. In other words, it affects to expound them as they should be; or it affects to expound them as they ought to be; or it affects to expound them as they would be if they were good or worthy of praise; or it affects to expound them as they would be if they conformed to an assumed measure.

The science of ethics (or, simply and briefly, ethics) consists of two departments: one relating specially to positive law, the other relating specially to positive morality. The department which relates specially to positive law, is commonly styled *the science of legislation*, or, simply and briefly, *legislation*. The department which relates specially to positive morality, is commonly styled *the science of morals*, or, simply and briefly, *morals*.

Meaning of the epithet *good* or *bad* as applied to a human law.

The foregoing attempt to define the science of ethics naturally leads me to offer the following explanatory remark.

When we say that a human law is good or bad, or is worthy of praise or blame, or is what it should be or what it should not be, or is what it ought to be or what it ought not to be, we mean (unless we intimate our mere liking or aversion) this: namely, that the law agrees with or differs from a something to which we tacitly refer it as to a measure or test.

For example, According to either of the hypotheses which I stated in preceding lectures, a human law is good or bad as it agrees or does not agree with the law of God: that is to say, with the law of God as indicated by the principle of utility, or with the law of God as indicated by the moral sense. To the adherent of the theory of utility, a human law is good if it be generally useful, and a human law is bad if it be generally pernicious. For, in *his* opinion, it is consonant or not with the law of God, inasmuch as it is consonant or not with the principle of general utility. To the adherent of the hypothesis of a moral sense, a human law is good if he likes it he knows not why, and a human law is bad if he hates it he knows not wherefore. For, in *his* opinion, that his inexplicable feeling of liking or aversion shows that the human law pleases or offends the Deity.

To the atheist, a human law is good if it be generally useful, and a human law is bad if it be generally pernicious. For the principle of general utility would serve as a measure or test, although it were not an index to an ulterior measure or test. But if he call the law a good one without believing it useful, or if he call the law a bad one without believing it pernicious, the atheist simply intimates his mere liking or aversion. For, unless it be thought an index to the law set by the Deity, an inexplicable feeling of approbation or disapprobation can hardly be considered a measure or test. And, in the opinion of the atheist, there is no law of God which his inexplicable feeling can point at.

To the believer in a supposed revelation, a human law is good or bad as it agrees with or differs from the terms wherein the revelation is expressed.

In short, the goodness or badness of a human law is

a phrase of relative and varying import. A law which is good to one man is bad to another, in case they tacitly refer it to different and adverse tests.

Meaning of the epithet *good* as applied to the law of God.

The Divine laws may be styled good, in the sense with which the atheist may apply the epithet to human. We may style them good, or worthy of praise, inasmuch as they agree with utility considered as an ultimate test. And this is the only meaning with which we can apply the epithet to the laws of God. Unless we refer them to utility considered as an ultimate test, we have no test by which we can try them. To say that they are good because they are set by the Deity, is to say that they are good as measured or tried by themselves. But to say this is to talk absurdly: for every object which is measured, or every object which is brought to a test, is compared with a given object other than itself.—If the laws set by the Deity were not generally useful, or if they did not promote the general happiness of his creatures, or if their great Author were not wise and benevolent, they would not be good, or worthy of praise, but were devilish and worthy of execration.

Before I conclude the present digression, I must submit this further remark to the attention of the reader.

The expression *law of nature*, or *natural law*, has two disparate meanings. It signifies the law of God, or a portion of positive law and positive morality.

I have intimated in the course of this digression, that the phrase *law of nature*, or the phrase *natural law*, often signifies the law of God.

Natural law as thus understood, and the *natural law* which I mentioned in my fourth lecture, are disparate expressions. The *natural law* which I there mentioned, is a portion of positive law and positive morality. It consists of the human rules, legal and moral, which have obtained at all times and obtained at all places.

According to the compound hypothesis which I mentioned in my fourth lecture, these human rules, legal and moral, have been fashioned on the law of God as indicated by *the moral sense*. Or, adopting the language of the classical Roman jurists, these human rules, legal and moral, have been fashioned on the Divine law as known by *natural reason.*

But, besides the human rules which have obtained with all mankind, there are human rules, legal and moral, which have been limited to peculiar times, or limited to peculiar places.

Now, according to the compound hypothesis which I mentioned in my fourth lecture, these last have not been fashioned on the law of God, or have been fashioned on the law of God as conjectured by the light of utility.

Being fashioned on the law of God as known by an infallible guide, human rules of the first class are styled *the law of nature*: For they are not of human position purely or simply, but are laws of God or Nature clothed with human sanctions. As obtaining at all times and obtaining at all places, they are styled by the classical jurists *jus gentium*, or *jus omnium gentium.*

But human rules of the second class are styled *positive.* For, not being fashioned on the law of God, or being fashioned on the law of God as merely conjectured by utility, they, certainly or probably, are of purely human position. They are not laws of God or Nature clothed with human sanctions.

As I stated in my fourth lecture, and shall show completely hereafter, the distinction of human rules into natural and positive involves the compound hypothesis which I mentioned in that discourse.

The connection of the present (the fifth) lecture with the first, second, third, fourth, and sixth.

Positive laws, the appropriate matter of jurisprudence, are related in the way of resemblance, or by a close or remote analogy, to the following objects:— 1. In the way of resemblance, they are related to the laws of God. 2. In the way of resemblance, they are related to those rules of positive morality which are laws properly so called. 3. By a close or strong analogy, they are related to those rules of positive morality which are merely opinions or sentiments held or felt by men in regard to human conduct. 4. By a remote or slender analogy, they are related to laws merely metaphorical, or laws merely figurative.

To distinguish positive laws from the objects now enumerated, is the purpose of the present attempt to determine the province of jurisprudence.

In pursuance of the purpose to which I have now adverted, I stated, in my first lecture, the essentials of a *law* or *rule* (taken with the largest signification which can be given to the term *properly*).

In my second, third, and fourth lectures, I stated the marks or characters by which the laws of God are distinguished from other laws. And, stating those marks or characters, I explained the nature of the index to his unrevealed laws, or I explained and examined the hypotheses which regard the nature of that index. I made this explanation at a length which may seem disproportionate, but which I have deemed necessary because these laws, and the index by which they are known, are the standard or measure to which all other laws should conform, and the standard measure or test by which they should be tried.

But before I can complete the purpose to which I have adverted above, I must examine or discuss especially the following principal topics (and must touch upon other topics of secondary or subordinate importance):—1. I must examine the marks or characters by which positive laws are distinguished from other laws. 2. I must examine the distinguishing marks of those positive moral rules which are laws properly so called. 3. I must examine the distinguishing marks of those positive moral rules which are styled *laws* or *rules* by an analogical extension of the term. 4. I must examine the distinguishing marks of laws merely metaphorical, or laws merely figurative.

In order to an explanation of the marks which distinguish positive laws, I must analyse the expression *sovereignty*, the correlative expression *subjection*, and the inseparably connected expression *independent political society*. For the essential difference of a positive law (or the difference that severs it from a law which is not a positive law) may be stated thus. Every positive law, or every law simply and strictly so called, is set by a sovereign person, or a sovereign body of persons, to a member or members of the independent political society wherein that person or body is sovereign or supreme. Or (changing the expression) it is set by a monarch, or sovereign number, to a person or persons in a state of subjection to its author.

But my analysis of those expressions occupies so large a space, that, in case I placed it in the lecture which I am now delivering, the lecture which I am now delivering would run to insufferable length.

The purpose mentioned above will, therefore, be completed in the following order.

Excluding from my present discourse my analysis of those expressions, I shall complete, in my present discourse, the purpose mentioned above, so far as I can complete it consistently with that exclusion. In my present discourse, I shall examine or discuss especially the following principal topics: namely, the distinguishing marks of those positive moral rules which are laws properly so called: the distinguishing marks of those positive moral rules which are styled *laws* or *rules* by an analogical extension of the term: the distinguishing marks of the laws which are styled *laws* by a metaphor.

I shall complete, in my sixth lecture, the purpose mentioned above, by explaining the marks or characters which distinguish positive laws, or laws strictly so called: an explanation involving an analysis of the capital expression *sovereignty*, the correlative expression *subjection*, and the inseparably connected expression *independent political society*.

Having shown the connection of my present discourse with foregoing and following lectures, I proceed to examine or discuss its appropriate topics or subjects.

The essentials of a law properly so called, together with certain consequences which those essentials import.

In my first lecture, I endeavoured to resolve a *law* (taken with the largest signification which can be given to the term *properly*) into the necessary or essential elements of which it is composed.

Now those essentials of a law proper, together with certain consequences which those essentials import, may be stated briefly in the following manner:—1. Laws properly so called are a species of *commands*. But, being a *command*, every law properly so called flows from a *determinate* source, or emanates from a *determinate* author. In other words, the author from whom it proceeds is a *determinate* rational being, or a *determinate* body or aggregate of rational beings. For whenever a *command* is expressed or intimated, one party signifies a wish that another shall do or forbear: and the latter is obnoxious to an evil which the former intends to inflict in case the wish be disregarded. But every *signification* of a wish made by a single individual, or made by a body of individuals *as a body or collective whole*, supposes that the individual or body is *certain* or *determinate*. And every *intention* or *purpose* held by a single individual, or held by a body of individuals *as a body or collective whole*, involves the same supposition. 2. Every sanction properly so called is an eventual evil *annexed to a command*. Any eventual evil may operate as a *motive* to conduct: but, unless the conduct be commanded and the evil be annexed to the command purposely to enforce obedience, the evil is not a *sanction* in the proper acceptation of the term. 3. Every duty properly so called supposes a *command* by which it is created. For every sanction properly so called is an eventual evil *annexed to a command*. And duty properly so called is obnoxiousness to evils of the kind.

The laws of God, and positive laws, are laws properly so called.

Now it follows from these premises, that the laws of God, and positive laws, are laws proper, or laws properly so called.

The laws of God are laws proper, inasmuch as they are *commands* express or tacit, and therefore emanate from a *certain* source.

Positive laws, or laws strictly so called, are established directly or immediately by authors of three kinds:—by monarchs, or sovereign bodies, as supreme political superiors: by men in a state of subjection, as subordinate political superiors: by subjects, as private persons, in pursuance of legal rights. But every positive law, or every law strictly so called, is a direct or circuitous command of a monarch or sovereign number in the character of political superior: that is to say, a direct or circuitous command of a monarch or sovereign number to a person or persons in a state of subjection to its author. And being a *command* (and therefore flowing from a *determinate* source), every positive law is a law proper, or a law properly so called.

The generic character of positive moral rules.

Besides the human laws which I style positive law, there are human laws which I style positive morality, rules of positive morality, or positive moral rules.

The generic character of laws of the class may be stated briefly in the following negative manner:—No law belonging to the class is a direct or circuitous command of a monarch or sovereign number in the character of political superior. In other words, no law belonging to the class is a direct or circuitous command of a monarch or sovereign number to a person or persons in a state of subjection to its author.

Of positive moral rules, some are

But of positive moral rules, some are laws proper, or laws properly so called: others are laws improper, or laws improperly so called. Some have all the essentials of an *imperative* law or rule: others are deficient in some of those essentials, and are styled *laws* or *rules* by an analogical extension of the term.

laws proper, but others are laws improper.

The positive moral rules which are laws properly so called, are distinguished from other laws by the union of two marks:—1. They are imperative laws or rules set by men to men. 2. They are not set by men as political superiors, nor are they set by men as private persons, in pursuance of legal rights.

The positive moral rules which are laws properly so called, are *commands.*

Inasmuch as they bear the latter of these two marks, they are not commands of sovereigns in the character of political superiors. Consequently, they are not positive laws: they are not clothed with legal sanctions, nor do they oblige legally the persons to whom they are set. But being *commands* (and therefore being established by *determinate* individuals or bodies), they are laws properly so called: they are armed with sanctions, and impose duties, in the proper acceptation of the terms.

It will appear from the following distinctions, that positive moral rules which are laws properly so called may be reduced to three kinds.

Of positive moral rules which are laws properly so called, some are established by men who are not subjects, or are not in a state of subjection: Meaning by 'subjects,' or by 'men in a state of subjection,' men in a state of subjection to a monarch or sovereign number.—Of positive moral rules which are laws properly so called, and are not established by men in a state of subjection, some are established by men living in the negative state which is styled a state of nature or a state of anarchy: that is to say, by men who are *not* in the state which is styled a state of government, or are *not* members, sovereign or subject, of any political society. —Of positive moral rules which are laws properly so called, and are not established by men in a state of subjection, others are established by sovereign individuals or bodies, but are not established by sovereigns in the character of political superiors. Or a positive moral rule of this kind may be described in the following manner: It is set by a monarch or sovereign number, but not to a person or persons in a state of subjection to its author.

Of laws properly so called which are set by subjects, some are set by subjects as subordinate political superiors. But of laws properly so called which are set by subjects, others are set by subjects as private persons: Meaning by 'private persons,' subjects not in the class of subordinate political superiors, or subordinate political superiors not considered as such.—Laws set by subjects as subordinate political superiors, are positive laws: they are clothed with legal sanctions, and impose legal duties. They are set by sovereigns or states in the character of political superiors, although they are set by sovereigns circuitously or remotely. Although they are made directly by subject or subordinate authors, they are made through legal rights granted by sovereigns or states, and held by those subject authors as mere trustees for the granters.—Of laws set by subjects as private persons, some are not established by sovereign or supreme authority. And these are rules of positive morality: they are not clothed with legal sanctions, nor do they oblige legally the parties to whom they are set.—But of laws set by subjects as private persons, others are set or established in pursuance of legal rights residing in the subject authors. And these are positive laws or laws strictly so called. Although they are made directly by subject authors, they are made in pursuance of rights granted or conferred by sovereigns in the character of political superiors: they legally oblige the parties to whom they are set, or are clothed with legal sanctions. They are commands of sovereigns as political superiors, although they are set by sovereigns circuitously or remotely.[7]

It appears from the foregoing distinctions, that positive moral rules which are laws properly so called are of three kinds:—1. Those which are set by men living in a state of nature. 2. Those which are set by sovereigns,

Laws set by men, as private persons, in pursuance of legal rights.

[7] A law set by a subject as a private person, but in pursuance of a legal right residing in the subject author, is either a positive law purely or simply, or is compounded of a positive law and a rule of positive morality. Or (changing the expression) it is either a positive law purely or simply, or it is a positive law as viewed from one aspect, and a rule of positive morality as viewed from another.

The person who makes the law in pursuance of the legal right, is either legally bound to make the law, or he is not. In the first case, the law is a positive law purely or simply. In the second case, the law is compounded of a positive law and a positive moral rule.

For example, A guardian may have a right over his pupil or ward, which he is legally bound to exercise, for the benefit of the pupil or ward, in a given or specified manner. In other words, a guardian may be clothed with a right, over his pupil or ward, in trust to exercise the same, for the benefit of the pupil or ward, in a given or specified manner. Now if, in pursuance of his right, and agreeably to his duty or trust, he sets a law or rule to the pupil or ward, the law is a positive law purely or simply. It is properly a law which the state sets to the ward through its minister or instrument the guardian. It is not made by the guardian of his own spontaneous movement, or is made in pursuance of a duty which the state has imposed upon him. The position of the guardian is closely analogous to the position of subordinate political superiors; who hold their delegated powers of direct or judicial legislation as mere trustees for the sovereign granters.

Again: the master has legal rights, over or against his slave, which are conferred by the state upon the master for his own benefit. And, since they are conferred upon him for his own benefit, he is not legally bound to exercise or use them. Now if, in pursuance of these rights, he sets a law to his slave, the law is compounded of a positive law and a positive moral rule. Being made by sovereign authority, and clothed by the sovereign with

but not by sovereigns as political superiors. 3. Those which are set by subjects as private persons, and are not set by the subject authors in pursuance of legal rights.

To cite an example of rules of the first kind were superfluous labour. A man living in a state of nature may impose an imperative law: though, since the man *is* in

sanctions, the law made by the master is properly a positive law. But, since it is made by the master of his own spontaneous movement, or is not made by the master in pursuance of a legal duty, it is properly a rule of positive morality, as well as a positive law. Though the law set by the master is set circuitously by the sovereign, it is set or established by the sovereign at the pleasure of the subject author. The master is not the instrument of the sovereign or state, but the sovereign or state is rather the instrument of the master.

Before I dismiss the subject of the present note, I must make two remarks.

1. Of laws made by men as private persons, some are frequently styled 'laws *autonomic*.' Or it is frequently said of some of those laws, that they are made through an αὐτονομία residing in the subject authors. Now laws *autonomic*, or *autonomical*, are laws made by subjects, as private persons, in pursuance of legal rights: that is to say, in pursuance of legal rights which they are free to exercise or not, or in pursuance of legal rights which are not saddled with trusts. A law of the kind is styled *autonomic*, because it is made by its author of his own spontaneous disposition, or not in pursuance of a duty imposed upon him by the state.

It is clear, however, that the term *autonomic* is not exclusively applicable to laws of the kind in question. The term will apply to every law which is not made by its author in pursuance of a legal duty. It will apply, for instance, to every law which is made immediately or directly by a monarch or sovereign number: independence of legal duty being of the essence of sovereignty.

2. Laws which are positive law as viewed from one aspect, but which are positive morality as viewed from another, I place simply or absolutely in the first of those capital classes. If affecting exquisite precision, I placed them in each of those classes, I could hardly indicate the boundary by which those classes are severed without resorting to expressions of repulsive complexity and length.

a state of nature, he cannot impose the law in the character of sovereign, and cannot impose the law in pursuance of a legal right. And the law being *imperative* (and therefore proceeding from a *determinate* source) is a law properly so called: though, for want of a sovereign author proximate or remote, it is not a positive law but a rule of positive morality.

An imperative law set by a sovereign to a sovereign, or by one supreme government to another supreme government, is an example of rules of the second kind. Since no supreme government is in a state of subjection to another, an imperative law set by a sovereign to a sovereign is not set by its author in the character of political superior. Nor is it set by its author in pursuance of a legal right: for every legal right is conferred by a supreme government, and is conferred on a person or persons in a state of subjection to the granter. Consequently, an imperative law set by a sovereign to a sovereign is not a positive law or a law strictly so called. But being *imperative* (and therefore proceeding from a *determinate* source), it amounts to a law in the proper signification of the term, although it is purely or simply a rule of positive morality.

If they be set by subjects as private persons, and be not set by their authors in pursuance of legal rights, the laws following are examples of rules of the third kind: namely, imperative laws set by parents to children; imperative laws set by masters to servants; imperative laws set by lenders to borrowers; imperative laws set by patrons to parasites. Being *imperative* (and therefore proceeding from *determinate* sources), the laws foregoing are laws properly so called: though, if they be set by subjects as private persons, and be not set by their authors in pursuance of legal rights, they are not positive laws but rules of positive morality.

Again: A club or society of men, signifying its

collective pleasure by a vote of its assembled members, passes or makes a law to be kept by its members severally under pain of exclusion from its meetings. Now if it be made by subjects as private persons, and be not made by its authors in pursuance of a legal right, the law voted and passed by the assembled members of the club is a further example of rules of the third kind. If it be made by subjects as private persons, and be not made by its authors in pursuance of a legal right, it is not a positive law or a law strictly so called. But being an *imperative* law (and the body by which it is set being therefore *determinate*), it may be styled a *law* or *rule* with absolute precision or propriety, although it is purely or simply a rule of positive morality.

The positive moral rules which are laws improperly so called, are *laws set or imposed by general opinion.*

The positive moral rules which are laws improperly so called, are *laws set* or *imposed by general opinion*: that is to say, by the general opinion of any class or any society of persons. For example, Some are set or imposed by the general opinion of persons who are members of a profession or calling: others, by that of persons who inhabit a town or province: others, by that of a nation or independent political society: others, by that of a larger society formed of various nations.

A few species of the laws which are set by general opinion have gotten appropriate names.—For example, There are laws or rules imposed upon gentlemen by opinions current amongst gentlemen. And these are usually styled *the rules of honour*, or *the laws* or *law of honour*.—There are laws or rules imposed upon people of fashion by opinions current in the fashionable world. And these are usually styled *the law set by fashion*.—There are laws which regard the conduct of independent political societies in their various relations to one another: Or, rather, there are laws which regard the conduct of sovereigns or supreme governments in their various relations to one another. And laws or rules of this species, which are imposed upon nations or sovereigns by opinions current amongst nations, are usually styled *the law of nations* or *international law*.

A law set or imposed by general opinion, is merely the *opinion* or *sentiment* of an *indeterminate* body of persons in regard to a kind of conduct.

Now a law set or imposed by general opinion is a law improperly so called. It is styled a *law* or *rule* by an analogical extension of the term. When we speak of a law set by general opinion, we denote, by that expression, the following fact:—Some *indeterminate* body or *uncertain* aggregate of persons regards a kind of conduct with a sentiment of aversion or liking: Or (changing the expression) that indeterminate body opines unfavourably or favourably of a given kind of conduct. In *consequence* of that sentiment, or in *consequence* of that opinion, it is likely that they or some of them will be displeased with a party who shall pursue or not pursue conduct of that kind. And, in *consequence* of that displeasure, it is likely that *some* party (*what* party being undetermined) will visit the party provoking it with some evil or another.

The body by whose opinion the law is said to be set, does not *command*, expressly or tacitly, that conduct of the given kind shall be forborne or pursued. For, since it is not a body precisely determined or certain, it cannot, *as a body*, express or intimate a wish. *As a body*, it cannot *signify* a wish by oral or written words, or by positive or negative deportment. The so called *law* or *rule* which its opinion is said to impose, is merely the *sentiment* which it feels, or is merely the *opinion* which it holds, in regard to a kind of conduct.

A determinate member of the body, who opines or feels with the body, may doubtless be moved or impelled, by that very opinion or sentiment, to *command* that conduct of the kind shall be forborne or pursued. But the command expressed or intimated by that determinate party is not a law or rule imposed by general opinion. It is a law properly so called, set by a determinate author.—For example, The so called law of nations consists of opinions or sentiments current among nations generally. It therefore is not law properly so called. But one supreme government may doubtless *command* another to forbear from a kind of conduct which the law of nations condemns. And, though it is fashioned on law which is law improperly so called, this command is a law in the proper signification of the term. Speaking precisely, the command is a rule of positive morality set by a determinate author. For, as no supreme government is in a state of subjection to another, the government commanding does not command in its character of political superior. If the government receiving the command were in a state of subjection to the other, the command, though fashioned on the law of nations, would amount to a positive law.

The foregoing description of a law set by general opinion imports the following consequences:—that the party who will enforce it against any future transgressor is never determinate and assignable. The party who actually enforces it against an actual transgressor is, of necessity, certain. In other words, if an actual transgressor be harmed in consequence of the breach of the law, and in consequence of that displeasure which the breach of the law has provoked, he receives the harm from a party, who, of necessity, is certain. But that certain party is not the executor of a *command* proceeding from the uncertain body. He has not been authorised by that uncertain body to enforce that so called law which its opinion is said to establish. He is not in the position of a minister of justice appointed by the sovereign or state to execute commands which it issues. He harms the actual offender against the so called law or (to speak in analogical language) he applies the sanction annexed to it, of his own spontaneous movement. Consequently, though a party who actually enforces it is, of necessity, certain, the party who will enforce it against any future offender is never determinate and assignable.

A brief statement of the analogy between a law proper and a law set or imposed by general opinion.

It follows from the foregoing reasons, that a so called law set by general opinion is not a law in the proper signification of the term. It also follows from the same reasons, that it is not armed with a sanction, and does not impose a duty, in the proper acceptation of the expressions. For a sanction properly so called is an evil annexed to a command. And duty properly so called is an obnoxiousness to evils of the kind.

But a so called law set by general opinion is closely analogous to a law in the proper signification of the term. And, by consequence, the so called sanction with which the former is armed, and the so called duty which the former imposes, are closely analogous to a sanction and a duty in the proper acceptation of the expressions.

The analogy between a law in the proper signification of the term and a so called law set by general opinion, may be stated briefly in the following manner: —1. In the case of a law properly so called, the determinate individual or body by whom the law is established wishes that conduct of a kind shall be forborne or pursued. In the case of a law imposed by general opinion, a wish that conduct of a kind shall be forborne or pursued is felt by the uncertain body whose general opinion imposes it. 2. If a party obliged by the law proper shall not comply with the wish of the determinate individual or body, he probably will suffer, in *consequence* of his not complying, the evil or inconvenience annexed to the law as a sanction. If a party obnoxious to their displeasure shall not comply with the wish of the uncertain body of persons, he probably will suffer, in *consequence* of his not complying, some evil or inconvenience from some party or another. 3. By the sanction annexed to the law proper, the parties obliged are inclined to act or forbear agreeably to its injunctions or prohibitions. By the evil which probably will follow the displeasure of the uncertain body, the parties obnoxious are inclined to act or forbear agreeably to the sentiment or opinion which is styled analogically a law. 4. In consequence of the law properly so called, the conduct of the parties obliged has a steadiness, constancy, or uniformity, which, without the existence of the law, their conduct would probaby want. In consequence of the sentiment or opinion which is styled analogically a law, the conduct of the parties obnoxious has a steadiness, constancy, or uniformity which, without the existence of that sentiment in the uncertain body of persons, their conduct would hardly present. For they who are obnoxious to the sanction which arms the law proper, commonly do or forbear from the acts which the law enjoins or forbids; whilst they who are obnoxious to the evil which will probably follow the displeasure of the uncertain body of persons, commonly do or forbear from the acts which the body approves or dislikes.—Many of the applications of the term *law* which are merely metaphorical or figurative, were probably suggested (as I shall show hereafter) by that uniformity of conduct which is consequent on a law proper.

Distinction between a *determinate*, and an *indeterminate* body of single or individual persons.

In the foregoing analysis of a law set by general opinion, the meaning of the expression '*indeterminate* body of persons' is indicated rather than explained. To complete my analysis of a law set by general opinion (and to abridge that analysis of sovereignty which I shall place in my sixth lecture), I will here insert a concise exposition of the following pregnant distinction: namely, the distinction between a *determinate*, and an *indeterminate* body of single or individual persons.—If my exposition of the distinction shall appear obscure and crabbed, my hearers (I hope) will recollect that the distinction could hardly be expounded in lucid and flowing expressions.

I will first describe the distinction in general or abstract terms, and will then exemplify and illustrate the general or abstract description.

If a body of persons be determinate, *all* the persons who compose it are determined and assignable, or *every* person who belongs to it is determined and may be indicated.

But determinate bodies are of two kinds.

A determinate body of one of those kinds is distinguished by the following marks:—1. The body is composed of persons determined specifically or individually, or determined by characters or descriptions respectively appropriate to themselves. 2. Though every individual member must of necessity answer to many generic descriptions, every individual member is a member of the determinate body, not by reason of his answering to any generic description but by reason of his bearing his specific or appropriate character.

A determinate body of the other of those kinds is distinguished by the following marks:—1. It comprises *all* the persons who belong to a given class, or who belong respectively to two or more of such classes. In other words, *every* person who answers to a given generic description, or to any of two or more given generic descriptions, is also a member of the determinate body. 2. Though every individual member is of necessity determined by a specific or appropriate character, every individual member is a member of the determinate body, not by reason of his bearing his specific or appropriate character, but by reason of his answering to the given generic description.

If a body be indeterminate, *all* the persons who compose it are not determined and assignable. Or (changing

G

the expression) *every* person who belongs to it is not determined, and, therefore, cannot be indicated.—For an indeterminate body consists of *some* of the persons who belong to another and larger aggregate. But *how many of those persons* are members of the indeterminate body, or *which of those persons in particular* are members of the indeterminate body, is not and cannot be known completely and exactly.

For example, The trading firm or partnership of A B and C is a determinate body of the kind first described above. Every member of the firm is determined specifically, or by a character or description peculiar or appropriate to himself. And every member of the firm belongs to the determinate body, not by reason of his answering to any generic description, but by reason of his bearing his specific or appropriate character. It is as being that very individual person that A B or C is a limb of the partnership.

The British Parliament for the time being, is a determinate body of the kind lastly described above. It comprises the *only* person who answers for the time being to the generic description of king. It comprises *every* person belonging to the class of peers who are entitled for the time being to vote in the upper house. It comprises *every* person belonging to the class of commoners who for the time being represent the commons in parliament. And, though every member of the British Parliament is of necessity determined by a specific or appropriate character, he is not a member of the parliament by reason of his bearing that character, but by reason of his answering to the given generic description. It is not as being the individual George, but as being the individual who answers to the generic description of king, that George is king of Britain and Ireland, and a limb of the determinate body which is sovereign or supreme therein. It is not as being the individual

Grey, or as being the individual Peel, that Grey is a member of the upper house, or Peel a member of the lower. Grey is a member of the upper house, as belonging to the class of peers entitled to vote therein. Peel is a member of the lower house, as answering the generic description 'representative of the commons in parliament.'—The generic characters of the persons who compose the British Parliament, are here described generally, and, therefore, inaccurately. To describe those generic characters minutely and accurately, were to render a complete description of the intricate and perplexed system which is styled the British Constitution.—A maxim of that Constitution may illustrate the subject of the present paragraph. The meaning of the maxim, 'the king never dies,' may, I believe, be rendered in the following manner. Though an actual occupant of the kingly office is human, mortal, and transient, the duration of the office itself has no possible limit which the British Constitution can contemplate. And on the death of an actual occupant, the office instantly devolves to that individual person who bears the generic character which entitles to take the crown: to that individual person who is then heir to the crown, according to the generic description contained in the Act of Settlement.

To exemplify the foregoing description of an indeterminate body, I will revert to the nature of a law set by general opinion. Where a so called law is set by *general* opinion, *most* of the persons who belong to a determinate body or class opine or feel alike in regard to a kind of conduct. But the number of that majority, or the several individuals who compose it, cannot be fixed or assigned with perfect fulness or accuracy. For example, A law set or imposed by the *general* opinion of a nation, by the *general* opinion of a legislative assembly, by the *general* opinion of a profession, or by the *general* opinion of a club, is an opinion or sentiment, relating to conduct of a kind, which is held or felt by *most* of those who belong to that certain body. But how many of that body, or which of that body in particular, hold or feel that given opinion or sentiment, is not and cannot be known completely and correctly. Consequently, that majority of the certain body forms a body uncertain. Or (changing the expression) the body which is formed by that majority is an indeterminate portion of a determinate body or aggregate.—Generally speaking, therefore, an indeterminate body is an indeterminate portion of a body determinate or certain. But a body or class of persons may also be indeterminate, because it consists of persons of a vague generic character. For example, The body or class of gentlemen consists of individual persons whose generic character of gentleman cannot be described precisely. Whether a given man were a genuine gentleman or not, is a question which different men might answer in different ways.—An indeterminate body may therefore be indeterminate after a twofold manner. It may consist of an uncertain portion of an uncertain body or class. For example, A law set or imposed by the *general* opinion of gentlemen is an opinion or sentiment of *most* of those who are commonly deemed gentlemanly. But what proportion of the class holds the opinion in question, or what proportion of the class feels the sentiment in question, is not less indeterminate than the generic character of gentlemen. The body by whose opinion the so called law is set, is, therefore, an uncertain portion of an uncertain body or aggregate.—And here I may briefly remark, that a certain portion of a certain body is itself a body determinate. For example, The persons who answer the generic description 'representative of the commons in parliament,' are a certain portion of the persons who answer the generic description 'commoner of the united kingdom.' A select committee of the representative body, or any portion of the body happening to form a house, is a certain or determined portion of the representatives of the commons in parliament. And, in any of these or similar cases, the certain portion of the certain body is itself a body determinate.

A determinate body of persons is capable of *corporate* conduct, or is capable, *as a body*, of positive or negative deportment. Whether it consists of persons determined by specific characters, or of persons determined or defined by a character or characters generic, every person who belongs to it is determined and may be indicated. In the first case, every person who belongs to it may be indicated by his specific character. In the second case, every person who belongs to it is also knowable: For *every* person who answers to the given generic description, or who answers to any of the given generic descriptions, is therefore a member of the body. Consequently, the entire body, or any proportion of its members, is capable, *as a body*, of positive or negative deportment: As, for example, of meeting at determinate times and places; of issuing expressly or tacitly a law or other command; of choosing and deputing representatives to perform its intentions or wishes; of receiving obedience from others, or from any of its own members.

But an indeterminate body is incapable of *corporate* conduct, or is incapable, *as a body*, of positive or negative deportment. An indeterminate body is incapable of corporate conduct, inasmuch as the several persons of whom it consists cannot be known and indicated completely and correctly. In case a portion of its members act or forbear in concert, that given portion of its members is, by that very concert, a determinate or certain body. For example, A law set or imposed by the *general* opinion of barristers condemns the sordid practice of hugging or caressing attorneys. And as those whose opinion or sentiment sets the so called law are an indeterminate part of the determinate body of barristers, they form a body uncertain and incapable of corporate conduct. But in case a number or portion of that uncertain body assembled and passed a resolution to check the practice of hugging, that number or portion of that uncertain body would be, by the very act, a certain body or aggregate. It would form a determinate body consisting of the determined individuals who assembled and passed the resolution.—A law imposed by general opinion may be the cause of a law in the proper acceptation of the term. But the law properly so called, which is the consequent or effect, utterly differs from the so called law which is the antecedent or cause. The one is an opinion or sentiment of an uncertain body of persons; of a body essentially incapable of joint or corporate conduct. The other is set or established by the positive or negative deportment of a certain individual or aggregate.

For the purpose of rendering my exposition as little intricate as possible, I have supposed that a body of persons, forming a body determinate, either consists of persons determined by specific characters, or of persons determined or defined by a generic description or descriptions.—But a body of persons, forming a body determinate, may consist of persons determined by specific or appropriate characters, and also of persons determined by a character or characters generic. Let us suppose, for example, that the individual Oliver Cromwell was sovereign or supreme in England: or that the individual Cromwell, and the individuals Ireton and Fleetwood, formed a triumvirate which was sovereign in that country. Let us suppose, moreover, that Cromwell, or the triumvirs, convened a house of commons elected in the ancient manner: and that

Cromwell, or the triumvirs, yielded a part in the sovereignty to this representative body. Now the sovereign or supreme body formed by Cromwell and the house, or the sovereign and supreme body formed by the triumvirs and the house, would have consisted of a person or persons determined or defined specifically, and of persons determined or defined by a generic character or description. The members of the house of commons would have been members of the sovereign body, as answering the generic description 'representatives of the commons in parliament.' But it is as being the very individual Cromwell, or as being the very individuals Cromwell, Ireton, and Fleetwood, that he or they would have formed a limb of the sovereign or supreme body. It is not as answering to a given generic description, or as acquiring a part in the sovereignty by a given generic mode, that he or they would have shared the sovereignty with the body representing the people.—A body of persons, forming a body determinate, may also consist of persons determined or defined specifically, and determined or defined moreover by a character or characters generic. A select committee of a body representing a people or nation, consists of individual persons named or appointed specifically to sit on that given committee. But those specific individuals could not be members of the committee, unless they answered the generic description 'representative of the people or nation.'

It follows from the exposition immediately preceding that the one or the number which is sovereign in an independent political society is a *determinate* individual person or a *determinate* body of persons. If the sovereign one or number were not determinate or certain, it could not command expressly or tacitly, and could not be an object of obedience to the subject members of the community.—Inasmuch as this principle is amply explained by the exposition immediately preceding, I shall refer to it in my sixth lecture, as to a principle sufficiently known. The intricate and difficult analysis which I shall place in that discourse, will thus be somewhat facilitated, and not inconsiderably abridged.

As closely connected with the matter of the exposition immediately preceding, the following remark concerning supreme government may be put commodiously in the present place.—In order that a supreme government may possess much stability, and that the society wherein it is supreme may enjoy much tranquillity, the persons who take the sovereignty in the way of succession, must take or acquire by a given generic mode, or by given generic modes. Or (changing the expression) they must take by reason of their answering to a given generic description, or by reason of their respectively answering to given generic descriptions.—For example, the Roman Emperors or Princes (who were virtually monarchs or autocrators) did not succeed to the sovereignty of the Roman Empire or World by a given generic title: by a mode of acquisition given or preordained, and susceptible of generic description. It was neither as lineal descendant of Julius Cæsar or Augustus, nor by the testament or other disposition of the last possessor of the throne, nor by the appointment or nomination of the Roman people or senate, nor by the election of a determinate body formed of the military class, nor by any mode of acquisition generic and preordained, that every successive Emperor, or every successive Prince, acquired the virtual sovereignty of the Roman Empire or World. Every successive Emperor acquired by a mode of acquisition which was purely anomalous or accidental: which had not been predetermined by any law or custom, or by any positive law or rule of positive morality. Every actual occupant of the Imperial office or dignity (whatever may have been the manner wherein he had gotten possession) was obeyed, for the time, by the bulk of the military class; was acknowledged, of course, by the impotent and trembling senate; and received submission, of course, from the inert and helpless mass which inhabited the city and provinces. By reason of this irregularity in the succession to the virtual sovereignty, the demise of an Emperor was not uncommonly followed by a shorter or longer dissolution of the general supreme government. Since no one could claim to succeed by a given generic title, or as answering for the time being to a given generic description, a contest for the prostrate sovereignty almost inevitably arose between the more influential of the actual military chiefs. And till one of the military candidates had vanquished and crushed his rivals, and had forced with an armed hand his way to the vacant throne, the generality or bulk of the inhabitants in the Roman Empire or World could hardly render obedience to one and the same superior. By reason, also of this irregularity in the succession to the Imperial office, the general and habitual obedience to an actual occupant of the office was always extremely precarious. For, since he was not occupant by a given generic title, or by reason of his having answered to a given generic description, the title of any rebel, who might anyhow eject him, would not have been less legitimate or less constitutional than his own. Or (speaking with greater precision) there was no mode of acquiring the office, which could be styled legitimate, or which could be styled constitutional: which was susceptible of generic description, and which had been predetermined by positive law or morality. There was not, in the Roman World, any determinate person, whom positive law or morality had pointed out to its inhabitants as the exclusively appropriate object of general and habitual

G*

obedience.—The reasoning which applies in the case of a monarchy, will also apply, with few variations, in the case of a government by a number. Unless the members of the supreme body held their respective stations by titles generic and fixed, the given supreme government must be extremely unstable, and the given society wherein it is supreme must often be torn by contests for the possession of shares in the sovereignty.

Laws set by *general* opinion, or opinions or sentiments of *indeterminate bodies*, are the only opinions or sentiments that have gotten the name of *laws*. But an opinion or sentiment held or felt by an *individual*, or by *all* the members of a *certain aggregate*, may be as closely analogous to a law proper as the opinion or sentiment of an indeterminate body.

Before I close my analysis of those laws improperly so called which are closely analogous to laws in the proper acceptation of the term, I must advert to a seeming caprice of current or established language.

A law set or imposed by *general* opinion, is an opinion or sentiment, regarding conduct of a kind, which is held or felt by an *indeterminate body*: that is to say, an indeterminate portion of a certain or uncertain aggregate.

Now a like opinion or sentiment held or felt by an *individual*, or held or felt *universally* by the members of a *body determinate*, may be as closely analogous to a law proper as a so called law set by *general* opinion. It may bear an analogy to a law in the proper acceptation of the term, exactly or nearly resembling the analogy to a law proper which is borne by an opinion or sentiment of an *indeterminate body*. An opinion, for example, of a patron, in regard to conduct of a kind, may be a law or rule to his own dependent or dependants, just as a like opinion of an indeterminate body is a law or rule to all who might suffer by provoking its displeasure. And whether a like opinion be held by an uncertain aggregate, or be held by *every* member of a precisely determined body, its analogy to a law proper is exactly or nearly the same.

But when we speak of a law set or imposed by opinion, we always or commonly mean (I rather incline to believe) a law set or imposed by *general* opinion: that is to say, an opinion or sentiment, regarding conduct of a kind, which is held or felt by an uncertain body or class. The term *law*, or *law set by opinion*, is never or rarely applied to a like opinion or sentiment of a precisely determined party: that is to say, a like opinion or sentiment held or felt by an individual, or held or felt universally by the members of a certain aggregate.

This seeming caprice of current or established language probably arose from the following causes.

An opinion, regarding conduct, which is held by an individual person, or which is held universally by a *small* determinate body, is commonly followed by consequences of comparatively trifling importance. The circle of the persons to whom its influence reaches, or whose desires or conduct it affects or determines, is rarely extensive. The analogy which such opinions bear to laws proper, has, therefore, attracted little attention, and has, therefore, not gotten them the name of *laws*. —An opinion held universally by a *large* determinate body, is not less largely influential, or is more largely influential, than an opinion of an uncertain portion of the same certain aggregate. But since the determinate body is large or numerous, an opinion held by *all* its members can hardly be distinguished from an opinion held by *most* of its members. An opinion held *universally* by the members of the body determinate, is, therefore, equivalent in practice to a *general* opinion of the body, and is, therefore, classed with the laws which *general* opinion imposes.

Deferring to this seeming caprice of current or established language, I have forborne from ranking sentiments of precisely determined parties with the laws improperly so called which are closely analogous to the proper. I have restricted that description to sentiments, regarding conduct, of uncertain bodies or classes. My foregoing analysis or exposition of laws of that description, is, therefore, an analysis of laws set by *general* opinion.

If the description ought to embrace (as, I think, it certainly ought) opinions, regarding conduct, of precisely determined parties, my foregoing analysis or exposition will still be correct substantially. With a few slight and obvious changes, my foregoing analysis of a law set by *general* opinion will serve as an analysis of a law set by *any* opinion: of a law set by the opinion of an indeterminate body, and of a law set by the opinion of a precisely determined party.

For the character or essential difference of a law imposed by opinion, is this: that the law is not a *command*, issued expressly or tacitly, but is merely an *opinion* or *sentiment*, relating to conduct of a kind, which is held or felt by an uncertain body, or by a determinate party. A wish that conduct of the kind shall shall be pursued or forborne, is not *signified*, expressly or tacitly, by that uncertain body, or that determinate party: nor does that body or party *intend* to inflict an evil upon any whose conduct may deviate from the given opinion or sentiment. The opinion or sentiment is merely an opinion or sentiment, although it subjects a transgressor to the chance of a consequent evil, and may even lead to a command regarding conduct of the kind.

Between the opinion or sentiment of the indeterminate body, and the opinion or sentiment of the precisely determined party, there is merely the following difference:—The precisely determined party is *capable* of issuing a command in pursuance of the opinion or sentiment. But the uncertain body is not. For, being essentially incapable of joint or corporate conduct, it cannot, as a body, signify a wish or desire, and cannot, as a body, hold an intention or purpose.

The foregoing distribution

It appears from the expositions in the preceding portion of my discourse, that laws properly so called, with *of laws proper and of such improper laws as are closely analogous to the proper, briefly recapitulated.*

such improper laws as are closely analogous to the proper, are of three capital classes:—1. The law of God, or the laws of God. 2. Positive law, or positive laws. 3. Positive morality, rules of positive morality, or positive moral rules.

It also appears from the same expositions, that positive moral rules are of two species:—1. Those positive moral rules which are express or tacit commands, and which are therefore laws in the proper acceptation of the term. 2. Those laws improperly so called (but closely analogous to laws in the proper acceptation of the term) which are set by general opinion, or are set by opinion: which are set by opinions of uncertain bodies; or by opinions of uncertain bodies, and opinions of determinate parties.

The sanctions, proper and improper, by which those laws are respectively enforced; the duties, proper and improper, which those laws respectively impose; and the rights, proper and improper, which those laws respectively confer.

The sanctions annexed to the laws of God, may be styled *religious*.—The sanctions annexed to positive laws, may be styled, emphatically, *legal*: for the laws to which they are annexed, are styled, simply and emphatically, *laws* or *law*. Or, as every positive law supposes a πόλις or *civitas*, or supposes a society political and independent, the epithet *political* may be applied to the sanctions by which such laws are enforced.—Of the sanctions which enforce compliance with positive moral rules, some are sanctions properly so called, and others are styled *sanctions* by an analogical extension of the term: that is to say, some are annexed to rules which are laws imperative and proper, and others enforce the rules which are laws set by opinion. Since rules of either species may be styled positive morality, the sanctions which enforce compliance with rules of either species may be styled *moral* sanctions. Or (changing the expression) we may say of rules of either species, that they are sanctioned or enforced *morally*.[8]

[8] The term *morality*, *moral*, or *morally*, is often opposed tacitly to *immorality*, *immoral*, or *immorally*, and imports that

The duties imposed by the laws of God may be styled *religious*.—The duties imposed by positive laws, may be styled, emphatically, *legal*: or, like the laws by which they are imposed, they may be said to be sanctioned *legally*.—Of the duties imposed by positive moral rules, some are duties properly so called, and others are styled *duties* by an analogical extension of the term: that is to say, some are creatures of rules which are laws imperative and proper, and others are creatures of the rules which are laws set by opinion. Like the sanctions proper and improper by which they are respectively enforced, these duties proper and improper may be styled *moral*. Or we may say of the duties, as of the rules by which they are imposed, that they are sanctioned or enforced *morally*.

Every right supposes a duty incumbent on a party or parties other than the party entitled. Through the imposition of that corresponding duty, the right was conferred. Through the continuance of that corresponding duty, the right continues to exist. If that corresponding duty be the creature of a law imperative, the right is a right properly so called. If that corresponding duty be the creature of a law improper, the right is styled a *right* by an analogical extension of the term.—Consequently, a right existing through a duty imposed

the object to which it is applied or referred is approved of by the speaker or writer. But by the term *morality*, I merely denote the human rules which I style 'positive morality'. And by the terms '*moral* sanctions', 'rules sanctioned *morally*', '*moral* duties or rights', and 'duties or rights sanctioned *morally*', I merely mean that the rules to which the sanctions are annexed, or by which the duties or rights are imposed or conferred, are positive moral rules: rules bearing the generic character which I have stated and explained above. If I mean to praise or blame a positive human rule, or a duty or right which the rule imposes or confers, I style it consonant to the law of God, or contrary to the law of God. Or (what, in effect, is the same thing) I style it generally useful, or generally pernicious.

by the law of God, or a right existing through a duty imposed by positive law, is a right properly so called. Where the duty is the creature of a positive moral rule, the nature of the corresponding right depends upon the nature of the rule. If the rule imposing the duty be a law imperative and proper, the right is a right properly so called. If the rule imposing the duty be a law set by opinion, the right is styled a *right* through an analogical extension of the term.—Rights conferred by the law of God, or rights existing through duties imposed by the law of God, may be styled *Divine*.—Rights conferred by positive law, or rights existing through duties imposed by positive law, may be styled, emphatically, *legal*. Or it may be said of rights conferred by positive law, that they are sanctioned or protected *legally*.—The rights proper and improper which are conferred by positive morality, may be styled *moral*. Or it may be said of rights conferred by positive morality, that they are sanctioned or protected *morally*.[9]

The law of God, positive law, and positive morality, sometimes *coincide*, sometimes do *not* coincide, and sometimes *conflict*.

The body or aggregate of laws which may be styled the law of God, the body or aggregate of laws which may be styled positive law, and the body or aggregate of laws which may be styled positive morality, sometimes *coincide*, sometimes do *not* coincide, and sometimes *conflict*.

One of these bodies of laws *coincides* with another,

[9] Here I may briefly observe, that, in order to a complete determination of the appropriate province of jurisprudence, it is necessary to explain the import of the term *right*. For, as I have stated already, numerous positive laws proceed directly from subjects through *rights* conferred upon the authors by supreme political superiors. And, for various other reasons which will appear in my sixth lecture, the appropriate province of jurisprudence cannot be defined completely, unless an explanation of the term *right* constitute a part of the definition. But, in order to an explanation of right *in abstract* (or in order to an explanation of the nature which is common to *all* rights), I must previously explain the differences of the principal kinds of rights,

when acts, which are enjoined or forbidden by the former, are also enjoined, or are also forbidden by the latter.—For example, The killing which is styled *murder* is forbidden by the positive law of every political society: it is also forbidden by a so called law which the general opinion of the society has set or imposed: it is also forbidden by the law of God as known through the principle of utility. The murderer commits a crime, or he violates a positive law: he commits a conventional immorality, or he violates a so called law which general opinion has established: he commits a sin, or he violates the law of God. He is obnoxious to punishment, or other evil, to be inflicted by sovereign authority: he is obnoxious to the hate and the spontaneous ill-offices of the generality or bulk of the society: he is obnoxious to evil or pain to be suffered here or hereafter by the immediate appointment of the Deity.

One of these bodies of laws does *not* coincide with another, when acts, which are enjoined or forbidden by the former, are not enjoined, or are not forbidden by the latter.—For example, Though smuggling is forbidden by positive law, and (speaking generally) is not less pernicious than theft, it is not forbidden by the opinions or sentiments of the ignorant or unreflecting. Where the impost or tax is itself of pernicious tendency, smuggling is hardly forbidden by the opinions or sentiments

with the meaning of various terms which the term *right* implies. And as that previous explanation cannot be given with effect, till positive law is distinguished from the objects to which it is related, it follows that an explanation of the expression *right* cannot enter into the attempt to determine the province of jurisprudence.

At every step which he takes on his long and scabrous road, a difficulty similar to that which I have now endeavoured to suggest encounters the expositor of the science. As every department of the science is implicated with every other, any detached exposition of a single and separate department is inevitably a fragment more or less imperfect.

of any: And it is therefore practised by any without the slightest shame, or without the slightest fear of incurring general censure. Such, for instance, is the case where the impost or tax is laid upon the foreign commodity, not for the useful purpose of raising a public revenue, but for the absurd and mischievous purpose of protecting a domestic manufacture.—Offences against the game laws are also in point: for they are not offences against positive morality, although they are forbidden by positive law. A gentleman is not dishonoured, or generally shunned by gentlemen, though he shoots without a qualification. A peasant who wires hares escapes the censure of peasants, though the squires, as doing justiceship, send him to the prison and the tread-mill.

One of these bodies of laws *conflicts* with another, when acts, which are enjoined or forbidden by the former, are forbidden or enjoined by the latter.—For example, In most of the nations of modern Europe, the practice of duelling is forbidden by positive law. It is also at variance with the law which is received in most of those nations as having been set by the Deity in the way of express revelation. But in spite of positive law, and in spite of his religious convictions, a man of the class of gentlemen may be forced by the law of honour to give or to take a challenge. If he forebore from giving, or if he declined a challenge, he might incur the general contempt of gentlemen or men of honour, and might meet with slights and insults sufficient to embitter his existence. The negative *legal* duty which certainly is incumbent upon him, and the negative *religious* duty to which he believes himself subject, are therefore mastered and controlled by that positive *moral* duty which arises from the so-called law set by the opinion of his class.

The simple and obvious considerations to which I

have now adverted, are often overlooked by legislators. If they fancy a practice pernicious, or hate it they know not why, they proceed, without further thought, to forbid it by positive law. They forget that positive law may be superfluous or impotent, and therefore may lead to nothing but purely gratuitous vexation. They forget that the moral or the religious sentiments of the community may already suppress the practice as completely as it can be suppressed: or that, if the practice is favoured by those moral or religious sentiments the strongest possible fear which legal pains can inspire may be mastered by a stronger fear of other and conflicting sanctions.[10]

In consequence of the frequent coincidence of positive law and morality, and of positive law and the law

The acts and forbearances, which, according to the theory of utility, are objects of the law of God: and the acts and forbearances, which, according to the same theory, ought to be objects respectively of positive morality and law.

[10] There are classes of useful acts which it were useless to enjoin, and classes of mischievous acts which it were useless to forbid: for we are sufficiently prone to the useful, and sufficiently averse from the mischievous acts, without the incentives and restraints applied by religious sanctions, or by sanctions legal or moral. And, assuming that general utility is the index to the Divine commands, we may fairly infer that acts of such classes are not enjoined or forbidden by the law of God; that he no more enjoins or forbids acts of the classes in question, than he enjoins or forbids such acts as are generally pernicious or useful.

There are also classes of acts, generally useful or pernicious, which demand the incentives or restraints applied by religious sanctions or by sanctions legal or moral. Without the incentives and restraints applied by religious sanctions, or applied by sanctions legal or moral, we are not sufficiently prone to those which are generally useful, and are not sufficiently averse from those which are generally pernicious. And, assuming that general utility is the index to the Divine commands, all these classes of useful, and all these classes of pernicious acts, are enjoined and forbidden respectively by the law of God.

Being enjoined or being forbidden by the Deity, all these classes of useful, and all these classes of pernicious acts, ought to be enjoined or forbidden by positive morality: that is to say, by the positive morality which consists of opinions or sentiments. But, this notwithstanding, some of these classes of acts

of God, the true nature and fountain of positive law is often absurdly mistaken by writers upon jurisprudence. Where positive law has been fashioned on positive morality, or where positive law has been fashioned on the law of God, they forget that the copy is the creature of the sovereign, and impute it to the author of the model.

For example: Customary laws are positive laws fashioned by judicial legislation upon pre-existing customs. Now, till they become the grounds of judicial decisions upon cases, and are clothed with legal sanctions by the sovereign one or number, the customs are merely rules set by opinions of the governed, and sanctioned or enforced morally: Though, when they become the reasons of judicial decisions upon cases, and are clothed with legal sanctions by the sovereign one

ought not to be enjoined or forbidden by positive law. Some of these classes of acts ought not to be enjoined or forbidden even by the positive morality which consists of imperative rules.

Every act or forbearance that ought to be an object of positive law, ought to be an object of the positive morality which consists of opinions or sentiments. Every act or forbearance that ought to be an object of the latter, is an object of the law of God as construed by the principle of utility. But the circle embraced by the law of God, and which may be embraced to advantage by positive morality, is larger than the circle which can be embraced to advantage by positive law. Inasmuch as the two circles have one and the same centre, the whole of the region comprised by the latter is also comprised by the former. But the whole of the region comprised by the former is not comprised by the latter.

To distinguish the acts and forbearances that ought to be objects of law, from those that ought to be abandoned to the exclusive cognisance of morality, is, perhaps, the hardest of the problems which the science of ethics presents. The only existing approach to a solution of the problem, may be found in the writings of Mr. Bentham: who, in most of the departments of the two great branches of ethics, has accomplished more for the advancement of the science than all his predecessors put together.—See, in particular, his *Principles of Morals and Legislation*, ch. xvii.

or number, the customs are rules of positive law as well as of positive morality. But, because the customs were observed by the governed before they were clothed with sanctions by the sovereign one or number, it is fancied that customary laws exist *as positive laws* by the institution of the private persons with whom the customs originated.—Admitting the conceit, and reasoning by analogy, we ought to consider the sovereign the author of the positive morality which is often a consequence of positive law. Where a positive law, not fashioned on a custom, is favourably received by the governed, and enforced by their opinions or sentiments, we must deem the so called law, set by those opinions or sentiments, a law imperative and proper of the supreme political superior.

Again: The portion of positive law which is parcel of the *law of nature* (or, in the language of the classical jurists, which is parcel of the *jus gentium*) is often supposed to emanate, even as positive law, from a Divine or Natural source. But (admitting the distinction of positive law into law natural and law positive) it is manifest that law natural, considered as a portion of positive, is the creature of human sovereigns, and not of the Divine monarch. To say that it emanates, as positive law, from a Divine or Natural source, is to confound positive law with law whereon it is fashioned, or with law whereunto it conforms.

The foregoing distribution of laws proper, and of such improper laws as are closely analogous to the proper, tallies,

The foregoing distribution of laws proper, and of such improper laws as are closely analogous to the proper, tallies in the main, with a division of laws which is given incidentally by Locke in his Essay on Human Understanding. And since this division of laws, or of the sources of duties or obligations, is recommended by the great authority which the writer has justly acquired, I gladly append it to my own division or analysis. The passage of his essay in which the division occurs, is part of an inquiry into the nature of *relation*, and is therefore concerned indirectly with the nature and kinds of *law*. With the exclusion of all that is foreign to the nature and kinds of law, with the exclusion of a few expressions which are obviously redundant, and with the correction of a few expressions which are somewhat obscure, the passage containing the divisions may be rendered in the words following:[11]

in the main, with a division of laws which is given incidentally by Locke in his Essay on Human Understanding.

'The conformity or disagreement men's voluntary actions have to a rule to which they are referred, and by which they are judged of, is a sort of relation which may be called *moral relation*.

'Human actions, when with their various ends, objects, manners, and circumstances, they are framed into distinct complex ideas, are, as has been shown, so many *mixed modes*, a great part whereof have names annexed to them. Thus, supposing gratitude to be a readiness to acknowledge and return kindness received, or *polygamy* to be the having more wives than one at once, when we frame these notions thus in our minds, we have there so many determined ideas of mixed modes.

'But this is not all that concerns our actions. It is not enough to have determined ideas of them, and to

[11] Locke's division or analysis is far from being complete, and the language in which it is stated is often extremely unapt. It must, however, be remembered, that the nature of *relation* generally (and not the nature of *law*, with its principal kinds) is the appropriate object of his inquiry. Allowing for the defects, which, therefore, were nearly inevitable, his analysis is strikingly accurate. It evinces that matchless power of precise and just thinking, with that religious regard for general utility and truth, which marked the incomparable man who emancipated human reason from the yoke of mystery and jargon. And from this his incidental excursion into the field of law and morality, and from other passages of his essay wherein he touches upon them, we may infer the important services which he would have rendered to the science of ethics, if, complying with the instances of Molyneux, he had examined the subject exactly.

know what names belong to such and such combinations of ideas. We have a further and greater concernment. And that is, to know whether such actions are morally good or bad.

'Good or evil is nothing but pleasure or pain, or that which occasions or procures pleasure or pain to us. *Moral good or evil*, then, is only the conformity or disagreement of our voluntary actions to some law, whereby good or evil is drawn on us by the will and power of the law-maker: which good or evil, pleasure or pain, attending our observance or breach of the law, by the decree of the law-maker, is that we call reward or punishment.

'Of these moral rules or laws, to which men generally refer, and by which they judge of the rectitude or pravity of their actions, there seem to me to be three sorts, with their three different enforcements, or rewards and punishments. For since it would be utterly in vain to suppose a rule set to the free actions of man, without annexing to it some enforcement of good and evil to determine his will, we must, wherever we suppose a law, suppose also some reward or punishment annexed to that law. It would be in vain for one intelligent being to set a rule to the actions of another, if he had it not in his power to reward the compliance with, and punish deviation from his rule, by some good and evil that is not the natural product and consequence of the action itself: for that being a natural convenience or inconvenience, would operate of itself without a law. This, if I mistake not, is the true nature of all *law* properly so called.

'The laws that men generally refer their actions to, to judge of their rectitude or obliquity, seem to me to be these three: 1. The *Divine* law. 2. The *civil* law. 3. The law of *opinion* or *reputation*, if I may so call it.—By the relation they bear to the first of these, men judge whether their actions are sins or duties: by the second, whether they be criminal or innocent: and by the third, whether they be virtues or vices.

'By the *Divine* law, I mean that law which God hath set to the actions of men, whether promulgated to them by the light of nature, or the voice of revelation. This is the only true touchstone of *moral rectitude*. And by comparing them to this law, it is, that men judge of the most considerable *moral good* or *evil* of their actions: that is, whether as *duties* or *sins*, they are like to procure them happiness or misery from the hands of the Almighty.

'The *civil* law, the rule set by the commonwealth to the actions of those who belong to it, is a rule to which men refer their actions, to judge whether they be *criminal* or no. This law nobody overlooks, the rewards and punishments that enforce it being ready at hand, and suitable to the power that makes it: which is the force of the commonwealth, engaged to protect the lives, liberties and possessions of those who live according to its law, and has power to take away life, liberty or goods from him who disobeys.

'The law of *opinion* or *reputation* is another law that men generally refer their actions to, to judge of their rectitude or obliquity.

'*Virtue* and *vice* are names pretended, and supposed everywhere to stand for actions in their own nature right or wrong: and as far as they really are so applied, they so far are coincident with the Divine law above mentioned. But yet, whatever is pretended, this is visible, that these names *virtue* and *vice*, in the particular instances of their application through the several nations and societies of men in the world, are constantly attributed to such actions only as in each country and society are in reputation or discredit. Nor is it to be thought strange, that men everywhere should give the name of *virtue* to those actions which amongst them are judged praiseworthy, and call that *vice* which they account blameable; since they would condemn themselves, if they should think anything *right*, to which they allowed not commendation; anything *wrong*, which they let pass without blame.

'Thus the measure of what is everywhere called and esteemed *virtue* and *vice*, is this approbation or dislike, praise or blame, which by a secret and tacit consent establishes itself in the several societies, tribes, and clubs of men in the world; whereby several actions come to find credit or disgrace amongst them, according to the judgment, maxims, or fashions of that place. For though men uniting into politick societies have resigned up to the publick the disposing of all their force, so that they cannot employ it against any fellow-citizens any further than the law of the country directs, yet they retain still the power of thinking well or ill, approving or disapproving of the actions of those whom they live amongst and converse with: and by this approbation and dislike, they establish amongst themselves what they will call *virtue* and *vice.*

'That this is the common *measure of virtue and vice*, will appear to any one who considers, that, though that passes for *vice* in one country, which is counted *virtue* (or, at least, not *vice*) in another, yet everywhere *virtue* and praise, *vice* and blame go together. *Virtue* is everywhere that which is thought praiseworthy; and nothing but that which has the allowance of public esteem is called *virtue*. *Virtue* and praise are so united, that they are often called by the same name. "Sunt sua prœmia laudi," says Virgil. And, says Cicero, "nihil habet natura præstantius, quam *honestatem*, quam *laudem*, quam *dignitatem*, quam *decus*:" all which, he tells you, are names for the same thing. Such is the language of the heathen philosophers, who well understood wherein the notions of *virtue* and *vice* consisted.

'But though, by the different temper, education, fashion, maxims, or interest of different sorts of men, it fell out, that what was thought praiseworthy in one place, escaped not censure in another, and so in different societies *virtues* and *vices* were changed, yet, as to the main, they for the most part kept the same everywhere. For since nothing can be more natural, than to encourage with esteem and reputation that wherein everyone finds his advantage, and to blame and discountenance the contrary, it is no wonder that esteem and discredit, virtue and vice, should in a great measure everywhere correspond with the unchangeable rule of right and wrong which the law of God hath established: there being nothing that so directly and visibly secures and advances the general good of mankind in this world as obedience to the law He has set them, and nothing that breeds such mischiefs and confusion as the neglect of it. And therefore men, without renouncing all sense and reason, and their own interest, could not generally mistake in placing their commendation or blame on that side which really deserved it not. Nay, even those men, whose practice was otherwise, failed not to give their approbation right: few being depraved to that degree, as not to condemn, at least in others, the faults they themselves were guilty of. Whereby, even in the corruption of manners, the law of God, which ought to be the rule of virtue and vice, was pretty well observed.

'If any one shall imagine that I have forgotten my own notion of a law, when I make the law, whereby men judge of *virtue* and *vice*, to be nothing but the consent of private men who have not authority to make a law; especially wanting that which is so necessary and essential to a law, a power to enforce it: I think, I may say, that he who imagines commendation and disgrace not to be strong motives on men to accommodate themselves to the opinions and rules of those with whom they converse, seems little skilled in the nature or history of mankind: The greatest part whereof he shall find to govern themselves chiefly, if not solely, by this law of fashion: and so they do that which keeps them in reputation with their company, little regard the law of God or the magistrate. The penalties that attend the breach of God's law, some, nay, perhaps most men seldom seriously reflect on; and amongst those that do, many, whilst they break the law, entertain thoughts of future reconciliation, and making their peace for such breaches. And as to the punishments due from the law of the commonwealth, they frequently flatter themselves with the hope of impunity. But no man escapes the punishment of their censure and dislike, who offends against the fashion and opinion of the company he keeps, and would recommend himself to. Nor is there one of ten thousand, who is stiff and insensible enough to bear up under the constant dislike and condemnation of his own club. He must be of a strange and unusual constitution, who can content himself to live in constant disgrace and disrepute with his own particular society. Solitude many men have sought and been reconciled to: but nobody that has the least thought or sense of a man about him, can live in society under the constant dislike and ill opinion of his familiars, and those he converses with. This is a burthen too heavy for human sufferance: and he must be made up of irreconcileable contradictions, who can take pleasure in company, and yet be insensible of contempt and disgrace from his companions.

'The law of God, the law of politick societies, and the law of fashion or private censure, are, then, the three rules to which men variously compare their actions. And it is from their conformity or disagreement to one of these rules, that they judge of their rectitude or obliquity, and name them good or bad.

'Whether we take the rule, to which, as to a touchstone, we bring our voluntary actions, from the fashion of the country, or from the will of a law-maker, the mind is easily able to observe the relation any action hath to it, and to judge whether the action agrees or disagrees with the rule. And thus the mind hath a notion of *moral goodness or evil*: which is either conformity or not conformity of any action to that rule. If I find an action to agree or disagree with the esteem of the country I have been bred in, and to be held by most men there worthy of praise or blame, I call the action virtuous or vicious. If I have the will of a supreme invisible law-maker for my rule, then, as I suppose the action commanded or forbidden by God, I call it good or evil, duty or sin. And if I compare it to the civil law, the rule made by the legislative power of the country, I call it lawful or unlawful, no crime or a crime. So that whencesoever we take the rule of actions, or by what standard soever we frame in our minds the ideas of virtues or vices, their rectitude or obliquity consists in their agreement or disagreement with the patterns prescribed by some law.

'Before I quit this argument, I would observe that, in the relations which I call *moral relations*, I have a true notion of relation, by comparing the action with the rule, whether the rule be true or false. For if I measure any thing by a supposed yard, I know whether the thing I measure be longer or shorter than that supposed yard, though the yard I measure by be not exactly the standard. Measuring an action by a wrong rule, I shall judge amiss of its moral rectitude: but I shall not mistake the relation which the action bears to the rule whereunto I compare it.'—*Essay concerning Human Understanding*. Book II Chap. XXVIII.

Laws metaphorical or

The analogy borne to a law proper by a law which opinion imposes, lies mainly in the following point of

figurative. —The common and negative nature of laws of the class.

resemblance. In the case of a law set by opinion, as well as in the case of a law properly so called, a rational being or beings are obnoxious to contingent evil, in the event of their not complying with a known or presumed desire of another being or beings of a like nature. If, in either of the two cases, the contingent evil is suffered, it is suffered by a rational being, through a rational being: And it is suffered by a rational being, through a rational being, in consequence of the suffering party having disregarded a desire of a rational being or beings.—The analogy, therefore, by which the laws are related, mainly lies in the resemblance of the improper sanction and duty to the sanction and duty properly so called. The contingent evil in prospect which enforces the law improper, and the present obnoxiousness to that contingent evil, may be likened to the genuine sanction which enforces the law proper, and the genuine duty or obligation which the law proper imposes.—The analogy between a law in the proper acceptation of the term, and a law improperly so called which opinion sets or imposes, is, therefore, strong or close. The defect which excludes the latter from the rank of a law proper, merely consists in this: that the wish or desire of its authors has not been duly *signified*, and that they have no formed *intention* of inflicting evil or pain upon those who may break or transgress it.

But, beside the laws improper which are set or imposed by opinion, there are laws improperly so called which are related to laws proper by slender or remote analogies. And, since they have gotten the name of *laws* from their slender or remote analogies to laws properly so called, I style them laws metaphorical, or laws merely metaphorical.

The metaphorical applications of the term *law* are numerous and different. The analogies by which they are suggested, or by which metaphorical laws are related to laws proper, will, therefore, hardly admit of a common and positive description. But laws metaphorical, though numerous and different, have the following common and negative nature.—No property or character of any metaphorical law can be likened to a sanction or a duty. Consequently, every metaphorical law wants that point of resemblance which mainly constitutes the analogy between a law proper and a law set by opinion.

The common and negative nature of laws metaphorical or figurative, shown by examples.

To show that figurative laws want that point of resemblance, and are therefore remotely analogous to laws properly so called, I will touch slightly and briefly upon a few of the numberless cases in which the term *law* is extended and applied by a metaphor.

The most frequent and remarkable of those metaphorical applications is suggested by that uniformity, or that stability of conduct, which is one of the ordinary consequences of a law proper.—By reason of the sanction working on their wills or desires, the parties obliged by a law proper commonly adjust their conduct to the pattern which the law prescribes. Consequently, wherever we observe a uniform order of events, or a uniform order of coexisting phænomena, we are prone to impute that order to a *law* set by its author, though the case presents us with nothing that can be likened to a sanction or a duty.

For example: We say that the movements of lifeless bodies are determined by certain *laws*: though, since the bodies are lifeless and have no desires or aversions, they cannot be touched by aught which in the least resembles a sanction, and cannot be subject to aught which in the least resembles an obligation. We mean that they move in certain uniform modes, and that they move in those uniform modes through the pleasure and appointment of God: just as parties obliged behave in a uniform manner through the pleasure and appointment of the party who imposes the law and the duty.—Again: We say that certain actions of the lower and irrational animals are determined by certain *laws*: though, since they cannot understand the purpose and provisions of a law, it is impossible that sanctions should effectually move them to obedience, or that their conduct should be guided by a regard to duties or obligations. We mean that they act in certain uniform modes, either in consequence of instincts (or causes which we cannot explain), or else in consequence of hints which they catch from experience and observation: and that, since their uniformity of action is an effect of the Divine pleasure, it closely resembles the uniformity of conduct which is wrought by the authors of laws in those who are obnoxious to the sanctions.[12]—In short, whenever we talk of *laws* governing the irrational world, the metaphorical application of the term *law* is suggested by this double analogy. 1. The successive and synchronous phænomena composing the irrational world, happen and exist, for the most part, in uniform series: which uniformity of succession and coexistence resembles the uniformity of conduct produced by an imperative law. 2. That uniformity of succession and coexistence, like the uniformity of conduct produced by an imperative law, springs from the will and intention of an intelligent and rational author.—When an atheist speaks of *laws*

[12] Speaking with absolute precision, the lower animals, or the animals inferior to man, are not destitute of reason. Since their conduct is partly determined by conclusions drawn from experience, they observe, compare, abstract, and infer. But the intelligence of the lower animals is so extremely limited, that, adopting the current expression, I style them *irrational*. Some of the more sagacious are so far from being irrational, that they understand and observe laws set to them by human masters. But these laws being few and of little importance, I throw them, for the sake of simplicity, out of my account. I say universally of the lower animals, that they cannot understand a law, or guide their conduct by duty.

governing the irrational world, the metaphorical application is suggested by an analogy still more slender and remote that that which I have now analyzed. He means that the uniformity of succession and coexistence resembles the uniformity of conduct produced by an imperative rule. If, to draw the analogy closer, he ascribes those laws to an author, he personifies a verbal abstraction, and makes it play the legislator. He attributes the uniformity of succession and coexistence to *laws* set by *nature*: meaning, by *nature*, the world itself; or, perhaps, that very uniformity which he imputes to nature's commands.

Many metaphorical applications of the term *law* or *rule* are suggested by the analogy following.—An imperative law or rule guides the conduct of the obliged, or is a *norma*, model, or pattern, to which their conduct conforms. A proposed guide of human conduct, or a model or pattern offered to human imitation, is, therefore, frequently styled a *law* or *rule* of conduct, although there be not in the case a shadow of a sanction or a duty.

For example: To every law properly so called there are two distinct parties: a party by whom it is established, and a party to whom it is set. But, this notwithstanding, we often speak of a law set by a man to himself: meaning that he intends to pursue some given course of conduct as exactly as he would pursue it if he were bound to pursue it by a law. An intention of pursuing exactly some given course of conduct, is the only law or rule which a man can set to himself. The binding virtue of a law lies in the sanction annexed to it. But in the case of a so called law set by a man to himself, he is not constrained to observe it by aught that resembles a sanction. For though he may fairly purpose to inflict a pain on himself, if his conduct shall depart from the guide which he intends it shall follow, the infliction of the conditional pain depends upon his own will.—Again: When we talk of *rules* of art, the metaphorical application of the term *rules* is suggested by the analogy in question. By a *rule* of art, we mean a prescription or pattern which is offered to practitioners of an art, and which they are advised to observe when performing some given process. There is not the semblance of a sanction, nor is there the shadow of a duty. But the offered prescription or pattern may guide the conduct of practitioners, as a rule imperative and proper guides the conduct of the obliged.[13]

Laws metaphorical or figurative are often blended and confounded with laws imperative and proper.

The preceding disquisition on figurative laws is not so superfluous as some of my hearers may deem it. Figurative laws are not unfrequently mistaken for laws imperative and proper. Nay, attempts have actually been made, and by writers of the highest celebrity, to explain and illustrate the nature of laws imperative and proper, by allusions to so called laws which are merely such through a metaphor. Of these most gross and scarcely credible errors, various cases will be mentioned in future stages of my Course. For the present, the following examples will amply demonstrate that the errors are not impossible.

In an excerpt from Ulpian placed at the beginning of the Pandects, and also inserted by Justinian in the second title of his Institutes, a fancied *jus naturale*, common to all animals, is thus distinguished from the *jus naturale* or *gentium* to which I have adverted above. '*Jus naturale* est, quod natura omnia animalia docuit: nam jus istud non humani generis proprium, sed omnium animalium, quæ in terra, quæ in mari nascuntur, avium quoque commune est. Hinc descendit maris atque feminæ conjunctio, quam nos matrimonium appellamus; hinc liberorum procreatio, hinc educatio: videmus etenim cetera quoque animalia, feras etiam, istius juris peritia censeri. *Jus gentium* est, quo gentes

[13] Supposed difference between law and rule.—*MS. note.*

humanæ utuntur. Quod a *naturali* recedere, inde facile intelligere licet; quia illud omnibus animalibus, hoc solis hominibus inter se commune est.' The *jus naturale* which Ulpian here describes, and which he here distinguishes from the *jus naturale* or *gentium*, is a name for the instincts of animals. More especially, it denotes that instinctive appetite which leads them to propagate their kinds, with that instinctive sympathy which inclines parent animals to nourish and educate their young. Now the instincts of animals are related to laws by the slender or remote analogy which I have already endeavoured to explain. They incline the animals to act in certain uniform modes, and they are given to the animals for that purpose by an intelligent and rational Author. But these metaphorical laws which govern the lower animals, and which govern (though less despotically) the human species itself, should not have been blended and confounded, by a grave writer upon jurisprudence, with laws properly so called. It is true that the instincts of the animal man, like many of his affections which are not instinctive, are amongst the causes of laws in the proper acceptation of the term. More especially, the laws regarding the relation of husband and wife, and the laws regarding the relation of parent and child, are mainly caused by the instincts which Ulpian particularly points at. And that, it is likely, was the reason which determined this legal oracle to class the instincts of animals with laws imperative and proper. But nothing can be more absurd than the ranking with laws themselves the causes which lead to their existence. And if human instincts are laws because they are causes of laws, there is scarcely a faculty or affection belonging to the human mind, and scarcely a class of objects presented by the outward world, that must not be esteemed a law and an appropriate subject of jurisprudence.—I must, however, remark, that the *jus*

H

quod natura omnia animalia docuit is a conceit peculiar to Ulpian: and that this most foolish conceit, though inserted in Justinian's compilations, has no perceptible influence on the detail of the Roman law. The *jus naturale* of the classical jurists generally, and the *jus naturale* occurring generally in the Pandects, is equivalent to the *natural law* of modern writers upon jurisprudence, and is synonymous with the *jus gentium*, or the *jus naturale et gentium*, which I have tried to explain concisely at the end of a preceding note. It means those positive laws and those rules of positive morality, which are not peculiar or appropriate to any nation or age, but obtain, or are thought to obtain, in all nations and ages: and which, by reason of their obtaining in all nations and ages, are supposed to be formed or fashioned on the law of God or Nature as known by the moral sense. 'Omnes populi' (says Gaius), 'qui legibus et moribus reguntur, partim suo proprio, partim communi omnium hominum jure utuntur. Nam quod quisque populus ipse sibi jus constituit, id ipsius proprium est, vocaturque jus civile; quasi jus proprium ipsius civitatis. Quod vero naturalis ratio inter omnes homines constituit, id aput omnes populos peræque custoditur, vocaturque jus gentium; quasi quo jure omnes gentes utuntur.' The universal *leges et mores* here described by Gaius, and distinguished from the *leges et mores* peculiar to a particular nation, are styled indifferently, by most of the classical jurists, *jus gentium*, *jus naturale*, or *jus naturale et gentium*. And the law of nature, as thus understood, is not intrinsically absurd. For as some of the dictates of utility are always and everywhere the same, and are also so plain and glaring that they hardly admit of mistake, there are legal and moral rules which are nearly or quite *universal*, and the expediency of which must be seen by merely *natural* reason, or by reason without the lights of extensive experience and observation. The distinction of law and morality into natural and positive, is a needless and futile subtility: but still the distinction is founded on a real and manifest difference. The *jus naturale* or *gentium* would be liable to little objection, if it were not supposed to be the offspring of a moral instinct or sense, or of innate practical principles. But, since it is closely allied (as I shall show hereafter[14]) to that misleading and pernicious jargon, it ought to be expelled, with the *natural law* of the moderns, from the sciences of jurisprudence and morality.

The following passage is the first sentence in Montesquieu's *Spirit of Laws*. 'Les lois, dans la signification la plus étendue, sont les rapports nécessaires qui dérivent de la nature des choses: et dans ce sens tous les êtres ont leurs lois: la Divinité a ses lois; le monde matériel a ses lois; les intelligences supérieures à l'homme ont leurs lois; les bêtes ont leurs lois; l'homme a ses lois.' Now objects widely different, though bearing a common name, are here blended and confounded. Of the laws which govern the conduct of intelligent and rational creatures, some are laws imperative and proper, and others are closely analogous to laws of that description. But the so called laws which govern the material world, with the so called laws which govern the lower animals, are merely laws by a metaphor. And the so called laws which govern or determine the Deity are clearly in the same predicament. If his actions were governed or determined by laws imperative and proper, he would be in a state of dependence on another and superior being. When we say that the actions of the Deity are governed or determined by laws, we mean that they conform to intentions which the Deity himself has conceived, and which he pursues or observes with inflexible steadiness or constancy. To mix these

[14] Lect. xxxii. *post.*

figurative laws with laws imperative and proper, is to obscure, and not to elucidate, the nature or essence of the latter.—The beginning of the passage is worthy of the sequel. We are told that laws are the necessary relations which flow from the nature of things. But what, I would crave, are relations? What, I would also crave, is the nature of things? And how do the necessary relations which flow from the nature of things differ from those relations which originate in other sources? The terms of the definition are incomparably more obscure than the term which it affects to expound.

If you read the disquisition in Blackstone on the nature of laws in general, or the fustian description of law in Hooker's Ecclesiastical Polity, you will find the same confusion of laws imperative and proper with laws which are merely such by a glaring perversion of the term. The cases of this confusion are, indeed, so numerous, that they would fill a considerable volume.

Physical or natural sanctions.

From the confusion of laws metaphorical with laws imperative and proper, I turn to a mistake, somewhat similar, which, I presume to think, has been committed by Mr. Bentham.

Sanctions proper and improper are of three capital classes:—the sanctions properly so called which are annexed to the laws of God: the sanctions properly so called which are annexed to positive laws: the sanctions properly so called, and the sanctions closely analogous to sanctions properly so called, which respectively enforce compliance with positive moral rules. But to sanction religious, legal, and moral, this great philosopher and jurist adds a class of sanctions which he styles *physical* or *natural*.

When he styles these sanctions *physical*, he does not intend to intimate that they are distinguished from other sanctions by the mode wherein they operate: he does not intend to intimate that these are the only sanctions which affect the suffering parties through physical or material means. Any sanction of any class may reach the suffering party through means of that description. If a man were smitten with blindness by the immediate appointment of the Deity, and in consequence of a sin he had committed against the Divine law, he would suffer a religious sanction through his physical or bodily organs. The thief who is hanged or imprisoned by virtue of a judicial command, suffers a legal sanction through physical or material means. If a man of the class of gentlemen violates the law of honour, and happens to be shot in a duel arising from his moral delinquency, he suffers a moral sanction in a physical or material form.

The meaning annexed by Mr. Bentham to the expression 'physical sanction,' may, I believe, be rendered in the following manner:—A physical sanction is an evil brought upon the suffering party by an act or omission of his own. But, though it is brought upon the sufferer by an act or omission of his own, it is not brought upon the sufferer through any Divine law, or through any positive law, or rule of positive morality. For example: If your house be destroyed by fire through your neglecting to put out a light, you bring upon yourself, by your negligent omission, a *physical* or *natural* sanction: supposing, I mean, that your omission is not to be deemed a sin, and that the consequent destruction of your house is not to be deemed a punishment inflicted by the hand of the Deity. In short, though a physical sanction is an evil falling on a rational being, and brought on a rational being by an act or omission of his own, it is neither brought on the sufferer through a law imperative and proper, nor through an analogous law set or imposed by opinion. In case I borrowed the just, though tautological language of Locke, I should describe a physical sanction in such some terms as the following. 'It is an evil *naturally* produced by the conduct whereon it is consequent: and, being *naturally* produced by the conduct whereon it is consequent, it reaches the suffering party *without the intervention of a law*.'

Such physical or natural evils are related by the following analogy to sanctions properly so called. 1. When they are actually suffered, they are suffered by rational beings through acts or omissions of their own. 2. Before they are actually suffered, or whilst they exist in prospect, they affect the wills or desires of the parties obnoxious to them as sanctions properly so called affect the wills of the obliged. The parties are urged to the acts which may avert the evils from their heads, or the parties are deterred from the acts which may bring the evils upon them.

But in spite of the specious analogy at which I have now pointed, I dislike, for various reasons, the application of the term *sanction* to these physical or natural evils. Of those reasons I will briefly mention the following:—1. Although these evils are suffered by intelligent rational beings, and by intelligent rational beings through acts or omissions of their own, they are not suffered as consequences of their not complying with desires of intelligent rational beings. The acts or omissions whereon these evils are consequent, can hardly be likened to breaches of duties, or to violations of imperative laws. The analogy borne by these evils to sanctions properly so called, is nearly as remote as the analogy borne by laws metaphorical to laws imperative and proper. 2. By the term *sanction*, as it is now restricted, the evils enforcing compliance with laws imperative and proper, or with the closely analogous laws which opinion sets or imposes, are distinguished from other evils briefly and commodiously. If the term were commonly extended to these physical or natural evils, this advantage would be lost. The term would then comprehend every possible evil which a man may bring upon himself by his own voluntary conduct. The term would then comprehend every contingent evil which can work on the will or desires as a motive to action or forbearance.

In strictness, declaratory laws, laws repealing laws, and laws of imperfect obligation (in the sense of the Roman jurists), ought to be classed respectively with laws metaphorical or figurative, and rules of positive morality.

I close my disquisitions on figurative laws, and on those metaphorical sanctions which Mr. Bentham denominates *physical*, with the following connected remarks.

Declaratory laws, laws repealing laws, and laws of imperfect obligation (in the sense of the Roman jurists), are merely analogous to laws in the proper acceptation of the term. Like laws imperative and proper, declaratory laws, laws repealing laws, and laws of imperfect obligation (in the sense of the Roman jurists), are signs of pleasure or desire proceeding from law-makers. A law of imperfect obligation (in the sense of the Roman jurists) is also allied to an imperative law by the following point of resemblance. Like a law imperative and proper, it is offered as a *norma*, or guide of conduct, although it is not armed with a legal or political sanction.

Declaratory laws, and laws repealing laws, ought in strictness to be classed with laws metaphorical or figurative: for the analogy by which they are related to laws imperative and proper is extremely slender or remote. Laws of imperfect obligation (in the sense of the Roman jurists) are laws set or imposed by the opinions of the law-makers, and ought in strictness to be classed with rules of positive morality. But though laws of these three species are merely analogous to laws in the proper acceptation of the term, they are closely connected with positive laws, and are appropriate subjects of jurisprudence. Consequently I treat them as improper laws of anomalous or eccentric sorts, and exclude them from the classes of laws to which in strictness they belong.

Note—on the prevailing tendency to confound what is with what ought to be law or morality, that is, 1st, to confound positive law with the science of legislation, and positive morality with deontology; and 2ndly, to confound positive law with positive morality, and both with legislation and deontology.—(See page 164.)

1st. Tendency to confound positive law with the science of legislation and positive morality with deontology. Example from Blackstone.

The existence of law is one thing; its merit or demerit is another. Whether it be or be not is one enquiry; whether it be or be not conformable to an assumed standard, is a different enquiry. A law, which actually exists, is a law, though we happen to dislike it, or though it vary from the text, by which we regulate our approbation and disapprobation. This truth, when formally announced as an abstract proposition, is so simple and glaring that it seems idle to insist upon it. But simple and glaring as it is, when enunciated in abstract expressions the enumeration of the instances in which it has been forgotten would fill a volume.

Sir William Blackstone, for example, says in his 'Commentaries,' that the laws of God are superior in obligation to all other laws; that no human laws should be suffered to contradict them; that human laws are of no validity if contrary to them; and that all valid laws derive their force from that Divine original.

Now, he *may* mean that all human laws ought to conform to the Divine laws. If this be his meaning, I assent to it without hesitation. The evils which we are exposed to suffer from the hands of God as a consequence of disobeying His commands are the greatest evils to which we are obnoxious; the obligations which they impose are consequently paramount to those imposed by any other laws, and if human commands conflict with the Divine law, we ought to disobey the command which is enforced by the less powerful sanction; this is implied in the term *ought*: the proposition is identical, and therefore perfectly indisputable—it is our interest to choose the smaller and more uncertain evil, in preference to the greater and surer. If this be Blackstone's meaning, I assent to his proposition, and have only to object to it, that it tells us just nothing. Perhaps, again, he means that human lawgivers are themselves obliged by the Divine laws to fashion the laws which they impose by that ultimate standard, because if they do not, God will punish them. To this also I entirely assent: for if the index to the law of God be the principle of utility, that law embraces the whole of our voluntary actions in so far as motives applied from without are required to give them a direction conformable to the general happiness.

But the meaning of this passage of Blackstone, if it has a meaning, seems rather to be this: that no human law which conflicts with the Divine law is obligatory or binding; in other words, that no human law which conflicts with the Divine law *is a law*, for a law without an obligation is a contradiction in terms. I suppose this to be his meaning, because when we say of any transaction that it is invalid or void, we mean that it is not binding: as, for example, if it be a contract, we mean that the political law will not lend its sanction to enforce the contract.

Now, to say that human laws which conflict with the Divine law are not binding, that is to say, are not laws, is to talk stark nonsense. The most pernicious laws, and therefore those which are most opposed to the will of God, have been and are continually enforced as laws by judicial tribunals. Suppose an act innocuous, or positively beneficial, be prohibited by the sovereign under the penalty of death; if I commit this act, I shall be tried and condemned, and if I object to the sentence, that it is contrary to the law of God, who has commanded that human lawgivers shall not prohibit acts which have no evil consequences, the Court of Justice will demonstrate the inconclusiveness of my reasoning by hanging me up, in pursuance of the law of which I have impugned the validity. An exception, demurrer, or plea, founded on the law of God was never heard in a Court of Justice, from the creation of the world down to the present moment.

But this abuse of language is not merely puerile, it is mischievous. When it is said that a law ought to be disobeyed, what is meant is that we are urged to disobey it by motives more cogent and compulsory than those by which it is itself sanctioned. If the laws of God are certain,

H*

the motives which they hold out to disobey any human command which is at variance with them are paramount to all others. But the laws of God are not always certain. All divines, at least all reasonable divines, admit that no scheme of duties perfectly complete and unambiguous was ever imparted to us by revelation. As an index to the Divine will, utility is obviously insufficient. What appears pernicious to one person may appear beneficial to another. And as for the moral sense, innate practical principles, conscience, they are merely convenient cloaks for ignorance or sinister interest: they mean either that I hate the law to which I object and cannot tell why, or that I hate the law, and that the cause of my hatred is one which I find it incommodious to avow. If I say openly, I hate the law, *ergo*, it is not binding and ought to be disobeyed, no one will listen to me; but by calling my hate my conscience or my moral sense, I urge the same argument in another and more plausible form: I seem to assign a reason for my dislike, when in truth I have only given it a sounding and specious name. In times of civil discord the mischief of this detestable abuse of language is apparent. In quiet times the dictates of utility are fortunately so obvious that the anarchical doctrine sleeps, and men habitually admit the validity of laws which they dislike. To prove by pertinent reasons that a law is pernicious is highly useful, because such process may lead to the abrogation of the pernicious law. To incite the public to resistance by determinate views of *utility* may be useful, for resistance, grounded on clear and definite prospects of good, is sometimes beneficial. But to proclaim generally that all laws which are pernicious or contrary to the will of God are void and not to be tolerated, is to preach anarchy, hostile and perilous as much to wise and benign rule as to stupid and galling tyranny.

Another example from Blackstone.

In another passage of his 'Commentaries,' Blackstone enters into an argument to prove that a master cannot have a right to the labour of his slave. Had he contented himself with expressing his *disapprobation*, a very well-grounded one certainly, of the institution of slavery, no objection could have been made to his so expressing himself. But to dispute the existence or the possibility of the right is to talk absurdly. For in every age, and in almost every nation, the right has been given by positive law, whilst that pernicious disposition of positive law has been backed by the positive morality of the free or master classes.

Paley's definition of civil liberty.

Paley's admired definition of civil liberty appears to me to be obnoxious to the very same objection: it is a definition of civil liberty as it ought to be. 'Civil liberty,' he says, 'is the not being restrained by any law but which conduces in a greater degree to the public welfare;' and this is distinguished from *natural* liberty, which is the not being restrained at all. But when liberty is not exactly synonymous with right it means, and can mean nothing else, but exemption from restraint or obligation, and is therefore altogether incompatible with law, the very idea of which implies restraint and obligation. But restraint is restraint although it be useful, and liberty is liberty though it may be pernicious. You may, if you please, call a useful restraint *liberty*, and refuse the name liberty to exemption from restraint when restraint is for the public advantage. But by this abuse of language you throw not a ray of light upon the nature of political liberty; you only add to the ambiguity and indistinctness in which it is already involved. I shall have to define and analyze the notion of liberty hereafter, on account of its intimate connection with right, obligation, and sanction.

Example from the writers on international law.

Grotius, Puffendorf, and the other writers on the so-called law of nations, have fallen into a similar confusion of ideas: they have confounded positive international morality, or the rules which actually obtain among civilized nations in their mutual intercourse, with their own vague conceptions of international morality as it *ought to be*, with that indeterminate something which they conceived it would be, if it conformed to that indeterminate something which they call the law of nature. Professor Von Martens, of Göttingen, who died only a few years ago[15], is actually the first of the writers on the law

[15] This, it will be remembered, was spoken in the year 1830 or 1831.

of nations who has seized this distinction with a firm grasp, the first who has distinguished the rules which ought to be received in the intercourse of nations, or which would be received if they conformed to an assumed standard of whatever kind, from those which *are* so received, endeavoured to collect from the practice of civilized communities what are the rules actually recognized and acted upon by them, and gave to these rules the name of positive international law.

2nd. Tendency to confound positive law with positive morality, and both with legislation and deontology. Examples from the Roman jurists.

I have given several instances in which law and morality as they ought to be are confounded with the law and morality which actually exist. I shall next mention some examples in which positive law is confounded with positive morality, and both with the science of legislation and deontology.

Those who know the writings of the Roman lawyers only by hearsay are accustomed to admire their philosophy. Now this, in my estimation, is the only part of their writings which deserves contempt. Their extraordinary merit is evinced not in general speculation, but as expositors of the Roman law. They have seized its general principles with great clearness and penetration, have applied these principles with admirable logic to the explanation of details, and have thus reduced this positive system of law to a compact and coherent whole. But the philosophy which they borrowed from the Greeks, or which, after the examples of the Greeks, they themselves fashioned, is naught. Their attempts to define jurisprudence and to determine the province of the jurisconsult are absolutely pitiable, and it is hardly conceivable how men of such admirable discernment should have displayed such contemptible imbecility.

At the commencement of the digest is a passage attempting to define jurisprudence. I shall first present you with this passage in a free translation, and afterwards in the original. 'Jurisprudence,' says this definition, 'is the knowledge of things divine and human; the science which teaches men to discern the just from the unjust.' 'Jurisprudentia est divinarum atque humanarum rerum notitia, justi atque injusti scientia.' In the excerpt from Ulpian, which is placed at the beginning of the digest, it is attempted to define the office or province of the jurisconsult. 'Law,' says the passage, 'derives its name from justice, *justitia*, and is the science or skill in the good and the equitable. Law being the creature of justice, we the jurisconsults may be considered as her priests, for justice is the goddess whom we worship, and to whose service we are devoted. Justice and equity are our vocation; we teach men to know the difference between the just and the unjust, the lawful and the unlawful; we strive to reclaim them from vice, not only by the terrors of punishment, but also by the blandishment of rewards; herein, unless we flatter ourselves, aspiring to sound and real philosophy, and not like some whom we could mention, contenting ourselves with vain and empty pretension.' 'Juri operam daturum prius nosse oportet, unde nomen juris descendat. Est autem a justitia appellatum; nam, ut eleganter Celsus definit, jus est ars boni et æqui. Cujus merito quis nos sacerdotes appellet; justitiam namque colimus, et boni et æqui notitiam profitemur, æquum ab iniquo separantes, licitum ab illicito discernentes, bonos non solum metu pœnarum verum etiam prœmiorum quoque exhortatione efficere cupientes, veram, nisi fallor, philosophiam, non simulatam affectantes.'

Were I to present you with all the criticisms which these two passages suggest, I should detain you a full hour. I shall content myself with one observation on the scope and purpose of them both. That is, that they affect to define jurisprudence, or what comes exactly to the same thing, the office or province of the jurisconsult. Now jurisprudence, if it is anything, is the science of law, or at most the science of law combined with the art of applying it; but what is here given as a definition of it, embraces not only law, but positive morality, and even the test to which both these are to be referred. It therefore comprises the science of legislation and deontology. Further, it affirms that law is the creature of justice, which is as much as to say that it is the child of its own offspring. For when by *just* we mean anything but to express our own approbation we mean something which *accords with some given law.* True, we speak of law and justice, or of law and equity, as opposed to each other, but when we do so, we mean to express mere dislike of the law, or to intimate that it conflicts with another law, the law of God, which is its standard. According to this, every pernicious law is unjust. But, in truth, law is itself the standard of justice. What deviates from any law is unjust with reference to that law, though it may be just with reference to another law of superior authority. The terms just and unjust imply a standard, and conformity to that standard and a deviation from it; else they signify mere dislike, which it would be far better to signify by a grunt or a groan than by a mischievous and detestable abuse of articulate language. But justice is commonly erected into an entity, and spoken of as a legislator, in which character it is supposed to prescribe the law, conformity to which it should denote. The veriest dolt who is placed in a jury box, the merest old woman who happens to be raised to the bench, will talk finely of equity or justice—the justice of the case, the equity of the case, the imperious demands of justice, the plain dictates of equity. He forgets that he is there to enforce *the law of the land*, else he does not administer that justice or that equity with which alone he is immediately concerned.

Example from Lord Mansfield.

This is well known to have been a strong tendency of Lord Mansfield—a strange obliquity in so great a man. I will give an instance. By the English law, a promise to give something or to do something for the benefit of another is not binding without what is called a consideration, that is, a motive assigned for the promise, which motive must be of a particular kind. Lord Mansfield, however, overruled the distinct provisions of the law by ruling that moral obligation was a sufficient consideration. Now, moral obligation is an obligation imposed by opinion, or an obligation imposed by God: that is, moral obligation is anything which we choose to call so, for the precepts of positive morality are infinitely varying, and the will of God, whether indicated by utility or by a moral sense, is equally matter of dispute. This decision of Lord Mansfield, which assumes that the judge is to enforce morality enables the judge to enforce just whatever he pleases.

I must here observe that I am not objecting to Lord Mansfield for assuming the office of a legislator. I by no means disapprove of what Mr. Bentham has chosen to call by the disrespectful, and therefore, as I conceive, injudicious, name of judge-made law. For I consider it injudicious to call by any name indicative of disrespect what appears to me highly beneficial and even absolutely necessary. I cannot understand how any person who has considered the subject can suppose that society could possibly have gone on if judges had not legislated, or that there is any danger whatever in allowing them that power which they have in fact exercised, to make up for the negligence or the incapacity of the avowed legislator. That part of the law of every country which was made by judges has been far better made than that part which consists of statutes enacted by the legislative. Notwithstanding my great admiration for Mr. Bentham, I cannot but think that, instead of blaming judges for having legislated, he should blame them for the timid, narrow, and piecemeal manner in which they have legislated, and for legislating under cover of vague and indeterminate phrases, such as Lord Mansfield employed in the above example, and which would be censurable in any legislator.

Past - Part I - understanding

Future { Part II - application
Part III - evolution

HARVARD LAW REVIEW.

VOL. X. MARCH 25, 1897. NO. 8.

THE PATH OF THE LAW.[1]

WHEN we study law we are not studying a mystery but a well known profession. We are studying what we shall want in order to appear before judges, or to advise people in such a way as to keep them out of court. The reason why it is a profession, why people will pay lawyers to argue for them or to advise them, is that in societies like ours the command of the public force is intrusted to the judges in certain cases, and the whole power of the state will be put forth, if necessary, to carry out their judgments and decrees. People want to know under what circumstances and how far they will run the risk of coming against what is so much stronger than themselves, and hence it becomes a business to find out when this danger is to be feared. The object of our study, then, is prediction, the prediction of the incidence of the public force through the instrumentality of the courts.

The means of the study are a body of reports, of treatises, and of statutes, in this country and in England, extending back for six hundred years, and now increasing annually by hundreds. In these sibylline leaves are gathered the scattered prophecies of the past upon the cases in which the axe will fall. These are what properly have been called the oracles of the law. Far the most important and pretty nearly the whole meaning of every new effort of legal thought is to make these prophecies more precise, and to

[1] An Address delivered by Mr. Justice Holmes, of the Supreme Judicial Court of Massachusetts, at the dedication of the new hall of the Boston University School of Law, on January 8, 1897. Copyrighted by O. W. Holmes, 1897.

generalize them into a thoroughly connected system. The process is one, from a lawyer's statement of a case, eliminating as it does all the dramatic elements with which his client's story has clothed it, and retaining only the facts of legal import, up to the final analyses and abstract universals of theoretic jurisprudence. The reason why a lawyer does not mention that his client wore a white hat when he made a contract, while Mrs. Quickly would be sure to dwell upon it along with the parcel gilt goblet and the sea-coal fire, is that he forsees that the public force will act in the same way whatever his client had upon his head. It is to make the prophecies easier to be remembered and to be understood that the teachings of the decisions of the past are put into general propositions and gathered into text-books, or that statutes are passed in a general form. The primary rights and duties with which jurisprudence busies itself again are nothing but prophecies. One of the many evil effects of the confusion between legal and moral ideas, about which I shall have something to say in a moment, is that theory is apt to get the cart before the horse, and to consider the right or the duty as something existing apart from and independent of the consequences of its breach, to which certain sanctions are added afterward. But, as I shall try to show, a legal duty so called is nothing but a prediction that if a man does or omits certain things he will be made to suffer in this or that way by judgment of the court; — and so of a legal right.

The number of our predictions when generalized and reduced to a system is not unmanageably large. They present themselves as a finite body of dogma which may be mastered within a reasonable time. It is a great mistake to be frightened by the ever increasing number of reports. The reports of a given jurisdiction in the course of a generation take up pretty much the whole body of the law, and restate it from the present point of view. We could reconstruct the corpus from them if all that went before were burned. The use of the earlier reports is mainly historical, a use about which I shall have something to say before I have finished.

I wish, if I can, to lay down some first principles for the study of this body of dogma or systematized prediction which we call the law, for men who want to use it as the instrument of their business to enable them to prophesy in their turn, and, as bearing upon the study, I wish to point out an ideal which as yet our law has not attained.

The first thing for a business-like understanding of the matter is to understand its limits, and therefore I think it desirable at once to point out and dispel a confusion between morality and law, which sometimes rises to the height of conscious theory, and more often and indeed constantly is making trouble in detail without reaching the point of consciousness. You can see very plainly that a bad man has as much reason as a good one for wishing to avoid an encounter with the public force, and therefore you can see the practical importance of the distinction between morality and law. A man who cares nothing for an ethical rule which is believed and practised by his neighbors is likely nevertheless to care a good deal to avoid being made to pay money, and will want to keep out of jail if he can.

I take it for granted that no hearer of mine will misinterpret what I have to say as the language of cynicism. The law is the witness and external deposit of our moral life. Its history is the history of the moral development of the race. The practice of it, in spite of popular jests, tends to make good citizens and good men. When I emphasize the difference between law and morals I do so with reference to a single end, that of learning and understanding the law. For that purpose you must definitely master its specific marks, and it is for that that I ask you for the moment to imagine yourselves indifferent to other and greater things.

I do not say that there is not a wider point of view from which the distinction between law and morals becomes of secondary or no importance, as all mathematical distinctions vanish in presence of the infinite. But I do say that that distinction is of the first importance for the object which we are here to consider, — a right study and mastery of the law as a business with well understood limits, a body of dogma enclosed within definite lines. I have just shown the practical reason for saying so. If you want to know the law and nothing else, you must look at it as a bad man, who cares only for the material consequences which such knowledge enables him to predict, not as a good one, who finds his reasons for conduct, whether inside the law or outside of it, in the vaguer sanctions of conscience. The theoretical importance of the distinction is no less, if you would reason on your subject aright. The law is full of phraseology drawn from morals, and by the mere force of language continually invites us to pass from one domain to the other without perceiving it, as we are sure to do unless we have the boundary constantly before our minds. The law talks about rights, and duties, and malice, and intent, and negligence, and so forth, and nothing is easier, or, I may say, more common in legal reasoning, than to take these words in their moral sense, at some stage of the argument, and so to drop into fallacy. For instance, when we speak of the rights of man in a moral sense, we mean to mark the limits of interference with individual freedom which we think are prescribed by conscience, or by our ideal, however reached. Yet it is certain that many laws have been enforced in the past, and it is likely that some are enforced now, which are condemned by the most enlightened opinion of the time, or which at all events pass the limit of interference as many consciences would draw it. Manifestly, therefore, nothing but confusion of thought can result from assuming that the rights of man in a moral sense are equally rights in the sense of the Constitution and the law. No doubt simple and extreme cases can be put of imaginable laws which the statute-making power would not dare to enact, even in the absence of written constitutional prohibitions, because the community would rise in rebellion and fight; and this gives some plausibility to the proposition that the law, if not a part of morality, is limited by it. But this limit of power is not coextensive with any system of morals. For the most part it falls far within the lines of any such system, and in some cases may extend beyond them, for reasons drawn from the habits of a particular people at a particular time. I once heard the late Professor Agassiz say that a German population would rise if you added two cents to the price of a glass of beer. A statute in such a case would be empty words, not because it was wrong, but because it could not be enforced. No one will deny that wrong statutes can be and are enforced, and we should not all agree as to which were the wrong ones.

The confusion with which I am dealing besets confessedly legal conceptions. Take the fundamental question, What constitutes the law? You will find some text writers telling you that it is something different from what is decided by the courts of Massachusetts or England, that it is a system of reason, that it is a deduction from principles of ethics or admitted axioms or what not, which may or may not coincide with the decisions. But if we take the view of our friend the bad man we shall find that he does not care two straws for the axioms or deductions, but that he does want to know what the Massachusetts or English courts are likely to do in fact. I am much of his mind. The prophecies of what the courts will do in fact, and nothing more pretentious, are what I mean by the law.

Take again a notion which as popularly understood is the widest conception which the law contains; — the notion of legal duty, to which already I have referred. We fill the word with all the content which we draw from morals. But what does it mean to a bad man? Mainly, and in the first place, a prophecy that if he does certain things he will be subjected to disagreeable consequences by way of imprisonment or compulsory payment of money. But from his point of view, what is the difference between being fined and being taxed a certain sum for doing a certain thing? That his point of view is the test of legal principles is shown by the many discussions which have arisen in the courts on the very question whether a given statutory liability is a penalty or a tax. On the answer to this question depends the decision whether conduct is legally wrong or right, and also whether a man is under compulsion or free. Leaving the criminal law on one side, what is the difference between the liability under the mill acts or statutes authorizing a taking by eminent domain and the liability for what we call a wrongful conversion of property where restoration is out of the question? In both cases the party taking another man's property has to pay its fair value as assessed by a jury, and no more. What significance is there in calling one taking right and another wrong from the point of view of the law? It does not matter, so far as the given consequence, the compulsory payment, is concerned, whether the act to which it is attached is described in terms of praise or in terms of blame, or whether the law purports to prohibit it or to allow it. If it matters at all, still speaking from the bad man's point of view, it must be because in one case and not in the other some further disadvantages, or at least some further consequences, are attached to the act by the law. The only other disadvantages thus attached to it which I ever have been able to think of are to be found in two somewhat insignificant legal doctrines, both of which might be abolished without much disturbance. One is, that a contract to do a prohibited act is unlawful, and the other, that, if one of two or more joint wrongdoers has to pay all the damages, he cannot recover contribution from his fellows. And that I believe is all. You see how the vague circumference of the notion of duty shrinks and at the same time grows more precise when we wash it with cynical acid and expel everything except the object of our study, the operations of the law.

Nowhere is the confusion between legal and moral ideas more manifest than in the law of contract. Among other things, here again the so called primary rights and duties are invested with a mystic significance beyond what can be assigned and explained. The duty to keep a contract at common law means a prediction that you must pay damages if you do not keep it, — and nothing else. If you commit a tort, you are liable to pay a compensatory sum. If you commit a contract, you are liable to pay a compensatory sum unless the promised event comes to pass, and that is all the difference. But such a mode of looking at the matter stinks in the nostrils of those who think it advantageous to get as much ethics into the law as they can. It was good enough for Lord Coke, however, and here, as in many other cases, I am content to abide with him. In Bromage *v.* Genning,[1] a prohibition was sought in the King's Bench against a suit in the marches of Wales for the specific performance of a covenant to grant a lease, and Coke said that it would subvert the intention of the covenantor, since he intends it to be at his election either to lose the damages or to make the lease. Sergeant Harris for the plaintiff confessed that he moved the matter against his conscience, and a prohibition was granted. This goes further than we should go now, but it shows what I venture to say has been the common law point of view from the beginning, although Mr. Harriman, in his very able little book upon Contracts has been misled, as I humbly think, to a different conclusion.

I have spoken only of the common law, because there are some cases in which a logical justification can be found for speaking of civil liabilities as imposing duties in an intelligible sense. These are the relatively few in which equity will grant an injunction, and will enforce it by putting the defendant in prison or otherwise punishing him unless he complies with the order of the court. But I hardly think it advisable to shape general theory from the exception, and I think it would be better to cease troubling ourselves about primary rights and sanctions altogether, than to

[1] 1 Roll. Rep. 368.

describe our prophecies concerning the liabilities commonly imposed by the law in those inappropriate terms.

I mentioned, as other examples of the use by the law of words drawn from morals, malice, intent, and negligence. It is enough to take malice as it is used in the law of civil liability for wrongs, — what we lawyers call the law of torts, — to show you that it means something different in law from what it means in morals, and also to show how the difference has been obscured by giving to principles which have little or nothing to do with each other the same name. Three hundred years ago a parson preached a sermon and told a story out of Fox's Book of Martyrs of a man who had assisted at the torture of one of the saints, and afterward died, suffering compensatory inward torment. It happened that Fox was wrong. The man was alive and chanced to hear the sermon, and thereupon he sued the parson. Chief Justice Wray instructed the jury that the defendant was not liable, because the story was told innocently, without malice. He took malice in the moral sense, as importing a malevolent motive. But nowadays no one doubts that a man may be liable, without any malevolent motive at all, for false statements manifestly calculated to inflict temporal damage. In stating the case in pleading, we still should call the defendant's conduct malicious; but, in my opinion at least, the word means nothing about motives, or even about the defendant's attitude toward the future, but only signifies that the tendency of his conduct under the known circumstances was very plainly to cause the plaintiff temporal harm.[1]

In the law of contract the use of moral phraseology has led to equal confusion, as I have shown in part already, but only in part. Morals deal with the actual internal state of the individual's mind, what he actually intends. From the time of the Romans down to now, this mode of dealing has affected the language of the law as to contract, and the language used has reacted upon the thought. We talk about a contract as a meeting of the minds of the parties, and thence it is inferred in various cases that there is no contract because their minds have not met; that is, because they have intended different things or because one party has not known of the assent of the other. Yet nothing is more certain than that parties may be bound by a contract to things which neither of them intended, and when one does not know of the other's assent. Sup-

[1] See Hanson *v.* Globe Newspaper Co., 159 Mass. 293, 302.

pose a contract is executed in due form and in writing to deliver a lecture, mentioning no time. One of the parties thinks that the promise will be construed to mean at once, within a week. The other thinks that it means when he is ready. The court says that it means within a reasonable time. The parties are bound by the contract as it is interpreted by the court, yet neither of them meant what the court declares that they have said. In my opinion no one will understand the true theory of contract or be able even to discuss some fundamental questions intelligently until he has understood that all contracts are formal, that the making of a contract depends not on the agreement of two minds in one intention, but on the agreement of two sets of external signs, — not on the parties' having *meant* the same thing but on their having *said* the same thing. Furthermore, as the signs may be addressed to one sense or another, — to sight or to hearing, — on the nature of the sign will depend the moment when the contract is made. If the sign is tangible, for instance, a letter, the contract is made when the letter of acceptance is delivered. If it is necessary that the minds of the parties meet, there will be no contract until the acceptance can be read, — none, for example, if the acceptance be snatched from the hand of the offerer by a third person.

This is not the time to work out a theory in detail, or to answer many obvious doubts and questions which are suggested by these general views. I know of none which are not easy to answer, but what I am trying to do now is only by a series of hints to throw some light on the narrow path of legal doctrine, and upon two pitfalls which, as it seems to me, lie perilously near to it. Of the first of these I have said enough. I hope that my illustrations have shown the danger, both to speculation and to practice, of confounding morality with law, and the trap which legal language lays for us on that side of our way. For my own part, I often doubt whether it would not be a gain if every word of moral significance could be banished from the law altogether, and other words adopted which should convey legal ideas uncolored by anything outside the law. We should lose the fossil records of a good deal of history and the majesty got from ethical associations, but by ridding ourselves of an unnecessary confusion we should gain very much in the clearness of our thought.

So much for the limits of the law. The next thing which I wish to consider is what are the forces which determine its content and its growth. You may assume, with Hobbes and Bentham and Austin, that all law emanates from the sovereign, even when the first human beings to enunciate it are the judges, or you may think that law is the voice of the Zeitgeist, or what you like. It is all one to my present purpose. Even if every decision required the sanction of an emperor with despotic power and a whimsical turn of mind, we should be interested none the less, still with a view to prediction, in discovering some order, some rational explanation, and some principle of growth for the rules which he laid down. In every system there are such explanations and principles to be found. It is with regard to them that a second fallacy comes in, which I think it important to expose.

The fallacy to which I refer is the notion that the only force at work in the development of the law is logic. In the broadest sense, indeed, that notion would be true. The postulate on which we think about the universe is that there is a fixed quantitative relation between every phenomenon and its antecedents and consequents. If there is such a thing as a phenomenon without these fixed quantitative relations, it is a miracle. It is outside the law of cause and effect, and as such transcends our power of thought, or at least is something to or from which we cannot reason. The condition of our thinking about the universe is that it is capable of being thought about rationally, or, in other words, that every part of it is effect and cause in the same sense in which those parts are with which we are most familiar. So in the broadest sense it is true that the law is a logical development, like everything else. The danger of which I speak is not the admission that the principles governing other phenomena also govern the law, but the notion that a given system, ours, for instance, can be worked out like mathematics from some general axioms of conduct. This is the natural error of the schools, but it is not confined to them. I once heard a very eminent judge say that he never let a decision go until he was absolutely sure that it was right. So judicial dissent often is blamed, as if it meant simply that one side or the other were not doing their sums right, and, if they would take more trouble, agreement inevitably would come.

This mode of thinking is entirely natural. The training of lawyers is a training in logic. The processes of analogy, discrimination, and deduction are those in which they are most at home. The language of judicial decision is mainly the language of logic.

And the logical method and form flatter that longing for certainty and for repose which is in every human mind. But certainty generally is illusion, and repose is not the destiny of man. Behind the logical form lies a judgment as to the relative worth and importance of competing legislative grounds, often an inarticulate and unconscious judgment, it is true, and yet the very root and nerve of the whole proceeding. You can give any conclusion a logical form. You always can imply a condition in a contract. But why do you imply it? It is because of some belief as to the practice of the community or of a class, or because of some opinion as to policy, or, in short, because of some attitude of yours upon a matter not capable of exact quantitative measurement, and therefore not capable of founding exact logical conclusions. Such matters really are battle grounds where the means do not exist for determinations that shall be good for all time, and where the decision can do no more than embody the preference of a given body in a given time and place. We do not realize how large a part of our law is open to reconsideration upon a slight change in the habit of the public mind. No concrete proposition is self-evident, no matter how ready we may be to accept it, not even Mr. Herbert Spencer's Every man has a right to do what he wills, provided he interferes not with a like right on the part of his neighbors.

Why is a false and injurious statement privileged, if it is made honestly in giving information about a servant? It is because it has been thought more important that information should be given freely, than that a man should be protected from what under other circumstances would be an actionable wrong. Why is a man at liberty to set up a business which he knows will ruin his neighbor? It is because the public good is supposed to be best subserved by free competition. Obviously such judgments of relative importance may vary in different times and places. Why does a judge instruct a jury that an employer is not liable to an employee for an injury received in the course of his employment unless he is negligent, and why do the jury generally find for the plaintiff if the case is allowed to go to them? It is because the traditional policy of our law is to confine liability to cases where a prudent man might have foreseen the injury, or at least the danger, while the inclination of a very large part of the community is to make certain classes of persons insure the safety of those with whom they deal. Since the last words were written, I have seen the requirement of such insurance put forth as part of the programme of one of the best known labor organizations. There is a concealed, half conscious battle on the question of legislative policy, and if any one thinks that it can be settled deductively, or once for all, I only can say that I think he is theoretically wrong, and that I am certain that his conclusion will not be accepted in practice *semper ubique et ab omnibus.*

Indeed, I think that even now our theory upon this matter is open to reconsideration, although I am not prepared to say how I should decide if a reconsideration were proposed. Our law of torts comes from the old days of isolated, ungeneralized wrongs, assaults, slanders, and the like, where the damages might be taken to lie where they fell by legal judgment. But the torts with which our courts are kept busy to-day are mainly the incidents of certain well known businesses. They are injuries to person or property by railroads, factories, and the like. The liability for them is estimated, and sooner or later goes into the price paid by the public. The public really pays the damages, and the question of liability, if pressed far enough, is really the question how far it is desirable that the public should insure the safety of those whose work it uses. It might be said that in such cases the chance of a jury finding for the defendant is merely a chance, once in a while rather arbitrarily interrupting the regular course of recovery, most likely in the case of an unusually conscientious plaintiff, and therefore better done away with. On the other hand, the economic value even of a life to the community can be estimated, and no recovery, it may be said, ought to go beyond that amount. It is conceivable that some day in certain cases we may find ourselves imitating, on a higher plane, the tariff for life and limb which we see in the Leges Barbarorum.

I think that the judges themselves have failed adequately to recognize their duty of weighing considerations of social advantage. The duty is inevitable, and the result of the often proclaimed judicial aversion to deal with such considerations is simply to leave the very ground and foundation of judgments inarticulate, and often unconscious, as I have said. When socialism first began to be talked about, the comfortable classes of the community were a good deal frightened. I suspect that this fear has influenced judicial action both here and in England, yet it is certain that it is not a conscious factor in the decisions to which I refer. I think that something similar has led people who no longer hope to control the legislatures to look to the courts as expounders of the Constitutions, and that in some courts new principles have been discovered outside the bodies of those instruments, which may be generalized into acceptance of the economic doctrines which prevailed about fifty years ago, and a wholesale prohibition of what a tribunal of lawyers does not think about right. I cannot but believe that if the training of lawyers led them habitually to consider more definitely and explicitly the social advantage on which the rule they lay down must be justified, they sometimes would hesitate where now they are confident, and see that really they were taking sides upon debatable and often burning questions.

So much for the fallacy of logical form. Now let us consider the present condition of the law as a subject for study, and the ideal toward which it tends. We still are far from the point of view which I desire to see reached. No one has reached it or can reach it as yet. We are only at the beginning of a philosophical reaction, and of a reconsideration of the worth of doctrines which for the most part still are taken for granted without any deliberate, conscious, and systematic questioning of their grounds. The development of our law has gone on for nearly a thousand years, like the development of a plant, each generation taking the inevitable next step, mind, like matter, simply obeying a law of spontaneous growth. It is perfectly natural and right that it should have been so. Imitation is a necessity of human nature, as has been illustrated by a remarkable French writer, M. Tarde, in an admirable book, "Les Lois de l'Imitation." Most of the things we do, we do for no better reason than that our fathers have done them or that our neighbors do them, and the same is true of a larger part than we suspect of what we think. The reason is a good one, because our short life gives us no time for a better, but it is not the best. It does not follow, because we all are compelled to take on faith at second hand most of the rules on which we base our action and our thought, that each of us may not try to set some corner of his world in the order of reason, or that all of us collectively should not aspire to carry reason as far as it will go throughout the whole domain. In regard to the law, it is true, no doubt, that an evolutionist will hesitate to affirm universal validity for his social ideals, or for the principles which he thinks should be embodied in legislation. He is content if he can prove them best for here and now. He may be ready to admit that he knows nothing about an absolute best in the cosmos, and even that he knows next to nothing about a permanent best for men. Still it is true that a body of law is more rational and more civilized when every rule it contains is referred articulately and definitely to an end which it subserves, and when the grounds for desiring that end are stated or are ready to be stated in words.

At present, in very many cases, if we want to know why a rule of law has taken its particular shape, and more or less if we want to know why it exists at all, we go to tradition. We follow it into the Year Books, and perhaps beyond them to the customs of the Salian Franks, and somewhere in the past, in the German forests, in the needs of Norman kings, in the assumptions of a dominant class, in the absence of generalized ideas, we find out the practical motive for what now best is justified by the mere fact of its acceptance and that men are accustomed to it. The rational study of law is still to a large extent the study of history. History must be a part of the study, because without it we cannot know the precise scope of rules which it is our business to know. It is a part of the rational study, because it is the first step toward an enlightened scepticism, that is, toward a deliberate reconsideration of the worth of those rules. When you get the dragon out of his cave on to the plain and in the daylight, you can count his teeth and claws, and see just what is his strength. But to get him out is only the first step. The next is either to kill him, or to tame him and make him a useful animal. For the rational study of the law the black-letter man may be the man of the present, but the man of the future is the man of statistics and the master of economics. It is revolting to have no better reason for a rule of law than that so it was laid down in the time of Henry IV. It is still more revolting if the grounds upon which it was laid down have vanished long since, and the rule simply persists from blind imitation of the past. I am thinking of the technical rule as to trespass *ab initio*, as it is called, which I attempted to explain in a recent Massachusetts case.[1]

Let me take an illustration, which can be stated in a few words, to show how the social end which is aimed at by a rule of law is obscured and only partially attained in consequence of the fact that the rule owes its form to a gradual historical development, instead of being reshaped as a whole, with conscious articulate reference to the end in view. We think it desirable to prevent one man's property being misappropriated by another, and so we

[1] Commonwealth *v.* Rubin, 165 Mass. 453.

make larceny a crime. The evil is the same whether the misappropriation is made by a man into whose hands the owner has put the property, or by one who wrongfully takes it away. But primitive law in its weakness did not get much beyond an effort to prevent violence, and very naturally made a wrongful taking, a trespass, part of its definition of the crime. In modern times the judges enlarged the definition a little by holding that, if the wrongdoer gets possession by a trick or device, the crime is committed. This really was giving up the requirement of a trespass, and it would have been more logical, as well as truer to the present object of the law, to abandon the requirement altogether. That, however, would have seemed too bold, and was left to statute. Statutes were passed making embezzlement a crime. But the force of tradition caused the crime of embezzlement to be regarded as so far distinct from larceny that to this day, in some jurisdictions at least, a slip corner is kept open for thieves to contend, if indicted for larceny, that they should have been indicted for embezzlement, and if indicted for embezzlement, that they should have been indicted for larceny, and to escape on that ground.

Far more fundamental questions still await a better answer than that we do as our fathers have done. What have we better than a blind guess to show that the criminal law in its present form does more good than harm? I do not stop to refer to the effect which it has had in degrading prisoners and in plunging them further into crime, or to the question whether fine and imprisonment do not fall more heavily on a criminal's wife and children than on himself. I have in mind more far-reaching questions. Does punishment deter? Do we deal with criminals on proper principles? A modern school of Continental criminalists plumes itself on the formula, first suggested, it is said, by Gall, that we must consider the criminal rather than the crime. The formula does not carry us very far, but the inquiries which have been started look toward an answer of my questions based on science for the first time. If the typical criminal is a degenerate, bound to swindle or to murder by as deep seated an organic necessity as that which makes the rattlesnake bite, it is idle to talk of deterring him by the classical method of imprisonment. He must be got rid of; he cannot be improved, or frightened out of his structural reaction. If, on the other hand, crime, like normal human conduct, is mainly a matter of imitation, punishment fairly may be expected to help to keep it out of fashion. The study of criminals has been thought by some well known men of science to sustain the former hypothesis. The statistics of the relative increase of crime in crowded places like large cities, where example has the greatest chance to work, and in less populated parts, where the contagion spreads more slowly, have been used with great force in favor of the latter view. But there is weighty authority for the belief that, however this may be, "not the nature of the crime, but the dangerousness of the criminal, constitutes the only reasonable legal criterion to guide the inevitable social reaction against the criminal." [1]

The impediments to rational generalization, which I illustrated from the law of larceny, are shown in the other branches of the law, as well as in that of crime. Take the law of tort or civil liability for damages apart from contract and the like. Is there any general theory of such liability, or are the cases in which it exists simply to be enumerated, and to be explained each on its special ground, as is easy to believe from the fact that the right of action for certain well known classes of wrongs like trespass or slander has its special history for each class? I think that there is a general theory to be discovered, although resting in tendency rather than established and accepted. I think that the law regards the infliction of temporal damage by a responsible person as actionable, if under the circumstances known to him the danger of his act is manifest according to common experience, or according to his own experience if it is more than common, except in cases where upon special grounds of policy the law refuses to protect the plaintiff or grants a privilege to the defendant.[2] I think that commonly malice, intent, and negligence mean only that the danger was manifest to a greater or less degree, under the circumstances known to the actor, although in some cases of privilege malice may mean an actual malevolent motive, and such a motive may take away a permission knowingly to inflict harm, which otherwise would be granted on this or that ground of dominant public good. But when I stated my view to a very eminent English judge the

---

[1] Havelock Ellis, "The Criminal," 41, citing Garofalo. See also Ferri, "Sociologie Criminelle," *passim*. Compare Tarde, "La Philosophie Pénale."

[2] An example of the law's refusing to protect the plaintiff is when he is interrupted by a stranger in the use of a valuable way, which he has travelled adversely for a week less than the period of prescription. A week later he will have gained a right, but now he is only a trespasser. Examples of privilege I have given already. One of the best is competition in business.

other day, he said: "You are discussing what the law ought to be; as the law is, you must show a right. A man is not liable for negligence unless he is subject to a duty." If our difference was more than a difference in words, or with regard to the proportion between the exceptions and the rule, then, in his opinion, liability for an act cannot be referred to the manifest tendency of the act to cause temporal damage in general as a sufficient explanation, but must be referred to the special nature of the damage, or must be derived from some special circumstances outside of the tendency of the act, for which no generalized explanation exists. I think that such a view is wrong, but it is familiar, and I dare say generally is accepted in England.

Everywhere the basis of principle is tradition, to such an extent that we even are in danger of making the rôle of history more important than it is. The other day Professor Ames wrote a learned article to show, among other things, that the common law did not recognize the defence of fraud in actions upon specialties, and the moral might seem to be that the personal character of that defence is due to its equitable origin. But if, as I have said, all contracts are formal, the difference is not merely historical, but theoretic, between defects of form which prevent a contract from being made, and mistaken motives which manifestly could not be considered in any system that we should call rational except against one who was privy to those motives. It is not confined to specialties, but is of universal application. I ought to add that I do not suppose that Mr. Ames would disagree with what I suggest.

However, if we consider the law of contract, we find it full of history. The distinctions between debt, covenant, and assumpsit are merely historical. The classification of certain obligations to pay money, imposed by the law irrespective of any bargain as quasi contracts, is merely historical. The doctrine of consideration is merely historical. The effect given to a seal is to be explained by history alone. — Consideration is a mere form. Is it a useful form? If so, why should it not be required in all contracts? A seal is a mere form, and is vanishing in the scroll and in enactments that a consideration must be given, seal or no seal. — Why should any merely historical distinction be allowed to affect the rights and obligations of business men?

Since I wrote this discourse I have come on a very good example of the way in which tradition not only overrides rational policy, but overrides it after first having been misunderstood and having been given a new and broader scope than it had when it had a meaning. It is the settled law of England that a material alteration of a written contract by a party avoids it as against him. The doctrine is contrary to the general tendency of the law. We do not tell a jury that if a man ever has lied in one particular he is to be presumed to lie in all. Even if a man has tried to defraud, it seems no sufficient reason for preventing him from proving the truth. Objections of like nature in general go to the weight, not to the admissibility, of evidence. Moreover, this rule is irrespective of fraud, and is not confined to evidence. It is not merely that you cannot use the writing, but that the contract is at an end. What does this mean? The existence of a written contract depends on the fact that the offerer and offeree have interchanged their written expressions, not on the continued existence of those expressions. But in the case of a bond the primitive notion was different. The contract was inseparable from the parchment. If a stranger destroyed it, or tore off the seal, or altered it, the obligee could not recover, however free from fault, because the defendant's contract, that is, the actual tangible bond which he had sealed, could not be produced in the form in which it bound him. About a hundred years ago Lord Kenyon undertook to use his reason on this tradition, as he sometimes did to the detriment of the law, and, not understanding it, said he could see no reason why what was true of a bond should not be true of other contracts. His decision happened to be right, as it concerned a promissory note, where again the common law regarded the contract as inseparable from the paper on which it was written, but the reasoning was general, and soon was extended to other written contracts, and various absurd and unreal grounds of policy were invented to account for the enlarged rule.

I trust that no one will understand me to be speaking with disrespect of the law, because I criticise it so freely. I venerate the law, and especially our system of law, as one of the vastest products of the human mind. No one knows better than I do the countless number of great intellects that have spent themselves in making some addition or improvement, the greatest of which is trifling when compared with the mighty whole. It has the final title to respect that it exists, that it is not a Hegelian dream, but a part of the lives of men. But one may criticise even what one reveres. Law is the business to which my life is devoted, and I should show less than devotion if I did not do what in me lies to improve it, and, when I perceive what seems to me the ideal of its future, if I hesitated to point it out and to press toward it with all my heart.

Perhaps I have said enough to show the part which the study of history necessarily plays in the intelligent study of the law as it is to-day. In the teaching of this school and at Cambridge it is in no danger of being undervalued. Mr. Bigelow here and Mr. Ames and Mr. Thayer there have made important contributions which will not be forgotten, and in England the recent history of early English law by Sir Frederick Pollock and Mr. Maitland has lent the subject an almost deceptive charm. We must beware of the pitfall of antiquarianism, and must remember that for our purposes our only interest in the past is for the light it throws upon the present. I look forward to a time when the part played by history in the explanation of dogma shall be very small, and instead of ingenious research we shall spend our energy on a study of the ends sought to be attained and the reasons for desiring them. As a step toward that ideal it seems to me that every lawyer ought to seek an understanding of economics. The present divorce between the schools of political economy and law seems to me an evidence of how much progress in philosophical study still remains to be made. In the present state of political economy, indeed, we come again upon history on a larger scale, but there we are called on to consider and weigh the ends of legislation, the means of attaining them, and the cost. We learn that for everything we have to give up something else, and we are taught to set the advantage we gain against the other advantage we lose, and to know what we are doing when we elect.

There is another study which sometimes is undervalued by the practical minded, for which I wish to say a good word, although I think a good deal of pretty poor stuff goes under that name. I mean the study of what is called jurisprudence. Jurisprudence, as I look at it, is simply law in its most generalized part. Every effort to reduce a case to a rule is an effort of jurisprudence, although the name as used in English is confined to the broadest rules and most fundamental conceptions. One mark of a great lawyer is that he sees the application of the broadest rules. There is a story of a Vermont justice of the peace before whom a suit was brought by one farmer against another for breaking a churn. The justice took time to consider, and then said that he had looked through the statutes and could find nothing about churns, and gave judgment for the defendant. The same state of mind is shown in all our common digests and text-books. Applications of rudimentary rules of contract or tort are tucked away under the head of Railroads or Telegraphs or go to swell treatises on historical subdivisions, such as Shipping or Equity, or are gathered under an arbitrary title which is thought likely to appeal to the practical mind, such as Mercantile Law. If a man goes into law it pays to be a master of it, and to be a master of it means to look straight through all the dramatic incidents and to discern the true basis for prophecy. Therefore, it is well to have an accurate notion of what you mean by law, by a right, by a duty, by malice, intent, and negligence, by ownership, by possession, and so forth. I have in my mind cases in which the highest courts seem to me to have floundered because they had no clear ideas on some of these themes. I have illustrated their importance already. If a further illustration is wished, it may be found by reading the Appendix to Sir James Stephen's Criminal Law on the subject of possession, and then turning to Pollock and Wright's enlightened book. Sir James Stephen is not the only writer whose attempts to analyze legal ideas have been confused by striving for a useless quintessence of all systems, instead of an accurate anatomy of one. The trouble with Austin was that he did not know enough English law. But still it is a practical advantage to master Austin, and his predecessors, Hobbes and Bentham, and his worthy successors, Holland and Pollock. Sir Frederick Pollock's recent little book is touched with the felicity which marks all his works, and is wholly free from the perverting influence of Roman models.

The advice of the elders to young men is very apt to be as unreal as a list of the hundred best books. At least in my day I had my share of such counsels, and high among the unrealities I place the recommendation to study the Roman law. I assume that such advice means more than collecting a few Latin maxims with which to ornament the discourse, — the purpose for which Lord Coke recommended Bracton. If that is all that is wanted, the title "De Regulis Juris Antiqui" can be read in an hour. I assume that, if it is well to study the Roman law, it is well to study it as a working system. That means mastering a set of technicalities more difficult and less understood than our own, and studying another course of history by which even more than our own the Roman law must be explained. If any one doubts me, let him read Keller's "Der Römische Civil Process und die Actionen," a treatise on the prætor's edict, Muirhead's most interesting "Historical Introduction to the Private Law of Rome," and, to give him the best chance possible, Sohm's admirable Institutes. No. The way to gain a liberal view of your subject is not to read something else, but to get to the bottom of the subject itself. The means of doing that are, in the first place, to follow the existing body of dogma into its highest generalizations by the help of jurisprudence; next, to discover from history how it has come to be what it is; and, finally, so far as you can, to consider the ends which the several rules seek to accomplish, the reasons why those ends are desired, what is given up to gain them, and whether they are worth the price.

We have too little theory in the law rather than too much, especially on this final branch of study. When I was speaking of history, I mentioned larceny as an example to show how the law suffered from not having embodied in a clear form a rule which will accomplish its manifest purpose. In that case the trouble was due to the survival of forms coming from a time when a more limited purpose was entertained. Let me now give an example to show the practical importance, for the decision of actual cases, of understanding the reasons of the law, by taking an example from rules which, so far as I know, never have been explained or theorized about in any adequate way. I refer to statutes of limitation and the law of prescription. The end of such rules is obvious, but what is the justification for depriving a man of his rights, a pure evil as far as it goes, in consequence of the lapse of time? Sometimes the loss of evidence is referred to, but that is a secondary matter. Sometimes the desirability of peace, but why is peace more desirable after twenty years than before? It is increasingly likely to come without the aid of legislation. Sometimes it is said that, if a man neglects to enforce his rights, he cannot complain if, after a while, the law follows his example. Now if this is all that can be said about it, you probably will decide a case I am going to put, for the plaintiff; if you take the view which I shall suggest, you possibly will decide it for the defendant. A man is sued for trespass upon land, and justifies under a right of way. He proves that he has used the way openly and adversely for twenty years, but it turns out that the plaintiff had granted a license to a person whom he reasonably supposed to be the defendant's agent, although not so in fact, and therefore had assumed that the use of the way was permissive, in which case no right would be gained. Has the defendant gained a right or not? If his gaining it stands on the fault and neglect of the landowner in the ordinary sense, as seems commonly to be supposed, there has been no such neglect, and the right of way has not been acquired. But if I were the defendant's counsel, I should suggest that the foundation of the acquisition of rights by lapse of time is to be looked for in the position of the person who gains them, not in that of the loser. Sir Henry Maine has made it fashionable to connect the archaic notion of property with prescription. But the connection is further back than the first recorded history. It is in the nature of man's mind. A thing which you have enjoyed and used as your own for a long time, whether property or an opinion, takes root in your being and cannot be torn away without your resenting the act and trying to defend yourself, however you came by it. The law can ask no better justification than the deepest instincts of man. It is only by way of reply to the suggestion that you are disappointing the former owner, that you refer to his neglect having allowed the gradual dissociation between himself and what he claims, and the gradual association of it with another. If he knows that another is doing acts which on their face show that he is on the way toward establishing such an association, I should argue that in justice to that other he was bound at his peril to find out whether the other was acting under his permission, to see that he was warned, and, if necessary, stopped.

I have been speaking about the study of the law, and I have said next to nothing of what commonly is talked about in that connection, — text-books and the case system, and all the machinery with which a student comes most immediately in contact. Nor shall I say anything about them Theory is my subject, not practical details. The modes of teaching have been improved since my time, no doubt, but ability and industry will master the raw material with any mode. Theory is the most important part of the dogma of the law, as the architect is the most important man who takes part in the building of a house. The most important improvements of the last twenty-five years are improvements in theory. It is not to be feared as unpractical, for, to the competent, it simply means going to the bottom of the subject. For the incompetent, it sometimes is true, as has been said, that an interest in general ideas means an absence of particular knowledge. I remember in army days reading of a youth who, being examined for the lowest grade and being asked a question about squadron drill, answered that he never had considered the evolutions of less than ten thousand men. But the weak and foolish must be left to their folly. The danger is that the able and practical minded should look with indifference or distrust upon ideas the connection of which with their business is remote. I heard a story, the other day, of a man who had a valet to whom he paid high wages, subject to deduction for faults. One of his deductions was, "For lack of imagination, five dollars." The lack is not confined to valets. The object of ambition, power, generally presents itself nowadays in the form of money alone. Money is the most immediate form, and is a proper object of desire. "The fortune," said Rachel, "is the measure of the intelligence." That is a good text to waken people out of a fool's paradise. But, as Hegel says,[1] "It is in the end not the appetite, but the opinion, which has to be satisfied." To an imagination of any scope the most far-reaching form of power is not money, it is the command of ideas. If you want great examples read Mr. Leslie Stephen's "History of English Thought in the Eighteenth Century," and see how a hundred years after his death the abstract speculations of Descartes had become a practical force controlling the conduct of men. Read the works of the great German jurists, and see how much more the world is governed to-day by Kant than by Bonaparte. We cannot all be Descartes or Kant, but we all want happiness. And happiness, I am sure from having known many successful men, cannot be won simply by being counsel for great corporations and having an income of fifty thousand dollars. An intellect great enough to win the prize needs other food beside success. The remoter and more general aspects of the law are those which give it universal interest. It is through them that you not only become a great master in your calling, but connect your subject with the universe and catch an echo of the infinite, a glimpse of its unfathomable process, a hint of the universal law.

[1] Phil. des Rechts, § 190.

SOME FUNDAMENTAL LEGAL CONCEPTIONS AS APPLIED IN JUDICIAL REASONING

From very early days down to the present time the essential nature of trusts and other equitable interests has formed a favorite subject for analysis and disputation. The classical discussions of Bacon[1] and Coke are familiar to all students of equity, and the famous definition of the great chief justice (however inadequate it may really be) is quoted even in the latest text-books on trusts.[2] That the subject has had a peculiar fascination for modern legal thinkers is abundantly evidenced by the well known articles of Langdell[3] and Ames,[4] by the oft-repeated

---

[1] Bacon on Uses (Circa 1602; Rowe's ed. 1806), pp. 5-6: "The nature of an use is best discerned by considering what it is not, and then what it is. * * * First, an use is no right, title, or interest in law; and therefore master attorney, who read upon this statute, said well, that there are but two rights: *Jus in re*: *Jus ad rem.*

"The one is an estate, which is *jus in re;* the other a demand, which is *jus ad rems* but an use is neither. * * * So as now we are come by negatives to the affirmative, what an use is. * * * *Usus est dominium fiduciarium*: Use is an ownership in trust.

"So that *usus & status, sive possessio, potius differunt secundum rationem fori, quam secundum naturam rei,* for that one of them is in court of law, the other in court of conscience. * * *"

[2] Co. Lit. (1628) 272 b: "*Nota,* an use is a trust or confidence reposed in some other, which is not issuing out of the land, but as a thing collaterall, annexed in privitie to the estate of the land, and to the person touching the land, *scilicet,* that *cesty que use* shall take the profit, and that the terre-tenant shall make an estate according to his direction. So as *cesty que use* had neither *jus in re,* nor *jus ad rem,* but only a confidence and trust for which he had no remedie by the common law, but for the breach of trust, his remedie was only by *subpoena* in chancerie. * * *"

This definition is quoted and discussed approvingly in Lewin, Trusts (12th ed., 1911), p. 11. It is also noticed in Maitland, Lectures on Equity (1909), pp. 43, 116.

[3] See Langdell, Classification of Rights and Wrongs (1900), 13 Harv. L. Rev., 659, 673: "Can equity then create such rights as it finds to be necessary for the purposes of justice? As equity wields only physical power, it sems to be impossible that it should actually create anything. * * * It seems, therefore, that equitable rights exist only in contemplation of equity, *i. e.*, that they are a *fiction* invented by equity for the promotion of justice. * * *

"Shutting our eyes, then, to the fact that equitable rights are a fiction, and assuming them to have an actual existence, what is their nature, what

observations of Maitland in his Lectures on Equity,[5] by the very divergent treatment of Austin in his Lectures on Jurisprudence,[6] by the still bolder thesis of Salmond in his volume on Jurisprudence,[7] and by the discordant utterances of Mr. Hart[8] and Mr.

---

their extent, and what is the field which they occupy? * * * They must not violate the law. * * * Legal and equitable rights must, therefore, exist side by side, and the latter cannot interfere with, or in any manner affect, the former."

See also (1887) 1 Harv. L. Rev., 55, 60: "Upon the whole, it may be said that equity could not create rights *in rem* if it would, and that it would not if it could." Compare *Ibid.* 58; and Summary of Eq. Plead. (2nd ed., 1883) secs. 45, 182-184.

[4] See Ames, "Purchase for Value Without Notice" (1887), 1 Harv. L. Rev., 1, 9: "The trustee is the owner of the land, and, of course, two persons with adverse interests cannot be owners of the same thing. What the *cestui que trust* really owns is the obligation of the trustee; for an obligation is as truly the subject matter of property as any physical *res.* The most striking difference between property in a thing and property in an obligation is in the mode of enjoyment. The owner of a house or a horse enjoys the fruits of ownership without the aid of any other person. The only way in which the owner of an obligation can realize his ownership is by compelling its performance by the obligor. Hence, in the one case, the owner is said to have a right *in rem,* and in the other, a right *in personam.* In other respects the common rules of property apply equally to ownership of things and ownership of obligations. For example, what may be called the passive rights of ownership are the same in both cases. The general duty resting on all mankind not to destroy the property of another, is as cogent in favor of an obligee as it is in favor of the owner of a horse. And the violation of this duty is as pure a tort in the one case as in the other."

[5] Lect. on Eq. (1909), 17, 18, 112: "The thesis that I have to maintain is this, that equitable estates and interests are not *jura in rem.* For reasons that we shall perceive by and by, they have come to look very like *jura in rem;* but just for this very reason it is the more necessary for us to observe that they are essentially *jura in personam,* not rights against the world at large, but rights against certain persons."

See also Maitland, Trust and Corporation (1904), reprinted in 3 Collected Papers, 321, 325.

[6] (5th ed.) Vol. I, p. 378: "By the provisions of that part of the English law which is called equity, a contract to sell at once vests *jus in rem* or ownership in buyer, and the seller has only *jus in re aliena.* * * * To complete the transaction the legal interest of the seller must be passed to the buyer, in legal form. To this purpose the buyer has only *jus in personam*: a right to compel the seller to pass his legal interest; but speaking generally, he has *dominium* or *jus in rem,* and the instrument is a conveyance."

[7] (2nd ed., 1907) p. 230: "If we have regard to the essence of the matter rather than to the form of it, a trustee is not an owner at all, but

Whitlock[9] in their very recent contributions to our periodical literature.

It is believed that all of the discussions and analyses referred to are inadequate. Perhaps, however, it would have to be admitted that even the great intrinsic interest of the subject itself and the noteworthy divergence of opinion existing among thoughtful lawyers of all times would fail to afford more than a comparatively slight excuse for any further discussion considered as a mere end in itself. But, quite apart from the presumably practical consideration of endeavoring to "think straight" in relation to all legal problems, it is apparent that the true analysis of trusts and other equitable interests is a matter that should appeal to even the most extreme pragmatists of the law. It may well be that one's view as to the correct analysis of such interests would control the decision of a number of specific questions. This is obviously true as regards the solution of many difficult and delicate problems in constitutional law and in the conflict of laws.[10] So, too, in certain questions in the law of perpetuities, the intrinsic nature of equitable interests is of great significance, as attested

a mere agent, upon whom the law has conferred the power and imposed he duty of administering the property of another person. In legal theory, however, he is not a mere agent, but an owner. He is a person to whom the property of someone else is fictitiously attributed by the law, to the intent that the rights and powers thus rested in a *nominal* owner shall be used by him on behalf of the real owner."

[8] See Walter G. Hart (author of "Digest of Law of Trusts"), The Place of Trust in Jurisprudence (1912), 28 Law Quart. Rev., 290, 296. His position is substantially that of Ames and Maitland.

At the end of this article Sir Frederick Pollock, the editor, puts the query: "Why is Trust not entitled to rank as a head *sui generis?*"

[9] See A. N. Whitlock, Classification of the Law of Trusts (1913), 1 Calif. Law Rev., 215, 218: "It is submitted," says the writer, "that the *cestui* has in fact something more than a right *in personam,* that such a right might be more properly described as a right *in personam ad rem,* or, possibly, a right *in rem per personam.*"

Surely such nebulous and cumbrous expressions as these could hardly fail to make "confusion worse confounded."

[10] See Beale, Equitable Interests in Foreign Property, 20 Harv. L. Rev. (1907), 382; and compare the important cases, *Fall v. Eastin* (1905), 75 Neb., 104; S. C. (1909), 215 U. S., 1, 14-15 (especially concurring opinion of Holmes, J.); *Selover, Bates & Co. v. Walsh* (1912), 226 U. S., 112; *Bank of Africa Limited v. Cohen* (1909), 2 Ch. 129, 143.

by the well-known *Gomm* case[11] and others more or less similar. The same thing is apt to be true of a number of special questions relating to the subject of *bona fide* purchase for value. So on indefinitely.[12]

But all this may seem like misplaced emphasis; for the suggestions last made are not peculiarly applicable to equitable interests: the same points and the same examples seem valid in relation to all possible kinds of jural interests, legal as well as equitable,—and that too, whether we are concerned with "property," "contracts," "torts," or any other title of the law. Special reference has therefore been made to the subject of trusts and other equitable interests only for the reason that the striking divergence of opinion relating thereto conspicuously exemplifies the need for dealing somewhat more intensively and systematically than is usual with the nature and analysis of all types of jural interests. Indeed, it would be virtually impossible to consider the subject of trusts at all adequately without, at the very threshold analyzing and discriminating the various fundamental conceptions that are involved in practically every legal problem. In this connection the suggestion may be ventured that the usual discussions of trusts and other jural interests seem inadequate (and at times misleading) for the very reason that they are not founded on a sufficiently comprehensive and discriminating analysis of jural relations in general. Putting the matter in another way, the tendency—and the fallacy—has been to treat the specific problem as if it were far less complex than it really is; and this commendable effort to treat as simple that which is really complex has, it is believed, furnished a serious obstacle to the clear understanding, the orderly statement, and the correct solution of legal problems. In short, it is submmitted that the

---

[11] (1882) 20 Ch. D. 562, 580, per Sir George Jessel, M. R.: "If then the rule as to remoteness applies to a covenant of this nature, this covenant clearly is bad as extending beyond the period allowed by the rule. Whether the rule applies or not depends upon this, as it appears to me, does or does not the covenant give *an interest in the land?* * * * If it is a mere personal contract it cannot be enforced against the assignee. Therefore the company must admit that somehow it *binds the land.* But if it binds the land, it creates *an equitable interest in the land.*"

[12] Compare *Ball v. Milliken* (1910), 31 R. I., 36; 76 Atl., 789, 793, involving a point other than perpetuities, but quoting in support of the decision reached Sir George Jessel's language as to "equitable interests in land." See preceding note.

right kind of simplicity can result only from more searching and more discriminating analysis.

If, therefore, the title of this article suggests a merely philosophical inquiry as to the nature of law and legal relations,—a discussion regarded more or less as an end in itself,—the writer may be pardoned for repudiating such a connotation in advance. On the contrary, in response to the invitation of the editor of this journal, the main purpose of the writer is to emphasize certain oft-neglected matters that may aid in the understanding and in the solution of practical, every-day problems of the law. With this end in view, the present article and another soon to follow will discuss, as of chief concern, the basic conceptions of the law,—the legal elements that enter into all types of jural interests. A later article will deal specially with the analysis of certain typical and important interests of a complex character,—more particularly trusts and other equitable interests. In passing, it seems necessary to state that both of these articles are intended more for law school students than for any other class of readers. For that reason, it is hoped that the more learned reader may pardon certain parts of the discussion that might otherwise seem unnecessarily elementary and detailed. On the other hand, the limits of space inherent in a periodical article must furnish the excuse for as great a brevity of treatment as is consistent with clearness, and for a comparatively meager discussion—or even a total neglect—of certain matters the intrinsic importance of which might otherwise merit greater attention. In short, the emphasis is to be placed on those points believed to have the greatest practical value.

LEGAL CONCEPTIONS CONTRASTED WITH NON-LEGAL CONCEPTIONS.

At the very outset it seems necessary to emphasize the importance of differentiating purely legal relations from the physical and mental facts that call such relations into being. Obvious as this initial suggestion may seem to be, the arguments that one may hear in court almost any day and likewise a considerable number of judicial opinions afford ample evidence of the inveterate and unfortunate tendency to confuse and blend the legal and the non-legal quantities in a given problem. There are at least two special reasons for this.

For one thing, the association of ideas involved in the two sets of relations—the physical and the mental on the one hand, and the purely legal on the other—is in the very nature of the case, extremely close. This fact has necessarily had a marked influence upon the general doctrines and the specific rules of early systems of law. Thus, we are told by Pollock and Maitland:

"Ancient German law, like ancient Roman law, sees great difficulties in the way of an assignment of a debt or other benefit of a contract * * * men do not see how there can be a transfer of a right unless that right is embodied in some corporeal thing. The history of the incorporeal things has shown us this; they are not completely transferred until the transferee has obtained seisin, has turned his beasts onto the pasture, presented a clerk to the church or hanged a thief upon the gallows. A covenant or a warranty of title may be so bound up with land that the assignee of the land will be able to sue the covenantor or warrantor."[13]

In another connection, the same learned authors observe:

"The realm of mediæval law is rich with incorporeal things. Any permanent right which is of a transferable nature, at all events if it has what we may call a territorial ambit, is thought of as a thing that is very like a piece of land. Just because it is a thing it is transferable. This is no fiction invented by the speculative jurists. For the popular mind these things are things. The lawyer's business is not to make them things but to point out that they are incorporeal. The layman who wishes to convey the advowson of a church will say that he conveys the church; it is for Bracton to explain to him that what he means to transfer is not that structure of wood and stone which belongs to God and the saints, but a thing incorporeal, as incorporeal as his own soul or the *anima mundi*."[14]

A second reason for the tendency to confuse or blend non-legal and legal conceptions consists in the ambiguity and looseness of our legal terminology. The word "property" furnishes a striking example. Both with lawyers and with laymen this term has no definite or stable connotation. Sometimes it is employed to indicate the physical object to which various legal rights, privileges, etc., relate; then again—with far greater discrimination and accuracy—the word is used to denote the legal interest (or aggregate of legal relations) appertaining to such physical object. Frequently there is a rapid and fallacious shift from the one

[13] 2 Hist. Eng. Law (2nd ed., 1905), 226.

[14] *Ibid.*, 124.

meaning to the other. At times, also, the term is used in such a "blended" sense as to convey no definite meaning whatever.

For the purpose of exemplifying the looser usage just referred to, we may quote from *Wilson v. Ward Lumber Co.*:[15]

"The term 'property', as commonly used denotes any external object *over which* the *right* of property is exercised. In this sense it is a very wide term, and includes every class of acquisitions which a man can own or have an interest in."

Perhaps the ablest statement to exemplify the opposite and more accurate usage is that of Professor Jeremiah Smith (then Mr. Justice Smith) in the leading case of *Eaton v. B. C. & M. R. R. Co.*:[16]

"In a strict legal sense, land is not 'property', but the subject of property. The term 'property', although in common parlance frequently applied to a tract of land or a chattel, in its legal signification 'means only the rights of the owner in relation to it'. 'It denotes a right over a determinate thing'. 'Property is the right of any person to possess, use, enjoy, and dispose of a thing'. Selden, J., in *Wynehamer v. People*, 13 N. Y., 378, p. 433; 1 Blackstone's com., 138; 2 Austin's *Jurisprudence*, 3rd ed., 817, 818. * * * The right of indefinite user (or of using indefinitely) is an essential quality of absolute property, without which absolute property can have no existence. * * * This right of user necessarily includes the right and power of excluding others from using the land. See 2 *Austin on Jurisprudence*, 3rd ed., 836; Wells, J., in *Walker v. O. C. W. R. R.*, 103 Mass., 10, p. 14."

Another useful passage is to be found in the opinion of Sherwood, J., in *St. Louis v. Hall*:[17]

"Sometimes the term is applied to the thing itself, as a horse, or a tract of land; these things, however, though the subjects of

---

[15] (1895) 67 Fed. Rep., 674, 677. For a somewhat similar, and even more confusing, form of statement, see *In re Fixen* (1900), 102 Fed. Rep., 295, 296.

[16] 51 N. H., 504, 511. Se also the excellent similar statements of Comstock, J., in *Wynehamer v. People* (1856), 13 N. Y., 378, 396; Selden J., S. C., 13 N. Y., 378, 433-434; Ryan, C., in *Law v. Rees Printing Co.* (1894), 41 Neb., 127, 146; Magruder, J., in *Dixon v. People* (1897), 168 Ill., 179, 190.

[17] (1893) 116 Mo., 527, 533-534. That the last sentence quoted is not altogether adequate as an analysis of property will appear, it is hoped, from the latter part of the present discussion.

See also, as regards the term, "property," the opinion of Doe, C. J., in *Smith v. Fairloh* (1894), 68 N. H., 123, 144-145. ("By considering the property *dissolved* into the *legal rights* of which it consists" etc.)

property, are, when coupled with possession, but the *indicia,* the visible manifestation of invisible rights, 'the evidence of things not seen.'

"Property, then, in a determinate object, is composed of certain constituent elements, to wit: The unrestricted right of use, enjoyment, and disposal, of that object."

In connection with the ambiguities latent in the term "property", it seems well to observe that similar looseness of thought and expression lurks in the supposed (but false) contrast between "corporeal" and "incorporeal" property. The second passage above quoted from Pollock and Maitland exhibits one phase of this matter. For further striking illustration, reference may be made to Blackstone's well-known discussion of corporeal and incorporeal hereditaments. Thus, the great commentator tells us:

"But an hereditament, says Sir Edward Coke, is by much the largest and most comprehensive expression; for it includes not only lands and tenements, but whatsoever *may be inherited,* be it corporeal or incorporeal, real, personal, or mixed."[18]

It is clear that only *legal interests* as such can be inherited; yet in the foregoing quotation there is inextricable confusion between the physical or "corporeal" objects and the corresponding legal interests, all of which latter must necessarily be "incorporeal," or "invisible," to use the expression of Mr. Justice Sherwood. This ambiguity of thought and language continues throughout Blackstone's discussion; for a little later he says:

"Hereditaments, then, to use the largest expression, are of two kinds, corporeal and incorporeal. Corporeal consist of such as affect the senses, such as may be seen and handled by the body; incorporeal are not the objects of sensation, can neither be seen nor handled; are creatures of the mind, and exist only in contemplation."

Still further on he says:

"An incorporeal hereditament is a right issuing out of a thing corporate (whether real or personal), or concerning, or annexed to, or exercisable within, the same. * * *

"Incorporeal hereditaments are principally of ten sorts: advowsons, tithes, commons, ways, offices, dignities, franchises, corodies or pensions, annuities, and rents."

---

[18] 2 Black. Com. (1765), 16-43.

Since all legal interests are "incorporeal"—consisting, as they do, of more or less limited aggregates of *abstract* legal relations—such a supposed contrast as that sought to be drawn by Blackstone can but serve to mislead the unwary. The legal interest of the fee simple owner of land and the comparatively limited interest of the owner of a "right of way" over such land are alike so far as "incorporeality" is concerned; the true contrast consists, of course, primarily in the fact that the fee simple owner's aggregate of legal relations is far more extensive than the aggregate of the easement owner.

Much of the difficulty, as regards legal terminology, arises from the fact that many of our words were originally applicable only to physical things;[19] so that their use in connection with legal relations is, strictly speaking, figurative or fictional. The term, "transfer," is a good example. If X says that he has transferred his watch to Y, he may conceivably mean, quite literally, that he has physically handed over the watch to Y; or, more likely, that he has "transferred" his *legal interest,* without any delivery of possession,—the latter, of course, being a relatively figurative use of the term. This point will be reached again, when we come to treat of the "transfer" of legal interests. As another instance of this essentially metaphorical use of a term borrowed from the physical world, the word "power" may be mentioned. In legal discourse, as in daily life, it may frequently be used in the sense of physical or mental capacity to do a thing; but, more usually and aptly, it is used to indicate a *"legal* power", the connotation of which latter term is fundamentally different. The same observations apply, *mutatis mutandis,* to the term "liberty."

Passing to the field of contracts, we soon discover a similar inveterate tendency to confuse and blur legal discussions by failing to discriminate between the mental and physical facts involved in the so-called "agreement" of the parties, and the legal "contractual obligation" to which those facts give rise. Such

---

[19] Compare Poll. & Maitl. Hist. Eng. Law (2nd ed., 1905), Vol. II, p. 31: "Few, if any, of the terms in our legal vocabulary have always been technical terms. The license that the man of science can allow himself of coining new words is one which by the nature of the case is denied to lawyers. They have to take their terms out of the popular speech; gradually the words so taken are defined; sometimes a word continues to have both a technical meaning for lawyers and a different and vaguer meaning for laymen; sometimes the word that lawyers have adopted is abandoned by the laity." Compare also *Ibid.,* p. 33.

ambiguity and confusion are peculiarly incident to the use of the term "contract." One moment the word may mean *the agreement* of the parties; and then, with a rapid and unexpected shift, the writer or speaker may use the term to indicate the *contractual obligation* created by law as a result of the agrement. Further instances of this sort of ambiguity will be noticed as the discussion proceeds.

OPERATIVE FACTS CONTRASTED WITH EVIDENTIAL FACTS.

For the purpose of subsequent convenient reference, it seems necessary at this point to lay emphasis upon another important distinction inherent in the very nature of things. The facts important in relation to a given jural transaction may be either *operative* facts or *evidential* facts. Operative, constitutive, causal, or "dispositive" facts are those which, under the general legal rules that are applicable, suffice to change legal relations, that is, either to create a new relation, or to extinguish an old one, or to perform both of these functions simultaneously.[20] For

---

[20] Compare Waldo, C. J., in *White v. Multonomah Co.* (1886), 13 Ore., 317, 323: "A 'right' has been define dby Mr. Justice Holmes to be the legal consequence which attaches to certain facts. (The Common Law, 214). Every fact which forms one of the group of facts of which the right is the legal consequence appertains to the substance of the right."

The present writer's choice of the term "operative" has been suggested by the following passage from Thayer, Prelim. Treat. Evid. (1898), p. 393: "Another discrimination to be observed is that between documents which constitute a contract, fact, or transaction, and those which merely certify and evidence something outside of themselves,—a something valid and *operative,* independent of the writing."

Compare also Holland, Jurisp. (10th ed., 1906), 151: "A fact giving rise to a right has long been described as a 'title'; but no such well-worn equivalent can be found for a fact through which a right is transferred, or for one by which a right is extinguished. A new nomenclature was accordingly invented by Bentham, which is convenient for scientific use, although it has not found its way into ordinary language. He describes this whole class of facts as 'Dispositive'; distinguishing as 'Investitive' those by means of which a right comes into existence, as 'Divestitive' those through which it terminates, and as 'Translative' those through which it passes from one person to another."

The word "ultimate," sometimes used in this connection, does not seem to be so pointed and useful a term as either "operative" or "constitutive."

example, in the creation of a contractual obligation between A and B, the *affirmative* operative facts are, *inter alia,* that each of the parties is a human being, that each of them has lived for not less than a certain period of time, (is not "under age"), that A has made an "offer," that B has "accepted" it, etc. It is sometimes necessary to consider, also, what may, from the particular point of view, be regarded as *negative* operative facts. Thus, *e. g.,* the fact that A did not wilfully misrepresent an important matter to B, and the fact that A had not "revoked" his offer, must really be included as parts of the totality of operative facts in the case already put.

Taking another example,—this time from the general field of torts—if X commits an assault on Y by putting the latter in fear of bodily harm, this particular group of facts immediately create in Y the privilege of self-defense,—that is, the privilege of using sufficient force to repel X's attack; or, correlatively, the otherwise existing duty of Y to refrain from the application of force to the person of X is, by virtue of the special operative facts, immediately terminated or extinguished.

In passing, it may not be amiss to notice that the term, "facts in issue," is sometimes used in the present connection. If, as is usual, the term means "facts put in issue by the *pleadings,*" the expression is an unfortuante one. The operative facts alleged by the pleadings are more or less *generic* in character; and if the pleadings be sufficient, only such *generic* operative facts are "put in issue." The operative facts of real life are, on the other hand, very specific. That being so, it is clear that the *real* and *specific* facts finally relied on are comparatively seldom put in issue by the pleadings. Thus, if, in an action of tort, the declaration of A alleges that he was, through the carelessness, etc., of B, bitten by the latter's dog, the fact alleged is generic in character, and it matters not whether it was dog Jim or dog Dick that did the biting. Even assuming, therefore, that the biting was done by Jim, (rather than by Dick), it could not be said that this specific fact was put in issue by the pleadings. Similarly, and more obviously, the pleading in an ordinary action involving so-called negligence, is usually very generic in character,[21] so

[21] Compare, however, *Illinois Steel Co. v. Ostrowski* (1902), 194 Ill., 376, 384, correctly sustaining a declaration alleging the operative facts *specifically* instead of *generically,* as required by the more approved forms of pleading.

that any one of various possible groups of specific operative facts would suffice, so far as the defendant's obligation *ex delicto* is concerned. It therefore could not be said that any one of such groups had been put in issue by the pleadings. A common fallacy in this connection is to regard the *specific* operative facts established in a given case as being but "evidence" of the *generic* (or "ultimate") operative facts alleged in the pleadings.[22]

An evidential fact is one which, on being ascertained, affords some logical basis—not conclusive—for inferring some other fact. The latter may be either a constitutive fact or an intermediate evidential fact. Of all the facts to be ascertained by the tribunal, the operative are, of course, of primary importance; the evidential are subsidiary in their functions.[23] As a rule there is little danger of confusing evidential facts with operative facts. But there is one type of case that not infrequently gives rise to this sort of error. Suppose that in January last a contractual obligation was created by written agreement passing between A and B. In an action now pending between these parties, the physical *instrument* is offered for inspection by the tribunal. If one were thoughtless, he would be apt to say that this is a case where part of the operative facts creating the original obligation are directly presented to the senses of the tribunal. Yet a moment's reflection will show that such is not the case. The document, in its

---

The rules of pleading determining whether allegations must be generic or specific—and if the latter, to what degree—are, like other rules of law, based on considerations of policy and convenience. Thus the facts constituting *fraud* are frequently required to be alleged in comparatively specific form; and similarly as regards *cruelty* in an action for divorce based on that ground. The reasons of policy are obvious in each case.

[22] Compare *McCaughey v. Schuette* (1897), 117 Cal., 223. While the decision in this case can be supported, the statement that the specific facts pleaded were "evidentiary" seems inaccurate and misleading.

There are, of course, genuine instances of the fatally erroneous pleading of strictly evidential facts instead of either generic or specific operative facts. See *Rogers v. Milwaukee,* 13 Wis., 610; and contrast *Illinois Steel Co. v. Ostrowski, supra,* note 21.

[23] Both operative and evidential facts must, under the law, be *ascertained* in some one or more of four possible modes: 1. By judicial admissions (what is not disputed); 2. By judicial notice, or knowledge (what is known or easily knowable); 3. By judicial perception (what is ascertained directly through the senses; cf. "real evidence"); 4. By judicial inference (what is ascertained by reasoning from facts already ascertained by one or more of the four methods here outlined).

then existing shape, had, as regards its operative effect, spent its force as soon as it was delivered in January last. If, therefore, the unaltered document is produced for inspection, the facts thus ascertained must, as regards the alleged contractual agreement, be purely evidential in character. That is to say, the present existence of the piece of paper, its specific tenor, etc., may, along with other evidential facts (relating to absence of change) tend to prove the various operative facts of last January,—to wit, that such paper existed at that time; that its tenor was then the same as it now is; that it was delivered by A to B, and so forth.

It now remains to observe that in many situations a single convenient term is employed to designate (generically) certain miscellaneous groups of operative facts which, though differing widely as to their individual "ingredients," have, as regards a given matter, the same *net* force and effect. When employed with discrimination, the term "possession" is a word of this character; so also the term "capacity," the term "domicile," etc. But the general tendency to confuse legal and non-legal quantities is manifest here as elsewhere; so that only too frequently these words are used rather nebulously to indicate legal relations as such.[24]

FUNDAMENTAL JURAL RELATIONS CONTRASTED WITH ONE ANOTHER.

One of the greatest hindrances to the clear understanding, the incisive statement, and the true solution of legal problems frequently arises from the express or tacit assumption that all legal relations may be reduced to "rights" and "duties," and that these latter categories are therefore adequate for the purpose of analyzing even the most complex legal interests, such as trusts, options, escrows, "future" interests, corporate interests, etc. Even if the difficulty related merely to inadequacy and ambiguity of

[24] As an example of this, compare Lord Westbury, in *Bell v. Kennedy* (1868), L. R. 1 H. L. (Sc.), 307: "Domicile, therefore, is an idea of the law. It is the *relation* which the *law creates* between an individual and a particular locality or country."

Contrast the far more accurate language of Chief Justice Shaw, in *Abington v. Bridgewater* (1840), 23 Pick., 170: "The *fact* of domicile is often one of the highest importance to a person; it *determines* his civil and political rights and privileges, duties and obligations. * * *"

terminology, its seriousness would nevertheless be worthy of definite recognition and persistent effort toward improvement; for in any closely reasoned problem, whether legal or non-legal, chameleon-hued words are a peril both to clear thought and to lucid expression.[25] As a matter of fact, however, the above mentioned inadequacy and ambiguity of terms unfortunately reflect, all too often, corresponding paucity and confusion as regards actual legal conceptions. That this is so may appear in some measure from the discussion to follow.

---

[25] In this connection, the words of one of the great masters of the common law are significant. In his notable Preliminary Treatise on Evidence (1898), p. 190, Professor James Bradley Thayer said:

"As our law develops it becomes more and more important to give definiteness to its phraseology; discriminations multiply, new situations and complications of fact arise, and the old outfit of ideas, discriminations, and phrases has to be carefully revised. Law is not so unlike all other subjects of human contemplation that clearness of thought will not help us powerfully in grasping it. If terms in common legal use are used exactly, it is well to know it; if they are used inexactly, it is well to know that, and to remark just how they are used."

Perhaps the most characteristic feature of this author's great constructive contribution to the law of evidence is his constant insistence on the need for clarifying our legal terminology, and making careful "discriminations" between conceptions and terms that are constantly being treated as if they were one and the same. See, *e. g., Ibid.*, pp. vii, 183, 189-190, 278, 306, 351, 355, 390-393. How great the influence of those discriminations has been is well known to all students of the law of evidence.

The comparatively recent remarks of Professor John Chipman Gray, in his Nature and Sources of the Law (1909), Pref. p. viii, are also to the point:

"The student of Jurisprudence is at times troubled by the thought that he is dealing not with things, but with words, that he is busy with the shape and size of counters in a game of logomachy, but when he fully realizes how these words have been passed and are still being passed as money, not only by fools and on fools, but by and on some of the acutest minds, he feels that there is work worthy of being done, if only it can be done worthily."

No less significant and suggestive is the recent and charactistic utterance of one of the greatest jurists of our time, Mr. Justice Holmes. In *Hyde v. United States* (1911), 225 U. S., 347, 391, the learned judge very aptly remarked: "It is one of the misfortunes of the law that ideas become encysted in phrases and thereafter for a long time cease to provoke further analysis."

See also, Field, J., in *Morgan v. Louisiana* (1876), 93 U. S., 217, 223, and Peckham, J. in *Phoenix Ins. Co. v. Tennessee* (1895), 161 U. S., 174, 177, 178.

The strictly fundamental legal relations are, after all, *sui generis;* and thus it is that attempts at formal definition are always unsatisfactory, if not altogether useless. Accordingly, the most promising line of procedure seems to consist in exhibiting all of the various relations in a scheme of "opposites" and "correlatives," and then proceeding to exemplify their individual scope and application in concrete cases. An effort will be made to pursue this method:

Jural Opposites	rights no-rights	privilege duty	power disability	immunity liability
Jural Correlatives	right duty	privilege no-right	power liability	immunity disability

Rights and Duties. As already intimated, the term "rights" tends to be used indiscriminately to cover what in a given case may be a privilege, a power, or an immunity, rather than a right in the strictest sense; and this looseness of usage is occasionally recognized by the authorities. As said by Mr. Justice Strong in *People v. Dikeman*:[26]

"The word 'right' is defined by lexicographers to denote, among other things, *property, interest, power, prerogative, immunity, privilege* (Walker's Dict. word 'Right'). In law it is most frequently applied to property in its restricted sense, but it is often used to designate *power, prerogative,* and *privilege,* * * *."

Recognition of this ambiguity is also found in the language of Mr. Justice Jackson, in *United States v. Patrick*:[27]

"The words 'right' or 'privilege' have, of course, a variety of meanings, according to the connection or context in which they are used. Their definition, as given by standard lexicographers, include 'that which one has a *legal claim to do,' 'legal power,' 'authority,' 'immunity* granted by authority,' 'the investiture with special or peculiar rights.'"

And, similarly, in the language of Mr. Justice Sneed, in *Lonas v. State*:[28]

"The state, then, is forbidden from making and enforcing any law which shall abridge the *privileges* and *immunities* of citizens of the United States. It is said that the words *rights, privileges* and *immunities,* are abusively used, as if they were synonymous.

---

[26] (1852) 7 How. Pr., 124, 130.

[27] (1893) 54 Fed. Rep., 338, 348.

[28] (1871) 3 Heisk. (Tenn.), 287, 306-307.

The word *rights* is generic, common, embracing whatever may be lawfully claimed."[29]

It is interesting to observe, also, that a tendency toward discrimination may be found in a number of important constitutional and statutory provisions. Just how accurate the distinctions in the mind of the draftsman may have been it is, of course, impossible to say.[30]

Recognizing, as we must, the very broad and indiscriminate use of the term, "right," what clue do we find, in ordinary legal discourse, toward limiting the word in question to a definite and appropriate meaning. That clue lies in the correlative "duty," for it is certain that even those who use the word and the conception "right" in the broadest possible way are accustomed to thinking of "duty" as the invariable correlative. As said in *Lake Shore & M. S. R. Co. v. Kurtz*:[31]

---

[29] See also, for similar judicial observations, *Atchison & Neb. R. Co. v. Baty* (1877), 6 Neb., 37, 40. (The term *right* in civil society is defined to mean that which a man is entitled *to have,* or *to do,* or *to receive* from others within the limits prescribed by law.") ; *San Francisco v. S. V. Water Co.* ( ), 48 Cal., 531 ("We are to ascertain the *rights, privileges, powers, duties* and *obligations* of the Spring Valley Water Co., by reference to the general law.").

Compare also Gilbert, Evid. (4th ed., 1777), 126: "The men of one county, city, hundred, town, corporation, or parish are evidence in relation to the *rights privileges, immunities* and affairs of such town, city, etc."

[30] See *Kearns v. Cordwainers' Co.* (1859), 6 C. B. N. S., 388, 409 (construing The Thames Conservancy Act, 1857, 20 and 21 Vict. c. cxlvii., s. 179: "None of the powers by this act conferred * * * shall extend to, take away, alter or abridge any right, claim, privilege, franchise, exemption, or immunity to which any owners * * * of any lands * * * are now by law entitled.") ; *Fearon v. Mitchell* (1872), L. R. 7 Q. B., 690, 695 ("The other question remains to be disposed of, as to whether the case comes within the proviso of s. 50 of 21 and 22 Vict. c. 98, that 'no market shall be established in pursuance of this section so as to interfere with any rights, powers, or privileges enjoyed within the district by any person without his consent.' ") ; Cal. Civ. Code, sec. 648a: "Building and loan associations may be formed under this title with or without guarantee or other capital stock, with all the rights, powers, and privileges, and subject to all the restrictions and liabilities set forth in this title.") ; Tenn. Const. of 1834, Art. 9, sec. 7: "The legislature shall have no power to pass any law granting to any individual or individuals, rights, privileges and immunities or exemptions, other than * * *").

[31] (1894) 10 Ind. App., 60; 37 N. E., 303, 304.

"A duty or a legal obligation is that which one ought or ought not to do. 'Duty' and 'right' are correlative terms. When a right is invaded, a duty is violated."[32]

In other words, if X has a right against Y that he shall stay off the former's land, the correlative (and equivalent) is that Y is under a duty toward X to stay off the place. If, as seems desirable, we should seek a synonym for the term "right" in this limited and proper meaning, perhaps the word "claim" would prove the best. The latter has the advantage of being a monosyllable. In this connection, the language of Lord Watson in *Studd v. Cook*[33] is instructive:

"Any words which in a settlement of moveables would be recognized by the law of Scotland as sufficient to create a right *or claim* in favor of an executor * * * must receive effect if used with reference to lands in Scotland."

Privileges and "No-Rights." As indicated in the above scheme of jural relations, a privilege is the opposite of a duty, and the correlative of a "no-right." In the example last put, whereas X has a *right* or *claim* that Y, the other man, should stay off the land, he himself has the *privilege* of entering on the land; or, in equivalent words, X does not have a duty to stay off. The privilege of entering is the negation of a duty to stay off. As indicated by this case, some caution is necessary at this point, for, always, when it is said that a given privilege is the mere negation of a *duty,* what is meant, of course, is a duty having a content or tenor precisely *opposite* to that of the privilege in question. Thus, if, for some special reason, X has contracted with Y to go on the former's own land, it is obvious that X has, as regards Y, both the privilege of entering and the *duty of entering.* The privilege is perfectly consistent with this sort of duty,—

[32] See also *Howley Park Coal, etc., Co. v. L. & N. W. Ry.* (1913), A. C. 11, 25, 27 (per Viscount Haldane, L. C.: "There is an obligation (of lateral support) on the neighbor, and in that sense there is a correlative right on the part of the owner of the first piece of land;" per Lord Shaw: "There is a reciprocal right to lateral support for their respective lands and a reciprocal obligation upon the part of each owner. * * * No diminution of the right on the one hand or of the obligation on the other can be effected except as the result of a plain contract. * * *").

Compare, to similar effect, *Galveston, etc. Ry. Co. v. Harrigan* (1903), 76 S. W., 452, 453 (Tex. Civ. App.).

[33] (1883) 8 App. Cas., at p. 597.

for the latter is of the *same* content or tenor as the privilege;—but it still holds good that, as regards Y, X's privilege of entering is the precise negation of a duty *to stay off*. Similarly, if A has not contracted with B to perform certain work for the latter, A's privilege of *not* doing so is the very negation of a duty of *doing* so. Here again the duty contrasted is of a content or tenor exactly opposite to that of the privilege.

Passing now to the question of "correlatives," it will be remembered, of course, that a duty is the invariable correlative of that legal relation which is most properly called a right or claim. That being so, if further evidence be needed as to the fundamental and important difference between a right (or claim) and a privilege, surely it is found in the fact that the correlative of the latter relation is a "no-right," there being no single term available to express the latter conception. Thus, the correlative of X's right that Y shall not enter on the land is Y's duty not to enter; but the correlative of X's privilege of entering himself is manifestly Y's "no-right" that X shall not enter.

In view of the considerations thus far emphasized, the importance of keeping the conception of a right (or claim) and the conception of a privilege quite distinct from each other seems evident; and more than that, it is equally clear that there should be a separate term to represent the latter relation. No doubt, as already indicated, it is very common to use the term "right" indiscriminately, even when the relation designated is really that of privilege;[34] and only too often this identity of terms has involved for the particular speaker or writer a confusion or blurring of ideas. Good instances of this may be found even in unexpected places. Thus Professor Holland, in his work on Jurisprudence, referring to a different and well known sort of ambiguity inherent in the Latin *"Ius,"* the German *"Recht,"* the Italian *"Diritto,"* and the French *"Droit,"*—terms used to express "not only 'a right,' but also 'Law' in the abstract,"—very aptly observes:

"If the expression of widely different ideas by one and the same term resulted only in the necessity for * * * clumsy para-

[34] For merely a few out of numberless judicial instances of this loose usage, see *Pearce v. Scotcher* (1882), L. R. 9 Q. B., 162, 167; *Quinn v. Leathem* (1901), A. C. 495 (*passim*); *Allen v. Flood* (1898), A. C. 1 (*passim*); *Lindley v. Nat. Carbonic Acid Gas Co.* (1910), 220 U. S., 61, 75; *Smith v. Cornell Univ.* (1894), 45 N. Y. Supp., 640, 643; *Farnum v. Kern Valley Bk.* (1910), 107 Pac., 568. See also *post*, n. 38.

phrases, or obviously inaccurate paraphrases, no great harm would be done; but unfortunately the identity of terms seems irresistibly to suggest an identity between the ideas expressed by them."[35]

Curiously enough, however, in the very chapter where this appears,—the chapter on "Rights,"—the notions of right, privilege and power seem to be blended, and that, too, although the learned author states that "the correlative of * * * legal right is legal duty," and that "these pairs of terms express * * * in each case the same state of facts viewed from opposite sides." While the whole chapter must be read in order to appreciate the seriousness of this lack of discrimination a single passage must suffice by way of example:

"If * * * the power of the State will protect him in so carrying out his wishes, and will compel such acts or forbearances on the part of other people as may be necessary in order that his wishes may be so carried out, then he has a 'legal right' so to carry out his wishes."[36]

The first part of this passage suggests privileges, the middle part rights (or claims), and the last part privileges.

Similar difficulties seem to exist in Professor Gray's able and entertaining work on The Nature and Sources of Law. In his chapter on "Legal Rights and Duties" the distinguished author takes the position that a right always has a duty as its correlative;[37] and he seems to define the former relation substantially according to the more limited meaning of "claim." Legal privileges, powers, and immunities are *prima facie* ignored, and the impression conveyed that all legal relations can be comprehended under the conceptions, "right" and "duty." But, with the greatest hesitation and deference, the suggestion may be ventured that a number of his examples seem to show the inadequacy of such mode of treatment. Thus, *e. g.*, he says:

"The eating of shrimp salad is an interest of mine, and, if I can pay for it, the law will protect that interest, and it is therefore a right of mine to eat shrimp salad which I have paid for, although I know that shrimp salad always gives me the colic."[38]

This passage seems to suggest primarily two classes of relations: *first,* the party's respective privileges, as against A, B, C.

[35] El. Jurisp. (10th ed.), 83.

[36] *Ibid.*, 82.

[37] See Nat. and Sources of Law (1909), secs. 45, 184.

[38] *Ibid.*, sec. 48.

D and others in relation to eating the salad, or, correlatively, the respective "no-rights" of A. B. C. D and others that the party should not eat the salad; *second,* the party's respective rights (or claims) as against A. B. C. D and others that they should not interfere with the physical act of eating the salad, or, correlatively, the respective duties of A, B, C, D and others that they should not interfere.

These two groups of relations seem perfectly distinct; and the privileges could, in a given case exist even though the rights mentioned did not. A. B. C. and D, being the owners of the salad, might say to X: "Eat the salad, if you can; you have our license to do so, but we don't agree not to interfere with you." In such a case the privileges exist, so that if X succeeds in eating the salad, he has violated no rights of any of the parties. But it is equally clear that if A had succeeded in holding so fast to the dish that X couldn't eat the contents, no right of X would have been violated.[39]

Perhaps the essential character and importance of the distinction can be shown by a slight variation of the facts. Suppose that X, being already the legal owner of the salad, contracts with Y that he (X) will never eat this particular food. With A, B,

---

[39] Other instances in Professor Gray's work may be noted. In sec. 53, he says: "So again, a householder has the right to eject by force a trespasser from his 'castle.' That is, if sued by the trespasser for an assault, he can call upon the court to refuse the plaintiff its help. In other words, a man's legal rights include not only the power effectually to call for aid from an organized society against another, but also the power to call effectually upon the society to abstain from aiding others."

This, it is respectfully submitted, seems to confuse the householder's privilege of ejecting the trespasser (and the "no-right" of the latter) with a complex of *potential* rights, privileges, powers and immunities relating to the supposed action at law.

In sec. 102, the same learned author says: "If there is an ordinance that the town constable may kill all dogs without collars, the constable may have a legal right to kill such dogs, but the dogs are not under a legal duty to wear collars."

It would seem, however, that what the ordinance did was to create a privilege—the absence of the duty not to kill which otherwise would have existed in favor of the owner of the dog. Moreover, that appears to be the most natural connotation of the passage. The latter doesn't except very remotely, call up the idea of the constable's accompanying rights against all others that they shouldn't interfere with his actual killing of the dog.

See, also, secs. 145, 186.

C, D and others no such contract has been made. One of the relations now existing between X and Y is, as a consequence, fundamentally different from the relation between X and A. As regards Y, X has no privilege of eating the salad; but as regards either A or any of the others, X has such a privilege. It is to be observed incidentally that X's right that Y should not eat the food persists even though X's own privilege of doing so has been extinguished.[40]

On grounds already emphasized, it would seem that the line of reasoning pursued by Lord Lindley in the great case of *Quinn v. Leathem*[41] is deserving of comment:

"The plaintiff had the ordinary *rights* of the British subject. He was *at liberty* to earn his living in his own way, provided he did not violate some special law prohibiting him from so doing, and provided he did not infringe the rights of other people. This *liberty* involved *the liberty* to deal with other persons who were willing to deal with him. *This liberty* is *a right* recognized by law; its *correlative* is the general *duty* of every one not to prevent the free exercise of this *liberty* except so far as his own liberty of action may justify him in so doing. But a person's *liberty* or *right* to deal with others is nugatory unless they are at liberty to deal with him if they choose to do so. Any interference with their liberty to deal with him affects him."

A "liberty" considered as a legal relation (or "right" in the loose and generic sense of that term) must mean, if it have any definite content at all, precisely the same thing as *privilege*,[42] and certainly that is the fair connotation of the term as used the first three times in the passage quoted. It is equally clear, as already indicated, that such a privilege or liberty to deal with others at will might very conceivably exist without any peculiar concomitant rights against "third parties" as regards certain kinds of interference.[43] Whether there should be such concomitant rights (or claims) is ultimately a question of justice and policy; and it should be considered, as such, on its merits. The only correlative logically implied by the privileges or liberties in question are the "no-rights" of "third parties." It would therefore be a *non*

[40] It may be noted incidentally that a statute depriving a party of privileges as such may raise serious constitutional questions under the Fourteenth Amendment. Compare, *e. g., Lindley v. Nat. Carbonic Gas Co.* (1910), 220 U. S., 61.

[41] (1901) A. C., 495, 534.

[42] See *post*, pp. 38-44.

[43] Compare *Allen v. Flood* (1898), A. C., 1.

sequitur to conclude from the mere existence of such liberties that "third parties." are under a *duty* not to interfere, etc. Yet in the middle of the above passage from Lord Lindley's opinion there is a sudden and question-begging shift in the use of terms. First, the "liberty" in question is transmuted into a "right," and then, possibly under the seductive influence of the latter word, it is assumed that the "correlative" must be "the general duty of every one not to prevent," etc.

Another interesting and instructive example may be taken from Lord Bowen's oft-quoted opinion in *Mogul Steamship Co. v. McGregor.*[44]

"We are presented in this case with an apparent conflict or antinomy between two rights that are equally regarded by the law—the right of the plaintiffs to be protected in the legitimate exercise of their trade, and the right of the defendants to carry on their business as seems best to them, provided they commit no wrong to others."

As the learned judge states, the conflict or antinomy is only apparent; but this fact seems to be obscured by the very indefinite and rapidly shifting meanings with which the term "right" is used in the above quoted language. Construing the passage as a whole, it seems plain enough that by "the right of the plaintiffs" in relation to the defendants a legal right or claim in the strict sense must be meant; whereas by "the right of the defendants" in relation to the plaintiffs a legal privilege must be intended. That being so, the "two rights" mentioned in the beginning of the passage, being respectively claim and privilege, could not be in conflict with each other. To the extent that the defendants have privileges the plaintiffs have no rights; and conversely, to the extent that the plaintiffs have rights the defendants have no privileges ("no-privilege" equals duty of opposite tenor).[45]

---

[44] (1889) 23 Q. B. D., 59.

[45] Cases almost without number might be cited to exemplify similar blending of fundamental conceptions and rapid shifting in the use of terms;—and that, too, even when the problems involved have been such as to invite close and careful reasoning. For a few important cases of this character, see *Allen v. Flood* (1898), A. C, 1, (Hawkins, J., p. 16: "I know it may be asked, 'What is the legal right of the plaintiffs which is said to have been invaded?' My answer is, that right which should never be lost sight of, and which I have already stated—the right freely to pursue their lawful calling;" Lord Halsbury, p. 84: "To dig into one's own land

Thus far it has been assumed that the term "privilege" is the most appropriate and satisfactory to designate the mere negation of duty. Is there good warrant for this?

In Mackeldey's Roman Law[46] it is said:

"Positive laws either contain general principles embodied in the rules of law * * * or for especial reasons they establish something that differs from those general principles. In the first case they contain a common law (*jus commune*), in the second a special law (*jus singulare s. exorbitans*). The latter is either favorable or unfavorable * * * according as it enlarges or restricts, in opposition to the common rule, the rights of those for whom it is established. The favorable special law (*jus singulare*) as also the right created by it * * * in the Roman law is termed benefit of the law (*beneficium juris*) or privilege (*privilegium*) * * *"[47]

First a special law, and then by association of ideas, a special advantage conferred by such a law. With such antecedents, it is not surprising that the English word "privilege" is not infrequently used, even at the present time, in the sense of a special or peculiar legal advantage (whether right, privilege, power or immunity) belonging either to some individual or to some particular class of persons.[48] There are, indeed, a number of judicial opinions

under the circumstances stated requires no cause or excuse. He may act from mere caprice, but his right on his own land is absolute, so long as he does not interfere with the rights of others;" Lord Ashbourne, p. 112: "The plaintiff had, in my opinion, a clear right to pursue their lawful calling. * * * It would be, I think, an unsatisfactory state of the law that allowed the wilful invader of such a right without lawful leave or justification to escape from the consequences of his action."); *Quinn v. Leathem* (1901), A. C., 495, 533; *Lindsley v. Natural Carbonic Gas Co* (1910), 220 U. S., 61, 74; *Robertson v. Rochester Folding Box Co.* (1902), 171 N. Y., 538 (Parker, C. J., p. 544: "The so-called right of privacy is, as the phrase suggests, founded upon the claim that a man has the right to pass through this world, if he wills, without having his picture published."); *Wabash, St. L. & P. R. Co. v. Shacklet* (1883), 105 Ill., 364, 389.

In *Purdy v. State* (1901), 43 Fla., 538, 540, the anomalous expression "right of privilege" is employed.

[46] (Dropsie Tr.) secs. 196-197.

[47] The same matter is put somewhat less clearly in Sohm's Institutes (Ledlies Tr., 3rd ed.), 28.

See also *Rector, etc. of Christ Church v. Philadelphia* (1860), 24 How., 300, 301, 302.

[48] According to an older usage, the term "privilege" was frequently employed to indicate a "franchise," the latter being really a miscellaneous complex of special rights, privileges, powers, or immunities, etc. Thus, in an early book, *Termes de la Ley*, there is the following definition: "'Privi-

recognizing this as one of the meanings of the term in question.[49] That the word has a wider signification even in ordinary non-technical usage is sufficiently indicated, however, by the fact that the term *"special* privileges" is so often used to indicate a contrast to ordinary or general privileges. More than this, the dominant specific connotation of the term as used in popular speech seems to be more *negation of duty.* This is manifest in the terse and oft-repeated expression, "That is your privilege,"—meaning, of course, "You are under no duty to do otherwise."

Such being the case, it is not surprising to find, from a wide survey of judicial precedents, that the *dominant* technical meaning of the term is, similarly, negation of *legal duty.*[50] There are two very common examples of this, relating respectively to "privileged communications" in the law of libel and to "privileges against self-crimination" in the law of evidence. As regards the first case, it is elementary that if a certain group of operative facts are present, a privilege exists, which, without such facts, would not be recognized.[51] It is, of course, equally clear that even

---

leges' are liberties and franchises granted to an office, place, towne, or manor by the King's great charter, letters patent, or Act of Parliament, as toll, sake, socke, infangstheefe, outfangstheefe, turne, or delfe, and divers such like."

Compare *Blades v Higgs* (1865), 11 H. L. Cas., 621, 631, per Lord Westbury: "Property *ratione privilegii* is the right which by a peculiar franchise anciently granted by the Crown, by virtue of prerogative, one may have of taking animals *ferae naturae* on the land of another; and in like manner the game when taken by virtue of the privilege becomes the absolute property of the owner of the franchise."

[49] See *Humphrey v. Pegues* (1872), 16 Wall., 244, 247, per Hunt, J.: "All the 'privileges' as well as powers and rights of the prior company. were granted to the latter. A more imporant or more comprehensive privilege than a perpetual immunity from taxation can scarcely be imagined. It contains the essential idea of a peculiar benefit or advantage, of a special exemption from a burden falling upon others."

See also *Smith v. Floyd* (1893), 140 N. Y., 337, 342; *Lonas v. State* (1871). 3 Heisk., 287, 306,307; *Territory v Stokes* (1881), 2 N. M., 161, 169, 170; *Ripley v. Knight* (1878), 123 Mass., 515, 519; *Dike v. State* (1888), 38 Minn., 366; *Re Miller* (1893), 1 Q. B., 327.

Compare *Wisener v. Burrell* (1911), 28 Okla., 546.

[50] Compare *Louisville & N. R Co. v. Gaines* (1880), 3 Fed. Rep., 266, 278, per Baxter, Asso. J.: "Paschal says (the term privilege) is a special right belonging to an individual or class; *properly,* an *exemption* from some *duty."*

[51] For apt use of the terms, "privilege" and "privileged" in relation to libel, see Hawkins, J., in *Allen v. Flood* (1898), A. C. 1, 20-21.

though all such facts be present as last supposed, the superadded fact of malice will, in cases of so-called "conditional privilege," extinguish the privilege that otherwise would exist. It must be evident also, that whenever the privilege does exist, it is not special in the sense of arising from a special law, or of being conferred as a special favor on a particular individual. The same privilege would exist, by virtue of general rules, for any person whatever under similar circumstances. So, also, in the law of evidence, the privilege against self-crimination signifies the mere negation of a duty, to testify,—a duty which rests upon a witness in relation to all ordinary matters; and, quite obviously, such privilege arises, if at all, only by virtue of general laws.[52]

As already intimated, while both the conception and the term "privilege" find conspicuous exemplification under the law of libel and the law of evidence, they nevertheless have a much wider significance and utility as a matter of judicial usage. To make this clear, a few miscellaneous judicial precedents will now be noticed. In Dowman's Case,[53] decided in the year 1583, and reported by Coke, the court applied the term to the subject of waste:

> "And as to the objection which was made, that the said privilege to be without impeachment of waste cannot be without deed, etc. To that it was answered and resolved, that if it was admitted that a deed in such case should be requisite, yet without question all the estates limited would be good , although it is admitted, that the clause concerning the said privilege would be void."

In the great case of *Allen v. Flood*[54] the opinion of Mr. Justice Hawkins furnishes a useful passage for the purpose now in view:

---

[52] As regards the general duty to testify, specific performance may usually be had under duress of potential or actual contempt proceedings; and, apart from that, failure to testify might subject the wrongdoer either to a statutory liability for a penalty in favor of the injured party litigant or, in case of actual damage, to a common law action on the case.

The subject of witnesses is usually thought of as a branch of the so-called *adjective* law, as distinguished, from the so-called *substantive* law. But, as the writer has had occasion to emphasize on another occasion (The Relations betwen Equity and Law, 11 Mich. L. Rev., 537, 554, 556, 569), there seems to be no intrinsic or essential difference between those jural relations that relate to the "substantive" law and those that relate to the "adjective" law. This matter will be considered more fully in a later part of the discussion.

[53] (1583) 9 Coke, 1.

[54] (1898) A. C., 1, 19.

"Every person has a privilege * * * in the interests of public justice to put the criminal law in motion against another whom he *bona fide,* and upon reasonable and probable cause, believes to have been guilty of a crime. * * * It must not, however, be supposed that hatred and ill-will existing in the mind of a prosecutor must of necessity *destroy* the *privilege,* for it is not impossible that such hatred and ill-will may have very natural and pardonable reasons for existing. * * *"

Applying the term in relation to the subject of property, Mr. Justice Foster, of the Supreme Court of Maine, said in the case of *Pulitzer v. Lumgston*:[55]

"It is contrary to the policy of the law that there should be any outstanding titles, estates, or powers, by the existence, operation or exercise of which, at a period of time beyond lives in being and twenty-one years and a fraction thereafter, the complete and unfettered enjoyment of an estate, *with all the rights, privileges and powers incident to ownership,* should be qualified or impeded."

As a final example in the present connection, the language of Baron Alderson in *Hilton v. Eckerley*[56] may be noticed:

"*Prima facie* it is the privilege of a trader in a free country, in all matters not contrary to law, to regulate his own mode of carrying them on according to his discretion and choice."[57]

The closest synonym of legal "privilege" seems to be legal "liberty." This is sufficiently indicated by an unusually discriminating and instructive passage in Mr. Justice Cave's opinion in *Allen v. Flood*:[58]

"The personal rights with which we are most familiar are: 1. Rights of reputation; 2. Rights of bodily safety and freedom; 3. Rights of property; or, in other words, rights relating to mind, body and estate, * * *

"In my subsequent remarks the word 'right' will, as far as possible, always be used in the above sense; and it is the more

[55] (1896) 89 Me., 359.

[56] (1856) 6 E. & B., 47. 74.

[57] For other examples of apt use of the term in question, see *Borland v Boston* (1882), 132 Mass., 89 ("municipal rights, privileges, powers or duties"); *Hamilton v. Graham* (1871), L. R. 2 H. L. (Sc.), 167, 169, per Hatherley, L. C.; *Jones v. De Moss* (1911), 151 Ia., 112, 117; *Kripp v. Curtis* (1886), 71 Cal., 62, 63; *Lamer v. Booth* (1874), 50 Miss., 411, 413; *Weller v. Brown* (1911), Cal., ; 117 Pac., 517; *Mathews v. People* (1903), 202 Ill., 389, 401; *Abington v. North Bridgewater* (1840), 23 Pick., 170.

[58] (1898) A. C., 1, 29.

necessary to insist on this as during the argument at your Lordship's bar it was frequently used in a much wider and more indefinite sense. Thus it was said that a man has a perfect right to fire off a gun, when all that was meant, apparently, was that a man has a *freedom* or *liberty* to fire off a gun, so long as he does not violate or infringe any one's rights in doing so, which is a very different thing from a right, the violation or disturbance of which can be remedied or prevented by legal process."[59]

While there are numerous other instances of the apt use of the term "liberty," both in judicial opinions[60] and in conveyancing

---

[59] For the reference to Mr. Justice Cave's opinion, the present writer is indebted to Salmond's work on Jurisprudence. Citing this case and one other, *Starey v. Graham* (1899), 1 Q. B., 406, 411, the learned author adopts and uses exclusively the term "liberty" to indicate the opposite of "duty," and apparently overlooks the importance of *privilege* in the present connection. Curiously enough, moreover, in his separate Treatise on Torts, his discussion of the law of defamation gives no explicit intimation that *privilege* in relation to that subject represents merely *liberty*, or *"no-duty."*

Sir Frederick Pollock, in his volume on Jurisprudence (2nd ed., 1904), 62, seems in effect to deny that legal liberty represents any true legal relation as such. Thus, he says, *inter alia*: "The act may be right in the popular and rudimentary sense of not being forbidden, but freedom has not the character of legal right until we consider the risk of unauthorized interference. It is the duty of all of us not to interfere with our neighbors' lawful freedom. This brings the so-called primitive rights into the sphere of legal rule and protection. *Sometimes it is thought that lawful power or liberty is different from the right not to be interfered with; but for the reason just given this opinion, though plausible, does not seem correct.*" Compare also Pollock, Essays in Jurisp. & Ethics (1882), Ch. I.

It is difficult to see, however, why, as between X and Y, the "privilege + no-right" situation is not just as real a jural relation as the precisely opposite "duty + right" relation betwen any two parties. Perhaps the habit of recognizing exclusively the latter as a jural relation springs more or less from the traditional tendency to think of the law as consisting of "commands," or imperative rules. This, however, seems fallacious. A rule of law that *permits* is just as real as a rule of law that *forbids;* and, similarly,s aying that the law *permits* a given act to X as between himself and Y predicates just as genuine a legal relation as saying that the law *forbids* a certain act to X as between himself and Y. That this is so seems, in some measure, to be confirmed by the fact that the first sort of act would ordinarily be pronounced "lawful," and the second "unlawful." Compare *Thomas v. Sorrel* (1673), Vaughan, 331, 351.

[60] Compare *Dow v. Newborough* (1728), Comyns, 242 ("For the use is only a liberty to take the profits, but two cannot severally take the profits of the same land, therefore there cannot be an use upon a use." It should be observed that in this and the next case to be cited, along with the liberty

documents,[61] it is by no means so common or definite a word as "privilege." The former term is far more likely to be used in the sense of physical or personal freedom (*i. e.,* absence of physi-*cal* restraint), as distinguished from a legal relation; and very frequently there is the connotation of *general* political liberty, as distinguished from a particular relation between two definite individuals. Besides all this, the term "privilege" has the advantage of giving us, as a variable, the adjective "privileged". Thus, it is frequently convenient to speak of a privileged act, a privileged transaction, a privileged conveyance, etc.

The term "license", sometimes used as if it were synonymous with "privilege," is not strictly appropriate. This is simply another of those innumerable cases in which the mental and physical facts are so frequently confused with the legal relation which

---

or privilege there are associated powers and rights, etc.: for instance, the *power* to acquire a title to the things severed from the realty); *Bourne v. Taylor* (1808), 10 East., 189 (Ellenborough, C. J.): "The second question is whether the replication ought to have traversed the liberty of working the mines. * * * The word *liberty,* too, implies the same thing. It imports, *ex vi termini,* that it is a *privilege* to be exercised over another man's estates"); *Wickham v. Hawkes* (1840), 7 M. & W., 63, 78-79; *Quinn v. Leathem* (1901), A. C. 495, 534 (per Lord Lindley: see quotation *aent,* p.); *Pollock v. Farmers' Loan & Trust Co.* (1895), 157 U. S., 429, 652 (per White, J., "rights and liberties"); *Mathews v. People* (1903), 202 Ill., 389, 401 (Magruder, C. J.: "It is now well settled that the privilege of contracting is both a liberty, and a property right.").

For *legislative* use of the term in question, see the Copyright Act, 8 Anne (1709) c. 19 ("Shall have the sole right and liberty of printing each book and books for the term of * * *").

Like the word "privilege" (see *ante* p. 38, n. 48), the term "liberty" is occasionally used, especially in the older books, to indicate a franchise, or complex of special rights, privileges, powers, or immunities. Thus in Noy's Maxims (1641) there is this definition: "Liberty is a royal privilege in the hands of a subject;" and, similarly, Blackstone (2 Com. 37) says: "Franchise and liberty are used as synonymous terms; and their definition is, a royal privilege, or branch of the king's prerogative, subsisting in the hands of a subject."

This definition is quoted in *S. F. Waterworks v. Schottler* (1882), 62 Cal. 69, 106, and *Central R. & Banking Co. v. State* (1875), 54 Ga., 401, 409. Compare also *Rex v. Halifax & Co.* (1891), 2 Q. B., 263.

[61] Compare *Pond v. Bates,* 34 L. J. (N. S.), 406 ("With full power and free liberty to sink for, win and work the same, with all liberties, privileges, etc., necessary and convenient," etc.); *Hamilton v. Graham* (1871), L. R. 2 H. L. (Sc.), 166, 167; *Attersoll v. Stevens* (1808), 1 Taunt., 183; *Wickham v. Hawker* (1840), 7 M. & W., 63, 78-79.

they create. Accurately used, "license" is a generic term to indicate a group of *operative* facts required to create a particular privilege,—this being especially evident when the word is used in the common phrase "leave and license." This point is brought out by a passage from Mr. Justice Adams' opinion in *Clifford v. O'Neill*:[62]

"A license is merely a *permission* to do an act which, *without such permission,* would amount to a trespass * * * nor will the continuous enjoyment of the privilege *conferred,* for any period of t'me cause it to ripen into a tangible interest in the land affected."[63]

Powers and Liabilities. As indicated in the preliminary scheme of jural relations, a legal power (as distinguished, of course, from a mental or physical power) is the opposite of legal disability, and the correlative of legal liability. But what is the intrinsic nature of a legal power as such? Is it possible to analyze the conception represented by this constantly employed and very important term of legal discourse? Too close an analysis might seem metaphysical rather than useful; so that what is here presented is intended only as an approximate explanation sufficient for all practical purposes.

A change in a given legal relation may result (1) from some superadded fact or group of facts not under the volitional control of a human being (or human beings); or (2) from some superadded fact or group of facts which are under the volitional control of one or more human beings. As regards the second class of cases, the person (or persons) whose volitional control is paramount may be said to have the (legal) power to effect the particular change of legal relations that is involved in the problem.

The second class of cases—powers in the technical sense—

---

[62] (1896) 12 App. Div., 17; 42 N. Y. Sup., 607, 609.

[63] See, in accord, the oft-quoted passage from *Thomas v. Sorrell* (1673), Vaughan, 331, 351 ("A dispensation or license properly passes no interest, nor alters or transfers property in anything, but only makes an action lawful, which without it had been unlawful. As a license to go beyond the seas, to hunt in a man's park, to come into his house, are only actions, which without license, had been unlawful.").

Compare also *Taylor v. Waters* (1817), 7 Taunt., 374, 384 ("Those cases abundantly prove that a license to enjoy a beneficial privilege in land may be granted, and, notwithstanding the statue of frauds, without writing." In this case the license (operative facts) is more or less confused with privileges (the legal relation created); *Heap v. Hartley* (1889), 42 Ch. D., 461, 470.

must now be further considered. The nearest synonym for any ordinary case seems to be (legal) "ability,"[64]—the latter being obviously the opposite of "inability," or "disability." The term "right," so frequently and loosely used in the present connection, is an unfortunate term for the purpose,—a not unusual result being confusion of thought as well as ambiguity of expression.[65] The term "capacity" is equally unfortunate; for, as we have already seen, when used with discrimination, this word denotes a particular group of operative facts, and not a legal relation of any kind.

Many examples of legal powers may readily be given. Thus, X, the owner of ordinary personal property "in a tangible object" has the power to extinguish his own legal interest (rights, powers, immunities, etc.) through that totality of operative facts known as abandonment; and—simultaneously and correlatively—to create in other persons privileges and powers relating to the abandoned object,—*e. g.,* the power to acquire title to the later by appropriating it.[66] *Similarly,* X has the power to transfer his interest to Y,—that is, to extinguish his own interest and concomitantly create in Y a new and corresponding interest.[67] So

---

[64] Compare *Remington v. Parkins* (1873), 10 R. I., 550, 553, per Durfee, J.: "A power is an ability to do."

[65] See *People v. Dikeman* (1852), 7 Howard Pr., 124, 130; and *Lonas v. State* (1871), 3 Heisk. (Tenn.), 287 ,306-307, quoted *ante,* p.

See also *Mabre v. Whittaker* (1906), 10 Wash., 656, 663 (Washington Laws of 1871 provided in relation to community property: "The husband shall have the management of all the common property, but shall not have the *right* to sell or encumber real estate except he shall be joined in the sale or encumbrance by the wife. * * *" Per Scott, J.: "'Right' in the sense used there means power").

Compare also *St. Joseph Fire & Marine Ins. Co. v. Hanck* (1876), 63 Mo., 112, 118.

Numberless additional instances might be given of the use of the term "right," where the legal quantity involved is really a power rather than a right in the sense of claim.

[66] It is to be noted that abandonment would leave X himself with precisely the same sort of privileges and powers as any other person.

[67] Compare *Wynehamer v. People* (1856), 13 N. Y., 378, 396 (Comstock, J.: "I can form no notion of property which does not include the essential characteristics and attributes with which it is clothed by the laws of society * * * among which are, fundamentally the right of the occupant or owner to use and enjoy (the objects) exclusively, and his *absolute power to sell and dispose of them*"); *Bartemeyer v. Iowa* (1873), 18 Wall., 129, 137 (Field, J.: "The right of property in an article involves the *power*

also X has the power to create contractual obligations of various kinds. Agency cases are likewise instructive. By the use of some *metaphorical* expression such as the Latin, *qui facit per alium, facit per se,* the true nature of agency relations is only too frequently obscured. The creation of an agency relation involves, *inter alia,* the grant of legal powers to the so-called agent, and the creation of correlative liabilities in the principal.[68] That is to say, one party P has the power to create agency powers in another party A,—for example, the power to convey X's property, the power to impose (so-called) contractual obligations on P, the power to discharge a debt, owing to P, the power to "receive" title to property so that it shall vest in P, and so forth. In passing, it may be well to observe that the term "authority," so frequently used in agency cases, is very ambiguous and slippery in its connotation. Properly employed in the present connection, the word seems to be an abstract or qualitative term corresponding to the concrete "authorization,"—the latter consisting of a particular group of operative facts taking place between the principal and the agent. All too often, however, the term in question is so used as to blend and confuse these operative facts with the

---

to sell and dispose of such articles as well as to use and enjoy it"); *Low v. Rees Printing Co.* (1894), 41 Neb., 127, 146 (Ryan, C.: "Property, in its broad sense, is not the physical thing which may be the subject of ownership, but is the right of dominion, possession, and *power of disposition* which may be acquired over it.").

Since the power of alienation is frequently one of the fundamental elements of a complex legal interest (or property aggregate), it is obvious that a statute extinguishing such power may, in a given case be unconstitutional as depriving the owner of property without due prócess of law. See the cases just cited.

[68] For a leading case exhibiting the nature of agency powers, especially powers "coupled with an interest," see *Hunt v. Rousmanier* (1883), 8 Wheat., 173, 201.

It is interesting to note that in the German Civil Code the provisions relating to agency are expressed in terms of powers,—*e. g.,* sec. 168: "The expiration of the power is determined by the legal relations upon which the giving of the power is founded. The power is also revocable in the event of the continuance of the legal relation, unless something different results from the latter."

Incidentally, it may be noticed also, that as a matter of English usage, the term "power of attorney" has, by association of ideas, come to be used to designate the mere operative *instrument* creating the powers of an agent.

powers and privileges thereby created in the agent.[69] A careful discrimination in these particulars would, it is submitted, go far toward clearing up certain problems in the law of agency.[70]

Essentially similar to the powers of agents are powers of appointment in relation to property interests. So, too, the powers of public officers are, intrinsically considered, comparable to those of agents,—for example, the power of a sheriff to sell property under a writ of execution. The power of a donor, in a gift *causa mortis,* to revoke the gift and divest the title of the donee is another clear example of the legal quantities now being considered;[71] also a pledgee's statutory power of sale.[72]

There are, on the other hand, cases where the true nature of the relations involved has not, perhaps, been so clearly recognized. Thus, in the case of a conditional sale of personality, assuming

---

[69] For examples of the loose and confusing employment of the term "authority" in agency cases,—and that too, in problems of the conflict of laws requiring the closest reason,—see *Pope v. Nickerson* (1844), 3 Story, 465, 473, 476, 481, 483; *Lloyd v Guibert* (1865), 6 B. & S., 100, 117; *King v. Sarria* (1877), 69 N. Y., 24, 28, 30-32; *Risdon, etc., Works v. Furness* (1905), 1 K. B. 304; (1906) 1 K. B. 49.

For a criticism of these cases in relation to the present matter, see the writer's article The Individual Liability of Stockholders and the Conflict of Laws (1909), 9 Columb. L. Rev., 492, 512, n. 46, 521, n. 71; 10 Columb. L. Rev., 542-544.

[70] The clear understanding and recognition of the agency relation as involving the creation of legal powers may be of crucial importance in many cases,—especially, as already intimated, in regard to problems in the conflict of laws. Besides the cases in the preceding note, two others may be referred to, *Milliken v. Pratt* (1878), 125 Mass., 374, presenting no analysis of the agency problem; and, on the other hand, Freeman's Appeal (1897), 68 Conn., 533, involving a careful analysis of the agency relation by Baldwin, J. Led by this analysis to reach a decision essentially opposite to that of the Massachusetts case, the learned judge said, *inter alia*:

"Such was, in effect, the act by which Mrs. Mitchell undertook to do what she had no legal capacity to do, by making her husband her agent to deliver the guaranty to the bank. He had no more power to make it operative by delivery in Chicago to one of his creditors in Illinois, than he would have had to make it operative by delivery here, had it been drawn in favor of one of his creditors in Connecticut. It is not the place of delivery that controls, but the power of delivery."

[71] See *Emery v. Clough* (1885), 63 N. H., 552 ("right or power of defeasance").

[72] See *Hudgens v. Chamberlain* (1911), 161 Cal., 710, 713, 715. For another instance of statutory powers, see *Capital, etc., Bk. v. Rhodes* (1903), 1 Ch. 631, 655 (powers under registry acts.).

the vendee's agreement has been fully performed except as to the payment of the last installment and the time for the latter has arrived, what is the interest of such vendee as regards the property? Has he, as so often assumed, merely a contractual *right* to have title passed to him by consent of the vendor, on final payment being made; or has he, irrespective of the consent of the vendor the power to divest the title of the latter and to acquire a perfect title for himself? Though the language of the cases is not always so clear as it might be, the vendee seems to have precisely that sort of power.[73] Fundamentally considered, the typical escrow transaction in which the performance of conditions is within the volitional control of the grantee, is somewhat similar to the conditional sale of personalty; and, when reduced to its lowest terms, the problem seems easily to be solved in terms of legal powers. Once the "escrow" is formed, the grantor still has the legal title; but the grantee has an irrevocable power to divest that title by performance of certain conditions (*i. e.,* the addition of various operative facts), and concomitantly to vest title in himself. While such power is outstanding, the grantor is,

[73] Though the nebulous term "rights" is used by the courts, it is evident that powers are the actual quantities involved.

Thus, in the instructive case of *Carpenter v. Scott* (1881), 13 R. I., 477, 479, the court said, by Matteson, J.: "Under it (the conditional sale) the vendee acquires not only the right of possession and use, but the right to become the absolute owner upon complying with the terms of the contract. These are rights of which no act of the vendor can divest him, and which, in the absence of any stipulation in the contract restraining him, he can transfer by sale or mortgage. Upon performance of the conditions of the sale, the title to the property vests in the vendee, or in the event that he has sold, or mortgaged it, in his vendee, or mortgagee, without further bill of sale. * * * These rights constitute an actual, present interest in the property, which, as we have seen above, is capable of transfer by sale or mortgage."

It is interesting to notice that in the foregoing passage, the term "right" is first used to indicate *privileges* of possession and use; next the term is employed primarily in the sense of legal power, though possibly there is a partial blending of this idea with that of legal claim, or right (in the narrowest connotation); then the term (in plural form) is used for the third time so as to lump together the vendee's privileges, powers and claims.

For another case indicating in substance the true nature of the vendee's interest, see *Christensen v. Nelson* (1901), 38 Or. 473, 477, 479, indicating, in effect, that the vendee's powers as well as privileges may be transferred to another, and that a proper tender constitutes "the equivalen of payment."

of course, subject to a correlative liability to have his title divested.[74] Similarly, in the case of a conveyance of land in fee simple subject to condition subsequent, after the condition has been performed, the original grantor is commonly said to have a "*right* of entry." If, however, the problem is analyzed, it will be seen that, as of primary importance, the grantor has two legal quantities, (1) the privilege of entering, and (2) the power, by means of such entry, to divest the estate of the grantee.[75] The latter's estate endures, subject to the correlative liability of being divested, until such power is actually exercised.[76]

Passing now to the field of contracts, suppose A mails a letter to B offering to sell the former's land, Whiteacre, to the latter for ten thousand dollars, such letter being duly received. The operative facts thus far mentioned have created a power as regards B and a correlative liability as regards A. B, by dropping a letter of acceptance in the box, has the power to impose potential or inchoate[77] obligation *ex contractu* on A and himself; and, assuming that the land is worth fifteen thousand dollars, that particular legal quantity—the "power *plus* liability" relation between A and B—seems to be worth about five thousnad dollars to B. The liability of A will continue for a reasonable time unless, in exercise of his power to do so, A previously extinguishes it by that series of operative facts known as "revocation." These last matters are usually described by saying that A's "offer" will "con-

[74] See *Davis v. Clark* (1897), 58 Kan. 100; 48 Pac., 563, 565; *Leiter v. Pike* (1889), 127 Ill., 287, 326; *Welstur v. Trust Co.* (1895), 145 N. Y., 275, 283; *Furley v. Palmer* (1870), 20 Oh. St., 223, 225.

The proposition that the grantee's power is irrevocable is subject to the qualification that it might possibly be extinguished (or modified *pro tanto*) as the result of a transaction between the grantor and one having the position of *bona fide purchaser,* or the equivalent.

It is hardly necessary to add that the courts, instead of analyzing the problem of the escrow in terms of powers, as here indicated, are accustomed to stating the question and deciding it in terms of "delivery," "relation back," "performance of conditions," etc.

[75] In this connection it is worthy of note that Sugden, in his work on Powers (8th ed., 1861) 4, uses, contrary to general practice, the expression, "*power* of entry for condition broken."

[76] For miscellaneous instances of powers, see the good opinions in *Bk. of S. Australia v. Abrahams,* L. R. P. C., 265; *Barlow v. Ross* (1890), 24 Q. B. D., 381, 384.

[77] As to "inchoate" obligations, see *Frost v. Knight* (1872) L. R. 7 Ex. 111, per Cockburn, C. J. This matter will receive further attention in a later part of the discussion.

tinue" or "remain open" for a reasonable time, or for the definite time actually specified, unless A previously "withdraws" or "revokes" such offer.[78] While no doubt, in the great majority of cases no harm results from the use of such expressions, yet these forms of statement seem to represent a blending of non-legal and legal quantities which, in any problem requiring careful reasoning, should preferably be kept distinct. An offer, considered as a series of physical and mental operative facts, has spent its force as soon as such series has been completed by the "offeree's receipt." The real question is therefore as to the *legal effect,* if any, at that moment of time. If the latter consist of B's power and A's correlative liability, manifestly it is those *legal relations* that "continue" or "remain open" until modified by revocation or other operative facts. What has thus far been said concerning contracts completed by mail would seem to apply, *mutatis mutandis,* to every type of contract. Even where the parties are in the presence of each other, the offer creates a liability against the offerer, together with a correlative power in favor of the offeree. The only distinction for present purposes would be in the fact that such power and such liability would expire within a very short period of time.

Perhaps the practical justification for this method of analysis is somewhat greater in relation to the subject of options. In his able work on Contacts,[79] Langdell says:

> "If the offerer stipulates that his offer shall remain open for a specified time, the first question is whether such stipulation constitutes a binding contract. * * * When such a stipulation is binding, the further question arises, whether it makes the offer irrevocable. It has been a common opinion that it does, but that is clearly a mistake. * * * An offer is merely one of the elements of a contract; and it is indispensable to the making of a contract that the wills of the contracting parties do, in legal contemplation, concur at the moment of making it. An offer, therefore, which the party making it has no power to revoke, is a legal impos-

[78] Compare *Boston R. Co. v. Bartlett* (1849), 3 Cush., 225: "Though the writing signed by the defendant was but an offer, and an offer which might be revoked, yet while it remained in force and unrevoked, it was a continuing offer, during the time limited for acceptance, and during the whole of the rest of the time it was an offer every instant; but as soon as it was accepted, it ceased to be an offer merely.

Compare also the forms of statement in Ashley, Contr. (1911), 16 *et. seq.*

[79] Langdell, Sum. Contr. (2nd ed., 1880), sec. 178.

sibility. Moreover, if the stipulation should make the offer irrevocable, it would be a contract incapable of being broken; which is also a legal impossibility. The only effect, therefore, of such a stipulation is to give the offeree a claim for damages if the stipulation be broken by revoking the offer."[80]

The foregoing reasoning ignores the fact that an ordinary offer *ipso facto* creates a legal relation—a legal power and a legal liability,—and that it is this relation (rather than the physical and mental facts constituting the offer) that "remains open." If these points be conceded, there seems no difficulty in recognizing an unilateral option agreement supported by consideration or embodied in a sealed instrument as creating in the optionee an irrevocable power to create, at any time within the period specified, a bilateral obligation as between himself and the giver of the option. Correlatively to that power, there would, of course, be a liability against the option-giver which he himself would have no power to extinguish. The courts seem to have no difficulty in reaching precisely this result as a matter of substance; though their explanations are always in terms of "withdrawal of offer," and similar expressions savoring of physical and mental quantities.[81]

In connection with the powers and liabilities created respectively by an ordinary offer and by an option, it is interesting to consider the liabilities of a person engaged in a "public calling;" for, as it seems, such a party's characteristic position is, one might almost say, intermediate between that of an ordinary contractual

---

[80] Langdell's *a priori* premises and specific conclusions have been adopted by a number of other writers on the subject. See, for example, Ashley, Contr. (1911), 25 *et seq.*, R. L. McWilliams, Enforcement of Option Agreements (1913), 1 Calif. Law Rev., 122.

[81] For a recent judicial expression on the subject, see *W. G. Reese Co. v. House* (1912), 162 Cal., 740, 745 per Sloss J.: "Where there is a consideration, the option cannot be withdrawn during the time agreed upon for its duration, while, if there be no consideration the party who has given the option may revoke it at any time before acceptance, even though the time limited has not expired * * * such offer, duly accepted, constitutes a contract binding upon both parties and enforceable by either."

See, to the same effect, *Linn v. McLean* (1885), 80 Ala., 360, 364; *O'Brien v. Boland* (1896), 166 Mass., 481, 483 (sealed offer).

Most of the cases recognizing the irrevocable power of the optionee have arisen in equitable suits for specific performance; but there seems to be no reason for doubting that the same doctrine should be applied in a common law action for damages. See, in accord, *Baker v. Shaw* (1912), 68 Wash., 99 103 (*dicta* in an action for damages).

offerer and that of an option-giver. It has indeed been usual to assert that such a party is (generally speaking) under a present *duty* to all other parties; but this is believed to be erroneous. Thus, Professor Wyman, in his work on Public Service Companies,[82] says:

> "The duty placed upon every one exercising a public calling is primarily a duty to serve every man who is a member of the public. * * * It is somewhat difficult to place this exceptional duty in our legal system. * * * The truth of the matter is that the obligation resting upon one who has undertaken the performance of public duty is *sui generis*."[83]

It is submitted that the learned writer's difficulties arise primarily from a failure to see that the innkeeper, the common carrier and others similarly "holding out" are under present *liabilities* rather than present *duties*. Correlativly to those liabilities are the respective powers of the various members of the public. Thus, for example, a travelling member of the public has the legal power, by making proper application and sufficient tender, to impose a duty on the innkeeper to receive him as a guest. For breach of the duty *thus* created an action would of course lie. It would therefore seem that the innkeeper is, to some extent, like one who had given an option to every travelling member of the public. He differs, as regards net legal effect, only because he can extinguish his present liabilities and the correlative powers of the travelling members of the public *by going out of business*. Yet, on the other hand, his liabilities are more onerous than that of an ordinary contractual offerer, for he cannot extinguish his liabilities by any simple performance akin to revocation of offer.

As regards all the "legal powers" thus far considered, possibly some caution is necessary. If, for example, we consider the ordinary property owner's power of alienation, it is necessary to distinguish carefully between the *legal* power, the *physical* power to do the things necessary for the "exercise" of the legal power, and, finally, the *privilege* of doing these things—that is, if such privilege does really exist. It may or may not. Thus, if X, a landowner, has contracted with Y that the former will not alienate to Z, the acts of X necessary to exercise the power of alienating to Z are privileged as between X and every party other than Y; but, obviously, as between X and Y, the former has no

[82] Secs. 330-333.

[83] Compare, to the same effect, Keener, Quasi-Contr. (1893), p. 18.

privilege of doing the necessary acts; or conversely, he is under a duty to Y not to do what is necessary to exercise the power.

In view of what has already been said, very little may suffice concerning a *liability* as such. The latter, as we have seen, is the correlative of power, and the opposite of immunity (or exemption). While no doubt the term "liability" is often loosely used as a synonym for "duty," or "obligation," it is believed, from an extensive survey of judicial precedents, that the connotation already adopted as most appropriate to the word in question is fully justified. A few cases tending to indicate this will now be noticed. In *McNeer v. McNeer,*[84] Mr. Justice Magruder balanced the conceptions of power and liability as follows:

"So long as she lived, however, his interest in her land lacked those *elements of property,* such as *power of disposition* and *liability to sale on* execution which had formerly given it the character of a vested estate."

In *Booth v. Commonwealth,*[85] the court had to construe a Virginia statute providing "that all free white male persons who are twenty-one years of age and not over sixty, shall be *liable* to serve as jurors, except as hereinafter provided." It is plain that this enactment imposed only a *liability* and not a *duty.* It is a liability to have a duty created. The latter would arise only when, in exercise of their powers, the parties litigant and the court officers, had done what was necessary to impose a specific duty to perform the functions of a juror. The language of the court, by Moncure, J., is particularly apposite as indicating that liability is the opposite, or negative, of immunity (or exemption):

"The word both expressed and implied is 'liable,' which has a very different meaning from 'qualified * * *. It's meaning is 'bound' or 'obliged' * * *. A person exempt from serving on juries is not liable to serve, and a person not liable to serve is exempt from serving. The terms seem to be convertible."

A further good example of judicial usage is to be found in *Emery v. Clough.*[86] Referring to a gift *causa mortis* and the donee's liability to have his already vested interest divested by the donor's exercise of his power of revocation, Mr. Justice Smith said:

"The title to the gift *causa mortis* passed by the delivery, defeasible only in the lifetime of the donor, and his death perfects

[84] (1892) 142 Ill., 388, 397.

[85] 1861) 16 Grat., 519, 525.

[86] (1885) 63 N. H., 552.

the title in the donee by terminating the donor's right or *power of defeasance.* The property passes from the donor to the donee directly * * * and after his death it is *liable* to be divested only in favor of the donor's creditors. * * * His right and power ceased with his death."

Perhaps the nearest synonym of "liability" is "subjection" or "responsibility." As regards the latter word, a passage from Mr. Justice Day's opinion in *McElfresh v. Kirkendall*[87] is interesting:

"The words 'debt' and 'liability' are not synonymous, and they are not commonly so understood. As applied to the pecuniary relations of the parties, liability is a term of broader significance than debt. * * * Liability is responsibility."

While the term in question has the broad generic connotation already indicated, no doubt it very frequently indicates that specific form of liability (or complex of liabilities) that is correlative to a power (or complex of powers)[88] vested in a party litigant and the various court officers. Such was held to be the meaning of a certain California statute involved in the case of *Lattin v. Gillette.*[89] Said Mr. Justice Harrison:

"The word 'liability' is the condition in which an individual is placed after a breach of his contract, or a violation of any obligation resting upon him. It is defined by Bouvier to be responsibility."[90]

---

[87] (1873) 36 Ia., 224, 226.

[88] Compare *Attorney General v. Sudeley* (1896), 1 Q. B., 354, 359 (per Lord Esher: "What is called a 'right of action' is not the *power* of bringing an action. Anybody can bring an action though he has no right at all."); *Kroessin v. Keller* (1895), 60 Minn., 372 (per Collins, J.: "The power to bring such actions").

[89] (1892) 95 Cal., 317, 319.

[90] We are apt to think of liability as exclusively an onerous relation of one party to another. But, in its broad technical significance, this is not necessarily so. Thus X, the owner of a watch, has the power to abandon his property—that is, to extinguish his existing rights, powers, and immunities relating thereto (not, however, his privileges, for until someone else has acquired title to the abandoned watch, X would have the same privileges as before); and correlatively to X's power of abandonment there is a liability in every other person. But such a liability instead of being onerous or unwelcome, is quite the opposite. As regards another person M, for example, it is a *liability to have created in his favor (though against his will) a privilege and a power* relating to the watch,—that is, the privilege of taking possession and the power, by doing so, to vest a title in himself. See *Dougherty v. Creary* (1866), 30 Cal., 290, 298. Contrast with this agreeable form of liability the *liability to have a duty created*—for example the liability of one who has made or given an option in a case where the value of the property has greatly risen.

Immunities and Disabilities. As already brought out, immunity is the correlative of disability ("no-power"), and the opposite, or negation, of liability. Perhaps it will also be plain, from the preliminary outline and from the discussion down to this point, that a power bears the same general contrast to an immunity that a right does to a privilege. A right is one's affirmative claim against another, and a privilege is one's freedom from the right or claim of another. Similarly, a power is one's affirmative "control" over a given legal relation as against another; whereas an immunity is one's freedom from the legal power or "control" of another as regards some legal relation.

A few examples may serve to make this clear. X, a landowner, has, as we have seen, power to alienate to Y or to any other ordinary party. On the other hand, X has also various immunities as against Y, and all other ordinary parties. For Y is under a disability (*i. e.,* has no power) so far as shifting the legal interest either to himself or to a third party is concerned; and what is true of Y applies similarly to every one else who has not by virtue of special operative facts acquired a power to alienate X's property. If, indeed, a sheriff has been duly empowered by a writ of execution to sell X's interest, that is a very different matter: correlative to such sheriff's power would be the *liability* of X,—the very opposite of immunity (or exemption). It is elementary, too, that as against the sheriff, X might be immune or exempt in relation to certain parcels of property, and be liable as to others. Similarly, if an agent has been duly appointed by X to sell a given piece of property, then, as to the latter, X has, in relation to such agent, a liability rather than an immunity.

For over a century there has been, in this country, a great deal of important litigation involving immunities from powers of taxation. If there be any lingering misgivings as to the "practical" importance of accuracy and discrimination in legal conceptions and legal terms, perhaps some of such doubts would be dispelled by considering the numerous cases on valuable taxation exemptions coming before the United States Supreme Court. Thus, in *Phoenix Ins. Co. v. Tennessee,*[91] Mr. Justice Peckham expressed the views of the court as follows:

"In granting to the De Sota Company 'all the rights, privileges, and immunities' of the Bluff City Company, all words are used which could be regarded as necessary to carry the exemption from

[91] (1895) 161 U. S., 174, 177.

taxation possessed by the Bluff City Company; while in the next following grant, that of the charter of the plaintiff in error, the word 'immunity' is omitted. Is there any meaning to be attached to that omission, and if so, what? We think some meaning is to be attached to it. The word 'immunity' expresses more clearly and definitely an intention to include therein an exemption from taxation than does either of the other words. Exemption from taxation is more accurately described as an 'immunity' than as a privilege, although it is not to be denied that the latter word may sometimes and under some circumstances include such exemptions."

In *Morgan v. Louisiana*,[92] there is an instructive discussion from the pen of Mr. Justice Field. In holding that on a foreclosure sale of the franchise and property of a railroad corporation an immunity from taxation did not pass to the purchaser, the learned Judge said:

"As has been often said by this court, the whole community is interested in retaining the power of taxation undiminished * * *. The exemption of the property of the company from taxation, and the exemption of its officers and servants from jury and military duty, were both intended for the benefit of the company, and its benefit alone. In their personal character they are analogous to exemptions from execution of certain property of debtors, made by laws of several of the states."[93]

---

[92] (1876) 93 U. S., 217, 222.

[93] See, in accord, *Picard v. Tennessee, etc., R. Co.* (1888), 130 U. S., 637, 642, (Field, J.); *Rochester Railway Co. v. Rochester* (1906) 205 U. S., 236, 252 (Moody, J., reviewing the many other cases on the subject).

In *Internat. & G. N. Ry. Co. v. State* (1899), 75 Tex., 356, a different view was taken as to the *alienability* of an immunity from taxation. Speaking by Stayton, C. J., the court said:

"Looking at the provisions of the Act of March 10, 1875, we think there can be no doubt the exemption from taxation given by it, instead of being a right vesting only in appellant, is a right which inheres in the property to which it applies, and follows it into the hands of whosover becomes the owner. * * * The existence of this right enhances the value of the property to which it applies. Shareholders and creditors must be presumed to have dealt with the corporation on the faith of the contract which gave the exemption, and it cannot be taken away by legislation, by dissolution of the corporation, or in any other manner not sufficient to pass title to any other property from one person to another. The right to exemption from taxation is secured by the same guaranty which secures titles to those owning lands granted under the act, and though the corporation may be dissolved, will continue to exist in favor of persons owning the property to which the immunity applies. Lawful dissolution of a corporation will destroy all its corporate franchises or privileges vested by

So far as immunities are concerned ,the two judicial discussions last quoted concern respectively problems of interpretation and problems of alienability. In many other cases difficult constitutional questions have arisen as the result of statutes impairing or extending various kinds of immunities. Litigants have, from time to time, had occasion to appeal both to the clause against impairment of the obligation of contracts and to the provision against depriving a person of property without due process of law. This has been especially true as regards exemptions from taxation[94] and exemptions from execution.[95]

If a word may now be permitted with respect to mere terms as such, the first thing to note is that the word "right" is overworked in the field of immunities as elsewhere.[96] As indicated, however, by the judicial expressions already quoted, the best synonym is, of course, the term "exemption."[97] It is instructive legislature not to grant the benefit claimed by the bill."

---

the act of incorporation; but if it holds rights, privileges, and franchises in the nature of property, secured by contract based on valuable consideration, these will survive the dissolution of the corporation, for the benefit of those who may have a right to or just claim upon its assets."

Compare, as regard homestead exemptions, Sloss, J., in *Smith v. Bougham* (1909), 156 Cal., 359, 365: "A declaration of homestead * * * attaches certain privileges and immunities to such title as may at the time be held."

[94] See *Choate v. Trapp* (1912), 224 U. S., 665.

[95] See *Brearly School, Limited v. Ward* (1911), 201 N. Y., 358; 94 N. E., 1001 (an interesting decision, with three judges dissenting). The other cases on the subject are collected in Ann. Cas., 1912 B, 259.

[96] See *Brearly School, Limited v. Ward*, cited in preceding note; also *Internat. & G. N. Ry. Co. v. State* (1899), 75 Tex., 356, quoted from, *ante*, n. 91.

[97] Compare also *Wilson v. Gaines* (1877), 9 Baxt. (Tenn.), 546, 550-551, Turney, J.: "The use in the statutes of two only of the words of the constitution, *i. e.*, 'rights' and 'privileges,' and the omission to employ either of the other two following in immediate succession, viz.,' immunities' and 'exemptions,' either of which would have made clear the construction claimed by complainant, evidence a purposed intention on the part of the

Only very rarely is a court found seeking to draw a subtle distinction between an immunity and an exemption. Thus, in a recent case, *Strahan v. Wayne Co.* (June, 1913), 142 N. W., 678, 680 (Neb.), Mr. Justice Barnes said: "It has been held by the great weight of authority that dower is not immune (from the inheritance tax) because it is dower, but because it * * * belonged to her unchoately during (the husband's) life. * * * Strictly speaking, the widow's share should be considered as immune, rather than exempt, from an inheritance tax. It is free, rather than freed, from such tax."

to note, also, that the word "impunity" has a very similar connotation. This is made evident by the interesting discriminations of Lord Chancellor Finch in *Skelton v. Skelton,*[98] a case decided in 1677:

"But this I would by no means allow, that equity should enlarge the restraints of the disabilities introduced by act of parliament; and as to the granting of injunctions to stay waste, I took a distinction where the tenant hath only *impunitatem,* and where he hath *jus in arboribus.* If the tenant have only a bare indemnity or *exemption* from an action (at law), if he committed waste, there it is fit he should be restrained by injunction from committing it."[99]

In the latter part of the preceding discussion, eight conceptions of the law have been analyzed and compared in some detail, the purpose having been to exhibit not only their intrinsic meaning and scope, but also their relations to one another and the methods by which they are applied, in judicial reasoning, to the solution of concrete problems of litigation. Before concluding this branch of the discussion a general suggestion may be ventured as to the great practical importance of a clear appreciation of the distinctions and discriminations set forth. If a homely metaphor be permitted, these eight conceptions,—rights and duties, privileges and no-rights, powers and liabilities, immunities and disabilities,—seem to be what may be called "the lowest common denominators of the law." Ten fractions (1-3, 2-5, etc.) may, *superficially,* seem so different from one another as to defy comparison. If, however, they are expressed in terms of their lowest common denominators (5-15, 6-15, etc.), comparison becomes easy, and fundamental similarity may be discovered. The same thing is

[98] (1677) 2 Swanst., 170.

[99] In *Skelton v. Skelton,* it will be observed, the word *"impunity"* and the word *"exemption"* are used as the opposite of *liability* to the powers of a plaintiff in an action at law.

For similar recent instances, see *Vacher & Sons, Limited v. London Society of Compositors* (1913), A. C. 107, 118, 125 (per Lord Macnaghten: "Now there is nothing absurd in the notion of an association or body enjoying immunity from actions at law;" per Lord Atkinson: "Conferring on the trustees immunity as absolute," etc.).

Compare also *Baylies v. Bishop of London* (1913), 1 Ch., 127, 139, 140, per Hamilton, L. J.

For instances of the apt use of the term "disability" as equivalent to the negation of legal power, see *Poury v. Hordern* (1900), 1 Ch., 492, 495; *Sheridan v. Elden* (1862), 24 N. Y., 281, 384.

of course true as regards the lowest generic conceptions to which any and all "legal quantities" may be reduced.

Reverting, for example, to the subject powers, it might be difficult at first glance to discover any essential and fundamental similarity between conditional sales of personalty, escrow transactions, option agreements, agency relations, powers of appointment, etc. But if all these relations are reduced to their lowest generic terms, the conceptions of legal power and legal liability are seen to be dominantly, though not exclusively, applicable throughout the series. By such a process it becomes possible not only to discover essential similarities and illuminating analogies in the midst of what appears superficially to be infinite and hopeless variety, but also to discern common principles of justice and policy underlying the various jural problems involved. An indirect, yet very practical, consequence is that it frequently becomes feasible, by virtue of such analysis, to use as persuasive authorities judicial precedents that might otherwise seem altogether irrelevant. If this point be valid with respect to powers, it would seem to be equally so as regards all of the other basic conceptions of the law. In short, the deeper the analysis, the great become one's perception of fundamental unity and harmony in the law.[100]

Wesley Newcomb Hohfeld.

Stanford University, California.

---

[100] The next article in the present series will discuss the distinctions between legal and equitable jural relations; also the contrast between rights, etc., *in rem,* and rights, etc., *in personam.* The supposed distinctions betwen substantive and adjective jural relations will also be considered,—chiefly with the purpose of showing that, so far as the intrinsic and essential nature of those relations is concerned, the distinctions commonly assumed to exist are imaginary rather than real. Finally, some attention will be given to the nature and analysis of complex legal interests, or aggregates of jural relations.

HARVARD LAW REVIEW.

VOL. XXV. APRIL, 1912. NO. 6.

THE SCOPE AND PURPOSE OF SOCIOLOGICAL JURISPRUDENCE.

[*Concluded.*]

III.

SOCIOLOGICAL JURISPRUDENCE.

SOCIOLOGICAL Jurisprudence is still formative. In diversity of view the sociological jurists but reflect the differences that exist among sociologists. This is no more a ground for denying that there is a sociological school or denying that there is a sociological method in jurisprudence, than the differences among philosophical jurists are ground for denying that there is a philosophical method.

In common with sociology, sociological jurisprudence has its origin in the positivist philosophers in the sense that each subject has a continuous development from Comte's positive philosophy. But both have long got beyond this and are now wholly independent of it. Nevertheless, there are those who appear to insist that sociological jurisprudence must be identified with a philosophical jurisprudence of the positivist type.[1] Others, also, because sociological thought went through an anthropological-ethnological stage, both in the social sciences generally and in jurisprudence, assume that sociological jurisprudence can mean only

[1] Berolzheimer, System der Rechts und Wirthschaftsphilosophie, II, 385–386; Charmont, La renaissance du droit naturel, 122–127.

a science of law based on anthropology and ethnology.[2] In other words, some insist it must stand for a mechanical interpretation that regards law as the product of an inexorable mechanism of social forces. Others insist that it must stand for an ethnological interpretation; for a science of law developed from comparative study of primitive institutions or for a generalization from the jural materials gathered by a purely descriptive social science.[3] Today, such views are held chiefly by the critics of sociological jurisprudence. But they have a certain warrant in an unhappy tendency in the earlier stages of the development of the new school to insist exclusively upon some one phase of social science or some one mode of investigation or some one interpretation. It is to be remembered, however, that all the methods of jurisprudence have suffered from a like tendency; that extreme assertions of an imperative theory at one time brought analytical jurisprudence into disfavor, that historical jurisprudence is now under a cloud because it was so long identified with Savigny's views as to law-making, and that philosophical jurisprudence has still to recover in some countries the ground it lost when it became identified with the metaphysical method of the last century. Sociological jurisprudence did not find itself at once, and some assert it has not yet done so.[4] It has gone through several stages, of which some have

---

[2] Del Vecchio, I presupposti filosofici della nozione del diritto, 86–93.

[3] "What we call sociology is often no more than a mass of facts of experience which logically ought to belong to the science of universal comparative law, and, to speak more broadly, to the science of law from which they have only been excluded because of the over-narrow conception which has obtained heretofore. Institutions and phenomena of social life which, considered in a certain stage of evolution or under some better-known aspect, are indubitably of a juridical nature, are cast out of the official bounds of juridical science when they are presented in a more primitive form, among less civilized peoples or even among peoples of a different civilization. For example, a work upon the parental régime and the patrimonial régime of the Papuans or of the Bogos, and perhaps even of the Aztecs or of the Coreans, would have few chances of being taken into consideration by jurists, who do not like to go beyond the limits of the traditional culture. But such a work would easily find asylum in the often chaotic mass of facts and conjectures which we call sociology, which, in its defective systematization bears the mark of the imperfections of contemporary culture. The truth is that the only sociology which has a *raison d'être* is a treatise of the rules of method, common to different sciences, to be observed in the study of human facts." Del Vecchio, Sull' idea di una scienza del diritto universale comparato, 11 (1909).

[4] "We employ the expression 'science of law' as synonymous with juridical sociology. It is a science that has yet to be constituted." Rolin, Prolégomènes à la science du droit, 1.

been outgrown thoroughly, while others are still represented in current discussion. These stages must be distinguished and borne in mind if we are to understand either sociological jurisprudence or its critics. It is true that they can be distinguished only in a broad and general way. As in so many other cases where periods are to be set off, the lines must be drawn somewhat arbitrarily here and there, for the stages merge or overlap, and the whole course of development has not proceeded for half a century. But, with this reservation, there seems good warrant for holding that sociological jurisprudence has gone through three stages and has entered upon a fourth. These may be called (1) the mechanical stage, (2) the biological stage, (3) the psychological stage, and (4) the stage of unification.[5]

1. The Positivists — The Mechanical Stage.[6]

It has been said that Comte's sociology was a "technology of social machinery, a handbook of the soulless forces which turned the wheels of the ages."[7] Comte was a mathematician. Moreover, in the first half of the nineteenth century the central point in scientific thinking was the mechanism of the physical universe. Men's minds were fascinated by the idea of laws, mathematically demonstrable, which control the operations of nature, and for a season they took, as it were, a mathematical view; they sought to find mathematical or mechanical laws according to which all things came into existence and were governed in their course of existence. This type of thinking is to be seen in the first positive philosophies of law and in the first stage of sociological jurisprudence.[8] It was the obvious result of the mental bent of the founder of sociology. But in jurisprudence it was especially congenial and so lingered

---

[5] So far as they have to do with general sociology, the classification and the discussion following are based upon Small, The Meaning of Social Science, 71–85.

[6] Berolzheimer, System der Rechts und Wirthschaftsphilosophie, II, § 44; Gumplowicz, Philosophisches Staatsrecht (1877); Allgemeines Staatsrecht (3d edition of the former) (1907); Geschichte der Staatstheorien (1905) (see especially the appendix, Zur Kritik der juristischen Methode im Staatsrecht); Stein, Die soziale Frage im Lichte der Philosophie (1897, 2 ed., 1903) (especially the chapter, Ursprung und sozialer Charakter des Rechts).

[7] Small, The Meaning of Social Science, 74.

[8] A good account of this may be found in Carle, La vita del diritto, 2 ed., § 229. Compare Korkunov, General Theory of Law (transl. by Hastings) 265 *et seq.*

longer than elsewhere because of the influence of the historical school. Like the historical jurist, the first type of sociologist looked at law in its evolution, in its successive changes, and sought to relate these changes to the changes undergone by society itself.[9] The historical jurist found metaphysical laws behind them. The positivist substituted physical laws. The result was the same. Each eliminated the old idea of right and with it all idealism in jurisprudence or legislation.[10]

A later form of what is essentially the same type of juristic sociology is to be seen in attempts to state all jural experience solely in terms of economics. The economic interpretation has been spoken of heretofore. In combination with positivist ideas, it has given rise to a sort of fatalist natural law. The old natural law called for search for an eternal body of principles to which the positive law must be made to conform. This new natural law calls for search for a body of rules governing legal development to which law must and will conform, do what we may. Whatever exists in law exists because of the operation of these rules. The operation of these same rules will change it and will change it in accordance with fixed and definite rules in every way comparable to those which determine the events of nature. The doctrine has been set forth in its most extreme form in America:

> "Law is the resultant of the conflict of forces which arises from the struggle for existence among men. Ultimately these forces become fused under the necessity of obtaining expression through a single mouthpiece, and that fusion, effected under this pressure, we call the will of the sovereign. It is, however, the will of a sovereign precisely in the sense that the earth's orbit, which is a resultant of the conflict between centrifugal and centripetal force, is the will of a sovereign. *Both the law and the orbit are necessities*, and the one and the other have a like relation to an abstract idea of right and justice." [11]

---

[9] On this relation of the positivists to the historical jurists, see Charmont, La renaissance du droit naturel, 117.

[10] *Id.* 122. A similar coöperation with the type of analytical jurist who eliminates juridical idealism through insistence upon the imperative character of law and hence upon the sovereign will as the ultimate, self-sufficient source of legal rules, would have been possible had the two schools been brought in contact. Indeed a combination of positivism and of social utilitarianism may be seen in Vander Eycken, Méthode de l'interpretation juridique (1907).

[11] Brooks Adams, in Centralization and the Law, 23 (1906).

Again:

"Various forces being always in conflict, they become fused in the effort to obtain expression, and their fusion creates a *corpus juris*, *the corpus inclining in the direction of the predominant force in the precise degree in which it predominates*. . . .

"The sovereign being only a vent or mouthpiece, the form the mouthpiece takes, or the name given it, is immaterial. Whether the social resultant expresses itself through a prophet like Moses, or an emperor like Cæsar, or a moneyed oligarchy like the modern British Parliament, the result is the same. The dominant class, whether it be priests or usurers or soldiers or bankers, will shape the law to favor themselves, and that code will most nearly approach the ideal of justice of each particular age which favors most perfectly the dominant class." [12]

This is precisely the position of the mechanical period of sociology, a period long outgrown in the social sciences other than jurisprudence.[13] Professor Small says aptly that

"The sociological fashion set by Spencer was to treat social forces as though they were mills of the gods which men could at most learn to describe, but which they might not presume to organize and control." [14]

Thus in one of his earlier writings Gumplowicz, in discussing the aristocratic order, argues that criticism is futile.

"Sociology," he says, "must refrain from all such criticism of nature. For sociology, only the facts and their conformity to laws have an interest." His reason is that "*Social phenomena follow necessarily from the nature of men* and from the nature of their relationships." [15]

In this very spirit, the jurist I have been quoting says:

"With the moral or political aspects of this controversy, we, as lawyers, have nothing to do, for professionally the function of the lawyer is to accept that which exists and deal with exigencies as they arise. We are only concerned with the effect of the struggle upon the *corpus juris*,

---

[12] *Id.* 63–64.

[13] See Small, General Sociology, 80–87.

[14] *Id.* 84. Again: "While the Spencerian influence was uppermost, the tendency was to regard social progress as a sort of mechanically determined redistribution of energy which thought could neither accelerate nor retard." *Id.* 82.

[15] Grundriss der Sociologie, 133 (1885). I have used Professor Small's translation, in General Sociology, 86.

since the law, being the resultant of the forces in conflict, must ultimately be directed in the direction of the stronger, and be used to crown the victor." [16]

All that has been said as to the practical effects of the analytical and the historical methods, when made, as they usually come to be, the basis of a theory of legislation, applies with even greater force to this type of sociological jurisprudence.[17] Law is an inevitable resultant; in making or finding it, legislator or judge is merely bringing about "conformity to the *de facto* wishes of the dominant forces of the community." [18] The eighteenth-century doctrine, although it put the *fundamenta* beyond reach of change, at least moved us to scan the details of the superstructure and to endeavor to make each part conform to the fixed ideal plan. It admitted that legislator and jurist had each a function. The historical school denied any real function to the former. The positivist denies it to the latter. To the doctrine of legislative futility, which he accepts, though for other reasons, he adds a doctrine of juristic futility. Hence the achievements of this school have been purely negative. They have helped to clear away, but they have built nothing. For the "declaration of the dominant social organism by which a legal standard is created or imposed" [19] may or may not establish itself in the legal system. The Roman law of juristic acts has not become the law of the world nor is the Anglo-American law of torts becoming a law of the world because either has behind it a dominant social force. Much that has such a force behind it leaves but a faint mark upon the law. A theory that leaves out of account the quest of jurists and judges for an ideal of an absolute, eternal justice, well or ill conceived, to which they seek to make the rules enforced in tribunals approximate so far as possible, and juris-

[16] Centralization and the Law, 132–133.

[17] The mechanical sociology has been so thoroughly criticized from so many quarters, and by none more effectively than by sociologists themselves, that even its persistence in a type of recent juristic thinking cannot justify giving much space to what is no more than a belated phase. But a reference to James, The Will to Believe, 216 (Great Men and their Environment), may be worth while.

[18] Holmes, J., in Lochner *v.* New York, 198 U. S. 45, 75, 25 Sup. Ct. 539, 547 (1905). Here, however, the Spencerian jurisprudence is invoked against the traditional historical jurisprudence. The notion that social forces working through legislation cannot make law is met by the proposition that they can and will make the law, the means of expression being wholly immaterial, and that it is not for the lawyer to interfere.

[19] Gareis so defines legislation. Science of Law (transl. by Kocourek), 80.

tic tradition, that is traditional principles and traditional modes of reasoning therefrom, ignores the chief influences in determining the bulk of the rules actually in force in any legal system at any given time. No doubt the ideal of justice is affected by training and associations which reflect class-interest. On the other hand the conscious endeavor to adhere to the ideal is a powerful check on the operation of class-interest.[20] Self-interest of the dominant class in the community for the time being affects chiefly the imperative element in legal systems, that is, legislation. Perhaps for that very reason legislation, as a means of making law, has played the least part in legal development.[21]

If, however, the earlier type of sociological jurist on one side brought us by another path to the position of the futility of effort to which the historical school had led us, on another side he performed a service which Berolzheimer rightly pronounces invaluable.[22] This service was twofold: (1) in displacing the individualist starting-point and the atomistic standpoint of nineteenth-century jurisprudence by insisting upon the importance of the group, of the class, of "the compact plurality,"[23] and (2) in compelling us to relate the law more critically to other social phenomena. In urging that the form of social organization was not an arbitrary and artificial fact, that society was not a mere human invention, that the development of society took place according to fixed principles analogous to those which govern the physical universe, and hence that laws and legal institutions develop in accordance with similar principles, they drove the other schools to seek a broader foundation and furnished much of the impetus which produced the social-philosophical school.

2. The Biological Stage.[24]

In the last third of the nineteenth century many jurists began to look at all things literally or figuratively in terms of biology.

---

[20] See particularly Professor Burdick's demonstration of this in his paper, Is Law the Expression of Class Selfishness?, 25 HARV. L. REV. 349.

[21] An excellent critique of the theory of law as the expression of the interest of the dominant class may be found in Tanon, L'évolution du droit et la conscience sociale, 3 ed., 180–189.

[22] System der Rechts und Wirthschaftsphilosophie, II, 384.

[23] Berolzheimer, *loc. cit.*

[24] Berolzheimer, System der Rechts und Wirthschaftsphilosophie, II, §§ 47, 51;

The epoch-making work of Darwin had made evolution the central idea in scientific thought. From the natural sciences the conception invaded and remade philology, was applied to the history of social and religious institutions, and ultimately came into jurisprudence. A natural science of the state and a natural science of the law succeeded the attempts to work out a physical science of the state. A biological sociology succeeded the mechanical sociology. For a time, indeed, the two overlapped. This is true of Spencer's sociology, which, as has been pointed out by many critics, was not at all evolutionist.[25] It is true also of the first attempts at sociological jurisprudence from the biological standpoint. Jurists were attracted by the conception of natural selection. The struggle for existence seemed to afford a fundamental principle for jurisprudence which confirmed the beliefs they had formed under the influence of the historical school or of the positivists. Accordingly they brought us to the same position to which the latter had led us previously, but by this route: The end of law is to give free play in an orderly and regulated manner to the elimination of the unfit, to further selection by a well-ordered social struggle for existence. Revolt of the social conscience against such theories has been an important factor in the juristic movement for the socialization of law.[26]

In its biological stage, sociological jurisprudence exhibits four types: (1) a mechanical type, which has just been considered, (2) an ethnological type, (3) a philosophical type, and (4) an organismic type. The three last deserve special consideration.

Attempts to develop and apply theories of evolution led for a time to exaggerated reliance upon primitive law. A school of jurists

---

Kuhlenbeck, Natürliche Grundlagen des Rechts; Matzat, Philosophie der Anpassung mit besonderer Berücksichtigung des Rechtes und des Staates; Ruppin, Darwinismus und Sozialwissenschaft; Hasse, Natur und Gesellschaft; Michaelis, Prinzipien der natürlichen und sozialen Entwickelungsgeschichte des Menschen; Coker, Organismic Theories of the State, chaps. 3, 4; Tourtoulon, Principes philosophiques de l'histoire du droit, 80–173; Letourneau, Évolution juridique; D'Aguanno, La genesi e l'evoluzione del diritto civile; Cogliolo, Saggi sopra l'evoluzione del diritto privato; Cogliolo, La teoria dell' evoluzione darwinista nel diritto privato.

[25] "While Spencer was popularizing the notion of evolution, he was also circulating a theory of society which was in effect as fatalistic as the hyper-Calvinistic dogma of foreordination. . . . Society, in Spencer's version, was simply a gigantic organism endowed with an unalterable amount of energy, and this energy would inexorably redistribute itself according to laws lodged in itself." Small, The Meaning of Social Science, 82.

[26] See especially Tanon, L'évolution du droit et la conscience sociale, 116–166.

arose who expected study of the social and legal institutions of the most primitive peoples to reveal the fundamental data of jurisprudence and the fundamental laws of jural development. They conceived that they could find in primitive man all the materials which were needed to explain the social man in general, and hence in primitive social institutions the materials needed to explain the legal systems of today. I have referred elsewhere to the writings of this school and to the good work its adherents did in broadening the historical and philosophical schools.[27] Here it is enough to say that their influence gave rise on the one hand to attempts to interpret jurisprudence and legal history in terms of race, considered in another connection heretofore,[28] and on the other hand to an opinion that the true method of jurisprudence was that which sociologists have called the demographic; that legal science was to be founded upon generalization from a descriptive sociology.[29] The kernel of truth in each case is that juristic study in the past, both historical and philosophical, had been too restricted in its materials.[30] Beyond this, ethnological and demographic methods are no more the chief tools of the sociological jurists than they have proved to be in the case of the general sociologists. As one of the latter says:

> " It is a grotesque hallucination that men in stages of arrested development — men about whom, moreover, all available evidence is woefully meager — furnish the only clues to human nature." [31]

It is no less grotesque to suppose that the social institutions of such men furnish the only or even the chief clues to the principles of legal systems. Yet the reaction recently from the exaggerated

---

[27] 24 HARV. L. REV. 614–617.

[28] 25 HARV. L. REV. 165. See also Tourtoulon, Les principes philosophiques de l'histoire du droit, 85–86.

[29] "There are determinate laws according to which all organic structures, which are formed over men in the human race, are developed, and these laws may be disclosed by comparison of the corresponding periods of development of all the generic organisms upon the earth, living and past. To determine these laws is the next task of the political and legal science of the future. For the determination of these laws, a mighty mass of material lies before us which needs only collection and collation in order to produce the most fruitful ideas for the jurisprudence of the future." Post, Der Ursprung des Rechts, 7 (1876).

[30] See Del Vecchio, Sull' idea di una scienza del diritto universale comparatc, 11; Kohler, Rechtsphilosophie und Universalrechtsgeschichte, §§ 8, 11.

[31] Small, General Sociology, 100.

claims once made for the so-called ethnological jurisprudence may well have gone too far. Thus it has been said:

"While equally with the individual each race depends on its heredity and bears the consequences thereof, the law is no more individual than any other social fact. It is the product of the group. The thought which emanates from the group is freed from physiological influence, since it emanates from other thoughts and not from an organic body. Consequently race has no influence upon institutions. White, yellow, or black of the same degree of development, placed in the same conditions, would reproduce exactly the same law, while remaining in their private psychology white, yellow, and black." [32]

As Tourtoulon says of this, it is true that individual characters combine in the group, but they are not lost there. The argument that seeks to prove that race has nothing to do with law would demonstrate that the laws enacted by an assembly of drunk men would carry no trace of the merely personal drunkenness of each individual.[33] More thorough study is required. But enough has been done at one point to yield valuable results. The problem of the relation of law and mixed races is becoming acute in some parts of the world, and the effect upon the law of a mixed race, whose members are moved by diverse ideals and are incapable of concerted action toward a common goal, is becoming manifest.[34] Comparative study of primitive law is showing also that the relativity of jural principles has been much overrated since the downfall of the law-of-nature school. After a comparison of the laws of Hammurabi (B. C. 2285–2242) with the Salic Law (A. D. 466–511), Fehr says:

"Over and above race and nation there must be conditions of general validity governing the production of law. The fundamental forms of spiritual social life, from which the law springs, are more independent of race and nation than the historical school conceded. The likeness of law in cases of the most striking unlikeness of race can only be explained by a common human basis." [35]

The philosophical type of bio-sociological theory of law proceeds in one form or another upon the idea of selection. In one form, the development of law is conceived as resulting from a conflict or

[32] Tourtoulon, Les principes philosophiques de l'histoire du droit, 85, stating Durkheim's view.

[33] *Id.* 86.

[34] *Id.* 125.

[35] Hammurapi und das Salisches Recht, 136.

competition of legal institutions or of legal doctrines, from which those emerge which are most adapted to further the progress of the race. Accordingly law is held to be an aggregate of the means by which each group protects itself against hindrances to its continuance and to its progress found in the actions of certain of its members or in the hostility of other groups.[36] A complete legal system is worked out in this way after a fashion that reminds one forcibly of the method of the metaphysical jurists. Thus with Richard the starting-point in every case is prohibitive intervention designed to obviate conflict. For example, society forbids its members to possess themselves by force or fraud of a good already possessed; it punishes theft, robbery, and plundering and so creates ownership. In the same way contract is developed by opposition from measures taken to repress deceit, fraud, abuse of trust and the like, the validity of an agreement concluded honestly and fairly being deduced ultimately by way of consequence.[37] This type of sociological jurisprudence is quite as barren as the metaphysical jurisprudence which it imitates. Indeed, that sociological jurisprudence should take such a turn at all is but one more illustration of the influence of propinquity upon juristic thought. We must remember that the metaphysical school was still alive and not without vigor in France at the very end of the nineteenth century.

In another form of the philosophical type under consideration race-conflict or conflict of race ideas is made the basis. Enough has been said of ethnological interpretations heretofore. In still another form, which has had no little currency, class-conflict is taken as the basis, not, however, as in the mechanical sociology, by conceiving of class-conflict as fixing mechanically the whole

---

[36] Richard, Origines de l'idée du droit, 5. Compare: "To my mind sociology is the study of adaptations of men (these are principally mental adaptations) to life in society. Law is one of these adaptations; the one which has for its end to combat by constraint the effects or the causes of certain defaults of adaptation which are considered intolerable. Juridical sociology is, then, the *study of the mental adaptations of men living in society, which adaptations are destined to struggle by means of constraint against certain inadaptations of the same men.* Considered from this point of view, the science of law appears a chapter of the natural history of man." Rolin, Prolégomènes à la science du droit, 4–5. The italics are in the original.

Korkunov gives us the best version of this type of theory: "Legal development as a whole is a struggle of old law, unconsciously established, against new law consciously adopted." General Theory of Law (transl. by Hastings) 165.

[37] Richard, Origines de l'idée du droit, 54–55.

content of legal systems, but by conceiving of it as resulting in a process of selection by which, as it were, the unfit institution and the unfit rule are weeded out or by which the race or nation falls behind or is eliminated which does not develop and preserve the fit institution and the fit rule.[38] The idea of selection through class-conflict has been urged chiefly by Vaccaro.[39] In his view, law grows out of the struggle of social classes for supremacy. He does not deduce therefrom, however, that the sole function of law is to express the will of the dominant class for the time being — "to crown the victor." [40] In quite another spirit from those who adhere to the imperative form of the economic interpretation,[41] he says that its function is to adapt men to the social environment by determining the conditions of their coexistence.[42] This is simply a sociological version of an idea which is to be found frequently in the writings of the metaphysical and historical jurists.[43] The most important difference is in the insistence upon relativity. Thus, Vaccaro says:

> "The conditions of coexistence imposed by law are not those that ought to be in order to assure the greatest possible prosperity of all the associates, but *those which result from the action and reaction of men as they are at a given historical moment*." [44]

---

[38] "The institutions of civilized peoples have been considered as the product of a selection because societies which have not disciplined or organized themselves, which have practiced theft, violence, assassination, have been eliminated." Charmont, La renaissance du droit naturel, 119. It is noteworthy that Montesquieu had an idea not unlike this. See his description of the Troglodytes, who perished utterly because they wilfully violated contracts. Lettres Persanes, Lettre XIV *et seq.*

[39] Le basi del diritto e dello stato (1893), translated by Gaure as Les bases sociologiques du droit et de l'état (1898). For an appreciation and critique, see Gumplowicz, Geschichte der Staatstheorien, § 137.

[40] Brooks Adams in Centralization and the Law, 132.

[41] Here again the influence of propinquity upon juristic thought is manifest. Brooks Adams wrote in a country where analytical jurisprudence was one of the two prevailing methods. His lectures are full of attacks upon the orthodox analytical position. Yet his sociological theory is essentially analytical. Vaccaro wrote in a country where natural law was far from dead and the analytical theory almost unheard of.

[42] Les bases sociologiques du droit et de l'état, 452.

[43] *E. g.*: — "The sum of the conditions of social co-existence with regard to the activity of the community and of individuals." Pulszky, Theory of Law and Civil Society, 312 (1888). "The power of coercion . . . necessary for the harmonious co-existence of the individual with the whole." Lioy, Philosophy of Right with Special Reference to the Principles and Development of Law (transl. by Hastie), II, 122 (1891).

[44] Les bases sociologiques du droit et de l'état, 452. The point will be more clear if

Perhaps enough has been said to indicate that this idea of relativity, valuable as it is in enabling us to combat absolute ideas of justice and hard and fast schemes of supposed fundamental jural principles, may itself be carried too far. No action and reaction of men as they have been at any given moment since republican Rome will explain the long history of the doctrine of impossible and illegal conditions precedent in testaments; no theory of the power of a creditor class will explain the *beneficium excussionis*, its long and involved history in the modern world, and its tendency to disappear in favor of creditors at the very time when both law and public opinion are becoming more and more tender of debtors. But such matters are of more importance in legal systems and have more significance for jurisprudence than the short-lived penal legislation from which most of the data for the theories of class-struggle as the determining factor in legal history have been drawn. Such theories, however, have had an important consequence in directing attention to the unequal operation of doctrines derived by the nineteenth-century method of abstraction, when applied to a society in which industrial progress has resulted in sharply differentiated classes. A group of socialist-jurists has worked upon this matter with zeal and effect.[45]

Foremost among those who have examined actual legal systems with a view of ascertaining the relation of existing rules and doctrines to the interests of the industrial class is Anton Menger.[46] The law of modern Continental Europe was reformulated in codes which, except in the case of the new code of the German Empire, for the most part antedate modern industrial conditions. Hence in this juristic new start the laborer was not taken into account at all.[47]

---

we compare this with Trendelenburg's formula: "The sum of those *universal* determinations of action through which it happens that the ethical whole and its parts may be preserved and further developed." Naturrecht, § 46.

[45] See Berolzheimer, System der Rechts und Wirthschaftsphilosophie, § 40; Charmont, Le droit et l'esprit démocratique, chap. 2 (la socialisation du droit); Gumplowicz, Die soziologische Staatsidee, 115 *et seq.*; Stein, Die soziale Frage im Lichte der Philosophie, 2 ed., 336 *et seq.*

[46] Das Recht auf den vollen Arbeitsertrag (1886, 3 ed., 1904); Das bürgerliche Recht und die besitzlosen Klassen (1889, 3 ed., 1904); Ueber die sozialen Aufgaben der Rechtswissenschaft (1895, 2 ed., 1905).

[47] Compare Glasson's observations upon the French code: Le code civil et la question ouvrière, 6. Also Tissier, Le code civil et les classes ouvrières, Livre du centennaire du code civil, 71–94.

Menger's comparisons of the interests which the law secures with those which it leaves unsecured showed that a situation had arisen for which the codes had made no provision. Indeed from the standpoint of class-struggle, it is said that the working class was left wholly out of the reckoning in the drawing up of the codes. This can hardly be maintained. The French code, which served as a model, was based chiefly upon the juristic writing of the century before and represents the law of a period when there was no such class to attract attention. But it is true of the codes of Continental Europe, as of our Anglo-American common law, that their abstractions, proceeding upon a theoretical equality, do not fit at all points a society divided into classes by conditions of industry. Much of what has been written in Europe from this standpoint might have been written by American social workers. Thus:

"Insanitary housing, exorbitant rent, payment in advance, subjection to shop regulations, fixing of the method and the duration of work, fines, the sweating system, — all is covered by the fiction of liberty of contract. Meanwhile in fact liberty is suppressed." [48]

In compelling study of the relation of law to social classes and so making for a socialization of the law, the group of socialist jurists has done a considerable service.

The organismic type of bio-sociological theory of law is in reality a philosophical theory couched in bio-sociological terminology. Thus Fouillé says:

"The laws of natural history are valid for nations, for at the same time that a nation is a work of voluntary consent it is also a natural organism." [49]

Hence, he holds, the same laws of natural history obtain for national institutions, including legal systems. In application, however, his method is that of the metaphysical jurists, and his formula of law —

"The concrete and complete law, at the same time ideal and real, becomes *the maximum of liberty, equal for all individuals,* which is compatible with the maximum of liberty, of force and of interest for the social organism" [50] —

[48] Andler, preface to the French version of Menger's Recht auf den vollen Arbeitsertrag (Droit au product integral du travail).

[49] L'idée moderne du droit, 6 ed., 402 (1909).

[50] *Id.* 394.

is but a familiar formula of the metaphysical school superficially socialized.

So Kuhlenbeck's essay at a "legal-philosophical and critical estimation of the theory of descent"[51] is to be classed with philosophical rather than with sociological systems.

Now that "the heroic period of socio-biology" in jurisprudence has passed[52] and this phase of sociological jurisprudence comes to be reviewed, the liberalizing effect of the idea of evolution, as soon as it was freed from the hard and fast mechanical systems of those who first applied it, and the loosening effect of biological terminology upon the absolute ideas which the historical school had left unshaken and upon some which that school had set up of its own motion, must be conceded to have marked a step forward. Beyond this, little has been achieved. Biological facts are indirectly and remotely among the causes of law. But they are not the proximate causes which the jurist must investigate. Justice, in the sense of the end of legal administration, public order, the jural order, or *Friedensordnung* as the Germans put it, may be regarded as a sort of directing and debrutalizing of the process of selection, a mode of requiring the struggle for existence to be carried out according to rule. Criminal law particularly may be looked upon as performing a function of selection. Yet when we have looked at these institutions in this way we have not been looking at those features which are significant for sociology or for jurisprudence. Tourtoulon says rightly:

> "The idea of selection does not suffice to constitute the basis, theoretical or practical, of any part of the law."[53]

3. The Psychological Stage.[54]

Three influences combined to turn the attention of sociological jurists toward psychology. They may be summed up in three

[51] Natürliche Grundlagen des Rechts und der Politik. Ein Beitrag zur rechtsphilosophischen und kritischen Würdigung der sogenanten Deszendenztheorie (1905).

[52] These words are Tourtoulon's. Les principes philosophiques de l'histoire du droit, 82.

[53] *Id.* 166.

[54] Berolzheimer, System der Rechts und Wirthschaftsphilosophie, II, § 49; Tarde, Les lois de l'imitation, chap. 7, § 4, Parsons' transl. 310–322 (1890, 2 ed. 1895); Tarde,

names, Gierke, Ward, and Tarde. More precisely they were (1) study of group personality and group will, leading to a psychological movement in legal and political philosophy, (2) the complete change in method in the social sciences which resulted from Ward's thesis that "psychic forces are as real and natural as physical forces . . . and that they are the true causes of all social phenomena,"[55] and (3) Tarde's demonstration of the extent to which imitation is a factor in the development of legal institutions and his working out of the psychological or sociological laws of imitation.

As a Germanist, Gierke[56] was at outs with the orthodox historical school, which was then wholly Romanist. To this fortunate circumstance we may owe it, in part at least, that while his method is primarily and truly historical, he had broken with the metaphysics of the historical school as well as with its learned tradition. Hence, in contrast with the method, then prevalent, of beginning all juristic discussion with the individual will, he struck the sociological note in his first sentence:

> "What man is, he owes to the union of man with man. The possibility of creating associations, which not only enhance the power of those who live contemporaneously but above all, through their permanence, surviving the personality of the individual, bind the past of the race to those to come, gives us the possibility of the development of history."[57]

His theory of associations thus became as strong an attack upon the individualist jurisprudence of the nineteenth century upon one side as Jhering's theory of interests was upon another. That the group or association has a real personality, that in fact and not merely in legal fiction it is more than an aggregation of individuals, that there is a group will, which is something real, apart from the wills of the associated individuals, that the law does not create but merely recognizes personality, exactly as in the case of the human being, and does not create but merely gives legal effect

Les transformations du droit (1894, 6 ed. 1909); Tourtoulon, Les principes philosophiques de l'histoire du droit, 174–331 (1908); Tanon, L'Évolution du droit et la conscience sociale, 3 ed., 143–176 (1911); Vanni, Lezioni di filosofia del diritto, 3 ed., 29 *et seq.* (1908, 1 ed. 1901).

[55] Small, The Meaning of Social Science, 84; Ward, Dynamic Sociology, I, 457 *et seq.*

[56] Das deutsche Genossenschaftsrecht, vol. I, 1868, vol. II, 1873, vol. III, 1881.

[57] *Id.* I, 1.

to the powers of action of the group or association, again exactly as in the case of the human being, — these ideas of Gierke's not only revolutionized theories of the juristic person but they compelled new theories of the greatest of all these groups, namely, the state.[58] Accordingly the group will became no less important — indeed in a sense more important — than the individual will; group motives had to be sought and explained no less than individual motives. As Wundt put it, the state is not necessary to law. What is necessary is an association or society which is capable of producing a collective will because of correspondence of ideas and interests.[59] The significance of this proposition for the theory of International Law is manifest.

One effect of the shifting of emphasis in the philosophy of law from individual will to group will, and so from individual psychology to group psychology, was to give prominence to the idea of relativity, which, as we have seen, other modes of juristic thought were fostering at the same time. Wundt, in a brief sketch of a philosophy of law, lays especial stress upon this. The development of law, he says, is a process of the psychology of peoples.[60] Hence, like all psychical creations, law has been and will forever continue to be in a process of becoming. He adds:

> "Thus we see that law is as variable as man himself; and the attempt to include it in an abstract and absolutely valid system has about as much chance of success as the attempt to introduce an universal language." [61]

Another effect was to give a social-psychological turn to theories of legal obligation, or, in other words, to produce social psychological theories of sanction. Thus Jellinek, who defines society as the "aggregate of the psychological relations between men which are manifest in the external world," [62] begins with the analytical view which characterizes all recent German writing. The essential marks of rules of law, he says, are three:

---

[58] Gierke, Die Grundbegriffe des Staatsrechts und die neuesten Staatstheorien, Zeitschrift für die gesamte Staatswissenschaft, XXX, 304. See also his Die Genossenschaftstheorie und die deutsche Rechtssprechung (1887), particularly pp. 10 *et seq.*

[59] Logik, II^2, 2 ed., 543 (1895).

[60] *Id.* 533.

[61] Ethics (transl. by Titchener and others), III, 161 (1892).

[62] Allgemeine Staatslehre, 2 ed., 89 (1905). This was also in the first edition (1900).

"1. They are norms for the external conduct of men toward one another. 2. They are norms which proceed from a known external authority. 3. They are norms whose binding force is guaranteed by external power." [63]

But what makes a rule law, he says, is that it obtains as a rule, and what makes a right is that the rule which stands behind it obtains in action. This means that its psychological efficiency is guaranteed, that is, that the authority which has prescribed it is so backed by social-psychological power as to be in a position to give effect to the rule, as a motive for action, in spite of counteracting individual motives.[64] Jellinek's doctrine of the relation of state to law and of the nature of sanction is a needed corrective of the imperative ideas which have sprung up in the wake of German legislation. His conception of the social-psychological guarantee, whereby rules are made effective and so are made law, is one of the most important contributions of the psychological movement.[65]

While juristic thought was developing a psychological tendency from within, a psychological movement was going on without which was presently to develop this tendency still further and to give it a new direction. In the biological stage, as we have seen, the static conception of the mechanical sociology persisted. The change of front which involved complete abandonment of that conception begins with Ward.[66] As far back as 1883, when Spencer's sociology was in possession of the field, Ward took the position that social forces were essentially psychic.[67] Whereas social science had been content to study the laws by which social progress took place and had believed it possible to do no more than to observe nature realize itself, Ward conceived that nature might realize itself by "action of its conscious parts upon its unconscious

---

[63] Jellinek, Allgemeine Staatslehre, 325.

[64] *Id.* 326.

[65] For numerous examples from American law of today of the way in which judge-made as well as statutory rules fail because they have no such guarantee, see my paper, Law in Books and Law in Action, 44 Am. L. Rev. 12.

[66] Dynamic Sociology (1883); Pure Sociology (1903); The Psychic Factors of Civilization (1901); Applied Sociology (1906). For a juristic discussion of Ward, see Gumplowicz, Geschichte der Staatstheorien, §§ 119–120.

[67] Dynamic Sociology, chaps. 5, 7, 9, 11. "The truth comes forth that the social forces are essentially psychic. It is this that has made it imperative that the foundations of sociology be sought in psychology." The Psychic Factors of Civilization, 120.

parts."[68] Hence it is not enough to study and observe: "the attitude of man toward nature should be two-fold: first, that of a student; second, that of a master."[69] We must study and thus come to know the efficient social forces, but we do this not to know beforehand the results of their inexorable working, but to be able ultimately to apply them consciously to social ends.[70] Summarily stated, his doctrine was that sociology rests upon psychology, and not directly upon biology,[71] that we must know not only how non-sentient nature works, but "how mind combines its work with the non-sentient factors of human conditions,"[72] and that this part of nature may be harnessed to man's use as so much of physical nature has been so harnessed. Perhaps nothing has done so much to create world-wide dissatisfaction with law and to make problems of law reform acute almost everywhere as the persistence in juristic thinking and judicial decision of nineteenth-century ideas of the futility of effort at a time when the efficacy of effort had become part of the sociological and the political creed.[73]

A more immediate effect upon jurisprudence was produced by the work of Gabriel Tarde (1843–1904).[74] Tarde, a trained lawyer, was *juge d'instruction* for eighteen years, afterwards head of the statistical department of the French ministry of justice, and professor of philosophy in the Collége de France. Besides the works referred to in the note, he wrote a Penal Philosophy, which is translating for the Modern Criminal Science Series. His most important writings have to do with philosophy and sociology: While Ward was showing us that the psychic factors are those of

---

[68] Small, General Sociology, 86.

[69] Dynamic Sociology, II, 11.

[70] "The most important principle of social dynamics is effort. But its dynamic effect, from the standpoint of pure sociology, is unconscious, unintended, and undesired. The social development that results from it is spontaneous. Applied sociology assumes that effort is consciously and intentionally directed to the improvement of social conditions." Applied Sociology, 13.

[71] The Psychic Factors of Civilization, chap. 18.

[72] Small, General Sociology, 85.

[73] "Every beneficent change in legislation comes from a fresh study of social conditions and of social ends, and from some rejection of obsolete law to make room for a rule which fits the new facts. One can hardly escape from the conclusion that a lawyer who has not studied economics and sociology is very apt to become a public enemy." Professor Henderson in American Journal of Sociology, XI, 847.

[74] For Tarde's writings that bear more immediately upon jurisprudence see *supra*, note 54.

first importance, Tarde was studying these factors and seeking to discover the fundamental principle by which they are governed. This principle, as one of cosmic philosophy, he took to be universal, endless repetition, of which the social form is imitation. Reviewing the development of civilization, the evolution of language, art, law, and institutions, he found that imitation was a constant factor. Accordingly he undertook to find the psychological and sociological laws of imitation.

Tarde was the first sociologist to give us an adequate theory of what is in reality the most significant part of legal systems. To the lay eye, legislation commonly occupies the whole stage. Tarde, as a practical lawyer, knew the importance of doctrinal writing and judicial decision, of the traditional element in law, of the modes of juristic thinking that give continuity to legal systems. Although rules have disappeared, have altered, have sprung up, developed and decayed, and from small beginnings have grown into whole departments of the law since the seventeenth century, our common law has a real unity from the age of Coke to the present. As a mode of thinking, as a mode of reasoning upon legal subjects, it is the same in England, the United States, Canada, and Australia, the same in substance in one century as in the next. In the same way the Roman tradition has continuity and essential identity from the third century to the twentieth, and as that tradition gives form and color to all the new elements in the law of Continental Europe, so with us the common-law tradition has put its mark upon equity, admiralty, and the law merchant, and has been able to fit legislation, fashioned by whatever force, into its own system. Explanation of this toughness of jural tradition is much more worth while than theories of formal law-making.

To sum up, the earlier psychological movement made possible a reconciliation of Jhering's insistence upon conscious law-making and the historical view, Ward gave the deathblow to the static theory of the positivists and Tarde gave us the leading principle by which, subconsciously, the direction of law-making and law-finding is chiefly determined. Not only does social psychology occupy a chief place in recent sociological jurisprudence [75] but modes of

[75] Brugeilles, Le droit et la sociologie, chap. 6; Les phénomènes interpsychologiques (1910).

juristic thought, the world-view [76] of judges and doctrinal writers and the psychology of juridical methods are coming to be the subjects of special study.[77] With us, unhappily, what studies of the sort have been attempted have been the work of laymen. Such a book as Professor Ross' Social Psychology, written by a lawyer with Anglo-American law for its subject, would be worth many volumes of the conventional analytical and historical jurisprudence.

4. The Stage of Unification.[78]

At the very end of the last century sociologists were coming to see that no one of the methods theretofore worked out was the whole of sociology and that none of the solving ideas put forward was equal to the task of unfolding all the social sciences.[79] A few years later, Ward enumerated twelve "leading sociological conceptions or unitary principles," each of which had been "put forward with large claims to being in and of itself the science of sociology." [80] In another place, after repeating this enumeration, he said:

> "No single one of these conceptions is to be rejected. All are legitimate parts of the science. . . . All these various lines, together with all others that have been or shall be followed out, may be compared to so many minor streams, all tending in a given direction and converging so as ultimately to unite in one great river that represents the whole science of sociology as it will be finally established." [81]

---

[76] I adopt Baldwin's rendering of *Weltanschauung*, Dictionary of Philosophy and Psychology, II, 822.

[77] Wurzel, Das juristische Denken (1904); Bozi, Die Weltanschauung der Jurisprudenz (1907); Les méthodes juridiques (lectures by a number of French professors of law, 1911).

[78] Brugeilles, Le droit et la sociologie (1910); Ward, Contemporary Sociology (1902); Gumplowicz, Geschichte der Staatstheorien, § 122 (1905); Small, General Sociology, 90–97 (1905); Small, The Meaning of Social Science, Lects. I, III, X (1910).

[79] See the papers cited in Small, General Sociology, 90, note 39.

[80] Contemporary Sociology (reprint of three papers published in American Journal of Sociology, vii, 475 *et seq.*, 629 *et seq.*, 749 *et seq.* "Thus designated these unitary principles, forming the basis of so many systems or schools of sociology, were the following: — Sociology as: I, Philanthropy; II, Anthropology; III, Biology (the organic theory); IV, Political Economy; V, The Philosophy of History; VI, The Special Social Sciences; VII, The Description of Social Facts; VIII, Association; IX, The Division of Labor; X, Imitation; XI, Unconscious Social Constraint; XII, The Struggle of Races." Pure Sociology, 13–14 (1903). It is worth noting that all of these except the first and the fifth, in one form or another, have been put forward in the same way in sociological jurisprudence.

[81] Pure Sociology, 14.

Presently it was seen also that not only was it needful to combine the several methods that had been employed in sociology and to unify the science, but that it was equally needful to put the science into relation with the other social sciences; to unify the social sciences by recognizing that they are "merely methodological divisions of societary science in general." [82]

Both of the foregoing conceptions have come into sociological jurisprudence. It is now recognized that each of the directions which sociological jurisprudence has taken has something for the science as a whole and that no one of them must be pursued exclusively and undeviatingly.[83] It has been felt for some time that the entire separation of jurisprudence from the other social sciences, the leaving of it to itself on the one hand and the conviction of its self-sufficiency on the other hand, was not merely unfortunate for the science of law on general considerations, in that it necessitated a narrow and partial view but was in large part to be charged with the backwardness of law in meeting social ends, the tardiness of lawyers in admitting or even perceiving such ends, and the gulf between legal thought and popular thought on matters of social reform.[84] Not a little of the world-wide discontent with our present legal order is due to modes of juristic thought and juridical method which result from want of "team-work" between jurisprudence and the other social sciences.[85] The first movement toward a better relation between these sciences grew out of the political interpretation of jurisprudence and of legal history, for which the historical school stood, especially in England. Jurisprudence and politics were thus brought into coöperation. In the same way the culture interpretation, adhered to by the Neo-Hegelians, has led to a

[82] Small, General Sociology, 91. "Social science cannot be many. It must be one. The next stage of social science must be marked by a drawing together of the parallel or diverging lines of research in which it has been broken up. We must use the knowledge which we have already gained of parts or aspects or details of human experience to construct a more adequate general survey of the whole of human experience." The Meaning of Social Science, 87.

[83] Brugeilles, Le droit et la sociologie, 160 *et seq.*

[84] Tarde, Les Transformations du droit, Introduction.

[85] Ross, Social Psychology, 223–224; Ely, Economic Theory and Labor Legislation, 18; Bruce, Laissez Faire and the Supreme Court of the United States, 20 Green Bag 546. "So far as any direct influence upon our courts is concerned, our modern textbooks upon economics might as well be written in Chinese." Humble, Economics from a Legal Standpoint, 42 Am. L. Rev. 379.

closer relation between jurisprudence and economics, as shown by treatment of the philosophy of law and the philosophy of economics as parts of a larger subject.[86] The unity of the social sciences and the impossibility of a self-centered, self-sufficing science of law are now insisted upon by sociological jurists.[87] But much remains to be done everywhere in this direction,[88] and in America we have yet to make the very beginning, except as we have learned to harness history for the purposes of legal science. For it is not long since a seventeenth-century legal history was as orthodox as an eighteenth-century philosophy of law and nineteenth-century economics are still. Freeman tells of a teacher of law who

"required the candidates for degrees to say that William the Conqueror introduced the feudal system at the great Gemot of Salisbury in 1086."

When the historian protested, the lawyer replied in all sincerity that he was examiner in law, not in history:

"Facts might be found in chronicles, but law was to be found in Blackstone; it was to be found in Blackstone as an infallible source; what Blackstone said, he, as a law-examiner could not dispute." [89]

---

[86] Berolzheimer, System der Rechts und Wirthschaftsphilosophie, ii, viii. The very title of Dr. Berolzheimer's book is suggestive. Compare also the title and scope of the Archiv für Rechts und Wirthschaftsphilosophie. In the same spirit, Professor Humble says: "In spite of this indifference and lack of co-operation . . . the subject matter of the two studies [*i. e.* law and economics] is largely common ground." Economics from a Legal Standpoint, 42 Am. L. Rev. 379, 380.

[87] "The error of the classical conception was in looking upon law as a science isolated from the others, self-sufficient, furnishing a certain number of propositions the combination whereof ought to provide for all needs. In reality the law is only a resultant. Its explanation is outside of itself. Its sources must be sought elsewhere." Vander Eycken, Méthode positive de l'interprétation, 112 (1907). "Nothing is more fallacious than to believe that one may give an account of the law by means of the law itself." Roguin, Le règle de droit, 8 (1905). See also Bosanquet, Philosophical Theory of the State, 36 *et seq.* (1899).

[88] Kantorowicz, Rechtswissenschaft und Soziologie, 8 (1911).

[89] Freeman, Methods of Historical Study, 73–74. Compare with the foregoing: "The report of the commission . . . is based upon a most voluminous array of statistical tables, extracts from the works of philosophical writers and the industrial laws of many countries, all of which are designed to show that our own system of dealing with industrial accidents is economically, morally, and legally unsound. Under our form of government, however, courts must regard all economic, philosophical, and moral theories, attractive and desirable though they may be, as subordinate to the primary question whether they can be molded into statutes without infringing upon the letter or spirit of our written constitutions." Ives *v.* South Buffalo R. Co., 201 N. Y. 271, 287, 94 N. E. 431, 437 (1911). Of course, economic, moral, and philosophical

Holmes and Bigelow and Thayer and Ames and Maitland have made us wiser with respect to law and history. But it is still good form for the lawyer to look upon our eighteenth-century Bills of Rights as authoritative text-books of politics,[90] of ethics,[91] and of economics.[92]

The Present Status of Sociological Jurisprudence.[93]

The main problem to which sociological jurists are addressing themselves today is to enable and to compel law-making, and also

theories of today could have no more bearing on the reading of the text than historical study of today, in the mind of Freeman's teacher, could have upon the legal dogma as to what was legal history!

[90] People *v.* Coler, 166 N. Y. 1, 14, 59 N. E. 716, 720 (1901); Low *v.* Rees Printing Co., 41 Neb. 127, 135, 59 N. W. 362, 364 (1894); State *ex rel.* Zillmer *v.* Kreutzberg, 114 Wis. 530, 537, 90 N. W. 1098, 1101 (1902).

[91] Durkin *v.* Kingston Coal Co., 171 Pa. St. 193, 202, 33 Atl. 237, 238 (1895); Hoxie *v.* New York, etc. R. Co., 82 Conn. 352, 359; 73 Atl. 754, 757 (1909). I am indebted to Professor Munroe Smith for calling my attention to a notable example in the minority report of a committee of the Bar Association of the City of New York upon a proposition for amendment of the state constitution so as to permit the enactment of a Workmen's Compensation Act. The report says: "We must begin by ourselves understanding that the constitutional provisions which are contained in our bill of rights in the state and federal constitutions are moral principles, as weighty in moral authority and as vital to the safety of society as any that have ever been promulgated, not even excepting the golden rule. After that, we must teach the people. We must make *them* understand that constitutional rights are moral rights, and that whatever experiments they may try in modes of social organization, they must never try any experiments which will imperil those moral rights. We must make them understand that once they tamper with the security of those moral rights they will, like Samson, wreck the social structure and be themselves crushed in the ruins. There is no duty resting upon the lawyers of today which is higher than the duty to resist to the uttermost any effort at amendment of our constitutions which shall endanger in the slightest degree the moral principles in the bill of rights, or which shall permit any man's property to be taken under any pretext without due process of law, or which shall extend to any man anything less than the absolutely equal protection of the law." Report of Special Committee . . . to consider the Question of an Amendment to the Constitution of the State of New York Empowering the Legislature to Enact a Workmen's Compensation Law (Dated 27 December, 1911) p. 17.

[92] "A law that restricts the freedom of contract on the part of both the master and servant can not in the end operate to the benefit of either." People *v.* Coler, 166 N. Y. 1, 16, 59 N. E. 716, 721 (1901). See for many other examples the papers referred to *supra*, note 85.

[93] Ehrlich, Soziologie und Jurisprudenz (1906); Kantorowicz, Rechtswissenschaft und Soziologie (1911); Kelsen, Ueber Grenzen zwischen juristischer und soziologischer Methode (1911); Brugeilles, Le droit et la sociologie (1910).

interpretation and application of legal rules, to take more account, and more intelligent account, of the social facts upon which law must proceed and to which it is to be applied.[94] More specifically, they insist upon six points:

(1) The first is study of the actual social effects of legal institutions and legal doctrines. Thus Kantorowicz says:

"I advise one who does not believe this to read a section of the German Civil Code in the following way: Let him ask himself with respect to each statement . . . what harms would social life undergo if instead of this statement the opposite were enacted. And then let him turn to all text-books, commentaries, monographs, and reports of decisions and see how many questions of this sort he will find answered and how many he will find even put. Characteristically, also, statistics upon civil law are almost wholly wanting, so that we can be sure of almost nothing as to the social function of civil law, particularly as to the measure of its realization. For instance, we only know that the Civil Code governs five forms of matrimonial property régime, but we have not the least suggestion in what numerical relation and in what geographical subdivisions the several forms occur now in social life." [95]

---

[94] "No glance strays over this Chinese wall into the region of social life for the regulation whereof these precepts were promulgated; that troubles the orthodox jurists as little as the uses which the builders of a machine may chance sometime to make of his formula troubles the pure mathematician." Kantorowicz, Rechtswissenschaft und Soziologie, 5. "So this means only remains: look over the Chinese wall into the region of social life in which it is the task of every rule of law to bring forth some sort of consequences." *Id.* 7. See also Vander Eycken, Méthode positive de l'interprétation, 109 *et seq.*; Holmes, The Path of the Law, 10 HARV. L. REV. 457, 467.

Perhaps the most effective study in this direction has been done in Professor Ehrlich's "Seminar for Living Law." See Ehrlich, Die Erforschung des lebenden Rechts, Schmollers Jahrbuch, xxxv, 129 (1911). With us, a sign of a new tendency to take more account of the social facts involved in application of legal rules may be seen in the opinion of Winslow, C. J., in Borgnis *v.* Falk Co., 133 N. W. 209 (Wis., 1911). Reference should be made also to the well-known briefs of Mr. Brandeis in Muller *v.* State of Oregon, 208 U. S. 412, 28 Sup. Ct. 324 (1908), and Ritchie *v.* Wayman, 244 Ill. 509, 91 N. E. 695 (1910), and to the brief in State *v.* Cramer (Supreme Court of Ohio, Jan. 16, 1912). See Boyd, the Economic and Legal Basis of Compulsory Industrial Insurance for Workmen, 10 Mich. L. Rev. 345.

[95] Rechtswissenschaft und Soziologie, 8. In the United States we are even more backward. Proper statistics of the administration of civil justice, which are a prerequisite of intelligent reform of procedure, are not to be had except for the Municipal Court of Chicago. As to criminal law, see Robinson, History and Organization of Criminal Statistics in the United States (1911); Mayo-Smith, Statistics and Sociology, chap. 12 (1907); Ralston, The Delay in the Execution of Murderers, Paper Read Before the Pennsylvania Bar Association (1911).

(2) The second is sociological study in connection with legal study in preparation for legislation. The accepted scientific method has been to study other legislation analytically. Comparative legislation has been taken to be the best foundation for wise law-making. But it is not enough to compare the laws themselves. It is much more important to study their social operation and the effects which they produce, if any, when put in action.[96]

(3) The third is study of the means of making legal rules effective. This has been neglected almost entirely in the past. We have studied the making of law sedulously. It seems to have been assumed that, when made, law will enforce itself. This is true not only of legislation but also of that more important part of our law which rests in the reports. Almost the whole energy of our judicial system is employed in working out a consistent, logical, minutely precise body of precedents. The important part of our system is not the trial judge who dispenses justice to litigants but the judge of the appellate court who uses the litigation as a means of developing the law; and we judge the system by the output of written opinions and not by the actual results *inter partes* in concrete causes. But the life of the law is in its enforcement. Serious scientific study of how to make our huge annual output of legislation and judicial interpretation effective is imperative.[97]

(4) A means toward the end last considered is a sociological legal history; that is, study not merely of how doctrines have evolved and developed, considered solely as jural materials, but of what social effects the doctrines of the law have produced in the past and how they have produced them.[98] Accordingly Kantorowicz

---

[96] Legislative reference bureaus are beginning to do this work. See Reinsch, Bestrebungen zur Verbesserung der gesetzgeberischen Tätigkeit, Blätter für verglichende Rechtswissenschaft, viii, 246. Kantorowicz gives as an example: in preparation for housing legislation there should be inquiry as to "how far the statutory law of tenancy is silenced by contracts of leasing." *Id.* 9. See some sensible, practical remarks upon this phase of sociological jurisprudence in Tanon, L'évolution du droit et la conscience sociale, 3 ed., 196–202. An important recent work, largely from this standpoint, is Jethro Brown, The Underlying Principles of Modern Legislation (1912).

[97] See my papers, the Need of a Sociological Jurisprudence, 19 Green Bag 607; Law in Books and Law in Action, 44 Am. L. Rev. 12.

[98] "What method shall we employ in studying juridical phenomena? We shall have to investigate: what juridical phenomena are, their classification, the necessary and sufficient conditions in order that they be obligatory, their generality and their permanence. Comparative law can teach us already as to the comparative generality of a phenomenon. . . . Legal history makes us aware of the comparative permanence

calls for a legal history which shall not deal with rules and doctrines apart from the economic and social history of their time, as if the causes of change in the law were always to be found in the legal phenomena of the past; a legal history that shall not try to show that the law of the past can give us an answer to every question, by systematic deduction, as if it were a system without hiatus and without antinomies.[99] Instead it is to show us how the law of the past grew out of social, economic, and psychological conditions, how it accorded with or accommodated itself to them, and how far we can proceed upon that law as a basis, or in disregard of it, with well-grounded expectations of producing the results desired.[100]

(5) Another point is the importance of reasonable and just solutions of individual causes, too often sacrificed in the immediate past to the attempt to bring about an impossible degree of certainty. A whole literature has grown up in recent years upon this subject. In general the sociological jurists stand for what has been called equitable application of law; that is, they conceive of the legal rule as a general guide to the judge, leading him toward the just result, but insist that within wide limits he should be free to deal with the individual case, so as to meet the demands of justice between the parties and accord with the general reason of ordinary men.[101]

(6) Finally, the end, toward which the foregoing points are but some of the means, is to make effort more effective in achieving the purposes of law.[102]

---

of these phenomena. . . . One may seek to verify how far the degree of generality of a juridical phenomenon accords with its degree of permanence." Brugeilles, Le droit et la sociologie, 160.

[99] Rechtswissenschaft und Sociologie, 30–34.

[100] Dicey's Law and Public Opinion in England (1905) is a history of legislation from this standpoint. Compare Wigmore's history of the law of confessions. Evidence, I, § 865.

[101] See some account of this doctrine in my paper, The Enforcement of Law, 20 Green Bag 401 (1908).

Out of the great mass of writing upon this subject in the past ten years, reference may be made to the following: Ehrlich, Freie Rechtsfindung und freie Rechtswissenschaft (1903); Gnæus Flavius (Kantorowicz), Der Kampf um die Rechtswissenschaft (1906); Fuchs, Recht und Wahrheit in unserer heutigen Justiz (1908); Oertmann, Gesetzeszwang und Richterfreiheit (1909); Gmelin, Quousque? Beiträge zur soziologischen Rechtsfindung (1910); Kantorowicz, Rechtswissenschaft und Soziologie, 11 *et seq.* (1911).

[102] "The jurist must study the law teleologically; he must observe how the elements of law turn out in their respective working; whether their operation leads to useful or to harmful consequences, to consequences which accord with culture or to those which

Summarily stated, the sociological jurist pursues a comparative study of legal systems, legal doctrines, and legal institutions as social phenomena, and criticizes them with respect to their relation to social conditions and social progress. Comparing sociological jurists with jurists of the other schools, we may say:

1. They look more to the working of the law than to its abstract content.

2. They regard law as a social institution which may be improved by intelligent human effort, and hold it their duty to discover the best means of furthering and directing such effort.

3. They lay stress upon the social purposes which law subserves rather than upon sanction.

4. They urge that legal precepts are to be regarded more as guides to results which are socially just and less as inflexible molds.

5. Their philosophical views are very diverse. Beginning as positivists, recently they have adhered to some one of the groups of the social philosophical school, from which, indeed, the sociological school, on many essential points, is not easily distinguishable. While Professor Moore tells us that the time has come "in the development of the pragmatic movement for systematic and detailed applications of pragmatic conceptions and methods to specific problems, rather than further discussion of general principles,"[103] unhappily discussion of general principles goes on and a pragmatist philosophy of law is yet to come. When it is promulgated it may expect many adherents from the sociological jurists.

Roscoe Pound.

HARVARD LAW SCHOOL.

---

oppose it; to consequences whereby values are appraised justly or unjustly." Kohler, Introduction to Rogge's Methodologische Vorstudien zu einer Kritik des Rechts, viii (1911).

[103] Pragmatism and its Critics, Preface.

COLUMBIA LAW REVIEW

VOL. XXXV JUNE, 1935 NO. 6

TRANSCENDENTAL NONSENSE AND THE FUNCTIONAL APPROACH

I. THE HEAVEN OF LEGAL CONCEPTS

Some fifty years ago a great German jurist had a curious dream. He dreamed that he died and was taken to a special heaven reserved for the theoreticians of the law. In this heaven one met, face to face, the many concepts of jurisprudence in their absolute purity, freed from all entangling alliances with human life. Here were the disembodied spirits of good faith and bad faith, property, possession, *laches,* and rights *in rem.* Here were all the logical instruments needed to manipulate and transform these legal concepts and thus to create and to solve the most beautiful of legal problems. Here one found a dialectic-hydraulic-interpretation press, which could press an indefinite number of meanings out of any text or statute, an apparatus for constructing fictions, and a hair-splitting machine that could divide a single hair into 999,999 equal parts and, when operated by the most expert jurists, could split each of these parts again into 999,999 equal parts. The boundless opportunities of this heaven of legal concepts were open to all properly qualified jurists, provided only they drank the Lethean draught which induced forgetfulness of terrestrial human affairs. But for the most accomplished jurists the Lethean draught was entirely superfluous. They had nothing to forget.[1]

Von Jhering's dream has been retold, in recent years, in the chapels of sociological, functional, institutional, scientific, experimental, realistic, and neo-realistic jurisprudence. The question is raised, "How much of contemporary legal thought moves in the pure ether of Von Jhering's heaven of legal concepts?" One turns to our leading legal textbooks and to the opinions of our courts for answer. May the Shade of Von Jhering be our guide.

1. *Where Is a Corporation?*

Let us begin our survey by observing an exceptionally able court as it deals with a typical problem in legal procedure. In the case of *Tauza v. Susquehanna Coal Company,*[2] a corporation which had been

[1] VON JHERING, IM JURISTISCHEN BEGRIFFSHIMMEL, IN SCHERZ UND ERNST IN DER JURISPRUDENZ (11th ed. 1912) 245.

[2] 220 N. Y. 259, 115 N. E. 915 (1917).

chartered by the State of Pennsylvania was sued in New York. Summons and complaint were served upon an officer of the corporation in New York in the manner prescribed by New York law. The corporation raised the objection that it *could not* be sued in New York. The New York Court of Appeals disagreed with this contention and held that the corporation could be sued in that State. What is of interest for our purposes is not the particular decision of the court but the mode of reasoning by which this decision was reached.

The problem which the Court of Appeals faced was a thoroughly practical one. If a competent legislature had considered the problem of when a corporation incorporated in another State should be subject to suit, it would probably have made some factual inquiry into the practice of modern corporations in choosing their sovereigns[3] and into the actual significance of the relationship between a corporation and the state of its incorporation. It might have considered the difficulties that injured plaintiffs may encounter if they have to bring suit against corporate defendants in the state of incorporation. It might have balanced, against such difficulties, the possible hardship to corporations of having to defend actions in many states, considering the legal facilities available to corporate defendants. On the basis of *facts* revealed by such an inquiry, and on the basis of certain political or ethical *value judgments* as to the propriety of putting financial burdens upon corporations, a competent legislature would have attempted to formulate some rule as to when a foreign corporation should be subject to suit.

The Court of Appeals reached its decision without avowedly considering any of these matters. It does not appear that scientific evidence on any of these issues was offered to the court. Instead of addressing itself to such economic, sociological, political, or ethical questions as a competent legislature might have faced, the court addressed itself to the question, "Where is a corporation?" Was this corporation *really* in Pennsylvania or in New York, or could it be in two places at once?

Clearly the question of *where a corporation is,* when it incorporates in one state and has agents transacting corporate business in another state, is not a question that can be answered by empirical observation. Nor is it a question that demands for its solution any analysis of political considerations or social ideals. It is, in fact, a question identical in metaphysical status with the question which scholastic theologians are supposed to have argued at great length, "How many angels can stand on the point of a needle?" Now it is extremely doubtful whether any of the scholastics ever actually discussed this question.[4] Yet the ques-

[3] See Berle, *Investors and the Revised Delaware Corporation Act* (1929) 29 Columbia Law Rev. 563; Ripley, Main Street and Wall Street (1927).

[4] Several students of scholastic philosophy inform me that they have never found any evidence of such discussion more reliable than the hearsay testimony of Rabelais.

tion has become, for us, a symbol of an age in which thought without roots in reality was an object of high esteem.

Will future historians deal more charitably with such legal questions as "Where is a corporation?" Nobody has ever seen a corporation. What right have we to believe in corporations if we don't believe in angels? To be sure, some of us have seen corporate funds, corporate transactions, etc. (just as some of us have seen angelic deeds, angelic countenances, etc.). But this does not give us the right to hypostatize, to "thingify," the corporation, and to assume that it travels about from State to State as mortal men travel. Surely we are qualifying as inmates of Von Jhering's heaven of legal concepts when we approach a legal problem in these essentially supernatural terms.

Yet it is exactly in these terms of transcendental nonsense that the Court of Appeals approached the question of whether the Susquehanna Coal Company could be sued in New York State. "The essential thing," said Judge Cardozo, writing for a unanimous court, "is that the corporation shall have come into the State."[5] Why this journey is *essential,* or how it is *possible,* we are not informed. The opinion notes that the corporation has an office in the State, with eight salesmen and eleven desks, and concludes that the corporation is really "in" New York State. From this inference it easily follows that since a person who is in New York can be sued here, and since a corporation is a person, the Susquehanna Coal Company is subject to suit in a New York court.

The same manner of reasoning can be used by the same court to show that the Dodge Bros. Motor Corporation "cannot" be sued in New York because the corporation (as distinguished from its corps of New York employees and dealers) is not "in" New York.[6]

Strange as this manner of argument will seem to laymen, lawyers trained by long practice in believing what is impossible,[7] will accept this reasoning as relevant, material, and competent. Indeed, even the great protagonist of sociological jurisprudence, Mr. Justice Brandeis, has invoked this supernatural approach to the problem of actions against foreign corporations, without betraying any doubt as to the factual reference of the question, "Where is a corporation?" Thus, in the leading case of *Bank of America v. Whitney Central National Bank,*[8] the

[5] See 220 N. Y. at 268, 115 N. E. at 918.

[6] Holzer v. Dodge Bros. Motor Corp., 233 N. Y. 216, 135 N. E. 268 (1922).

[7] "I can't believe *that*!" said Alice.

"Can't you?" the Queen said, in a pitying tone. "Try again: draw a long breath, and shut your eyes."

Alice laughed. "There's no use trying," she said; "one can't believe impossible things."

"I dare say you haven't had much practice," said the Queen. "When I was your age I always did it for half an hour a day. Why, sometimes I've believed as many as six impossible things before breakfast." (Lewis Carroll, Through the Looking Glass, c. 5.)

[8] 261 U. S. 171 (1923).

United States Supreme Court faced the question of whether a banking corporation incorporated in Louisiana could be sued in New York, where it carried on numerous financial transactions and where its president had been served, but where it did not own any desks. The Supreme Court held that although the defendant "had what would popularly be called a large New York business," the action could not be maintained, and offered, per Brandeis, J., the following justification of this curious conclusion:[9]

> "The jurisdiction taken of foreign corporations, in the absence of statutory requirement or express consent, does not rest upon a fiction of constructive presence, like *qui facit per alium facit per se*. It flows from the fact that the corporation itself does business in the State or district in such a manner and to such an extent that its actual presence there is established. That the defendant was not in New York, and, hence, was not found within the district, is clear."

Of course, it would be captious to criticize courts for delivering their opinions in the language of transcendental nonsense. Logicians sometimes talk as if the only function of language were to convey ideas. But anthropologists know better and assure us that "language is primarily a pre-rational function."[10] Certain words and phrases are useful for the purpose of releasing pent-up emotions, or putting babies to sleep, or inducing certain emotions and attitudes in a political or a judicial audience. The law is not a science but a practical activity, and myths may impress the imagination and memory where more exact discourse would leave minds cold.

Valuable as is the language of transcendental nonsense for many practical legal purposes, it is entirely useless when we come to study, describe, predict, and criticize legal phenomena. And although judges and lawyers need not be legal scientists, it is of some practical importance that they should recognize that the traditional language of argument and opinion neither explains nor justifies court decisions. When the vivid fictions and metaphors of traditional jurisprudence are thought of as reasons for decisions, rather than poetical or mnemonic devices for formulating decisions reached on other grounds, then the author, as well as the reader, of the opinion or argument, is apt to forget the social forces which mold the law and the social ideals by which the law is to be judged. Thus it is that the most intelligent judges in America can deal with a concrete practical problem of procedural law and corporate responsibility without any appreciation of the economic, social, and ethical issues which it involves.

---

[9] *Id.*, at 173.
[10] Sapir, Language (1921) 14.

2. *When is a Corporation?*

The field of corporation law offers many illuminating examples of the traditional supernatural approach to practical legal problems. In the famous *Coronado* case,[11] the question was presented to the United States Supreme Court, whether employers whose business had been injured in the course of a strike could recover a judgment against a labor union which had "encouraged" the strike, or whether suit could be brought only against particular individuals charged with committing or inducing the injury. So far as appears from the printed record, counsel for the union defendants did not attempt to show that labor unions would be seriously handicapped by the imposition of financial responsibility for damage done in strikes, that it would be impossible for labor unions to control *agents provocateurs,* and that labor unions served a very important function in modern industrial society which would be seriously endangered by the type of liability in question. Instead of offering any such argument to support the claim of the labor union to legal immunity for the torts of its members, counsel for the union advanced the metaphysical argument that a labor union, being an unincorporated association, is not a person and, therefore, cannot be subject to tort liability. This is a very ancient and respectable argument in procedural law. Pope Innocent IV used it in the middle of the Thirteenth Century to prove that the treasuries of religious bodies could not be subject to tort liability.[12] Unfortunately, the argument that a labor union is not a person is one of those arguments that remain true only so long as they are believed.[13] When the court rejected the argument and held the union liable, the union became a person—to the extent of being suable as a legal entity—and the argument ceased to be true.

The Supreme Court argued, "A labor union can be sued because it is, in essential aspects, a person, a quasi-corporation." The realist will say, "A labor union is a person or quasi-corporation because it can be sued; to call something a person in law, is merely to state, in metaphorical language, that it can be sued."

---

[11] United Mine Workers of America v. Coronado Coal Co., 259 U. S. 344 (1922). The British prototype of this case, Taff-Vale Ry. Co. v. Amalg. Soc. of Railway Servants, [1901] A. C. 426, reached a similar decision, professedly upon similar transcendental grounds, but this was soon upset by special legislation. See WEBB, HISTORY OF TRADE UNIONISM (Rev. ed. 1920) 600 ff.

[12] *Cf.* DEWEY, *"Corporate Personality"* in PHILOSOPHY AND CIVILIZATION (1931), 154; and see 3 GIERKE, DAS DEUTSCHE GENOSSENSCHAFTRECHT 279-285; *cf.* 3 HOLDSWORTH, HISTORY OF ENGLISH LAW (3d ed. 1923) 470-474.

[13] Compare the case of Wild Modesty, a flower found on certain islands of the South Seas, which is really white but turns red when any one looks at it (reported in Traprock's "The Cruise of the Kawa" [1921] 10).

There is a significant difference between these two ways of describing the situation. If we say that a court acts in a certain way "because a labor union is a person," we *appear to justify the court's action,* and to justify that action, moreover, in transcendental terms, by asserting something that sounds like a proposition but which *can not be confirmed or refuted by positive evidence or by ethical argument.* If, on the other hand, we say that a labor union is a person "because the courts allow it to be sued," we recognize that the action of the courts has not been justified at all, and that the question of whether the action of the courts is justifiable calls for an answer in non-legal terms. To justify or criticize legal rules in purely legal terms is always to argue in a vicious circle.[14]

3. *What's in a Trade Name?*

The divorce of legal reasoning from questions of social fact and ethical value is not a product of crusty legal fictions inherited from darker ages. Even in the most modern realms of legal development one finds the thought of courts and of legal scholars trapezing around in cycles and epicycles without coming to rest on the floor of verifiable fact. Modern developments in the law of unfair competition offer many examples of such circular reasoning.

There was once a theory that the law of trade marks and tradenames was an attempt to protect the consumer against the "passing off" of inferior goods under misleading labels.[15] Increasingly the courts have departed from any such theory and have come to view this branch of law as a protection of property rights in divers economically valuable sale devices.[16] In practice, injunctive relief is being extended today to realms where no actual danger of confusion to the consumer is present, and this extension has been vigorously supported and encouraged by leading writers in the field.[17] Conceivably this extension might be justified by a demonstration that privately controlled sales devices serve as a psychologic base for the power of business monopolies, and that such monopolies are socially valuable in modern civilization. But no such line of argument has ever been put forward by courts or scholars advocating increased legal protection of trade names and similar de-

[14] *Cf.* Roguin, La Regle du Droit (1889): "Nothing is more fallacious than to believe that one may give an account of the law by means of the law itself."

[15] See Nims, Unfair Competition and Trade-Marks (3d ed. 1929) § 8, and cases cited.

[16] See American Washboard Co. v. Saginaw Mfg. Co., 103 Fed. 281, 285 (C. C. A. 6th, 1900).

[17] Nims, *op. cit. supra* note 15, § 9a; Handler and Pickett, *Trade-Marks and Trade Names—An Analysis and Synthesis* (1930) 30 Columbia Law Rev. 168, 759; Schechter, *The Rational Basis of Trade-Mark Protection* (1927) 40 Harv. L. Rev. 813.

vices. For if they advanced any such argument, it might seem that they were taking sides upon controversial issues of politics and economics. Courts and scholars, therefore, have taken refuge in a vicious circle to which no obviously extra-legal facts can gain admittance. The current legal argument runs: One who by the ingenuity of his advertising or the quality of his product has induced consumer responsiveness to a particular name, symbol, form of packaging, etc., has thereby created a thing of value; a thing of value is property; the creator of property is entitled to protection against third parties who seek to deprive him of his property.[18] This argument may be embellished, in particular cases, with animadversions upon the selfish motives of the infringing defendant, a summary of the plaintiff's evidence (naturally uncontradicted) as to the amount of money he has spent in advertising, and insinuations (seldom factually supported) as to the inferiority of the infringing defendant's product.

The vicious circle inherent in this reasoning is plain. It purports to base legal protection upon economic value, when, as a matter of actual fact, the economic value of a sales device depends upon the extent to which it will be legally protected. If commercial exploitation of the word "Palmolive" is not restricted to a single firm, the word will be of no more economic value to any particular firm than a convenient size, shape, mode of packing, or manner of advertising, common in the trade. Not being of economic value to any particular firm, the word would be regarded by courts as "not property," and no injunction would be issued. In other words, the fact that courts did not protect the word would make the word valueless, and the fact that it was valueless would then be regarded as a reason for not protecting it. Ridiculous as this vicious circle seems, it is logically as conclusive or inconclusive as the opposite vicious circle, which accepts the fact that courts do protect private exploitation of a given word as a reason why private exploitation of that word should be protected.

The circularity of legal reasoning in the whole field of unfair competition is veiled by the "thingification" of *property*. Legal language portrays courts as examining commercial words and finding, somewhere inhering in them, *property rights*. It is by virtue of the property right which the plaintiff has acquired in the word that he is entitled to an injunction or an award of damages. According to the recognized authorities on the law of unfair competition, courts are not *creating* property, but are merely *recognizing* a pre-existent Something.

[18] *Cf.* American Agricultural Chemical Co. v. Moore, 17 F.(2d) 196 (M.D. Ala. 1927) in which an interesting implication of the current theory is carried to its logical conclusion. A fertilizer company is granted an injunction against state officials seeking to prevent the use of a misleading trade name. The argument is: The plaintiff expected to do a large business under this trade name; such expectations are property, and must be protected against governmental interference.

The theory that judicial decisions in the field of unfair competition law are merely recognitions of a supernatural Something that is immanent in certain trade names and symbols is, of course, one of the numerous progeny of the theory that judges have nothing to do with making the law, but merely recognize pre-existent truths not made by mortal men.[19] The effect of this theory, in the law of unfair competition as elsewhere, is to dull lay understanding and criticism of what courts do in fact.

What courts are actually doing, of course, in unfair competition cases, is to create and distribute a new source of economic wealth or power. Language is socially useful apart from law, as air is socially useful, but neither language nor air is a source of economic wealth unless some people are prevented from using these resources in ways that are permitted to other people. That is to say, property is a function of inequality.[20] If courts, for instance, should prevent a man from breathing any air which had been breathed by another (within, say, a reasonable statute of limitations), those individuals who breathed most vigorously and were quickest and wisest in selecting desirable locations in which to breathe (or made the most advantageous contracts with such individuals) would, by virtue of their property right in certain volumes of air, come to exercise and enjoy a peculiar economic advantage, which might, through various modes of economic exchange, be turned into other forms of economic advantage, e.g. the ownership of newspapers or fine clothing. So, if courts prevent a man from exploiting certain forms of language which another has already begun to exploit, the second user will be at the economic disadvantage of having to pay the first user for the privilege of using similar language or else of having to use less appealing language (generally) in presenting his commodities to the public.

Courts, then, in establishing inequality in the commercial exploitation of language are creating economic wealth and property, creating property not, of course, *ex nihilo,* but out of the materials of social fact, commercial custom, and popular moral faiths or prejudices. It does not follow, except by the fallacy of composition,[21] that in creating

[19] See M. R. COHEN, *The Process of Judicial Legislation,* in LAW AND THE SOCIAL ORDER (1933) 112, also printed in (1914) 48 AM. L. REV. 161.

[20] See M. R. COHEN, *Property and Sovereignty,* in LAW AND THE SOCIAL ORDER (1933) 41; R. L. Hale, *Coercion and Distribution in a Supposedly Non-Coercive State* (1923) 38 POL. SCI. Q. 470; R. L. Hale, *Rate Making and the Revision of the Property Concept* (1922) 22 COLUMBIA LAW REV. 209.

[21] "Composition is the passage from a statement about *each* or *every* member of a collection, taken severally, in one of the premises, to a statement about the collection as a whole in the conclusion." EATON, GENERAL LOGIC (1931) 340. An instance of the commission of this fallacy, in the present context, would be the statement that the court is adding to the wealth of society because it is adding to the wealth of the particular individuals whose control over the sales device it protects.

new private property courts are benefiting society. Whether they are benefiting society depends upon a series of questions which courts and scholars dealing with this field of law have not seriously considered. Is there, for practical purposes, an unlimited supply of equally attractive words under which any commodity can be sold, so that the second seller of the commodity is at no commercial disadvantage if he is forced to avoid the word or words chosen by the first seller? If this is not the case, i.e. if peculiar emotional contexts give one word more sales appeal than any other word suitable for the same product, should the peculiar appeal of that word be granted by the state, without payment, to the first occupier? Is this homestead law for the English language necessary in order to induce the first occupier to use the most attractive word in selling his product? If, on the other hand, all words are originally alike in commercial potentiality, but become differentiated by advertising and other forms of commercial exploitation, is this type of business pressure a good thing, and should it be encouraged by offering legal rewards for the private exploitation of popular linguistic habits and prejudices? To what extent is differentiation of commodities by trade names a help to the consumer in buying wisely? To what extent is the exclusive power to exploit an attractive word, and to alter the quality of the things to which the word is attached, a means of deceiving consumers into purchasing inferior goods?

Without a frank facing of these and similar questions,[22] legal reasoning on the subject of trade names is simply economic prejudice masquerading in the cloak of legal logic. The prejudice that identifies the interests of the plaintiff in unfair competition cases with the interests of business[23] and identifies the interests of business with the interests of society, will not be critically examined by courts and legal scholars until it is recognized and formulated. It will not be recognized or formulated so long as the hypostatization of "property rights" conceals the circularity of legal reasoning.

4. *How High Is Fair Value?*

Perhaps the most notorious example of circular reasoning in contemporary jurisprudence is that involved in judicial determination of the returns to which public utilities are entitled "under the Constitution."[24]

---

[22] An example of realistic analysis of consequences in this field is Legis., The Vestal Bill for the Copyright Registration of Designs (1931) 31 COLUMBIA LAW REV. 477.

[23] See Schechter, *supra* note 17, at 831.

[24] The circularity of judicial reasoning in this field is discussed in R. L. Hale, *Value and Vested Rights* (1927) 27 COLUMBIA LAW REV. 523; D. R. Richberg, *Value by Judicial Fiat* (1927) 40 HARV. L. REV. 567; J. C. Bonbright, *The Problem of Judicial Valuation* (1927) 27 COLUMBIA LAW REV. 493.

What courts purport to do in rate cases is to ascertain the "value" of the utility's property and then to fix a price to the consumer which assures the utility a fair rate of return upon that value. This would be an understandable procedure if the courts meant by "value" either actual cost or replacement cost. For almost forty years, however, since the famous case of *Smyth v. Ames*,[25] the courts have insisted that it may be "unconstitutional" to allow a utility merely a fair return on the actual cost or replacement cost of its property; it must be allowed a fair return on the "actual value" of the property.

What is the actual value of a utility's property? Obviously it is the capitalization at current market rates of the allowed and expected profit. In a six per cent money market, an enterprise which is allowed to take six million dollars profit per annum will be valued at one hundred million dollars, one that is allowed three millions per annum, at fifty million dollars. *The actual value of a utility's property, then, is a function of the court's decision,* and the court's decision cannot be based in fact upon the actual value of the property. That value is created by the court; prior to the court's decision and aside from information or belief as to what the court will decide, it is not an economic fact. Nor is it avowedly an ethical fact based upon a determination of the amount which a given utility ought, in the light of social facts and social policies, to be allowed to charge its patrons. Judicial reasoning in this field is thus entirely mythical, and the actual motivation of courts in reaching given decisions is effectively concealed, from all true believers in the orthodox legal theology.

5. *When Is Legal Process "Due"?*

Legal reasoning carries a peculiar freight of human hopes and human suffering in that realm where the phrase "due process of law" serves as a text for judicial review of social legislation. Here, at least, one might hope that a "decent respect to the opinions of mankind" would lead courts to formulate with some clarity their own conception of what it is that they are doing. Yet in no realm does logomachy offer more stubborn resistance to realistic analysis.

What is due process of law?

One might have supposed from the language of certain cases[26] that "due process of law" meant such law as was familiar to the Founding Fathers of the Constitution. Thus conceived, the phrase would denote a fairly definite concept, and the function of the courts in applying that concept to legislation would be that of objective scholarly inquiry into

[25] 169 U. S. 466 (1898).

[26] See Murray v. Hoboken Land and Improvement Co., 18 How. 272, 280 (U. S. 1855); Robertson v. Baldwin, 165 U. S. 275 (1897), and cases cited.

legal history. It is clear, however, that the modern judicial use of the due process clauses is not based upon any such historical inquiry. Regulation of wages and prices, against which these clauses have been directed with particular severity, finds ample historical precedent in early colonial and English legislation.[27]

Recent judicial utterances suggest a second conception of due process: Legislation falls within the "due process" clauses when it is such as rational men may approve. Taken seriously, this conception makes of our courts lunacy commissions sitting in judgment upon the mental capacity of legislators and, occasionally, of judicial brethren. Some such conception served as the major premise for the famous brief of Mr. Brandeis in the case of *Muller v. Oregon,*[28] which marshaled the favorable opinions entertained by individuals of undisputed sanity towards legislation restricting the hours of industrial labor for women. But subsequent applications of this technique have found less favor in the eyes of the courts, and when Mr. Frankfurter presented to the Supreme Court a similar anthology of opinions in favor of minimum wage legislation for women, the reply of the Supreme Court was that one might also make an impressive compilation of unfavorable opinions.[29] The fact, then, that reasonable men approve of specific legislation does not prevent it from being a violation of "due process of law."

The phrase "due process of law," then, denotes neither an historical nor a psychiatric fact. Does it, perhaps, denote a moral ideal? Whether legislation is due or undue or overdue may seem to laymen to be a question of social ethics or morality. But such a conception has been vigorously repudiated by the courts. Thus Mr. Frankfurter's analysis of the social evils which minimum wage legislation might eliminate was characterized by the United States Supreme Court as "interesting but only mildly persuasive," and the Court went on to say:

> "These are all proper enough for the consideration of the lawmaking bodies, since their tendency is to establish the desirability or undesirability of the legislation; but they reflect no legitimate light upon the question of its validity, and that is what we are called upon to decide."[30]

"Due process of law," then, can no more be defined in social ethical terms than in terms of legal history or abnormal psychology.

---

[27] See, for instance, the New York act of April 3, 1778, "An act to regulate the wages of mechanicks and labourers, the prices of goods and commodities, and the charges of inn holders within this State, and for other purposes therein mentioned," and other statutes cited in Handler, *Constitutionality of Investigations by the Federal Trade Commission* (1928) 28 Columbia Law Rev. 708, 712 n. 14; see also 2 Boudin, Government by Judiciary (1932) 401, 447.

[28] 208 U. S. 412 (1908).

[29] Adkins v. Children's Hospital, 261 U. S. 525, 559 (1923).

[30] *Ibid.*

In practice, the Supreme Court professes to consider, in a "due process" case, primarily its own former adjudications on the subject, apparently believing, with the Bellman,[31] that what it says three times must be true. But this process of self-fertilization will scarcely account for actual decisions. And one may suspect that a court would not consistently hide behind a barrage of transcendental nonsense if the grounds of its decisions were such as could be presented without shame to the public.

6. *The Nature of Legal Nonsense*

It would be tedious to prolong our survey; in every field of law we should find the same habit of ignoring practical questions of value or of positive fact and taking refuge in "legal problems" which can always be answered by manipulating legal concepts in certain approved ways. In every field of law we should find peculiar concepts which are not defined either in terms of empirical fact or in terms of ethics but which are used to answer empirical and ethical questions alike, and thus bar the way to intelligent investigation of social fact and social policy. *Corporate entity, property rights, fair value,* and *due process* are such concepts. So too are *title, contract, conspiracy, malice, proximate cause,* and all the rest of the magic "solving words" of traditional jurisprudence. Legal arguments couched in these terms are necessarily circular, since these terms are themselves creations of law, and such arguments add precisely as much to our knowledge as Moliere's physician's discovery that opium puts men to sleep because it contains a dormitive principle.

Now the proposition that opium puts men to sleep *because* it contains a dormitive principle is scientifically useful if "dormitive principle" is defined physically or chemically. Otherwise it serves only to obstruct the path of understanding with the pretense of knowledge. So, too, the proposition that a law is unconstitutional *because* it deprives persons of property without due process of law would be scientifically useful if "property" and "due process" were defined in non-legal terms; otherwise such a statement simply obstructs study of the relevant facts.

If the foregoing instances of legal reasoning are typical, we may

---

[31] "Just the place for a Snark!" the Bellman cried,
As he landed his crew with care;
Supporting each man on the top of the tide
By a finger entwined in his hair.
"Just the place for a Snark! I have said it twice:
That alone should encourage the crew.
"Just the place for a Snark! I have said it thrice:
What I tell you three times is true."
Lewis Carroll, The Hunting of the Snark, Fit the First.

summarize the basic assumptions of traditional legal theory in the following terms:

Legal concepts (for example, *corporations* or *property rights*) are supernatural entities which do not have a verifiable existence except to the eyes of faith. *Rules of law,* which refer to these legal concepts, are not descriptions of empirical social facts (such as the customs of men or the customs of judges) nor yet statements of moral ideals, but are rather theorems in an independent system. It follows that a *legal argument* can never be refuted by a moral principle nor yet by any empirical fact. *Jurisprudence,* then, as an autonomous system of legal concepts, rules, and arguments, must be independent both of ethics and of such positive sciences as economics or psychology. In effect, it is a special branch of the science of transcendental nonsense.

II. The Functional Method

That something is radically wrong with our traditional legal thought-ways has long been recognized. Holmes, Gray, Pound, Brooks Adams, M. R. Cohen, T. R. Powell, Cook, Oliphant, Moore, Radin, Llewellyn, Yntema, Frank, and other leaders of modern legal thought in America, are in fundamental agreement in their disrespect for "mechanical jurisprudence," for legal magic and word-jugglery.[32] But mutual agreement is less apparent when we come to the question of what to do: How are we going to get out of this tangle? How are we going to substitute a realistic, rational, scientific account of legal happenings for the classical theological jurisprudence of concepts?

Attempts to answer this question have made persistent use of the phrase "functional approach." Unfortunately, this phrase has often been used with as little meaning as any of the magical legal concepts against which it is directed. Many who use the term "functional" intend no more than the vague connotation which the word "practical"

[32] See Holmes, *"The Path of the Law"* (1897) 10 Harv. L. Rev. 457, Collected Legal Papers (1920) 167; Gray, Nature and Sources of the Law (1909) c. 4-5; Pound, *Law in Books and Law in Action* (1910) 44 Am. L. Rev. 12; Pound, Mechanical Jurisprudence (1908) 8 Columbia Law Rev. 605; Brooks Adams, *Law under Inequality: Monopoly,* in Centralization and the Law (1906) Lecture 2; M. R. Cohen, *The Process of Judicial Legislation* (1914) 48 Am. L. Rev. 161, Law and the Social Order (1933) 112; T. R. Powell, *The Judiciality of Minimum Wage Legislation* (1924) 37 Harv. L. Rev. 545; Cook, *Logical and Legal Bases of the Conflict of Laws* (1924) 33 Yale L. J. 457; Oliphant, *A Return to Stare Decisis* (1928) 6 Am. L. School Rev. 215; U. Moore, *Rational Basis of Legal Institutions* (1923) 23 Columbia Law Rev. 609; M. Radin, *Case Law and Stare Decisis: Concerning Präjudizienrecht in Amerika* (1933) 33 Columbia Law Rev. 199; Llewellyn, *A Realistic Jurisprudence—The Next Step* (1930) 30 Columbia Law Rev. 431; Llewellyn, *Some Realism about Realism: Responding to Dean Pound* (1931) 44 Harv. L. Rev. 1222; Yntema, *The Hornbook Method and the Conflict of Laws* (1928) 37 Yale L. J. 468; Frank, Law and the Modern Mind (1930).

conveys to the "practical" man. Again, the term "functional approach" is sometimes used to designate a modern form of animism, according to which every social institution or biological organ has a "purpose" in life, and is to be judged good or bad as it achieves or fails to achieve this "purpose." I shall not attempt to be faithful to these vague usages in using the term "functional." I shall use the term rather to designate certain principles or tendencies which appear most clearly in modern physical and mathematical science and in modern philosophy. For it is well to note that the problem of eliminating supernatural terms and meaningless questions and redefining concepts and problems in terms of verifiable realities is not a problem peculiar to law. It is a problem which has been faced in the last two or three centuries, and more especially in the last four or five decades, by philosophy, mathematics, and physics, as well as by psychology, economics, anthropology, and doubtless other sciences as well. Functionalism, operationalism, pragmatism, logical positivism, all these and many other terms have been used in diverse fields, with differing overtones of meaning and emphasis, to designate a certain common approach to this general task of redefining traditional concepts and traditional problems.

It may perhaps clarify the significance of the functional approach in law to trace some of the basic contributions which the functional method has made in modern science and philosophy.

1. *The Eradication of Meaningless Concepts*

On its negative side (naturally of special prominence in a protestant movement), functionalism represents an assault upon all dogmas and devices that cannot be translated into terms of actual experience.

In physics, the functional or operational method is an assault upon such supernatural concepts as absolute space and absolute time; in mathematics, upon supernatural concepts of real and imaginary, rational and irrational, positive and negative numbers. In psychology, William James inaugurates the functional method (of which behaviorism is an extreme form) by asking the naive question: "Does consciousness exist?"[33] Modern "functional grammar" is an assault upon grammatical theories and distinctions which, as applied to the English language, simply have no verifiable significance—such empty concepts, for instance, as that of noun syntax, with its unverifiable distinction between a nominative, an objective, and a possessive case.[34] And passing to the field

[33] ESSAYS IN RADICAL EMPIRICISM (1912) 1. Answering this question, James asserts, "There is . . . no aboriginal stuff or quality of being, contrasted with that of which material objects are made, out of which our thoughts of them are made; but there is a function in experience which thoughts perform . . ." (pp. 3-4).

[34] See H. N. RIVLIN, FUNCTIONAL GRAMMAR (1930); and *cf.* L. BLOOMFIELD, LANGUAGE (1933), p. 266 *et passim.*

of art, we find that functional architecture is likewise a repudiation of outworn symbols and functionless forms that have no meaning,—hollow marble pillars that do not support, fake buttresses, and false fronts.[35]

So, too, in law. Our legal system is filled with supernatural concepts, that is to say, concepts which cannot be defined in terms of experience, and from which all sorts of empirical decisions are supposed to flow. Against these unverifiable concepts modern jurisprudence presents an ultimatum. Any word that cannot pay up in the currency of fact, upon demand, is to be declared bankrupt, and we are to have no further dealings with it. Llewellyn has filed an involuntary petition in bankruptcy against the concept Title,[36] Oliphant against the concept Contract,[37] Haines, Brown, T. R. Powell, Finkelstein, and Cushman against Due Process, Police Power, and similar word-charms of constitutional law,[38] Hale, Richberg, Bonbright, and others against the concept of Fair Value in rate regulation,[39] Cook and Yntema against the concept of Vested Rights in the conflict of laws.[40] Each of these men has tried to expose the confusions of current legal thinking engendered by these concepts and to reformulate the problems in his field in terms which show the concrete relevance of legal decisions to social facts.

2. *The Abatement of Meaningless Questions*

It is a consequence of the functional attack upon unverifiable concepts that many of the traditional problems of science, law, and philosophy are revealed as pseudo-problems devoid of meaning. As the protagonist of logical positivism, Wittgenstein, says of the traditional problems of philosophy:

> "Most propositions and questions, that have been written about philosophical matters, are not false, but senseless. We cannot, therefore, answer questions of this kind at all, but only state their senselessness. Most questions and propositions of the philosophers result from the fact that we do not understand the logic of our language. (They are of the same kind as the question whether

---

[35] See F. L. Wright, Modern Architecture (1931).

[36] Llewellyn, Cases and Materials on the Law of Sales (1930).

[37] Oliphant, *Mutuality of Obligation in Bilateral Contracts at Law* (1925) 25 Columbia Law Rev. 705; (1928) 28 Columbia Law Rev. 997.

[38] C. G. Haines, *General Observations on the Effects of Personal, Political and Economic Influences in the Decisions of Judges* (1922) 17 Ill. L. Rev. 96; R. A. Brown, *Police Power—Legislation for Health and Personal Safety* (1929) 42 Harv. L. Rev. 866; T. R. Powell, *The Judiciality of Minimum Wage Legislation* (1924) 37 Harv. L. Rev. 545; M. Finkelstein, *Judicial Self-Limitation* (1924) 37 Harv. L. Rev. 338; R. E. Cushman, *The Social and Economic Interpretation of the Fourteenth Amendment* (1922) 20 Mich. L. Rev. 737.

[39] See note 24, *supra*.

[40] Cook, *Logical and Legal Bases of the Conflict of Laws* (1924) 33 Yale L. J. 457; Yntema, *The Hornbook Method and the Conflict of Laws* (1928) 37 Yale L. J. 468.

the Good is more or less identical than the Beautiful.) And so it is not to be wondered at that the deepest problems are really no problems."[41]

The same thing may be said of the problems of traditional jurisprudence. As commonly formulated, such "problems" as, "What is the holding or *ratio decidendi* of a case?"[42] or "Which came first,—the law or the state?"[43] or "What is the essential distinction between a crime and a tort?"[44] or "Where is a corporation?" are in fact meaningless, and can serve only as invitations to equally meaningless displays of conceptual acrobatics.

Fundamentally there are only two significant questions in the field of law. One is, "How do courts actually decide cases of a given kind?" The other is, "How ought they to decide cases of a given kind?" Unless a legal "problem" can be subsumed under one of these forms, it is not a meaningful question and any answer to it must be nonsense.[45]

3. *The Redefinition of Concepts*

Although the negative aspect of the functional method is apt to assume peculiar prominence in polemic controversy, the value of the method depends, in the last analysis, upon its positive contributions to the advancement of knowledge. Judged from this standpoint, I think it is fair to say that the functional method has justified itself in every scientific field to which it has been actually applied, and that functional redefinition of scientific concepts has been the keynote of most significant theoretical advances in the sciences during the last half century.

The tremendous advance made in our understanding of the foundations of pure mathematics, achieved through the work of such men as Frege, Peano, Whitehead, and Russell,[46] offers an illuminating example of the functional method in action.

---

[41] WITTGENSTEIN, TRACTATUS LOGICO-PHILOSOPHICUS (1922) prop. 4.003. And *cf.* JAMES, PRAGMATISM (1908): "The pragmatic method is primarily a method of settling metaphysical disputes that otherwise might be interminable. . . . The pragmatic method in such cases is to try to interpret each notion by tracing its respective practical consequences. . . . If no practical differences whatever can be traced, then the alternatives mean practically the same thing, and all dispute is idle. . . . It is astonishing to see how many philosophical disputes collapse into insignificance the moment you subject them to this simple test of tracing a practical consequence." (pp. 45-49.)

[42] See Goodhart, *Determining the Ratio Decidendi of a Case* (1930) 40 YALE L. J. 161; and *cf.* LLEWELLYN, BRAMBLE BUSH (1930) 47.

[43] Fortunately there is very little literature in the English language on this problem. German jurists, however, are inordinately fond of it.

[44] See C. K. ALLEN, LEGAL DUTIES AND OTHER ESSAYS IN JURISPRUDENCE (1931) 226. And *cf.* W. W. Cook, Book Review (1932) 42 YALE L. J. 299.

[45] *Cf.* F. S. Cohen, *What Is a Question?* (1929) 39 MONIST 350.

[46] See RUSSELL, PRINCIPLES OF MATHEMATICS (1903); INTRODUCTION TO MATHEMATICAL PHILOSOPHY (1919); RUSSELL AND WHITEHEAD, PRINCIPIA MATHEMATICA (1910); FREGE, DIE GRUNDLAGEN DER ARITHMETIK (1884).

Mathematics, fifty years ago, contained as many unanalyzed "fictions," supernatural concepts, unreal questions, and unjustified operations as classical jurisprudence. High school students are still taught to subtract the integer seven from the integer two, which is logically impossible. An integer is the number of a class, and obviously a class of seven members cannot be contained in, or subtracted from, a class of two members. The student who refuses to believe in such supernatural subtraction is entirely justified, although he must expect scant mercy from ignorant teachers and examiners (as must the law student who refuses to answer senseless questions of law and merely points out their senselessness). Nevertheless, the mathematical fiction, like the legal fiction (*e.g.* the spatial location of a corporation), represents a confused perception of a significant fact, and it is the province of functional analysis to untangle the confusion and find the fact. It is a fact that if you move seven units in one direction—in the direction of bankruptcy, say, or in the direction of lowered temperature—and call that direction "minus"—and then move two units in the opposite direction—"plus"—you have in effect moved five units in the first—the "minus"—direction. Undoubtedly, it is useful to invent or define mathematical terms which will describe these two *motions* or *operations* and the relation between them (as it is useful to invent legal terms to describe the corporate activities of human beings). But such mathematical terms, it is important to recognize, are not numbers, as "number" is ordinarily defined (*i.e.* they are not integers). What, then, are these novel entities? Classical mathematics conceived of these entities as integers acting, under a special dispensation, in supernatural ways. Modern mathematics shows that these entities, known as "sign numbers," are not integers at all, but rather *constructs* or *functions* of integers. The number "—7" is the operation of moving from any integer to its immediate predecessor in the series of integers, repeated seven times. The number "+7" is the converse operation, *i.e.,* the operation of moving from any integer to its immediate successor, repeated seven times. The number "+7" is therefore something quite different from the integer "7." It is, however, a logical function or construct of the integer seven, since the integer seven appears in the definition of "+7" as an operation repeated "seven" times.

Similarly, modern advances in mathematics have made it clear that rational and irrational, real and imaginary, numbers are not numbers at all, in the original sense of the term, but are functions of such numbers.[47] The so-called arithmetization of mathematics, and the definition of the concepts of mathematics by Whitehead and Russell, as con-

---

[47] See RUSSELL, INTRODUCTION TO MATHEMATICAL PHILOSOPHY (1919) c. 7.

structs of certain simple logical terms, have stripped mathematical terms of their supernatural significations, illumined and eliminated hidden inconsistencies, and clarified the relationships of mathematical concepts not only to each other but to the material world.

A similar use of the functional method has characterized the most significant advances of modern philosophy. The attack upon transcendental conceptions of God, matter, the Absolute, essence and accident, substance and attribute, has been vigorously pressed by C. S. Peirce, James, Dewey, Russell, Whitehead, C. I. Lewis, C. D. Broad, and most recently by the Viennese School, primarily by Wittgenstein and Carnap.[48] These men fall into various schools,—pragmatism, pragmaticism (which is the word Peirce shifted to when he saw what his followers were doing to the word "pragmatism"), neo-realism, critical realism, functional realism, and logical positivism. It would be unfair to minimize the real differences between some of these schools, but in one fundamental respect they assume an identical position. This is currently expressed in the sentence, "A thing is what it does." More precise is the language of Peirce: "In order to ascertain the meaning of an intellectual conception one should consider what practical consequences might conceivably result by necessity from the truth of that conception; and the sum of these consequences will constitute the entire meaning of the conception."[49] The methodological implications of this maxim are summed up by Russell in these words:

> "The supreme maxim in scientific philosophising is this: *Wherever possible, logical constructions are to be substituted for inferred entities.*"[50]

In other words, instead of assuming hidden causes or transcendental principles behind everything we see or do, we are to redefine the concepts of abstract thought as constructs, or functions, or complexes, or patterns, or arrangements, of the things that we do actually see or do. All concepts that cannot be defined in terms of the elements of actual experience are meaningless.

---

[48] See C. S. Peirce, Chance, Love and Logic (1923); Collected Papers (1931-1934), especially vol. 5; James, Pragmatism (1908); Essays in Radical Empiricism (1912); Dewey, *Appearing and Appearance,* in Philosophy and Civilization (1931) 51; Russell, Our Knowledge of the External World as a Field for Scientific Method in Philosophy (1914); Mysticism and Logic (1918); Whitehead, The Principles of Natural Knowledge (1919); The Concept of Nature (1920); C. I. Lewis, Mind and the World-Order (1929); C. D. Broad, Scientific Thought (1923); Wittgenstein, Tractatus Logico-Philosophicus (1922); Carnap, *Ueberwindung der Metaphysik durch logische Analyse der Sprache* (1932) 2 Erkenntnis no. 4; J. E. Boodin, *Functional Realism* (1934) 43 Philosophical Review 147.

[49] 5 C. S. Peirce, Collected Papers 6.

[50] Russell, Mysticism and Logic (1918) 155.

The task of modern philosophy is the salvaging of whatever significance attaches to the traditional concepts of metaphysics, through the redefinition of these concepts as functions of actual experience. Whatever differences may exist among modern philosophers in the choice of experiential terms which are to serve as the basic terms of functional analysis—"events," "sensa," and "atomic facts" are but a few of these basic terms—few would disagree with the point of view expressed by William James when he says that in our investigation of any abstract concept the central question must be: "What is its cash value in terms of particular experience? and what special differences would come into the world if it were true or false?"[51]

A similar use of the functional method characterizes recent advances in physics. Instead of conceiving of space as something into which physical things fit, but which somehow exists, unverifiably, apart from the things that fill it (as the Common Law is supposed to exist apart from and prior to actual decisions), and then assuming that there is an ether that fills space when it is empty, modern physicists conceive space as a manifold of relations between physical objects or events. The theory of relativity begins with the recognition that relations between physical objects or events involve a temporal as well as a spatial aspect. Thus it becomes convenient for certain purposes to substitute the notion of space-time for that of space, or even to substitute a notion which includes mass as well as space and time.

The parallel between the functional method of modern physics and the program of realistic jurisprudence is so well sketched by a distinguished Chinese jurist that I can only offer a quotation without comment:[52]

> "Professor Eddington, in a recent book on "The Nature of the Physical World," observes: "A thing must be defined according to the way in which it is in practice recognized and not according to some ulterior significance that we suppose it to possess." So Professor Bridgman, in "The Logic of Modern Physics":
>
> > "Hitherto many of the concepts of physics have been defined in terms of their properties." But now, "in general, we mean by any concept nothing more than a set of operations; *the concept is synonymous with the corresponding set of operations.* If the concept is physical, as of length, the operations are actual physical operations, namely, those by which length is measured; or if the concept is mental, as of mathematical continuity, the operations are mental operations, namely those by which we determine whether a given aggregate of magnitudes is continuous."
>
> Now, this way of dealing with concepts was precisely what Holmes introduced into the science of law early in the '80's. Before discussing the significance

---

[51] James, *The Pragmatic Method* (1904) 1 Jour. of Philosophy 673.

[52] John C. H. Wu, *Realistic Analysis of Legal Concepts: A Study in the Legal Method of Mr. Justice Holmes* (1932) 5 China L. Rev. 1, 2.

and possibilities of the new method, let me list here some of his definitions of things juridic:

> Law: "The prophecies of what the courts will do in fact, and nothing more pretentious, are what I mean by the law."
>
> * * * *
>
> "But for legal purposes a right is only the hypostasis of a prophecy—the imagination of a substance *supporting* the fact that the public force will be brought to bear upon those who do things said to contravene it—just as we talk of the force of gravitation accounting for the conduct of bodies in space."
>
> Duty: "A legal duty so called is nothing but a prediction that if a man does or omits certain things he will be made to suffer in this or that way by judgment of the court; and so of a legal right."
>
> * * * *
>
> Contract: "The duty to keep a contract at common law means a prediction that you must pay damages if you do not keep it and nothing else. If you commit a tort, you are liable to pay a compensatory sum. If you commit a contract, you are liable to pay a compensatory sum unless the promised event comes to pass, and that is all the difference."

"It may be conceded at the outset that all these definitions are capable of being further developed or improved upon: The important point to note is the complete departure from the way the old Classical Jurisprudence defined things. Hostile as he was to the traditional logic, Holmes touched the springs of the neo-realistic logic in his analysis of legal concepts. He departed entirely from the subject-predicate form of logic, and employed a logic of relations. He did not try to show how a legal entity possesses certain inherent properties. What he was trying everywhere to bring out is: If a certain group of facts is true of a person, then the person will receive a certain group of consequences attached by the law to that group of facts. Instead of treating a legal concept as a substance which in its nature necessarily contains certain inherent properties, we have here a logic which regards it as a mere signpost of a real relation subsisting between an antecedent and a consequent, and, as one of the New Realists so aptly puts it, all signposts must be kept up to date, with their inscriptions legible and their pointing true. In short, by turning the juristic logic from a subject-predicate form to an antecedent-consequent form, Holmes virtually created an inductive science of law. For both the antecedent and the consequent are to be proved and ascertained empirically."

In brief, Holmes and, one should add, Hohfeld[53] have offered a logical basis for the redefinition of every legal concept in empirical terms, *i.e.* in terms of judicial decisions. The ghost-world of supernatural legal entities to whom courts delegate the moral responsibility of deciding cases vanishes; in its place we see legal concepts as patterns of judicial behavior, behavior which affects human lives for better or

[53] See HOHFELD, FUNDAMENTAL LEGAL CONCEPTIONS (1919).

worse and is therefore subject to moral criticism. Of the functional method in legal science, one may say, as Russell has said of the method in contemporary philosophy, "Our procedure here is precisely analogous to that which has swept away from the philosophy of mathematics the useless menagerie of metaphysical monsters with which it used to be infested."[54]

4. *The Redirection of Research*

It is often easier to distinguish a school of thought by asking not, "What basic theory does it defend?" but rather, "What basic question does it propound?"

A failure to recognize that the law is a vast field, in which different students are interested in diverse problems, has the unfortunate effect of making every school of legal thought an *ex officio* antagonist of every other school. Dean Pound's classification of jurists into mutually exclusive "analytical," "historical," "philosophical," and "sociological" schools, with sub-species too numerous to mention,[55] has given a good deal of prestige to the idea that a new school of jurisprudence must offer a revolutionary threat to all existing schools. It would be unfortunate to regard "functionalism" in law as a substitute for all other "isms." Rather, we must regard functionalism, in law as in anthropology, economics, and other fields, as a call for the study of problems which have been neglected by other scientific methods of investigation.

In general, when one comes upon a strange fact and seeks to understand it, there are four inquiries he can pursue.

In the first place, our investigator can *classify* the fact—either by putting an arbitrary label upon it or by discerning in the fact to be explained the significant similarities and differences which relate it to other facts.

Again, one may seek to discover the *genesis* of the fact in question, to trace its historical antecedents.

In the third place, one may inquire into the *nature* of the fact presented, endeavoring by logical analysis to resolve it into simpler elements.

A fourth possible approach seeks to discover the *significance* of the fact through a determination of its implications or consequences in a given mathematical, physical or social context.

It is this last approach to which the term "functional" has been applied. Obviously, it is not the *only* way of gathering useful information, and obviously, it is largely dependent upon the results of classificatory or taxonomic investigation, genetic or historical research, and

---

[54] RUSSELL, *loc. cit. supra* note 50.

[55] See POUND, OUTLINES OF LECTURES ON JURISPRUDENCE (4th ed. 1928) c. 1.

analytical inquiries. Finally, it must be remarked that the functional method is not a recent invention. Plato's attempt to define "justice" by assessing the activities of a just state,[56] and Aristotle's conception of the soul as the way a living body behaves[57] are illustrious examples of functional analysis. So, too, Hume's analysis of causation in terms of uniformity of succession, and Berkeley's analysis of matter in terms of its appearances, are significant attempts to redefine supernatural concepts in natural terms,[58] to wash ideas in cynical acid (borrowing Holmes' suggestive phrase).[59]

If functional analysis seems novel in the law, this is perhaps traceable to the general backwardness of legal science, which is the product of social factors that cannot be exorcised by new slogans.

With these caveats against the notion that the functional approach is a new intellectual invention which will solve all the problems of law (or of anthropology, economics, or any other science), we may turn to the significant question: "What are the new directions which the functional method will give to our scientific research?"

In attempting to answer this question for the field of law we may find suggestive precedents in other social sciences.

Applied to the study of religion, for instance, the functional approach has meant a shift of emphasis away from the attempt to systematize and compare religious beliefs, away from concern with the genesis and evolution of religions, and towards a study of the consequences of various religious beliefs in terms of human motivation and social structure. Outstanding examples of this focus are Weber's and Tawney's studies of the influence of Protestantism in the development of modern capitalism,[60] and James' essays on the psychological significance for the individual of various religious beliefs.[61] The functional approach asks of every religious dogma or ritual: How does it work? How does it serve to mould men's lives, to deter from certain avenues of conduct and expression, to sanction accepted patterns of behavior, to produce or alleviate certain emotional stresses, to induce social solidarity, to

[56] PLATO, REPUBLIC.

[57] ARISTOTLE, DE ANIMA, I, 1; II, 1.

[58] *Cf.* JAMES, PRAGMATISM (1908): "There is absolutely nothing new in the pragmatic method. Socrates was an adept at it. Aristotle used it methodically. Locke, Berkeley, and Hume made momentous contributions to truth by its means" (at p. 50). See, also, James, *The Pragmatic Method* (1904) 1 JOUR. OF PHILOSOPHY 673.

[59] ". . . the vague circumference of the notion of duty shrinks and at the same time grows more precise when we wash it with cynical acid and expel everything except the object of our study, the operations of the law." Holmes, "*The Path of the Law*" (1897) 10 HARV. L. REV. 457, 462.

[60] MAX WEBER, THE PROTESTANT ETHIC AND THE SPIRIT OF CAPITALISM (tr. by Parsons, 1930); R. H. TAWNEY, RELIGION AND THE RISE OF CAPITALISM (1926).

[61] JAMES, THE VARIETIES OF RELIGIOUS EXPERIENCE (1902).

lay a basis for culture accumulation by giving life after death to the visions, thoughts and achievements of mortal men.[62] The significance of a religious dogma is found not in a system of theological propositions but in a mode of human conduct. The functional approach demands objective description of this conduct, in which the empirical significance of the religious belief is embodied. Just so, the functional approach in physics captures the significance of a physical concept in the actual processes and operations of the physicist, rather than in the theological or metaphysical interpretations which physicists put upon their own activities. It is an application of this same approach that discovers the significance of a legal principle in the actual behavior of judges, sheriffs and litigants rather than in conventional accounts of the principles that judges, sheriffs and litigants are "supposed" to follow.

In anthropology, the functional method represents a movement away from two types of study: the naive reporting and classification of striking human peculiarities; and the more sophisticated attempt to trace the historical origin, evolution and diffusion of "complexes." Those who have embraced the functional approach (not all of whom have invoked the word "functional"), have been primarily concerned to trace the social consequences of diverse customs, beliefs, rituals, social arrangements, and patterns of human conduct. This approach has led to fertile fields that most earlier investigators missed. In the study of primitive art, the new focus has brought into the foreground the question of the craftsman's motivations and purposes, the significance of art as an individualizing or socializing force, the whole problem of interplay between materials, techniques, and social needs.[63] The study of primitive social organization comes increasingly to deal with the functional significance of family, clan, and tribal groupings as social determinants in the production, distribution, and use of property, as well as in the non-economic human relationships of education, religion, play, sex, and companionship.[64] In the study of primitive law, the functional approach raises to the fore the problem of incentives to obedience and the efficacy of these incentives, the techniques of law

---

[62] *Cf.* KAPLAN, JUDAISM AS A CIVILIZATION (1934), c. 26 *(Functional Method of Interpretation)*; Elwang, THE SOCIAL FUNCTION OF RELIGIOUS BELIEF (UNIV. OF MO. STUDIES, SOCIAL SCIENCE SERIES, vol. 2, no. 1, 1908); FOSTER, THE FUNCTION OF RELIGION IN MAN'S STRUGGLE FOR EXISTENCE (1909).

[63] See BOAS, PRIMITIVE ART (1927).

[64] See Boas, *The Social Organization and the Secret Societies of the Kwakiutl Indians* (1895) REPORT OF U. S. NAT. MUSEUM, at 315; MALINOWSKI, THE FAMILY AMONG THE AUSTRALIAN ABORIGINES (1913); LOWIE, PRIMITIVE SOCIETY (1920); GOLDENWEISER, HISTORY, PSYCHOLOGY AND CULTURE (1933) Part III *(Totemism)*; W. C. McKern, *Functional Families of the Patwin* (UNIV. OF CALIF. PUB. IN AMER. ARCHAEOLOGY AND ETHNOLOGY, vol. 13, no. 7).

enforcement, and the relations of rivalry or supplementation between legal sanctions and other social forces.[65]

A similar use of the functional approach is characteristic of modern political science, in which revolt against the classical supernatural conception of sovereignty is a point of agreement uniting the most diverse schools of contemporary thought. Typical is the following statement:

> "By institutions we merely mean collective behavior patterns, the ways in which a community carries on the innumerable activities of social life. . . . Society achieves certain results through collective political actions. The means that it uses are the behavior patterns which we call courts, legislative bodies, commissions, electorates, administration. We idealize these institutions collectively and personify them in the State. But this idealization is pure fancy. The State as a juristic or ideal person is the veriest fiction. It is real only as a collective name for governmental institutions."[66]

Under the influence of the functional approach political theory ceases to be a science of pure forms, and comes increasingly to grips with the psychological motives and the technological forces that function through political instruments.

In economics we have witnessed a similar shift of research from the taxonomic or systematic analysis of economic "norms" to the study of the actual economic behavior of men and nations. Veblen's indictment of classical economic theory may be applied word for word to classical jurisprudence, if we merely substitute for the terms "economic" and "economist" the terms "legal" and "jurist":

> "The standpoint of the classical *economists,* in their higher or definitive syntheses and generalizations, may not inaptly be called the standpoint of ceremonial adequacy. . . . In effect, this preconception imputes to things a tendency to work out what the instructed common sense of the time accepts as the adequate or worthy end of human effort. . . . This ideal of conduct is made to serve as a canon of truth . . ."
>
> "The metaphors are effective, both in their homiletical use and as a labor-saving device,—more effective than their user designs them to be. By their use the theorist is enabled serenely to enjoin himself from following out an elusive train of causal sequence. . . . The scheme so arrived at is spiritually binding on the behavior of the phenomena contemplated. . . . Features of the

---

[65] See MALINOWSKI, CRIME AND CUSTOM IN SAVAGE SOCIETY (1926); HOGBIN, LAW AND ORDER IN POLYNESIA (1934). In his introduction to the latter volume, Malinowski writes: "Modern anthropology concentrates, above all, on what is now usually called the function of a custom, belief or institution. By function we mean the part which is played by any one factor of a culture within the general scheme."

[66] W. J. Shepard, *Democracy in Transition* (1935) 29 AM. POL. SCI. REV. 1; *cf.* H. J. LASKI, GRAMMAR OF POLITICS (2d ed. 1929); W. Y. ELLIOTT, THE PRAGMATIC REVOLT IN POLITICS (1928).

process that do not lend themselves to interpretation in terms of the formula are abnormal cases and are due to disturbing causes. In all this the agencies or forces causally at work in the *economic* life process are neatly avoided. The outcome of the method, at its best, is a body of logically consistent propositions concerning the normal relations of things—a system of *economic* taxonomy."[67]

The same "standpoint of ceremonial adequacy" has to some extent characterized the works of our classical jurists,—such masters of the law as Beale, Williston, and even Wigmore. For them, as for the classical economists, it was easy to avoid "an elusive train of causal sequence." Principles, conceived as "spiritually binding on the behavior of the phenomena contemplated," diverted their attention from the hard facts of the legal world,—the human motivations and social prejudices of judges, the stretching or shrinking of precedents in every washing, the calculations of juries, and the fact of legislation,—and at the same time diverted attention from the task of legal criticism.[68]

The age of the classical jurists is over, I think. The "Restatement of the Law" by the American Law Institute is the last long-drawn-out gasp of a dying tradition.[69] The more intelligent of our younger law teachers and students are not interested in "restating" the dogmas of legal theology. There will, of course, be imitators and followers of the classical jurists, in the years ahead. But I think that the really creative legal thinkers of the future will not devote themselves, in the manner of Williston, Wigmore, and their fellow masters, to the taxonomy of legal concepts and to the systematic explication of principles of "justice" and "reason," buttressed by "correct" cases. Creative legal thought will more and more look behind the pretty array of "correct" cases to the actual facts of judicial behavior, will make increasing use of statistical methods in the scientific description and prediction of judicial behavior, will more and more seek to map the hidden springs of judicial decision and to weigh the social forces which are represented on the bench. And on the critical side, I think that creative legal thought will more and more look behind the traditionally accepted principles of "justice" and "reason" to appraise in ethical terms the social values at stake in any choice between two precedents.

---

[67] VEBLEN, *Why Is Economics Not an Evolutionary Science?* in THE PLACE OF SCIENCE in MODERN CIVILIZATION (1919) 56, 65-67.

[68] To say this is not to deny that such legal scholars have performed yeoman service in clarifying the logical implications and inconsistencies of judicial doctrines. Such analysis is useful, but it is not the sum and substance of legal science. *Cf.* F. S. COHEN, ETHICAL SYSTEMS AND LEGAL IDEALS (1933) 235-237.

[69] See M. Franklin, *The Historic Function of the American Law Institute: Restatement as Transitional to Codification* (1934) 47 HARV. L. REV. 1367; and *cf.* Patterson, *The Restatement of the Law of Contracts* (1933) 33 COLUMBIA LAW REV. 397; E. S. Robinson, *Law—An Unscientific Science* (1935) 44 YALE L. J. 235, 261.

"Social policy" will be comprehended not as an emergency factor in legal argument but rather as the gravitational field that gives weight to any rule or precedent, whether it be in constitutional law, in the law of trade-marks, or in the most technical details of legal procedure.

There is implied in this shifting of the paths of legal research a change in the equipment needs of the student of law. Familiarity with the words of past judicial opinions and skill in the manipulation of legal concepts are not enough for the student who seeks to understand the social forces that control judicial behavior, nor for the lawyer who seeks to use these forces.[70]

The vested interests of our law schools in an "independent" science of law are undermined by every advance in our knowledge of the social antecedents and consequences of judicial decision. It becomes the part of discretion, in law schools aware of such advances, to admit that legal science necessarily involves us in psychology, economics, and political theory. Courses in our more progressive law schools are beginning to treat, most gingerly, of the psychological doctrines embedded in our rules of evidence, the sociological theories assumed in our criminal law, the economic assumptions embalmed in our doctrines of constitutional law, and the psychological, sociological, and economic *facts* which give force and significance to rules and decisions in these and other fields of law. The first steps taken are clumsy and evoke smiles of sympathy or roars of laughter from critics of diverse temperaments. The will to walk persists.

For the lawyer, no less than for the legal scholar, handling of materials hitherto considered "non-legal" assumes increasing importance. And courts that shut their doors to such non-legal materials, laying the taboos of evidence law upon facts and arguments that reveal the functional social significance of a legal claim or a legal precedent, will eventually learn that society has other organs—legislatures and legislative committees and administrative commissions of many sorts—that are willing to handle, in straightforward fashion, the materials, statistical and descriptive, that a too finicky judiciary disdains.

III. The Uses of the Functional Method in Law

The significance of the functional method in the field of law is clarified if we consider the bearings of this method upon four traditional legal problems: (1) The definition of law; (2) The nature of legal rules and concepts; (3) The theory of legal decisions; and (4) The role of legal criticism.

[70] The implications of the functional method for legal education are carefully traced in Keyserling, *Social Objectives in Legal Education* (1933) 33 Columbia Law Rev. 437.

1. *The Definition of Law*

The starting point of functional analysis in American jurisprudence is found in Justice Holmes' definition of law as "prophecies of what the courts will do in fact." It is in "The Path of the Law,"[71] that this realistic conception of law is first clearly formulated:

> "If you want to know the law and nothing else, you must look at it as a bad man, who cares only for the material consequences which such knowledge enables him to predict, not as a good one, who finds his reasons for conduct, whether inside the law or outside of it, in the vaguer sanctions of conscience. . . . Take the fundamental question, What constitutes the law? You will find some text writers telling you that it is something different from what is decided by the courts of Massachusetts or England, that it is a system of reason, that it is a deduction from principles of ethics or admitted axioms or what not, which may or may not coincide with the decisions. But if we take the view of our friend the bad man we shall find that he does not care two straws for the axioms or deductions, but that he does want to know what the Massachusetts or English courts are likely to do in fact. I am much of his mind. The prophecies of what the courts will do in fact, and nothing more pretentious, are what I mean by the law."

A good deal of fruitless controversy has arisen out of attempts to show that this definition of law as the way courts actually decide cases is either true or false.[72] A definition of law is *useful* or *useless*. It is not *true* or *false*, any more than a New Year's resolution or an insur-

---

[71] HOLMES, *Path of the Law* (1897) 10 HARV. L. REV. 457, 459-461; COLLECTED LEGAL PAPERS (1921) p. 167, 171-173. A more precise definition, following Holmes, is given in C. J. Keyser, *On the Study of Legal Science* (1929) 38 YALE L. J. 413.

[72] For examples of such argument see Dickinson, *Legal Rules: Their Function in the Process of Decision* (1931) 79 U. OF PA. LAW REV. 833; H. Kantorowicz, *Some Rationalism about Realism* (1934) 43 YALE L. J. 1240; FRANK, LAW AND THE MODERN MIND (1930) 127-128. The vicious circle in Dickinson's attempted refutation of the realistic definition of law I have elsewhere analyzed. See F. S. COHEN, ETHICAL SYSTEMS AND LEGAL IDEALS (1933) 12, n. 16. Kantorowicz repeats the same argument, emphasizing the charge that a definition of law in terms of court decisions "puts the cart before the horse" and is as ridiculous as a definition of medicine in terms of the behavior of doctors. The parallel, though witty, is inapt: The correct analogy to a definition of the science of law as description of the behavior of judges would be a definition of the science of medicine as a description of the behavior of certain parasites, etc. Kantorowicz accepts uncritically the metaphysical assumption that definition is a one-way passage from the more general to the less general. But modern logic has demonstrated the hollowness of this assumption. It is useful for certain purposes to define points as functions of lines. For other purposes it is useful to define lines as functions of points. It is just as logical to define law in terms of courts as the other way about. The choice is a matter of convenience, not of logic or truth.

The same metaphysical fallacy vitiates the opposite argument of Frank, namely, that "primary" reality is particular and concrete, so that a definition of law must necessarily be in terms of actual decisions. To the eyes of modern logic, the world contains things *and* relations, neither of which can claim a superior grade of reality. One can start a fight or a scientific inquiry *either* with a concrete fact *or* with a general principle.

ance policy. A definition is in fact a type of insurance against certain risks of confusion. It cannot, any more than can a commercial insurance policy, eliminate all risks. Absolute certainty is as foreign to language as to life. There is no final insurance against an insurer's insolvency. And the words of a definition always carry their own aura of ambiguity. But a definition is useful if it insures against risks of confusion more serious than any that the definition itself contains.

"What courts do" is not entirely devoid of ambiguity. There is room for disagreement as to what a *court* is, whether, for instance, the Interstate Commerce Commission or the Hague Tribunal or the Council of Tesuque Pueblo is a court, and whether a judge acting in excess of those powers which the executive arm of the government will recognize acts as a court. There may even be disagreement as to the line of distinction between what courts *do* and what courts *say,* in view of the fact that most judicial behavior is verbal. But these sources of ambiguity in Holmes' definition of law are peripheral rather than central, and easily remedied. They are, therefore, far less dangerous sources of confusion than the basic ambiguity inherent in classical definitions of law which involve a confusion between what is and what ought to be.

The classical confusion against which realistic jurisprudence is a protest is exemplified in Blackstone's classical definition of law as "a rule of civil conduct, prescribed by the supreme power in a State, commanding what is right, and prohibiting what is wrong."[73]

In this definition we have an attempt to unite two incompatible ideas which, in the tradition of English jurisprudence, are most closely associated with the names of Hobbes and Coke, respectively.

Hobbes, the grandfather of realistic jurisprudence, saw in law the commands of a body to whom private individuals have surrendered their force. In a state of nature there is war of all against all. In order to achieve peace and security, each individual gives up something of his freedom, something of his power, and the commands of the collective power, that is the state, constitute law.

Hobbes' theory of law has been very unpopular with respectable citizens, but I venture to think that most of the criticism directed against it, in the last two and a half centuries, has been based upon a misconception of what Hobbes meant by a state of nature. So far as I know, Hobbes never refers to the state of nature as an actual historical era, at the end of which men came together and signed a social contract. The state of nature is a stage in analysis rather than a stage of history. It exists today and has always existed, to a greater or lesser degree, in

---

[73] BL. COMM.* 44.

various realms of human affairs. To the extent that any social relationship is exempt from governmental control it presents what Hobbes calls a state of nature.

In international relations today, at least to the extent that nations have not effectively surrendered their power through compacts establishing such rudimentary agencies of international government as the League of Nations or the Universal Postal Union, there is in fact a state of nature and a war of all against all. This war, as Hobbes insists, is present potentially before actual hostilities break out. Not only in international relations, but in industrial relations today do we find war of all against all, in regions to which governmental control has not been extended, or from which it has been withdrawn—if it existed.

Mutual concessions and delegations of power involved in an arbitration contract, an international treaty, an industrial "code," a corporate merger, or a collective labor agreement, are steps in the creation of government, and call into operation new rules of law and new agencies of law enforcement. Governments do not arise once and for all. Government is arising today in many regions of social existence, and it arises wherever individuals find the conflicts inherent in a state of nature unendurable. The process by which government is created and its commands formulated is a process of human bargaining, based upon mutual consent but weighted by the relative power of conflicting individuals or groups.

In all this conception of law, there is no appeal to reason or goodness. Law commands obedience not because of its goodness, or its justice, or its rationality, but because of the power behind it. While this power does rest to a real extent upon popular beliefs about the value of certain legal ideals, it remains true today, as Hobbes says in his *Dialogue on the Common Law,* "In matter of government, when nothing else is turned up, clubs are trump."[74]

Quite different from this realistic conception of law is the theory made famous by Coke that law is only the perfection of reason.[75] This is a notion which has had considerable force in American constitutional history, having served first as a basis for popular revolution against tyrannical violations of "natural law" and the "natural rights" of Englishmen, and serving more recently as a judicial ground for denying legality to statutes that judges consider "unreasonable." It would be absurd to deny the importance of this concept of natural law or justice as a standard by which to judge the acts of rulers, legislative, executive or judicial. It is clear, however, that the validity of this concept of law

[74] HOBBES, DIALOGUE BETWEEN A PHILOSOPHER AND A STUDENT OF THE COMMON LAWS OF ENGLAND (1681), *Of Punishments.*

[75] CO. LITT.* 976.

lies in a realm of values, which is not identical with the realm of social actualities.

The confusion and ambiguity which infest the classical conception of law, as formulated by Blackstone and implicitly accepted by most modern legal writers, arise from the attempt to throw together two inconsistent ideas. Blackstone attempts in effect to superimpose the picture of law drawn by the tender-minded hypocrite, Coke, upon the picture executed by the tough-minded cynic, Hobbes, and to give us a composite photograph. Law, says Blackstone, is "a rule of civil conduct prescribed by the supreme power in a State (Hobbes speaking) commanding what is right and prohibiting what is wrong (Coke speaking)"[76] Putting these two ideas together, we have a fertile source of confusion, which many important legal scholars since Blackstone have found about as useful in legal polemics as the ink with which a cuttlefish befuddles his enemies.

Those theorists who adhere to the Blackstonian definition of law are able to spin legal theories to the heart's content without fear of refutation. If legislatures or courts disagree with a given theory, it is a simple matter to show that this disagreement is unjust, unreasonable, monstrous and, therefore, not "sound law." On the other hand, the intruding moralist who objects to a legal doctrine on the ground that it is unjust or undesirable can be told to go back to the realm of morality he came from, since the law is the command of the sovereign and not a matter of moral theory. Perhaps the chief usefulness of the Blackstonian theory is the gag it places upon legal criticism. Obviously, if the law is something that commands what is right and prohibits what is wrong, it is impossible to argue about the goodness or badness of any law, and any definition that deters people from criticism of the law is very useful to legal apologists for the existing order of society. As a modern authority on legal reasoning declares, "Thus all things made legal are at the same time legally ethical because it is law, and the law must be deemed ethical or the system itself must perish."[77]

2. *The Nature of Legal Rules and Concepts*

If the functionalists are correct, the meaning of a definition is found in its consequences. The definition of a general term like "law" is significant only because it affects all our definitions of specific legal concepts.

---

[76] That "right" and "wrong" are used in this definition as ethical, rather than strictly legal, terms is made clear in Blackstone's own exegesis upon his definition. COMM.* 54-55.

[77] BRUMBAUGH, LEGAL REASONING AND BRIEFING (1917), 7.

The consequence of defining law as a function of concrete judicial decisions is that we may proceed to define such concepts as "contract," "property," "title," "corporate personality," "right," and "duty," similarly as functions of concrete judicial decisions.

The consequence of defining law as a hodge-podge of political force and ethical value ambiguously amalgamated is that every legal concept, rule or question will present a similar ambiguity.

Consider the elementary legal question: "Is there a contract?"

When the realist asks this question, he is concerned with the actual behavior of courts. For the realist, the contractual relationship, like law in general, is a function of legal decisions. The question of what courts *ought* to do is irrelevant here. Where there is a promise that will be legally enforced there is a contract. So conceived, any answer to the question "Is there a contract" must be in the nature of a prophecy, based, like other prophecies, upon past and present facts. So conceived, the question "Is there a contract?" or for that matter any other legal question, may be broken up into a number of subordinate questions, each of which refers to the actual behavior of courts: (1) What courts are likely to pass upon a given transaction and its consequences? (2) What elements in this transaction will be viewed as relevant and important by these courts? (3) How have these courts dealt with transactions in the past which are *similar* to the given transaction, that is, *identical in those respects which the court will regard as important?* (4) What forces will tend to compel judicial conformity to the precedents that appear to be in point (*e.g.* inertia, conservatism, knowledge of the past, or intelligence sufficient to acquire such knowledge, respect for predecessors, superiors or brothers on the bench, a habit of deference to the established expectations of the bar or the public) and how strong are these forces? (5) What factors will tend to evoke new judicial treatment for the transaction in question (*e.g.* changing public opinion, judicial idiosyncrasies and prejudices, newly accepted theories of law, society or economics, or the changing social context of the case) and how powerful are these factors?

These are the questions which a successful practical lawyer faces and answers in any case. The law, as the realistic lawyer uses the term, is the body of answers to such questions. The task of prediction involves, in itself, no judgment of ethical value. Of course, even the most cynical practitioner will recognize that the positively existing ethical beliefs of judges are material facts in any case because they determine what facts the judge will view as important and what past rules he will regard as reasonable or unreasonable and worthy of being extended or restricted. But judicial beliefs about the values of life and the ideals of society are *facts,* just as the religious beliefs of the Andaman Islanders are facts, and the truth or falsity of such moral beliefs is a matter of complete unconcern to the practical lawyer, as to the scientific observer.

Washed in cynical acid, every legal problem can thus be interpreted as a question concerning the positive behavior of judges.

There is a second and radically different meaning which can be given to our type question, "Is there a contract?" When a judge puts this question, in the course of writing his opinion, he is not attempting to predict his own behavior. He is in effect raising the question, in an obscure way, of whether or not liability *should* be attached to certain acts. This is inescapably an ethical question. What a judge ought to do in a given case is quite as much a moral issue as any of the traditional problems of Sunday School morality.[78]

It is difficult for those who still conceive of morality in other-worldly terms to recognize that every case presents a moral question to the court. But this notion has no terrors for those who think of morality in earthly terms. Morality, so conceived, is vitally concerned with such facts as human expectations based upon past decisions, the stability of economic transactions, and even the maintenance of order and simplicity in our legal system. If ethical values are inherent in all realms of human conduct, the ethical appraisal of a legal situation is not to be found in the spontaneous outpourings of a sensitive conscience unfamiliar with the social context, the background of precedent, and the practices and expectations, legal and extra-legal, which have grown up around a given type of transaction.

It is the great disservice of the classical conception of law that it hides from judicial eyes the ethical character of every judicial question, and thus serves to perpetuate class prejudices and uncritical moral assumptions which could not survive the sunlight of free ethical controversy.

The Blackstonian conception of law as half-mortal and half-divine gives us a mythical conception of contract. When a master of classical jurisprudence like Williston asks the question "Is there a contract?", he has in mind neither the question of scientific prediction which the practical lawyer faces, nor the question of values which the conscientious judge faces. If he had in mind the former question, his studies would no doubt reveal the extent to which courts actually enforce various types of contractual obligation.[79] His conclusions would be in terms of prob-

[78] *Cf.* F. S. Cohen, *Modern Ethics and the Law* (1934) 4 BROOKLYN L. REV. 33, on the conception of "Sunday School morality."

[79] So hallowed is the juristic tradition of ignoring the actual facts of cases that a distinguished jurist, Professor Goodhart, can argue in all seriousness that the practice adopted by some American law libraries of putting the records of cases on file is very dangerous. Students might be distracted from the official *ratio decidendi* of the case, and might try to discover what the actual facts of the case were, which would be a death-blow to traditional jurisprudence. See Goodhart, *Determining Ratio Decidendi of a Case* (1930) 40 YALE L. J. 161, 172.

ability and statistics. On the other hand, if Professor Williston were interested in the ethical aspects of contractual liability, he would undoubtedly offer a significant account of the human values and social costs involved in different types of agreements and in the means of their enforcement. In fact, however, the discussions of a Williston will oscillate between a theory of what courts actually do and a theory of what courts ought to do, without coming to rest either on the plane of social actualities or on the plane of values long enough to come to grips with significant problems. This confused wandering between the world of fact and the world of justice vitiates every argument and every analysis.

Intellectual clarity requires that we carefully distinguish between the two problems of (1) objective description, and (2) critical judgment, which classical jurisprudence lumps under the same phrase. Such a distinction realistic jurisprudence offers with the double-barreled thesis: (1) that every legal rule or concept is simply a function of judicial decisions to which all questions of value are irrelevant, and (2) that the problem of the judge is not whether a legal rule or concept actually exists but whether it *ought* to exist. Clarity on two fronts is the result. Description of legal facts becomes more objective, and legal criticism becomes more critical.

The realistic lawyer, when he attempts to discover how courts are actually dealing with certain situations, will seek to rise above his own moral bias and to discount the moral bias of the legal author whose treatise he consults.

The realistic author of textbooks will not muddy his descriptions of judicial behavior with wishful thinking; if he dislikes a decision or line of decisions, he will refrain from saying, "This cannot be the law because it is contrary to sound principle," and say instead, "This is the law, but I don't like it," or more usefully, "This rule leads to the following results, which are socially undesirable for the following reasons * * *."

The realistic advocate, if he continues to use ritual language in addressing an unrealistic court, will at least not be fooled by his own words: he will use his "patter" to induce favorable judicial attitudes and at the same time to distract judicial attention from precedents and facts that look the wrong way (as the professional magician uses his "patter" to distract the attention of his audience from certain facts). Recognizing the circularity of conceptual argument, the realistic advocate will contrive to bring before the court the human values that favor his cause, and since the rules of evidence often stand in the way, he will perforce bring his materials to judicial attention by sleight-of-hand—through the appeal of a "sociological brief" to "judicial notice," through discussion of the background and consequences of past cases cited as precedents, through elaboration and exegesis upon admissible evidence, or even through a political speech or a lecture on economics in the summation of his case or argument.

The realistic judge, finally, will not fool himself or anyone else by basing decisions upon circular reasoning from the presence or absence of corporations, conspiracies, property rights, titles, contracts, proximate causes, or other legal derivatives of the judicial decision itself. Rather, he will frankly assess the conflicting human values that are opposed in every controversy, appraise the social importance of the precedents to which each claim appeals, open the courtroom to all evidence that will bring light to this delicate practical task of social adjustment, and consign to Von Jhering's heaven of legal concepts all attorneys whose only skill is that of the conceptual acrobat.

3. *The Theory of Legal Decisions*

The uses of the functional approach are not exhausted by "realistic jurisprudence." "Realistic jurisprudence," as that term is currently used,[80] is a theory of the nature of law, and therefore a theory of the nature of legal rules, legal concepts, and legal questions. Its essence is the definition of law as a function of judicial decisions. This definition is of tremendous value in the development of legal science, since it enables us to dispel the supernatural mists that envelop the legal order and to deal with the elements of the legal order in objective, scientific terms. But this process of definition and clarification is only a preliminary stage in the life of legal science. When we have analyzed legal rules and concepts as patterns of decisions, it becomes relevant to ask, "What are judicial decisions made of?"

If we conceive of legal rules and concepts as functions of judicial decisions, it is convenient, for purposes of this analysis, to think of these decisions as hard and simple facts. Just as every physical object may be analyzed as a complex of positive and negative electrons, so every legal institution, every legal rule or concept may be analyzed as a complex of plaintiff decisions and defendant decisions. But simplicity is relative to the level of analysis. For the chemist, the atom is the lowest term of analysis. But the physicist cannot stop the process of analysis with the atom or even the electron. It would be heresy to the faith of science to endow either with final simplicity and perpet-

[80] See K. N. LLEWELLYN, *A Realistic Jurisprudence—The Next Step* (1930) 30 COLUMBIA LAW REV. 431; Pound, *The Call for a Realist Jurisprudence* (1931) 44 HARV. L. REV. 697; Llewellyn, *Some Realism about Realism: Responding to Dean Pound* (1931) 44 HARV. L. REV. 1222.

ual immunity from further analysis. Unfortunately, certain advocates of realistic jurisprudence, after using the functional method to break down rules and concepts into atomic decisions, refuse to go any further with the analytic process. They are willing to look upon decisions as simple unanalyzable products of judicial hunches or indigestion.

The "hunch" theory of law,[81] by magnifying the personal and accidental factors in judicial behavior, implicitly denies the relevance of significant, predictable, social determinants that govern the course of judicial decision. Those who have advanced this viewpoint have performed a real service in indicating the large realm of uncertainty in the actual law. But actual experience does reveal a significant body of predictable uniformity in the behavior of courts. Law is not a mass of unrelated decisions nor a product of judicial bellyaches. Judges are human, but they are a peculiar breed of humans, selected to a type and held to service under a potent system of governmental controls. Their acts are "judicial" only within a system which provides for appeals, rehearings, impeachments, and legislation. The decision that is "peculiar" suffers erosion—unless it represents the first salient manifestation of a new social force, in which case it soon ceases to be peculiar. It is more useful to analyze a judicial "hunch" in terms of the continued impact of a judge's study of precedents, his conversations with associates, his reading of newspapers, and his recollections of college courses, than in strictly physiological terms.

A truly realistic theory of judicial decisions must conceive every decision as something more than an expression of individual personality, as concomitantly and even more importantly a function of social forces, that is to say, as a product of social determinants and an index of social consequences. A judicial decision is a social event. Like the enactment of a Federal statute, or the equipping of police cars with radios, a judicial decision is an intersection of social forces: Behind the decision are social forces that play upon it to give it a resultant momentum and direction; beyond the decision are human activities affected by it. The decision is without significant social dimensions when it is viewed simply at the moment in which it is rendered. Only by probing behind the decision to the forces which it reflects, or projecting beyond the decision the lines of its force upon the future, do we come to an understanding of the meaning of the decision itself. The distinction between "holding" and "dictum" in any decision is not to be discovered

[81] See Hutcheson, *The Judgment Intuitive: The Function of the "Hunch" in Judicial Decisions* (1929) 14 CORN. L. Q. 274; Hutcheson, *Lawyer's Law and the Little, Small Dice* (1932) 7 TULANE L. REV. 1; FRANK, LAW AND THE MODERN MIND (1930) c. 12-13; T. Schroeder, *The Psychologic Study of Judicial Opinions* (1918) 6 CALIF. L. REV. 89.

by logical inspection of the opinion or by historical inquiry into the actual facts of the case.[82] That distinction involves us in a prediction, a prophecy of the weight that courts will give to future citations of the decision rendered. This is a question not of pure logic but of human psychology, economics and politics.

What is the meaning of a judicial decision, summed up in the words, "Judgment for the plaintiff"? Obviously, the significance of the decision, even for the parties directly involved in the case, depends upon certain predictable uniformities of official behavior, *e.g.* that a sheriff or marshall will enforce the decision, in one way or another, over a period of time, that the given decision will be respected or followed in the same court or other courts if the question at issue is relitigated, and that certain procedures will be followed in the event of an appeal, etc. When we go beyond the merely private significance of an actual decision, we are involved in a new set of predictions concerning the extent to which other cases, similar in certain respects, are likely to receive the same treatment in the same courts or in other courts within a given jurisdiction. Except in the context of such predictions the announcement of a judicial decision is only a noise. If reasonably certain predictions of this sort could never be made, as Jerome Frank at times seems to say,[83] then all legal decisions would be simply noises, and no better grist for science than the magical phrases of transcendental jurisprudence.

If the understanding of any decision involves us necessarily in prophecy (and thus in history), then the notion of law as something that exists completely and systematically at any given moment in time is false.[84] Law is a social process, a complex of human activities, and an adequate legal science must deal with human activity, with cause and effect, with the past and the future. Legal science, as traditionally conceived, attempts to give an instantaneous snapshot of an existing and completed system of rights and duties. Within that system there are no temporal processes, no cause and no effect, no past and no future. A legal decision is thus conceived as a logical deduction from fixed principles. Its meaning is expressed only in terms of its logical consequences. A legal system, thus viewed, is as far removed from temporal activity as a

---

[82] Compare the orthodox wild goose chase of Goodhart after a formula which will determine the "real" *ratio decidendi* of a case (Goodhart, *Determining the Ratio Decidendi of a Case* (1930) 40 YALE L. J. 161) with the sane description by Llewellyn of the way in which cases come to stand for propositions of narrow or wide scope. THE BRAMBLE BUSH (1930) 47, 61-66. *Cf.* also Oliphant, *A Return to Stare Decisis* (1928) 6 AM. L. SCHOOL REV. 215, 217-218; F. S. Cohen, ETHICAL SYSTEMS AND LEGAL IDEALS (1933) 33-37.

[83] See FRANK, LAW AND THE MODERN MIND (1930), 7, 53, 104-111, 132-134.

[84] In this, law is no different from other social institutions or physical objects. *Cf.* C. I. LEWIS, *op. cit. supra* note 48, c. 5.

system of pure geometry. In fact, jurisprudence is as much a part of pure mathematics as is algebra, unless it be conceived as a study of human behavior,—human behavior as it molds and is molded by judicial decisions. Legal systems, principles, rules, institutions, concepts, and decisions can be understood only as functions of human behavior.[85]

Such a view of legal science reveals gaps in our legal knowledge to which, I think, legal research will give increasing attention.

We are still in the stage of guesswork and accidentally collected information, when it comes to formulating the social forces which mold the course of judicial decision. We know, in a general way, that dominant economic forces play a part in judicial decision, that judges usually reflect the attitudes of their own income class on social questions, that their views on law are molded to a certain extent by their past legal experience as counsel for special interests, and that the impact of counsel's skill and eloquence is a cumulative force which slowly hammers the law into forms desired by those who can best afford to hire legal skill and eloquence; but nobody has ever charted, in scientific fashion, the extent of such economic influences.[86] We know, too, that judges are craftsmen, with aesthetic ideals,[87] concerned with the aesthetic judgments that the bar and the law schools will pass upon their awkward or skillful, harmonious or unharmonious, anomalous or satisfying, actions and theories; but again we have no specific information on the extent of this aesthetic bias in the various branches of the law. We know that courts are, at least in this country, a generally conservative social force, and more like a brake than a motor in the social mechanism, but we have no scientific factual comparison of judicial, legislative, and executive organs of government, from the standpoint of social engineering. Concretely and specifically, we know that Judge So-and-so, a former attorney for a non-union shop, has very definite ideas about labor injunctions, that another judge, who has had an unfortunate sex life, is parsimonious in the fixing of alimony; that another judge

[85] "To say that a legal institution,—private property, the federal government of the United States, Columbia University,—exists is to say that a group of persons is doing something, is acting in some way. It is to point to a particular aspect of human behavior. . . . But a legal institution is something more than the way men act on a single occasion. . . . A legal institution is the happening over and over again of the same kind of behavior." U. Moore, *loc. cit. supra* note 32.

[86] Promising first steps towards such a study have been taken in: Brooks Adams, *op. cit. supra* note 32; GUSTAVUS MYERS, HISTORY OF THE SUPREME COURT (1912); Boudin, *op. cit. supra* note 27 (1932); Walter Nelles, *Commonwealth v. Hunt* (1932) 32 COLUMBIA LAW REV. 1128; Nelles, *The First American Labor Case* (1931) 41 YALE L. J. 165; Max Lerner, *The Supreme Court and American Capitalism* (1933) 42 YALE L. J. 668; W. Hamilton, *Judicial Tolerance of Farmers' Cooperatives* (1929) 38 YALE L. J. 936; articles of Haines, Brown, and Cushman cited *supra* note 38.

[87] *Cf.* F. S. COHEN, ETHICAL SYSTEMS AND LEGAL IDEALS (1933) 56-61; *Modern Ethics and the Law* (1934) 4 BROOKLYN L. REV. 33, 48-50.

can be "fixed" by a certain political "boss"; that a series of notorious kidnappings will bring about a wave of maximum sentences in kidnapping cases. All this knowledge is useful to the practicing lawyer, to the public official, to the social reformer, and to the disinterested student of society. But it is most meager, and what little of it we have, individually, is not collectively available. There is at present no publication showing the political, economic, and professional background and activities of our various judges. Such a reference work would be exceedingly valuable, not only to the practical lawyer who wants to bring a motion or try a case before a sympathetic court, but also to the disinterested student of the law. Such a Judicial Index is not published, however, because it would be disrespectable.[88] According to the classical theory, these things have nothing to do with the way courts decide cases. A witty critic of the functional approach regards it as a *reductio ad absurdum* of this approach that law schools of the future may investigate judicial psychology, teach the art of bribery, and produce graduate detectives.[89] This is far from a *reductio ad absurdum*. Our understanding of the law will be greatly enriched when we learn more about how judges think, about the exact extent of judicial corruption, and about the techniques for investigating legally relevant facts. Of course, this knowledge may be used for improper purposes, but cannot the same be said of the knowledge which traditional legal education distributes?

If we know little today of the motivating forces which mold legal decisions, we know even less of the human consequences of these decisions. We do not even know how far the appellate cases, with which legal treatises are almost exclusively concerned, are actually followed in the trial courts.[90] Here, again, the experienced practitioner is likely to have accumulated a good deal of empirical information, but the young law clerk, just out of a first-rate law school, is not even aware that such a problem exists. Likewise, the problem of the actual enforcement of judgments has received almost no critical study. Discussion of the extent to which various statutes are actually enforced regularly moves in

---

[88] Frank reports (LAW AND THE MODERN MIND, 112-115) the discontinuance of a statistical study of the decisions of various New York magistrates which revealed startling differences in the treatment of certain offenses.

[89] Kantorowicz, *Some Rationalism about Realism* (1934) 43 YALE L. J. 1240.

[90] The Institute of Law of Johns Hopkins broke the ice in the modern study of trial court decisions. See STUDY OF CIVIL JUSTICE IN NEW YORK (1931). See also MARSHALL, STUDY OF JUDICIAL SYSTEM OF MARYLAND (1932); C. E. Clark, *Fact Research in Law Administration* (1928) 2 CONN. BAR J. 211; B. L. Shientag and F. S. Cohen, *Summary Judgments in the Supreme Court of New York* (1932) 32 COLUMBIA LAW REV. 825, and works cited therein, notes 6 and 7; Saxe, *Summary Judgments in New York—A Statistical Study* (1934) 19 CORN. L. Q. 237; B. L. Shientag, *Summary Judgment* (1935) 4 FORDHAM L. REV. 186.

the thin air of polemic theory. It is usually practically impossible to find out whether a given statute has ever been enforced unless its enforcement has raised a legal tangle for appellate courts.

When we advance beyond the realm of official conduct and seek to discover the social consequences of particular statutes or decisions, we find a few promising programs of research[91] but almost no factual studies.[92] Today the inclusion of factual annotations in a code, showing the extent and effects of law enforcement, would strike most lawyers as almost obscene. But notions of obscenity change, and every significant intellectual revolution raises to prominence facts once obscure and disrespectable. It is reasonable to expect that some day even the impudencies of Holmes and Llewellyn will appear sage and respectable.

4. *Legal Criticism*

It is perhaps the chief service of the functional approach that in cleansing legal rules, concepts, and institutions of the compulsive flavors of legal logic or metaphysics, room is made for conscious ethical criticism of law. In traditional jurisprudence, criticism, where it exists, is found masked in the protective camouflage of transcendental nonsense: "The law *must* (or *cannot*) be thus and so, because the *nature* of contracts, corporations or contingent remainders so requires." The functional approach permits ethics to come out of hiding. When we recognize that legal rules are simply formulae describing uniformities of judicial decision, that legal concepts likewise are patterns or functions of judicial decisions, that decisions themselves are not products of logical parthenogenesis born of pre-existing legal principles but are social events with social causes and consequences, then we are ready for the serious business of appraising law and legal institutions in terms of some standard of human values.

The importance for legal criticism of clear, objective description of judicial behavior, its causes and its consequences, is coming to be

---

[91] See, for example, Pound, *The Scope and Purpose of Sociological Jurisprudence* (1911-1912) 24 HARV. L. REV. 591, 25 *id.* 140, 489; F. K. Beutel, *Some Implications of Experimental Jurisprudence* (1934) 48 HARV. L. REV. 169, 191-194.

[92] Notable exceptions are: MCCRACKEN, STRIKE INJUNCTIONS IN THE NEW SOUTH (1931); Brissenden and Swayzee, *The Use of the Labor Injunction in the New York Needle Trades* (1929) 44 POL. SCI. Q. 548, (1930) 45 *id.* 87. In addition to these direct studies of the effects of legal rules or decisions, there is a growing literature on the social materials with which law is concerned. Examples of such work are: POUND AND FRANKFURTER, CRIMINAL JUSTICE IN CLEVELAND (1922); R. R. Powell and Looker, *Decedents' Estates: Illumination from Probate and Tax Records* (1930) 30 COLUMBIA LAW REV. 919; Smith, Lilly and Dowling, *Compensation for Automobile Accidents: A Symposium* (1932) 32 COLUMBIA LAW REV. 785; S. and E. T. Glueck, *Predictability in the Administration of Criminal Justice* (1929) 42 HARV. L. REV. 297.

generally recognized. What is not so easily recognized is the importance for objective legal science of legal criticism.

Since the brilliant achievements of Bentham, descriptive legal science has made almost no progress in determining the consequences of legal rules.[93] This failure of scholarship, in the light of the encouraging progress of modern research into the antecedents and social context of judicial decision, calls for explanation.

Possibly this gap is to be explained in terms of an inherited assumption that statutes and decisions are self-executing, that the consequences of a law or a judgment are, therefore, clearly indicated by the language of the statute or decision itself, and that factual research is therefore a work of supererogation. Possibly this failure of research is to be explained in terms of the dominance of the private lawyer in our legal education. The private attorney is interested in the *causes* of judicial decisions, but his interest in consequences is likely to stop with the payment of a fee. I am inclined to think, however, that the failure of our legal scholarship in this direction may be attributed to a more fundamental difficulty. The prospect of determining the consequences of a given rule of law appears to be an infinite task, and is indeed an infinite task unless we approach it with some discriminating criterion of what consequences are *important*. Now a criterion of *importance* presupposes a criterion of values, which is precisely what modern thinkers of the "sociological" and "realistic" schools of jurisprudence have never had. Dean Pound has talked for many years of the "balancing" of interests, but without ever indicating which interests are more important than others or how a standard of weight or fineness can be constructed for the appraisal of "interests."[94] Contemporary "realists" have, in general, either denied absolutely that absolute standards of importance can exist,[95] or else insisted that we must thoroughly understand the facts as they are before we begin to evaluate them. Such a postponement of the problem of values is equivalent to its repudiation. We never shall thoroughly understand the facts as they are, and we are

[93] The following spiritual exercise is recommended by Professor Kantorowicz. Let the unconverted lawyer or law student read a code of laws in the following way: "Let him ask himself with respect to each statement . . . what harms would social life undergo if instead of this statement the opposite were enacted. And then let him turn to all textbooks, commentaries, monographs and reports of decisions and see how many questions of this sort he will find answered and how many he will find even put." RECHTSWISSENSCHAFT UND SOCIOLOGIE (1911) 8, quoted in Pound, *supra* note 91, 25 HARV. L. REV. 489, 513.

[94] *Cf.* W. L. Grossman, *The Legal Philosophy of Roscoe Pound* (1935) 44 YALE L. J. 605, 608-611; John C. H. Wu, *The Juristic Philosophy of Roscoe Pound* (1924) 18 ILL. LAW REV. 285, 294-304.

[95] See U. Moore, *Rational Basis of Legal Institutions* (1923) 23 COLUMBIA LAW REV. 609, 612; W. Nelles, Book Review (1933) 33 COLUMBIA LAW REV. 763, 765-768.

not likely to make much progress towards such understanding unless we at the same time bring into play a critical theory of values. In terms of such a theory, particular human desires and habits are important, and the task of research into legal consequences passes from the realm of vague curiosity to the problem form: How do these rules of law strengthen or change these important habits and satisfy or impede these important desires?

The positive task of descriptive legal science cannot, therefore, be entirely separated from the task of legal criticism. The collection of social facts without a selective criterion of human values produces horrid wilderness of useless statistics.[96] The relation between positive legal science and legal criticism is not a relation of temporal priority, but of mutual dependence.[97] Legal criticism is empty without objective description of the causes and consequences of legal decisions. Legal description is blind without the guiding light of a theory of values. It is through the union of objective legal science and a critical theory of social values that our understanding of the human significance of law will be enriched. It is loyalty to this union of distinct disciplines that will mark whatever is of lasting importance in contemporary legal science and legal philosophy.

FELIX S. COHEN

WASHINGTON, D. C.

---

[96] See Pound, *The Call for a Realist Jurisprudence* (1931) 44 HARV. L. REV. 697, 701.

[97] I have attempted to trace these relations in some detail in ETHICAL SYSTEMS AND LEGAL IDEALS (1933) and again, more briefly and in words of one and two syllables, in *Modern Ethics and the Law* (1934) 4 BROOKLYN L. REV. 33.

COLUMBIA LAW REVIEW

VOL. XXX APRIL, 1930 NO. 4

A REALISTIC JURISPRUDENCE—THE NEXT STEP*

The problem of defining law; focus versus confines

The difficulty in framing any concept of "law" is that there are so many things to be included, and the things to be included are so unbelievably different from each other. Perhaps it is possible to get them all under one verbal roof. But I do not see what you have accomplished if you do. For a concept, as I understand it, is built for a purpose. It is a thinking tool. It is to make your data more manageable in doing something, in getting somewhere with them. And I have not yet met the job, or heard of it, to which all the data that associate themselves with this loosest of suggestive symbols, "law," are relevant at once. We do and have too many disparate things and thinkings to which we like to attach that name. For instance, legislators pass "a law," by which we mean that they officially put a new form of words on the statute books. That calls up associations with regard to attorneys and judges, and to suits being brought "under the statute." But it also calls up associations with regard to those sets of practices and expectations and people which we call political parties and machines and lobbies. The former we should want, in some way, to include under the head "law," I suspect. If we did not, we ought to stop defining and think a little further. The latter—the parties and lobbies—we might have more doubt about, even if we did stop and think. Again, it seems fairly clear that there has been something we could not well dissociate from our symbol "law" in places and times when there was no legislature and even no state—indeed when there was no organization we can call "political" that was distinct from any other organization. You cannot study the simpler forms of society nor "the law" of such forms without looking into the mechanisms of organized control at such times and places; but today you will be likely to distinguish such types of control as *non-legal*. Of course, you would not disregard them, if you wanted to

* The substance of this paper was presented at the Round Table on Current Trends in Political and Legal Thought of the American Association of Political Science, December, 1929, under the title *Modern Concepts of Law*.

know anything about "law" that was worth knowing. But you would regard them as background, or foreground, or underground, to your center of interest. They would be something that you would compare and contrast with "law," I suspect, in the present order of society. And yet I also suspect you would have your hands full if you set about to draw the line between "the two." Or again, there are gentlemen who spend a good deal of time discussing "the ends of law," or "what law ought to be." Are they talking about "law"? Certainly their postulates and conclusions, in gross and in detail, have no need to look like anything any judge ever did; and at times some of those gentlemen seem to avail themselves of that freedom; but it would be a case-hardened person who denied that what they are dealing with is closely connected with this same loose suggestive symbol. What interests me about that is when a judge is working in a "well-settled field" he is likely to pay no attention to what such gentlemen say, and to call it irrelevant speculation; whereas when he is working in an "unsettled field" he seems to pay a lot of attention to their ideas, or to ideas of much the same order. This I take to mean that *for some purposes* they are talking something very close to "law," under any definition; and for *other* purposes, they are talking something whose connection with "law" as just used is fairly remote. And this problem of the word calling up wide-scattered and disparate references, *according to the circumstance,* seems to me vital.

So that I am not going to attempt a definition of law. Not anybody's definition; much less my own. A definition both excludes and includes. It marks out a field. It makes some matters fall inside the field; it makes some fall outside. And the exclusion is almost always rather arbitrary. I have no desire to exclude anything from matters legal. In one aspect law is as broad as life, and for some purposes one will have to follow life pretty far to get the bearings of the legal matters one is examining. I say again, therefore, that I shall not attempt a definition. I shall not describe a periphery, a stopping place, a barrier. I shall instead devote my attention to the *focus* of matters legal. I shall try to discuss a *point of reference*; a point of reference to which I believe all matters legal can most usefully be referred, if they are to be seen with intelligence and with appreciation of their bearings. A focus, a core, a center—with the bearings and boundaries outward unlimited. Pardon my saying it so often; but I find it very hard to make people understand that I am not talking about putting or pushing anything *out of* the field or concept of law. People are so much used to definitions—although definitions have not always been of so much use to people. I am, therefore, going to talk about substituting a somewhat unfamiliar, but more exciting and more useful focus, for the focus that most thinking about law in the past has had.

Two references to the course that thought has taken will help to set the perspective: one, to the tenets of the nineteenth century schools of jurisprudence; one, to the development of the concepts of rights and of interests.

For the nineteenth century schools I am content to accept one of Pound's summaries.[1] It fits with what reading in the field I have done; it is based upon vastly more reading in the field than I shall ever do. With regard to the analytical jurists, Pound stresses their interest in a body of established precepts whereby a definite legal result is supposed to be fitted to a definite set of facts; he stresses the centering of their definition upon the "aggregate of authoritative legal precepts applied by tribunals as such in a given time and place," and their presupposition of a state to make precepts and tribunals authoritative. The historical jurists, on the other hand, he finds making little distinction between law and other forms of social control; with them customary precepts, irrespective of whether they originate in the organs of politically organized societies, come in for heavy attention; central in their picture of law are the traditional techniques of decision and the traditional or customary notions of rightness. (All this, it may be added, without any too close analysis as to what is meant by "custom.") For the philosophical jurists, finally, Pound finds that "philosophical, political and ethical ideas as to the end of law and as to what legal precepts should be in view thereof" occupy the center of the stage.

I have no wish to put the tenets of these schools to the test, nor to pursue them further. Their value here is limited, but great within its limits: taken together, they hammer home the complexity of law. Each school was reaching for a single definition of all that was significant about law. Each school wound up with a definition which stressed some phases and either overlooked or greatly understressed others. Each had a definition with which, for its purposes, and especially in the hands of its creative thinkers, it made striking headway. But too close attention to any one of the definitions—in its exclusion aspects—for too long, would have meant ultimate barrenness. And I gather that one lesson Pound has drawn from his study of these and other schools has been to insist rather on what goes into the idea of law than on what is to be kept out of it.

---

[1] LAW AND MORALS (1924), 25 *et seq.*

Precepts as the Heart and Core of Most Thinking About Law

Moreover, you will have noted running through his summary of their views the word "precepts." This is traditional. When men talk or think about law, they talk and think about *rules.* "Precepts" as used by Pound, for instance, I take to be roughly synonymous with rules and principles, the principles being wider in scope and proportionately vaguer in connotation, with a tendency toward idealization of some portion of the *status quo* at any given time. And I think you will find as you read Pound that the precepts are *central* to his thinking about law. Along with rules and principles—along with precepts proper, may I say?—he stresses for instance "standards" as a part of the subject matter of law. These standards seem to be those vague but useful pictures with which one approaches a wide and varied field of conduct to measure the rights of a particular situation: a conception of what a reasonable man would do in the circumstances, or of what good faith requires, and similar pictures. They differ from rules, though not from principles, partly in their vagueness; they differ from both in being not propositions in themselves, but normative approaches to working out the application of some one *term* in a major proposition. The principle, let us say, would read: a man must answer for what good faith requires. But a standard (like a concept; like any class-term, loose or sharp) functions chiefly or exclusively as *part* of a precept. Consequently, it belongs in much the same world. It, too, *centers* on precepts. But Pound mentions more as law than precepts and standards. Along with the standards he stresses also ideals as to "the end" of law. These I take to be in substance standards on a peculiarly vague and majestic scale; standards, perhaps, to be applied to rules rather than to individual transactions.[2] Finally, he stresses—and we meet here a very different order of phenomena—"the traditional techniques of developing and applying" precepts. Only a man gifted with insight would have added to the verbal formulae and verbalized (though vague) conceptual pictures thus far catalogued, such an element *of practices,* of habits and techniques of action, of *behavior.* But only a man partially caught in the traditional precept-thinking of an age that is passing would have focussed that behavior on, have given it a major reference to, have belittled its importance by dealing with it as a phase of, those merely verbal formulae: precepts. I have no wish to argue the point. It will appeal, or it will not, and argument will be of little service.

[2] Not only ideals, but standards, not only standards, but concepts, not only concepts, but rules, involve of course generalized mental pictures which play a part in shaping both rules and the actions of courts. But as traditionally dealt with, this ideal element, even where observed, is promptly related in the first instance to rules.

But not only this particular bit of phrasing (which might be accidental), but the use made in Pound's writings of the idea, brings out vigorously the limitations of rules, of precepts, of *words,* when made the focus, the *center of reference,* in thinking about law.[3]

Remedies, Rights and Interests: A Developing Insight

Indeed, those limitations appear throughout the current analysis of law in terms of interests, rights and remedies. The growth of that analysis requires a short digression, but one that I believe worth making. It has to do with the *subject matter* of the rules and pre-

[3] Pound's work in this aspect is as striking in its values as in its limitations. It is full to bursting of magnificent insight. It is to Pound we owe the suggestion of "the limits of effective legal action" (worked out in terms of *court* decisions). It is to Pound we owe the contrast of law-in-books and law-in-action (the latter limited again, in his working out of it, to what *courts* do; though in other places he insists upon *administrative* organs as the present center of legal growth). It is to Pound we owe the formulation "individualization of treatment of an offender," and the reference to the proceedings of the Conference on Charities and Corrections to see what the criminal law is really doing. And so it goes. I am not concerned here with whether prior writers may have contributed to, or anticipated, some or all of these ideas. Pound saw them, he formulated them, he drove them home. But these brilliant buddings have in the main not come to fruition. No one thinks them through in their relation either to each other or to the bulk of received jurisprudence. "Balancing of interests" remains with no indication of how to tell an interest when you see one, much less with any study of how they are or should be balanced. "Sociological jurisprudence" remains bare of most that is significant in sociology. "Law-in-action" is left as a suggestion, while further discussion of "the law" centers on "precept." "The limits of effective legal action" —a formulation that fairly shrieks for study of the habit and control set-up of society (that *complex,* industrialized, [partially] urban, indirect-cooperation society he has given us words for)—is left without study of the society to which law is supposed to have relation. The more one learns, the more one studies, the more light and stimulus Pound's writings give. But always peculiarly on a fringe of insight which fails to penetrate at all to the more systematic set-up of the material. One is tempted to see in the thinking of the one man and of the American school of sociological jurisprudence a parallel to the development of case law as a whole: accepting in the main what has been handed down; systematizing compartment-wise; innovating where need shows, powerfully and surely—but *ad hoc* only, with little drive toward or interest in incorporating the innovation into or aligning it with the mass of the material as received.

Critical reading of Pound's work, it may be noted in passing, and especially the phrasing of any concrete criticism, are embarrassed by the constant indeterminacy of the level of his discourse. At times the work purports clearly to travel on the level of considered and buttressed scholarly discussion; at times on the level of bed-time stories for the tired bar; at times on an intermediate level, that of the thoughtful but unproved essay. Most often, it is impossible to tell the intended level of any chapter or passage, and the writing seems to pass without notice from one to another. Now it is obvious that three successive, mutually inconsistent generalizations, though no one of them sustainable as the deliberate propositions of a scholar, may all be illuminating and indeed all true at once—on the level of the after-dinner speech, or even of the thought-provoking essay. All of which gags the critic at the same time that it perhaps stimulates his critical faculties. There is value in this. There is value, even, in the legal bed-time story. But there is greater value to be had. What would one not give for the actual appearance of the long-awaited *Sociological Jurisprudence,* if its author would integrate it in terms of those pioneering thoughts of his which thus far have been waiting to be called together in a Constituent Assembly?

cepts of which men regarded the legal system as made up. Both with us and in the Roman system that subject matter has in the course of time undergone striking changes.

In the earlier stages the rules were thought of almost exclusively as rules of remedies.[4] Remedies were few and specific. There were a few certain ways to lug a man into court and a few certain things that you or the court could do with him when you got him there. We are concerned here not with why that was (why "can" a court of law give no injunctive relief today?) but only with *that* it was. The question for the man of that day took this shape: on what facts could one man make use of any specific one of the specific ways of making the court bother another man? And the rules of law were rules about that. They clustered around each remedy. In those terms people thought.[5] They thought about what they could see and do. Their crude minds dealt only with what they could observe. What they observed, they described.

---

[4] I am presupposing the presence of "rules of law," *i.e.*, at least assuming law as a semi-specialized activity of control distinguished from other mechanisms of control; and also presupposing generalization to have set in. Just how far this first assumption reaches I am sure I do not know; I should be inclined to regard any special assembly held for the purpose of adjusting disputes, by say village elders otherwise without official position or authority (*cf.* GUTMAN, DAS RECHT DER DSCHAGGA, DER SPRUCHRASEN), as one instance of its presence. The second assumption presupposes that prior decision has begun to be dealt with as precedent; that *Themis* is not merely an oracle, but marks a norm. But I am insisting that it be a norm *of law.* Vinogradoff cogently points out that Maine's *Themis* is not a pure creation of the judgment maker; before the *Themis* was a societal life in which norms were both explicit and implicit. I hesitate, however, to call the *implicit* norms either "rules" or "legal," and see nothing but confusion to be had from so doing. I see only *practices,* more or less definite, more or less conscious, plus a generalized attitude that whatever is practice is right, and whatever varies widely enough is wrong. Certainly the process of making the implicit norm express calls for difficult creative work (two pieces of gold as the reward, on the shield of Achilles!) though any man can *recognize* the result once arrived at *as* right, if it is right (the crowd will award the gold!). Certainly also the "explicit-making" permits a twisting. Finally, once the judgment is made, it is both clearer to see, firmer in outline, more rigid, and perhaps more authoritative than it was before. If authoritative at all *because of who made it,* or the circumstances of its making, moreover, it has certainly begun the differentiation out of the general social matrix into the specific character of legality. (Malinowski's analysis in *Crime and Custom in Savage Society* (1926) is somewhat similar; but it moves in terms of dominant authoritativeness of the norm, not of the functionary. If, *when appealed to,* a norm will prevail over an inconsistent norm of common practice, he thinks of it as legal. An illuminating discrimination.)

[5] Here and in the following I am talking about the thinking of what my friend T. R. Powell calls the "postmortemizers," those who hash over events that are past, and write books about them, or build taught law. Such persons typically show a wider range of thought than the practical man of similar ability, but a greater naiveté. The practical man seems to think in two water-tight compartments. One half of his mind grinds out the ideology of the day, as gospel, over pippins and cheese or from the rostrum; that half belongs to the postmortemizers. The other half deals cannily with existing institutions, of whatever holiness, to shape (at times it verges on twisting) them to the needs of the practical man or of

To later writers this seemed primitive. The later thinkers find a different kind of order in the field of law. Remedies seem to them to have a *purpose,* to be protections of something else. They could imagine these somethings and give them a name: *rights,* substantive rights. Thus the important, the substantial rules of law become rules defining rights. Remedies are relegated to the periphery of attention. They are "adjective law" merely—devices more or less imperfect for giving effect to the important things, the substantive rights which make up the substance of the law. The relation of rights to rules is fairly clear: the two are aspects of the same thing. When a rule runs in favor of a person, he has a right, as measured by the rule. Or, if he has a right, that can be phrased by setting out a rule ascribing to him and persons in like situation with him the benefits connoted by the rights. Rights are thus precise counterparts of rules, when the rights are ascribed generally to all persons in a class in given circumstances; and this is the typical postmortemizer's line of discourse. Or rights, when ascribed to particular individuals in specific circumstances, are deductions which presuppose the rule; the major premise is the general rule on rights; the minor is the proposition hooking up this individual and these circumstances with that general rule. Rights and rules are therefore for present purposes pretty much interchangeable; the right is a shorthand symbol for the rule.[6]

Substantive rights and rules are spoken of as prevailing between people, laymen: one has, *e.g.,* a right to the performance of a contract. It is a heresy when Coke or Holmes speaks of a man having liberty under the law to perform his contract, or pay damages, at his option. It would likewise be a heresy to argue that the vital real evidence of this supposed "right" lies in an action for damages, and that the right could rather more accurately be phrased somewhat as follows: if the other party does not perform as agreed, you can sue, and *if* you have a fair lawyer, and nothing goes wrong with your witnesses or the jury, *and* you give up four or five days of time and some ten to thirty percent of

---

his client. This side of the practical man's mind must have been at work in every legal system from the days of the most formal rigidity. (Compare the whole preparation and sequence of the lawsuit in Dasent's *Njals-Saga.*) And some persons—conscious creators—must have taken thought of the relation of interest and remedy since there has been law. (Compare the protection of the Church in the old English laws.) But the tone and ideas of the postmortemizers have changed from age to age, and while not altering the basic attitudes of the practical man, have changed his words and his stock of ideas, his tools, seemingly with powerful effects on his results.

[6] For present purposes the dubious distinction taken by the German thinkers: "objective *Recht*" (rather "law" than "right") and "subjective *Recht*" (close to our pre-Hohfeldian "right") can be disregarded. It fits the discussion in that the subjective *Recht* is viewed first of all as a deduction from the rule of law, and then as an independent something.

the proceeds, and wait two to twenty months, you will *probably* get a judgment for a sum considerably less than what the performance would have been worth—which, if the other party is solvent and has not secreted his assets, you can in further due course collect with six percent interest for delay. To argue thus would be to confuse the remedy (which you can see) with the substantive right (which you cannot see, but which you know is there—somewhere; people tell you so). The substantive right in this body of thought has a shape and scope independent of the accidents of remedies. And herein lies the scientific advance involved in the concept. You are freed of any necessity of observing what courts do, and of limiting your discussion to that. You get back into the ultimate realities behind their doing. Obviously you can think more clearly among those ultimate realities. They are not so much obscured by inconsistency and divergence of detail. They are not answerable to fact.

Most lay thinking, it may be noted in passing, is on this level today. Typical is the current acceptance of a paper rule or statute as meaning something simply because it has paper authority—indeed, as meaning all it says, or all it is supposed to have been intended to say, simply because it has paper authority.

Far be it from me to dispute that the concepts of substantive rights and of rules of substantive law have had great value.[7] They moved definitely and sharply toward fixing the attention of thinkers on the idea that procedure, remedies, existed not merely because they existed, nor because they had value in themselves, but because they had a purpose. From which follows immediate inquiry into what the purpose is, and criticism, if the means to its accomplishment be poor. They moved, moreover, to some extent, toward sizing up the law by situations, instead of under the categories of historically conditioned, often archaic remedy-law: a new base for a new synthesis; a base for law reform.

The Ambiguities in the Concepts of Rules and Rights

But that should not obscure the price that was paid for the advance. A price first, as already described, of moving discussion away from the checkup of fact. To a legal reformer in his campaigning, in his getting of new views across, this may have value, if "the fact" in question be existing positive law. He may move more comfortably if he can keep people from observing that his moves mean change. To a scientist, observing, or to a reformer engaged not in selling his reform,

[7] Neither would I be understood to deny practical consequences to this mode of thinking, in our case results, in constitutional law, limitation of actions, etc., or to urge that describing the remedy describes the whole situation, today. It *does* describe the most important, and a much neglected aspect of the situation.

in propaganding, in putting ideas over, but in inquiring what is before him, where he wants to get, and how to get there, this obfuscation of the facts is another matter.

Secondly, a price was paid, of ambiguity—indeed of multiguity. "Rules" is a term sufficiently ambiguous. A rule may be prescriptive: "this is what *ought* to be; what the judges *ought* to do in such cases." Or it may be descriptive: "this is what *is;* what the judges *actually* do in such cases." Or it may be both at once: "this is *both* what they do *and* what they ought to do."[7a] And when theorists discuss, they will move from one of these meanings into another without notice, and with all and any gradations of connotations. In the particular case of rules "of law" a further ambiguity affects the word "rule": whether descriptive or prescriptive, there is little effort to make out *whose* action and *what* action is prescribed or described. The statement "this is the rule" typically means: "I find this formula of words in authoritative books."[8] Does this connote: *Courts are actually proceeding* according to this formula"; or *"Courts* always *rehearse* this formula in this connection?" Does it connote: *"People* are conducting themselves in the light of this formula"; or even "People are conducting themselves as this formula suggests that they ought to." The theorist will rarely trouble to tell you how many (if any) of these connotations are implicit in his statement: "this is the rule." But he will reason, on the next page, from some one of such implications. Which means: confusion, profuse and inevitable.[9]

The confusion is stirred blacker with the concept "right" poured in. "Right" adds nothing to descriptive power. But it gives a specious

[7a] Put another way, prescriptive rules are rules *for* doing something; descriptive rules are so-called rules *of* doing something—statements of observed regularity. But "rules *of*" in common speech includes both aspects at once, and "rules *for*" as often as not connotes the presence of a corresponding practice. I shall limit my term "rules" to "rules for," and shall not *imply* any such connotation.

[8] I omit from discussion here one other troublesome confusion: whenever rules are discussed in their prescriptive aspect, it is frequently difficult to tell whether a writer is giving *his own view* of what ought to be, or, on the other hand, a view sanctioned by authority—the prevailingly accepted prescriptive rules. In this last case the *prevalence* of a given prescriptive rule is a fact capable of description (or misdescription); but it always remains to be noted whether that prevailing prescriptive rule has any counterpart in *practice,* or remains in the paper or lip-service stage.

[9] Refinement of terms goes some distance to avoid this confusion. "Rule" is well confined to the *pre*scriptive sphere. "Paper rule" is a fair name for a rule to which no counterpart in practice is ascribed. "Working rule" indicates a rule with counterpart in practice, or else a practice *consciously* normatized. *Cf. supra* note 4. "Practice" indicates an observable course of action, with no necessary ascription of conscious normatizing about it. In an earlier paper (15 Am. Ec. Rev. 671) I failed to make this last distinction; it seems obvious, however, that it refines one's descriptive and reasoning technique in an important detail. Consider, *e.g.,* the double value Ehrlich's work would have had, if his stock of terms had served to keep such distinctions clear, and to let his magnificent thinking work itself out free of confusion.

appearance of substance to prescriptive rules. They seem to be *about* some *thing*. So that to clothe one's statement about what rules of law are in terms of rights, is to double the tendency to disregard the limitations actually put on rules or rights by practice and by remedies. At the vital core of thought about law, at the very place where one thought impinges on another, or where one part of law impinges on another, one sees the impingement in terms of idealized somethings which may not, which mostly *do* not, reflect men's actions. In terms of words, and not in terms of conduct; in terms of what *apparently* is understandable *without* checking up in life. So that one makes the assumption—without the urge to inquiry—that one is dealing with reality when he talks of rights, and proceeds to use these unchecked words for further building.

There is another confusion, found in dealing with rules, and strengthened by the associated idea of rights, within the field of doctrine itself. Having come to regard words as sound bases for further thinking, the tendency is well nigh inevitable to simplify the formulations more and more: to rub out of the formulations even the discrepancies in paper doctrine which any growing system of law contains in heaping measure; doubly so because the word "rights" introduces *sub rosa* at this point the additional notion of "rightness" (in the sense of what ought to be)—before which unwanted discrepancies must fall. I am speaking here of the effects of the idea of rightness on the rejection of some of the existent purely doctrinal materials in favor of other equally doctrinal materials, the case of conflicts in and within legal doctrine—a matter of vast concern to a lawyer, though perhaps of no great moment to a political scientist.

But the same tendency carries over quite as well into the confusion of legal with non-legal materials, where it concerns political scientist and lawyer in common; and here the idea of "rights" seems to be the heavy tool of confusion, with no help at all from the idea of "rules." "Right" eternally suggests its connotation of inherent "rightness"—social, political, economic, and especially moral. It takes more careful self-analysis than most have been interested in giving to keep the *non-legal* "right" (which was a reason for claiming or striving toward or awarding a legal right) distinguished from the "legal right" which was conceived, I take it, as something not quite a mere description of an available remedy, but at least an official recognition that some kind of remedy could be had. The threat of ambiguous middle is obvious.[9a] The natural rights theorists did little to make it less.

[9a] Wherever the plaintiff has a [legal] right to recover, he can recover at law. This plaintiff has a [social, moral, economic] right to recover. Therefore this plaintiff can recover in this action at law. This may improve the law. It has. It is not, for that, any the better thinking for a scientist *to use*.

Interests

This third confusion (but, be it noted, neither the second nor the first) was cleared up by the controversy that centered about Ihering. Since that controversy we take some care to limit our term "rights" to legal rights ("substantive," if nothing more be said), and are thereby aided in keeping the legal separate from the social factors at work in a situation. The term *interests,* on the other hand, comes in to focus attention on the presence of social factors, and to urge that substantive rights themselves, like remedies, exits only for a purpose. Their purpose is now perceived to be the protection of the interests. To be sure, we do not know what interests are. Hence, behind substantive rights (which we need not check against anything courts *do*) we now have interests (which we need not check against anything at all, and about whose presence, extent, nature and importance, whether the interests be taken absolutely or taken relatively one to another, no two of us seem to be able to agree). The scientific advance should again be obvious. Complete subjectivity has been achieved.

At this stage of the development, then, one arrives at a double chain of purposes. One starts with the interest. That is a social fact or factor of some kind, existing dependent of the law.[9b] And it has value independent of the law. Indeed, its protection is the purpose of substantive legal rights, of legal rules, of precepts of substantive law. "Security of transactions" is such an interest. The rules and rights of contract law exist to protect and effectuate it. The rules and rights are not ends, but means. But they are means which in another aspect (like most means) themselves become ends: remedies exist as means to effectuate the substantive rights, to realize the substantive rules. Obviously the means may be inadequate, badly chosen, wasteful, even self-defeating, at either stage. They may be so, cumulatively, at both stages. The rule that consideration is necessary to make an offer irrevocable for three days, even when the offer is fully intended, business like, signed, in writing, and expressed to be irrevocable for three days, may be thought not adapted to further security of transactions. The rule that certain oral and essential terms of an agreement are without force, if the balance of the agreement has been committed to writing, and looks on its face to be complete, raises considerable doubts as to its furtherance of security of transactions—sufficiently so as to have made our rules on the subject rather intricate and uncertain, and our judicial practices at times highly uncertain.

[9b] This is an overstatement. Past law may have contributed much to the present existence of an interest, and to its shape and extent.

The rules standardizing the remedies in contracts for the sale of goods, limiting the remedy to a suit before a jury, and for damages, and measuring the damages in the great body of cases by arbitrary standards which presuppose a frictionless market, may be thought to give inadequate remedy, even if the basis of supposed substantive rules and rights be thought wholly adequate to *its* purposes. The means, I say, may be inadequate; but the analysis invites discovery of the inadequacy. Hence, whatever one thinks of the sufficiency in the large of the analysis in the threefold terms of interests, substantive rights and rules, and remedies, one can but pay homage to the sureness with which it forces law on the attention as something man-made, something capable of criticism, of change, of reform—and capable of criticism, change, and reform not only according to standards found inside law itself (inner harmony, logical consistence of rules, parts and tendencies, *elegantia juris*) but also according to standards vastly more vital found *outside* law itself, in the society law purports both to govern *and to serve.*

On the other hand, the set-up in these terms has carried over its full measure of confusion, as I have tried to indicate above. And the confusion thus carried over is not—like the virtues of the analysis—familiar, well understood, and regularly taken account of. Which brings me again to the suggestion made above, that the use of precepts, or rules, or of rights which are logical counterparts of rules—of *words,* in a word—as the *center* of reference in thinking about law, is a block to clear thinking about matters legal. I want again to make sure that I am not misunderstood. (1) I am not arguing that "rules of substantive law" are without importance. (2) I am not arguing that it is not humanly *possible* to use the interests-rights and rules-remedies analysis and still think clearly and usefully about law. (3) Least of all, am I attempting to urge the exclusion of substantive rights and rules from the field of "law." Instead of these things, I am arguing (1) that rules of substantive law are of far less importance than most legal theorizers have assumed in most of their thinking and writing, and that they are *not* the most useful center of reference for discussion of law; (2) that the presence of the term "rights and rules" in the interest set-up (a) has persistent tendency to misfocus attention on that term; (b) that the avoidance of that tendency is a great gain in clarity; and (c) that to both attempt such avoidance and retain the term is to cumber all discussion with embarrassing and quite unnecessary baggage; (3) that substantive rights and rules should be removed from their present position at the *focal point* of legal discussion, in favor the *area of contact* between judicial (or official) *behavior* and the *behavior* of laymen; that the substantive rights and rules should be studied not as self-existent, nor as a major point of reference, but themselves with constant reference to that area of behavior-contacts. Let me take up the second and third of these positions together, and turn then to the first.

The Interests-Rights-Remedies Analysis: Words v. Practice

I see no value to be gained from the interests-rights and rules-remedies set up except to bring out, to underscore, that law is not all, nor yet the major part of, society; and to force attention to the relations and interactions of law and the rest of society; and as a matter of method, to provide words which keep legal and non-legal aspects of the situation and the interactions distinct. And it would seem to go without demonstration that *the most significant* (I do *not* say the *only* significant) aspects of the relations of law and society lie in the field of behavior, and that words take on importance either because and insofar as they are behavior, or because and insofar as they demonstrably reflect or influence other behavior. This statement seems not worth making. Its truth is absurdly apparent. For all that, it reverses, it upsets, the whole traditional approach to law. It turns accepted theory on its head. The traditional approach is in terms of words; it centers on words; it has the utmost difficulty in getting beyond words. If nothing be said about behavior, the *tacit* assumption is that the words do reflect behavior, and if they be the words of rules of law, do influence behavior, even influence behavior effectively and precisely to conform completely to those words. Here lies the key to the muddle. The "rules" are laid down; in the type-case they are "ought" rules, prescriptive rules: the writer's prescriptions, the writer's oughts, individually proclaimed oughts—the true rule is that judges should give judgment for the plaintiff on these facts.[10] From this we jump without necessary notice into equivalent oughts as *accepted* in the legal system under discussion: prevailing oughts—the authorities agree that judges should give judgment for the plaintiff on these facts. Here, again without notice and without inquiry, we *assume* that *practice* of the judges conforms to the accepted oughts on the books; that the verbal formulations of oughts *describe* precisely the is-es of practice; that they *do* give such judgment on such facts. A toothed bird of a situation, in law or any other walk of life. Where is men's ideology about their doing, about what is good prac-

[10] How joyously sharp, under this addressing of the rule to the judge becomes the distinction between a rule telling him what to *do,* himself, and one telling him how to instruct a jury!

tice—where is that ideology or has it ever been an adequate description of their *working* practice?

This is the first tacit imputation of factuality to the rules of ought. A second such imputation follows forthwith—again without explicitness, again without inquiry, again (save in odd instances) without challenge or suggestion or doubt. The paper rule of ought which has now been *assumed* to *describe* the judges' *working* rule of ought (*i.e.*, to correspond with the judges' practice of decision) is now further assumed to *control* the practice of the interested laymen, to *govern* people's conduct. Pray for the storm-tossed mariner on a night like this! What hope is there for clarity of reasoning with such a waste of billowing to build on?

Do I suggest that (to cut in at one crucial point) the "accepted rules," the rules the judges say that they apply, are without influence upon their actual behavior? I do not. I do not even say that, *sometimes*, these "accepted rules" may not be a very accurate description of the judges' actual behavior. What I say is that such accuracy of description is rare. The question is how, and how much, and in what direction, do the accepted rule and the practice of decision diverge? More: how, and how much, *in each case?* You cannot generalize on this, *without investigation.* Your guesses may be worth something, in the large. *They are worth nothing at all, in the particular.* The one thing we know now for certain is, that different rules have totally different relations to the behavior of judges, of other officials, and of the particular persons "governed" (optimistic word!) by those different rules. The approach here argued for admits, then, out of hand, *some* relation between *any* accepted rule and judicial behavior; and then proceeds to deny that that admission involves anything but a problem for investigation in the case in hand; and to argue that the significance of the particular rule will appear only *after* the investigation of the vital, focal, phenomenon: the behavior. And if an empirical *science* of law is to have any realistic basis, any responsibility to the facts, I see no escape from moving to this position. Thus, and only thus, is the real gain sought by the interests-rights and rules-remedies analysis to be made tangible. I do not deny, be it noted, that those who have cast their thinking in that set-up are from time to time aware of the importance of what is here urged. "Law-in-books and law-in-action." Indeed, whenever challenged on the point, any one of them will proceed to remodel his emphasis *ad hoc;* he will, for a moment, fix his stress on the remedy, even on the effects of the remedy, as used, in life. *But* it is an *ad hoc* remodelling. It is forgotten when the immediate issue is passed. It is no part of the standard equipment of investigation, discussion, synthesis; it is a part only of the equipment of defense. When used apart from combat, as a result of a worker's own curiosity or of some sudden fact-stimulus from outside, it flares like a shooting star, and disappears. Always the night of words will close again in beauty over the wild, streaked disturbance.

Interests: What Are They?

This emphasis on behavior, on the observable, on *attempts* at objective cross-check on the data under discussion, on *attempts* to find words which describe and do not misdescribe those data, ought to bear fruit in the discussion of interests, as well. The attribution of "interest" quality to anything of necessity involves a value-judgment over and above those value-judgments inherent in any scientific inquiry.[11] At that point the behavior approach ceases to promise objective agreement, except in this—that isolation of the value-judgement, in presentation, from the observed phenomena on which it in part rests, would clarify much discussion. Above all, such an approach to interests would move in terms of *demonstrating the existence of groupings* of behavior claimed to be significant, as the part of scientific decency when any "interest" is set up for discussion. The present approach tends instead to set up the broadest of formulae about interests, and to attribute them to situations in magisterial unconcern for the specific facts. I have paid my respects briefly above to some aspects of "security of transactions." I would not be understood thereby to deny that those three words are highly useful, or that they refer to very significant aspects of our life. But I am very eager to be understood as questioning how much is accomplished, for any given specific problem, by resting merely on the magic of those words. I think my friend Patterson has wisely described the interest-concept, in its present stage of development, as merely a red flag to *challenge investigation* in certain general directions—as leaving in any concrete situation most of the fact gathering and most of the fact weighing still to be done. "Security of transactions," in the contract cases I have put above would, to him, mean the most useful raising of a query: what kind of transactions is involved? Better, what *kinds* of transactions are involved? How many? What results, at present? What disappointments? What effects would any proposed change have? What possible undesired effects, in the hands of interested parties? And

[11] As, *e.g.*, that it is worth while finding out; that it is worth while checking conclusions constantly by facts; and striving to state conclusions which stay within the observed facts; probably also that it is worth while to publish such conclusions for discussion irrespective of what prejudices they may affront, or what accepted values they may disturb.

so on. "Security of transactions" would settle nothing. It would, as facts become clear, suggest one line of policy which has come in many phases of the law to be regarded as important; but it would leave the importance of that line of policy in any case to be illumined by the facts relevant to the situation in that instant case. No elimination of the subjective value-judgment, then; but an illumination by objective data of the basis and bearings of a subjective value-judgment. Insofar, a comparison of *facts* with *facts,* and not of *words* with *words.* Not a comparison of a mere formula of words about an interest with a formula of words said to be a "rule of law," a precept with no man knows what unexamined meaning in life. Nay, rather the objective data, the *specific* data, *claimed* to represent an interest, compared with the *actual doings* of the judges and the *actual effects* of their doings *on the data claimed to represent an interest.* If the judges' *sayings* have *demonstrable* effects, add those to the comparison. What else is relevant? Better: is anything else anything like *so* relevant?

I have said above that this can be done under the more cumbersome three-fold analytical set-up.[12] I have said that it semi-occasionlly

---

[12] Throughout this paper I am speaking primarily from the viewpoint of the postmortemizer, the observer, the orderer, the scientist. But in passing let me pay my respects to four other lines of legal thinking in which the utility of the suggested approach seems equally striking. (a) That of the practicing lawyer. In his moments of action, in his actual handling of a case or situation, the measure of his success is the measure in which he actually uses this approach. (The question of how far he uses it consciously, how far intuitively, is immaterial.) His job is either to guide a specific client through the difficulties of action in a concrete situation, or to bring the personnel of a specific tribunal to a specific result. The desired results, and not formulae, are his focus, and he uses formulae as he uses his knowledge of both judicial tradition and individual peculiarity: as tools to reach his desired result. He can be more effective, as any other practical man or artist can, if his technique be consciously studied. This is not to say that all that goes to make up his technique can be laid down or be consciously imparted. Still less is it to urge that he is himself a trustworthy reporter of his own technique.

(b) That of the legislator. Here is a man who wants results. How can one doubt the added utility to be derived from his wrestling with the observable facts of official action and lay action as those facts exist? Indeed, the successful practitioner and the successful politician are precisely the men whose grasp of the realities of law puts the word-beclouded theorist to shame.

(c) That of the philosopher of law—on the side of the "ends of law" and social values. He takes his data for philosophizing from somewhere. The worthwhileness of his philosophy is to a considerable degree conditioned on those data. If they be data of life, his problems become more real, his check-up easier, his basis of thinking more actual. This means at least, when he comes to the application of his chosen values to the criticism of "positive law," that he would bridge to the law-in-action of his day, not merely to the books. If he be a pure mystic, this may be immaterial; otherwise the gain seems inevitable.

For the devotee of formal logic in the law the picture is somewhat different. He will be concerned with words, with propositions. Probably almost wholly with propositions which move within the realm of ought—of doctrine—presumably the accepted doctrine of the system. Once he has his propositions, he runs free of the

has been done. I have said that it is rarely done, and that the definite tendency of that set-up is to block off the doing of it. I venture to predict that without the shift of emphasis, of focus, to behavior, that tendency will continue cheerfully in evidence.

Meaning of Rules and Rights Under the Behavior Analysis

What now, is the place of rules and rights, under such an approach? To attempt their excision from the field of law would be to fly in the face of fact. I should like to begin by distinguishing real "rules" and rights from paper rules and rights. The former

approach here discussed. He meets that approach in two places: the first, when he puts concrete content into his symbols, to start with. He will be no more accurate a logician, but a more useful one, if he reaches into observed fact, not merely into paper words, for that life content. And again, when the logical process is over, and he wishes to compare his results with something, to see whether he would not prefer another line of systematizing, he can use the behavior-area effectively for his comparison.

But what I have said of the logician suggests the making express of a matter implicit throughout the paper. To say that the area of behavior contact is the most useful point of reference for all matters legal is *not* to say that a specialist may not do the most useful of work, conceivably, without even reaching to that point of reference. A careful study of the formal logic of judicial opinions would be a useful study. But I would urge that even its usefulness would be hugely increased by an equally careful study of the instrumentalism, the pragmatic and socio-psychological decision elements in the same cases. And that an equally geometric increase in illumination would follow a further careful study of the effects on the society concerned of the same cases. Under the present "words" and "rules" appproach, all the tendency would be to stop with, or slightly modify, the first of these hypothetical studies. Under the behavior-contact approach each would be welcome, but the insistent drive would be toward completing the last before the significance of the others would be thought even measurably understood.

(d) That of the judge. His approach as one member of a bench to his colleagues does not seem to me to differ significantly for the present purpose from that of the practicing lawyer. His approach *for himself* involves (as does the approach of the philosopher) his forming a value-judgment on the case in hand, in addition to observation and predicition. How his value-judgment can fail of higher utility if he sees his problem not as the mere making of an abstract paper formula, but as the devising of a *way of working* in court *which will in due course affect people* is hard for me to see. The latter approach will certainly force him toward using all facilities he has available to *visualize* in advance the effects of the decision. Such visualization has been thought—and, I conceive, rightly—to be the essence of case-law wisdom-in-action. The approach described should make this wisdom-in-action a reality in a higher percentage of cases. I have developed elsewhere that whereas the net effect is undoubtedly an expansion of the traditional field of discretion and judicial law-making, yet this should give even a conservative no cause for alarm: first, because even when expanded, that field remains amazingly narrow, taken in relation to law as a whole, or to the movement of law—only cumulative changes over decades being in the main of much note; second, because it involves the introduction of no technique of change not already hallowed by conservative tradition, but only a reorganization, for conscious utilization, of techniques accepted for centuries as good; third (this an article of faith, not a matter capable as yet of proof) because the type of change produced under these circumstances is change which moves official action more into keeping with current needs; and another type of change, now constantly occurring, though hidden, tends to be eliminated: change by way of over-simplification of verbal formulae and over-"application" of such formulae to cases they never had before been applied to, and do not fit. Das Amerikanische Präjudizienrecht (in preparation).

are conceived in terms of behavior; they are but other names, convenient shorthand symbols, for the remedies, the actions of the courts. They are descriptive, not prescriptive, except in so far as there may occasionally be implied that courts *ought to* continue in their practices.[13] "Real rules," then, if I had my way with words, would by legal scientists be called the practices of the courts, and not "rules" at all. And statements of "rights" would be statements of likelihood that in a given situation a certain type of court action loomed in the offing. Factual terms. No more. This use of "rights," at least, has already considerable standing among the followers of Hohfeld. This concept of "real rule" has been gaining favor since it was first put into clarity by Holmes. "Paper rules" are what have been treated, traditionally, as rules of law: the accepted *doctrine* of the time and place—what the books there say "the law" is. The "real rules" and rights—"what the courts will do in a given case, and nothing more pretentious"—are then predictions. They are, I repeat, on the level of isness and not of oughtness; they seek earnestly to go no whit, in their suggestion, beyond the remedy actually available. Like all shorthand symbols, they are dangerous in connotation, when applied to situations which are not all quite alike. But their intent and effort is to describe. And one can borrow for them Max Weber's magnificent formulation in terms of probability: a right (or practice, or "real rule") exists *to the extent that* a likelihood exists that *A* can induce a court to squeeze, out of *B*, *A*'s damages; more: *to the extent that* the likely collections will cover *A's* damage. In this aspect *substantive* rights and "rules," as distinct from adjective, simply disappear—on the descriptive level. The measure of a "rule," the measure of a right, becomes what can be done about the situation. *Accurate* statement of a "real rule" or of a right includes all procedural limitations on what can be done about the situation. What is left, in the realm of *description,* are at the one end the facts, the groupings of conduct (and demonstrable expectations) which may be claimed to constitute an interest; and on the other the practices of courts in their effects upon the conduct and expectations of the laymen in question. Facts, in the world of isness, to be compared directly with other facts, also in the world of isness.

A reversion, do you say, to the crude and out-moded thinking of rules in terms of remedies only, to confining legal thinking to the vagaries of tradition-bound procedure? Not quite. It is a reversion

[13] Eliminating such an implication would to my mind be pure gain. The question of desirability of continuing a given practice, when it comes up for discussion at all, is better made express.

to the realism of that primitive point of view. But a sophisticated reversion to a sophisticated realism. Gone is the ancient assumption that law is because law is; there has come since, and remains, the inquiry into the purpose of what courts are doing, the criticism in terms of searching out purposes and criticizing means. Here value-judgments reenter the picture, and should. Observing particular, concrete facts of conduct and of expectation which suggest the presence of "an interest," one arrives at his value conclusion that something in those facts calls for protection at the hands of state officials. What protection is called for, and called for in terms of what *action* of the state officials? Again a matter of judgment—but a matter of judgment which at least foots on reality and comes to results in terms of action. With that hypothetical action, the actual conduct of those officials can be directly compared. Room for error, in plenty, in diagnosing interests, and in imagining the forms of official conduct suited to their protection. But realism in discussion; realism at each end of the comparison; a narrowing as far as the present state of knowledge will permit, of the field for obstructing eyes with words that masquerade as things without a check-up.

The Place and Treatment of Paper Rules

Are "rules of law" in the accepted sense eliminated in such a course of thought? Somewhat obviously not. Whether they be pure paper rules, or are the accepted patter of the law officials, they remain present, and their presence remains an actuality—an actuality of importance—but an actuality whose *precise* importance, whose bearing and influence become clear. First of all they appear as what they are: rules of authoritative ought, addressed *to* officials, telling *officials* what the *officials* ought to do.[14] To which telling the officials either pay no heed at all (the pure paper rule; the dead-letter statute; the obsolete case) or listen partly (the rule "construed" out of recognition; the rule to which lip-service only is paid, while practice runs another course) or listen with all care (the rule with which the official practice pretty accurately coincides). I think that every such official precept-on-the-books (statute, doctrine laid down in the decision of a court, administrative regulation) tacitly contains an element of pseudo-

[14] This I think holds true of *all* official ought-rules, irrespective of their form. I speak of their effects, not of their purposes. And the rights of laymen result through the screen of the official's practice, by a kind of social reflex. Ehrlich described the phenomenon cogently, so far as concerned the rules governing the set-up of the state governmental machine. A legal philosopher or a normatizer, with his mind fixed on the purpose of rules to ultimately affect the conduct of the "governed," will quarrel with this. A sociologist is content to see and describe what happens—and *compare* that with what is purposed.

description along with its statement of what officials ought to do; a tacit statement that officials do act according to the tenor of the rule; a tacit prediction that officials will act according to its tenor. Neither statement nor prediction is often true *in toto*. And the first point of the approach here made is skepticism as to the truth of either in the case in hand. Yet it is an accepted convention to act and talk as if this statement and prediction were most solemn truth: a tradition marked peculiarly among the legal profession when engaged officially. It is indeed of first importance to remember that such a tradition contains a tendency to verify itself.[15] But no more so than to remember that such a tendency is no more powerful than its opposite: that other tendency to move quietly into falsifying the prediction in fact, while laying on an ointment of conventional words to soothe such as wish to believe the prediction has worked out.

Thus the problem of official formulations of rules and rights becomes complex. First, as to formulations already present, already existent: the accepted doctrine. There, I repeat, one lifts an eye canny and skeptical as to whether judicial behavior is in fact what the paper rule purports (implicitly) to state. One seeks the real practice on the subject, by study of how the cases do in fact eventuate. One seeks to determine how far the paper rule is real, how far *merely* paper.[16] One seeks an understanding of *actual* judicial behavior, in that comparison of rule with practice; one follows also the use made of the paper rule in argument by judges and by counsel, and the apparent influence of its official presence on decisions. One seeks to determine when it is stated, but ignored; when it is stated and followed; when and why it is *expressly* narrowed or extended or modified, so that a new paper rule is created. One observes the level of *silent* application or modification or escape, in the "interpretation" of the facts of a case, in contrast to that other and quite distinct level of express wrestling with the language of the paper rule. One observes how strongly ingrained is the tradition of requiring a good paper justification, in terms of officially accepted paper rules, before any decision, however appealing on the facts, can be regarded as likely of acceptance. And by the same token, one observes the importance of the

---

[15] Ehrlich, again, brings this out beautifully.

[16] And on moving into the further fields of contact between judicial or official behavior and lay behavior, one gets into much deeper water: how does the paper rule work out (*i.e.*, have a reflection or a counterpart in behavior) in lower court cases, unappealed? How often does it have any influence? What influence on administrative officials? On transactions between laymen which never reach any officials? All signs point to this being vastly more important than the set-up of doctrine, or even than the actual practices of higher courts. What is documented takes on a specious appearance of value, as against the unexplored.

official formulae as tools of argument and persuasion; one observes both the stimuli to be derived from, and the limitations set by, their language. Very rapidly, too, one perceives that neither are all official formulae alike in these regards, nor are all courts, nor are all times and circumstances for the same formula in the same court. The *handling* of the official formulae to influence court behavior then comes to appear as an art, capable only to a limited extent of routinization or (to date) of accurate and satisfying description. And the discrepancy, great or small, between the official formula and what actually results, obtains the limelight attention it deserves.

Paper Rules and New Control

I am tempted, however, to regard the *new* formulation of official rules as even more vitally affected by the approach here suggested than is the dealing with existing formulations. For such new formulation is always with a purpose.[17] The effectuation of this purpose (one recalls "the protection of an interest," *supra*) *must be sought by means of verbal formulation.* In part the need is based on our legal tradition: our officials move to a great extent on the stimulus of and in the light of verbally formulated rules.[18] In part, moreover, verbal formulations, and especially those in regard to *new, planned* change in action, are an inherently essential tool of communication in a complex society; they are peculiarly important in a society which depends in good part upon written records to maintain continuity of practice between successive incumbents of an office, and between suc-

[17] This hopelessly over-simplifies. There may be as many divergent purposes as there are participants. Almost regularly the formulator's purpose and the purpose he publicly assigns are in part disparate.

[18] This factor has by no means the exclusive importance the devotees of paper rules tend to attribute to it. The keener observers constantly stress this: what other meaning has the emphasis on the traditional techniques "for developing and applying precepts"; the *practice* of the office, or of the Constitution, which shift emphases, and often create or abrogate whole institutions; the "interpreting away" of a rule; the importance of experience in the office, of the "trained" incumbent. And so forth.

On the other hand the factor of verbally formulated rules has enough importance to explain why they have so long been considered the core of even the substance of law. They are not the sole machinery for *producing* regularity. Habit, practice, unverbalized experience and tradition, are vital to regularity. But they are *a* factor in *producing* it—to the extent that officials react to words, and read words, alike. They are, moreover, the main device for *checking* regularity, for letting outsiders get an idea that officials are staying within the due limits of discretion. And they are, as indicated, a most vital element in introducing change in regularity. Where official behavior occurs *without* regularity, the older views tend to deny it the character of law (the assumed irregularity or caprice of cadi-justice, and the like). On this I differ. I should of course stress as the more perfect illustration of the concept *regular* official behavior; but I regard the behavior as more vital than the regularity, and the mere paper expression of desired regularity—save so far as it expresses an ideal—well, as paper.

cessive generations. But since the ultimate effectuation of a purpose is in terms of action, of behavior, the verbal formulation, to be an efficient tool, must be such as will produce the behavior[19] desired. *This turns on the relevant prevailing practices and attitudes of the relevant persons.* In one familiar doctrinal illustration, language used in a statute "will be read" in the light both of the existing common law, and of prior judicial construction of that language. But that is a matter of the top, the most superficial, level. Below that are the more vital practices prevalent as to *handling* official rules, described roughly above; practices, *i.e.,* of courts and of lawyers.

But in regard to the new (and especially the statutory) formulation, the behavior problem goes much deeper than such practices of the legal elect. The ways of appellate courts in handling existing official rules presuppose the cracking of the toughest nut the statutory draftsman has to crack: the case is already in court; someone is already making an appeal to the official formula. Whereas one of the statutory draftsman's major problems is to look into existent behavior beforehand, to make sure that his formula, when it becomes an official rule, will not merely bask in the sun upon the books. He must so shape it as to *induce its application* (with all the discrepancies that may entail) or else (for any purpose save that of pacifying clamorous constituents content with words) his blow is spent in air.[20]

Only as a second job does he have to wrestle with making his formula so impinge upon judicial tradition that the results in action will be those desired *if* a case gets into court. Again there is little to be gained by laboring the point. It seems patent that only a gain in realism and effectiveness of thinking can come from consistently (not occasionally) regarding the official formulation as a tool, not as a thing of value in itself; as a means without meaning save in terms of its workings, and of meaning in its workings only when these last are compared with the results desired. In the terms used above: as *prima facie* pure paper until the contrary is demonstrated; and as at best a new piece of an established but moving environment, one single element in a complex of practices, ideas and institutions without whose study the one element

[19] I have not attempted in this paper to define conduct, action, behavior. I have no desire to exclude such things as the arousing and disappointment of expectations, the creation of hopes and fears, etc. The approach advocated would, however, go vigorously to inquiring into the grounds for claiming the arousing or disappointment of expectations in any given case,—as also to inquiring into what expectations, and whose. So, too, for example, with the thought processes of judges, the influence of ideology on judges and laymen, etc. *Cf.* 15 AM. EC. REV. 670, n. 17, 675, n. 32.

[20] Other aspects are developed in PROCEEDINGS OF CONFERENCE OF SOCIAL WORK (1928), at 129 *et seq.*

means nothing. Hence: not the elimination of rules, but the setting of words and paper in perspective.

The Place and Treatment of Concepts

Like rules, concepts are not to be eliminated; it cannot be done. Behavior is too heterogeneous to be dealt with except after some artificial ordering. The sense impressions which make up what we call observation are useless unless gathered into some arrangement. Nor can thought go on without categories.

A realistic approach would, however, put forward two suggestions on the making of such categories. The first of them rests primarily upon the knowledge that to classify is to disturb. It is to build emphases, to create stresses, which obscure some of the data under observation and give fictitious value to others—a process which can be excused only insofar as it is necessary to the accomplishing of a purpose. The data to be singled out in reference to that purpose are obviously those which appear most relevant. But true relevancy can be determined only as the inquiry advances. For this reason a realistic approach to any new problem would begin by scepticism as to the adequacy of the *received* categories for ordering the phenomena effectively toward a solution of the new problem. It is quite possible that the received categories as they already stand are perfect for the purpose. It is, however, altogether unlikely. The suggestion then comes to this: that with the new purpose in mind one approach the data afresh, taking them in as raw a condition as possible, and discovering how far and how well the available traditional categories really cover the most relevant of the raw data. And that before proceeding one undertake such modifications in the categories as may be necessary or look promising. In view of the tendency toward over-generalization in the past this is likely to mean the making of smaller categories—which may be either sub-groupings inside the received categories, or may cut across them.

The other suggestion of a realistic approach rests on the observation that categories and concepts, once formulated and once they have entered into thought processes, tend to take on an appearance of solidity, reality and inherent value which has no foundation in experience. More than this: although orginally formulated on the model of at least some observed data, they tend, once they have entered into the organization of thinking, both to suggest the presence of corresponding data when these data are not in fact present, and to twist any fresh observation of data into conformity with the terms of the categories. This has been discussed above in its application to rules; it holds true, however, of any concept. It is peculiarly troublesome in regard to legal concepts, because of the tendency of the crystallized legal concept to persist after the fact model from which the concept was once derived has disappeared or changed out of recognition. A simple but striking instance is the resistance opposed by the "master-servant" concept to each readjustment along the lines of a new industrial labor situation. The counsel of the realistic approach here, then, would be the constant back-checking of the category against the data, to see whether the data are still present *in the form suggested by the category-name.* This slows up thinking. But it makes for results which means something when one gets them.

Background of the Behavior Approach

All this is nothing new in social science. It is of a piece with the work of the modern ethnographer. He substitutes painstaking objective description of practice, for local *report* of what the practice is, or for (what is worse) a report either of local practice or of local ideology pleasantly distorted by the observor's own home-grown conventions. It is of a piece with the development of objective method in psychology. It fits into the pragmatic and instrumental developments in logic.[21] It seeks to capitalize the methodological worries that have been working through in these latter years to new approaches in sociology, economics, political science. The only novel feature is the application to that most conventionalized and fiction-ridden of disciplines, the law. In essence the historical school of jurists from the one side, and Bentham and later Ihering from the other, were approaching the lines of theorizing here put forth. Holmes' mind had travelled most of the road two generations back. What has been done in the last decades that has some touch of novelty, is for theorizers to go beyond theorizing, to move, along such lines as these, into the gathering and interpretation of facts about legal behavior: Ehrlich, Nussbaum, Hedemann, Brandeis, Frankfurter, Moore, Clark, Douglas, Moley, Yntema, Klaus, Handler, Lambert[22]—I name only enough to show that neither a single country nor a

---

[21] Mortimer Adler suggests to me that the operational approach to modern physics is a classic analogue and precursor.

[22] The work of the different men moves in somewhat different fields, and is uneven in value. The same holds often of different work of the same man. And an exhaustive bibliography of all that has been done along the lines discussed would be long. Probably most titles would fall in the useful but less advanced field of discovering the appellate courts' real practice as distinct from the paper pattern of courts or writers. The names listed were chosen with reference to work at the next stage beyond: facts as to lower court operations, and the beginnings of inquiry into the contact-area between official and layman's conduct. EHRLICH (Czernowitz), GRUNDLEGUNG EINER SOZIOLOGIE DES RECHTS, and see PAGE, PRO. ASSN. AM. L. S. (1914), 46. Unfortunately most of the findings of his investigations into "living law" are inaccessible. NUSSBAUM (Berlin), in his RECHTSTATSACHEN-FORSCHUNG; HEDEMANN (Jena), REICHSGERICHT UND WIRTSCHAFSRECHT; Brandeis, the brief in *Muller v. Oregon*, and his opinions, repeatedly; FRANKFURTER

single school is involved, and to make clear that the point of view has moved beyond the stage of chatter and has proved itself in operation. That out of the way, I should like to glance at a few further implications of the approach.

Administrative Action as Law

Three of them appear together. First, to focus on the area of contact between judicial behavior and the behavior of the "governed" is to stress *interactions.* Second, central as are the judges' actions in disputed cases, there is a vast body of other officials whose actions are of no less importance; quantitatively their actions are of vastly greater importance, though it may well be that the judge's position gives him a leverage of peculiar power. In what has preceded I have somewhat lightly argued as if judge and court were the be-all and end-all of the legal focus. It is time to reformulate, to grow at once more accurate and more inclusive.[23] The actions of these other officials touch the interested layman more often than do those of the judge; increasingly so, and apparently increasing at a rising rate of increase as the administrative machine gains in force and function. More often than not, administrative action is, *to the layman affected,* the last expression of the law on the case. In such a situation, I think it highly useful to regard it as the law of the case. I see no gain whatever, and much loss, from setting up a fictitious unity in the law, when some officials do one thing, some another, and the courts now and again a third. Realistically, the law is then not one, but at least three, and by no means three-in-one. If what the courts do ultimately prevails *and is translated into* administrative practice, that is that. If such an event is predictable in advance, I find it vastly more useful to think of that event as the emerging unity of the law, which until it happens may be an ought, and is already an opportunity (at a price) for him with gumption and money to reach for it, but is not *yet* the probable law for the ordinary case. What—more

AND LANDIS (Harvard), THE BUSINESS OF THE SUPREME COURT (1928); FRANKFURTER AND GREEN, THE LABOR INJUNCTION (1930); Underhill Moore (Yale), mimeographed and MS. materials on banking in relation to the law of banking; Moore and Shamos, *Interest on the Balances of Checking Accounts* (1927) 27 COLUMBIA LAW REV. 633; C. E. Clark (Yale), MS. materials on the actual practice of litigation in Connecticut and New York; partial results appear in the CONN. BAR J. for July, 1928, April and July, 1929, and the W. VA. L. J. for Dec. 1929; Wm. Douglas (Yale), study in bankruptcy and insolvency practice, still under way; Moley (Columbia), the crime surveys, generally; Yntema and Theo. Hope (Johns Hopkins), pending investigations into the use of federal jurisdiction and into the actual course of litigation in state courts; Klaus (Columbia), *Sale, Agency and Price Maintenance* (1928) 28 COLUMBIA LAW REV. 312, 441; Handler (Columbia), *False and Misleading Advertising* (1929) 39 YALE L. J. 22; IHIGAHI, LE DROIT CORPORATIF INTERNATIONAL DE LA VENTE DE SOILS (1928); and Klaus' excellent review (1928) 28 COLUMBIA LAW REV. 991.

[23] The reformulation would complicate the preceding argument, but would not essentially change it. Except insofar as the argument would thereby gain cogency.

than one law, on a single point, in a single jurisdiction, according to the whim or practice of an official, or according to the funds or temperament or political complexion of the layman affected? Just that. What else expresses the facts? Why blink and squint because the paper tradition is annoyed? As long as there are words to describe the court rule which will ultimately prevail (in a case where it will!), and to describe the situation differently before and after the victory, what is gained in a *science of observation* by using the same words to describe both conditions—except a sure confusion?[24]

Hence I argue that the focus, the center of law, is not merely what the judge does, in the impact of that doing on the interested layman, but what *any* state official does, officially.[25] Lawyers are curious. As to a *court* of first instance, though it be a justice's court, they would have no difficulty seeing this. They could even see that a wrong decision below, appealed from and reversed, would be part of the troubles of a litigant, would reduce his effective rights—how often do they jockey the case to bring about a settlement, by trading on just such friction-factors! But to say that the decision of the eighteen hundred dollar clerk in Bureau *B* that certain expenses are not deductible from my income tax return *is* the law in my case, gives a lawyer's ideology the same shock that it gives to a political scientist to urge that for purposes of that decision, that official *is* the State. One needs again to wash the matter down with Holmes' "cynical acid" and see what is left. In the same manner, if the official's decision is adverse and erroneous, I should include as a subtraction from my effective rights, if I proceeded to get a reversal, the ill-will and subsequent trouble I might incur at the hands of that official; as a part of the law, if I won; and its predictability as a determining part of the law, if I decided not to fight.

---

[24] On the *normative* side of law no confusion or doubt would exist in this case. The "right rule" would be the same all along. But that is no reason for obscuring the divergence in the results, on the level of description and prediction. We need, precisely for such purposes, to sever the normative from the descriptive aspects of law. Moreover, results affect norms, quite as much as norms affect results. If the outcome were going to be the overthrow of the judicial by the administrative practice, in the case put, the norm would pending outcome be in considerable doubt. And one of the (quite incidental) advantages of the approach contended for is to make explicit, understandable, *and non-shocking* the fact and realm of occurrence of such doubts as to norm.

[25] If we were dealing with a society which lacked political organization, this obviously would be a bad terminology. But another of the futilities of overgeneralization in the law has been the attempt to find *one* set of terms to cover the institutions of disparate societies. Before political organization we find control, and often specialized or semi-specialized control institutions. But in describing a politically organized society it is exceedingly convenient to limit the term to the official Big Stick. A convenient term for the closely similar "law" of the subgroup in such a society is "by-law." Sociologically the two are often more similar than dissimilar. *Cf.* Max Weber, Wirtschaft u. Gesellschaft, 16, 17, 27 etc.; and 15 Am. Ec. Rev. 672 *et seq.*

Laymen's Behavior as a Part of Law

Interactions between official behavior and laymen's behavior, first; and second, the recognition of official behavior of all officials as part of the core of law. Third, and an immediate part of both, the recognition of what Nicholas Spykman so strongly and properly stresses: that the word "official" tacitly presupposes, connotes, reaches out to include, all those patterns of action (ordering, initiative) and obedience (including passivity) on the part both of the official and of all laymen affected which *make up* the official's position and authority as such. Something of this sort is the idea underlying "consent of the governed," "ultimate dependence upon public opinion," and the like; but these older phrasings have no neatness of outline; they do not even suggest the need of sharp-edged drawing, which I take to be the reason why they act as a soporific, while the Spykman formulation acts as a stimulant to the curiosity and imagination. In a passing it is well to note that here, too, Max Weber's method of formulation becomes classic: the official exists as such precisely *insofar as* such patterns of action and obedience prevail.[26] I agree whole-heartedly that these patterns are an essential part of any phenomena we call law. The more whole-heartedly because Spykman's formulation brings out with fresh emphasis the difference between paper rules and resultant behavior, and the extent to which the behavior which results (if any) from the official formulation of a rule depends on the patterns of thought and action of the persons whose behavior is in question.

The Need for Narrower, More Concrete Study

How far these patterns can be presupposed, how far they require specific examination, depends on the individual case. Here as throughout we run into the need for reexamining the majestic categories of the romantic period of jurisprudence. The old categories are imposing in their purple, but they are all too big to handle. They hold too many heterogeneous items to be of any use. What is true of some law simply will not hold of other law. What is true of some persons as to some law will not hold of other persons, even as to the same or similar law.[27] I care not how reclassification be made, so long as it is in terms of observation and of organizing the data usably, *and* with back-check to the facts. But reclassification is called for. From another angle, what we

[26] In the same way (borrowing Spykman again) *to the extent that* the official's behavior plays into these interlocking patterns of action it becomes "official" rather than personal behavior, and so of direct interest here. "Purely" personal behavior of an official approaches inconceivability; but substantially personal behavior may take up a great bulk of a given official's time.

[27] *Cf.* PRO. CONF. SOCIAL WORK (1928), 129, 131, *et seq.*

need is patience to look and see what is there; and to do that we must become less ambitious as to how much we are going to look at all at once.

An illustration may make the point clearer. Some "rules" are aimed at controlling and affecting the behavior of persons whose whole set and interest is opposed to making the adjustment desired; others are aimed at affecting behavior of persons who are not only willing to adjust, but have an existing effective machinery for accomplishing the adjustment. A type of the first is almost any phase of professional crime; a type of the second, perhaps, would be some change in the law affecting city real estate transactions which happens to be desired by the dealers. Most cases are compounded of both elements. If city real estate alone is involved, much might be said at first blush for law reform being peculiarly easy and quick, because the practice is firmly entrenched of never entering a real estate deal without consulting a lawyer. But other practices are also entrenched, such as relying upon first mortgage finance from a particular type of concern which in turn insists upon a title policy which in turn is under control of companies whose interest runs counter to certain types of law reform. The troubles of Torrens titles in New York City are an instance. They are substantially unmarketable; no mortgage company will loan on them because no title company will insure them.[28] That is, however, an instance of attempted "helpful-device" legal innovation. It is a different problem from the "ordering-and-forbidding" legal innovation. Barring questions of constitutionality, and barring the political question of how far legislation running counter to the desires of a well organized and powerful group can be achieved at all, it is obvious that enforcement of a new prescribed style of doing business upon New York City title companies would be *prima facie* a promising problem of legal engineering, precisely because their business is localized, well organized, and run by relatively few business units. Unlike the professional criminal, they could not dive underground and survive. The problem of detection would therefore be one of detecting not persons, but infractions by known units; and their deals could almost certainly be forced into the open. The major policing problem would therefore in all likelihood become one of anticipating and barring out in advance "evasions" undertaken by changing the methods of business under advice of counsel: *i.e.*, a problem of initially or subsequently so framing the official formulae of ordering and forbidding that transactions could not be accomplished (at a profit, after deducting fines, etc.) except along lines of the general purposes of the legislation. True,

---

[28] Thus one Torrens title to one lot in a block makes the block unavailable for large scale improvement. R. R. B. Powell tells me that Torrens titles have even on occasion been de-registered, in order to gain access to mortgage money.

unless the engineering were so successful that a somewhat comparably profitable new turn to the business developed, the legislator would have to reckon not only with initial, but with persistent and highly skilled resistance—which might even take the line it once did with the railroads, of seeking to capture the governmental machine. And it is of course this type of resistance which would in fact (contrary to our hypothesis) keep the constitutional issue in the forefront of the fight. The parallels and the divergencies from regulation or prohibition of liquor traffic would be instructive. As one moves to bank robberies or jewelry thefts the parallels begin to fade out and the divergencies to sharpen. I have purposely chosen an illustration from a field in which I am blankly ignorant, in order to bring out the lines of thought and inquiry which open, under the approach, *even before the gathering of data is begun.* It is obvious that the set or attitude of those affected or sought to be affected by any piece of "law" is at the heart of the problem of control; it should be equally obvious that the style of organization of those persons, their group ways of action—whether among themselves or with regard to society at large—is equally vital. Behavior effects depend upon present behavior conditions.

The Narrow Application of Most Rules—and Its Implications

This leads directly into the next point: most pieces of law affect only a *relatively* small number of persons ever or at all, with any directness—or are intended to. Where that is the case, the *organization, attitude, present and probable behavior of the persons sought to be affected* is what needs major consideration, from the angle of getting results (or of understanding results). Indeed, the very *identification* of those persons may be a precondition calling for much study. Which is a somewhat absurdly roundabout way of saying that unless those matters are studied, the rules drawn, and the administrative behavior adapted to the persons in question, results will be an accident. *"To the persons in question,"* and, indeed, "to those persons *under the conditions in question.*" It cannot be too strongly insisted that our attitude toward "rules" of law, treating them as universal in *application,* involves a persistent twisting of observation. "Rules" in the realm of action *mean* what rules *do;* "rules" in the realm of action *are* what they do. The *possible* application and applicability are not without importance, but the *actual* application and applicability are of controlling importance. To think of rules as universals—especially, to think of them as being applicable to "all persons who bring themselves within their terms"—is to muffle one's eyes in a constitutional fiction before beginning a survey of the scene. To be sure, constitutions purport to require rules of law to be "equal and general."[29] But most rules, however general as to the few they cover, are highly special, when viewed from the angle of how many citizens there are. And most rules "applying" to "all who come within their terms" (all those who set up barber shops, or are tempted to commit murder, or to bribe officials, or to embezzle from banks or certify checks without the drawer having funds, or to adopt a child, or run a manufacturing establishment employing five or more persons) do not and will not, realistically considered, ever be "applicable" in any meaningful sense of the term, to *most* people in the community. Such rules are indeed open. Persons do move in and out of the sphere of their applicability. But that sphere is much more clearly seen, when viewed (as compared with the community) as narrow, as special, as peculiar. Obviously even more special is the sphere of *real* application: of official *behavior* with reference to application. (And is it not clear that this most special sphere is the one of greatest consequence to the persons on whose behavior any results depend: the objects of the "regulation?")[30]

I know of no consequence of the approach here contended for—the approach in terms of organized behavior interacting with organized behavior—no consequence more illuminating than this immediate opening up for study of the sub-group and institutional structure both of "governors" and of "governed." Its opening up for study as a first essential to any understanding at all, as making the study of law a study in first instance of particularized situations and what happens in or can be done about them.[31]

---

[29] In practice this comes to: *"equable* in the choice of the very limited class to be affected." *Equality* of rule is impossible in a specialized society. It is true that some few of the lines of discrimination which are under our system excluded from consideration, are suggested by the word "equality." But it is not particularly significant, save historically.

[30] I have stressed elsewhere that the vital problem in such cases is that of creating in the conduct of the relevant persons new *practices* (folkways) which conform to the purposes sought *via* the new legal rules. PROC. CONF. SOC. WORK (1928), at 132 *et seq.* And that the effectiveness of legal rules, old or new, is not to be measured simply by how often officials act in accordance with them. *Ibid.*, and 15 AM. EC. REV. 682. Indeed the ideal effectiveness is not achieved until officials do not have to act at all. But if the rules are of the kind which coincide roughly with ancient, established lay practice *(mores)* it becomes a serious problem how far we have in such cases effectiveness of the *legal rule,* or of the occasional official behavior with reference to the rule. Contrast the extreme opposite case: an entire organized line of activity all units of which are prepared to move or not to move along lines newly prescribed, according to the outcome in court of a deliberately chosen test case. It is behavior of officials *alone,* but behavior of officials in its *interaction* with that of the relevant laymen.

[31] What is wanted in the way of generalization must come from a resynthesis of such particularized studies, when we have them. Meantime, we have our common sense and tradition-given understanding of *some* of the regularities of official behavior, and sufficient traditional skills in predicting, influencing, managing official or other behavior to get on after a fashion, in practice, while we learn more.

Realism as to "Society"

"What can be done," and by whom? I have spoken of law as a means: *whose* means, to *whose* end? Discussions of law, like discussions of "social control," tend a little lightly to assume "*a* society" and to assume the antecedent discovery of "social" objectives. Either is hard to find in any sense which corresponds with the facts of control. Where is the unity, the single coherent group? Where is the demonstrable objective which is social, and not opposed by groups well nigh as important as those which support it? And law in particular presents over most, if not all of its bulk, the phenomenon of clashing interests, of antagonistic persons or groups, with officials stepping in to favor some as against some others. Either to line up the dissenter in the interests of his own group; that is one broad phase. Or to regulate the relations between two groups, or to alter the terms of the struggle (competitive or other) between them. Hence the eternal fight for the control of the machinery of law, and of law making, whereby the highly interested *A*s can hope partially to force their will upon the equally but adversely interested *B*s, and to put behind that control the passive approval and support of the great body of *C*s—who happen to be disinterested, or, what is equally to the point, uninterested. To the truth of this observation it makes little difference whether the ends of the *A*s are material or idealistic whether wholly selfish, or dedicated most altruistically to some concept of the welfare of the whole. And while this welter with regard to change in law may, if you will, be thought of as political, the presence of the welter raises problems in defining "interests." One must also recur to the fact that it is on the same welter that official behavior is expected to be brought to bear when the new "rule" has been proclaimed.[32] Thus raising all the problems raised above, with this addition: the possibility, not there mentioned, of a group of laymen pushing to help the official program through.

One matter does need mention here, however: the eternal dilemna of the law, indeed of society; and of the law because the law purports peculiarly among our institutions to "represent" the whole. There is, amid the welter of self-serving groups, clamoring and struggling over this machine that will give power over others, the recurrent emergence of some wholeness, some sense of responsibility which outruns enlightened self-interest, and results in action apparently headed (often purposefully) for the common good. To affirm this is to confess no Hege-

[32] Not quite the same. The fight and victory may have somewhat changed the picture. And the enactment of a new formula has some consequences in itself: among others, that the formula chosen imposes temporary (though sometimes wide) limits upon what the officials can do, whereas the prior struggle is typically in terms of policies, not measures.

lian mysticism of the State. It leaves quite open any question of the existence of some "life principle" in a society. It merely notes that, lacking such a self-sanation in terms of the whole, the whole would not indefinitely continue as a whole. And to deny that would be folly. It would be to carry emancipation from the idle ideology of "representation of the whole" into blindness to the half-truth around which that once-precious ideology was built. But to deny the emancipation, to worship the half truth without dire and specific concern for the details of the welter, would be a folly quite as great.[33]

What Law is Thought to Be: Folk-Law

In all the emphasis placed upon behavior I may have created the impression that a "realistic" approach would make itself unrealistic by disregarding what people *think* law is. Not so. But a realistic approach would cut at once into analysis and subdivision of the terms "people," "think," and "law" in such a phrase. For the great mass of persons not particularly concerned, I suspect that "law" in this aspect, *so far as* it concerns themselves, means "what I ought to do" and is not much distinguished from those selective slight idealizations of current practice we think of as morals. At times the issue certainly gets closer: "I want this contract to stick"—and doubtless I will then think of putting it in writing, and will meditate on reciting a formula I saw somewhere (in a deed, was it?): "for one dollar and other good and valuable considerations"; I may get a witness to the signing, too. In the field of private law we know singularly little of this folk-law-in-action. In that of criminal law we can suspect a very rough coincidence of folk-law-in-action with folk-morality-in-action,[34] except that here and there the thought of cop

[33] It is along the same line that I feel strongly the unwisdom, when turning the spotlight on behavior, of throwing overboard emphasis on rules, concepts, ideology, and ideological stereotypes or patterns. These last are, by themselves, confusing, misleading, inadequate to describe or explain. But a jurisprudence which was practically workable could not have been built in terms of them, if they had not contained a goodly core of truth and sense. To be sure, it was not the precept-ideology of jurisprudence, but the practice that jurisprudence only partly mirrored, which actually worked. But one thing sociological study ought to do for the advance of science is to school the advocates of new insight no longer to junk wholesale the old insight against which they are rebelling. The rebelling indicates inadequacy in the old. It does not indicate that the old did not have much solid basis. The bare fact that the old exists, could come into existence and persist, evidences that it had. If we can examine it for what it has, and carry that with us into a new alignment, we shall do much to reduce the well-known pendulum swing from exaggeration to exaggeration. This is of less moment in the early stages of a new movement. The innovator carries over willy-nilly the virtues of the same training against which he is in intellectual revolt. But those newly trained in the new school will be half-trained unsound exaggerators, if the original innovators fail to incorporate *in their doctrine as in their practice* the life-power of the older school, even while attacking the latter's false emphases and implications.

[34] May I insist again at this point that "folk morality" really means at least as many important varieties in specific details as there are sub-groups within the main group?

and jail will work deterrently when plain external and internal non-official social sanctions might not wholly click; we can suspect further that over considerable fields criminal law is too new and too specialized to have much background or counterpart in folk-morality; and, finally, that some fairly wide bodies of non-moral (or not yet moral) criminal law aspects will have percolated into folk-law: I think of traffic law (as known to the traffickers) as distinctly in advance in most places of traffic morality, and of similar discrepancies in regard to liquor, gambling, and sex matters, as to some portions of a population with variant morals. Now clearly what people think law to be, as regards themselves, has some effect at times upon their action. My guess is, however, the effect on the side of forbidding is much slighter than the lawyer is likely to imagine, whenever any important pressure of self-interest is present, except for a relatively small minority, or over relatively small areas of action for any particular person. On the other hand, my guess is that in the field in which law provides "helpful devices"—the attempt to use which presupposes concurrent self-interest—folk-law has very considerable influence in shaping conduct. The problem calls for exploration, from the realist's angle, by cautious study of detail. Even more important, I suspect, is the problem of what law is supposed to be with regard to others than the supposer. But important in accounting less for action than for inaction. For it seems likely that in this aspect law is mainly conceived simply as being all right, without concern for detail; and that this aspect of folk-law is close to the heart of the grand-scale passive cooperation of the uninterested which makes control of the political machinery a prize.

Ideals as to What Law Ought to Be

No less important than what people think law is, is what people conceive that law should be. Any change in law is in good part a reflection of someone's desire to produce a difference. And just as attitudes and expectations must be taken into account along with overt behavior, so must purposes and the ideal pictures toward which purposes drive. Thus far, even from the angle of a purely descriptive science.

Into another aspect of ideals as to what law ought to be this paper does not attempt to go. I make no effort here to indicate either the proper rule, or the proper action on any legal subject. I do, however, argue, and with some vigor, that as soon as one turns from the *formulation* of ideals to their *realization,* the approach here indicated is vital to his making headway. It is only in terms of a sound descriptive science of law (or of what is roughly equivalent, a soundly built working art, which takes equal account of conditions) that ideals move beyond the stage of dreams. Moreover, as has so often been pointed out, both the feasibility of accomplishing a policy and the cost of its accomplishment are in a world of limited possibilities vital elements in arriving at a judgment of the worthwhileness of the policy itself.

Conclusion

In conclusion, then, may I repeat that I have been concerned not at all with marking a periphery of law, with defining "it," with *excluding* anything at all from its field. I have argued that the trend of the most fruitful thinking about law has run steadily toward regarding law as an engine (a heterogenous multitude of engines) having purposes, not values in itself; and that the clearer visualization of the problems involved moves toward ever-decreasing emphasis on words, and ever-increasing emphasis on observable behavior (in which any demonstrably probable attitudes and thought-patterns should be included). Indeed that the focus of study, the point of reference for all things legal has been shifting, and should now be consciously shifted to the area of contact, of interaction, between official regulatory behavior and the behavior of those affecting or affected by official regulatory behavior; and that the rules and precepts and principles which have hitherto tended to keep the limelight should be displaced, and treated with severe reference to their bearing upon that area of contact—in order that paper rules may be revealed for what they are, and rules with real behavior correspondences come into due importance. That the complex phenomena which are lumped under the term "law" have been too broadly treated in the past, and that a realistic understanding, possible only in terms of observable behavior, is again possible only in terms of study of the way in which persons and institutions are organized in our society, and of the cross-bearings of any particular *part* of law and of any particular *part* of the social of the social organization.

Included in the field of law under such an approach is everything currently included, and a vast deal more. At the very heart, I suspect, is the behavior of judges, peculiarly, that part of their behavior which marks them as judges—those practices which establish the continuity of their office with their predecessors and successors, and which make their official contacts with other persons; but that suspicion on my part may be a relic of the case law tradition in which we American lawyers have been raised. Close around it on the one hand lies the behavior of other government officials. On the other, the sets of accepted formulae which judges recite, seek light from, try to follow. Distinguishing here the formulae with close behavior-correspondences from others; those of frequent application from those of infrequent. Close around these again, lie various persons' ideas of what the law is; and especially their views of what it or some part of it ought to accomplish. At first hand contact with officials' behavior, from another angle, lies the social set-up where the official's acts impinge directly on it; and behind that the social set-up which resists or furthers or reflects the impingement of his acts. Farther from the center lies legal and social philosophy—approaching that center more directly in proportion as the materials with which it deals are taken directly from the center. Part of law, in many aspects, is all of society, and all of man in society. But that is a question of periphery and not of center, of the reach of a specific problem in hand, not of a general discussion. As to the overlapping of the field as thus sketched with that of other social sciences, I should be sorry if no overlapping were observable. The social sciences are not staked out like real estate. Even in law the sanctions for harmless trespass are not heavy.

KARL N. LLEWELLYN

COLUMBIA LAW SCHOOL

WHAT IS A LEGAL ACT?*

HANS KELSEN

Translated by Bonnie Paulson and Stanley L. Paulson

How is it decided that an act is, indeed, a legal act? Alfred Verdross, like Hans Kelsen and Adolf Merkl a leading writer in the Vienna School of Legal Philosophy, puts this question in his paper "An Antinomy of Legal Theory." Kelsen replies to Verdross in the paper translated here, dividing Verdross's question into two parts: a conceptual question—What is a legal act?—and a concrete legal question—Is this particular act a legal act? The first question is for legal theorists, the second, for legal officials. In answer to the first question, Kelsen argues that a legal act is an act by means of which a legal norm is issued or applied. The second question is more difficult, at least in the case of revolutionary acts and in the case of acts of legal officials who have in a particular instance overstepped the bounds of their authority. These kinds of cases give rise to conceptual issues, which Kelsen considers at length. He also touches on efficacy, the basic norm, the significance of a constitutive determination of facts, judicial review, a court's examination of the legal act apart from any exercise of review powers, etc.

In a very interesting essay, "An Antimony of Legal Theory,"[1] Professor Alfred Verdross considers the question of how an act is legitimated [*legitimieren*] as a legal act. He grants that legitimation normally takes place in a legal proceeding established to examine the act in question, that it is normally the result of an act of [recognition

*["Was ist ein Rechtsakt?" first appeared in the *Oesterreichische Zeitschrift für öffentcliches Recht*, vol. 4 (1952), pp. 263-274, and was reprinted in *Die Wiener Rechtstheoretische Schvle*, H. Klecatsky, R. Marcic, and H. Schambeck, eds. (Vienna: Europa Verlag, 1968), vol. 2, pp. 1381-1393, and in the *Internationale Festschrift für Alfred Verdross zum 80. Geburtstag*, R. Marcic, H. Mosler, E. Suy, and K. Zemanek, eds. (Munich and Salzburg: Wilhelm Fink Verlag, 1971), pp. 153-165. The translation is printed with the kind permission of Mrs. Maria K. Feder, Kensington, California, and the Springer-Verlag, Vienna.

The translators' footnotes, in brackets, are flagged with letters in the text; Kelsen's own footnotes are numbered.]

1. Alfred Verdross, "Eine Antinomie der Rechtstheorie," 73 *Juristische Blätter* (1951), pp. 169-171 [reprinted in *Die Wiener Rechtstheoretische Schule*, H. Klecatsky, R. Marcic, and H. Schambeck, eds. (Vienna: Europa Verlag, 1968), vol. 2, pp. 1375-1380. References to Verdross in the footnotes below are abbreviated, using "*Jur. Bl.*" for the original printing and "*Wiener Schule*" for the reprinting.]

by] a duly authorized legal organ.[b] Since, however, this process of review must come to an end and since there will be, at the end, a legal act that cannot be reviewed further, an act protected in other words by the doctrine of finality, the question arises: "Who, then, decides whether the act of an authorized legal organ is indeed an act protected by the doctrine of finality?"[c] Verdross concludes that in the last analysis this question is not answered on the basis of the legal system, neither by means of another legal act in a legal proceeding, as one theory claims, nor, as another claims, through the discipline of legal theory. This question is not answered on the basis of the legal system at all but rather through the discipline of sociology. In what follows, I would like to comment on Verdross's position.

First of all, I believe that two different questions must be kept straight. One question is: What is a legal act? Or: According to what criteria can one distinguish a legal act from an act not having the character of a legal act? This first question aims at defining the abstract concept of the legal act. The second question, different from the first, is this: Who decides? Or, put more generally, how is it decided that a certain act representing itself subjectively as a legal act, that is, claiming to be a legal act, is objectively a legal act? How, in other words, is it decided in a concrete case that the criteria distinguishing the legal act are met?

The first question is answered by legal theory, which has the task of defining the concept of the legal act as well as all other legal concepts. The question may well be answered differently in different schools of legal theory. The Pure Theory of Law defines the concept of the legal act as follows: A legal act is an act by means of which a legal norm is issued (figuratively speaking, "created") or applied. Moreover, the Pure Theory claims that an act is a law-creating or law-applying act only if it corresponds to the norms that govern the creation and application of the law within the legal system, that is, only if the act in question is based on the legal system. That the law governs its own creation and application is a characteristic of the normative order as a dynamic system. This characteristic is described in the hierarchical

---

a. [Here and at a number of points below Kelsen uses "*legitimieren*" in contexts where one might have expected forms of the verb "to recognize" ("*anerkennen*"). In fact, Kelsen appears to be assuming that legal recognition is sufficient for legitimation of an act as a legal act; see, *e.g.*, p. 208 *infra*. Verdross for his part does not use "*legitimieren*" at all in the paper "*Eine Antinomie der Rechtstheorie.*"]

b. [See, on the concept of the legal organ, Hans Kelsen, *Reine Rechtslehre*, 2d ed. (Vienna: Franz Deuticke Verlag, 1960), § 30 (c); Felix Ermacora, *Allgemeine Staatslehre* (West Berlin: Duncker & Humblot, 1970), vol. 2, pp. 912-923.]

c. [Verdross, *Jur. Bl.*, p. 169; *Wiener Schule*, p. 1376.]

theory [*Stufentheorie*] developed by Adolf Merkl, according to which the legal system consists of higher-order and lower-order norms. Higher-order norms govern the creation of [lower-order][d] norms, while lower-order norms correspond to—that is, are created on the basis of—the higher-order norms. If legal norms can be created only in correspondence to other norms, that is, only on the basis of the legal system, then the formation of law is also the application of law, and law-creating acts are also law-applying acts. The definition of the legal act as a law-applying act presupposes, however, that the norms in question, which both govern the creation of law and are applied in that creation, are understood to include not just positive norms, that is, norms issued by means of legal acts in a legal proceeding. The norms of, historically speaking, the first constitution, especially of a constitution established by revolution, are not created in correspondence to pre-existing, positive norms, that is, norms issued by means of legal acts. Constitutional norms are set in correspondence to a basic norm, a norm that is not issued but only presupposed. And the presupposition is: One ought to act as the constitution prescribes.

It should be noted, however, that the basic norm has reference only to an efficacious constitution. For, as the Pure Theory emphasizes, a constitution is considered binding only if it is for the most part efficacious, that is, only if the individuals whose behavior is regulated by the constitution do in fact generally behave in accordance with it. This is the principle of *efficacy*, which therefore must be included in the formulation of the basic norm.[2] The definition of the legal act as an act based on the legal system can be maintained, then, only if the concept of the legal system is not limited to positive norms but is understood to include, along with positive norms based on the constitution, the norms of the constitution itself—including the presupposed basic norm, the foundation of the constitution. And the concept of the legal system must be spelled out in this way, for a constitution cannot be conceived of as a binding norm apart from its foundation, the basic norm. If the norms of the constitution are components of

---

d. [We are reading, here, "lower-order norms" where Kelsen in fact writes "other norms" ("*andere Normen*"); this reading makes it clear that the expression "lower-order norms" at the point of the insertion and again later in the same sentence refers to one and the same body of norms.]

2. This is correct insofar as the legal system is isolated as a domestic legal system and is not considered within the framework of the international legal order. In the latter, the principle of efficacy is a component of positive international law. (See my *General Theory of Law and State* [Cambridge, Mass.: Harvard University Press, 1945], pp. 121ff.) The following discussion, however, takes as its point of departure the first of the perspectives mentioned here.

the legal system, then the basic norm, too, must be seen as belonging to the legal system. If legal positivism is understood to mean that only positive norms—only norms issued by means of human acts—can be considered law, then the principle of legal positivism is possible only with this qualification. To say this much is not to yield ground to the natural law theory, for the basic norm formulated by legal theory has only a formal, not a material character. The basic norm is the foundation of every efficacious constitution, whatever the content of legal norms issued on the basis of this constitution may be, even if they conflict with norms regarded as part of the natural law. Accordingly, legal theory is to define the law as a system of (coercive) norms issued by means of human acts on the basis of the constitution and, if the constitution is for the most part efficacious, presupposed as binding. Here the constitution is to be understood as a norm (or plurality of norms) established by means of human acts and governing the creation of other norms.

The second question asks whether a particular act is a legal act. If this question involves nothing other than the logical subsumption of a concrete state of affairs under an abstract concept, then—like the question of whether a certain living being is a person or whether a certain metal is gold—it can be answered by anyone endowed with reason. Therefore the legal theorist, too, can answer the question of whether a particular act is a legal act, or, as it is sometimes put, reason can answer the question, reason as exercised by the legal theorist. The answer, however, can vary greatly, not only if there is no consensus on the definition of the concept but also if the existence of the concrete state of affairs is doubtful. There is, in the case of subsumption of a particular act under the concept of the legal act, an additional consideration. If the concept of the legal act is defined such that a legal act is an act based on the legal system, then subsumption is impossible without an interpretation of the legal system. And usually several, indeed, often conflicting interpretations are available. But the specifically legal problem, whether a particular act is a legal act, is not aimed at a purely logical subsumption at all. What matters is a *decision*, an authentic, constitutive, legally binding decision, to which the legal system attaches very specific consequences. Such a decision is not a mere function of reason but rather a function of the will; therefore, neither legal theory nor any other discipline is competent to take the decision. To take a legally binding decision means to issue a norm (an individual norm).

Legal theory as a discipline cannot produce norms. It can only describe and reproduce descriptively norms that have been produced by legal organs in legal proceedings, and it does this by formulating legal *propositions* (not to be confused with the legal *norms* issued by legal organs, which norms are the object of inquiry for legal theory). The jurist or legal theorist provides a representation of the law, while the legal organ creates and applies the law. The relation between legal theorist and legal organ is like that between musician and composer. The musician reproduces on an instrument a piece of music that the composer first produced. To be sure, one also says that the musician "interprets" the piece of music. And the legal theorist can express a view as to whether an act presenting itself subjectively as a legal act is objectively a legal act; expressing a view on the question is of course not precluded by the fact that legal theory cannot "decide" the question. When the United States Congress passes a law, anyone can express a view on whether the act is constitutional, on whether or not it is a binding legal act. But a view expressed in this way is legally irrelevant, for the legal system attaches to it no consequences whatever. Suppose, however, that the law passed by Congress is to be applied in a judicial proceeding according to a judge's subjective view of the matter, and suppose the judge is of the view that the statute is unconstitutional, that this congressional enactment is not, in other words, a binding legal act. Then the judge, in accordance with the present legal system, is to forbear from applying the enactment, passed by Congress and presenting itself subjectively as law. The judge is to decide the case at hand as though this enactment had never been passed, as though the act did not exist. Only if the judge is of the view that the congressional enactment is constitutional, that it is a binding legal act, only then is he to apply it as law to the case at hand. The judge's view on the constitutionality or unconstitutionality of the congressional enactment, his view, that is to say, of the legal character of the act in question, is not the mere logical subsumption of a concrete state of affairs under an abstract concept. It is not an intellectual operation; anyone, including the legal theorist, can undertake an intellectual operation. Rather, it is a decision that the judge alone is authorized to take and to which the legal system attaches consequences of the greatest significance.

Attaching certain consequences to certain facts qua conditions is the essence of the legal system. When, however, the legal system attaches in a general scheme certain consequences to certain facts qua conditions, then, in order that these consequences can be realized, the legal system must also specify how, in a concrete case, the existence of the facts qua conditions is reliably to be determined. It is therefore not the facts themselves but rather the constitutive determination of the facts, as arrived at in a legal proceeding, that is the decisive condition to which legal consequences are attached. Such a determination, in accordance with standing procedures, of the facts qua conditions is therefore unavoidable. If the fact qua condition is a legal act, then the existence of this legal act must in every case be ascertained in a legal proceeding, that is, by a legal organ. In this way it must be *decided* whether the act in question is a legal act, whether it is precisely that act to which the legal system attaches consequences. This means, again, that the legal organ responsible for bringing about the consequences must in every case examine whether the act in question is a legal act, even if the legal system has regulations that we speak of, most imprecisely, as precluding judicial review.

If the constitution directs the courts to apply the laws passed by parliament, it can, to be sure, also specify that the question of the constitutionality of such laws is not to be heard in the courts. The constitution cannot, however, forbid the courts to consider whether something representing itself subjectively as law has been passed by parliament and not by a private association. The legal system can prohibit ordinary courts from reviewing the constitutionality of an administrative act, reserving such review to a specific organ, for example, an administrative court. But the legal system cannot prevent ordinary courts from considering whether an act that serves as a presupposition of their decisions is indeed an administrative act, whether, that is to say, it is the act of an administrative official and not that of a private party. Consider a trespass complaint, brought by a property owner against someone who used a path on the property without permission. The defendant contends that the path had been declared public by the appropriate administrative official. Now the court cannot hand down a judgment for the plaintiff on the basis of a decision that the declaration of public use was illegal. It can, however, hold for the plaintiff on the basis of a decision that the act declaring the path public, while appearing to be an administrative act, is not really an administrative act since it was not the act of an administrative official at all. If the court decides that the act in question is an administrative act, that is, a legal act, then the court must reject the complaint. Even if not expressly formulated, this decision is included in the rejection of the complaint. In both of these instances—namely, the application of the congressional enactment as law in the one instance and the rejection of the trespass complaint in the other—the legal consequence specified by the legal system is attached not directly to the legal act in question but rather to the reliable determination of the act by the law-applying organ. Such a determination, however, is not possible without an examination of the act. This examination can be limited but never wholly precluded. Put generally: The consequences attached to a legal act cannot ensue without an examination of the act in question and a decision on its legal character.

This sort of examination and decision, however, is not to be identified with that special procedure whereby the legal system in certain cases provides for the examination of and a decision on questions of legality [*Rechtsmässigkeit*], that is, questions about the objective legal character of particular acts claiming subjectively to be legal acts. Such a procedure simply represents a special form of regulation, a special instance of what is necessary in all cases, namely, the examination of and a decision on the legal character of an act with which legal consequences are coupled. For example, one such special procedure is the appeals procedure, to which adjudicative decisions and certain administrative acts are subject. Since the appeals procedure is necessarily limited, it must lead to an act of the highest court, an act not subject to further review [*Ueberprüfung*] in the appeals procedure and customarily characterized in terms of the doctrine of finality. When, however, the legal system attaches consequences to a final act such as this, then this act too must be examined in a subsequent proceeding and its legal character must be reliably determined. (The legal system will always attach consequences to a final act, for the act is introduced into the law only for the sake of its consequences.) Verdross's very instructive example here is a final judgment of the highest court, which judgment must be carried out by the executory court and can be carried out only if the executory court validates the judgment as a final judgment of the highest court. The final act, protected by the doctrine of finality from further review, is therefore no argument against the thesis that the legal character of an act can be decided only in a legal proceeding and cannot be reliably determined by legal theory (though it must be reliably determined so that its consequences can ensue). At any rate, the question formulated by Verdross—"Who, then, decides whether the act of an authorized legal organ is indeed an act protected by the doctrine of finality?"[e]—cannot be answered by saying that the decision is left to legal theory, for legal theory, as already pointed out, cannot "decide" anything at all. The question can only be decided as follows: Either examination and a decision, aimed at repeal of or a change in the act, are rejected by the organ that performed the act or by other legal organs. Or, alternatively, the legal consequences attached to the act are in fact realized by the appropriate organs.

e. [Verdross, *Jur. Bl.*, p. 169; *Wiener Schule*, p. 1376.]

When an act representing itself according to its subjective meaning as a legal act is then legitimated in the subsequent legal proceeding as objectively a legal act, such legitimation can take place only on the basis of the legal system within which the act claims validity. Verdross, however, contends that there are acts that cannot, in a subsequent legal proceeding, be legitimated on the basis of the legal system. Or, as he puts it, there are cases where the nature of the [legal] organ comprising the acting individuals "can be determined only in a way other than on the basis of a legal system,"[f] the acts in question "cannot on the basis of the legal system be recognized as legal acts,"[g] their qualification as acts of a [legal] organ can "be recognized not by means of legal theory based on the legal system but only by means of a social theory that considers what actually happens socially."[h]

Verdross mentions two categories of such acts. One category comprises "acts of persons who are indeed [legal] organs otherwise but who have in a particular instance overstepped the bounds of their authority."[i] Verdross contends that these acts, "to the extent that they are not set right by other legal norms, cannot on the basis of the legal system be recognized as legal acts. Their subsequent qualification as acts of a [legal] organ can therefore . . . be attained only if they are considered binding [legal] acts in the subsequent legal proceeding and are thereby incorporated into the legal system." Verdross goes on to point out that this, however, is a determination that can be made only by sociology and not by legal theory.

Counting against Verdross's view, it is problematic to assume that the acting persons have "in a particular instance overstepped the bounds of their authority," problematic if the other assumption is correct, namely, that the acts are "considered binding [legal] acts" in the subsequent legal proceeding of the authorized [legal] organs. In whose view have the persons in question overstepped their authority? According to a provision of the Constitution of the United States, the President may conclude treaties only with the approval of the Senate. In fact the President has concluded many politically significant treaties without the approval of the Senate, and these treaties have been executed unreservedly by the appropriate organs of the federal system. Can one say, legally speaking, that the President has overstepped the bounds of his authority? Is such a judgment, if expressed by one who writes

---

f. [Verdross, *Jur. Bl.*, p. 170; *Wiener Schule*, p. 1379.]
g. [Verdross, *Jur. Bl.*, p. 170; *Wiener Schule*, p. 1380.]
h. [*Ibid.*]
i. [*Ibid.*]
j. [*Ibid.*]

about the law, anything but a legally irrelevant interpretation of the United States Constitution, opposed by the legally relevant interpretation arrived at by the President himself, who is authorized to apply the Constitution and therefore also to interpret it? Even if, contrary to fact, the Supreme Court had not declared constitutional certain treaties concluded by the President without the approval of the Senate, would it not be nonsense, legally speaking, to claim in such circumstances that the President has overstepped the bounds of his authority? How, in the subsequent proceeding of the legal organs, can an act be considered "binding" if at the same time it is considered illegal because it is the act of an unauthorized organ? And how, other than "on the basis of the legal system," can these [legal] organs consider the act binding, that is, consider themselves legally bound to realize the consequences attached to the act by the legal system? The administrative organs and courts of the United States, insofar as they execute treaties that have been concluded by the President without the approval of the Senate, decide that these presidential acts are binding legal acts, that they are not null and void. And that means the administrative organs and courts accept the President's interpretation of the Constitution, the interpretation the President himself sees as underlying his function as a [legal] organ authorized to conclude treaties. In these circumstances it is hardly possible to contend that the acts in question originally stood outside the legal system and were "incorporated into the legal system" only through the subsequent legal proceeding. But even if this description of the process in question were correct, the "subsequent qualification as acts of a [legal] organ" is still possible only "on the basis of the legal system" into which the acts in question are "incorporated." And the description of the process whereby the legal character of an act is decided by legal organs in the subsequent legal proceeding—not by legal theory or any other discipline—stays strictly within the framework of legal theory, [understood] as cognition of the legal system qua normative system.

The second category of acts that cannot on the basis of the legal system be legitimated in a subsequent legal proceeding comprises, according to Verdross, revolutionary acts. These acts take place in violation of the existing constitution, and insofar as the norms issued thereby become efficacious, the existing constitution is entirely or partly replaced by a new constitution. Verdross offers this example: Replacing a supreme court with a revolutionary organ that successfully claims the same competence represents only a partly revolutionary change in the constitution. A totally revolutionary change in the constitution, however, reveals far more clearly the peculiarities of the process whereby a revolutionary act is legitimated, namely, through the acquisition of efficacy on the part of the norm issued by means of that act. Such a total change should therefore be presupposed in what follows.

First of all, there is the question as to the basis of the assumption made in describing this process, the assumption that the act in question violates the existing constitution. Such an assumption is defensible only if the act presents itself, according to its subjective meaning, not as an application of the existing constitution (as does the above-mentioned act of the President of the United States) but rather as an act directed toward the establishment of a new system, a system that cannot be brought about through a change in the constitution made according to the rules of the constitution. The assumption requires furthermore that the individuals whose behavior is regulated by the new constitution behave in accordance with it, making clear by their behavior that they regard the act giving birth to the constitution as binding in itself, fully aware that the act is in no way the result of an application of the earlier constitution.

It is therefore obvious that the act establishing the constitution cannot, in the subsequent proceeding, be legitimated on the basis of the legal system prevailing at the moment the act is performed. As noted earlier, the act in no way represents itself according to its subjective meaning as a legal act in the sense of this legal system. It makes no claim whatever to exist legally within the framework of this legal system. It does not ask, so to speak, to be evaluated and legitimated on the basis of this legal system. The act establishing the constitution claims subjectively to be a legal act in the sense of the new legal system that it inaugurates. If the act, in the subsequent proceeding of the organs appointed pursuant to the new legal system, is recognized [*anerkennen*] objectively as a legal act and is thereby legitimated [*legitimieren*], such legitimation can only be based on the new legal system. This appears to involve a *petitio principii*, for the system in which the act is to be recognized as a legal act becomes a legal system only through general recognition of the act, that is to say, only through actual conformity to the system created by the act, conformity by the individuals whose behavior is regulated in that system. Or, put still another way, only when the system becomes efficacious does it become a legal system. The system in question is a legal system *in statu nascendi*; it is not an actual but a potential legal system. If one takes it as such, then there is no *petitio principii* in the claim that the act establishing the constitution is recognized as a legal act on the basis of the potential legal system inaugurated by that act.

We have here the same logical problem familiar from the question of which came first, the chicken or the egg, a problem shown to be a pseudo problem once the egg is seen as a potential chicken. The individuals addressed by the constitution that is established through a revolutionary act are given a choice between carrying out the old or the new constitution. In deciding in favor of the new constitution, in deciding, that is, that the old constitution has ceased to be binding and that the new one is binding on them, they make the new system efficacious, thereby transforming it into a legal system. If they were conscious of the significance of this process, they would have to grant that they can recognize the new constitution as binding only by *presupposing* that one ought to act as the new constitution, not the old, prescribes. That is, they no longer presuppose a basic norm that serves as the foundation of the old constitution but rather a basic norm that serves as the foundation of the new. Legal theory—and only legal theory, not any other discipline—describes the process and makes us conscious of this underlying presupposition.

It is therefore not entirely correct to say, as I myself have no doubt said on occasion, that legal theory presupposes the basic norm. Just as legal theory cannot *issue* any norm, so it cannot *presuppose* any norm either. Legal theory simply determines that if—and only if—the basic norm is presupposed in the proceeding subsequent to the act establishing the constitution, then the constitution can be recognized as a binding legal norm and the act giving rise to the constitution can be recognized as a legal act. Therein lies the *hypothetical* character of the basic norm, which I have always emphasized to the utmost. Since, as already remarked above, the constitution and the norms issued on the basis of it form a legal system only when coupled with the basic norm qua foundation of the constitution, the act establishing the constitution can be legitimated as a legal act on the basis of the legal system inaugurated by the act. That this actually happens is also shown by the fact that the individuals whose act establishes the constitution—for example, the parties to the constitutional convention—are seen as standing inside, not outside the founding community ("founding" by means of the constitution),[k] are seen as an organ of this community,

---

k. [The translation is faithful to Kelsen's German ("*innerhalb der durch die Verfassung konstituierenden Gemeinschaft*"), with "founding" standing in for "constituting" to avoid a clash with "constitution." The question here is whether the bootstrap operation Kelsen is describing—that the presupposition of the basic norm in connection with subsequent legal acts serves *post-facto* to legitimate the constitution—warrants speaking *both* of the "founding [constituting] community" (here) and also (following sentence) of this "constituted community", *i.e.*, "the [legal] system constituting this community" ("*unter der diese Gemeinschaft konstituierenden* [*Rechts-*] *ordnung*").]

as its first legislative organ. These individuals are seen and must be seen as subject to the [legal] system constituting this community. The process whereby the act establishing the constitution becomes efficacious and is thereby legitimated is similar to the process giving rise to a norm of customary law: A norm, held to be binding (*opinio necessitatis*) but not yet a legal norm, becomes a legal norm in that the individuals whose behavior the norm regulates generally behave in conformity to the norm, that is to say, the norm becomes a legal norm in that it becomes efficacious. And, in that this norm becomes efficacious, behavior corresponding to it becomes legal retroactively, even if such behavior was originally illegal owing to a conflict with a previously valid legal norm. The principle of customary law is only one application of the general principle of efficacy, a principle that plays such a decisive role in the legal development of, historically speaking, a first constitution—in particular, a revolutionary constitution whose emergence marks a rupture in the existing constitution.

Verdross characterizes the "successful instituting of a revolutionary organ" as an institution "not based on the legal system,"[l] which can only mean that it is not based on the old legal system. And he says that the success of such an institution means "nothing other than that the acts of these persons are built into the chain of the legal process insofar as these acts form the positive basis for still further steps in the process."[m] If, however, the process that the revolutionary acts "are built into" is a "legal process," then that process must be based on a legal system. And what other legal system could this be than the new, potential legal system, existing *in statu nascendi*, the system inaugurated by the revolutionary act? If one fails to recognize that legal theory, in its description of the process, has as its object of inquiry a potential legal system, then one cannot develop this description free of contradiction. Verdross goes on to say: "It is not a matter here of acts that are, on the basis of the legal system, already qualified *ab initio* as acts of [legal] organs, but rather a matter of acts that are only 'subsequently' qualified as acts of [legal] organs in that they constitute the presupposition of further phases of a legal process, the process in which, for example, [quasi-adjudicative] judgments handed down by these individuals are carried out by the executory organs."[n] This description is correct only insofar as the acts in question acquire *ab initio* their [legal] quality from legal organs, and not on the basis of

---

l. [Verdross, *Jur. Bl.*, p. 170; *Wiener Schule*, p. 1379.]
m. [*Ibid.*]
n. [*Verdross, Jur. Bl.*, p. 170; *Wiener Schule*, pp. 1379-1380.]

an actual legal system but rather on the basis of a nascent, that is, potential legal system. Verdross concludes: "Such qualification [of acts as legal] by [legal] organs cannot, however, be recognized by means of legal theory, which takes as its point of departure the legal system; such qualification can be recognized only through a social theory that takes account of what actually happens socially."[o]

I cannot agree with this conclusion. From Verdross's own statement it follows that recognition of the revolutionary act as a legal act takes place in the subsequent legal proceeding by means of acts of legal organs and not by way of some academic discipline or other. Neither legal theory nor any other academic discipline is asked to decide whether the old constitution or the new one established by revolution is to be recognized as binding and therefore carried out. A discipline, in particular legal theory, and legal theory alone, can only describe this process, and it can do so without having to borrow from social theory. If Verdross finds it necessary to appeal to social theory, it is clearly because he assumes that, in describing the process, reference must be made to "what actually happens socially." But such reference is possible only in social theory and not in legal theory, which "takes as its point of departure the legal system." The difference between legal theory and social theory is not, however, that only the latter and not the former has actual human behavior as its object of inquiry.The difference is rather that legal theory has actual human behavior as its object of inquiry only insofar as this behavior is regulated by legal norms as condition or consequence, while social theory has reference to actual human behavior insofar as this behavior, as cause or effect, is subject to the laws of causality. As Verdross himself assumes, actual acts that create and apply the law are the object of inquiry in legal theory. That legal theory has positive law as its object of inquiry means that its object of inquiry comprises only those norms that are in fact issued and applied through human acts—in short, only an efficacious normative system. These norms attach to actual acts as conditions and to actual acts as consequences. Therefore the legal propositions in which legal theory describes its object of inquiry are hypothetical judgments, as are the laws of nature in which natural science describes its object of inquiry. But the object of inquiry in legal theory comprises actual acts as regulated by legal norms, and it comprises social occurrences only insofar as they take place in that specific context, created by norms,

---

o. [*Verdross, Jur. Bl.*, p. 170; *Wiener Schule*, p. 1380.]

that I characterize as *imputation*, while social theory describes human behavior in its *causal* context.[3] The principle of efficacy, which as the content [*Inhalt*] of the basic norm is a principle of specifically legal cognition, offers an adequate guarantee that legal theory cannot ever lose sight of the connection between legal norms and what we call "social reality."

---

3. See my essay "Causality and Imputation," 51 *Ethics* (1950), pp. 1-11 [reprinted in Hans Kelsen, *What is Justice*? (Berkeley and Los Angeles: University of California Press, 1957), pp. 324-349, 394-397].

Vol 10 No 2
July 1990

Legal Studies

On the theory of interpretation

Hans Kelsen*
(translated by Bonnie Litschewski Paulson and Stanley L Paulson)

§1. The legal system is not a system of co-ordinate norms, found at one and the same level. Rather, it is a hierarchical structure of superordinate and subordinate legal norms, whose reciprocal relations are illuminated by the structural analysis undertaken by the Pure Theory of Law. The enquiry into the hierarchical structure of the legal system has significant consequences for the problem of *interpretation*. Interpretation is an intellectual activity accompanying the law-creating process as it moves from a higher level of the hierarchical structure to the lower level governed by this higher level. In the standard case, that of interpreting statutes, the question to be answered is how, in applying the general norm (the statute) to a concrete material fact, one is to arrive at a corresponding individual norm (a judicial decision or an administrative act). There is, in addition, interpretation of the constitution in so far as the constitution is to be applied, in, say, the legislative process, or in issuing emergency regulations or other decrees stemming directly from the constitution – that is, in so far as the constitution is to be implemented at a lower level of the hierarchy. And there is also interpretation of individual norms, of judicial decisions, administrative directives, private law transactions, and the like. There is, in short, interpretation of all norms in so far as they are to be implemented, that is, in so far as the process of creating and implementing the law moves from one level of the hierarchy to the next.

§2. The relation between a higher and a lower level of the legal system – as between constitution and statute, or between statute and judicial

* Kelsen's paper '*Zur Theorie der Interpretation*' first appeared in the Czech journal *Internationale Zeitschrift für Theorie des Rechts*, volume 8 (1934), at pp 9–17, and was reprinted in the second volume of *Die Wiener rechtstheoretische Schule*, edited by Hans Klecatsky *et al* (Vienna: Europa Verlag, 1968), at pp 1363–1373.

Kelsen wrote the paper without footnotes; in a handful of cases, where terms are not obviously familiar or where references might be useful, we have added footnotes.

decision – is a relation of determining or binding. The higher-level norm governs the act whereby the lower-level norm is created (or simply governs the realisation of the coercive act if pure implementation of the higher-level norm is what is called for). In governing the creation of the lower-level norm, the higher-level norm determines not only the procedure whereby the lower-level norm is created but possibly the content of the norm to be created as well. In the relation between constitution and statute, procedural regulation is predominant. Nonetheless, the content of future statutes is determined here, too; the constitutional guarantee of basic rights and liberties is one such attempt to determine the content of future statutes – at least negatively – by precluding certain other content (interference with personal liberty and with property). In the relation between statute and judicial decision or administrative act, procedural regulation and regulation of the content of the future norm are balanced; just as the procedure for creating the individual norm is determined, so likewise the content of the individual norm (in the substantive law, [including] civil law, criminal law, and administrative law) is determined.

This determination, however, is never complete, for a norm cannot be binding with respect to every detail of the act putting it into practice. There must always remain a range of discretion, sometimes wider, sometimes narrower, so that the higher-level norm, in relation to the act implementing it (an act of lower-level norm creation or of pure implementation), has simply the character of a frame to be filled in by way of the act. Even a meticulously detailed command must leave a number of determinations to those carrying it out. If official *A* orders official *B* to arrest subject *C*, *B* must use his own discretion to decide when, where, and how he will carry out the warrant to arrest *C*; and these decisions depend upon external circumstances that *A* has not foreseen and for the most part cannot foresee.

§3. What emerges from the above is that every legal act implementing a norm – be it an act of law creation or an act of pure implementation – is determined only in part by this norm and remains indeterminate for the rest. This indeterminacy can pertain to the conditioning material fact as well as to the conditioned consequence, that is, to the 'why' as well as to the 'what' of the prescribed act. Indeterminacy can be directly intended, that is, can be part of the intention of the norm-issuing authority. Thus, the issuance of a general norm always proceeds (in keeping with its essence) on the presupposition that the individual norm issued in implementing the general norm will continue the process of determination, the process underlying the hierarchical ordering of legal norms. Likewise for delegation. Accompanied by a sanction for violation, a health law determines that upon outbreak of an epidemic the residents of the affected city are to take certain precautions to prevent the disease from spreading; administrative agencies are empowered to determine these precautions in various ways depending on the various diseases. Or, the criminal law provides for a fine or a jail sentence for a specified delict; in the concrete case, the judge is left both to decide in favour of one sanction or the other and to determine its severity, for which determination an upper and a lower limit may be established in the statute itself.

§4. Indeterminacy of the legal act can also be the unintended consequence of properties of the norm to be implemented by the act in question. First of all, there is the ambiguity of a word or a phrase used in expressing the norm; the linguistic sense of the norm is not unequivocal, and whoever is to implement the norm is faced with several possible readings. The same situation exists where the official implementing the norm believes he can assume a discrepancy between the linguistic expression of the norm and the will of the norm-issuing authority, while the question of how the authority's will is to be discovered may well be left completely open. In any case, where the linguistic expression of the norm may be assumed not to correspond to the will of the norm-issuer, there must be the possibility of enquiring into his will by appealing to sources other than the linguistic expression itself. Traditional jurisprudence generally recognises that the so-called will of the legislator or the intention of the parties entering into a legal transaction might not correspond to the words used in the statute or in the legal transaction. The discrepancy between will and expression can be total, but it may also be merely partial, for example, where the will of the legislator or the intention of the parties corresponds to at least one of the several possible readings of the linguistic expression of the norm. Finally, indeterminacy of the prescribed legal act can result from the fact that two purportedly valid contemporaneous norms – both contained, say, in one and the same statute – contradict one another wholly or in part.

§5. In all these cases, several possibilities for implementing the higher-level norm suggest themselves. The legal act implementing the legal norm can be made to correspond to one or another of the various possible readings of the norm. Or it can be made to correspond to the norm-issuer's will, however discovered, or to the expression he chooses. Or, in the case of two [contemporaneous] norms contradicting each other, the legal act can be made to correspond to one or the other of them, or it can be so fashioned that decisions are taken as if the norms abrogated one another. In all these cases, the norm to be implemented is simply a frame within which several possibilities for implementation are given, and every act that stays within this frame, filling it out in some possible sense, is in conformity with the norm.

If 'interpretation' is understood as discovering the sense of the norm to be implemented, its result can only be the discovery of the frame that the norm to be interpreted represents and, within this frame, the cognition of several possibilities for implementation. Interpreting a statute, then, leads not necessarily to a single decision as the only correct decision but possibly to several decisions, all of them of equal standing measured solely against the norm to be applied, even if only a single one of them becomes, in the act of the judicial decision, positive law. That a judicial decision is based on a statute means in truth only that the decision stays within the frame the statute represents, means only that the decision is one of the individual norms possible within the frame of the general norm, not that it is the only individual norm possible.

In traditional jurisprudence, however, more is expected from interpretation than simply the discovery of the frame for the prescribed legal act. The additional task to be accomplished, which traditional jurisprudence is inclined to see even as the main task of interpretation, is the development of a method for filling in the frame correctly. The familiar theory of interpretation would have us believe that the statute, applied in the concrete case, can provide only *one* correct decision and that the 'correctness' of this decision – its correctness in terms of the positive law – is based on the statute itself. Traditional theory represents the process of arriving at this interpretation as though it were an intellectual act of clarification or understanding, as though the interpreter had only to set into motion his mind and not his will, as though by sheer mental activity he could choose from among the existing possibilities one that corresponds to the positive law, and so make a correct choice in terms of the positive law.

§6. From the standpoint of the positive law, however, there is no criterion on the basis of which one of the possibilities given within the frame of the norm to be applied could be favoured over the other possibilities. In terms of the positive law, there is simply no method according to which only one of the several readings of a norm could be distinguished as 'correct' – assuming, of course, that several readings of the meaning of the norm are possible in the context of all other norms of the statute or of the legal system. In spite of every effort, traditional jurisprudence has not yet found an objectively plausible way to settle the conflict between will and the expression of will. Every method of interpretation developed thus far invariably leads merely to a possible result, never to a single correct result. From the standpoint of the positive law, it is a matter of complete indifference whether one neglects the text in order to stick to the presumed will of the legislator or strictly observes the text in order to avoid worrying about the usually problematic will of the legislator. Given the case where two simultaneously valid norms contradict one another, each of the three (previously mentioned) logical possibilities for implementation[1] has the very same standing in terms of the positive law. It is futile to try to establish 'legally' one possibility by excluding the others. Both familiar means of interpretation, *argumentum a contrario*[2] and analogy, are worthless, if only because they lead to opposite results and there is no criterion for deciding when to use one or the other. Even the principle of the so-called balancing of interests is merely a formulation of the problem here and not a solution. It does not supply

1. See the first paragraph of §5, above.

2. The *argumentum a contrario*, deployed as a parry to the argument by analogy (thus, Kelsen's juxtaposition of the two in the text immediately following), in effect says: because the statute expressly specifies (only) *A* as falling within its scope, then *B, C, D*, etc do not fall within its scope, notwithstanding their similarity to *A*.

the objective standard according to which competing interests can be compared with one another as a means of settling conflicts of interest. In particular, this standard is not to be drawn from the norm to be interpreted, or from the statute containing the norm, or from the legal system as a whole, as the doctrine of the so-called balancing of interests suggests it can be. The necessity of an 'interpretation' arises precisely because the norm to be applied – or the system of norms – leaves open several possibilities, which is really to say that neither the norm nor the system of norms provides a decision as to which of the interests involved is of greater value. This decision, this ranking of interests, is left instead to a future act of norm creation – to the judicial decision, for example.

§7. The notion underlying the traditional theory of interpretation is that in so far as the prescribed legal act is indeterminate, the determination not provided by the applicable higher-level norm can be arrived at through some sort of cognition of existing law. This self-contradictory notion flies in the face of the very assumption that interpretation is possible. For if a norm can be interpreted, then the question as to which is the 'correct' choice from among the possibilities given within the frame of the norm is hardly a question of cognition directed to the positive law; it is a problem not of legal theory but rather of legal policy.[3] The task of getting the correct judgment or the correct administrative act out of the statute is essentially the same task as creating the correct statute within the framework of the constitution. Just as one cannot get correct statutes out of the constitution by way of interpretation, so likewise one cannot get correct judgments out of the statute by way of interpretation. Certainly there is a difference between these two cases, but it is only a quantitative not a qualitative difference, consisting simply in the fact that the legislator is far less bound materially than the judge – that the legislator, in other words, enjoys far greater freedom in creating law. But even the judge creates law, even he is relatively free in this capacity. And precisely for this reason, it is a function of will to arrive at the individual norm in the process of implementing a statute, provided that the frame of the general norm is filled in thereby. 'Theoretical' commentaries supposedly assisting in implementing a statute are in fact thoroughly political, making suggestions for the legislator to consider, attempting to influence the creative function of the courts and administrative agencies. In applying a statute, there may well be room for cognitive activity beyond discovering the frame within which the act of application is to be confined; this is not cognition of the positive law, however, but cognition of other norms that can now make their way into the law-creating process, the norms, namely, of morality, of justice – social value judgments customarily characterised with the catch-phrases 'welfare of the people', 'public interest', 'progress', and the like. From the standpoint of

3. 'Legal policy' or '*Rechtspolitik*', while comparable to 'foreign policy', 'monetary policy', and the like, is broader in scope, referring generally to the various considerations – in respect of both means and ends – raised by legislators about what ought to be enacted as law.

the positive law, nothing can be said about their validity and whether or not they can be identified. From this vantage point, all such determinations can only be characterised negatively, that is to say, these determinations do not stem from the positive law itself. In relation to the positive law, the legal act is free of such constraints, that is, the authority called upon to act is free to do so according to his own discretion unless the positive law itself authorises some metalegal norm or other, such as morality or justice. This norm, however, would be transformed thereby into a norm of the positive law.

§8. The view that interpretation is cognition of the positive law, and as such is a way of deriving new norms from prevailing norms, is the foundation of the so-called jurisprudence of concepts (*Begriffsjurisprudenz*),[4] which the Pure Theory of Law also rejects. The Pure Theory decimates the view that norms can be created by way of cognition, a view that arises in the end from the need to imagine the law as a fixed system governing every aspect of human behaviour, and governing in particular the activity of the organs that apply the law, above all the courts. Their function – and thus, interpretation too – is to be seen simply as the discovery of existing norms, norms, then, that are simply to be uncovered in a certain way. The illusion of legal certainty is what traditional legal theory, wittingly or not, is striving to maintain.

§9. Interpretation is given a special role to play in filling gaps in the law. Genuine gaps, however, do not exist. A genuine gap would mean that a legal dispute could not be decided in accordance with prevailing norms because the statute lacked a provision speaking to the case and therefore could not be applied. Every legal dispute consists in one party making a claim against another party, and the decision granting or rejecting the claim depends on whether the statute – that is, a valid norm to be applied in the concrete case – establishes or does not establish the alleged legal obligation. Since there is no third possibility, a decision can always be made and, indeed, always on the basis of the statute, that is, by applying the statute. Even a decision rejecting the claim is made by appeal to the prevailing legal system. By imposing obligations on individuals to behave in certain ways, the legal system guarantees them freedom outside those obligations. If *A* demands that *B* behave in a way not established as obligatory by the prevailing legal system, then that legal system grants *B* the 'right' to forbear from this behaviour, a 'right' in the sense of legally guaranteed freedom. The legal system embraces not only the principle that one is obligated to behave in a certain way (in that behaving in the opposite way is set as a condition for

4. 'Jurisprudence of concepts' or '*Begriffsjurisprudenz*' is the name of the early nineteenth century view, associated with Puchta and the early Jhering, to the effect that legal science, 'identifying legal norms as systematically related to one another', brings them to light 'as the product of a scientific deduction [*einer wissenschaftlichen Deduktion*]'. Georg Puchta, *Cursus der Institutionen*, vol 1 (Leipzig, 1841), 36.

the specific consequence of an unlawful act), but also the principle that where one is not obligated to do or to forbear from doing, there one is free. It is this negative norm that is applied in a decision rejecting a claim directed to behaviour not established as obligatory.

If in certain cases one nevertheless speaks of a 'gap', this does not mean, as the expression misleadingly suggests, that a decision is logically impossible for want of a norm. Rather, it simply means that the decision granting or rejecting a claim, while logically possible, is felt to be too impractical or too unjust by the official called upon to take the decision, that is, called upon to apply the statute. Indeed, the decision is felt to be so impractical or so unjust that the official is inclined to assume that the legislator did not consider this case at all and that, if he had, he would have decided it differently than it would have to be decided on the basis of the statute. Whether or not the official's assumption is correct probably cannot be shown; in the face of his constitutionally established obligation to apply the statute, however, his assumption is irrelevant. Even the statute that is bad in the view of the official applying it is to be applied, quite apart from the fact that what some regard as bad appears to others to be good. The so-called 'gap', then, is nothing but the difference between the positive law and a system held to be better, more just, more nearly right. Only by placing this 'better' system alongside the system of positive law and thereby ascertaining the latter's shortcomings, only thus can one claim something like a 'gap'. The fact that it cannot be filled by way of interpretation is obvious as soon as one recognises its nature. Interpretation here does not serve to bring about application of the interpreted norm; on the contrary, interpretation here serves to eliminate the interpreted norm and to replace it with a norm that is better, more just, more nearly right – in short, the norm desired by the official applying it. Under the pretext that the original norm is being supplemented to make up for its deficiencies, it is overturned in the course of being applied and is replaced by a new norm. This fiction is useful particularly where statutory revision of general norms is, for whatever reason, difficult or impossible – because, say, customary law is involved, which cannot be modified in a rational procedure, or because the prevailing statutes are regarded as inviolable or of divine origin, or because the legislative machinery is, for whatever other reasons, difficult or impossible to set into motion.

§10. Alongside gaps proper, one occasionally distinguishes technical gaps. Technical gaps are regarded as possible even by those who, from a positivistic standpoint, deny the existence of genuine gaps, and the filling of technical gaps by way of interpretation is declared admissible. Technical gaps are said to exist where the legislator fails to regulate something that he would have to regulate to make technically possible the application of a statute. What is characterised as a technical gap, however, is either a gap in the original sense of the word, that is, a difference between the positive law and desired law, or it is that indeterminacy that stems from the frame-like character of the norm. An example of the first alternative: a statute establishes the binding force of a sale, but determines nothing on the question of who is at risk if the item sold is ruined, before delivery, through no fault of either party. It is not the case, however, that the legislator determines 'nothing' on the question. Rather, it is that he does not determine that the seller is freed from the obligation to deliver the goods or to provide a substitute, a determination obviously regarded as desirable by the individual claiming a 'gap' here. The very fact that the statute makes no exceptions to the seller's obligation to deliver the goods—no exceptions in the case mentioned here either—means that it determines that the seller bear the risk. An example of the second alternative with respect to what is characterised as a technical gap: a statute determines that an agency is to be created by way of an election, but does not regulate the election procedure. This means that any sort of election whatever is lawful, whether it be based on proportional or majority vote, whether it be conducted in public or in secret, and so on. The official empowered to carry out the election can use his discretion to determine the election procedure; in other words, the determination of the election procedure is left to a lower-level norm. Another example: a statute determines that in order to take action, a committee must be convened by its chairman; at the same time, the statute determines that the committee itself is to elect its chairman but determines nothing about how the committee is to assemble when there is no chairman. Either this norm means that when there is no chairman, any sort of assembly whatever is lawful, or it means simply that in this case, too, the committee is to be convened by its chairman, in which case the committee cannot function lawfully at all. Even here, however, no 'gap' exists. For the statute does provide that the committee is to be convened by its chairman – [and the provision stands] even when the committee has no chairman. If the statute prescribed nothing about how the committee is to assemble, then any sort of assembly whatever would be lawful. To be sure, the statute determines something nonsensical here, but that can happen; statutes are, after all, the handiwork of human beings. A norm can even be lacking in sense altogether, and then no interpretation can wring sense out of it. For interpretation cannot extract from a norm what the norm does not have.

§11. Theoretically, then, there are no gaps in the law. The legislator, however, influenced by a mistaken theory, may nevertheless presuppose the existence of 'gaps', even though these are not what the legislator himself perhaps considers them to be. The legislator may – and indeed frequently does – establish provisions that speak to cases where no decision can be derived from the statute, provisions like [article 7] of the Austrian Civil Code[5]

5. Austrian General Civil Code, art 7: 'If a case cannot be decided either from the language or from the natural sense of the statute, then consideration must be given to similar cases decided with certainty in the statutes and to the basis of other statutes related to the statute in question. Should the case still remain doubtful, then it must be decided with reference to the carefully compiled and well-considered circumstances, this in accordance with the principles of natural law.' (Kelsen refers in the German language text to article 6, but this is clearly a typographical error or a slip, since article 6, addressed to 'plain meaning' and legislative intent, speaks to cases where a decision can be drawn from the statute – precisely the opposite of Kelsen's context, in which the statutory provision speaks to 'cases where no decision can be derived from the statute'.)

and article 1 of the Swiss Civil Code.[6] If, as in the latter, the statute instructs the judge to decide in case of a 'gap' as he would decide *qua* legislator, this amounts to empowering the judge, in cases where he considers application of the statute unacceptable, to decide according to his own discretion instead of on the basis of the statute. The good legislator is not in a position to dispense with what might well be a necessary correction of his statute, for since he must reckon from the beginning with material facts he has not foreseen and cannot foresee, he can only address his general norms to the ordinary run of cases. Precisely for this reason, he cannot even specify those cases where he intends that the official applying the statute stand in for him; were he able to specify such cases, he would have no need for a stand-in. The legislator has no alternative but to leave this decision to the official applying the statute and to take the unavoidable risk that the 'delegated legislator' will also decide cases where the legislator would have his statute applied. The risk here, of course, is that questions arise about the principle of lawfulness in the application of those general norms that are issued expressly to be applied by courts and administrative agencies, and thus, questions arise as to the very validity of those norms. The full import of law creation threatens to shift from the general to the individual level, that is, from the legislator to the official applying the statute. To minimise this risk as much as possible, the empowerment to circumvent the statute is formulated in such a way that the official applying the statute is not aware of the extraordinary power that is in fact delegated to him. He is to believe that he may forbear from applying the statute only in those cases where it cannot be applied because it is in and of itself impossible to apply. He is to believe that he is free only where he himself is to function as legislator, but not free with respect to when he is to stand in for the legislator. The fact that he is in truth free even in this latter respect is concealed from him by the fiction of the 'gap'. It is the intention of the legislator that this formula, wittingly or unwittingly false, should encourage the official applying a statute to make only the most sparing use of his conceded freedom not to apply the statute in a concrete case. For to the official applying a statute, only the greatest divergence between the statute and his own sense of the law will appear to be a real 'gap', that is, a case that the legislator himself did not wish to regulate and that the statute therefore does not regulate; the logical premises are lacking, then, for the conclusion from general to particular represented in every act of law application. The formula of so-called 'gaps in the law' is typically ideological, depicting the application of a statute in a concrete case as logically impossible under the law, while – judged according to the discretion of the official applying the statute – it may simply be impractical in terms of legal policy.

6. Swiss Civil Code, art 1: 'The statute applies to all legal questions for which, in its terms or its exposition, it contains a provision. If no directive can be derived from the statute, then the judge shall decide in accordance with customary law or, failing that, the rule that he as a legislator would adopt. He should be guided therein by established doctrine and tradition.'

VOLUME 71 FEBRUARY 1958 NUMBER 4

HARVARD LAW REVIEW

POSITIVISM AND THE SEPARATION OF LAW AND MORALS †

H. L. A. Hart *

Professor Hart defends the Positivist school of jurisprudence from many of the criticisms which have been leveled against its insistence on distinguishing the law that is from the law that ought to be. He first insists that the critics have confused this distinction with other Positivist theories about law which deserved criticism, and then proceeds to consider the merits of the distinction.

IN this article I shall discuss and attempt to defend a view which Mr. Justice Holmes, among others, held and for which he and they have been much criticized. But I wish first to say why I think that Holmes, whatever the vicissitudes of his American reputation may be, will always remain for Englishmen a heroic figure in jurisprudence. This will be so because he magically combined two qualities: one of them is imaginative power, which English legal thinking has often lacked; the other is clarity, which English legal thinking usually possesses. The English lawyer who turns to read Holmes is made to see that what he had taken to be settled and stable is really always on the move. To make this discovery with Holmes is to be with a guide whose words may leave you unconvinced, sometimes even repelled, but never mystified. Like our own Austin, with whom Holmes shared many ideals and thoughts, Holmes was sometimes clearly wrong; but again like Austin, when this was so he was always wrong clearly. This surely is a sovereign virtue in jurisprudence. Clarity I know is said not to be enough; this may be true, but there are still questions in jurisprudence where the issues are confused because

† The original version of this article was delivered in April 1957 as the Oliver Wendell Holmes Lecture at the Harvard Law School.

* Professor of Jurisprudence and Fellow of University College, Oxford; Visiting Professor of Law, Harvard Law School, 1956–57.

they are discussed in a style which Holmes would have spurned for its obscurity. Perhaps this is inevitable: jurisprudence trembles so uncertainly on the margin of many subjects that there will always be need for someone, in Bentham's phrase, "to pluck the mask of Mystery" from its face.[1] This is true, to a pre-eminent degree, of the subject of this article. Contemporary voices tell us we must recognize something obscured by the legal "positivists" whose day is now over: that there is a "point of intersection between law and morals,"[2] or that what *is* and what *ought* to be are somehow indissolubly fused or inseparable,[3] though the positivists denied it. What do these phrases mean? Or rather which of the many things that they *could* mean, *do* they mean? Which of them do "positivists" deny and why is it wrong to do so?

I.

I shall present the subject as part of the history of an idea. At the close of the eighteenth century and the beginning of the nineteenth the most earnest thinkers in England about legal and social problems and the architects of great reforms were the great Utilitarians. Two of them, Bentham and Austin, constantly insisted on the need to distinguish, firmly and with the maximum of clarity, law as it is from law as it ought to be. This theme haunts their work, and they condemned the natural-law thinkers precisely because they had blurred this apparently simple but vital distinction. By contrast, at the present time in this country and to a lesser extent in England, this separation between law and morals is held to be superficial and wrong. Some critics have thought that it blinds men to the true nature of law and its roots in social life.[4]

---

[1] BENTHAM, *A Fragment on Government*, in 1 WORKS 221, 235 (Bowring ed. 1859) (preface, 41st para.).

[2] D'ENTRÈVES, NATURAL LAW 116 (2d ed. 1952).

[3] FULLER, THE LAW IN QUEST OF ITSELF 12 (1940); Brecht, *The Myth of Is and Ought*, 54 HARV. L. REV. 811 (1941); Fuller, *Human Purpose and Natural Law*, 53 J. PHILOS 697 (1953).

[4] See FRIEDMANN, LEGAL THEORY 154, 294–95 (3d ed. 1953). Friedmann also says of Austin that "by his sharp distinction between the science of legislation and the science of law," he "inaugurated an era of legal positivism and self-sufficiency which enabled the rising national State to assert its authority undisturbed by juristic doubts." *Id.* at 416. Yet, "the existence of a highly organised State which claimed sovereignty and unconditional obedience of the citizen" is said to be "the political condition which makes analytical positivism possible." *Id.* at 163. There is therefore some difficulty in determining which, in this account, is to be hen and which egg (analytical positivism or political condition). Apart from this, there seems to be little evidence that any national State rising in or after 1832 (when the *Province*

Others have thought it not only intellectually misleading but corrupting in practice, at its worst apt to weaken resistance to state tyranny or absolutism,[5] and at its best apt to bring law into disrespect. The nonpejorative name "Legal Positivism," like most terms which are used as missiles in intellectual battles, has come to stand for a baffling multitude of different sins. One of them is the sin, real or alleged, of insisting, as Austin and Bentham did, on the separation of law as it is and law as it ought to be.

How then has this reversal of the wheel come about? What are the theoretical errors in this distinction? Have the practical consequences of stressing the distinction as Bentham and Austin did been bad? Should we now reject it or keep it? In considering these questions we should recall the social philosophy which went along with the Utilitarians' insistence on this distinction. They stood firmly but on their own utilitarian ground for all the principles of liberalism in law and government. No one has ever combined, with such even-minded sanity as the Utilitarians, the passion for reform with respect for law together with a due recognition of the need to control the abuse of power even when power is in the hands of reformers. One by one in Bentham's works you can identify the elements of the *Rechtstaat* and all the principles for the defense of which the terminology of natural law has in our day been revived. Here are liberty of speech, and of press, the right of association,[6] the need that laws should be published and made widely known before they are enforced,[7] the need to control administrative agencies,[8] the insistence that there should be no criminal liability without fault,[9] and the importance of the prin-

---

of Jurisprudence Determined was first published) was enabled to assert its authority by Austin's work or "the era of legal positivism" which he "inaugurated."

[5] See Radbruch, *Die Erneuerung des Rechts*, 2 DIE WANDLUNG 8 (Germany 1947); Radbruch, *Gesetzliches Unrecht und Übergesetzliches Recht*, 1 SÜDDEUTSCHE JURISTEN-ZEITUNG 105 (Germany 1946) (reprinted in RADBRUCH, RECHTSPHILOSOPHIE 347 (4th ed. 1950)). Radbruch's views are discussed at pp. 617–21 *infra*.

[6] BENTHAM, *A Fragment on Government*, in 1 WORKS 221, 230 (Bowring ed. 1859) (preface, 16th para.); BENTHAM, *Principles of Penal Law*, in 1 WORKS 365, 574–75, 576–78 (Bowring ed. 1859) (pt. III, c. XXI, 8th para., 12th para.).

[7] BENTHAM, *Of Promulgation of the Laws*, in 1 WORKS 155 (Bowring ed. 1859); BENTHAM, *Principles of the Civil Code*, in 1 WORKS 297, 323 (Bowring ed. 1859) (pt. I, c. XVII, 2d para.); BENTHAM, *A Fragment on Government*, in 1 WORKS 221, 233 n.[*m*] (Bowring ed. 1859) (preface, 35th para.).

[8] BENTHAM, *Principles of Penal Law*, in 1 WORKS 365, 576 (Bowring ed. 1859) (pt. III, c. XXI, 10th para., 11th para.).

[9] BENTHAM, *Principles of Morals and Legislation*, in 1 WORKS 1, 84 (Bowring ed. 1859) (c. XIII).

ciple of legality, *nulla poena sine lege.*[10] Some, I know, find the political and moral insight of the Utilitarians a very simple one, but we should not mistake this simplicity for superficiality nor forget how favorably their simplicities compare with the profundities of other thinkers. Take only one example: Bentham on slavery. He says the question at issue is not whether those who are held as slaves can reason, but simply whether they suffer.[11] Does this not compare well with the discussion of the question in terms of whether or not there are some men whom Nature has fitted only to be the living instruments of others? We owe it to Bentham more than anyone else that we have stopped discussing this and similar questions of social policy in that form.

So Bentham and Austin were not dry analysts fiddling with verbal distinctions while cities burned, but were the vanguard of a movement which laboured with passionate intensity and much success to bring about a better society and better laws. Why then did they insist on the separation of law as it is and law as it ought to be? What did they mean? Let us first see what they said. Austin formulated the doctrine:

> The existence of law is one thing; its merit or demerit is another. Whether it be or be not is one enquiry; whether it be or be not conformable to an assumed standard, is a different enquiry. A law, which actually exists, is a law, though we happen to dislike it, or though it vary from the text, by which we regulate our approbation and disapprobation. This truth, when formally announced as an abstract proposition, is so simple and glaring that it seems idle to insist upon it. But simple and glaring as it is, when enunciated in abstract expressions the enumeration of the instances in which it has been forgotten would fill a volume.
>
> Sir William Blackstone, for example, says in his "Commentaries," that the laws of God are superior in obligation to all other laws; that no human laws should be suffered to contradict them; that human laws are of no validity if contrary to them; and that all valid laws derive their force from that Divine original.
>
> Now, he *may* mean that all human laws ought to conform to the Divine laws. If this be his meaning, I assent to it without hesitation. . . . Perhaps, again, he means that human lawgivers are themselves obliged by the Divine laws to fashion the laws which

[10] BENTHAM, *Anarchical Fallacies*, in 2 WORKS 489, 511–12 (Bowring ed. 1859) (art. VIII); BENTHAM, *Principles of Morals and Legislation*, in 1 WORKS 1, 144 (Bowring ed. 1859) (c. XIX, 11th para.).

[11] *Id.* at 142 n.§ (c. XIX, 4th para. n.§).

> they impose by that ultimate standard, because if they do not, God will punish them. To this also I entirely assent . . . .
>
> But the meaning of this passage of Blackstone, if it has a meaning, seems rather to be this: that no human law which conflicts with the Divine law is obligatory or binding; in other words, that no human law which conflicts with the Divine law *is a law* . . . .[12]

Austin's protest against blurring the distinction between what law is and what it ought to be is quite general: it is a mistake, whatever our standard of what ought to be, whatever "the text by which we regulate our approbation or disapprobation." His examples, however, are always a confusion between law as it is and law as morality would require it to be. For him, it must be remembered, the fundamental principles of morality were God's commands, to which utility was an "index": besides this there was the actual accepted morality of a social group or "positive" morality. Bentham insisted on this distinction without characterizing morality by reference to God but only, of course, by reference to the principles of utility. Both thinkers' prime reason for this insistence was to enable men to see steadily the precise issues posed by the existence of morally bad laws, and to understand the specific character of the authority of a legal order. Bentham's general recipe for life under the government of laws was simple: it was "*to obey punctually*; *to censure freely*."[13] But Bentham was especially aware, as an anxious spectator of the French revolution, that this was not enough: the time might come in any society when the law's commands were so evil that the question of resistance had to be faced, and it was then essential that the issues at stake at this point should neither be oversimplified nor obscured.[14] Yet, this was precisely what the confusion between law and morals had done and Bentham found that the confusion had spread symmetrically in two different directions. On the one hand

[12] AUSTIN, THE PROVINCE OF JURISPRUDENCE DETERMINED 184–85 (Library of Ideas ed. 1954).

[13] BENTHAM, *A Fragment on Government*, in 1 WORKS 221, 230 (Bowring ed. 1859) (preface, 16th para.).

[14] See BENTHAM, *Principles of Legislation*, in THE THEORY OF LEGISLATION 1, 65 n.* (Ogden ed. 1931) (c. XII, 2d para. n.*).

> Here we touch upon the most difficult of questions. If the law is not what it ought to be; if it openly combats the principle of utility; ought we to obey it? Ought we to violate it? Ought we to remain neuter between the law which commands an evil, and morality which forbids it?

See also BENTHAM, *A Fragment on Government*, in 1 WORKS 221, 287–88 (Bowring ed. 1859) (c. IV, 20th–25th paras.).

Bentham had in mind the anarchist who argues thus: "This ought not to be the law, therefore it is not and I am free not merely to censure but to disregard it." On the other hand he thought of the reactionary who argues: "This is the law, therefore it is what it ought to be," and thus stifles criticism at its birth. Both errors, Bentham thought, were to be found in Blackstone: there was his incautious statement that human laws were invalid if contrary to the law of God,[15] and "that spirit of obsequious *quietism* that seems constitutional in our Author" which "will scarce ever let him recognise a difference" between what is and what ought to be.[16] This indeed was for Bentham the occupational disease of lawyers: "[I]n the eyes of lawyers — not to speak of their dupes — that is to say, as yet, the generality of non-lawyers — the *is* and *ought to be* . . . were one and indivisible."[17] There are therefore two dangers between which insistence on this distinction will help us to steer: the danger that law and its authority may be dissolved in man's conceptions of what law ought to be and the danger that the existing law may supplant morality as a final test of conduct and so escape criticism.

In view of later criticisms it is also important to distinguish several things that the Utilitarians did not mean by insisting on their separation of law and morals. They certainly accepted many of the things that might be called "the intersection of law and morals." First, they never denied that, as a matter of historical fact, the development of legal systems had been powerfully influenced by moral opinion, and, conversely, that moral standards had been profoundly influenced by law, so that the content of many legal rules mirrored moral rules or principles. It is not in fact always easy to trace this historical causal connection, but Bentham was certainly ready to admit its existence; so too Austin

---

[15] 1 BLACKSTONE, COMMENTARIES *41. Bentham criticized "this dangerous maxim," saying "the natural tendency of such a doctrine is to impel a man, by the force of conscience, to rise up in arms against any law whatever that he happens not to like." BENTHAM, *A Fragment on Government*, in 1 WORKS 221, 287 (Bowring ed. 1859) (c. IV, 19th para.). See also BENTHAM, A COMMENT ON THE COMMENTARIES 49 (1928) (c. III). For an expression of a fear lest anarchy result from such a doctrine, combined with a recognition that resistance may be justified on grounds of utility, see AUSTIN, *op. cit. supra* note 12, at 186.

[16] BENTHAM, *A Fragment on Government*, in 1 WORKS 221, 294 (Bowring ed. 1859) (c. V, 10th para.).

[17] BENTHAM, *A Commentary on Humphreys' Real Property Code*, in 5 WORKS 389 (Bowring ed. 1843).

spoke of the "frequent coincidence"[18] of positive law and morality and attributed the confusion of what law is with what law ought to be to this very fact.

Secondly, neither Bentham nor his followers denied that by explicit legal provisions moral principles might at different points be brought into a legal system and form part of its rules, or that courts might be legally bound to decide in accordance with what they thought just or best. Bentham indeed recognized, as Austin did not, that even the supreme legislative power might be subjected to legal restraints by a constitution[19] and would not have denied that moral principles, like those of the fifth amendment, might form the content of such legal constitutional restraints. Austin differed in thinking that restraints on the supreme legislative power could not have the force of law, but would remain merely political or moral checks;[20] but of course he would have recognized that a statute, for example, might confer a delegated legislative power and restrict the area of its exercise by reference to moral principles.

What both Bentham and Austin were anxious to assert were the following two simple things: first, in the absence of an expressed constitutional or legal provision, it could not follow from the mere fact that a rule violated standards of morality that it was not a rule of law; and, conversely, it could not follow from the mere fact that a rule was morally desirable that it was a rule of law.

The history of this simple doctrine in the nineteenth century is too long and too intricate to trace here. Let me summarize it by saying that after it was propounded to the world by Austin it dominated English jurisprudence and constitutes part of the framework of most of those curiously English and perhaps unsatisfactory productions — the omnibus surveys of the whole field of jurisprudence. A succession of these were published after a full text of Austin's lectures finally appeared in 1863. In each of them the utilitarian separation of law and morals is treated as something that enables lawyers to attain a new clarity. Austin was said by one of his English successors, Amos, "to have delivered the law from the dead body of morality that still clung to

[18] AUSTIN, *op. cit. supra* note 12, at 162.

[19] BENTHAM, *A Fragment on Government*, in 1 WORKS 221, 289–90 (Bowring ed. 1859) (c. IV, 33d–34th paras.).

[20] See AUSTIN, *op. cit. supra* note 12, at 231.

it"; [21] and even Maine, who was critical of Austin at many points, did not question this part of his doctrine. In the United States men like N. St. John Green,[22] Gray, and Holmes considered that insistence on this distinction had enabled the understanding of law as a means of social control to get off to a fruitful new start; they welcomed it both as self-evident and as illuminating — as a revealing tautology. This distinction is, of course, one of the main themes of Holmes' most famous essay "The Path of the Law," [23] but the place it had in the estimation of these American writers is best seen in what Gray wrote at the turn of the century in *The Nature and Sources of the Law.* He said:

> The great gain in its fundamental conceptions which Jurisprudence made during the last century was the recognition of the truth that the Law of a State . . . is not an ideal, but something which actually exists. . . . [I]t is not that which ought to be, but that which is. To fix this definitely in the Jurisprudence of the Common Law, is the feat that Austin accomplished.[24]

II.

So much for the doctrine in the heyday of its success. Let us turn now to some of the criticisms. Undoubtedly, when Bentham and Austin insisted on the distinction between law as it is and as it ought to be, they had in mind *particular* laws the meanings of which were clear and so not in dispute, and they were concerned to argue that such laws, even if morally outrageous, were still laws. It is, however, necessary, in considering the criticisms which later developed, to consider more than those criticisms which were directed to this particular point if we are to get at the root of the dissatisfaction felt; we must also take account of the objection that, even if what the Utilitarians said on this particular point were true, their insistence on it, in a terminology suggesting a general cleavage between what is and ought to be law, obscured the fact

[21] AMOS, THE SCIENCE OF LAW 4 (5th ed. 1881). See also MARKBY, ELEMENTS OF LAW 4–5 (5th ed. 1896):

> Austin, by establishing the distinction between positive law and morals, not only laid the foundation for a science of law, but cleared the conception of law . . . of a number of pernicious consequences to which . . . it had been supposed to lead. Positive laws, as Austin has shown, must be legally binding, and yet a law may be unjust. . . . He has admitted that law itself may be immoral, in which case it may be our moral duty to disobey it . . . .

Cf. HOLLAND, JURISPRUDENCE 1–20 (1880).

[22] See Green, Book Review, 6 AM. L. REV. 57, 61 (1871) (reprinted in GREEN, ESSAYS AND NOTES ON THE LAW OF TORT AND CRIME 31, 35 (1933)).

[23] 10 HARV. L. REV. 457 (1897).

[24] GRAY, THE NATURE AND SOURCES OF THE LAW 94 (1st ed. 1909) (§ 213).

that at other points there is an essential point of contact between the two. So in what follows I shall consider not only criticisms of the particular point which the Utilitarians had in mind, but also the claim that an essential connection between law and morals emerges if we examine how laws, the meanings of which are in dispute, are interpreted and applied in concrete cases; and that this connection emerges again if we widen our point of view and ask, not whether every particular rule of law must satisfy a moral minimum in order to be a law, but whether a system of rules which altogether failed to do this could be a legal system.

There is, however, one major initial complexity by which criticism has been much confused. We must remember that the Utilitarians combined with their insistence on the separation of law and morals two other equally famous but distinct doctrines. One was the important truth that a purely analytical study of legal concepts, a study of the meaning of the distinctive vocabulary of the law, was as vital to our understanding of the nature of law as historical or sociological studies, though of course it could not supplant them. The other doctrine was the famous imperative theory of law — that law is essentially a command.

These three doctrines constitute the utilitarian tradition in jurisprudence; yet they are distinct doctrines. It is possible to endorse the separation between law and morals and to value analytical inquiries into the meaning of legal concepts and yet think it wrong to conceive of law as essentially a command. One source of great confusion in the criticism of the separation of law and morals was the belief that the falsity of any one of these three doctrines in the utilitarian tradition showed the other two to be false; what was worse was the failure to see that there were three quite separate doctrines in this tradition. The indiscriminate use of the label "positivism" to designate ambiguously each one of these three separate doctrines (together with some others which the Utilitarians never professed) has perhaps confused the issue more than any other single factor.[25] Some of the early American critics of the Austinian doctrine were, however,

[25] It may help to identify five (there may be more) meanings of "positivism" bandied about in contemporary jurisprudence:

(1) the contention that laws are commands of human beings, see pp. 602–06 *infra*,

(2) the contention that there is no necessary connection between law and morals or law as it is and ought to be, see pp. 594–600 *supra*,

(3) the contention that the analysis (or study of the meaning) of legal con-

admirably clear on just this matter. Gray, for example, added at the end of the tribute to Austin, which I have already quoted, the words, "He may have been wrong in treating the Law of the State as being the command of the sovereign"[26] and he touched shrewdly on many points where the command theory is defective. But other critics have been less clearheaded and have thought that the inadequacies of the command theory which gradually came to light were sufficient to demonstrate the falsity of the separation of law and morals.

This was a mistake, but a natural one. To see how natural it was we must look a little more closely at the command idea. The famous theory that law is a command was a part of a wider and more ambitious claim. Austin said that the notion of a command was "the *key* to the sciences of jurisprudence and morals,"[27] and contemporary attempts to elucidate moral judgments in terms of "imperative" or "prescriptive" utterances echo this ambitious claim. But the command theory, viewed as an effort to identify even the quintessence of law, let alone the quintessence of morals, seems breathtaking in its simplicity and quite inadequate. There is much, even in the simplest legal system, that is distorted if presented as a command. Yet the Utilitarians thought that the essence of a legal system could be conveyed if the notion of a command were supplemented by that of a habit of obedience. The simple scheme was this: What is a command? It is simply an expression by one person of the desire that another person should do or abstain from some action, accompanied by a threat of punishment which is likely to follow disobedience. Commands are laws if two conditions are satisfied: first, they must be general;

cepts is (a) worth pursuing and (b) to be distinguished from historical inquiries into the causes or origins of laws, from sociological inquiries into the relation of law and other social phenomena, and from the criticism or appraisal of law whether in terms of morals, social aims, "functions," or otherwise, see pp. 608–10 *infra*,

(4) the contention that a legal system is a "closed logical system" in which correct legal decisions can be deduced by logical means from predetermined legal rules without reference to social aims, policies, moral standards, see pp. 608–10 *infra*, and

(5) the contention that moral judgments cannot be established or defended, as statements of facts can, by rational argument, evidence, or proof ("noncognitivism" in ethics), see pp. 624–26 *infra*.

Bentham and Austin held the views described in (1), (2), and (3) but not those in (4) and (5). Opinion (4) is often ascribed to analytical jurists, see pages pp. 608–10 *infra*, but I know of no "analyst" who held this view.

[26] GRAY, THE NATURE AND SOURCES OF THE LAW 94–95 (2d ed. 1921).

[27] AUSTIN, *op. cit. supra* note 12, at 13.

second, they must be commanded by what (as both Bentham and Austin claimed) exists in every political society whatever its constitutional form, namely, a person or a group of persons who are in receipt of habitual obedience from most of the society but pay no such obedience to others. These persons are its sovereign. Thus law is the command of the uncommanded commanders of society — the creation of the legally untrammelled will of the sovereign who is by definition outside the law.

It is easy to see that this account of a legal system is threadbare. One can also see why it might seem that its inadequacy is due to the omission of some essential connection with morality. The situation which the simple trilogy of command, sanction, and sovereign avails to describe, if you take these notions at all precisely, is like that of a gunman saying to his victim, "Give me your money or your life." The only difference is that in the case of a legal system the gunman says it to a large number of people who are accustomed to the racket and habitually surrender to it. Law surely is not the gunman situation writ large, and legal order is surely not to be thus simply identified with compulsion.

This scheme, despite the points of obvious analogy between a statute and a command, omits some of the most characteristic elements of law. Let me cite a few. It is wrong to think of a legislature (and a fortiori an electorate) with a changing membership, as a group of persons habitually obeyed: this simple idea is suited only to a monarch sufficiently long-lived for a "habit" to grow up. Even if we waive this point, nothing which legislators do makes law unless they comply with fundamental accepted rules specifying the essential lawmaking procedures. This is true even in a system having a simple unitary constitution like the British. These fundamental accepted rules specifying what the legislature must do to legislate are not commands habitually obeyed, nor can they be expressed as habits of obedience to persons. They lie at the root of a legal system, and what is most missing in the utilitarian scheme is an analysis of what it is for a social group and its officials to accept such rules. This notion, not that of a command as Austin claimed, is the "key to the science of jurisprudence," or at least one of the keys.

Again, Austin, in the case of a democracy, looked past the legislators to the electorate as "the sovereign" (or in England as part of it). He thought that in the United States the mass of the electors to the state and federal legislatures were the sovereign whose commands, given by their "agents" in the legislatures, were law. But on this footing the whole notion of the sovereign outside the law being "habitually obeyed" by the "bulk" of the population must go: for in this case the "bulk" obeys the bulk, that is, it obeys itself. Plainly the general acceptance of the authority of a lawmaking procedure, irrespective of the changing individuals who operate it from time to time, can be only distorted by an analysis in terms of mass habitual obedience to certain persons who are by definition outside the law, just as the cognate but much simpler phenomenon of the general social acceptance of a rule, say of taking off the hat when entering a church, would be distorted if represented as habitual obedience by the mass to specific persons.

Other critics dimly sensed a further and more important defect in the command theory, yet blurred the edge of an important criticism by assuming that the defect was due to the failure to insist upon some important connection between law and morals. This more radical defect is as follows. The picture that the command theory draws of life under law is essentially a simple relationship of the commander to the commanded, of superior to inferior, of top to bottom; the relationship is vertical between the commanders or authors of the law conceived of as essentially outside the law and those who are commanded and subject to the law. In this picture no place, or only an accidental or subordinate place, is afforded for a distinction between types of legal rules which are in fact radically different. Some laws require men to act in certain ways or to abstain from acting whether they wish to or not. The criminal law consists largely of rules of this sort: like commands they are simply "obeyed" or "disobeyed." But other legal rules are presented to society in quite different ways and have quite different functions. They provide facilities more or less elaborate for individuals to create structures of rights and duties for the conduct of life within the coercive framework of the law. Such are the rules enabling individuals to make contracts, wills, and trusts, and generally to mould their legal relations with others. Such rules, unlike the criminal law, are not factors designed to obstruct wishes and choices of an antisocial sort. On the contrary, these rules provide facilities for the realization of wishes and choices. They do not say (like commands) "do this whether you wish it or not," but rather "if you wish to do this, here is the way to do it." Under these rules we exercise powers, make claims, and assert rights. These phrases mark off characteristic features of laws that confer rights and powers; they are laws which are, so to speak, put at the disposition of individuals in a way in which the criminal law is not. Much ingenuity has gone into the task of "reducing" laws of this second sort to some complex variant of laws of the first sort. The effort to show that laws conferring rights are "really" only conditional stipulations of sanctions to be exacted from the person ultimately under a legal duty characterizes much of Kelsen's work.[28] Yet to urge this is really just to exhibit dogmatic determination to suppress one aspect of the legal system in order to maintain the theory that the stipulation of a sanction, like Austin's command, represents the quintessence of law. One might as well urge that the rules of baseball were "really" only complex conditional directions to the scorer and that this showed their real or "essential" nature.

One of the first jurists in England to break with the Austinian tradition, Salmond, complained that the analysis in terms of commands left the notion of a right unprovided with a place.[29] But he confused the point. He argued first, and correctly, that if laws are merely commands it is inexplicable that we should have come to speak of legal rights and powers as conferred or arising under them, but then wrongly concluded that the rules of a legal system must necessarily be connected with moral rules or principles of justice and that only on this footing could the phenomenon of legal rights be explained. Otherwise, Salmond thought, we would have to say that a mere "verbal coincidence" connects the concepts of legal and moral right. Similarly, continental critics of the Utilitarians, always alive to the complexity of the notion of a subjective right, insisted that the command theory gave it no place. Hägerström insisted that if laws were merely commands the notion of an individual's right was really inexplicable, for commands are, as he said, something which we either obey or we do not obey; they do not confer rights.[30] But he, too, concluded that

[28] See, *e.g.*, KELSEN, GENERAL THEORY OF LAW AND STATE 58–61, 143–44 (1945). According to Kelsen, all laws, not only those conferring rights and powers, are reducible to such "primary norms" conditionally stipulating sanctions.

[29] SALMOND, THE FIRST PRINCIPLES OF JURISPRUDENCE 97–98 (1893). He protested against "the creed of what is termed the English school of jurisprudence," because it "attempted to deprive the idea of law of that ethical significance which is one of its most essential elements." *Id.* at 9, 10.

[30] HÄGERSTRÖM, INQUIRIES INTO THE NATURE OF LAW AND MORALS 217 (Olivecrona ed. 1953): "[T]he whole theory of the subjective rights of private individuals . . . is incompatible with the imperative theory." See also *id.* at 221:

> The description of them [claims to legal protection] as rights is wholly derived from the idea that the law which is concerned with them is a true ex-

moral, or, as he put it, common-sense, notions of justice must therefore be necessarily involved in the analysis of any legal structure elaborate enough to confer rights.[31]

Yet, surely these arguments are confused. Rules that confer rights, though distinct from commands, need not be moral rules or coincide with them. Rights, after all, exist under the rules of ceremonies, games, and in many other spheres regulated by rules which are irrelevant to the question of justice or what the law ought to be. Nor need rules which confer rights be just or morally good rules. The rights of a master over his slaves show us that. "Their merit or demerit," as Austin termed it, depends on how rights are distributed in society and over whom or what they are exercised. These critics indeed revealed the inadequacy of the simple notions of command and habit for the analysis of law; at many points it is apparent that the social acceptance of a rule or standard of authority (even if it is motivated only by fear or superstition or rests on inertia) must be brought into the analysis and cannot itself be reduced to the two simple terms. Yet nothing in this showed the utilitarian insistence on the distinction between the existence of law and its "merits" to be wrong.

III.

I now turn to a distinctively American criticism of the separation of the law that is from the the law that ought to be. It emerged from the critical study of the judicial process with which American jurisprudence has been on the whole so beneficially occupied. The most skeptical of these critics — the loosely named "Realists" of the 1930's — perhaps too naïvely accepted the conceptual framework of the natural sciences as adequate for the characterization of law and for the analysis of rule-guided action of which a living system of law at least partly consists. But they opened men's eyes to what actually goes on when courts decide cases, and the contrast they drew between the actual facts of judicial decision and the traditional terminology for describing it as if it were a wholly logical operation was usually illuminating; for in spite of some exaggeration the "Realists" made us acutely conscious of one cardinal feature of human language and human

pression of rights and duties in the sense in which the popular notion of justice understands these terms.

[31] *Id.* at 218.

thought, emphasis on which is vital not only for the understanding of law but in areas of philosophy far beyond the confines of jurisprudence. The insight of this school may be presented in the following example. A legal rule forbids you to take a vehicle into the public park. Plainly this forbids an automobile, but what about bicycles, roller skates, toy automobiles? What about airplanes? Are these, as we say, to be called "vehicles" for the purpose of the rule or not? If we are to communicate with each other at all, and if, as in the most elementary form of law, we are to express our intentions that a certain type of behavior be regulated by rules, then the general words we use — like "vehicle" in the case I consider — must have some standard instance in which no doubts are felt about its application. There must be a core of settled meaning, but there will be, as well, a penumbra of debatable cases in which words are neither obviously applicable nor obviously ruled out. These cases will each have some features in common with the standard case; they will lack others or be accompanied by features not present in the standard case. Human invention and natural processes continually throw up such variants on the familiar, and if we are to say that these ranges of facts do or do not fall under existing rules, then the classifier must make a decision which is not dictated to him, for the facts and phenomena to which we fit our words and apply our rules are as it were *dumb*. The toy automobile cannot speak up and say, "I am a vehicle for the purpose of this legal rule," nor can the roller skates chorus, "We are not a vehicle." Fact situations do not await us neatly labeled, creased, and folded, nor is their legal classification written on them to be simply read off by the judge. Instead, in applying legal rules, someone must take the responsibility of deciding that words do or do not cover some case in hand with all the practical consequences involved in this decision.

We may call the problems which arise outside the hard core of standard instances or settled meaning "problems of the penumbra"; they are always with us whether in relation to such trivial things as the regulation of the use of the public park or in relation to the multidimensional generalities of a constitution. If a penumbra of uncertainty must surround all legal rules, then their application to specific cases in the penumbral area cannot be a matter of logical deduction, and so deductive reasoning, which for generations has been cherished as the very perfection of human reasoning, cannot serve as a model for what judges, or indeed anyone, should do in bringing particular cases under general rules. In this area men cannot live by deduction alone. And it follows that if legal arguments and legal decisions of penumbral questions are to be rational, their rationality must lie in something other than a logical relation to premises. So if it is rational or "sound" to argue and to decide that for the purposes of this rule an airplane is not a vehicle, this argument must be sound or rational without being logically conclusive. What is it then that makes such decisions correct or at least better than alternative decisions? Again, it seems true to say that the criterion which makes a decision sound in such cases is some concept of what the law ought to be; it is easy to slide from that into saying that it must be a moral judgment about what law ought to be. So here we touch upon a point of necessary "intersection between law and morals" which demonstrates the falsity or, at any rate, the misleading character of the Utilitarians' emphatic insistence on the separation of law as it is and ought to be. Surely, Bentham and Austin could only have written as they did because they misunderstood or neglected this aspect of the judicial process, because they ignored the problems of the penumbra.

The misconception of the judicial process which ignores the problems of the penumbra and which views the process as consisting pre-eminently in deductive reasoning is often stigmatized as the error of "formalism" or "literalism." My question now is, how and to what extent does the demonstration of this error show the utilitarian distinction to be wrong or misleading? Here there are many issues which have been confused, but I can only disentangle some. The charge of formalism has been leveled both at the "positivist" legal theorist and at the courts, but of course it must be a very different charge in each case. Leveled at the legal theorist, the charge means that he has made a theoretical mistake about the character of legal decision; he has thought of the reasoning involved as consisting in deduction from premises in which the judges' practical choices or decisions play no part. It would be easy to show that Austin was guiltless of this error; only an entire misconception of what analytical jurisprudence is and why he thought it important has led to the view that he, or any other analyst, believed that the law was a closed logical system in which judges deduced their decisions from premises.[32] On the

[32] This misunderstanding of analytical jurisprudence is to be found in, among others, STONE, THE PROVINCE AND FUNCTION OF LAW 141 (1950):

contrary, he was very much alive to the character of language, to its vagueness or open character;[33] he thought that in the penumbral situation judges must necessarily legislate,[34] and, in accents that sometimes recall those of the late Judge Jerome Frank, he berated the common-law judges for legislating feebly and timidly and for blindly relying on real or fanciied analogies with past cases instead of adapting their decisions to the growing needs of society as revealed by the moral standard of utility.[35] The villains of

---

> In short, rejecting the implied assumption that all propositions of all parts of the law must be logically consistent with each other and proceed on a single set of definitions . . . he [Cardozo, J.,] denied that the law is actually what the analytical jurist, *for his limited purposes*, assumes it to be.

See also *id.* at 49, 52, 138, 140; FRIEDMANN, LEGAL THEORY 209 (3d ed. 1953). This misunderstanding seems to depend on the unexamined and false belief that analytical studies of the meaning of legal terms would be impossible or absurd if, to reach sound decisions in particular cases, more than a capacity for formal logical reasoning from unambiguous and clear predetermined premises is required.

[33] See the discussion of vagueness and uncertainty in law, in AUSTIN, *op. cit. supra* note 12, at 202–05, 207, in which Austin recognized that, in consequence of this vagueness, often only "fallible tests" can be provided for determining whether particular cases fall under general expressions.

[34] See AUSTIN, *op. cit. supra* note 12, at 191: "I cannot understand how any person who has considered the subject can suppose that society could possibly have gone on if judges had not legislated . . . ." As a corrective to the belief that the analytical jurist must take a "slot machine" or "mechanical" view of the judicial process it is worth noting the following observations made by Austin:

(1) Whenever law has to be applied, the " 'competition of opposite analogies' " may arise, for the case "may resemble in some of its points" cases to which the rule has been applied in the past and in other points "cases from which the application of the law has been withheld." 2 AUSTIN, LECTURES ON JURISPRUDENCE 633 (5th ed. 1885).

(2) Judges have commonly decided cases and so derived new rules by "building" on a variety of grounds including sometimes (in Austin's opinion too rarely) their views of what law ought to be. Most commonly they have derived law from preexisting law by "consequence founded on analogy," *i.e.*, they have made a new rule "in *consequence* of the existence of a similar rule applying to subjects which are *analogous* . . . ." 2 *id.* at 638–39.

(3) "[I]f every rule in a system of law were perfectly definite or precise," these difficulties incident to the application of law would not arise. "But the ideal completeness and correctness I now have imagined is not attainable in fact. . . . though the system had been built and ordered with matchless solicitude and skill." 2 *id.* at 997–98. Of course he thought that much could and should be done by codification to eliminate uncertainty. See 2 *id.* at 662–81.

[35] 2 *id.* at 641:

> Nothing, indeed, can be more natural, than that legislators, direct or judicial (especially if they be narrow-minded, timid and unskillful), should lean as much as they can on the examples set by their predecessors.

See also 2 *id.* at 647:

> But it is much to be regretted that Judges of capacity, experience and weight, have not seized every opportunity of introducing a new rule (a rule beneficial for the future) . . . . This is the reproach I should be inclined to make against Lord Eldon. . . . [T]he Judges of the Common Law Courts would not do what

this piece, responsible for the conception of the judge as an automaton, are not the Utilitarian thinkers. The responsibility, if it is to be laid at the door of any theorist, is with thinkers like Blackstone and, at an earlier stage, Montesquieu. The root of this evil is preoccupation with the separation of powers and Blackstone's "childish fiction" (as Austin termed it) that judges only "find," never "make," law.

But we are concerned with "formalism" as a vice not of jurists but of judges. What precisely is it for a judge to commit this error, to be a "formalist," "automatic," a "slot machine"? Curiously enough the literature which is full of the denunciation of these vices never makes this clear in concrete terms; instead we have only descriptions which cannot mean what they appear to say: it is said that in the formalist error courts make an excessive use of logic, take a thing to "a dryly logical extreme,"[36] or make an excessive use of analytical methods. But just how in being a formalist does a judge make an excessive use of logic? It is clear that the essence of his error is to give some general term an interpretation which is blind to social values and consequences (or which is in some other way stupid or perhaps merely disliked by critics). But logic does not prescribe interpretation of terms; it dictates neither the stupid nor intelligent interpretation of any expression. Logic only tells you hypothetically that *if* you give a certain term a certain interpretation then a certain conclusion follows. Logic is silent on how to classify particulars — and this is the heart of a judicial decision. So this reference to logic and to logical extremes is a misnomer for something else, which must be this. A judge has to apply a rule to a concrete case — perhaps the rule that one may not take a stolen "vehicle" across state lines, and in this case an airplane has been taken.[37] He either does not see or pretends not to see that the general terms of this rule are susceptible of different interpretations and that he has a choice left open uncontrolled by linguistic conventions. He ignores, or is blind to, the fact that he is in the area of the penumbra and is not dealing with a standard case. Instead of

---

they ought to have done, namely to model their rules of law and of procedure to the growing exigencies of society, instead of stupidly and sulkily adhering to the old and barbarous usages.

[36] Hynes v. New York Cent. R.R., 231 N.Y. 229, 235, 131 N.E. 898, 900 (1921); see POUND, INTERPRETATIONS OF LEGAL HISTORY 123 (2d ed. 1930); STONE, *op. cit. supra* note 32, at 140–41.

[37] See McBoyle v. United States, 283 U.S. 25 (1931).

choosing in the light of social aims, the judge fixes the meaning in a different way. He either takes the meaning that the word most obviously suggests in its ordinary nonlegal context to ordinary men, or one which the word has been given in some other legal context, or, still worse, he thinks of a standard case and then arbitrarily identifies certain features in it — for example, in the case of a vehicle, (1) normally used on land, (2) capable of carrying a human person, (3) capable of being self-propelled — and treats these three as always necessary and always sufficient conditions for the use in all contexts of the word "vehicle," irrespective of the social consequences of giving it this interpretation. This choice, not "logic," would force the judge to include a toy motor car (if electrically propelled) and to exclude bicycles and the airplane. In all this there is possibly great stupidity but no more "logic," and no less, than in cases in which the interpretation given to a general term and the consequent application of some general rule to a particular case is consciously controlled by some identified social aim.

Decisions made in a fashion as blind as this would scarcely deserve the name of decisions; we might as well toss a penny in applying a rule of law. But it is at least doubtful whether any judicial decisions (even in England) have been quite as automatic as this. Rather, either the interpretations stigmatized as automatic have resulted from the conviction that it is fairer in a criminal statute to take a meaning which would jump to the mind of the ordinary man at the cost even of defeating other values, and this itself is a social policy (though possibly a bad one); or much more frequently, what is stigmatized as "mechanical" and "automatic" is a determined choice made indeed in the light of a social aim but of a conservative social aim. Certainly many of the Supreme Court decisions at the turn of the century which have been so stigmatized [38] represent clear choices in the penumbral area to give effect to a policy of a conservative type. This is peculiarly true of Mr. Justice Peckham's opinions defining the spheres of police power and due process.[39]

---

[38] See, *e.g.*, Pound, *Mechanical Jurisprudence*, 8 COLUM. L. REV. 605, 615–16 (1908).

[39] See, *e.g.*, Lochner v. New York, 198 U.S. 45 (1905). Justice Peckham's opinion that there were no reasonable grounds for interfering with the right of free contract by determining the hours of labour in the occupation of a baker may indeed be a wrongheaded piece of conservatism but there is nothing automatic or mechanical about it.

But how does the wrongness of deciding cases in an automatic and mechanical way and the rightness of deciding cases by reference to social purposes show that the utilitarian insistence on the distinction between what the law is and what it ought to be is wrong? I take it that no one who wished to use these vices of formalism as proof that the distinction between what is and what ought to be is mistaken would deny that the decisions stigmatized as automatic are law; nor would he deny that the system in which such automatic decisions are made is a legal system. Surely he would say that they are law, but they are bad law, they ought not to be law. But this would be to use the distinction, not to refute it; and of course both Bentham and Austin used it to attack judges for failing to decide penumbral cases in accordance with the growing needs of society.

Clearly, if the demonstration of the errors of formalism is to show the utilitarian distinction to be wrong, the point must be drastically restated. The point must be not merely that a judicial decision to be rational must be made in the light of some conception of what ought to be, but that the aims, the social policies and purposes to which judges should appeal if their decisions are to be rational, are themselves to be considered as part of the law in some suitably wide sense of "law" which is held to be more illuminating than that used by the Utilitarians. This restatement of the point would have the following consequence: instead of saying that the recurrence of penumbral questions shows us that legal rules are essentially incomplete, and that, when they fail to determine decisions, judges must legislate and so exercise a creative choice between alternatives, we shall say that the social policies which guide the judges' choice are in a sense there for them to discover; the judges are only "drawing out" of the rule what, if it is properly understood, is "latent" within it. To call this judicial legislation is to obscure some essential continuity between the clear cases of the rule's application and the penumbral decisions. I shall question later whether this way of talking is salutory, but I wish at this time to point out something obvious, but likely, if not stated, to tangle the issues. It does not follow that, because the opposite of a decision reached blindly in the formalist or literalist manner is a decision intelligently reached by reference to some conception of what ought to be, we have a junction of law and morals. We must, I think, beware of thinking in a too simple-minded fashion about the word "ought." This is not because there is no distinction to be made between law as it is and ought to be. Far from it. It is because the distinction should be between what is and what from many different points of view ought to be. The word "ought" merely reflects the presence of some standard of criticism; one of these standards is a moral standard but not all standards are moral. We say to our neighbour, "You ought not to lie," and that may certainly be a moral judgment, but we should remember that the baffled poisoner may say, "I ought to have given her a second dose." The point here is that intelligent decisions which we oppose to mechanical or formal decisions are not necessarily identical with decisions defensible on moral grounds. We may say of many a decision: "Yes, that is right; that is as it ought to be," and we may mean only that some accepted purpose or policy has been thereby advanced; we may not mean to endorse the moral propriety of the policy or the decision. So the contrast between the mechanical decision and the intelligent one can be reproduced inside a system dedicated to the pursuit of the most evil aims. It does not exist as a contrast to be found only in legal systems which, like our own, widely recognize principles of justice and moral claims of individuals.

An example may make this point plainer. With us the task of sentencing in criminal cases is the one that seems most obviously to demand from the judge the exercise of moral judgment. Here the factors to be weighed seem clearly to be moral factors: society must not be exposed to wanton attack; too much misery must not be inflicted on either the victim or his dependents; efforts must be made to enable him to lead a better life and regain a position in the society whose laws he has violated. To a judge striking the balance among these claims, with all the discretion and perplexities involved, his task seems as plain an example of the exercise of moral judgment as could be; and it seems to be the polar opposite of some mechanical application of a tariff of penalties fixing a sentence careless of the moral claims which in our system have to be weighed. So here intelligent and rational decision is guided however uncertainly by moral aims. But we have only to vary the example to see that this need not necessarily be so and surely, if it need not necessarily be so, the Utilitarian point remains unshaken. Under the Nazi regime men were sentenced by courts for criticism of the regime. Here the choice of sentence might be guided exclusively by consideration of what was needed to maintain the state's tyranny effectively. What sentence would both terrorize the public at large and keep the friends and family of the prisoner in suspense so that both hope and fear would cooperate as factors making for subservience? The prisoner of such a system would be regarded simply as an object to be used in pursuit of these aims. Yet, in contrast with a mechanical decision, decision on these grounds would be intelligent and purposive, and from one point of view the decision would be as it ought to be. Of course, I am not unaware that a whole philosophical tradition has sought to demonstrate the fact that we cannot correctly call decisions or behavior truly rational unless they are in conformity with moral aims and principles. But the example I have used seems to me to serve at least as a warning that we cannot use the errors of formalism as something which per se demonstrates the falsity of the utilitarian insistence on the distinction between law as it is and law as *morally* it ought to be.

We can now return to the main point. If it is true that the intelligent decision of penumbral questions is one made not mechanically but in the light of aims, purposes, and policies, though not necessarily in the light of anything we would call moral principles, is it wise to express this important fact by saying that the firm utilitarian distinction between what the law is and what it ought to be should be dropped? Perhaps the claim that it is wise cannot be theoretically refuted for it is, in effect, an *invitation* to revise our conception of what a legal rule is. We are invited to include in the "rule" the various aims and policies in the light of which its penumbral cases are decided on the ground that these aims have, because of their importance, as much right to be called law as the core of legal rules whose meaning is settled. But though an invitation cannot be refuted, it may be refused and I would proffer two reasons for refusing this invitation. First, everything we have learned about the judicial process can be expressed in other less mysterious ways. We can say laws are incurably incomplete and we must decide the penumbral cases rationally by reference to social aims. I think Holmes, who had such a vivid appreciation of the fact that "general propositions do not decide concrete cases," would have put it that way. Second, to insist on the utilitarian distinction is to emphasize that the hard core of settled meaning is law in some centrally important sense and that even if there are borderlines, there must first be lines. If this were not so the notion of rules controlling courts' decisions would be senseless as some of the "Realists" — in their most extreme moods, and, I think, on bad grounds — claimed.[40] By contrast, to soften the distinction, to assert mysteriously that there is some fused identity between law as it is and as it ought to be, is to suggest that all legal questions are fundamentally like those of the penumbra. It is to assert that there is no central element of actual law to be seen in the core of central meaning which rules have, that there is nothing in the nature of a legal rule inconsistent with *all* questions being open to reconsideration in the light of social policy. Of course, it is good to be occupied with the penumbra. Its problems are rightly the daily diet of the law schools. But to be occupied with the penumbra is one thing, to be preoccupied with it another. And preoccupation with the penumbra is, if I may say so, as rich a source of confusion in the American legal tradition as formalism in the English. Of course we might abandon the notion that rules have authority; we might cease to attach force or even meaning to an argument that a case falls clearly within a rule and the scope of a precedent. We might call all such reasoning "automatic" or "mechanical," which is already the routine invective of the courts. But until we decide that this *is* what we want, we should not encourage it by obliterating the Utilitarian distinction.

IV.

The third criticism of the separation of law and morals is of a very different character; it certainly is less an intellectual argument against the Utilitarian distinction than a passionate appeal supported not by detailed reasoning but by reminders of a terrible experience. For it consists of the testimony of those who have descended into Hell, and, like Ulysses or Dante, brought back a message for human beings. Only in this case the Hell was not

[40] One recantation of this extreme position is worth mention in the present context. In the first edition of *The Bramble Bush*, Professor Llewellyn committed himself wholeheartedly to the view that "what these officials do about disputes is, to my mind, the law itself" and that "*rules* . . . are important so far as they help you . . . predict what judges will do . . . . That is all their importance, except as pretty playthings." LLEWELLYN, THE BRAMBLE BUSH 3, 5 (1st ed. 1930). In the second edition he said that these were "unhappy words when not more fully developed, and they are plainly at best a very partial statement of the whole truth. . . . [O]ne office of law is to control officials in some part, and to guide them even . . . where no thoroughgoing control is possible, or is desired. . . . [T]he words fail to take proper account . . . of the office of the institution of law as an instrument of conscious shaping . . . ." LLEWELLYN, THE BRAMBLE BUSH 9 (2d ed. 1951).

beneath or beyond earth, but on it; it was a Hell created on earth by men for other men.

This appeal comes from those German thinkers who lived through the Nazi regime and reflected upon its evil manifestations in the legal system. One of these thinkers, Gustav Radbruch, had himself shared the "positivist" doctrine until the Nazi tyranny, but he was converted by this experience and so his appeal to other men to discard the doctrine of the separation of law and morals has the special poignancy of a recantation. What is important about this criticism is that it really does confront the particular point which Bentham and Austin had in mind in urging the separation of law as it is and as it ought to be. These German thinkers put their insistence on the need to join together what the Utilitarians separated just where this separation was of most importance in the eyes of the Utilitarians; for they were concerned with the problem posed by the existence of morally evil laws.

Before his conversion Radbruch held that resistance to law was a matter for the personal conscience, to be thought out by the individual as a moral problem, and the validity of a law could not be disproved by showing that its requirements were morally evil or even by showing that the effect of compliance with the law would be more evil than the effect of disobedience. Austin, it may be recalled, was emphatic in condemning those who said that if human laws conflicted with the fundamental principles of morality then they cease to be laws, as talking "stark nonsense."

> The most pernicious laws, and therefore those which are most opposed to the will of God, have been and are continually enforced as laws by judicial tribunals. Suppose an act innocuous, or positively beneficial, be prohibited by the sovereign under the penalty of death; if I commit this act, I shall be tried and condemned, and if I object to the sentence, that it is contrary to the law of God . . . the court of justice will demonstrate the inconclusiveness of my reasoning by hanging me up, in pursuance of the law of which I have impugned the validity. An exception, demurrer, or plea, founded on the law of God was never heard in a Court of Justice, from the creation of the world down to the present moment.[41]

These are strong, indeed brutal words, but we must remember that they went along — in the case of Austin and, of course,

[41] AUSTIN, THE PROVINCE OF JURISPRUDENCE DETERMINED 185 (Library of Ideas ed. 1954).

Bentham — with the conviction that if laws reached a certain degree of iniquity then there would be a plain moral obligation to resist them and to withhold obedience. We shall see, when we consider the alternatives, that this simple presentation of the human dilemma which may arise has much to be said for it.

Radbruch, however, had concluded from the ease with which the Nazi regime had exploited subservience to mere law — or expressed, as he thought, in the "positivist" slogan "law as law" (*Gesetz als Gesetz*) — and from the failure of the German legal profession to protest against the enormities which they were required to perpetrate in the name of law, that "positivism" (meaning here the insistence on the separation of law as it is from law as it ought to be) had powerfully contributed to the horrors. His considered reflections led him to the doctrine that the fundamental principles of humanitarian morality were part of the very concept of *Recht* or Legality and that no positive enactment or statute, however clearly it was expressed and however clearly it conformed with the formal criteria of validity of a given legal system, could be valid if it contravened basic principles of morality. This doctrine can be appreciated fully only if the nuances imported by the German word *Recht* are grasped. But it is clear that the doctrine meant that every lawyer and judge should denounce statutes that transgressed the fundamental principles not as merely immoral or wrong but as having no legal character, and enactments which on this ground lack the quality of law should not be taken into account in working out the legal position of any given individual in particular circumstances. The striking recantation of his previous doctrine is unfortunately omitted from the translation of his works, but it should be read by all who wish to think afresh on the question of the interconnection of law and morals.[42]

It is impossible to read without sympathy Radbruch's passionate demand that the German legal conscience should be open to the demands of morality and his complaint that this has been too little the case in the German tradition. On the other hand there is an extraordinary naïveté in the view that insensitiveness

[42] See Radbruch, *Gesetzliches Unrecht und Übergesetzliches Recht*, 1 SÜDDEUTSCHE JURISTEN-ZEITUNG 105 (Germany 1946) (reprinted in RADBRUCH, RECHTSPHILOSOPHIE 347 (4th ed. 1950)). I have used the translation of part of this essay and of Radbruch, *Die Erneuerung des Rechts*, 2 DIE WANDLUNG 8 (Germany 1947), prepared by Professor Lon Fuller of the Harvard Law School as a mimeographed supplement to the readings in jurisprudence used in his course at Harvard.

to the demands of morality and subservience to state power in a people like the Germans should have arisen from the belief that law might be law though it failed to conform with the minimum requirements of morality. Rather this terrible history prompts inquiry into why emphasis on the slogan "law is law," and the distinction between law and morals, acquired a sinister character in Germany, but elsewhere, as with the Utilitarians themselves, went along with the most enlightened liberal attitudes. But something more disturbing than naïveté is latent in Radbruch's whole presentation of the issues to which the existence of morally iniquitous laws give rise. It is not, I think, uncharitable to say that we can see in his argument that he has only half digested the spiritual message of liberalism which he is seeking to convey to the legal profession. For everything that he says is really dependent upon an enormous overvaluation of the importance of the bare fact that a rule may be said to be a valid rule of law, as if this, once declared, was conclusive of the final moral question: "Ought this rule of law to be obeyed?" Surely the truly liberal answer to any sinister use of the slogan "law is law" or of the distinction between law and morals is, "Very well, but that does not conclude the question. Law is not morality; do not let it supplant morality."

However, we are not left to a mere academic discussion in order to evaluate the plea which Radbruch made for the revision of the distinction between law and morals. After the war Radbruch's conception of law as containing in itself the essential moral principle of humanitarianism was applied in practice by German courts in certain cases in which local war criminals, spies, and informers under the Nazi regime were punished. The special importance of these cases is that the persons accused of these crimes claimed that what they had done was not illegal under the laws of the regime in force at the time these actions were performed. This plea was met with the reply that the laws upon which they relied were invalid as contravening the fundamental principles of morality. Let me cite briefly one of these cases.[43]

In 1944 a woman, wishing to be rid of her husband, denounced him to the authorities for insulting remarks he had made about Hitler while home on leave from the German army. The wife was

[43] Judgment of July 27, 1949, Oberlandesgericht, Bamberg, 5 SÜDDEUTSCHE JURISTEN-ZEITUNG 207 (Germany 1950), 64 HARV. L. REV. 1005 (1951); see FRIEDMANN, LEGAL THEORY 457 (3d ed. 1953).

under no legal duty to report his acts, though what he had said was apparently in violation of statutes making it illegal to make statements detrimental to the government of the Third Reich or to impair by any means the military defense of the German people. The husband was arrested and sentenced to death, apparently pursuant to these statutes, though he was not executed but was sent to the front. In 1949 the wife was prosecuted in a West German court for an offense which we would describe as illegally depriving a person of his freedom (*rechtswidrige Freiheitsberaubung*). This was punishable as a crime under the German Criminal Code of 1871 which had remained in force continuously since its enactment. The wife pleaded that her husband's imprisonment was pursuant to the Nazi statutes and hence that she had committed no crime. The court of appeal to which the case ultimately came held that the wife was guilty of procuring the deprivation of her husband's liberty by denouncing him to the German courts, even though he had been sentenced by a court for having violated a statute, since, to quote the words of the court, the statute "was contrary to the sound conscience and sense of justice of all decent human beings." This reasoning was followed in many cases which have been hailed as a triumph of the doctrines of natural law and as signaling the overthrow of positivism. The unqualified satisfaction with this result seems to me to be hysteria. Many of us might applaud the objective — that of punishing a woman for an outrageously immoral act — but this was secured only by declaring a statute established since 1934 not to have the force of law, and at least the wisdom of this course must be doubted. There were, of course, two other choices. One was to let the woman go unpunished; one can sympathize with and endorse the view that this might have been a bad thing to do. The other was to face the fact that if the woman were to be punished it must be pursuant to the introduction of a frankly retrospective law and with a full consciousness of what was sacrificed in securing her punishment in this way. Odious as retrospective criminal legislation and punishment may be, to have pursued it openly in this case would at least have had the merits of candour. It would have made plain that in punishing the woman a choice had to be made between two evils, that of leaving her unpunished and that of sacrificing a very precious principle of morality endorsed by most legal systems. Surely if we have learned anything from the history of morals it is that the thing to do with a moral quandary is not to hide it. Like nettles, the occasions when life forces us to choose between the lesser of two evils must be grasped with the consciousness that they are what they are. The vice of this use of the principle that, at certain limiting points, what is utterly immoral cannot be law or lawful is that it will serve to cloak the true nature of the problems with which we are faced and will encourage the romantic optimism that all the values we cherish ultimately will fit into a single system, that no one of them has to be sacrificed or compromised to accommodate another.

> "All Discord Harmony not understood
> All Partial Evil Universal Good"

This is surely untrue and there is an insincerity in any formulation of our problem which allows us to describe the treatment of the dilemma as if it were the disposition of the ordinary case.

It may seem perhaps to make too much of forms, even perhaps of words, to emphasize one way of disposing of this difficult case as compared with another which might have led, so far as the woman was concerned, to exactly the same result. Why should we dramatize the difference between them? We might punish the woman under a new retrospective law and declare overtly that we were doing something inconsistent with our principles as the lesser of two evils; or we might allow the case to pass as one in which we do not point out precisely where we sacrifice such a principle. But candour is not just one among many minor virtues of the administration of law, just as it is not merely a minor virtue of morality. For if we adopt Radbruch's view, and with him and the German courts make our protest against evil law in the form of an assertion that certain rules cannot be law because of their moral iniquity, we confuse one of the most powerful, because it is the simplest, forms of moral criticism. If with the Utilitarians we speak plainly, we say that laws may be law but too evil to be obeyed. This is a moral condemnation which everyone can understand and it makes an immediate and obvious claim to moral attention. If, on the other hand, we formulate our objection as an assertion that these evil things are not law, here is an assertion which many people do not believe, and if they are disposed to consider it at all, it would seem to raise a whole host of philosophical issues before it can be accepted. So perhaps the most important single lesson to be learned from this form of the denial of the Utilitarian distinction is the one that the Utilitarians were most concerned to teach: when we have the ample resources of plain speech we must not present the moral criticism of institutions as propositions of a disputable philosophy.

V.

I have endeavored to show that, in spite of all that has been learned and experienced since the Utilitarians wrote, and in spite of the defects of other parts of their doctrine, their protest against the confusion of what is and what ought to be law has a moral as well as an intellectual value. Yet it may well be said that, though this distinction is valid and important if applied to any particular law of a system, it is at least misleading if we attempt to apply it to "law," that is, to the notion of a legal system, and that if we insist, as I have, on the narrower truth (or truism), we obscure a wider (or deeper) truth. After all, it may be urged, we have learned that there are many things which are untrue of laws taken separately, but which are true and important in a legal system considered as a whole. For example, the connection between law and sanctions and between the existence of law and its "efficacy" must be understood in this more general way. It is surely not arguable (without some desperate extension of the word "sanction" or artificial narrowing of the word "law") that every law in a municipal legal system must have a sanction, yet it is at least plausible to argue that a legal system must, to be a legal system, provide sanctions for certain of its rules. So too, a rule of law may be said to exist though enforced or obeyed in only a minority of cases, but this could not be said of a legal system as a whole. Perhaps the differences with respect to laws taken separately and a legal system as a whole are also true of the connection between moral (or some other) conceptions of what law ought to be and law in this wider sense.

This line of argument, found (at least in embryo form) in Austin, where he draws attention to the fact that every developed legal system contains certain fundamental notions which are "necessary" and "bottomed in the common nature of man,"[44] is worth pursuing — up to a point — and I shall say briefly why and how far this is so.

[44] AUSTIN, *Uses of the Study of Jurisprudence*, in THE PROVINCE OF JURISPRUDENCE DETERMINED 365, 373, 367–69 (Library of Ideas ed. 1954).

We must avoid, if we can, the arid wastes of inappropriate definition, for, in relation to a concept as many-sided and vague as that of a legal system, disputes about the "essential" character, or necessity to the whole, of any single element soon begin to look like disputes about whether chess could be "chess" if played without pawns. There is a wish, which may be understandable, to cut straight through the question whether a legal system, to be a legal system, must measure up to some moral or other standard with simple statements of fact: for example, that no system which utterly failed in this respect has ever existed or could endure; that the normally fulfilled assumption that a legal system aims at some form of justice colours the whole way in which we interpret specific rules in particular cases, and if this normally fulfilled assumption were not fulfilled no one would have any reason to obey except fear (and probably not that) and still less, of course, any moral obligation to obey. The connection between law and moral standards and principles of justice is therefore as little arbitrary and as "necessary" as the connection between law and sanctions, and the pursuit of the question whether this necessity is logical (part of the "meaning" of law) or merely factual or causal can safely be left as an innocent pastime for philosophers.

Yet in two respects I should wish to go further (even though this involves the use of a philosophical fantasy) and show what could intelligibly be meant by the claim that certain provisions in a legal system are "necessary." The world in which we live, and we who live in it, may one day change in many different ways; and if this change were radical enough not only would certain statements of fact now true be false and vice versa, but whole ways of thinking and talking which constitute our present conceptual apparatus, through which we see the world and each other, would lapse. We have only to consider how the whole of our social, moral, and legal life, as we understand it now, depends on the contingent fact that though our bodies do change in shape, size, and other physical properties they do not do this so drastically nor with such quicksilver rapidity and irregularity that we cannot identify each other as the same persistent individual over considerable spans of time. Though this is but a contingent fact which may one day be different, on it at present rest huge structures of our thought and principles of action and social life. Similarly, consider the following possibility (not because it is more than a possibility but because it reveals why we think certain things necessary in a legal system and what we mean by this): suppose that men were to become invulnerable to attack by each other, were clad perhaps like giant land crabs with an impenetrable carapace, and could extract the food they needed from the air by some internal chemical process. In such circumstances (the details of which can be left to science fiction) rules forbidding the free use of violence and rules constituting the minimum form of property — with its rights and duties sufficient to enable food to grow and be retained until eaten — would not have the necessary nonarbitrary status which they have for us, constituted as we are in a world like ours. At present, and until such radical changes supervene, such rules are so fundamental that if a legal system did not have them there would be no point in having any other rules at all. Such rules overlap with basic moral principles vetoing murder, violence, and theft; and so we can add to the factual statement that all legal systems in fact coincide with morality at such vital points, the statement that this is, in this sense, necessarily so. And why not call it a "natural" necessity?

Of course even this much depends on the fact that in asking what content a legal system must have we take this question to be worth asking only if we who consider it cherish the humble aim of survival in close proximity to our fellows. Natural-law theory, however, in all its protean guises, attempts to push the argument much further and to assert that human beings are equally devoted to and united in their conception of aims (the pursuit of knowledge, justice to their fellow men) other than that of survival, and these dictate a further necessary content to a legal system (over and above my humble minimum) without which it would be pointless. Of course we must be careful not to exaggerate the differences among human beings, but it seems to me that above this minimum the purposes men have for living in society are too conflicting and varying to make possible much extension of the argument that some fuller overlap of legal rules and moral standards is "necessary" in this sense.

Another aspect of the matter deserves attention. If we attach to a legal system the minimum meaning that it must consist of general rules — general both in the sense that they refer to courses of action, not single actions, and to multiplicities of men, not single individuals — this meaning connotes the principle of treating like cases alike, though the criteria of when cases are alike will be, so far, only the general elements specified in the rules. It is, however, true that *one* essential element of the concept of justice is the principle of treating like cases alike. This is justice in the administration of the law, not justice of the law. So there is, in the very notion of law consisting of general rules, something which prevents us from treating it as if morally it is utterly neutral, without any necessary contact with moral principles. Natural procedural justice consists therefore of those principles of objectivity and impartiality in the administration of the law which implement just this aspect of law and which are designed to ensure that rules are applied only to what are genuinely cases of the rule or at least to minimize the risks of inequalities in this sense.

These two reasons (or excuses) for talking of a certain overlap between legal and moral standards as necessary and natural, of course, should not satisfy anyone who is really disturbed by the Utilitarian or "positivist" insistence that law and morality are distinct. This is so because a legal system that satisfied these minimum requirements might apply, with the most pedantic impartiality as between the persons affected, laws which were hideously oppressive, and might deny to a vast rightless slave population the minimum benefits of protection from violence and theft. The stink of such societies is, after all, still in our nostrils and to argue that they have (or had) no legal system would only involve the repetition of the argument. Only if the rules failed to provide these essential benefits and protection for anyone — even for a slave-owning group — would the minimum be unsatisfied and the system sink to the status of a set of meaningless taboos. Of course no one denied those benefits would have any reason to obey except fear and would have every moral reason to revolt.

VI.

I should be less than candid if I did not, in conclusion, consider something which, I suspect, most troubles those who react strongly against "legal positivism." Emphasis on the distinction between law as it is and law as it ought to be may be taken to depend upon and to entail what are called "subjectivist" and "relativist" or "noncognitive" theories concerning the very nature of moral judgments, moral distinctions, or "values." Of course the Utilitarians themselves (as distinct from later positivists like Kelsen) did not countenance any such theories, however unsatisfactory their moral philosophy may appear to us now. Austin thought ultimate moral principles were the commands of God, known to us by revelation or through the "index" of utility, and Bentham thought they were verifiable propositions about utility. Nonetheless I think (though I cannot prove) that insistence upon the distinction between law as it is and ought to be has been, under the general head of "positivism," confused with a moral theory according to which statements of what is the case ("statements of fact") belong to a category or type radically different from statements of what ought to be ("value statements"). It may therefore be well to dispel this source of confusion.

There are many contemporary variants of this type of moral theory: according to some, judgments of what ought to be, or ought to be done, either are or include as essential elements expressions of "feeling," "emotion," or "attitudes" or "subjective preferences"; in others such judgments both express feelings or emotions or attitudes and enjoin others to share them. In other variants such judgments indicate that a particular case falls under a general principle or policy of action which the speaker has "chosen" or to which he is "committed" and which is itself not a recognition of what is the case but analogous to a general "imperative" or command addressed to all including the speaker himself. Common to all these variants is the insistence that judgments of what ought to be done, because they contain such "non-cognitive" elements, cannot be argued for or established by rational methods as statements of fact can be, and cannot be shown to follow from any statement of fact but only from other judgments of what ought to be done in conjunction with some statement of fact. We cannot, on such a theory, demonstrate, *e.g.*, that an action was wrong, ought not to have been done, merely by showing that it consisted of the deliberate infliction of pain solely for the gratification of the agent. We only show it to be wrong if we add to those verifiable "cognitive" statements of fact a general principle not itself verifiable or "cognitive" that the infliction of pain in such circumstances is wrong, ought not to be done. Together with this general distinction between statements of what is and what ought to be go sharp parallel distinctions between statements about means and statements of moral ends. We can rationally discover and debate what are appropriate means to given ends, but ends are not rationally discoverable or debatable; they are "fiats of the will," expressions of "emotions," "preferences," or "attitudes."

Against all such views (which are of course far subtler than this crude survey can convey) others urge that all these sharp distinctions between is and ought, fact and value, means and ends, cognitive and noncognitive, are wrong. In acknowledging ultimate ends or moral values we are recognizing something as much imposed upon us by the character of the world in which we live, as little a matter of choice, attitude, feeling, emotion as the truth of factual judgments about what is the case. The characteristic moral argument is not one in which the parties are reduced to expressing or kindling feelings or emotions or issuing exhortations or commands to each other but one by which parties come to acknowledge after closer examination and reflection that an initially disputed case falls within the ambit of a vaguely apprehended principle (itself no more "subjective," no more a "fiat of our will" than any other principle of classification) and this has as much title to be called "cognitive" or "rational" as any other initially disputed classification of particulars.

Let us now suppose that we accept this rejection of "noncognitive" theories of morality and this denial of the drastic distinction in type between statements of what is and what ought to be, and that moral judgments are as rationally defensible as any other kind of judgments. What would follow from this as to the nature of the connection between law as it is and law as it ought to be? Surely, from this alone, nothing. Laws, however morally iniquitous, would still (so far as this point is concerned) be laws. The only difference which the acceptance of this view of the nature of moral judgments would make would be that the moral iniquity of such laws would be something that could be demonstrated; it would surely follow merely from a statement of what the rule required to be done that the rule was morally wrong and so ought not to be law or conversely that it was morally desirable and ought to be law. But the demonstration of this would not show the rule not to be (or to be) law. Proof that the principles by which we evaluate or condemn laws are rationally discoverable, and not mere "fiats of the will," leaves untouched the fact that there are laws which may have any degree of iniquity or stupidity and still be laws. And conversely there are rules that have every moral qualification to be laws and yet are not laws.

Surely something further or more specific must be said if disproof of "noncognitivism" or kindred theories in ethics is to be relevant to the distinction between law as it is and law as it ought to be, and to lead to the abandonment at some point or some softening of this distinction. No one has done more than Professor Lon Fuller of the Harvard Law School in his various writings to make clear such a line of argument and I will end by criticising what I take to be its central point. It is a point which again emerges when we consider not those legal rules or parts of legal rules the meanings of which are clear and excite no debate but the interpretation of rules in concrete cases where doubts are initially felt and argument develops about their meaning. In no legal system is the scope of legal rules restricted to the range of concrete instances which were present or are believed to have been present in the minds of legislators; this indeed is one of the important differences between a legal rule and a command. Yet, when rules are recognized as applying to instances beyond any that legislators did or could have considered, their extension to such new cases often presents itself not as a deliberate choice or fiat on the part of those who so interpret the rule. It appears neither as a decision to give the rule a new or extended meaning nor as a guess as to what legislators, dead perhaps in the eighteenth century, would have said had they been alive in the twentieth century. Rather, the inclusion of the new case under the rule takes its place as a natural elaboration of the rule, as something implementing a "purpose" which it seems natural to attribute (in some sense) to the rule itself rather than to any particular person dead or alive. The Utilitarian description of such interpretative extension of old rules to new cases as judicial legislation fails to do justice to this phenomenon; it gives no hint of the differences between a deliberate fiat or decision to treat the new case in the same way as past cases and a recognition (in which there is little that is deliberate or even voluntary) that inclusion of the new case under the rule will implement or articulate a continuing and identical purpose, hitherto less specifically apprehended.

Perhaps many lawyers and judges will see in this language something that precisely fits their experience; others may think it a romantic gloss on facts better stated in the Utilitarian language of judicial "legislation" or in the modern American terminology of "creative choice."

To make the point clear Professor Fuller uses a nonlegal example from the philosopher Wittgenstein which is, I think, illuminating.

> Someone says to me: "Show the children a game." I teach them gaming with dice and the other says "I did not mean that sort of game." Must the exclusion of the game with dice have come before his mind when he gave me the order? [45]

Something important does seem to me to be touched on in this example. Perhaps there are the following (distinguishable) points. First, we normally do interpret not only what people are trying to do but what they say in the light of assumed common human objectives so that unless the contrary were expressly indicated we would not interpret an instruction to show a young child a game as a mandate to introduce him to gambling even though in other contexts the word "game" would be naturally so interpreted. Second, very often, the speaker whose words are thus interpreted might say: "Yes, that's what I mean [or "that's what I meant all along"] though I never thought of it until you put this particular case to me." Third, when we thus recognize, perhaps after argument or consultation with others, a particular case not specifically envisaged beforehand as falling within the ambit of some vaguely expressed instruction, we may find this experience falsified by description of it as a mere decision on our part so to treat the particular case, and that we can only describe this faithfully as coming to realize and to articulate what we "really" want or our "true purpose" — phrases which Professor Fuller uses later in the same article.[46]

I am sure that many philosophical discussions of the character of moral argument would benefit from attention to cases of the sort instanced by Professor Fuller. Such attention would help to provide a corrective to the view that there is a sharp separation between "ends" and "means" and that in debating "ends" we can only work on each other nonrationally, and that rational argument is reserved for discussion of "means." But I think the relevance of his point to the issue whether it is correct or wise to insist on the distinction between law as it is and law as it ought to be is very small indeed. Its net effect is that in interpreting legal rules there are some cases which we find after reflection to be so natural an elaboration or articulation of the rule that to think of and

---

[45] Fuller, *Human Purpose and Natural Law*, 53 J. PHILOS. 697, 700 (1956).

[46] *Id.* at 701, 702.

refer to this as "legislation," "making law," or a "fiat" on our part would be misleading. So, the argument must be, it would be misleading to distinguish in such cases between what the rule is and what it ought to be — at least in some sense of ought. We think it ought to include the new case and come to see after reflection that it really does. But even if this way of presenting a recognizable experience as an example of a fusion between is and ought to be is admitted, two caveats must be borne in mind. The first is that "ought" in this case need have nothing to do with morals for the reasons explained already in section III: there may be just the same sense that a new case will implement and articulate the purpose of a rule in interpreting the rules of a game or some hideously immoral code of oppression whose immorality is appreciated by those called in to interpret it. They too can see what the "spirit" of the game they are playing requires in previously unenvisaged cases. More important is this: after all is said and done we must remember how rare in the law is the phenomenon held to justify this way of talking, how exceptional is this feeling that one way of deciding a case is imposed upon us as the only natural or rational elaboration of some rule. Surely it cannot be doubted that, for most cases of interpretation, the language of choice between alternatives, "judicial legislation" or even "fiat" (though not arbitrary fiat), better conveys the realities of the situation.

Within the framework of relatively well-settled law there jostle too many alternatives too nearly equal in attraction between which judge and lawyer must uncertainly pick their way to make appropriate here language which may well describe those experiences which we have in interpreting our own or others' principles of conduct, intention, or wishes, when we are not conscious of exercising a deliberate choice, but rather of recognising something awaiting recognition. To use in the description of the interpretation of laws the suggested terminology of a fusion or inability to separate what is law and ought to be will serve (like earlier stories that judges only find, never make, law) only to conceal the facts, that here if anywhere we live among uncertainties between which we have to choose, and that the existing law imposes only limits on our choice and not the choice itself.

POSITIVISM AND FIDELITY TO LAW — A REPLY TO PROFESSOR HART

Lon L. Fuller *

Rephrasing the question of "law and morals" in terms of "order and good order," Professor Fuller criticizes Professor H. L. A. Hart for ignoring the internal "morality of order" necessary to the creation of all law. He then rejects Professor Hart's theory of statutory interpretation on the ground that we seek the objectives of entire provisions rather than the meanings of individual words which are claimed to have "standard instances."

PROFESSOR HART has made an enduring contribution to the literature of legal philosophy. I doubt if the issues he discusses will ever again assume quite the form they had before being touched by his analytical powers. His argument is no mere restatement of Bentham, Austin, Gray, and Holmes. Their views receive in his exposition a new clarity and a new depth that are uniquely his own.

I must confess that when I first encountered the thoughts of Professor Hart's essay, his argument seemed to me to suffer from a deep inner contradiction. On the one hand, he rejects emphatically any confusion of "what is" with "what ought to be." He will tolerate no "merger" of law and conceptions of what law ought to be, but at the most an antiseptic "intersection." Intelligible communication on any subject, he seems to imply, becomes impossible if we leave it uncertain whether we are talking about "what is" or "what ought to be." Yet it was precisely this uncertainty about Professor Hart's own argument which made it difficult for me at first to follow the thread of his thought. At times he seemed to be saying that the distinction between law and morality is something that exists, and will continue to exist, however we may talk about it. It expresses a reality which, whether we like it or not, we must accept if we are to avoid talking nonsense. At other times, he seemed to be warning us that the reality of the distinction is itself in danger and that if we do not mend our ways of thinking and talking we may lose a "precious moral

* Carter Professor of General Jurisprudence, Harvard Law School. A.B., Stanford, 1924, J.D., 1926.

ideal," that of fidelity to law. It is not clear, in other words, whether in Professor Hart's own thinking the distinction between law and morality simply "is," or is something that "ought to be" and that we should join with him in helping to create and maintain.

These were the perplexities I had about Professor Hart's argument when I first encountered it. But on reflection I am sure any criticism of his essay as being self-contradictory would be both unfair and unprofitable. There is no reason why the argument for a strict separation of law and morality cannot be rested on the double ground that this separation serves both intellectual clarity and moral integrity. If there are certain difficulties in bringing these two lines of reasoning into proper relation to one another, these difficulties affect also the position of those who reject the views of Austin, Gray, and Holmes. For those of us who find the "positivist" position unacceptable do ourselves rest our argument on the double ground that its intellectual clarity is specious and that its effects are, or may be, harmful. On the one hand, we assert that Austin's definition of law, for example, violates the reality it purports to describe. Being false in fact, it cannot serve effectively what Kelsen calls "an interest of cognition." On the other hand, we assert that under some conditions the same conception of law may become dangerous, since in human affairs what men mistakenly accept as real tends, by the very act of their acceptance, to become real.

It is a cardinal virtue of Professor Hart's argument that for the first time it opens the way for a truly profitable exchange of views between those whose differences center on the distinction between law and morality. Hitherto there has been no real joinder of issue between the opposing camps. On the one side, we encounter a series of definitional fiats. A rule of law is — that is to say, it really and simply and always is — the command of a sovereign, a rule laid down by a judge, a prediction of the future incidence of state force, a pattern of official behavior, etc. When we ask what purpose these definitions serve, we receive the answer, "Why, no purpose, except to describe accurately the social reality that corresponds to the word 'law.' " When we reply, "But it doesn't look like that to me," the answer comes back, "Well, it does to me." There the matter has to rest.

This state of affairs has been most unsatisfactory for those of us who are convinced that "positivistic" theories have had a distorting effect on the aims of legal philosophy. Our dissatisfaction arose not merely from the impasse we confronted, but because this impasse seemed to us so unnecessary. All that was needed to surmount it was an acknowledgment on the other side that its definitions of "what law really is" are not mere images of some datum of experience, but direction posts for the application of human energies. Since this acknowledgment was not forthcoming, the impasse and its frustrations continued. There is indeed no frustration greater than to be confronted by a theory which purports merely to describe, when it not only plainly prescribes, but owes its special prescriptive powers precisely to the fact that it disclaims prescriptive intentions. Into this murky debate, some shafts of light did occasionally break through, as in Kelsen's casual admission, apparently never repeated, that his whole system might well rest on an emotional preference for the ideal of order over that of justice.[1] But I have to confess that in general the dispute that has been conducted during the last twenty years has not been very profitable.

Now, with Professor Hart's paper, the discussion takes a new and promising turn. It is now explicitly acknowledged on both sides that one of the chief issues is how we can best define and serve the ideal of fidelity to law. Law, as something deserving loyalty, must represent a human achievement; it cannot be a simple fiat of power or a repetitive pattern discernible in the behavior of state officials. The respect we owe to human laws must surely be something different from the respect we accord to the law of gravitation. If laws, even bad laws, have a claim to our respect, then law must represent some general direction of human effort that we can understand and describe, and that we can approve in principle even at the moment when it seems to us to miss its mark.

If, as I believe, it is a cardinal virtue of Professor Hart's argument that it brings into the dispute the issue of fidelity to law, its chief defect, if I may say so, lies in a failure to perceive and accept the implications that this enlargement of the frame of argument necessarily entails. This defect seems to me more or less to permeate the whole essay, but it comes most prominently to the fore in his discussion of Gustav Radbruch and the Nazi regime.[2]

---

[1] Kelsen, *Die Idee des Naturrechtes*, 7 ZEITSCHRIFT FÜR ÖFFENTLICHES RECHT 221, 248 (Austria 1927).

[2] Hart, *Positivism and the Separation of Law and Morals*, 71 HARV. L. REV. 593, 615–21 (1958).

Without any inquiry into the actual workings of whatever remained of a legal system under the Nazis, Professor Hart assumes that something must have persisted that still deserved the name of law in a sense that would make meaningful the ideal of fidelity to law. Not that Professor Hart believes the Nazis' laws should have been obeyed. Rather he considers that a decision to disobey them presented not a mere question of prudence or courage, but a genuine moral dilemma in which the ideal of fidelity to law had to be sacrificed in favor of more fundamental goals. I should have thought it unwise to pass such a judgment without first inquiring with more particularity what "law" itself meant under the Nazi regime.

I shall present later my reasons for thinking that Professor Hart is profoundly mistaken in his estimate of the Nazi situation and that he gravely misinterprets the thought of Professor Radbruch. But first I shall turn to some preliminary definitional problems in which what I regard as the central defect in Professor Hart's thesis seems immediately apparent.

I. The Definition of Law

Throughout his essay Professor Hart aligns himself with a general position which he associates with the names of Bentham, Austin, Gray, and Holmes. He recognizes, of course, that the conceptions of these men as to "what law is" vary considerably, but this diversity he apparently considers irrelevant in his defense of their general school of thought.

If the only issue were that of stipulating a meaning for the word "law" that would be conducive to intellectual clarity, there might be much justification for treating all of these men as working in the same direction. Austin, for example, defines law as the command of the highest legislative power, called the sovereign. For Gray, on the other hand, law consists in the rules laid down by judges. A statute is, for Gray, not a law, but only a source of law, which becomes law only after it has been interpreted and applied by a court. Now if our only object were to obtain that clarity which comes from making our definitions explicit and then adhering strictly to those definitions, one could argue plausibly that either conception of the meaning of "law" will do. Both conceptions appear to avoid a confusion of morals and law, and both writers let the reader know what meaning they propose to attribute to the word "law."

The matter assumes a very different aspect, however, if our interest lies in the ideal of fidelity to law, for then it may become a matter of capital importance what position is assigned to the judiciary in the general frame of government. Confirmation for this observation may be found in the slight rumbling of constitutional crisis to be heard in this country today. During the past year readers of newspapers have been writing to their editors urging solemnly, and even apparently with sincerity, that we should abolish the Supreme Court as a first step toward a restoration of the rule of law. It is unlikely that this remedy for our governmental ills derives from any deep study of Austin or Gray, but surely those who propose it could hardly be expected to view with indifference the divergent definitions of law offered by those two jurists. If it be said that it is a perversion of Gray's meaning to extract from his writings any moral for present controversies about the role of the Supreme Court, then it seems to me there is equal reason for treating what he wrote as irrelevant to the issue of fidelity to law generally.

Another difference of opinion among the writers defended by Professor Hart concerns Bentham and Austin and their views on constitutional limitations on the power of the sovereign. Bentham considered that a constitution might preclude the highest legislative power from issuing certain kinds of laws. For Austin, on the other hand, any legal limit on the highest lawmaking power was an absurdity and an impossibility. What guide to conscience would be offered by these two writers in a crisis that might some day arise out of the provision of our constitution to the effect that the amending power can never be used to deprive any state without its consent of its equal representation in the Senate? [3] Surely it is not only in the affairs of everyday life that we need clarity about the obligation of fidelity to law, but most particularly and urgently in times of trouble. If all the positivist school has to offer in such times is the observation that, however you may choose to define law, it is always something different from morals, its teachings are not of much use to us.

I suggest, then, that Professor Hart's thesis as it now stands is essentially incomplete and that before he can attain the goals

[3] U.S. CONST. art. V.

he seeks he will have to concern himself more closely with a definition of law that will make meaningful the obligation of fidelity to law.

II. The Definition of Morality

It is characteristic of those sharing the point of view of Professor Hart that their primary concern is to preserve the integrity of the concept of law. Accordingly, they have generally sought a precise definition of law, but have not been at pains to state just what it is they mean to exclude by their definitions. They are like men building a wall for the defense of a village, who must know what it is they wish to protect, but who need not, and indeed cannot, know what invading forces those walls may have to turn back.

When Austin and Gray distinguish law from morality, the word "morality" stands indiscriminately for almost every conceivable standard by which human conduct may be judged that is not itself law. The inner voice of conscience, notions of right and wrong based on religious belief, common conceptions of decency and fair play, culturally conditioned prejudices — all of these are grouped together under the heading of "morality" and are excluded from the domain of law. For the most part Professor Hart follows in the tradition of his predecessors. When he speaks of morality he seems generally to have in mind all sorts of extralegal notions about "what ought to be," regardless of their sources, pretensions, or intrinsic worth. This is particularly apparent in his treatment of the problem of interpretation, where uncodified notions of what ought to be are viewed as affecting only the penumbra of law, leaving its hard core untouched.

Toward the end of the essay, however, Professor Hart's argument takes a turn that seems to depart from the prevailing tenor of his thought. This consists in reminding us that there is such a thing as an immoral morality and that there are many standards of "what ought to be" that can hardly be called moral.[4] Let us grant, he says, that the judge may properly and inevitably legislate in the penumbra of a legal enactment, and that this legislation (in default of any other standard) must be guided by the judge's notions of what ought to be. Still, this would be true even in a society devoted to the most evil ends, where the judge would

[4] Hart, *supra* note 2, at 624.

supply the insufficiencies of the statute with the iniquity that seemed to him most apt for the occasion. Let us also grant, says Professor Hart toward the end of his essay, that there is at times even something that looks like discovery in the judicial process, when a judge by restating a principle seems to bring more clearly to light what was really sought from the beginning. Again, he reminds us, this could happen in a society devoted to the highest refinements of sin, where the implicit demands of an evil rule might be a matter for discovery when the rule was applied to a situation not consciously considered when it was formulated.

I take it that this is to be a warning addressed to those who wish "to infuse more morality into the law." Professor Hart is reminding them that if their program is adopted the morality that actually gets infused may not be to their liking. If this is his point it is certainly a valid one, though one wishes it had been made more explicitly, for it raises much the most fundamental issue of his whole argument. Since the point is made obliquely, and I may have misinterpreted it, in commenting I shall have to content myself with a few summary observations and questions.

First, Professor Hart seems to assume that evil aims may have as much coherence and inner logic as good ones. I, for one, refuse to accept that assumption. I realize that I am here raising, or perhaps dodging, questions that lead into the most difficult problems of the epistemology of ethics. Even if I were competent to undertake an excursus in that direction, this is not the place for it. I shall have to rest on the assertion of a belief that may seem naïve, namely, that coherence and goodness have more affinity than coherence and evil. Accepting this belief, I also believe that when men are compelled to explain and justify their decisions, the effect will generally be to pull those decisions toward goodness, by whatever standards of ultimate goodness there are. Accepting these beliefs, I find a considerable incongruity in any conception that envisages a possible future in which the common law would "work itself pure from case to case" toward a more perfect realization of iniquity.

Second, if there is a serious danger in our society that a weakening of the partition between law and morality would permit an infusion of "immoral morality," the question remains, what is the most effective protection against this danger? I cannot myself believe it is to be found in the positivist position espoused by Austin, Gray, Holmes, and Hart. For those writers seem to me to falsify the problem into a specious simplicity which leaves untouched the difficult issues where real dangers lie.

Third, let us suppose a judge bent on realizing through his decisions an objective that most ordinary citizens would regard as mistaken or evil. Would such a judge be likely to suspend the letter of the statute by openly invoking a "higher law"? Or would he be more likely to take refuge behind the maxim that "law is law" and explain his decision in such a way that it would appear to be demanded by the law itself?

Fourth, neither Professor Hart nor I belong to anything that could be said in a significant sense to be a "minority group" in our respective countries. This has its advantages and disadvantages to one aspiring to a philosophic view of law and government. But suppose we were both transported to a country where our beliefs were anathemas, and where we, in turn, regarded the prevailing morality as thoroughly evil. No doubt in this situation we would have reason to fear that the law might be covertly manipulated to our disadvantage; I doubt if either of us would be apprehensive that its injunctions would be set aside by an appeal to a morality higher than law. If we felt that the law itself was our safest refuge, would it not be because even in the most perverted regimes there is a certain hesitancy about writing cruelties, intolerances, and inhumanities into law? And is it not clear that this hesitancy itself derives, not from a separation of law and morals, but precisely from an identification of law with those demands of morality that are the most urgent and the most obviously justifiable, which no man need be ashamed to profess?

Fifth, over great areas where the judicial process functions, the danger of an infusion of immoral, or at least unwelcome, morality does not, I suggest, present a real issue. Here the danger is precisely the opposite. For example, in the field of commercial law the British courts in recent years have, if I may say so, fallen into a "law-is-law" formalism that constitutes a kind of belated counterrevolution against all that was accomplished by Mansfield.[5] The matter has reached a stage approaching crisis as commercial cases are increasingly being taken to arbitration. The chief

[5] For an outstanding example, see G. Scammell and Nephew, Ltd. v. Ouston, [1941] A.C. 251 (1940). I personally would be inclined to put under the same head Victoria Laundry, Ltd. v. Newman Industries, Ltd., [1949] 2 K.B. 528 (C.A.).

reason for this development is that arbitrators are willing to take into account the needs of commerce and ordinary standards of commercial fairness. I realize that Professor Hart repudiates "formalism," but I shall try to show later why I think his theory necessarily leads in that direction.[6]

Sixth, in the thinking of many there is one question that predominates in any discussion of the relation of law and morals, to the point of coloring everything that is said or heard on the subject. I refer to the kind of question raised by the Pope's pronouncement concerning the duty of Catholic judges in divorce actions.[7] This pronouncement does indeed raise grave issues. But it does not present a problem of the relation between law, on the one hand, and, on the other, generally shared views of right conduct that have grown spontaneously through experience and discussion. The issue is rather that of a conflict between two pronouncements, both of which claim to be authoritative; if you will, it is one kind of law against another. When this kind of issue is taken as the key to the whole problem of law and morality, the discussion is so denatured and distorted that profitable exchange becomes impossible. In mentioning this last aspect of the dispute about "positivism," I do not mean to intimate that Professor Hart's own discussion is dominated by any *arrière-pensée*; I know it is not. At the same time I am quite sure that I have indicated accurately the issue that will be uppermost in the minds of many as they read his essay.

In resting content with these scant remarks, I do not want to seem to simplify the problem in a direction opposite to that taken by Professor Hart. The questions raised by "immoral morality" deserve a more careful exploration than either Professor Hart or I have offered in these pages.

III. The Moral Foundations of a Legal Order

Professor Hart emphatically rejects "the command theory of law," according to which law is simply a command backed by a force sufficient to make it effective. He observes that such a command can be given by a man with a loaded gun, and "law surely

[6] See Hart, *supra* note 2, at 608–12.

[7] See N.Y. Times, Nov. 8, 1949, p. 1, col. 4 (late city ed.) (report of a speech made on November 7, 1949 to the Central Committee of the Union of Catholic Italian Lawyers).

is not the gunman situation writ large."[8] There is no need to dwell here on the inadequacies of the command theory, since Professor Hart has already revealed its defects more clearly and succinctly than I could. His conclusion is that the foundation of a legal system is not coercive power, but certain "fundamental accepted rules specifying the essential lawmaking procedures."[9]

When I reached this point in his essay, I felt certain that Professor Hart was about to acknowledge an important qualification on his thesis. I confidently expected that he would go on to say something like this: I have insisted throughout on the importance of keeping sharp the distinction between law and morality. The question may now be raised, therefore, as to the nature of these fundamental rules that furnish the framework within which the making of law takes place. On the one hand, they seem to be rules, not of law, but of morality. They derive their efficacy from a general acceptance, which in turn rests ultimately on a perception that they are right and necessary. They can hardly be said to be law in the sense of an authoritative pronouncement, since their function is to state when a pronouncement is authoritative. On the other hand, in the daily functioning of the legal system they are often treated and applied much as ordinary rules of law are. Here, then, we must confess there is something that can be called a "merger" of law and morality, and to which the term "intersection" is scarcely appropriate.

Instead of pursuing some such course of thought, to my surprise I found Professor Hart leaving completely untouched the nature of the fundamental rules that make law itself possible, and turning his attention instead to what he considers a confusion of thought on the part of the critics of positivism. Leaving out of account his discussion of analytical jurisprudence, his argument runs something as follows: Two views are associated with the names of Bentham and Austin. One is the command theory of law, the other is an insistence on the separation of law and morality. Critics of these writers came in time to perceive — "dimly" Professor Hart says — that the command theory is untenable. By a loose association of ideas they wrongly supposed that in advancing reasons for rejecting the command theory they had also refuted the view that law and morality must be sharply separated. This was a "natural mistake," but plainly a mistake just the same.

[8] Hart, *supra* note 2, at 603.

[9] *Ibid.*

I do not think any mistake is committed in believing that Bentham and Austin's error in formulating improperly and too simply the problem of the relation of law and morals was part of a larger error that led to the command theory of law. I think the connection between these two errors can be made clear if we ask ourselves what would have happened to Austin's system of thought if he had abandoned the command theory.

One who reads Austin's Lectures V and VI [10] cannot help being impressed by the way he hangs doggedly to the command theory, in spite of the fact that every pull of his own keen mind was toward abandoning it. In the case of a sovereign monarch, law is what the monarch commands. But what shall we say of the "laws" of succession which tell who the "lawful" monarch is? It is of the essence of a command that it be addressed by a superior to an inferior, yet in the case of a "sovereign many," say, a parliament, the sovereign seems to command itself since a member of parliament may be convicted under a law he himself drafted and voted for. The sovereign must be unlimited in legal power, for who could adjudicate the legal bounds of a supreme lawmaking power? Yet a "sovereign many" must accept the limitation of rules before it can make law at all. Such a body can gain the power to issue commands only by acting in a "corporate capacity"; this it can do only by proceeding "agreeably to the modes and forms" established and accepted for the making of law. Judges exercise a power delegated to them by the supreme lawmaking power, and are commissioned to carry out its "direct or circuitous commands." Yet in a federal system it is the courts which must resolve conflicts of competence between the federation and its components.

All of these problems Austin sees with varying degrees of explicitness, and he struggles mightily with them. Over and over again he teeters on the edge of an abandonment of the command theory in favor of what Professor Hart has described as a view that discerns the foundations of a legal order in "certain fundamental accepted rules specifying the essential lawmaking procedures." Yet he never takes the plunge. He does not take it because he had a sure insight that it would forfeit the black-and-white distinction between law and morality that was the whole object of his Lectures — indeed, one may say, the enduring ob-

---

[10] 1 AUSTIN, LECTURES ON JURISPRUDENCE 167–341 (5th ed. 1885).

ject of a dedicated life. For if law is made possible by "fundamental accepted rules" — which for Austin must be rules, not of law, but of positive morality — what are we to say of the rules that the lawmaking power enacts to regulate its own lawmaking? We have election laws, laws allocating legislative representation to specific geographic areas, rules of parliamentary procedure, rules for the qualification of voters, and many other laws and rules of similar nature. These do not remain fixed, and all of them shape in varying degrees the lawmaking process. Yet how are we to distinguish between those basic rules that owe their validity to acceptance, and those which are properly rules of law, valid even when men generally consider them to be evil or ill-advised? In other words, how are we to define the words "fundamental" and "essential" in Professor Hart's own formulation: "certain fundamental accepted rules specifying the essential lawmaking procedure"?

The solution for this problem in Kelsen's theory is instructive. Kelsen does in fact take the plunge over which Austin hesitated too long. Kelsen realizes that before we can distinguish between what is law and what is not, there must be an acceptance of some basic procedure by which law is made. In any legal system there must be some fundamental rule that points unambiguously to the source from which laws must come in order to be laws. This rule Kelsen called "the basic norm." In his own words,

> The basic norm is not valid because it has been created in a certain way, but its validity is assumed by virtue of its content. It is valid, then, like a norm of natural law . . . . The idea of a pure positive law, like that of natural law, has its limitations.[11]

It will be noted that Kelsen speaks, not as Professor Hart does, of "fundamental rules" that regulate the making of law, but of a single rule or norm. Of course, there is no such single rule in any modern society. The notion of the basic norm is admittedly a symbol, not a fact. It is a symbol that embodies the positivist quest for some clear and unambiguous test of law, for some clean, sharp line that will divide the rules which owe their validity to their source and those which owe their validity to acceptance and intrinsic appeal. The difficulties Austin avoided by sticking with the command theory, Kelsen avoids by a fiction which simplifies reality into a form that can be absorbed by positivism.

[11] KELSEN, GENERAL THEORY OF LAW AND STATE 401 (3d ed. 1949).

A full exploration of all the problems that result when we recognize that law becomes possible only by virtue of rules that are not law, would require drawing into consideration the effect of the presence or absence of a written constitution. Such a constitution in some ways simplifies the problems I have been discussing, and in some ways complicates them. In so far as a written constitution defines basic lawmaking procedure, it may remove the perplexities that arise when a parliament in effect defines itself. At the same time, a legislature operating under a written constitution may enact statutes that profoundly affect the lawmaking procedure and its predictable outcome. If these statutes are drafted with sufficient cunning, they may remain within the frame of the constitution and yet undermine the institutions it was intended to establish. If the "court-packing" proposal of the 'thirties does not illustrate this danger unequivocally, it at least suggests that the fear of it is not fanciful. No written constitution can be self-executing. To be effective it requires not merely the respectful deference we show for ordinary legal enactments, but that willing convergence of effort we give to moral principles in which we have an active belief. One may properly work to amend a constitution, but so long as it remains unamended one must work with it, not against it or around it. All this amounts to saying that to be effective a written constitution must be accepted, at least provisionally, not just as law, but as good law.

What have these considerations to do with the ideal of fidelity to law? I think they have a great deal to do with it, and that they reveal the essential incapacity of the positivistic view to serve that ideal effectively. For I believe that a realization of this ideal is something for which we must plan, and that is precisely what positivism refuses to do.

Let me illustrate what I mean by planning for a realization of the ideal of fidelity to law. Suppose we are drafting a written constitution for a country just emerging from a period of violence and disorder in which any thread of legal continuity with previous governments has been broken. Obviously such a constitution cannot lift itself unaided into legality; it cannot be law simply because it says it is. We should keep in mind that the efficacy of our work will depend upon general acceptance and that to make this acceptance secure there must be a general belief that the constitution itself is necessary, right, and good. The provisions of the constitution should, therefore, be kept simple and understandable, not only in language, but also in purpose. Preambles and other explanations of what is being sought, which would be objectionable in an ordinary statute, may find an appropriate place in our constitution. We should think of our constitution as establishing a basic procedural framework for future governmental action in the enactment and administration of laws. Substantive limitations on the power of government should be kept to a minimum and should generally be confined to those for which a need can be generally appreciated. In so far as possible, substantive aims should be achieved procedurally, on the principle that if men are compelled to act in the right way, they will generally do the right things.

These considerations seem to have been widely ignored in the constitutions that have come into existence since World War II. Not uncommonly these constitutions incorporate a host of economic and political measures of the type one would ordinarily associate with statutory law. It is hardly likely that these measures have been written into the constitution because they represent aims that are generally shared. One suspects that the reason for their inclusion is precisely the opposite, namely, a fear that they would not be able to survive the vicissitudes of an ordinary exercise of parliamentary power. Thus, the divisions of opinion that are a normal accompaniment of lawmaking are written into the document that makes law itself possible. This is obviously a procedure that contains serious dangers for a future realization of the ideal of fidelity to law.

I have ventured these remarks on the making of constitutions not because I think they can claim any special profundity, but because I wished to illustrate what I mean by planning the conditions that will make it possible to realize the ideal of fidelity to law. Even within the limits of my modest purpose, what I have said may be clearly wrong. If so, it would not be for me to say whether I am also wrong clearly. I will, however, venture to assert that if I am wrong, I am wrong significantly. What disturbs me about the school of legal positivism is that it not only refuses to deal with problems of the sort I have just discussed, but bans them on principle from the province of legal philosophy. In its concern to assign the right labels to the things men do, this school seems to lose all interest in asking whether men are doing the right things.

IV. The Morality of Law Itself

Most of the issues raised by Professor Hart's essay can be restated in terms of the distinction between order and good order. Law may be said to represent order *simpliciter*. Good order is law that corresponds to the demands of justice, or morality, or men's notions of what ought to be. This rephrasing of the issue is useful in bringing to light the ambitious nature of Professor Hart's undertaking, for surely we would all agree that it is no easy thing to distinguish order from good order. When it is said, for example, that law simply represents that public order which obtains under all governments — democratic, Fascist, or Communist [12] — the order intended is certainly not that of a morgue or cemetery. We must mean a functioning order, and such an order has to be at least good enough to be considered as functioning by some standard or other. A reminder that workable order usually requires some play in the joints, and therefore cannot be too orderly, is enough to suggest some of the complexities that would be involved in any attempt to draw a sharp distinction between order and good order.

For the time being, however, let us suppose we can in fact clearly separate the concept of order from that of good order. Even in this unreal and abstract form the notion of order itself contains what may be called a moral element. Let me illustrate this "morality of order" in its crudest and most elementary form. Let us suppose an absolute monarch, whose word is the only law known to his subjects. We may further suppose him to be utterly selfish and to seek in his relations with his subjects solely his own advantage. This monarch from time to time issues commands, promising rewards for compliance and threatening punishment for disobedience. He is, however, a dissolute and forgetful fellow, who never makes the slightest attempt to ascertain who have in fact followed his directions and who have not. As a result he habitually punishes loyalty and rewards disobedience. It is apparent that this monarch will never achieve even his own selfish aims until he is ready to accept that minimum self-restraint that will create a meaningful connection between his words and his actions.

[12] *E.g.*, Friedmann, *The Planned State and the Rule of Law*, 22 Austr. L.J. 162, 207 (1948).

Let us now suppose that our monarch undergoes a change of heart and begins to pay some attention to what he said yesterday when, today, he has occasion to distribute bounty or to order the chopping off of heads. Under the strain of this new responsibility, however, our monarch relaxes his attention in other directions and becomes hopelessly slothful in the phrasing of his commands. His orders become so ambiguous and are uttered in so inaudible a tone that his subjects never have any clear idea what he wants them to do. Here, again, it is apparent that if our monarch for his own selfish advantage wants to create in his realm anything like a system of law he will have to pull himself together and assume still another responsibility.

Law, considered merely as order, contains, then, its own implicit morality. This morality of order must be respected if we are to create anything that can be called law, even bad law. Law by itself is powerless to bring this morality into existence. Until our monarch is really ready to face the responsibilities of his position, it will do no good for him to issue still another futile command, this time self-addressed and threatening himself with punishment if he does not mend his ways.

There is a twofold sense in which it is true that law cannot be built on law. First of all, the authority to make law must be supported by moral attitudes that accord to it the competency it claims. Here we are dealing with a morality external to law, which makes law possible. But this alone is not enough. We may stipulate that in our monarchy the accepted "basic norm" designates the monarch himself as the only possible source of law. We still cannot have law until our monarch is ready to accept the internal morality of law itself.

In the life of a nation these external and internal moralities of law reciprocally influence one another; a deterioration of the one will almost inevitably produce a deterioration in the other. So closely related are they that when the anthropologist Lowie speaks of "the generally accepted ethical postulates underlying our . . . legal institutions as their ultimate sanction and guaranteeing their smooth functioning,"[13] he may be presumed to have both of them in mind.

What I have called "the internal morality of law" seems to be almost completely neglected by Professor Hart. He does make

[13] LOWIE, THE ORIGIN OF THE STATE 113 (1927).

brief mention of "justice in the administration of the law," which consists in the like treatment of like cases, by whatever elevated or perverted standards the word "like" may be defined.[14] But he quickly dismisses this aspect of law as having no special relevance to his main enterprise.

In this I believe he is profoundly mistaken. It is his neglect to analyze the demands of a morality of order that leads him throughout his essay to treat law as a datum projecting itself into human experience and not as an object of human striving. When we realize that order itself is something that must be worked for, it becomes apparent that the existence of a legal system, even a bad or evil legal system, is always a matter of degree. When we recognize this simple fact of everyday legal experience, it becomes impossible to dismiss the problems presented by the Nazi regime with a simple assertion: "Under the Nazis there was law, even if it was bad law." We have instead to inquire how much of a legal system survived the general debasement and perversion of all forms of social order that occurred under the Nazi rule, and what moral implications this mutilated system had for the conscientious citizen forced to live under it.

It is not necessary, however, to dwell on such moral upheavals as the Nazi regime to see how completely incapable the positivistic philosophy is of serving the one high moral ideal it professes, that of fidelity to law. Its default in serving this ideal actually becomes most apparent, I believe, in the everyday problems that confront those who are earnestly desirous of meeting the moral demands of a legal order, but who have responsible functions to discharge in the very order toward which loyalty is due.

Let us suppose the case of a trial judge who has had an extensive experience in commercial matters and before whom a great many commercial disputes are tried. As a subordinate in a judicial hierarchy, our judge has of course the duty to follow the law laid down by his supreme court. Our imaginary Scrutton has the misfortune, however, to live under a supreme court which he considers woefully ignorant of the ways and needs of commerce. To his mind, many of this court's decisions in the field of commercial law simply do not make sense. If a conscientious judge caught in this dilemma were to turn to the positivistic philosophy what succor could he expect? It will certainly do no good to

[14] Hart, *supra* note 2, at 623–24.

remind him that he has an obligation of fidelity to law. He is aware of this already and painfully so, since it is the source of his predicament. Nor will it help to say that if he legislates, it must be "interstitially," or that his contributions must be "confined from molar to molecular motions." [15] This mode of statement may be congenial to those who like to think of law, not as a purposive thing, but as an expression of the dimensions and directions of state power. But I cannot believe that the essentially trite idea behind this advice can be lifted by literary eloquence to the point where it will offer any real help to our judge; for one thing, it may be impossible for him to know whether his supreme court would regard any particular contribution of his as being wide or narrow.

Nor is it likely that a distinction between core and penumbra would be helpful. The predicament of our judge may well derive, not from particular precedents, but from a mistaken conception of the nature of commerce which extends over many decisions and penetrates them in varying degrees. So far as his problem arises from the use of particular words, he may well find that the supreme court often uses the ordinary terms of commerce in senses foreign to actual business dealings. If he interprets those words as a business executive or accountant would, he may well reduce the precedents he is bound to apply to a logical shambles. On the other hand, he may find great difficulty in discerning the exact sense in which the supreme court used those words, since in his mind that sense is itself the product of a confusion.

Is it not clear that it is precisely positivism's insistence on a rigid separation of law as it is from law as it ought to be that renders the positivistic philosophy incapable of aiding our judge? Is it not also clear that our judge can never achieve a satisfactory resolution of his dilemma unless he views his duty of fidelity to law in a context which also embraces his responsibility for making law what it ought to be?

The case I have supposed may seem extreme, but the problem it suggests pervades our whole legal system. If the divergence

[15] Southern Pac. Co. v. Jensen, 244 U.S. 205, 221 (1917) (Holmes, J., dissenting), paraphrasing Storti v. Commonwealth, 178 Mass. 549, 554, 60 N.E. 210, 211 (1901) (Holmes, C.J.), in which it was held that a statute providing for electrocution as a means of inflicting the punishment of death was not cruel or unusual punishment within the Massachusetts Declaration of Rights, MASS. CONST. pt. First, art. XXVI, simply because it accomplished its object by molecular, rather than molar, motions.

of views between our judge and his supreme court were less drastic, it would be more difficult to present his predicament graphically, but the perplexity of his position might actually increase. Perplexities of this sort are a normal accompaniment of the discharge of any adjudicative function; they perhaps reach their most poignant intensity in the field of administrative law.

One can imagine a case — surely not likely in Professor Hart's country or mine — where a judge might hold profound moral convictions that were exactly the opposite of those held, with equal attachment, by his supreme court. He might also be convinced that the precedents he was bound to apply were the direct product of a morality he considered abhorrent. If such a judge did not find the solution for his dilemma in surrendering his office, he might well be driven to a wooden and literal application of precedents which he could not otherwise apply because he was incapable of understanding the philosophy that animated them. But I doubt that a judge in this situation would need the help of legal positivism to find these melancholy escapes from his predicament. Nor do I think that such a predicament is likely to arise within a nation where both law and good law are regarded as collaborative human achievements in need of constant renewal, and where lawyers are still at least as interested in asking "What is good law?" as they are in asking "What is law?"

V. The Problem of Restoring Respect for Law and Justice After the Collapse of a Regime That Respected Neither

After the collapse of the Nazi regime the German courts were faced with a truly frightful predicament. It was impossible for them to declare the whole dictatorship illegal or to treat as void every decision and legal enactment that had emanated from Hitler's government. Intolerable dislocations would have resulted from any such wholesale outlawing of all that occurred over a span of twelve years. On the other hand, it was equally impossible to carry forward into the new government the effects of every Nazi perversity that had been committed in the name of law; any such course would have tainted an indefinite future with the poisons of Nazism.

This predicament — which was, indeed, a pervasive one, affecting all branches of law — came to a dramatic head in a series of cases involving informers who had taken advantage of the Nazi terror to get rid of personal enemies or unwanted spouses. If all Nazi statutes and judicial decisions were indiscriminately "law," then these despicable creatures were guiltless, since they had turned their victims over to processes which the Nazis themselves knew by the name of law. Yet it was intolerable, especially for the surviving relatives and friends of the victims, that these people should go about unpunished, while the objects of their spite were dead, or were just being released after years of imprisonment, or, more painful still, simply remained unaccounted for.

The urgency of this situation does not by any means escape Professor Hart. Indeed, he is moved to recommend an expedient that is surely not lacking itself in a certain air of desperation. He suggests that a retroactive criminal statute would have been the least objectionable solution to the problem. This statute would have punished the informer, and branded him as a criminal, for an act which Professor Hart regards as having been perfectly legal when he committed it.[16]

On the other hand, Professor Hart condemns without qualification those judicial decisions in which the courts themselves undertook to declare void certain of the Nazi statutes under which the informer's victims had been convicted. One cannot help raising at this point the question whether the issue as presented by Professor Hart himself is truly that of fidelity to law. Surely it would be a necessary implication of a retroactive criminal statute against informers that, for purposes of that statute at least, the Nazi laws as applied to the informers or their victims were to be regarded as void. With this turn the question seems no longer to be whether what was once law can now be declared not to have been law, but rather who should do the dirty work, the courts or the legislature.

But, as Professor Hart himself suggests, the issues at stake are much too serious to risk losing them in a semantic tangle. Even if the whole question were one of words, we should remind ourselves that we are in an area where words have a powerful effect on human attitudes. I should like, therefore, to undertake a defense of the German courts, and to advance reasons why, in my opinion, their decisions do not represent the abandonment of

---

[16] See Hart, *supra* note 2, at 619–20.

legal principle that Professor Hart sees in them. In order to understand the background of those decisions we shall have to move a little closer within smelling distance of the witches' caldron than we have been brought so far by Professor Hart. We shall have also to consider an aspect of the problem ignored in his essay, namely, the degree to which the Nazis observed what I have called the inner morality of law itself.

Throughout his discussion Professor Hart seems to assume that the only difference between Nazi law and, say, English law is that the Nazis used their laws to achieve ends that are odious to an Englishman. This assumption is, I think, seriously mistaken, and Professor Hart's acceptance of it seems to me to render his discussion unresponsive to the problem it purports to address.

Throughout their period of control the Nazis took generous advantage of a device not wholly unknown to American legislatures, the retroactive statute curing past legal irregularities. The most dramatic use of the curative powers of such a statute occurred on July 3, 1934, after the "Roehm purge." When this intraparty shooting affair was over and more than seventy Nazis had been — one can hardly avoid saying — "rubbed out," Hitler returned to Berlin and procured from his cabinet a law ratifying and confirming the measures taken between June 30, and July 1, 1934, without mentioning the names of those who were now considered to have been lawfully executed.[17] Some time later Hitler declared that during the Roehm purge "the supreme court of the German people . . . consisted of myself,"[18] surely not an overstatement of the capacity in which he acted if one takes seriously the enactment conferring retroactive legality on "the measures taken."

Now in England and America it would never occur to anyone to say that "it is in the nature of law that it cannot be retroactive," although, of course, constitutional inhibitions may prohibit certain kinds of retroactivity. We would say it is normal for a law to operate prospectively, and that it may be arguable that it ought never operate otherwise, but there would be a certain occult unpersuasiveness in any assertion that retroactivity violates the very nature of law itself. Yet we have only to imagine a country in which *all* laws are retroactive in order to see that retroactivity

[17] N.Y. Times, July 4, 1934, p. 3, col. 3 (late city ed.).

[18] See N.Y. Times, July 14, 1934, p. 5, col. 2 (late city ed.).

presents a real problem for the internal morality of law. If we suppose an absolute monarch who allows his realm to exist in a constant state of anarchy, we would hardly say that he could create a regime of law simply by enacting a curative statute conferring legality on everything that had happened up to its date and by announcing an intention to enact similar statutes every six months in the future.

A general increase in the resort to statutes curative of past legal irregularities represents a deterioration in that form of legal morality without which law itself cannot exist. The threat of such statutes hangs over the whole legal system, and robs every law on the books of some of its significance. And surely a general threat of this sort is implied when a government is willing to use such a statute to transform into lawful execution what was simple murder when it happened.

During the Nazi regime there were repeated rumors of "secret laws." In the article criticized by Professor Hart, Radbruch mentions a report that the wholesale killings in concentration camps were made "lawful" by a secret enactment.[19] Now surely there can be no greater legal monstrosity than a secret statute. Would anyone seriously recommend that following the war the German courts should have searched for unpublished laws among the files left by Hitler's government so that citizens' rights could be determined by a reference to these laws?

The extent of the legislator's obligation to make his laws known to his subjects is, of course, a problem of legal morality that has been under active discussion at least since the Secession of the Plebs. There is probably no modern state that has not been plagued by this problem in one form or another. It is most likely to arise in modern societies with respect to unpublished administrative directions. Often these are regarded in quite good faith by those who issue them as affecting only matters of internal organization. But since the procedures followed by an administrative agency, even in its "internal" actions, may seriously affect the rights and interests of the citizen, these unpublished, or "secret," regulations are often a subject for complaint.

---

[19] Radbruch, *Die Erneuerung des Rechts*, 2 DIE WANDLUNG 8, 9 (Germany 1947). A useful discussion of the Nazi practice with reference to the publicity given laws will be found in Giese, *Verkündung und Gesetzeskraft*, 76 ARCHIV DES ÖFFENTLICHEN RECHTS 464, 471–72 (Germany 1951). I rely on this article for the remarks that follow in the text.

But as with retroactivity, what in most societies is kept under control by the tacit restraints of legal decency broke out in monstrous form under Hitler. Indeed, so loose was the whole Nazi morality of law that it is not easy to know just what should be regarded as an unpublished or secret law. Since unpublished instructions to those administering the law could destroy the letter of any published law by imposing on it an outrageous interpretation, there was a sense in which the meaning of every law was "secret." Even a verbal order from Hitler that a thousand prisoners in concentration camps be put to death was at once an administrative direction and a validation of everything done under it as being "lawful."

But the most important affronts to the morality of law by Hitler's government took no such subtle forms as those exemplified in the bizarre outcroppings I have just discussed. In the first place, when legal forms became inconvenient, it was always possible for the Nazis to bypass them entirely and "to act through the party in the streets." There was no one who dared bring them to account for whatever outrages might thus be committed. In the second place, the Nazi-dominated courts were always ready to disregard any statute, even those enacted by the Nazis themselves, if this suited their convenience or if they feared that a lawyer-like interpretation might incur displeasure "above."

This complete willingness of the Nazis to disregard even their own enactments was an important factor leading Radbruch to take the position he did in the articles so severely criticized by Professor Hart. I do not believe that any fair appraisal of the action of the postwar German courts is possible unless we take this factor into account, as Professor Hart fails completely to do.

These remarks may seem inconclusive in their generality and to rest more on assertion than evidentiary fact. Let us turn at once, then, to the actual case discussed by Professor Hart.[20]

In 1944 a German soldier paid a short visit to his wife while under travel orders on a reassignment. During the single day he was home, he conveyed privately to his wife something of his opinion of the Hitler government. He expressed disapproval of (*sich abfällig geäussert über*) Hitler and other leading personalities of the Nazi party. He also said it was too bad Hitler had not met his end in the assassination attempt that had occurred on

[20] Judgment of July 27, 1949, Oberlandesgericht, Bamberg, 5 SÜDDEUTSCHE JURISTEN-ZEITUNG 207 (Germany 1950), 64 HARV. L. REV. 1005 (1951).

July 20th of that year. Shortly after his departure, his wife, who during his long absence on military duty "had turned to other men" and who wished to get rid of him, reported his remarks to the local leader of the Nazi party, observing that "a man who would say a thing like that does not deserve to live." The result was a trial of the husband by a military tribunal and a sentence of death. After a short period of imprisonment, instead of being executed, he was sent to the front again. After the collapse of the Nazi regime, the wife was brought to trial for having procured the imprisonment of her husband. Her defense rested on the ground that her husband's statements to her about Hitler and the Nazis constituted a crime under the laws then in force. Accordingly, when she informed on her husband she was simply bringing a criminal to justice.

This defense rested on two statutes, one passed in 1934, the other in 1938. Let us first consider the second of these enactments, which was part of a more comprehensive legislation creating a whole series of special wartime criminal offenses. I reproduce below a translation of the only pertinent section:

> The following persons are guilty of destroying the national power of resistance and shall be punished by death: Whoever publicly solicits or incites a refusal to fulfill the obligations of service in the armed forces of Germany, or in armed forces allied with Germany, or who otherwise publicly seeks to injure or destroy the will of the German people or an allied people to assert themselves stalwartly against their enemies.[21]

It is almost inconceivable that a court of present-day Germany would hold the husband's remarks to his wife, who was barred from military duty by her sex, to be a violation of the final catch-all provision of this statute, particularly when it is recalled that the text reproduced above was part of a more comprehensive enactment dealing with such things as harboring deserters, escaping military duty by self-inflicted injuries, and the like. The question arises, then, as to the extent to which the interpretive principles applied by the courts of Hitler's government should be accepted in determining whether the husband's remarks were indeed unlawful.

---

[21] The passage translated is § 5 of a statute creating a Kriegssonderstrafrecht. Law of Aug. 17, 1938, [1939] 2 REICHSGESETZBLATT pt. I, at 1456. The translation is mine.

This question becomes acute when we note that the act applies only to *public* acts or utterances, whereas the husband's remarks were in the privacy of his own home. Now it appears that the Nazi courts (and it should be noted we are dealing with a special military court) quite generally disregarded this limitation and extended the act to all utterances, private or public.[22] Is Professor Hart prepared to say that the legal meaning of this statute is to be determined in the light of this apparently uniform principle of judicial interpretation?

Let us turn now to the other statute upon which Professor Hart relies in assuming that the husband's utterance was unlawful. This is the act of 1934, the relevant portions of which are translated below:

> (1) Whoever publicly makes spiteful or provocative statements directed against, or statements which disclose a base disposition toward, the leading personalities of the nation or of the National Socialist German Workers' Party, or toward measures taken or institutions established by them, and of such a nature as to undermine the people's confidence in their political leadership, shall be punished by imprisonment.
> (2) Malicious utterances not made in public shall be treated in the same manner as public utterances when the person making them realized or should have realized they would reach the public.
> (3) Prosecution for such utterances shall be only on the order of the National Minister of Justice; in case the utterance was directed against a leading personality of the National Socialist German Workers' Party, the Minister of Justice shall order prosecution only with the advice and consent of the Representative of the Leader.
> (4) The National Minister of Justice shall, with the advice and consent of the Representative of the Leader, determine who shall belong to the class of leading personalities for purposes of Section 1 above.[23]

Extended comment on this legislative monstrosity is scarcely called for, overlarded and undermined as it is by uncontrolled administrative discretion. We may note only: first, that it offers no justification whatever for the death penalty actually imposed on the husband, though never carried out; second, that if the wife's

---

[22] See 5 SÜDDEUTSCHE JURISTEN-ZEITUNG 207, 210 (Germany 1950).

[23] The translated passage is article II of A Law Against Malicious Attacks on the State and the Party and for the Protection of the Party Uniform, Law of Dec. 20, 1934, [1934] 1 REICHSGESETZBLATT 1269. The translation is mine.

act in informing on her husband made his remarks "public," there is no such thing as a private utterance under this statute. I should like to ask the reader whether he can actually share Professor Hart's indignation that, in the perplexities of the postwar reconstruction, the German courts saw fit to declare this thing not a law. Can it be argued seriously that it would have been more beseeming to the judicial process if the postwar courts had undertaken a study of "the interpretative principles" in force during Hitler's rule and had then solemnly applied those "principles" to ascertain the meaning of this statute? On the other hand, would the courts really have been showing respect for Nazi law if they had construed the Nazi statutes by their own, quite different, standards of interpretation?

Professor Hart castigates the German courts and Radbruch, not so much for what they believed had to be done, but because they failed to see that they were confronted by a moral dilemma of a sort that would have been immediately apparent to Bentham and Austin. By the simple dodge of saying, "When a statute is sufficiently evil it ceases to be law," they ran away from the problem they should have faced.

This criticism is, I believe, without justification. So far as the courts are concerned, matters certainly would not have been helped if, instead of saying, "This is not law," they had said, "This is law but it is so evil we will refuse to apply it." Surely moral confusion reaches its height when a court refuses to apply something it admits to be law, and Professor Hart does not recommend any such "facing of the true issue" by the courts themselves. He would have preferred a retroactive statute. Curiously, this was also the preference of Radbruch.[24] But unlike Professor Hart, the German courts and Gustav Radbruch were living participants in a situation of drastic emergency. The informer problem was a pressing one, and if legal institutions were to be rehabilitated in Germany it would not do to allow the people to begin taking the law into their own hands, as might have occurred while the courts were waiting for a statute.

As for Gustav Radbruch, it is, I believe, wholly unjust to say that he did not know he was faced with a moral dilemma. His postwar writings repeatedly stress the antinomies confronted in the effort to rebuild decent and orderly government in Germany.

[24] See Radbruch, *Die Erneuerung des Rechts*, 2 DIE WANDLUNG 8, 10 (Germany 1947).

As for the ideal of fidelity to law, I shall let Radbruch's own words state his position:

> We must not conceal from ourselves — especially not in the light of our experiences during the twelve-year dictatorship — what frightful dangers for the rule of law can be contained in the notion of "statutory lawlessness" and in refusing the quality of law to duly enacted statutes.[25]

The situation is not that legal positivism enables a man to know when he faces a difficult problem of choice, while Radbruch's beliefs deceive him into thinking there is no problem to face. The real issue dividing Professors Hart and Radbruch is: How shall we state the problem? What is the nature of the dilemma in which we are caught?

I hope I am not being unjust to Professor Hart when I say that I can find no way of describing the dilemma as he sees it but to use some such words as the following: On the one hand, we have an amoral datum called law, which has the peculiar quality of creating a moral duty to obey it. On the other hand, we have a moral duty to do what we think is right and decent. When we are confronted by a statute we believe to be thoroughly evil, we have to choose between those two duties.

If this is the positivist position, then I have no hesitancy in rejecting it. The "dilemma" it states has the verbal formulation of a problem, but the problem it states makes no sense. It is like saying I have to choose between giving food to a starving man and being mimsy with the borogoves. I do not think it is unfair to the positivistic philosophy to say that it never gives any coherent meaning to the moral obligation of fidelity to law. This obligation seems to be conceived as sui generis, wholly unrelated to any of the ordinary, extralegal ends of human life. The fundamental postulate of positivism — that law must be strictly severed from morality — seems to deny the possibility of any bridge between the obligation to obey law and other moral obligations. No mediating principle can measure their respective demands on conscience, for they exist in wholly separate worlds.

While I would not subscribe to all of Radbruch's postwar views — especially those relating to "higher law" — I think he

[25] Radbruch, *Gesetzliches Unrecht und Übergesetzliches Recht*, 1 SÜDDEUTSCHE JURISTEN-ZEITUNG 105, 107 (Germany 1946) (reprinted in RADBRUCH, RECHTSPHILOSOPHIE 347, 354 (4th ed. 1950)). The translation is mine.

saw, much more clearly than does Professor Hart, the true nature of the dilemma confronted by Germany in seeking to rebuild her shattered legal institutions. Germany had to restore both respect for law and respect for justice. Though neither of these could be restored without the other, painful antinomies were encountered in attempting to restore both at once, as Radbruch saw all too clearly. Essentially Radbruch saw the dilemma as that of meeting the demands of order, on the one hand, and those of good order, on the other. Of course no pat formula can be derived from this phrasing of the problem. But, unlike legal positivism, it does not present us with opposing demands that have no living contact with one another, that simply shout their contradictions across a vacuum. As we seek order, we can meaningfully remind ourselves that order itself will do us no good unless it is good for something. As we seek to make our order good, we can remind ourselves that justice itself is impossible without order, and that we must not lose order itself in the attempt to make it good.

VI. The Moral Implications of Legal Positivism

We now reach the question whether there is any ground for Gustav Radbruch's belief that a general acceptance of the positivistic philosophy in pre-Nazi Germany made smoother the route to dictatorship. Understandably, Professor Hart regards this as the most outrageous of all charges against positivism.

Here indeed we enter upon a hazardous area of controversy, where ugly words and ugly charges have become commonplace. During the last half century in this country no issue of legal philosophy has caused more spilling of ink and adrenalin than the assertion that there are "totalitarian" implications in the views of Oliver Wendell Holmes, Jr. Even the most cautiously phrased criticisms of that grand old figure from the age of Darwin, Huxley, and Haeckel seem to stir the reader's mind with the memory of past acerbities.[26] It does no good to suggest that perhaps Holmes did not perceive all the implications of his own philosophy, for this is merely to substitute one insult for another. Nor does it help much to recall the dictum of one of the closest companions of Holmes' youth — surely no imperceptive observer — that Holmes

[26] See, *e.g.*, Howe, *The Positivism of Mr. Justice Holmes*, 64 Harv. L. Rev. 529 (1951).

was "composed of at least two and a half different people rolled into one, and the way he keeps them together in one tight skin, without quarreling any more than they do, is remarkable." [27]

In venturing upon these roughest of all jurisprudential waters, one is not reassured to see even so moderate a man as Professor Hart indulging in some pretty broad strokes of the oar. Radbruch disclosed "an extraordinary naïveté" in assessing the temper of his own profession in Germany and in supposing that its adherence to positivism helped the Nazis to power.[28] His judgment on this and other matters shows that he had "only half digested the spiritual message of liberalism" he mistakenly thought he was conveying to his countrymen.[29] A state of "hysteria"[30] is revealed by those who see a wholesome reorientation of German legal thinking in such judicial decisions as were rendered in the informer cases.

Let us put aside at least the blunter tools of invective and address ourselves as calmly as we can to the question whether legal positivism, as practiced and preached in Germany, had, or could have had, any causal connection with Hitler's ascent to power. It should be recalled that in the seventy-five years before the Nazi regime the positivistic philosophy had achieved in Germany a standing such as it enjoyed in no other country. Austin praised a German scholar for bringing international law within the clarity-producing restraints of positivism.[31] Gray reported with pleasure that the "abler" German jurists of his time were "abjuring all '*nicht positivisches Recht*,'" and cited Bergbohm as an example.[32] This is an illuminating example, for Bergbohm was a scholar whose ambition was to make German positivism live up to its own pretensions. He was distressed to encounter vestigial traces of natural-law thinking in writings claiming to be positivistic. In particular, he was disturbed by the frequent recurrence of such notions as that law owes its efficacy to a perceived moral need for order, or that it is in the nature of man that he requires a legal order, etc. Bergbohm announced a program, never realized, to drive from positivistic thinking these last miasmas from the swamp

---

[27] See 1 PERRY, THE THOUGHT AND CHARACTER OF WILLIAM JAMES 297 (1935) (quoting a letter written by William James in 1869).

[28] Hart, *supra* note 2, at 617–18.

[29] *Id.* at 618.

[30] *Id.* at 619.

[31] 1 AUSTIN, LECTURES ON JURISPRUDENCE 173 (5th ed. 1885) (Lecture V).

[32] GRAY, THE NATURE AND SOURCES OF THE LAW 96 (2d ed. 1921).

of natural law.[33] German jurists generally tended to regard the Anglo-American common law as a messy and unprincipled conglomerate of law and morals.[34] Positivism was the only theory of law that could claim to be "scientific" in an Age of Science. Dissenters from this view were characterized by positivists with that epithet modern man fears above all others: "naïve." The result was that it could be reported by 1927 that "to be found guilty of adherence to natural law theories is a kind of social disgrace."[35]

To this background we must add the observation that the Germans seem never to have achieved that curious ability possessed by the British, and to some extent by the Americans, of holding their logic on short leash. When a German defines law, he means his definition to be taken seriously. If a German writer had hit upon the slogan of American legal realism, "Law is simply the behavior patterns of judges and other state officials," he would not have regarded this as an interesting little conversation-starter. He would have believed it and acted on it.

German legal positivism not only banned from legal science any consideration of the moral ends of law, but it was also indifferent to what I have called the inner morality of law itself. The German lawyer was therefore peculiarly prepared to accept as "law" anything that called itself by that name, was printed at government expense, and seemed to come "*von oben herab*."

In the light of these considerations I cannot see either absurdity or perversity in the suggestion that the attitudes prevailing in the German legal profession were helpful to the Nazis. Hitler did not come to power by a violent revolution. He was Chancellor before he became the Leader. The exploitation of legal forms started cautiously and became bolder as power was consolidated. The first attacks on the established order were on ramparts which, if they were manned by anyone, were manned by lawyers and judges. These ramparts fell almost without a struggle.

Professor Hart and others have been understandably distressed by references to a "higher law" in some of the decisions concerning informers and in Radbruch's postwar writings. I suggest that if German jurisprudence had concerned itself more with the inner morality of law, it would not have been necessary to invoke

---

[33] 1 BERGBOHM, JURISPRUDENZ UND RECHTSPHILOSOPHIE 355–552 (1892).

[34] See, *e.g.*, Heller, *Die Krisis der Staatslehre*, 55 ARCHIV FÜR SOZIALWISSENSCHAFT UND SOZIALPOLITIK 289, 309 (Germany 1926).

[35] Voegelin, *Kelsen's Pure Theory of Law*, 42 POL. SCI. Q. 268, 269 (1927).

any notion of this sort in declaring void the more outrageous Nazi statutes.

To me there is nothing shocking in saying that a dictatorship which clothes itself with a tinsel of legal form can so far depart from the morality of order, from the inner morality of law itself, that it ceases to be a legal system. When a system calling itself law is predicated upon a general disregard by judges of the terms of the laws they purport to enforce, when this system habitually cures its legal irregularities, even the grossest, by retroactive statutes, when it has only to resort to forays of terror in the streets, which no one dares challenge, in order to escape even those scant restraints imposed by the pretence of legality — when all these things have become true of a dictatorship, it is not hard for me, at least, to deny to it the name of law.

I believe that the invalidity of the statutes involved in the informer cases could have been grounded on considerations such as I have just outlined. But if you were raised with a generation that said "law is law" and meant it, you may feel the only way you can escape one law is to set another off against it, and this perforce must be a "higher law." Hence these notions of "higher law," which are a justifiable cause for alarm, may themselves be a belated fruit of German legal positivism.

It should be remarked at this point that it is chiefly in Roman Catholic writings that the theory of natural law is considered, not simply as a search for those principles that will enable men to live together successfully, but as a quest for something that can be called "a higher law." This identification of natural law with a law that is above human laws seems in fact to be demanded by any doctrine that asserts the possibility of an authoritative pronouncement of the demands of natural law. In those areas affected by such pronouncements as have so far been issued, the conflict between Roman Catholic doctrine and opposing views seems to me to be a conflict between two forms of positivism. Fortunately, over most of the area with which lawyers are concerned, no such pronouncements exist. In these areas I think those of us who are not adherents of its faith can be grateful to the Catholic Church for having kept alive the rationalistic tradition in ethics.

I do not assert that the solution I have suggested for the informer cases would not have entailed its own difficulties, particularly the familiar one of knowing where to stop. But I think it demonstrable that the most serious deterioration in legal morality under Hitler took place in branches of the law like those involved in the informer cases; no comparable deterioration was to be observed in the ordinary branches of private law. It was in those areas where the ends of law were most odious by ordinary standards of decency that the morality of law itself was most flagrantly disregarded. In other words, where one would have been most tempted to say, "This is so evil it cannot be a law," one could usually have said instead, "This thing is the product of a system so oblivious to the morality of law that it is not entitled to be called a law." I think there is something more than accident here, for the overlapping suggests that legal morality cannot live when it is severed from a striving toward justice and decency.

But as an actual solution for the informer cases, I, like Professors Hart and Radbruch, would have preferred a retroactive statute. My reason for this preference is not that this is the most nearly lawful way of making unlawful what was once law. Rather I would see such a statute as a way of symbolizing a sharp break with the past, as a means of isolating a kind of cleanup operation from the normal functioning of the judicial process. By this isolation it would become possible for the judiciary to return more rapidly to a condition in which the demands of legal morality could be given proper respect. In other words, it would make it possible to plan more effectively to regain for the ideal of fidelity to law its normal meaning.

VII. The Problem of Interpretation: The Core and the Penumbra

It is essential that we be just as clear as we can be about the meaning of Professor Hart's doctrine of "the core and the penumbra," [36] because I believe the casual reader is likely to misinterpret what he has to say. Such a reader is apt to suppose that Professor Hart is merely describing something that is a matter of everyday experience for the lawyer, namely, that in the interpretation of legal rules it is typically the case (though not universally so) that there are some situations which will seem to fall rather clearly within the rule, while others will be more doubtful. Professor Hart's thesis takes no such jejune form. His extended discussion of the core and the penumbra is not just a complicated way of recognizing that some cases are hard, while others are

[36] Hart, *supra* note 2, at 606–08.

easy. Instead, on the basis of a theory about language meaning generally, he is proposing a theory of judicial interpretation which is, I believe, wholly novel. Certainly it has never been put forward in so uncompromising a form before.

As I understand Professor Hart's thesis (if we add some tacit assumptions implied by it, as well as some qualifications he would no doubt wish his readers to supply) a full statement would run something as follows: The task of interpretation is commonly that of determining the meaning of the individual words of a legal rule, like "vehicle" in a rule excluding vehicles from a park. More particularly, the task of interpretation is to determine the range of reference of such a word, or the aggregate of things to which it points. Communication is possible only because words have a "standard instance," or a "core of meaning" that remains relatively constant, whatever the context in which the word may appear. Except in unusual circumstances, it will always be proper to regard a word like "vehicle" as embracing its "standard instance," that is, that aggregate of things it would include in all ordinary contexts, within or without the law. This meaning the word will have in any legal rule, whatever its purpose. In applying the word to its "standard instance," no creative role is assumed by the judge. He is simply applying the law "as it is."

In addition to a constant core, however, words also have a penumbra of meaning which, unlike the core, will vary from context to context. When the object in question (say, a tricycle) falls within this penumbral area, the judge is forced to assume a more creative role. He must now undertake, for the first time, an interpretation of the rule in the light of its purpose or aim. Having in mind what was sought by the regulation concerning parks, ought it to be considered as barring tricycles? When questions of this sort are decided there is at least an "intersection" of "is" and "ought," since the judge, in deciding what the rule "is," does so in the light of his notions of what "it ought to be" in order to carry out its purpose.

If I have properly interpreted Professor Hart's theory as it affects the "hard core," then I think it is quite untenable. The most obvious defect of his theory lies in its assumption that problems of interpretation typically turn on the meaning of individual words. Surely no judge applying a rule of the common law ever followed any such procedure as that described (and, I take it, prescribed) by Professor Hart; indeed, we do not normally even think of his problem as being one of "interpretation." Even in the case of statutes, we commonly have to assign meaning, not to a single word, but to a sentence, a paragraph, or a whole page or more of text. Surely a paragraph does not have a "standard instance" that remains constant whatever the context in which it appears. If a statute seems to have a kind of "core meaning" that we can apply without a too precise inquiry into its exact purpose, this is because we can see that, however one might formulate the precise objective of the statute, *this* case would still come within it.

Even in situations where our interpretive difficulties seem to head up in a single word, Professor Hart's analysis seems to me to give no real account of what does or should happen. In his illustration of the "vehicle," although he tells us this word has a core of meaning that in all contexts defines unequivocally a range of objects embraced by it, he never tells us what these objects might be. If the rule excluding vehicles from parks seems easy to apply in some cases, I submit this is because we can see clearly enough what the rule "is aiming at in general" so that we know there is no need to worry about the difference between Fords and Cadillacs. If in some cases we seem to be able to apply the rule without asking what its purpose is, this is not because we can treat a directive arrangement as if it had no purpose. It is rather because, for example, whether the rule be intended to preserve quiet in the park, or to save carefree strollers from injury, we know, "without thinking," that a noisy automobile must be excluded.

What would Professor Hart say if some local patriots wanted to mount on a pedestal in the park a truck used in World War II, while other citizens, regarding the proposed memorial as an eyesore, support their stand by the "no vehicle" rule? Does this truck, in perfect working order, fall within the core or the penumbra?

Professor Hart seems to assert that unless words have "standard instances" that remain constant regardless of context, effective communication would break down and it would become impossible to construct a system of "rules which have authority." [37] If in every context words took on a unique meaning, peculiar to that context, the whole process of interpretation would become

---

[37] See *id.* at 607.

so uncertain and subjective that the ideal of a rule of law would lose its meaning. In other words, Professor Hart seems to be saying that unless we are prepared to accept his analysis of interpretation, we must surrender all hope of giving an effective meaning to the ideal of fidelity to law. This presents a very dark prospect indeed, if one believes, as I do, that we cannot accept his theory of interpretation. I do not take so gloomy a view of the future of the ideal of fidelity to law.

An illustration will help to test, not only Professor Hart's theory of the core and the penumbra, but its relevance to the ideal of fidelity to law as well. Let us suppose that in leafing through the statutes, we come upon the following enactment: "It shall be a misdemeanor, punishable by a fine of five dollars, to sleep in any railway station." We have no trouble in perceiving the general nature of the target toward which this statute is aimed. Indeed, we are likely at once to call to mind the picture of a disheveled tramp, spread out in an ungainly fashion on one of the benches of the station, keeping weary passengers on their feet and filling their ears with raucous and alcoholic snores. This vision may fairly be said to represent the "obvious instance" contemplated by the statute, though certainly it is far from being the "standard instance" of the physiological state called "sleep."

Now let us see how this example bears on the ideal of fidelity to law. Suppose I am a judge, and that two men are brought before me for violating this statute. The first is a passenger who was waiting at 3 A.M. for a delayed train. When he was arrested he was sitting upright in an orderly fashion, but was heard by the arresting officer to be gently snoring. The second is a man who had brought a blanket and pillow to the station and had obviously settled himself down for the night. He was arrested, however, before he had a chance to go to sleep. Which of these cases presents the "standard instance" of the word "sleep"? If I disregard that question, and decide to fine the second man and set free the first, have I violated a duty of fidelity to law? Have I violated that duty if I interpret the word "sleep" as used in this statute to mean something like "to spread oneself out on a bench or floor to spend the night, or as if to spend the night"?

Testing another aspect of Professor Hart's theory, is it really ever possible to interpret a word in a statute without knowing the aim of the statute? Suppose we encounter the following incomplete sentence: "All improvements must be promptly reported to . . . ." Professor Hart's theory seems to assert that even if we have only this fragment before us we can safely construe the word "improvement" to apply to its "standard instance," though we would have to know the rest of the sentence before we could deal intelligently with "problems of the penumbra." Yet surely in the truncated sentence I have quoted, the word "improvement" is almost as devoid of meaning as the symbol "X."

The word "improvement" will immediately take on meaning if we fill out the sentence with the words, "the head nurse," or, "the Town Planning Authority," though the two meanings that come to mind are radically dissimilar. It can hardly be said that these two meanings represent some kind of penumbral accretion to the word's "standard instance." And one wonders, parenthetically, how helpful the theory of the core and the penumbra would be in deciding whether, when the report is to be made to the planning authorities, the word "improvement" includes an unmortgageable monstrosity of a house that lowers the market value of the land on which it is built.

It will be instructive, I think, to consider the effect of other ways of filling out the sentence. Suppose we add to, "All improvements must be promptly reported to . . ." the words, "the Dean of the Graduate Division." Here we no longer seem, as we once did, to be groping in the dark; rather, we seem now to be reaching into an empty box. We achieve a little better orientation if the final clause reads, "to the Principal of the School," and we feel completely at ease if it becomes, "to the Chairman of the Committee on Relations with the Parents of Children in the Primary Division."

It should be noted that in deciding what the word "improvement" means in all these cases, we do not proceed simply by placing the word in some general context, such as hospital practice, town planning, or education. If this were so, the "improvement" in the last instance might just as well be that of the teacher as that of the pupil. Rather, we ask ourselves, What can this rule be for? What evil does it seek to avert? What good is it intended to promote? When it is "the head nurse" who receives the report, we are apt to find ourselves asking, "Is there, perhaps, a shortage of hospital space, so that patients who improve sufficiently are sent home or are assigned to a ward where they will receive less attention?" If "Principal" offers more orientation than "Dean of the Graduate Division," this must be because we know something about the differences between primary education and education on the postgraduate university level. We must have some minimum acquaintance with the ways in which these two educational enterprises are conducted, and with the problems encountered in both of them, before any distinction between "Principal" and "Dean of the Graduate Division" would affect our interpretation of "improvement." We must, in other words, be sufficiently capable of putting ourselves in the position of those who drafted the rule to know what they thought "ought to be." It is in the light of this "ought" that we must decide what the rule "is."

Turning now to the phenomenon Professor Hart calls "preoccupation with the penumbra," we have to ask ourselves what is actually contributed to the process of interpretation by the common practice of supposing various "borderline" situations. Professor Hart seems to say, "Why, nothing at all, unless we are working with problems of the penumbra." If this is what he means, I find his view a puzzling one, for it still leaves unexplained why, under his theory, if one is dealing with a penumbral problem, it could be useful to think about other penumbral problems.

Throughout his whole discussion of interpretation, Professor Hart seems to assume that it is a kind of cataloguing procedure. A judge faced with a novel situation is like a library clerk who has to decide where to shelve a new book. There are easy cases: the *Bible* belongs under Religion, *The Wealth of Nations* under Economics, etc. Then there are hard cases, when the librarian has to exercise a kind of creative choice, as in deciding whether *Das Kapital* belongs under Politics or Economics, *Gulliver's Travels* under Fantasy or Philosophy. But whether the decision where to shelve is easy or hard, once it is made all the librarian has to do is to put the book away. And so it is with judges, Professor Hart seems to say, in all essential particulars. Surely the judicial process is something more than a cataloguing procedure. The judge does not discharge his responsibility when he pins an apt diagnostic label on the case. He has to do something about it, to treat it, if you will. It is this larger responsibility which explains why interpretative problems almost never turn on a single word, and also why lawyers for generations have found the putting of imaginary borderline cases useful, not only "on the penumbra," but in order to know where the penumbra begins.

These points can be made clear, I believe, by drawing again on our example of the statutory fragment which reads, "All improvements must be promptly reported to . . . ." Whatever the concluding phrase may be, the judge has not solved his problems simply by deciding what kind of improvement is meant. Almost all of the words in the sentence may require interpretation, but most obviously this is so of "promptly" and "reported." What kind of "report" is contemplated: a written note, a call at the office, entry in a hospital record? How specific must it be? Will it be enough to say "a lot better," or "a big house with a bay window"?

Now it should be apparent to any lawyer that in interpreting words like "improvement," "prompt," and "report," no real help is obtained by asking how some extralegal "standard instance" would define these words. But, much more important, when these words are all parts of a single structure of thought, they are in interaction with one another during the process of interpretation. "What is an 'improvement'? Well, it must be something that can be made the subject of a report. So, for purposes of this statute 'improvement' really means 'reportable improvement.' What kind of 'report' must be made? Well, that depends upon the sort of 'improvement' about which information is desired and the reasons for desiring the information."

When we look beyond individual words to the statute as a whole, it becomes apparent how the putting of hypothetical cases assists the interpretative process generally. By pulling our minds first in one direction, then in another, these cases help us to understand the fabric of thought before us. This fabric is something we seek to discern, so that we may know truly what it is, but it is also something that we inevitably help to create as we strive (in accordance with our obligation of fidelity to law) to make the statute a coherent, workable whole.

I should have considered all these remarks much too trite to put down here if they did not seem to be demanded in an answer to the theory of interpretation proposed by Professor Hart, a theory by which he puts such store that he implies we cannot have fidelity to law in any meaningful sense unless we are prepared to accept it. Can it be possible that the positivistic philosophy demands that we abandon a view of interpretation which sees as its central concern, not words, but purpose and structure? If so, then the stakes in this battle of schools are indeed high.

I am puzzled by the novelty Professor Hart attributes to the lessons I once tried to draw from Wittgenstein's example about teaching a game to children.[38] I was simply trying to show the role reflection plays in deciding what ought to be done. I was trying to make such simple points as that decisions about what ought to be done are improved by reflection, by an exchange of views with others sharing the same problems, and by imagining various situations that might be presented. I was assuming that all of these innocent and familiar measures might serve to sharpen our perception of what we were trying to do, and that the product of the whole process might be, not merely a more apt choice of means for the end sought, but a clarification of the end itself. I had thought that a famous judge of the English bench had something like this in mind when he spoke of the common law as working "itself pure." [39] If this view of the judicial process is no longer entertained in the country of its origin, I can only say that, whatever the vicissitudes of Lord Mansfield's British reputation may be, he will always remain for us in this country a heroic figure of jurisprudence.

I have stressed here the deficiencies of Professor Hart's theory as that theory affects judicial interpretation. I believe, however, that its defects go deeper and result ultimately from a mistaken theory about the meaning of language generally. Professor Hart seems to subscribe to what may be called "the pointer theory of meaning," [40] a theory which ignores or minimizes the effect on the

---

[38] Fuller, *Human Purpose and Natural Law*, 53 J. PHILOS. 697, 700 (1956).

[39] Omychund v. Barker, 1 Atk. 21, 33, 26 Eng. Rep. 15, 22–23 (Ch. 1744) (argument of Solicitor-General Murray, later Lord Mansfield):

> All occasions do not arise at once; . . . a statute very seldom can take in all cases, therefore the common law, *that works itself pure* by rules drawn from the fountain of justice, is for this reason superior to an act of parliament.

[40] I am speaking of the linguistic theory that seems to be implied in the essay under discussion here. In Professor Hart's brilliant inaugural address, *Definition and Theory in Jurisprudence*, 70 L.Q. REV. 37 (1954), the most important point made is that terms like "rule," "right," and "legal person" cannot be defined by pointing to correspondent things or actions in the external world, but can only be understood in terms of the function performed by them in the larger system, just as one cannot understand the umpire's ruling, "Y're out!" without having at least a general familiarity with the rules of baseball. Even in the analysis presented in the inaugural address, however, Professor Hart seems to think that the dependence of meaning on function and context is a peculiarity of formal and explicit systems, like those of a game or a legal system. He seems not to recognize that what he has to say about explicit systems is also true of the countless informal and overlapping systems that run through language as a whole. These implicit systematic or structural elements in language often enable us to understand at once the meaning of a word used in a wholly novel sense, as in the statement, "Experts regard

meaning of words of the speaker's purpose and the structure of language. Characteristically, this school of thought embraces the notion of "common usage." The reason is, of course, that it is only with the aid of this notion that it can seem to attain the inert datum of meaning it seeks, a meaning isolated from the effects of purpose and structure.

It would not do to attempt here an extended excursus into linguistic theory. I shall have to content myself with remarking that the theory of meaning implied in Professor Hart's essay seems to me to have been rejected by three men who stand at the very head of modern developments in logical analysis: Wittgenstein, Russell, and Whitehead. Wittgenstein's posthumous *Philosophical Investigations* constitutes a sort of running commentary on the way words shift and transform their meanings as they move from context to context. Russell repudiates the cult of "common usage," and asks what "instance" of the word "word" itself can be given that does not imply some specific intention in the use of it.[41] Whitehead explains the appeal that "the deceptive identity of the repeated word" has for modern philosophers; only by assuming some linguistic constant (such as the "core of meaning") can validity be claimed for procedures of logic which of necessity move the word from one context to another.[42]

VIII. The Moral and Emotional Foundations of Positivism

If we ignore the specific theories of law associated with the positivistic philosophy, I believe we can say that the dominant tone of positivism is set by a fear of a purposive interpretation of law and legal institutions, or at least by a fear that such an interpretation may be pushed too far. I think one can find confirmatory traces of this fear in all of those classified as "positivists" by Professor Hart, with the outstanding exception of

---

the English Channel as the most difficult swim in the world." In the essay now being discussed, Professor Hart seems nowhere to recognize that a rule or statute has a structural or systematic quality that reflects itself in some measure into the meaning of every principal term in it.

[41] Russell, *The Cult of "Common Usage,"* in Portraits From Memory and Other Essays 166, 170–71 (1956).

[42] Whitehead, *Analysis of Meaning*, in Essays in Science and Philosophy 122, 127 (1947).

Bentham, who is in all things a case apart and who was worlds removed from anything that could be called *ethical* positivism.

Now the belief that many of us hold, that this fear of purpose takes a morbid turn in positivism, should not mislead us into thinking that the fear is wholly without justification, or that it reflects no significant problem in the organization of society.

Fidelity to law *can* become impossible if we do not accept the broader responsibilities (themselves purposive, as all responsibilities are and must be) that go with a purposive interpretation of law. One can imagine a course of reasoning that might run as follows: This statute says absinthe shall not be sold. What is its purpose? To promote health. Now, as everyone knows, absinthe is a sound, wholesome, and beneficial beverage. Therefore, interpreting the statute in the light of its purpose, I construe it to direct a general sale and consumption of that most healthful of beverages, absinthe.

If the risk of this sort of thing is implicit in a purposive interpretation, what measures can we take to eliminate it, or to reduce it to bearable proportions? One is tempted to say, "Why, just use ordinary common sense." But this would be an evasion, and would amount to saying that although we know the answer, we cannot say what it is. To give a better answer, I fear I shall have to depart from those high standards of clarity Professor Hart so rightly prizes and so generally exemplifies. I shall have to say that the answer lies in the concept of *structure.* A statute or a rule of common law has, either explicitly, or by virtue of its relation with other rules, something that may be called a structural integrity. This is what we have in mind when we speak of "the intent of the statute," though we know it is men who have intentions and not words on paper. Within the limits of that structure, fidelity to law not only permits but demands a creative role from the judge, but beyond that structure it does not permit him to go. Of course, the structure of which I speak presents its own "problems of the penumbra." But the penumbra in this case surrounds something real, something that has a meaning and integrity of its own. It is not a purposeless collocation of words that gets its meaning on loan from lay usage.

It is one of the great virtues of Professor Hart's essay that it makes explicit positivism's concern for the ideal of fidelity to law. Yet I believe, though I cannot prove, that the basic reason why positivism fears a purposive interpretation is not that it may lead to anarchy, but that it may push us too far in the opposite direction. It sees in a purposive interpretation, carried too far, a threat to human freedom and human dignity.

Let me illustrate what I mean by supposing that I am a man without religious beliefs living in a community of ardent Protestant Christian faith. A statute in this community makes it unlawful for me to play golf on Sunday. I find this statute an annoyance and accept its restraints reluctantly. But the annoyance I feel is not greatly different from that I might experience if, though it were lawful to play on Sunday, a power failure prevented me from taking the streetcar I would normally use in reaching the course. In the vernacular, "it is just one of those things."

What a different complexion the whole matter assumes if a statute compels me to attend church, or, worse still, to kneel and recite prayers! Here I may feel a direct affront to my integrity as a human being. Yet the purpose of both statutes may well be to increase church attendance. The difference may even seem to be that the first statute seeks its end slyly and by indirection, the second, honestly and openly. Yet surely this is a case in which indirection has its virtues and honesty its heavy price in human dignity.

Now I believe that positivism fears that a too explicit and uninhibited interpretation in terms of purpose may well push the first kind of statute in the direction of the second. If this is a basic concern underlying the positivistic philosophy, that philosophy is dealing with a real problem, however inept its response to the problem may seem to be. For this problem of the impressed purpose is a crucial one in our society. One thinks of the obligation to bargain "in good faith" imposed by the National Labor Relations Act.[43] One recalls the remark that to punish a criminal is less of an affront to his dignity than to reform and improve him. The statutory preamble comes to mind: the increasing use made of it, its legislative wisdom, the significance that should be accorded to it in judicial interpretation. The flag salute cases[44] will, of course, occur to everyone. I myself recall the splendid analysis by Professor von Hippel of the things that were fundamentally wrong about Nazism, and his conclusion that the grossest

[43] § 8(d), added by 61 Stat. 142 (1947), 29 U.S.C. § 158(d) (1952); see NLRA §§ 8(a)(5), (b)(3), as amended, 61 Stat. 141 (1947), 29 U.S.C. §§ 158(a)(5), (b)(3) (1952).

[44] Minersville School Dist. v. Gobitis, 310 U.S. 586 (1940), *overruled*, West Virginia State Bd. of Educ. v. Barnette, 319 U.S. 624 (1943).

of all Nazi perversities was that of coercing acts, like the putting out of flags and saying, "Heil Hitler!" that have meaning only when done voluntarily, or, more accurately, have a meaning when coerced that is wholly parasitic on an association of them with past voluntary expressions.[45]

Questions of this sort are undoubtedly becoming more acute as the state assumes a more active role with respect to economic activity. No significant economic activity can be organized exclusively by "don'ts." By its nature economic production requires a co-operative effort. In the economic field there is special reason, therefore, to fear that "This you may not do" will be transformed into "This you must do — but willingly." As we all know, the most tempting opportunity for effecting this transformation is presented by what is called in administrative practice "the prehearing conference," in which the negative threat of a statute's sanctions may be used by its administrators to induce what they regard, in all good conscience, as "the proper attitude."

I look forward to the day when legal philosophy can address itself earnestly to issues of this sort, and not simply exploit them to score points in favor of a position already taken. Professor Hart's essay seems to me to open the way for such a discussion, for it eliminates from the positivistic philosophy a pretense that has hitherto obscured every issue touched by it. I mean, of course, the pretense of the ethical neutrality of positivism. That is why I can say in all sincerity that, despite my almost paragraph-by-paragraph disagreement with the views expressed in his essay, I believe Professor Hart has made an enduring contribution to legal philosophy.

---

[45] VON HIPPEL, DIE NATIONALSOZIALISTISCHE HERRSCHAFTSORDNUNG ALS WARNUNG UND LEHRE 6–7 (1946).

The Model of Rules

Ronald M. Dworkin

I. Embarrassing Questions

Lawyers lean heavily on the connected concepts of legal right and legal obligation. We say that someone has a legal right or duty, and we take that statement as a sound basis for making claims and demands, and for criticizing the acts of public officials. But our understanding of these concepts is remarkably fragile, and we fall into trouble when we try to say what legal rights and obligations are. We say glibly that whether someone has a legal obligation is determined by applying "the law" to the particular facts of his case, but this is not a helpful answer, because we have the same difficulties with the concept of law.

We are used to summing up our troubles in the classic questions of jurisprudence: What is "the law"? When two sides disagree, as often happens, about a proposition "of law," what are they disagreeing about, and how shall we decide which side is right? Why do we call what "the law" says a matter of legal "obligation"? Is "obligation" here just a term of art, meaning only "what the law says"? Or does legal obligation have something to do with moral obligation? Can we say that we have, in principle at least, the same reasons for meeting our legal obligations that we have for meeting our moral obligations?

These are not puzzles for the cupboard, to be taken down on rainy days for fun. They are sources of continuing embarrassment, and they nag at our attention. They embarrass us in dealing with particular problems that we must solve, one way or another. Suppose a novel right-of-privacy case comes to court, and there is no statute or precedent either granting or denying the particular right of anonymity claimed by the plaintiff. What role in the court's decision should be played by the fact that most people in the community think that private individuals are "morally" entitled to that particular privacy? Suppose the Supreme Court orders some prisoner freed because the police used procedures that the Court now says are constitutionally forbidden, although the Court's earlier decisions upheld these pro-

Ronald Dworkin is Professor of Law at Yale University. This article is adapted from a chapter in a forthcoming book.

cedures. Must the Court, to be consistent, free all other prisoners previously convicted through these same procedures?[1] Conceptual puzzles about "the law" and "legal obligation" become acute when a court is confronted with a problem like this.

These eruptions signal a chronic disease. Day in and day out we send people to jail, or take money away from them, or make them do things they do not want to do, under coercion of force, and we justify all of this by speaking of such persons as having broken the law or having failed to meet their legal obligations, or having interfered with other people's legal rights. Even in clear cases (a bank robber or a willful breach of contract), when we are confident that someone had a legal obligation and broke it, we are not able to give a satisfactory account of what that means, or why that entitles the state to punish or coerce him. We may feel confident that what we are doing is proper, but until we can identify the principles we are following we cannot be sure that they are sufficient, or whether we are applying them consistently. In less clear cases, when the issue of whether an obligation has been broken is for some reason controversial, the pitch of these nagging questions rises, and our responsibility to find answers deepens.

Certain lawyers (we may call them "nominalists") urge that we solve these problems by ignoring them. In their view the concepts of "legal obligation" and "the law" are myths, invented and sustained by lawyers for a dismal mix of conscious and subconscious motives. The puzzles we find in these concepts are merely symptoms that they are myths. They are unsolvable because unreal, and our concern with them is just one feature of our enslavement. We would do better to flush away the puzzles and the concepts altogether, and pursue our important social objectives without this excess baggage.

This is a tempting suggestion, but it has fatal drawbacks. Before we can decide that our concepts of law and of legal obligation are myths, we must decide what they are. We must be able to state, at least roughly, what it is we all believe that is wrong. But the nerve of our problem is that we have great difficulty in doing just that. Indeed, when we ask what law is and what legal obligations are, we are asking for a theory of how we use those concepts and of the conceptual commitments our use entails. We cannot conclude, before we have such a general theory, that our practices are stupid or superstitious.

Of course, the nominalists think they know how the rest of us

---

1 *See* Linkletter v. Walker, 381 U.S. 618 (1965).

use these concepts. They think that when we speak of "the law," we mean a set of timeless rules stocked in some conceptual warehouse awaiting discovery by judges, and that when we speak of legal obligation we mean the invisible chains these mysterious rules somehow drape around us. The theory that there are such rules and chains they call "mechanical jurisprudence," and they are right in ridiculing its practitioners. Their difficulty, however, lies in finding practitioners to ridicule. So far they have had little luck in caging and exhibiting mechanical jurisprudents (all specimens captured—even Blackstone and Joseph Beale—have had to be released after careful reading of their texts).

In any event, it is clear that most lawyers have nothing like this in mind when they speak of the law and of legal obligation. A superficial examination of our practices is enough to show this, for we speak of laws changing and evolving, and of legal obligation sometimes being problematical. In these and other ways we show that we are not addicted to mechanical jurisprudence.

Nevertheless, we do use the concepts of law and legal obligation, and we do suppose that society's warrant to punish and coerce is written in that currency. It may be that when the details of this practice are laid bare, the concepts we do use will be shown to be as silly and as thick with illusion as those the nominalists invented. If so, then we shall have to find other ways to describe what we do, and either provide other justifications or change our practices. But until we have discovered this and made these adjustments, we cannot accept the nominalists' premature invitation to turn our backs on the problems our present concepts provide.

Of course the suggestion that we stop talking about "the law" and "legal obligation" is mostly bluff. These concepts are too deeply cemented into the structure of our political practices—they cannot be given up like cigarettes or hats. Some of the nominalists have half-admitted this and said that the myths they condemn should be thought of as Platonic myths and retained to seduce the masses into order. This is perhaps not so cynical a suggestion as it seems; perhaps it is a covert hedging of a dubious bet.

If we boil away the bluff, the nominalist attack reduces to an attack on mechanical jurisprudence. Through the lines of the attack, and in spite of the heroic calls for the death of law, the nominalists themselves have offered an analysis of how the terms "law" and "legal obligation" should be used which is not very different from that of more classical philosophers. Nominalists present their analysis as a model of how legal institutions (particularly courts) "really operate."

But their model differs mainly in emphasis from the theory first made popular by the nineteenth century philosopher John Austin, and now accepted in one form or another by most working and academic lawyers who hold views on jurisprudence. I shall call this theory, with some historical looseness, "positivism." I want to examine the soundness of positivism, particularly in the powerful form that Professor H. L. A. Hart of Oxford has given to it. I choose to focus on his position, not only because of its clarity and elegance, but because here, as almost everywhere else in legal philosophy, constructive thought must start with a consideration of his views.

II. Positivism

Positivism has a few central and organizing propositions as its skeleton, and though not every philosopher who is called a positivist would subscribe to these in the way I present them, they do define the general position I want to examine. These key tenets may be stated as follows:

(a) The law of a community is a set of special rules used by the community directly or indirectly for the purpose of determining which behavior will be punished or coerced by the public power. These special rules can be identified and distinguished by specific criteria, by tests having to do not with their content but with their *pedigree* or the manner in which they were adopted or developed. These tests of pedigree can be used to distinguish valid legal rules from spurious legal rules (rules which lawyers and litigants wrongly argue are rules of law) and also from other sorts of social rules (generally lumped together as "moral rules") that the community follows but does not enforce through public power.

(b) The set of these valid legal rules is exhaustive of "the law," so that if someone's case is not clearly covered by such a rule (because there is none that seems appropriate, or those that seem appropriate are vague, or for some other reason) then that case cannot be decided by "applying the law." It must be decided by some official, like a judge, "exercising his discretion," which means reaching beyond the law for some other sort of standard to guide him in manufacturing a fresh legal rule or supplementing an old one.

(c) To say that someone has a "legal obligation" is to say that his case falls under a valid legal rule that requires him to do or to forbear from doing something. (To say he has a legal right, or has a legal power of some sort, or a legal privilege or immunity, is to assert, in a shorthand way, that others have actual or hypothetical legal obligations to act or not to act in certain ways touching him.) In the absence of such a valid legal rule there is no legal obligation; it follows that when the judge decides an issue by exercising his discretion, he is not enforcing a legal obligation as to that issue.

This is only the skeleton of positivism. The flesh is arranged differently by different positivists, and some even tinker with the bones. Different versions differ chiefly in their description of the fundamental test of pedigree a rule must meet to count as a rule of law.

Austin, for example, framed his version of the fundamental test as a series of interlocking definitions and distinctions.[2] He defined having an obligation as lying under a rule, a rule as a general command, and a command as an expression of desire that others behave in a particular way, backed by the power and will to enforce that expression in the event of disobedience. He distinguished classes of rules (legal, moral or religious) according to which person or group is the author of the general command the rule represents. In each political community, he thought, one will find a sovereign—a person or a determinate group whom the rest obey habitually, but who is not in the habit of obeying anyone else. The legal rules of a community are the general commands its sovereign has deployed. Austin's definition of legal obligation followed from this definition of law. One has a legal obligation, he thought, if one is among the addressees of some general order of the sovereign, and is in danger of suffering a sanction unless he obeys that order.

Of course, the sovereign cannot provide for all contingencies through any scheme of orders, and some of his orders will inevitably be vague or have furry edges. Therefore (according to Austin) the sovereign grants those who enforce the law (judges) discretion to make fresh orders when novel or troublesome cases are presented. The judges then make new rules or adapt old rules, and the sovereign either overturns their creations, or tacitly confirms them by failing to do so.

Austin's model is quite beautiful in its simplicity. It asserts the first tenet of positivism, that the law is a set of rules specially selected to govern public order, and offers a simple factual test—what has the sovereign commanded?—as the sole criterion for identifying those special rules. In time, however, those who studied and tried to apply Austin's model found it too simple. Many objections were raised, among which were two that seemed fundamental. First, Austin's key assumption that in each community a determinate group or institu-

2 J. Austin, The Province of Jurisprudence Determined (1832).

tion can be found, which is in ultimate control of all other groups, seemed not to hold in a complex society. Political control in a modern nation is pluralistic and shifting, a matter of more or less, of compromise and cooperation and alliance, so that it is often impossible to say that any person or group has that dramatic control necessary to qualify as an Austinian sovereign. One wants to say, in the United States for example, that the "people" are sovereign. But this means almost nothing, and in itself provides no test for determining what the "people" have commanded, or distinguishing their legal from their social or moral commands.

Second, critics began to realize that Austin's analysis fails entirely to account for, even to recognize, certain striking facts about the attitudes we take toward "the law." We make an important distinction between law and even the general orders of a gangster. We feel that the law's strictures—and its sanctions—are different in that they are obligatory in a way that the outlaw's commands are not. Austin's analysis has no place for any such distinction, because it defines an obligation as subjection to the threat of force, and so founds the authority of law entirely on the sovereign's ability and will to harm those who disobey. Perhaps the distinction we make is illusory—perhaps our feelings of some special authority attaching to the law is based on religious hangover or another sort of mass self-deception. But Austin does not demonstrate this, and we are entitled to insist that an analysis of our concept of law either acknowledge and explain our attitudes, or show why they are mistaken.

H. L. A. Hart's version of positivism is more complex than Austin's, in two ways. First, he recognizes, as Austin did not, that rules are of different logical kinds (Hart distinguishes two kinds, which he calls "primary" and "secondary" rules). Second, he rejects Austin's theory that a rule is a kind of command, and substitutes a more elaborate general analysis of what rules are. We must pause over each of these points, and then note how they merge in Hart's concept of law.

Hart's distinction between primary and secondary rules is of great importance.[3] Primary rules are those that grant rights or impose obligations upon members of the community. The rules of the criminal law that forbid us to rob, murder or drive too fast are good examples of primary rules. Secondary rules are those that stipulate how, and by whom, such primary rules may be formed, recognized, modified or extinguished. The rules that stipulate how Congress is composed, and how it enacts legislation, are examples of secondary rules. Rules about forming contracts and executing wills are also secondary rules because

3 *See* H. L. A. Hart, The Concept of Law 89-96 (1961).

they stipulate how very particular rules governing particular legal obligations (*i.e.*, the terms of a contract or the provisions of a will) come into existence and are changed.

His general analysis of rules is also of great importance.[4] Austin had said that every rule is a general command, and that a person is obligated under a rule if he is liable to be hurt should he disobey it. Hart points out that this obliterates the distinction between being *obliged* to do something and being *obligated* to do it. If one is bound by a rule he is obligated, not merely obliged, to do what it provides, and therefore being bound by a rule must be different from being subject to an injury if one disobeys an order. A rule differs from an order, among other ways, by being *normative*, by setting a standard of behavior that has a call on its subject beyond the threat that may enforce it. A rule can never be binding just because some person with physical power wants it to be so. He must have *authority* to issue the rule or it is no rule, and such authority can only come from another rule which is already binding on those to whom he speaks. That is the difference between a valid law and the orders of a gunman.

So Hart offers a general theory of rules that does not make their authority depend upon the physical power of their authors. If we examine the way different rules come into being, he tells us, and attend to the distinction between primary and secondary rules, we see that there are two possible sources of a rule's authority.[5]

(a) A rule may become binding upon a group of people because that group through its practices *accepts* the rule as a standard for its conduct. It is not enough that the group simply conforms to a pattern of behavior: even though most Englishmen may go to the movies on Saturday evening, they have not accepted a rule requiring that they do so. A practice constitutes the acceptance of a rule only when those who follow the practice regard the rule as binding, and recognize the rule as a reason or justification for their own behavior and as a reason for criticizing the behavior of others who do not obey it.

(b) A rule may also become binding in quite a different way, namely by being enacted in conformity with some *secondary* rule that stipulates that rules so enacted shall be binding. If the constitution of a club stipulates, for example, that by-laws may be adopted by a majority of the members, then particular by-laws so voted are binding upon all the members, not because of any practice of acceptance of these particular by-laws, but because the constitution says so. We use the concept of *validity* in this connection: rules binding because they

4 *Id.* at 79-88.
5 *Id.* at 97-107.

have been created in a manner stipulated by some secondary rule are called "valid" rules. Thus we can record Hart's fundamental distinction this way: a rule may be binding (a) because it is accepted or (b) because it is valid.

Hart's concept of law is a construction of these various distinctions.[6] Primitive communities have only primary rules, and these are binding entirely because of practices of acceptance. Such communities cannot be said to have "law," because there is no way to distinguish a set of legal rules from amongst other social rules, as the first tenet of positivism requires. But when a particular community has developed a fundamental secondary rule that stipulates how legal rules are to be identified, the idea of a distinct set of legal rules, and thus of law, is born.

Hart calls such a fundamental secondary rule a "rule of recognition." The rule of recognition of a given community may be relatively simple ("What the king enacts is law") or it may be very complex (the United States Constitution, with all its difficulties of interpretation, may be considered a single rule of recognition). The demonstration that a particular rule is valid may therefore require tracing a complicated chain of validity back from that particular rule ultimately to the fundamental rule. Thus a parking ordinance of the city of New Haven is valid because it is adopted by a city council, pursuant to the procedures and within the competence specified by the municipal law adopted by the state of Connecticut, in conformity with the procedures and within the competence specified by the constitution of the state of Connecticut, which was in turn adopted consistently with the requirements of the United States Constitution.

Of course, a rule of recognition cannot itself be valid, because by hypothesis it is ultimate, and so cannot meet tests stipulated by a more fundamental rule. The rule of recognition is the sole rule in a legal system whose binding force depends upon its acceptance. If we wish to know what rule of recognition a particular community has adopted or follows, we must observe how its citizens, and particularly its officials, behave. We must observe what ultimate arguments they accept as showing the validity of a particular rule, and what ultimate arguments they use to criticize other officials or institutions. We can apply no mechanical test, but there is no danger of our confusing the rule of recognition of a community with its rules of morality. The rule of recognition is identified by the fact that its province is the operation of the governmental apparatus of legislatures, courts, agencies, policemen, and the rest.

---

6 *Id. passim*, particularly ch. VI.

In this way Hart rescues the fundamentals of positivism from Austin's mistakes. Hart agrees with Austin that valid rules of law may be created through the acts of officials and public institutions. But Austin thought that the authority of these institutions lay only in their monopoly of power. Hart finds their authority in the background of constitutional standards against which they act, constitutional standards that have been accepted, in the form of a fundamental rule of recognition, by the community which they govern. This background legitimates the decisions of government and gives them the cast and call of obligation that the naked commands of Austin's sovereign lacked. Hart's theory differs from Austin's also, in recognizing that different communities use different ultimate tests of law, and that some allow other means of creating law than the deliberate act of a legislative institution. Hart mentions "long customary practice" and "the relation [of a rule] to judicial decisions" as other criteria that are often used, though generally along with and subordinate to the test of legislation.

So Hart's version of positivism is more complex than Austin's, and his test for valid rules of law is more sophisticated. In one respect, however, the two models are very similar. Hart, like Austin, recognizes that legal rules have furry edges (he speaks of them as having "open texture") and, again like Austin, he accounts for troublesome cases by saying that judges have and exercise discretion to decide these cases by fresh legislation.[7] (I shall later try to show why one who thinks of law as a special set of rules is almost inevitably drawn to account for difficult cases in terms of someone's exercise of discretion.)

III. Rules, Principles, and Policies

I want to make a general attack on positivism, and I shall use H. L. A. Hart's version as a target, when a particular target is needed. My strategy will be organized around the fact that when lawyers reason or dispute about legal rights and obligations, particularly in those hard cases when our problems with these concepts seem most acute, they make use of standards that do not function as rules, but operate differently as principles, policies, and other sorts of standards. Positivism, I shall argue, is a model of and for a system of rules, and its central notion of a single fundamental test for law forces us to miss the important roles of these standards that are not rules.

I just spoke of "principles, policies, and other sorts of standards." Most often I shall use the term "principle" generically, to refer to the

---

[7] *Id.* ch. VII.

whole set of these standards other than rules; occasionally, however, I shall be more precise, and distinguish between principles and policies. Although nothing in the present argument will turn on the distinction, I should state how I draw it. I call a "policy" that kind of standard that sets out a goal to be reached, generally an improvement in some economic, political, or social feature of the community (though some goals are negative, in that they stipulate that some present feature is to be protected from adverse change). I call a "principle" a standard that is to be observed, not because it will advance or secure an economic, political, or social situation deemed desirable, but because it is a requirement of justice or fairness or some other dimension of morality. Thus the standard that automobile accidents are to be decreased is a policy, and the standard that no man may profit by his own wrong a principle. The distinction can be collapsed by construing a principle as stating a social goal (*i.e.*, the goal of a society in which no man profits by his own wrong), or by construing a policy as stating a principle (*i.e.*, the principle that the goal the policy embraces is a worthy one) or by adopting the utilitarian thesis that principles of justice are disguised statements of goals (securing the greatest happiness of the greatest number). In some contexts the distinction has uses which are lost if it is thus collapsed.[8]

My immediate purpose, however, is to distinguish principles in the generic sense from rules, and I shall start by collecting some examples of the former. The examples I offer are chosen haphazardly; almost any case in a law school casebook would provide examples that would serve as well. In 1889 a New York court, in the famous case of *Riggs v. Palmer*,[9] had to decide whether an heir named in the will of his grandfather could inherit under that will, even though he had murdered his grandfather to do so. The court began its reasoning with this admission: "It is quite true that statutes regulating the making, proof and effect of wills, and the devolution of property, if literally construed, and if their force and effect can in no way and under no circumstances be controlled or modified, give this property to the murderer."[10] But the court continued to note that "all laws as well as all contracts may be controlled in their operation and effect by general, fundamental maxims of the common law. No one shall be permitted to profit by his own fraud, or to take advantage of his own wrong, or to found any claim upon his own iniquity, or to ac-

---

8 *See* Dworkin, *Wasserstrom: The Judicial Decision*, 75 ETHICS 47 (1964), reprinted as *Does Law Have a Function?*, 74 YALE L.J. 640 (1965).

9 115 N.Y. 506, 22 N.E. 188 (1889).

10 *Id.* at 509, 22 N.E. at 189.

quire property by his own crime."[11] The murderer did not receive his inheritance.

In 1960, a New Jersey court was faced, in *Henningsen v. Bloomfield Motors, Inc.*,[12] with the important question of whether (or how much) an automobile manufacturer may limit his liability in case the automobile is defective. Henningsen had bought a car, and signed a contract which said that the manufacturer's liability for defects was limited to "making good" defective parts—"this warranty being expressly in lieu of all other warranties, obligations or liabilities." Henningsen argued that, at least in the circumstances of his case, the manufacturer ought not to be protected by this limitation, and ought to be liable for the medical and other expenses of persons injured in a crash. He was not able to point to any statute, or to any established rule of law, that prevented the manufacturer from standing on the contract. The court nevertheless agreed with Henningsen. At various points in the court's argument the following appeals to standards are made: (a) "[W]e must keep in mind the general principle that, in the absence of fraud, one who does not choose to read a contract before signing it cannot later relieve himself of its burdens."[13] (b) "In applying that principle, the basic tenet of freedom of competent parties to contract is a factor of importance."[14] (c) "Freedom of contract is not such an immutable doctrine as to admit of no qualification in the area in which we are concerned."[15] (d) "In a society such as ours, where the automobile is a common and necessary adjunct of daily life, and where its use is so fraught with danger to the driver, passengers and the public, the manufacturer is under a special obligation in connection with the construction, promotion and sale of his cars. Consequently, the courts must examine purchase agreements closely to see if consumer and public interests are treated fairly."[16] (e) " '[I]s there any principle which is more familiar or more firmly embedded in the history of Anglo-American law than the basic doctrine that the courts will not permit themselves to be used as instruments of inequity and injustice?' "[17] (f) " 'More specifically, the courts generally refuse to lend themselves to the enforcement of a "bargain" in which one party has unjustly taken advantage of the economic necessities of other . . . .' "[18]

11 *Id.* at 511, 22 N.E. at 190.

12 32 N.J. 358, 161 A.2d 69 (1960).

13 *Id.* at 386, 161 A.2d at 84.

14 *Id.*

15 *Id.* at 388, 161 A.2d at 86.

16 *Id.* at 387, 161 A.2d at 85.

17 *Id.* at 389, 161 A.2d at 86 (quoting Frankfurter, J., in United States v. Bethlehem Steel, 315 U.S. 289, 326 (1942)).

18 *Id.*

The standards set out in these quotations are not the sort we think of as legal rules. They seem very different from propositions like "The maximum legal speed on the turnpike is sixty miles an hour" or "A will is invalid unless signed by three witnesses." They are different because they are legal principles rather than legal rules.

The difference between legal principles and legal rules is a logical distinction. Both sets of standards point to particular decisions about legal obligation in particular circumstances, but they differ in the character of the direction they give. Rules are applicable in an all-or-nothing fashion. If the facts a rule stipulates are given, then either the rule is valid, in which case the answer it supplies must be accepted, or it is not, in which case it contributes nothing to the decision.

This all-or-nothing is seen most plainly if we look at the way rules operate, not in law, but in some enterprise they dominate—a game, for example. In baseball a rule provides that if the batter has had three strikes, he is out. An official cannot consistently acknowledge that this is an accurate statement of a baseball rule, and decide that a batter who has had three strikes is not out. Of course, a rule may have exceptions (the batter who has taken three strikes is not out if the catcher drops the third strike). However, an accurate statement of the rule would take this exception into account, and any that did not would be incomplete. If the list of exceptions is very large, it would be too clumsy to repeat them each time the rule is cited; there is, however, no reason in theory why they could not all be added on, and the more that are, the more accurate is the statement of the rule.

If we take baseball rules as a model, we find that rules of law, like the rule that a will is invalid unless signed by three witnesses, fit the model well. If the requirement of three witnesses is a valid legal rule, then it cannot be that a will has been signed by only two witnesses and is valid. The rule might have exceptions, but if it does then it is inaccurate and incomplete to state the rule so simply, without enumerating the exceptions. In theory, at least, the exceptions could all be listed, and the more of them that are, the more complete is the statement of the rule.

But this is not the way the sample principles in the quotations operate. Even those which look most like rules do not set out legal consequences that follow automatically when the conditions provided are met. We say that our law respects the principle that no man may profit from his own wrong, but we do not mean that the law never permits a man to profit from wrongs he commits. In fact, people often profit, perfectly legally, from their legal wrongs. The most notorious case is adverse possession—if I trespass on your land long enough, some day I will gain a right to cross your land whenever I please. There are many less dramatic examples. If a man leaves one job, breaking a contract, to take a much higher paying job, he may have to pay damages to his first employer, but he is usually entitled to keep his new salary. If a man jumps bail and crosses state lines to make a brilliant investment in another state, he may be sent back to jail, but he will keep his profits.

We do not treat these—and countless other counter-instances that can easily be imagined—as showing that the principle about profiting from one's wrongs is not a principle of our legal system, or that it is incomplete and needs qualifying exceptions. We do not treat counter-instances as exceptions (at least not exceptions in the way in which a catcher's dropping the third strike is an exception) because we could not hope to capture these counter-instances simply by a more extended statement of the principle. They are not, even in theory, subject to enumeration, because we would have to include not only these cases (like adverse possession) in which some institution has already provided that profit can be gained through a wrong, but also those numberless imaginary cases in which we know in advance that the principle would not hold. Listing some of these might sharpen our sense of the principle's weight (I shall mention that dimension in a moment), but it would not make for a more accurate or complete statement of the principle.

A principle like "No man may profit from his own wrong" does not even purport to set out conditions that make its application necessary. Rather, it states a reason that argues in one direction, but does not necessitate a particular decision. If a man has or is about to receive something, as a direct result of something illegal he did to get it, then that is a reason which the law will take into account in deciding whether he should keep it. There may be other principles or policies arguing in the other direction—a policy of securing title, for example, or a principle limiting punishment to what the legislature has stipulated. If so, our principle may not prevail, but that does not mean that it is not a principle of our legal system, because in the next case, when these contravening considerations are absent or less weighty, the principle may be decisive. All that is meant, when we say that a particular principle is a principle of our law, is that the principle is one which officials must take into account, if it is relevant, as a consideration inclining in one direction or another.

The logical distinction between rules and principles appears more clearly when we consider principles that do not even look like rules. Consider the proposition, set out under "(d)" in the excerpts from the *Henningsen* opinion, that "the manufacturer is under a special obligation in connection with the construction, promotion and sale of his cars." This does not even purport to define the specific duties such a special obligation entails, or to tell us what rights automobile consumers acquire as a result. It merely states—and this is an essential link in the *Henningsen* argument—that automobile manufacturers must be held to higher standards than other manufacturers, and are less entitled to rely on the competing principle of freedom of contract. It does not mean that they may never rely on that principle, or that courts may rewrite automobile purchase contracts at will; it means only that if a particular clause seems unfair or burdensome, courts have less reason to enforce the clause than if it were for the purchase of neckties. The "special obligation" counts in favor, but does not in itself necessitate, a decision refusing to enforce the terms of an automobile purchase contract.

This first difference between rules and principles entails another. Principles have a dimension that rules do not—the dimension of weight or importance. When principles intersect (the policy of protecting automobile consumers intersecting with principles of freedom of contract, for example), one who must resolve the conflict has to take into account the relative weight of each. This cannot be, of course, an exact measurement, and the judgment that a particular principle or policy is more important than another will often be a controversial one. Nevertheless, it is an integral part of the concept of a principle that it has this dimension, that it makes sense to ask how important or how weighty it is.

Rules do not have this dimension. We can speak of rules as being *functionally* important or unimportant (the baseball rule that three strikes are out is more important than the rule that runners may advance on a balk, because the game would be much more changed with the first rule altered than the second). In this sense, one legal rule may be more important than another because it has a greater or more important role in regulating behavior. But we cannot say that one rule is more important than another within the system of rules, so that when two rules conflict one supercedes the other by virtue of its greater weight. If two rules conflict, one of them cannot be a valid rule. The decision as to which is valid, and which must be abandoned or recast, must be made by appealing to considerations beyond the rules themselves. A legal system might regulate such conflicts by other rules, which prefer the rule enacted by the higher authority, or the rule enacted later, or the more specific rule, or something of that sort. A legal system may also prefer the rule supported by the more important principles. (Our own legal system uses both of these techniques.)

It is not always clear from the form of a standard whether it is a rule or a principle. "A will is invalid unless signed by three witnesses" is not very different in form from "A man may not profit from his own wrong," but one who knows something of American law knows that he must take the first as stating a rule and the second as stating a principle. In many cases the distinction is difficult to make—it may not have been settled how the standard should operate, and this issue may itself be a focus of controversy. The first amendment to the United States Constitution contains the provision that Congress shall not abridge freedom of speech. Is this a rule, so that if a particular law does abridge freedom of speech, it follows that it is unconstitutional? Those who claim that the first amendment is "an absolute" say that it must be taken in this way, that is, as a rule. Or does it merely state a principle, so that when an abridgement of speech is discovered, it is unconstitutional unless the context presents some other policy or principle which in the circumstances is weighty enough to permit the abridgement? That is the position of those who argue for what is called the "clear and present danger" test or some other form of "balancing."

Sometimes a rule and a principle can play much the same role, and the difference between them is almost a matter of form alone. The first section of the Sherman Act states that every contract in restraint of trade shall be void. The Supreme Court had to make the decision whether this provision should be treated as a rule in its own terms (striking down every contract "which restrains trade," which almost any contract does) or as a principle, providing a reason for striking down a contract in the absence of effective contrary policies. The Court construed the provision as a rule, but treated that rule as containing the word "unreasonable," and as prohibiting only "unreasonable" restraints of trade.[19] This allowed the provision to function logically as a rule (whenever a court finds that the restraint is "unreasonable" it is bound to hold the contract invalid) and substantially as a principle (a court must take into account a variety of other principles and policies in determining whether a particular restraint in particular economic circumstances is "unreasonable").

Words like "reasonable," "negligent," "unjust," and "significant" often perform just this function. Each of these terms makes the application of the rule which contains it depend to some extent upon principles or policies lying beyond the rule, and in this way makes that rule itself more like a principle. But they do not quite turn the

[19] Standard Oil v. United States, 221 U.S. 1, 60 (1911); United States v. American Tobacco Co., 221 U.S. 106, 180 (1911).

rule into a principle, because even the least confining of these terms restricts the *kind* of other principles and policies on which the rule depends. If we are bound by a rule that says that "unreasonable" contracts are void, or that grossly "unfair" contracts will not be enforced, much more judgment is required than if the quoted terms were omitted. But suppose a case in which some consideration of policy or principle suggests that a contract should be enforced even though its restraint is not reasonable, or even though it is grossly unfair. Enforcing these contracts would be forbidden by our rules, and thus permitted only if these rules were abandoned or modified. If we were dealing, however, not with a rule but with a policy against enforcing unreasonable contracts, or a principle that unfair contracts ought not to be enforced, the contracts could be enforced without alteration of the law.

IV. Principles and the Concept of Law

Once we identify legal principles as separate sorts of standards, different from legal rules, we are suddenly aware of them all around us. Law teachers teach them, lawbooks cite them, legal historians celebrate them. But they seem most energetically at work, carrying most weight, in difficult lawsuits like *Riggs* and *Henningsen*. In cases like these, principles play an essential part in arguments supporting judgments about particular legal rights and obligations. After the case is decided, we may say that the case stands for a particular rule (*e.g.*, the rule that one who murders is not eligible to take under the will of his victim). But the rule does not exist before the case is decided; the court cites principles as its justification for adopting and applying a new rule. In *Riggs,* the court cited the principle that no man may profit from his own wrong as a background standard against which to read the statute of wills and in this way justified a new interpretation of that statute. In *Henningsen,* the court cited a variety of intersecting principles and policies as authority for a new rule respecting manufacturer's liability for automobile defects.

An analysis of the concept of legal obligation must therefore account for the important role of principles in reaching particular decisions of law. There are two very different tacks we might take.

(a) We might treat legal principles the way we treat legal rules and say that some principles are binding as law and must be taken into account by judges and lawyers who make decisions of legal obligation. If we took this tack, we should say that in the United States, at least, the "law" includes principles as well as rules.

(b) We might, on the other hand, deny that principles can be binding the way some rules are. We would say, instead, that in cases like *Riggs* or *Henningsen* the judge reaches beyond the rules that he is bound to apply (reaches, that is, beyond the "law") for extra-legal principles he is free to follow if he wishes.

One might think that there is not much difference between these two lines of attack, that it is only a verbal question of how one wants to use the word "law." But that is a mistake, because the choice between these two accounts has the greatest consequences for an analysis of legal obligation. It is a choice between two *concept*s of a legal principle, a choice we can clarify by comparing it to a choice we might make between two concepts of a legal rule. We sometimes say of someone that he "makes it a rule" to do something, when we mean that he has chosen to follow a certain practice. We might say that someone has made it a rule, for example, to run a mile before breakfast because he wants to be healthy and believes in a regimen. We do not mean, when we say this, that he is *bound* by the rule that he must run a mile before breakfast, or even that he regards it as binding upon him. Accepting a rule as binding is something different from making it a rule to do something. If we use Hart's example again, there is a difference between saying that Englishmen make it a rule to see a movie once a week, and saying that the English have a rule that one must see a movie once a week. The second implies that if an Englishman does not follow the rule, he is subject to criticism or censure, but the first does not. The first does not exclude the possibility of a *sort* of criticism—we cay say that one who does not see movies is neglecting his education—but we do not suggest that he is doing something wrong *just* in not following the rule.[20]

If we think of the judges of a community as a group, we could describe the rules of law they follow in these two different ways. We could say, for instance, that in a certain state the judges make it a rule not to enforce wills unless there are three witnesses. This would not imply that the rare judge who enforces such a rule is doing anything wrong just for that reason. On the other hand we can say that in that state a rule of law requires judges not to enforce such wills; this does imply that a judge who enforces them is doing something wrong. Hart, Austin and other positivists, of course, would insist on this latter account of legal rules; they would not at all be satisfied with the "make it a rule" account. It is not a verbal question of which account is right. It is a question of which describes the social situation more

20 The distinction is in substance the same as that made by Rawls, *Two Concepts of Rules*, 64 PHILOSOPHICAL REV. 3 (1955).

accurately. Other important issues turn on which description we accept. If judges simply "make it a rule" not to enforce certain contracts, for example, then we cannot say, before the decision, that anyone is "entitled" to that result, and that proposition cannot enter into any justification we might offer for the decision.

The two lines of attack on principles parallel these two accounts of rules. The first tack treats principles as binding upon judges, so that they are wrong not to apply the principles when they are pertinent. The second tack treats principles as summaries of what most judges "make it a principle" to do when forced to go beyond the standards that bind them. The choice between these approaches will affect, perhaps even determine, the answer we can give to the question whether the judge in a hard case like *Riggs* or *Henningsen* is attempting to enforce pre-existing legal rights and obligations. If we take the first tack, we are still free to argue that because such judges are applying binding legal standards they are enforcing legal rights and obligations. But if we take the second, we are out of court on that issue, and we must acknowledge that the murderer's family in *Riggs* and the manufacturer in *Henningsen* were deprived of their property by an act of judicial discretion applied *ex post facto*. This may not shock many readers—the notion of judicial discretion has percolated through the legal community—but it does illustrate one of the most nettlesome of the puzzles that drive philosophers to worry about legal obligation. If taking property away in cases like these cannot be justified by appealing to an established obligation, another justification must be found, and nothing satisfactory has yet been supplied.

In my skeleton diagram of positivism, previously set out, I listed the doctrine of judicial discretion as the second tenet. Positivists hold that when a case is not covered by a clear rule, a judge must exercise his discretion to decide that case by what amounts to a fresh piece of legislation. There may be an important connection between this doctrine and the question of which of the two approaches to legal principles we must take. We shall therefore want to ask whether the doctrine is correct, and whether it implies the second approach, as it seems on its face to do. En route to these issues, however, we shall have to polish our understanding of the concept of discretion. I shall try to show how certain confusions about that concept, and in particular a failure to discriminate different senses in which it is used, account for the popularity of the doctrine of discretion. I shall argue that in the sense in which the doctrine does have a bearing on our treatment of principles, it is entirely unsupported by the arguments the positivists use to defend it.

V. Discretion

The concept of discretion was lifted by the positivists from ordinary language, and to understand it we must put it back *in habitat* for a moment. What does it mean, in ordinary life, to say that someone "has discretion"? The first thing to notice is that the concept is out of place in all but very special contexts. For example, you would not say that I either do or do not have discretion to choose a house for my family. It is not true that I have "no discretion" in making that choice, and yet it would be almost equally misleading to say that I do have discretion. The concept of discretion is at home in only one sort of context: when someone is in general charged with making decisions subject to standards set by a particular authority. It makes sense to speak of the discretion of a sergeant who is subject to orders of superiors, or the discretion of a sports official or contest judge who is governed by a rule book or the terms of the contest. Discretion, like the hole in a doughnut, does not exist except as an area left open by a surrounding belt of restriction. It is therefore a relative concept. It always makes sense to ask, "Discretion under which standards?" or "Discretion as to which authority?" Generally the context will make the answer to this plain, but in some cases the official may have discretion from one standpoint though not from another.

Like almost all terms, the precise meaning of "discretion" is affected by features of the context. The term is always colored by the background of understood information against which it is used. Although the shadings are many, it will be helpful for us to recognize some gross distinctions.

Sometimes we use "discretion" in a weak sense, simply to say that for some reason the standards an official must apply cannot be applied mechanically but demand the use of judgment. We use this weak sense when the context does not already make that clear, when the background our audience assumes does not contain that piece of information. Thus we might say, "The sergeant's orders left him a great deal of discretion," to those who do not know what the sergeant's orders were or who do not know something that made those orders vague or hard to carry out. It would make perfect sense to add, by way of amplification, that the lieutenant had ordered the sergeant to take his five most experienced men on patrol but that it was hard to determine which were the most experienced.

Sometimes we use the term in a different weak sense, to say only that some official has final authority to make a decision and cannot be reviewed and reversed by any other official. We speak this way when the official is part of a hierarchy of officials structured so that some have higher authority but in which the patterns of authority are different for different classes of decision. Thus we might say that in baseball certain decisions, like the decision whether the ball or the runner reached second base first, are left to the discretion of the second base umpire, if we mean that on this issue the head umpire has no power to substitute his own judgment if he disagrees.

I call both of these senses weak to distinguish them from a stronger sense. We use "discretion" sometimes not merely to say that an official must use judgment in applying the standards set him by authority, or that no one will review that exercise of judgment, but to say that on some issue he is simply not bound by standards set by the authority in question. In this sense we say that a sergeant has discretion who has been told to pick any five men for patrol he chooses or that a judge in a dog show has discretion to judge airedales before boxers if the rules do not stipulate an order of events. We use this sense not to comment on the vagueness or difficulty of the standards, or on who has the final word in applying them, but on their range and the decisions they purport to control. If the sergeant is told to take the five most experienced men, he does not have discretion in this strong sense because that order purports to govern his decision. The boxing referee who must decide which fighter has been the more aggressive does not have discretion, in the strong sense, for the same reason.[21]

If anyone said that the sergeant or the referee had discretion in these cases, we should have to understand him, if the context permitted, as using the term in one of the weak senses. Suppose, for example, the lieutenant ordered the sergeant to select the five men he deemed most experienced, and then added that the sergeant had discretion to choose them. Or the rules provided that the referee should award the round to the more aggressive fighter, with discretion in selecting him. We should have to understand these statements in the second weak sense, as speaking to the question of review of the decision. The first weak sense—that the decisions take judgment—would be otiose, and the third, strong sense is excluded by the statements themselves.

We must avoid one tempting confusion. The strong sense of discretion is not tantamount to license, and does not exclude criticism. Almost any situation in which a person acts (including those in which

21 I have not spoken of that jurisprudential favorite, "limited" discretion, because that concept presents no special difficulties if we remember the relativity of discretion. Suppose the sergeant is told to choose from "amongst" experienced men, or to "take experience into account." We might say either that he has (limited) discretion in picking his patrol, or (full) discretion to either pick amongst experienced men or decide what else to take into account.

there is no question of decision under special authority, and so no question of discretion) makes relevant certain standards of rationality, fairness, and effectiveness. We criticize each other's acts in terms of these standards, and there is no reason not to do so when the acts are within the center rather than beyond the perimeter of the doughnut of special authority. So we can say that the sergeant who was given discretion (in the strong sense) to pick a patrol did so stupidly or maliciously or carelessly, or that the judge who had discretion in the order of viewing dogs made a mistake because he took boxers first although there were only three airedales and many more boxers. An official's discretion means not that he is free to decide without recourse to standards of sense and fairness, but only that his decision is not controlled by a standard furnished by the particular authority we have in mind when we raise the question of discretion. Of course this latter sort of freedom is important; that is why we have the strong sense of discretion. Someone who has discretion in this third sense can be criticized, but not for being disobedient, as in the case of the soldier. He can be said to have made a mistake, but not to have deprived a participant of a decision to which he was entitled, as in the case of a sports official or contest judge.

We may now return, with these observations in hand, to the positivists' doctrine of judicial discretion. That doctrine argues that if a case is not controlled by an established rule, the judge must decide it by exercising discretion. We want to examine this doctrine and to test its bearing on our treatment of principles; but first we must ask in which sense of discretion we are to understand it.

Some nominalists argue that judges always have discretion, even when a clear rule is in point, because judges are ultimately the final arbiters of the law. This doctrine of discretion uses the second weak sense of that term, because it makes the point that no higher authority reviews the decisions of the highest court. It therefore has no bearing on the issue of how we account for principles, any more than it bears on how we account for rules.

The positivists do not mean their doctrine this way, because they say that a judge has no discretion when a clear and established rule is available. If we attend to the positivists' arguments for the doctrine we may suspect that they use discretion in the first weak sense to mean only that judges must sometimes exercise judgment in applying legal standards. Their arguments call attention to the fact that some rules of law are vague (Professor Hart, for example, says that all rules of law have "open texture"), and that some cases arise (like *Henningsen*) in which no established rule seems to be suitable. They emphasize that judges must sometimes agonize over points of law, and that two equally trained and intelligent judges will often disagree.

These points are easily made; they are commonplace to anyone who has any familiarity with law. Indeed, that is the difficulty with assuming that positivists mean to use "discretion" in this weak sense. The proposition that when no clear rule is available discretion in the sense of judgment must be used is a tautology. It has no bearing, moreover, on the problem of how to account for legal principles. It is perfectly consistent to say that the judge in *Riggs*, for example, had to use judgment, and that he was bound to follow the principle that no man may profit from his own wrong. The positivists speak as if their doctrine of judicial discretion is an insight rather than a tautology, and as if it does have a bearing on the treatment of principles. Hart, for example, says that when the judge's discretion is in play, we can no longer speak of his being bound by standards, but must speak rather of what standards he "characteristically uses."[22] Hart thinks that when judges have discretion, the principles they cite must be treated on our second approach, as what courts "make it a principle" to do.

It therefore seems that positivists, at least sometimes, take their doctrine in the third, strong sense of discretion. In that sense it does bear on the treatment of principles; indeed, in that sense it is nothing less than a restatement of our second approach. It is the same thing to say that when a judge runs out of rules he has discretion, in the sense that he is not bound by any standards from the authority of law, as to say that the legal standards judges cite other than rules are not binding on them.

So we must examine the doctrine of judicial discretion in the strong sense. (I shall henceforth use the term "discretion" in that sense.) Do the principles judges cite in cases like *Riggs* or *Henningsen* control their decisions, as the sergeant's orders to take the most experienced men or the referee's duty to choose the more aggressive fighter control the decisions of these officials? What arguments could a positivist supply to show that they do not?

(1) A positivist might argue that principles cannot be binding or obligatory. That would be a mistake. It is always a question, of course, whether any particular principle is *in fact* binding upon some legal official. But there is nothing in the logical character of a principle that renders it incapable of binding him. Suppose that the judge in *Henningsen* had failed to take any account of the principle that automobile manufacturers have a special obligation to their consumers,

22 H.L.A. Hart, The Concept of Law 144 (1961).

or the principle that the courts seek to protect those whose bargaining position is weak, but had simply decided for the defendant by citing the principle of freedom of contract without more. His critics would not have been content to point out that he had not taken account of considerations that other judges have been attending to for some time. Most would have said that it was his duty to take the measure of these principles and that the plaintiff was entitled to have him do so. We mean no more, when we say that a *rule* is binding upon a judge, than that he must follow it if it applies, and that if he does not he will on that account have made a mistake.

It will not do to say that in a case like *Henningsen* the court is only "morally" obligated to take particular principles into account, or that it is "institutionally" obligated, or obligated as a matter of judicial "craft," or something of that sort. The question will still remain why this type of obligation (whatever we call it) is different from the obligation that rules impose upon judges, and why it entitles us to say that principles and policies are not part of the law but are merely extra-legal standards "courts characteristically use."

(2) A positivist might argue that even though some principles are binding, in the sense that the judge must take them into account, they cannot determine a particular result. This is a harder argument to assess because it is not clear what it means for a standard to "determine" a result. Perhaps it means that the standard *dictates* the result whenever it applies so that nothing else counts. If so, then it is certainly true that individual principles do not determine results, but that is only another way of saying that principles are not rules. Only rules dictate results, come what may. When a contrary result has been reached, the rule has been abandoned or changed. Principles do not work that way; they incline a decision one way, though not conclusively, and they survive intact when they do not prevail. This seems no reason for concluding that judges who must reckon with principles have discretion because a set of principles *can* dictate a result. If a judge believes that principles he is bound to recognize point in one direction and that principles pointing in the other direction, if any, are not of equal weight, then he must decide accordingly, just as he must follow what he believes to be a binding rule. He may, of course, be wrong in his assessment of the principles, but he may also be wrong in his judgment that the rule is binding. The sergeant and the referee, we might add, are often in the same boat. No one factor dictates which soldiers are the most experienced or which fighter the more aggressive. These officials must make judgments of the relative weights of these various factors; they do not on that account have discretion.

(3) A positivist might argue that principles cannot count as law because their authority, and even more so their weight, are congenitally *controversial.* It is true that generally we cannot *demonstrate* the authority or weight of a particular principle as we can sometimes demonstrate the validity of a rule by locating it in an act of Congress or in the opinion of an authoritative court. Instead, we make a case for a principle, and for its weight, by appealing to an amalgam of practice and other principles in which the implications of legislative and judicial history figure along with appeals to community practices and understandings. There is no litmus paper for testing the soundness of such a case—it is a matter of judgment, and reasonable men may disagree. But again this does not distinguish the judge from other officials who do not have discretion. The sergeant has no litmus paper for experience, the referee none for aggressiveness. Neither of these has discretion, because he is bound to reach an understanding, controversial or not, of what his orders or the rules require, and to act on that understanding. That is the judge's duty as well.

Of course, if the positivists are right in another of their doctrines—the theory that in each legal system there is an ultimate *test* for binding law like Professor Hart's rule of recognition—it follows that principles are not binding law. But the incompatibility of principles with the positivists' theory can hardly be taken as an argument that principles must be treated any particular way. That begs the question; we are interested in the status of principles because we want to evaluate the positivists' model. The positivist cannot defend his theory of a rule of recognition by fiat; if principles are not amenable to a test he must show some other reason why they cannot count as law. Since principles seem to play a role in arguments about legal obligation (witness, again, *Riggs* and *Henningsen*), a model that provides for that role has some initial advantage over one that excludes it, and the latter cannot properly be inveighed in its own support.

These are the most obvious of the arguments a positivist might use for the doctrine of discretion in the strong sense, and for the second approach to principles. I shall mention one strong counter-argument against that doctrine and in favor of the first approach. Unless at least some principles are acknowledged to be binding upon judges, requiring them as a set to reach particular decisions, then no rules, or very few rules, can be said to be binding upon them either.

In most American jurisdictions, and now in England also, the higher courts not infrequently reject established rules. Common law rules—those developed by earlier court decisions—are sometimes overruled directly, and sometimes radically altered by further development. Statutory rules are subjected to interpretation and reinterpretation, sometimes even when the result is not to carry out what is called the "legislative intent."[23] If courts had discretion to change established rules, then these rules would of course not be binding upon them, and so would not be law on the positivists' model. The positivist must therefore argue that there are standards, themselves binding upon judges, that determine when a judge may overrule or alter an established rule, and when he may not.

When, then, is a judge permitted to change an existing rule of law? Principles figure in the answer in two ways. First, it is necessary, though not sufficient, that the judge find that the change would advance some policy or serve some principle, which policy or principle thus justifies the change. In *Riggs* the change (a new interpretation of the statute of wills) was justified by the principle that no man should profit from his own wrong; in *Henningsen* certain rules about automobile manufacturer's liability were altered on the basis of the principles and policies I quoted from the opinion of the court.

But not any principle will do to justify a change, or no rule would ever be safe. There must be some principles that count and others that do not, and there must be some principles that count for more than others. It could not depend on the judge's own preferences amongst a sea of respectable extra-legal standards, any one in principle eligible, because if that were the case we could not say that any rules were binding. We could always imagine a judge whose preferences amongst extra-legal standards were such as would justify a shift or radical reinterpretation of even the most entrenched rule.

Second, any judge who proposes to change existing doctrine must take account of some important standards that argue against departures from established doctrine, and these standards are also for the most part principles. They include the doctrine of "legislative supremacy," a set of principles and policies that require the courts to pay a qualified deference to the acts of the legislature. They also include the doctrine of precedent, another set of principles and policies reflecting the equities and efficiencies of consistency. The doctrines of legislative supremacy and precedent incline toward the *status quo*, each within its sphere, but they do not command it. Judges are not free, however, to pick and choose amongst the principles and policies that make up these doctrines—if they were, again, no rule could be said to be binding.

Consider, therefore, what someone implies who says that a particu-

23 *See* Wellington & Albert, *Statutory Interpretation and the Political Process: A Comment on Sinclair v. Atkinson*, 72 YALE L.J. 1547 (1963).

lar rule is binding. He may imply that the rule is affirmatively supported by principles the court is not free to disregard, and which are collectively more weighty than other principles that argue for a change. If not, he implies that any change would be condemned by a combination of conservative principles of legislative supremacy and precedent that the court is not free to ignore. Very often, he will imply both, for the conservative principles, being principles and not rules, are usually not powerful enough to save a common law rule or an aging statute that is entirely unsupported by substantive principles the court is bound to respect. Either of these implications, of course, treats a body of principles and policies as law in the sense that rules are; it treats them as standards binding upon the officials of a community, controlling their decisions of legal right and obligation.

We are left with this issue. If the positivists' theory of judicial discretion is either trivial because it uses "discretion" in a weak sense, or unsupported because the various arguments we can supply in its defense fall short, why have so many careful and intelligent lawyers embraced it? We can have no confidence in our treatment of that theory unless we can deal with that question. It is not enough to note (although perhaps it contributes to the explanation) that "discretion" has different senses that may be confused. We do not confuse these senses when we are not thinking about law.

Part of the explanation, at least, lies in a lawyer's natural tendency to associate laws and rules, and to think of "the law" as a collection or system of rules. Roscoe Pound, who diagnosed this tendency long ago, thought that English speaking lawyers were tricked into it by the fact that English uses the same word, changing only the article, for "a law" and "the law."[24] (Other languages, on the contrary, use two words: "loi" and "droit," for example, and "Gesetz" and "Recht.") This may have had its effect, with the English speaking positivists, because the expression "a law" certainly does suggest a rule. But the principal reason for associating law with rules runs deeper, and lies, I think, in the fact that legal education has for a long time consisted of teaching and examining those established rules that form the cutting edge of law.

In any event, if a lawyer thinks of law as a system of rules, and yet recognizes, as he must, that judges change old rules and introduce new ones, he will come naturally to the theory of judicial discretion in the strong sense. In those other systems of rules with which he has experience (like games), the rules are the only special authority that

24 R. Pound, An Introduction to the Philosophy of Law 56 (rev. ed. 1954).

govern official decisions, so that if an umpire could change a rule, he would have discretion as to the subject matter of that rule. Any principles umpires might mention when changing the rules would represent only their "characteristic" preferences. Positivists treat law like baseball revised in this way.

There is another, more subtle consequence of this initial assumption that law is a system of rules. When the positivists do attend to principles and policies, they treat them as rules *manque*. They assume that *if* they are standards of law they must be rules, and so they read them as standards that are trying to be rules. When a positivist hears someone argue that legal principles are part of the law, he understands this to be an argument for what he calls the "higher law" theory, that these principles are the rules of a law above the law.[25] He refutes this theory by pointing out that these "rules" are sometimes followed and sometimes not, that for every "rule" like "no man shall profit from his own wrong" there is another competing "rule" like "the law favors security of title," and that there is no way to test the validity of "rules" like these. He concludes that these principles and policies are not valid rules of a law above the law, which is true, because they are not rules at all. He also concludes that they are extra-legal standards which each judge selects according to his own lights in the exercise of his discretion, which is false. It is as if a zoologist had proved that fish are not mammals, and then concluded that they are really only plants.

VI. The Rule of Recognition

This discussion was provoked by our two competing accounts of legal principles. We have been exploring the second account, which the positivists seem to adopt through their doctrine of judicial discretion, and we have discovered grave difficulties. It is time to return to the fork in the road. What if we adopt the first approach? What would the consequences of this be for the skeletal structure of positivism? Of course we should have to drop the second tenet, the doctrine of judicial discretion (or, in the alternative, to make plain that the doctrine is to be read merely to say that judges must often exercise judgment). Would we also have to abandon or modify the first tenet, the proposition that law is distinguished by tests of the sort that can be set out in a master rule like Professor Hart's rule of recognition? If principles of the *Riggs* and *Henningsen* sort are to count as law, and

25 *See, e.g.*, Dickinson, *The Law Behind Law* (pts. 1 & 2), 29 Colum. L. Rev. 112, 254 (1929).

we are nevertheless to preserve the notion of a master rule for law, then we must be able to deploy some test that all (and only) the principles that do count as law meet. Let us begin with the test Hart suggests for identifying valid *rules* of law, to see whether these can be made to work for principles as well.

Most rules of law, according to Hart, are valid because some competent institution enacted them. Some were created by a legislature, in the form of statutory enactments. Others were created by judges who formulated them to decide particular cases, and thus established them as precedents for the future. But this test of pedigree will not work for the *Riggs* and *Henningsen* principles. The origin of these as legal principles lies not in a particular decision of some legislature or court, but in a sense of appropriateness developed in the profession and the public over time. Their continued power depends upon this sense of appropriateness being sustained. If it no longer seemed unfair to allow people to profit by their wrongs, or fair to place special burdens upon oligopolies that manufacture potentially dangerous machines, these principles would no longer play much of a role in new cases, even if they had never been overruled or repealed. (Indeed, it hardly makes sense to speak of principles like these as being "overruled" or "repealed." When they decline they are eroded, not torpedoed.)

True, if we were challenged to back up our claim that some principle is a principle of law, we would mention any prior cases in which that principle was cited, or figured in the argument. We would also mention any statute that seemed to exemplify that principle (even better if the principle was cited in the preamble of the statute, or in the committee reports or other legislative documents that accompanied it). Unless we could find some such institutional support, we would probably fail to make out our case, and the more support we found, the more weight we could claim for the principle.

Yet we could not devise any formula for testing how much and what kind of institutional support is necessary to make a principle a legal principle, still less to fix its weight at a particular order of magnitude. We argue for a particular principle by grappling with a whole set of shifting, developing and interacting standards (themselves principles rather than rules) about institutional responsibility, statutory interpretation, the persuasive force of various sorts of precedent, the relation of all these to contemporary moral practices, and hosts of other such standards. We could not bolt all of these together into a single "rule," even a complex one, and if we could the result would bear little relation to Hart's picture of a rule of recognition, which is the picture of a fairly stable master rule specifying "some feature or features possession of which by a suggested rule is taken as a conclusive affirmative indication that it is a rule . . . ."[26]

Moreover, the techniques we apply in arguing for another principle do not stand (as Hart's rule of recognition is designed to) on an entirely different level from the principles they support. Hart's sharp distinction between acceptance and validity does not hold. If we are arguing for the principle that a man should not profit from his own wrong, we could cite the acts of courts and legislatures that exemplify it, but this speaks as much to the principle's acceptance as its validity. (It seems odd to speak of a principle as being valid at all, perhaps because validity is an all-or-nothing concept, appropriate for rules, but inconsistent with a principle's dimension of weight.) If we are asked (as we might well be) to defend the particular doctrine of precedent, or the particular technique of statutory interpretation, that we used in this argument, we should certainly cite the practice of others in using that doctrine or technique. But we should also cite other general principles that we believe support that practice, and this introduces a note of validity into the chord of acceptance. We might argue, for example, that the use we make of earlier cases and statutes is supported by a particular analysis of the point of the practice of legislation or the doctrine of precedent, or by the principles of democratic theory, or by a particular position on the proper division of authority between national and local institutions, or something else of that sort. Nor is this path of support a one-way street leading to some ultimate principle resting on acceptance alone. Our principles of legislation, precedent, democracy, or federalism might be challenged too; and if they were we should argue for them, not only in terms of practice, but in terms of each other and in terms of the implications of trends of judicial and legislative decisions, even though this last would involve appealing to those same doctrines of interpretation we justified through the principles we are now trying to support. At this level of abstraction, in other words, principles rather hang together than link together.

So even though principles draw support from the official acts of legal institutions, they do not have a simple or direct enough connection with these acts to frame that connection in terms of criteria specified by some ultimate master rule of recognition. Is there any other route by which principles might be brought under such a rule?

Hart does say that a master rule might designate as law not only rules enacted by particular legal institutions, but rules established by

26 H.L.A. Hart, The Concept of Law 92 (1961).

custom as well. He has in mind a problem that bothered other positivists, including Austin. Many of our most ancient legal rules were never explicitly created by a legislature or a court. When they made their first appearance in legal opinions and texts, they were treated as already being part of the law because they represented the customary practice of the community, or some specialized part of it, like the business community. (The examples ordinarily given are rules of mercantile practice, like the rules governing what rights arise under a standard form of commercial paper.)[27] Since Austin thought that all law was the command of a determinate sovereign, he held that these customary practices were not law until the courts (as agents of the sovereign) recognized them, and that the courts were indulging in a fiction in pretending otherwise. But that seemed arbitrary. If everyone thought custom might in itself be law, the fact that Austin's theory said otherwise was not persuasive.

Hart reversed Austin on this point. The master rule, he says, might stipulate that some custom counts as law even before the courts recognize it. But he does not face the difficulty this raises for his general theory because he does not attempt to set out the criteria a master rule might use for this purpose. It cannot use, as its only criterion, the provision that the community regard the practice as *morally* binding, for this would not distinguish legal customary rules from moral customary rules, and of course not all of the community's long-standing customary moral obligations are enforced at law. If, on the other hand, the test is whether the community regards the customary practice as *legally* binding, the whole point of the master rule is undercut, at least for this class of legal rules. The master rule, says Hart, marks the transformation from a primitive society to one with law, because it provides a test for determining social rules of law other than by measuring their acceptance. But if the master rule says merely that whatever other rules the community accepts as legally binding are legally binding, then it provides no such test at all, beyond the test we should use were there no master rule. The master rule becomes (for these cases) a non-rule of recognition; we might as well say that every primitive society has a secondary rule of recognition, namely the rule that whatever is accepted as binding is binding. Hart himself, in discussing international law, ridicules the idea that such a rule could be

27 *See* Note, *Custom and Trade Usage: Its Application to Commercial Dealings and the Common Law*, 55 COLUM. L. REV. 1192 (1955), and materials cited therein at 1193 n.1. As that note makes plain, the actual practices of courts in recognizing trade customs follow the pattern of applying a set of general principles and policies rather than a test that could be captured as part of a rule of recognition.

a rule of recognition, by describing the proposed rule as "an empty repetition of the mere fact that the society concerned . . . observes certain standards of conduct as obligatory rules."[28]

Hart's treatment of custom amounts, indeed, to a confession that there are at least some rules of law that are not binding because they are valid under standards laid down by a master rule but are binding —like the master rule—because they are accepted as binding by the community. This chips at the neat pyramidal architecture we admired in Hart's theory: we can no longer say that only the master rule is binding because of its acceptance, all other rules being valid under its terms.

This is perhaps only a chip, because the customary rules Hart has in mind are no longer a very significant part of the law. But it does suggest that Hart would be reluctant to widen the damage by bringing under the head of "custom" all those crucial principles and policies we have been discussing. If he were to call these part of the law and yet admit that the only test of their force lies in the degree to which they are accepted as law by the community or some part thereof, he would very sharply reduce that area of the law over which his master rule held any dominion. It is not just that all the principles and policies would escape its sway, though that would be bad enough. Once these principles and policies are accepted as law, and thus as standards judges must follow in determining legal obligations, it would follow that *rules* like those announced for the first time in *Riggs* and *Henningsen* owe their force at least in part to the authority of principles and policies, and so not entirely to the master rule of recognition.

So we cannot adapt Hart's version of positivism by modifying his rule of recognition to embrace principles. No tests of pedigree, relating principles to acts of legislation, can be formulated, nor can his concept of customary law, itself an exception to the first tenet of positivism, be made to serve without abandoning that tenet altogether. One more possibility must be considered, however. If no rule of recognition can provide a test for identifying principles, why not say that principles are ultimate, and *form* the rule of recognition of our law? The answer to the general question "What is valid law in an American jurisdiction?" would then require us to state all the principles (as well as ultimate constitutional rules) in force in that jurisdiction at the time, together with appropriate assignments of weight. A positivist might then regard the complete set of these standards as the rule of recognition of the jurisdiction. This solution has the attraction of

28 H.L.A. Hart, The Concept of Law 230 (1961).

paradox, but of course it is an unconditional surrender. If we simply designate our rule of recognition by the phrase "the complete set of principles in force," we achieve only the tautology that law is law. If, instead, we tried actually to list all the principles in force we would fail. They are controversial, their weight is all important, they are numberless, and they shift and change so fast that the start of our list would be obsolete before we reached the middle. Even if we succeeded, we would not have a key for law because there would be nothing left for our key to unlock.

I conclude that if we treat principles as law we must reject the positivists' first tenet, that the law of a community is distinguished from other social standards by some test in the form of a master rule. We have already decided that we must then abandon the second tenet —the doctrine of judicial discretion—or clarify it into triviality. What of the third tenet, the positivists' theory of legal obligation?

This theory holds that a legal obligation exists when (and only when) an established rule of law imposes such an obligation. It follows from this that in a hard case—when no such established rule can be found—there is no legal obligation until the judge creates a new rule for the future. The judge may apply that new rule to the parties in the case, but this is *ex post facto* legislation, not the enforcement of an existing obligation.

The positivists' doctrine of discretion (in the strong sense) required this view of legal obligation, because if a judge has discretion there can be no legal right or obligation—no entitlement—that he must enforce. Once we abandon that doctrine, however, and treat principles as law, we raise the possibility that a legal obligation might be imposed by a constellation of principles as well as by an established rule. We might want to say that a legal obligation exists whenever the case supporting such an obligation, in terms of binding legal principles of different sorts, is stronger than the case against it.

Of course, many questions would have to be answered before we could accept that view of legal obligation. If there is no rule of recognition, no test for law in that sense, how do we decide which principles are to count, and how much, in making such a case? How do we decide whether one case is better than another? If legal obligation rests on an undemonstrable judgment of that sort, how can it provide a justification for a judicial decision that one party had a legal obligation? Does this view of obligation square with the way lawyers, judges and laymen speak, and is it consistent with our attitudes about moral obligation? Does this analysis help us to deal with the classical jurisprudential puzzles about the nature of law?

These questions must be faced, but even the questions promise more than positivism provides. Positivism, on its own thesis, stops short of just those puzzling, hard cases that send us to look for theories of law. When we reach these cases, the positivist remits us to a doctrine of discretion that leads nowhere and tells nothing. His picture of law as a system of rules has exercised a tenacious hold on our imagination, perhaps through its very simplicity. If we shake ourselves loose from this model of rules, we may be able to build a model truer to the complexity and sophistication of our own practices.

VOLUME 88 APRIL 1975 NUMBER 6

HARVARD LAW REVIEW

HARD CASES †

Ronald Dworkin *

Philosophers and legal scholars have long debated the means by which decisions of an independent judiciary can be reconciled with democratic ideals. The problem of justifying judicial decisions is particularly acute in "hard cases," those cases in which the result is not clearly dictated by statute or precedent. The positivist theory of adjudication — that judges use their discretion to decide hard cases — fails to resolve this dilemma of judicial decisionmaking. Professor Dworkin has been an effective critic of the positivist position and in this essay he provides an alternative theory of adjudication that is more consistent with democratic ideals. He first posits a distinction between arguments of principle and arguments of policy and suggests that decisions in hard cases should be and are based on arguments of principle. He then illustrates how this distinction is used in cases involving constitutional provisions, statutes, and common law precedents.

THIS essay is a revised form of an inaugural lecture given at Oxford in June of 1971. I should like to repeat what I said then about my predecessor in the Chair of Jurisprudence. The philosophers of science have developed a theory of the growth of science; it argues that from time to time the achievement of a single man is so powerful and so original as to form a new paradigm, that is, to change a discipline's sense of what its problems are and what counts as success in solving them. Professor H.L.A. Hart's work is a paradigm for jurisprudence, not just in his country and not just in mine, but throughout the world. The province of jurisprudence is now the province he has travelled; it extends from the modal logic of legal concepts to the details of the law of criminal responsibility, and in each corner his is the view that others must take as their point of departure. It is difficult to think of any serious writing in jurisprudence in recent years, certainly in Great Britain and America, that has not either claimed his support or taken him as a principal antagonist. This essay is no exception.

His influence has extended, I might add, to form as well as

---

* Professor of Jurisprudence and Fellow of University College, Oxford University. B.A., Harvard, 1953; B.A., Oxford, 1955; LL.B., Harvard, 1957.

substance. His clarity is famous and his diction contagious: other legal philosophers, for example, once made arguments, but now we only deploy them, and there has been a perfect epidemic of absent-mindedness in imitation of the master. How shall we account for this extraordinary influence? In him reason and passion do not contend, but combine in intelligence, the faculty of making clear what was dark without making it dull. In his hands clarity enhances rather than dissipates the power of an idea. That is magic, and it is the magic that jurisprudence needs to work.

* * *

I. Introduction

A. The Rights Thesis

Theories of adjudication have become more sophisticated, but the most popular theories still put judging in the shade of legislation. The main outlines of this story are familiar. Judges should apply the law that other institutions have made; they should not make new law. That is the ideal, but for different reasons it cannot be realized fully in practice. Statutes and common law rules are often vague and must be interpreted before they can be applied to novel cases. Some cases, moreover, raise issues so novel that they cannot be decided even by stretching or reinterpreting existing rules. So judges must sometimes make new law, either covertly or explicitly. But when they do, they should act as deputy to the appropriate legislature, enacting the law that they suppose the legislature would enact if seized of the problem.

That is perfectly familiar, but there is buried in this common story a further level of subordination not always noticed. When judges make law, so the expectation runs, they will act not only as deputy to the legislature but as a deputy legislature. They will make law in response to evidence and arguments of the same character as would move the superior institution if it were acting on its own. This is a deeper level of subordination because it makes any understanding of what judges do in hard cases parasitic on a prior understanding of what legislators do all the time. This deeper subordination is therefore conceptual as well as political.

In fact, however, judges neither should be nor are deputy legislators, and the familiar assumption, that when they go beyond political decisions already made by someone else they are legislating, is misleading. It misses the importance of a fundamental distinction within political theory, which I shall now introduce in a crude form. This is the distinction between arguments of principle on the one hand and arguments of policy on the other.[1]

Arguments of policy justify a political decision by showing that the decision advances or protects some collective goal of the community as a whole. The argument in favor of a subsidy for aircraft manufacturers, that the subsidy will protect national defense, is an argument of policy. Arguments of principle justify a political decision by showing that the decision respects or secures some individual or group right. The argument in favor of antidiscrimination statutes, that a minority has a right to equal respect and concern, is an argument of principle. These two sorts of argument do not exhaust political argument. Sometimes, for example, a political decision, like the decision to allow extra income tax exemptions for the blind, may be defended as an act of public generosity or virtue rather than on grounds of either policy or principle. But principle and policy are the major grounds of political justification.

The justification of a legislative program of any complexity will ordinarily require both sorts of argument. Even a program that is chiefly a matter of policy, like a subsidy program for important industries, may require strands of principle to justify its particular design. It may be, for example, that the program provides equal subsidies for manufacturers of different capabilities, on the assumption that weaker aircraft manufacturers have some right not to be driven out of business by government intervention, even though the industry would be more efficient without them. On the other hand, a program that depends chiefly on principle, like an antidiscrimination program, may reflect a sense that rights are not absolute and do not hold when the consequences for policy are very serious. The program may provide, for example, that fair employment practice rules do not apply when they might prove especially disruptive or dangerous. In the subsidy case we might say that the rights conferred are generated by policy and qualified by principle; in the antidiscrimination case they are generated by principle and qualified by policy.

It is plainly competent for the legislature to pursue arguments of policy and to adopt programs that are generated by such arguments. If courts are deputy legislatures, then it must be competent for them to do the same. Of course, unoriginal judicial decisions that merely enforce the clear terms of some plainly valid

[1] I discussed the distinction between principles and policies in an earlier article. *See* Dworkin, *The Model of Rules*, 35 U. Chi. L. Rev. 14, 22–29 (1967). The more elaborate formulation in Part II of this essay is an improvement; among other virtues it prevents the collapse of the distinction under the (artificial) assumptions described in the earlier article.

statute are always justified on arguments of principle, even if the statute itself was generated by policy. Suppose an aircraft manufacturer sues to recover the subsidy that the statute provides. He argues his right to the subsidy; his argument is an argument of principle. He does not argue that the national defense would be improved by subsidizing him; he might even concede that the statute was wrong on policy grounds when it was adopted, or that it should have been repealed, on policy grounds, long ago. His right to a subsidy no longer depends on any argument of policy because the statute made it a matter of principle.

But if the case at hand is a hard case, when no settled rule dictates a decision either way, then it might seem that a proper decision could be generated by either policy or principle. Consider, for example, the problem of the recent *Spartan Steel* case.[2] The defendant's employees had broken an electrical cable belonging to a power company that supplied power to the plaintiff, and the plaintiff's factory was shut down while the cable was repaired. The court had to decide whether to allow the plaintiff recovery for economic loss following negligent damage to someone else's property. It might have proceeded to its decision by asking either whether a firm in the position of the plaintiff had a right to a recovery, which is a matter of principle, or whether it would be economically wise to distribute liability for accidents in the way the plaintiff suggested, which is a matter of policy.

If judges are deputy legislators, then the court should be prepared to follow the latter argument as well as the former, and decide in favor of the plaintiff if that argument recommends. That is, I suppose, what is meant by the popular idea that a court must be free to decide a novel case like *Spartan Steel* on policy grounds; and indeed Lord Denning described his own opinion in that case in just that way.[3] I do not suppose he meant to distinguish an argument of principle from an argument of policy in the technical way I have, but he in any event did not mean to rule out an argument of policy in that technical sense.

I propose, nevertheless, the thesis that judicial decisions in civil cases, even in hard cases like *Spartan Steel*, characteristically are and should be generated by principle not policy. That thesis plainly needs much elaboration, but we may notice that certain arguments of political theory and jurisprudence support the thesis even in its abstract form. These arguments are not decisive, but they are sufficiently powerful to suggest the importance of the thesis, and to justify the attention that will be needed for a more careful formulation.

---

[2] Spartan Steel & Alley Ltd. v. Martin & Co., [1973] 1 Q.B. 27.

[3] *Id.* at 36.

B. Principles and Democracy

The familiar story, that adjudication must be subordinated to legislation, is supported by two objections to judicial originality. The first argues that a community should be governed by men and women who are elected by and responsible to the majority. Since judges are, for the most part, not elected, and since they are not, in practice, responsible to the electorate in the way legislators are, it seems to compromise that proposition when judges make law. The second argues that if a judge makes new law and applies it retroactively in the case before him, then the losing party will be punished, not because he violated some duty he had, but rather a new duty created after the event.

These two arguments combine to support the traditional ideal that adjudication should be as unoriginal as possible. But they offer much more powerful objections to judicial decisions generated by policy than to those generated by principle. The first objection, that law should be made by elected and responsible officials, seems unexceptionable when we think of law as policy; that is, as a compromise among individual goals and purposes in search of the welfare of the community as a whole. It is far from clear that interpersonal comparisons of utility or preference, through which such compromises might be made objectively, make sense even in theory; but in any case no proper calculus is available in practice. Policy decisions must therefore be made through the operation of some political process designed to produce an accurate expression of the different interests that should be taken into account. The political system of representative democracy may work only indifferently in this respect, but it works better than a system that allows nonelected judges, who have no mail bag or lobbyists or pressure groups, to compromise competing interests in their chambers.

The second objection is also persuasive against a decision generated by policy. We all agree that it would be wrong to sacrifice the rights of an innocent man in the name of some new duty created after the event; it does, therefore, seem wrong to take property from one individual and hand it to another in order just to improve overall economic efficiency. But that is the form of the policy argument that would be necessary to justify a decision in *Spartan Steel*. If the plaintiff had no right to the recovery and the defendant no duty to offer it, the court could be justified in taking the defendant's property for the plaintiff only in the interest of wise economic policy.

But suppose, on the other hand, that a judge successfully justifies a decision in a hard case, like *Spartan Steel*, on grounds not of policy but of principle. Suppose, that is, that he is able to show that the plaintiff has a *right* to recover its damages. The two arguments just described would offer much less of an objection to the decision. The first is less relevant when a court judges principle, because an argument of principle does not often rest on assumptions about the nature and intensity of the different demands and concerns distributed throughout the community. On the contrary, an argument of principle fixes on some interest presented by the proponent of the right it describes, an interest alleged to be of such a character as to make irrelevant the fine discriminations of any argument of policy that might oppose it. A judge who is insulated from the demands of the political majority whose interests the right would trump is, therefore, in a better position to evaluate the argument.

The second objection to judicial originality has no force against an argument of principle. If the plaintiff has a right against the defendant, then the defendant has a corresponding duty, and it is that duty, not some new duty created in court, that justifies the award against him. Even if the duty has not been imposed upon him by explicit prior legislation, there is, but for one difference, no more injustice in enforcing the duty than if it had been.

The difference is, of course, that if the duty had been created by statute the defendant would have been put on much more explicit notice of that duty, and might more reasonably have been expected to arrange his affairs so as to provide for its consequences. But an argument of principle makes us look upon the defendant's claim, that it is unjust to take him by surprise, in a new light. If the plaintiff does indeed have a right to a judicial decision in his favor, then he is entitled to rely upon that right. If it is obvious and uncontroversial that he has the right, the defendant is in no position to claim unfair surprise just because the right arose in some way other than by publication in a statute. If, on the other hand, the plaintiff's claim is doubtful, then the court must, to some extent, surprise one or another of the parties; and if the court decides that on balance the plaintiff's argument is stronger, then it will also decide that the plaintiff was, on balance, more justified in his expectations. The court may, of course, be mistaken in this conclusion; but that possibility is not a consequence of the originality of its argument, for there is no reason to suppose that a court hampered by the requirement that its decisions be unoriginal will make fewer mistakes of principle than a court that is not.

C. *Jurisprudence*

We have, therefore, in these political considerations, a strong reason to consider more carefully whether judicial arguments cannot be understood, even in hard cases, as arguments generated by principle. We have an additional reason in a familiar problem of jurisprudence. Lawyers believe that when judges make new law their decisions are constrained by legal traditions but are nevertheless personal and original. Novel decisions, it is said, reflect a judge's own political morality, but also reflect the morality that is embedded in the traditions of the common law, which might well be different. This is, of course, only law school rhetoric, but it nevertheless poses the problem of explaining how these different contributions to the decision of a hard case are to be identified and reconciled.

One popular solution relies on a spatial image; it says that the traditions of the common law contract the area of a judge's discretion to rely upon his personal morality, but do not entirely eliminate that area. But this answer is unsatisfactory on two grounds. First, it does not elucidate what is at best a provocative metaphor, which is that some morality is embedded in a mass of particular decisions other judges have reached in the past. Second, it suggests a plainly inadequate phenomenological account of the judicial decision. Judges do not decide hard cases in two stages, first checking to see where the institutional constraints end, and then setting the books aside to stride off on their own. The institutional constraints they sense are pervasive and endure to the decision itself. We therefore need an account of the interaction of personal and institutional morality that is less metaphorical and explains more successfully that pervasive interaction.

The rights thesis, that judicial decisions enforce existing political rights, suggests an explanation that is more successful on both counts. If the thesis holds, then institutional history acts not as a constraint on the political judgment of judges but as an ingredient of that judgment, because institutional history is part of the background that any plausible judgment about the rights of an individual must accommodate. Political rights are creatures of both history and morality: what an individual is entitled to have, in civil society, depends upon both the practice and the justice of its political institutions. So the supposed tension between judicial originality and institutional history is dissolved: judges must make fresh judgments about the rights of the parties who come before them, but these political rights reflect, rather than oppose, political decisions of the past. When a judge chooses between the rule established in precedent and some new rule thought to be fairer, he does not choose between history and justice. He rather makes a judgment that requires some compromise between considerations that ordinarily combine in any calculation of political right, but here compete.

The rights thesis therefore provides a more satisfactory explanation of how judges use precedent in hard cases than the explanation provided by any theory that gives a more prominent place to policy. Judges, like all political officials, are subject to the doctrine of political responsibility. This doctrine states, in its most general form, that political officials must make only such political decisions as they can justify within a political theory that also justifies the other decisions they propose to make. The doctrine seems innocuous in this general form; but it does, even in this form, condemn a style of political administration that might be called, following Rawls, intuitionistic.[4] It condemns the practice of making decisions that seem right in isolation, but cannot be brought within some comprehensive theory of general principles and policies that is consistent with other decisions also thought right. Suppose a Congressman votes to prohibit abortion, on the ground that human life in any form is sacred, but then votes to permit the parents of babies born deformed to withhold medical treatment that will keep such babies alive. He might say that he feels that there is some difference, but the principle of responsibility, strictly applied, will not allow him these two votes unless he can incorporate the difference within some general political theory he sincerely holds.

The doctrine demands, we might say, articulate consistency. But this demand is relatively weak when policies are in play. Policies are aggregative in their influence on political decisions and it need not be part of a responsible strategy for reaching a collective goal that individuals be treated alike. It does not follow from the doctrine of responsibility, therefore, that if the legislature awards a subsidy to one aircraft manufacturer one month it must award a subsidy to another manufacturer the next. In the case of principles, however, the doctrine insists on distributional consistency from one case to the next, because it does not allow for the idea of a strategy that may be better served by unequal distribution of the benefit in question. If an official believes, for example, that sexual liberty of some sort is a right of individuals, then he must protect that liberty in a way that distributes the benefit reasonably equally over the class of those whom he supposes to have the right. If he allows one couple to use contraceptives on the ground that this right would otherwise be invaded,

[4] *See generally* Dworkin, *The Original Position*, 40 U. Chi. L. Rev. 500 (1973).

then he must, so long as he does not recant that earlier decision, allow the next couple the same liberty. He cannot say that the first decision gave the community just the amount of sexual liberty it needed, so that no more is required at the time of the second.

Judicial decisions are political decisions, at least in the broad sense that attracts the doctrine of political responsibility. If the rights thesis holds, then the distinction just made would account, at least in a very general way, for the special concern that judges show for both precedents and hypothetical examples. An argument of principle can supply a justification for a particular decision, under the doctrine of responsibility, only if the principle cited can be shown to be consistent with earlier decisions not recanted, and with decisions that the institution is prepared to make in the hypothetical circumstances. That is hardly surprising, but the argument would not hold if judges based their decisions on arguments of policy. They would be free to say that some policy might be adequately served by serving it in the case at bar, providing, for example, just the right subsidy to some troubled industry, so that neither earlier decisions nor hypothetical future decisions need be understood as serving the same policy.

Consistency here, of course, means consistency in the application of the principle relied upon, not merely in the application of the particular rule announced in the name of that principle. If, for example, the principle that no one has the duty to make good remote or unexpected losses flowing from his negligence is relied upon to justify a decision for the defendant in *Spartan Steel*, then it must be shown that the rule laid down in other cases, which allows recovery for negligent misstatements, is consistent with that principle; not merely that the rule about negligent misstatements is a different rule from the rule in *Spartan Steel*.

D. Three Problems

We therefore find, in these arguments of political theory and jurisprudence, some support for the rights thesis in its abstract form. Any further defense, however, must await a more precise statement. The thesis requires development in three directions. It relies, first, on a general distinction between individual rights and social goals, and that distinction must be stated with more clarity than is provided simply by examples. The distinction must be stated, moreover, so as to respond to the following problem. When politicians appeal to individual rights, they have in mind grand propositions about very abstract and fundamental interests, like the right to freedom or equality or respect. These grand rights do not seem apposite to the decision of hard cases at law, except, perhaps, constitutional law; and even when they are apposite they seem too abstract to have much argumentative power. If the rights thesis is to succeed, it must demonstrate how the general distinction between arguments of principle and policy can be maintained between arguments of the character and detail that do figure in legal argument. In Part II of this essay I shall try to show that the distinction between abstract and concrete rights, suitably elaborated, is sufficient for that purpose.

The thesis provides, second, a theory of the role of precedent and institutional history in the decision of hard cases. I summarized that theory in the last section, but it must be expanded and illustrated before it can be tested against our experience of how judges actually decide cases. It must be expanded, moreover, with an eye to the following problem. No one thinks that the law as it stands is perfectly just. Suppose that some line of precedents is in fact unjust, because it refuses to enforce, as a legal right, some political right of the citizens. Even though a judge deciding some hard case disapproves of these precedents for that reason, the doctrine of articulate consistency nevertheless requires that he allow his argument to be affected by them. It might seem that his argument cannot be an argument of principle, that is, an argument designed to establish the political rights of the parties, because the argument is corrupted, through its attention to precedent, by a false opinion about what these rights are. If the thesis is to be defended, it must be shown why this first appearance is wrong. It is not enough to say that the argument may be an argument of principle because it establishes the legal, as distinguished from the political, rights of the litigants. The rights thesis supposes that the right to win a law suit is a genuine political right, and though that right is plainly different from other forms of political rights, like the right of all citizens to be treated as equals, just noticing that difference does not explain why the former right may be altered by misguided earlier decisions. It is necessary, in order to understand that feature of legal argument, to consider the special qualities of institutional rights in general, which I consider in Part III, and the particular qualities of legal rights, as a species of institutional rights, which I consider in Part IV.

But the explanation I give of institutional and legal rights exposes a third and different problem for the rights thesis. This explanation makes plain that judges must sometimes make judgments of political morality in order to decide what the legal rights of litigants are. The thesis may therefore be thought open, on that ground, to the first challenge to judicial originality that I mentioned earlier. It might be said that the thesis is indefensible because it cheats the majority of its right to decide questions of political morality for itself. I shall consider that challenge in Part V.

These, then, are three problems that any full statement of the rights thesis must face. If that full statement shows these objections to the thesis misconceived, then it will show the thesis to be less radical than it might first have seemed. The thesis presents, not some novel information about what judges do, but a new way of describing what we all know they do; and the virtues of this new description are not empirical but political and philosophical.

II. Rights and Goals

A. Types of Rights

Arguments of principle are arguments intended to establish an individual right; arguments of policy are arguments intended to establish a collective goal. Principles are propositions that describe rights; policies are propositions that describe goals. But what are rights and goals and what is the difference? It is hard to supply any definition that does not beg the question. It seems natural to say, for example, that freedom of speech is a right, not a goal, because citizens are entitled to that freedom as a matter of political morality, and that increased munitions manufacture is a goal, not a right, because it contributes to collective welfare, but no particular manufacturer is entitled to a government contract. This does not improve our understanding, however, because the concept of entitlement uses rather than explains the concept of a right.

In this essay I shall distinguish rights from goals by fixing on the distributional character of claims about rights, and on the force of these claims, in political argument, against competing claims of a different distributional character. I shall make, that is, a formal distinction that does not attempt to show which rights men and women actually have, or indeed that they have any at all. It rather provides a guide for discovering which rights a particular political theory supposes men and women to have. The formal distinction does suggest, of course, an approach to the more fundamental question: it suggests that we discover what rights people actually have by looking for arguments that would justify claims having the appropriate distributional character. But the distinction does not itself supply any such arguments.

I begin with the idea of a political aim as a generic political justification. A political theory takes a certain state of affairs as a political aim if, for that theory, it counts in favor of any political decision that the decision is likely to advance, or to protect, that state of affairs, and counts against the decision that it will retard or endanger it. A political right is an individuated political aim. An individual has a right to some opportunity or resource or liberty if it counts in favor of a political decision that the decision is likely to advance or protect the state of affairs in which he enjoys the right, even when no other political aim is served and some political aim is disserved thereby, and counts against that decision that it will retard or endanger that state of affairs, even when some other political aim is thereby served.[5] A goal is a nonindividuated political aim, that is, a state of affairs whose specification does not in this way call for any particular opportunity or resource or liberty for particular individuals.

Collective goals encourage trade-offs of benefits and burdens within a community in order to produce some overall benefit for the community as a whole. Economic efficiency is a collective goal: it calls for such distribution of opportunities and liabilities as will produce the greatest aggregate economic benefit defined in some way. Some conception of equality may also be taken as a collective goal; a community may aim at a distribution such that maximum wealth is no more than double minimum wealth, or, under a different conception, so that no racial or ethnic group is much worse off than other groups. Of course, any collective goal will suggest a particular distribution, given particular facts. Economic efficiency as a goal will suggest that a particular industry be subsidized in some circumstances, but taxed punitively in others. Equality as a goal will suggest immediate and complete redistribution in some circumstances, but partial and discriminatory redistribution in others. In each case distributional principles are subordinate to some conception of aggregate collective good, so that offering less of some benefit to one man can be justified simply by showing that this will lead to a greater benefit overall.

Collective goals may, but need not, be absolute. The community may pursue different goals at the same time, and it may compromise one goal for the sake of another. It may, for example, pursue economic efficiency, but also military strength. The suggested distribution will then be determined by the sum of the two policies, and this will increase the permutations and combinations of possible trade-offs. In any case, these permutations and combinations will offer a number of competing strategies for serving each goal and both goals in combination. Economic efficiency may be well served by offering subsidies to all farmers, and to no

[5] I count legal persons as individuals, so that corporations may have rights; a political theory that counts special groups, like racial groups, as having some corporate standing within the community may therefore speak of group rights.

manufacturers, and better served by offering double the subsidy to some farmers and none to others. There will be alternate strategies of pursuing any set of collective goals, and, particularly as the number of goals increases, it will be impossible to determine in a piecemeal or case-by-case way the distribution that best serves any set of goals. Whether it is good policy to give double subsidies to some farmers and none to others will depend upon a great number of other political decisions that have been or will be made in pursuit of very general strategies into which this particular decision must fit.

Rights also may be absolute: a political theory which holds a right to freedom of speech as absolute will recognize no reason for not securing the liberty it requires for every individual; no reason, that is, short of impossibility. Rights may also be less than absolute; one principle might have to yield to another, or even to an urgent policy with which it competes on particular facts. We may define the weight of a right, assuming it is not absolute, as its power to withstand such competition. It follows from the definition of a right that it cannot be outweighed by all social goals. We might, for simplicity, stipulate not to call any political aim a right unless it has a certain threshold weight against collective goals in general; unless, for example, it cannot be defeated by appeal to any of the ordinary, routine goals of political administration, but only by a goal of special urgency. Suppose, for example, some man says he recognizes the right of free speech, but adds that free speech must yield whenever its exercise would inconvenience the public. He means, I take it, that he recognizes the pervasive goal of collective welfare, and only such distribution of liberty of speech as that collective goal recommends in particular circumstances. His political position is exhausted by the collective goal; the putative right adds nothing and there is no point to recognizing it as a right at all.

These definitions and distinctions make plain that the character of a political aim — its standing as a right or goal — depends upon its place and function within a single political theory. The same phrase might describe a right within one theory and a goal within another, or a right that is absolute or powerful within one theory but relatively weak within another. If a public official has anything like a coherent political theory that he uses, even intuitively, to justify the particular decisions he reaches, then this theory will recognize a wide variety of different types of rights, arranged in some way that assigns rough relative weight to each.

Any adequate theory will distinguish, for example, between background rights, which are rights that provide a justification for political decisions by society in the abstract, and institutional rights, that provide a justification for a decision by some particular and specified political institution. Suppose that my political theory provides that every man has a right to the property of another if he needs it more. I might yet concede that he does not have a legislative right to the same effect; I might concede, that is, that he has no institutional right that the present legislature enact legislation that would violate the Constitution, as such a statute presumably would. I might also concede that he has no institutional right to a judicial decision condoning theft. Even if I did make these concessions, I could preserve my initial background claim by arguing that the people as a whole would be justified in amending the Constitution to abolish property, or perhaps in rebelling and overthrowing the present form of government entirely. I would claim that each man has a residual background right that would justify or require these acts, even though I concede that he does not have the right to specific institutional decisions as these institutions are now constituted.

Any adequate theory will also make use of a distinction between abstract and concrete rights, and therefore between abstract and concrete principles. This is a distinction of degree, but I shall discuss relatively clear examples at two poles of the scale it contemplates, and therefore treat it as a distinction in kind. An abstract right is a general political aim the statement of which does not indicate how that general aim is to be weighed or compromised in particular circumstances against other political aims. The grand rights of political rhetoric are in this way abstract. Politicians speak of a right to free speech or dignity or equality, with no suggestion that these rights are absolute, but with no attempt to suggest their impact on particular complex social situations.

Concrete rights, on the other hand, are political aims that are more precisely defined so as to express more definitely the weight they have against other political aims on particular occasions. Suppose I say, not simply that citizens have a right to free speech, but that a newspaper has a right to publish defense plans classified as secret provided this publication will not create an immediate physical danger to troops. My principle declares for a particular resolution of the conflict it acknowledges between the abstract right of free speech, on the one hand, and competing rights of soldiers to security or the urgent needs of defense on the other. Abstract rights in this way provide arguments for concrete rights, but the claim of a concrete right is more definitive than any claim of abstract right that supports it.[6]

[6] A complete political theory must also recognize two other distinctions that I

B. *Principles and Utility*

The distinction between rights and goals does not deny a thesis that is part of popular moral anthropology. It may be entirely reasonable to think, as this thesis provides, that the principles the members of a particular community find persuasive will be causally determined by the collective goals of that community. If many people in a community believe that each individual has a right to some minimal concern on the part of others, then this fact may be explained, as a matter of cultural history, by the further fact that their collective welfare is advanced by that belief. If some novel arrangement of rights would serve their collective welfare better, then we should expect, according to this thesis, that in due time their moral convictions will alter in favor of that new arrangement.

I do not know how far this anthropological theory holds in our own society, or any society. It is certainly untestable in anything like the simple form in which I have put it, and I do not see why its claim, that rights are psychologically or culturally determined by goals, is a priori more plausible that the contrary claim. Perhaps men and women choose collective goals to accommodate some prior sense of individual rights, rather than delineating rights according to collective goals. In either case, however, there must be an important time lag, so that at any given time most people will recognize the conflict between rights and goals, at least in particular cases, that the general distinction between these two kinds of political aims presupposes.

---

use implicitly in this essay. The first is the distinction between rights against the state and rights against fellow citizens. The former justify a political decision that requires some agency of the government to act; the latter justify a decision to coerce particular individuals. The right to minimum housing, if accepted at all, is accepted as a right against the state. The right to recover damages for a breach of contract, or to be saved from great danger at minimum risk of a rescuer, is a right against fellow citizens. The right to free speech is, ordinarily, both. It seems strange to define the rights that citizens have against one another as political rights at all; but we are now concerned with such rights only insofar as they justify political decisions of different sorts. The present distinction cuts across the distinction between background and institutional rights; the latter distinguishes among persons or institutions that must make a political decision, the former between persons or institutions whom that decision directs to act or forbear. Ordinary civil cases at law, which are the principal subject of this essay, involve rights against fellow citizens; but I also discuss certain issues of constitutional and criminal law and so touch on rights against the state as well.

The second distinction is between universal and special rights; that is, between rights that a political theory provides for all individuals in the community, with exceptions only for phenomena like incapacity or punishment, and rights it provides for only one section of the community, or possibly only one member. I shall assume, in this essay, that all political rights are universal.

The distinction presupposes, that is, a further distinction between the force of a particular right within a political theory and the causal explanation of why the theory provides that right. This is a formal way of putting the point, and it is appropriate only when, as I am now supposing, we can identify a particular political theory and so distinguish the analytical question of what it provides from the historical question of how it came to provide it. The distinction is therefore obscured when we speak of the morality of a *community* without specifying which of the many different conceptions of a community morality we have in mind. Without some further specification we cannot construct even a vague or abstract political theory as the theory of the community at any particular time, and so we cannot make the distinction between reasons and force that is analytically necessary to understand the concepts of principle and policy. We are therefore prey to the argument that the anthropological thesis destroys the distinction between the two; we speak as if we had some coherent theory in mind, as the community's morality, but we deny that it distinguishes principle from policy on the basis of an argument that seems plausible just because we do not have any particular theory in mind. Once we do make plain what we intend by some reference to the morality of a community, and proceed to identify, even crudely, what we take the principles of that morality to be, the anthropological argument is tamed.

There are political theories, however, that unite rights and goals not causally but by making the force of a right contingent upon its power, as a right, to promote some collective goal. I have in mind various forms of the ethical theory called rule utilitarianism. One popular form of that theory, for example, holds that an act is right if the general acceptance of a rule requiring that act would improve the average welfare of members of the community.[7] A political theory might provide for a right to free speech, for example, on the hypothesis that the general acceptance of that right by courts and other political institutions would promote the highest average utility of the community in the long run.

But we may nevertheless distinguish institutional rights, at least, from collective goals within such a theory. If the theory provides that an official of a particular institution is justified in making a political decision, and not justified in refusing to make it, whenever that decision is necessary to protect the freedom to speak of any individual, without regard to the impact of the decision on collective goals, the theory provides free speech as a

---

[7] *See* Brandt, *Toward a Credible Form of Utilitarianism*, in MORALITY AND THE LANGUAGE OF CONDUCT 107 (H. Castenada and G. Nakhnikian, eds. 1963).

right. It does not matter that the theory stipulates this right on the hypothesis that if all political institutions do enforce the right in that way an important collective goal will in fact be promoted. What is important is the commitment to a scheme of government that makes an appeal to the right decisive in particular cases.

So neither the anthropological thesis nor rule utilitarianism offers any objection to the distinction between arguments of principle and arguments of policy. I should mention, out of an abundance of caution, one further possible challenge to that distinction. Different arguments of principle and policy can often be made in support of the same political decision. Suppose that an official wishes to argue in favor of racial segregation in public places. He may offer the policy argument that mixing races causes more overall discomfort than satisfaction. Or he may offer an argument of principle appealing to the rights of those who might be killed or maimed in riots that desegregation would produce. It might be thought that the substitutibility of these arguments defeats the distinction between arguments of principle and policy, or in any case makes the distinction less useful, for the following reason. Suppose it is conceded that the right to equality between races is sufficiently strong that it must prevail over all but the most pressing argument of policy, and be compromised only as required by competing arguments of principle. That would be an empty concession if arguments of principle could always be found to substitute for an argument of policy that might otherwise be made.

But it is a fallacy to suppose that because some argument of principle can always be found to substitute for an argument of policy, it will be as cogent or as powerful as the appropriate argument of policy would have been. If some minority's claim to an antidiscrimination statute were itself based on policy, and could therefore be defeated by an appeal to overall general welfare or utility, then the argument that cites the majority's discomfort or annoyance might well be powerful enough. But if the claim cites a right to equality that must prevail unless matched by a competing argument of principle, the only such argument available may be, as here, simply too weak. Except in extraordinary cases, the danger to any particular man's life that flows from desegregation adequately managed and policed will be very small. We might therefore concede that the competing right to life offers some argument countervailing against the right to equality here, and yet maintain that that argument is of negligible weight; strong enough, perhaps to slow the pace of desegregation but not strong enough even to slow it very much.

C. Economics and Principle

The rights thesis, in its descriptive aspect, holds that judicial decisions in hard cases are characteristically generated by principle not policy. Recent research into the connections between economic theory and the common law might be thought to suggest the contrary: that judges almost always decide on grounds of policy rather than principle. We must, however, be careful to distinguish between two propositions said to be established by that research. It is argued, first, that almost every rule developed by judges in such disparate fields as tort, contract and property can be shown to serve the collective goal of making resource allocation more efficient.[8] It is argued, second, that in certain cases judges explicitly base their decisions on economic policy.[9] Neither of these claims subverts the rights thesis.

The first claim makes no reference to the intentions of the judges who decided the cases establishing rules that improve economic efficiency. It does not suppose that these judges were aware of the economic value of their rules, or even that they would have acknowledged that value as an argument in favor of their decisions. The evidence, for the most part, suggests the contrary. The courts that nourished the unfortunate fellow-servant doctrine, for example, thought that the rule was required by fairness, not utility, and when the rule was abolished it was because the argument from fairness, not the argument from utility, was found wanting by a different generation of lawyers.[10]

If this first claim is sound, it might seem to some an important piece of evidence for the anthropological thesis described in the last section. They will think that it suggests that judges and lawyers, reflecting the general moral attitudes of their time, thought that corporations and individuals had just those rights that an explicit rule utilitarian would legislate to serve the general welfare. But the first claim might equally well suggest the contrary conclusion I mentioned, that our present ideas of general welfare reflect our ideas of individual right. Professor Posner, for example, argues for that claim by presupposing a particular conception of efficient resource allocation. He says that the value of some scarce resource to a particular individual is measured by the amount of money he is willing to pay for it, so that community welfare is maximized when each resource is in the hands of some-

---

[8] *See, e.g.*, R. Posner, Economic Analysis of Law 10–104 (1972).

[9] *See, e.g.*, Coase, *The Problem of Social Cost*, 3 J. Law & Econ. 1, 19–28 (1960).

[10] *See* Posner, *A Theory of Negligence*, 1 J. Legal Stud. 29, 71 (1972).

one who would pay more than anyone else to have it.[11] But that is hardly a self-evident or neutral conception of value. It is congenial to a political theory that celebrates competition, but far less congenial to a more egalitarian theory, because it demotes the claims of the poor who are willing to spend less because they have less to spend. Posner's conception of value, therefore, seems as much the consequence as the cause of a theory of individual rights. In any case, however, the anthropological thesis of the first claim offers no threat to the rights thesis. Even if we concede that a judge's theory of rights is determined by some instinctive sense of economic value, rather than the other way about, we may still argue that he relies on that theory, and not economic analysis, to justify decisions in hard cases.

The second claim we distinguished, however, may seem to present a more serious challenge. If judges explicitly refer to economic policy in some cases, then these cases cannot be understood simply as evidence for the anthropological thesis. Learned Hand's theory of negligence is the most familiar example of this explicit reference to economics. He said, roughly, that the test of whether the defendant's act was unreasonable, and therefore actionable, is the economic test which asks whether the defendant could have avoided the accident at less cost to himself than the plaintiff was likely to suffer if the accident occurred, discounted by the improbability of the accident.[12] It may be said that this economic test provides an argument of policy rather than principle, because it makes the decision turn on whether the collective welfare would have been advanced more by allowing the accident to take place or by spending what was necessary to avoid it. If so, then cases in which some test like Hand's is explicitly used, however few they might be, would stand as counterexamples to the rights thesis.

But the assumption that an economic calculation of any sort must be an argument of policy overlooks the distinction between abstract and concrete rights. Abstract rights, like the right to speak on political matters, take no account of competing rights; concrete rights, on the other hand, reflect the impact of such competition. In certain kinds of cases the argument from competing abstract principles to a concrete right can be made in the language of economics. Consider the principle that each member of a community has a right that each other member treat him with the minimal respect due a fellow human being.[13] That is a very abstract

[11] R. Posner, *supra* note 8, at 4.

[12] United States v. Carroll Towing Co., 159 F.2d 169, 173 (2d Cir. 1947). Coase, *supra* note 9, at 22–23, gives other examples, mostly of nuisance cases interpreting the doctrine that a "reasonable" interference with the plaintiff's use of his property is not a nuisance.

[13] A more elaborate argument of principle might provide a better justification

principle: it demands some balance, in particular cases, between the interests of those to be protected and the liberty of those from whom the principle demands an unstated level of concern and respect. It is natural, particularly when economic vocabulary is in fashion, to define the proper balance by comparing the sum of the utilities of these two parties under different conditions. If one man acts in a way that he can foresee will injure another so that the collective utility of the pair will be sharply reduced by his act, he does not show the requisite care and concern. If he can guard or insure against the injury much more cheaply or effectively than the other can, for example, then he does not show care and concern unless he takes these precautions or arranges that insurance.

That character of argument is by no means novel, though perhaps its economic dress is. Philosophers have for a long time debated hypothetical cases testing the level of concern that one member of a community owes to another. If one man is drowning, and another may save him at minimal risk to himself, for example, then the first has a moral right to be saved by the second. That proposition might easily be put in economic form: if the collective utility of the pair is very sharply improved by a rescue, then the drowning man has a right to that rescue and the rescuer a duty to make it. The parallel legal proposition may, of course, be much more complex than that. It may specify special circumstances in which the crucial question is not whether the collective utility of the pair will be sharply advanced, but only whether it will be marginally advanced. It might put the latter question, for example, when one man's positive act, as distinct from a failure to act, creates a risk of direct and foreseeable physical injury to the person or property of another. If the rights thesis is sound, of course, then no judge may appeal to that legal proposition unless he believes that the principle of minimal respect states an abstract legal right; but if he does, then he may cast his argument in economic form without thereby changing its character from principle to policy.

Since Hand's test, and the parallel argument about rescuing a drowning man, are methods of compromising competing rights, they consider only the welfare of those whose abstract rights are at stake. They do not provide room for costs or benefits to the community at large, except as these are reflected in the

---

for Hand's test than does this simple principle. I described a more elaborate argument in a set of Rosenthal Lectures delivered at Northwestern University Law School in March, 1975. The simple principle, however, provides a sufficiently good justification for the present point.

welfare of those whose rights are in question. We can easily imagine an argument that does not concede these restrictions. Suppose someone argued that the principle requiring rescue at minimal risk should be amended so as to make the decision turn, not on some function of the collective utilities of the victim and rescuer, but on marginal utility to the community as a whole, so that the rescuer must take into account not only the relative risks to himself and the victim, but the relative social importance of the two. It might follow that an insignificant man must risk his life to save a bank president, but that a bank president need not even tire himself to save a nobody. The argument is no longer an argument of principle, because it supposes the victim to have a right to nothing but his expectations under general utility. Hand's formula, and more sophisticated variations, are not arguments of that character; they do not subordinate an individual right to some collective goal, but provide a mechanism for compromising competing claims of abstract right.

Negligence cases are not the only cases in which judges compromise abstract rights in defining concrete ones. If a judge appeals to public safety or the scarcity of some vital resource, for example, as a ground for limiting some abstract right, then his appeal might be understood as an appeal to the competing rights of those whose security will be sacrificed, or whose just share of that resource will be threatened if the abstract right is made concrete. His argument is an argument of principle if it respects the distributional requirements of such arguments, and if it observes the restriction mentioned in the last section: that the weight of a competing principle may be less than the weight of the appropriate parallel policy. We find a different sort of example in the familiar argument that certain sorts of law suits should not be allowed because to do so would "swamp" the courts with litigation. The court supposes that if it were to allow that type of suit it would lack the time to consider promptly enough other law suits aiming to vindicate rights that are, taken together, more important than the rights it therefore proposes to bar.

This is an appropriate point to notice a certain limitation of the rights thesis. It holds in standard civil cases, when the ruling assumption is that one of the parties has a right to win; but it holds only asymmetrically when that assumption cannot be made. The accused in a criminal case has a right to a decision in his favor if he is innocent, but the state has no parallel right to a conviction if he is guilty. The court may therefore find in favor of the accused, in some hard case testing rules of evidence, for example, on an argument of policy that does not suppose that the accused has any right to be acquitted. The

Supreme Court in *Linkletter v. Walker*[14] said that its earlier decision in *Mapp v. Ohio*[15] was such a decision. The Court said it had changed the rules permitting the introduction of illegally obtained evidence, not because Miss Mapp had any right that such evidence not be used if otherwise admissible, but in order to deter policemen from collecting such evidence in the future. I do not mean that a constitutional decision on such grounds is proper, or even that the Court's later description of its earlier decision was accurate. I mean only to point out how the geometry of a criminal prosecution, which does not set opposing rights in a case against one another, differs from the standard civil case in which the rights thesis holds symmetrically.

III. Institutional Rights

The rights thesis provides that judges decide hard cases by confirming or denying concrete rights. But the concrete rights upon which judges rely must have two other characteristics. They must be institutional rather than background rights, and they must be legal rather than some other form of institutional rights. We cannot appreciate or test the thesis, therefore, without further elaboration of these distinctions.

Institutional rights may be found in institutions of very different character. A chess player has a "chess" right to be awarded a point in a tournament if he checkmates an opponent. A citizen in a democracy has a legislative right to the enactment of statutes necessary to protect his free speech. In the case of chess, institutional rights are fixed by constitutive and regulative rules that belong distinctly to the game, or to a particular tournament. Chess is, in this sense, an autonomous institution; I mean that it is understood, among its participants, that no one may claim an institutional right by direct appeal to general morality. No one may argue, for example, that he has earned the right to be declared the winner by his general virtue. But legislation is only partly autonomous in that sense. There are special constitutive and regulative rules that define what a legislature is, and who belongs to it, and how it votes, and that it may not establish a religion. But these rules belonging distinctly to legislation are rarely sufficient to determine whether a citizen has an institutional right to have a certain statute enacted; they do not decide, for example, whether he has a right to minimum wage legislation. Citizens are expected to repair to general considerations of political morality when they argue for such rights.

[14] 381 U.S. 618 (1965).

[15] 367 U.S. 643 (1961).

The fact that some institutions are fully and others partly autonomous has the consequence mentioned earlier, that the institutional rights a political theory acknowledges may diverge from the background rights it provides. Institutional rights are nevertheless genuine rights. Even if we suppose that the poor have an abstract background right to money taken from the rich, it would be wrong, not merely unexpected, for the referees of a chess tournament to award the prize money to the poorest contestant rather than the contestant with the most points. It would provide no excuse to say that since tournament rights merely describe the conditions necessary for calling the tournament a chess tournament, the referee's act is justified so long as he does not use the word "chess" when he hands out the award. The participants entered the tournament with the understanding that chess rules would apply; they have genuine rights to the enforcement of these rules and no others.

Institutional autonomy insulates an official's institutional duty from the greater part of background political morality. But how far does the force of this insulation extend? Even in the case of a fully insulated institution like chess some rules will require interpretation or elaboration before an official may enforce them in certain circumstances. Suppose some rule of a chess tournament provides that the referee shall declare a game forfeit if one player "unreasonably" annoys the other in the course of play. The language of the rule does not define what counts as "unreasonable" annoyance; it does not decide whether, for example, a player who continually smiles at his opponent in such a way as to unnerve him, as the Russian grandmaster Tal once smiled at Fischer, annoys him unreasonably.

The referee is not free to give effect to his background convictions in deciding this hard case. He might hold, as a matter of political theory, that individuals have a right to equal welfare without regard to intellectual abilities. It would nevertheless be wrong for him to rely upon that conviction in deciding difficult cases under the forfeiture rule. He could not say, for example, that annoying behavior is reasonable so long as it has the effect of reducing the importance of intellectual ability in deciding who will win the game. The participants, and the general community that is interested, will say that his duty is just the contrary. Since chess is an intellectual game, he must apply the forfeiture rule in such a way as to protect, rather than jeopardize, the role of intellect in the contest.

We have, then, in the case of the chess referee, an example of an official whose decisions about institutional rights are understood to be governed by institutional constraints even when the force of these constraints is not clear. We do not think that he is free to legislate interstitially within the "open texture" of imprecise rules.[16] If one interpretation of the forfeiture rule will protect the character of the game, and another will not, then the participants have a right to the first interpretation. We may hope to find, in this relatively simple case, some general feature of institutional rights in hard cases that will bear on the decision of a judge in a hard case at law.

I said that the game of chess has a character that the referee's decisions must respect. What does that mean? How does a referee know that chess is an intellectual game rather than a game of chance or an exhibition of digital ballet? He may well start with what everyone knows. Every institution is placed by its participants in some very rough category of institution; it is taken to be a game rather than a religious ceremony or a form of exercise or a political process. It is, for that reason, definitional of chess that it is a game rather than an exercise in digital skill. These conventions, exhibited in attitudes and manners and in history, are decisive. If everyone takes chess to be a game of chance, so that they curse their luck and nothing else when a piece *en prise* happens to be taken, then chess is a game of chance, though a very bad one.

But these conventions will run out, and they may run out before the referee finds enough to decide the case of Tal's smile. It is important to see, however, that the conventions run out in a particular way. They are not incomplete, like a book whose last page is missing, but abstract, so that their full force can be captured in a concept that admits of different conceptions; that is, in a *contested* concept.[17] The referee must select one or another of these conceptions, not to supplement the convention, but to enforce it. He must *construct* the game's character by putting to himself different sets of questions. Given that chess is an intellectual game, is it, like poker, intellectual in some sense that includes ability at psychological intimidation? Or is it, like mathematics, intellectual in some sense that does not include that ability? This first set of questions asks him to look more closely at the game, to determine whether its features support one rather than the other of these conceptions of intellect. But he must also ask a different set of questions. Given that chess is an intellectual game of some sort, what follows about reasonable behavior in a chess game? Is ability at psychological intimidation, or ability

[16] *See generally* H.L.A. HART, THE CONCEPT OF LAW 121–32 (1961).

[17] *See* Gallie, *Essentially Contested Concepts*, 56 PROCEEDINGS OF THE ARISTOTELIAN SOCIETY 167, 167–68 (1955–56). *See also* Dworkin, *The Jurisprudence of Richard Nixon*, NEW YORK REVIEW OF BOOKS, May 4, 1972, at 27.

to resist such intimidation, really an intellectual quality? These questions ask him to look more closely at the concept of intellect itself.

The referee's calculations, if they are self-conscious, will oscillate between these two sets of questions, progressively narrowing the questions to be asked at the next stage. He might first identify, by reflecting on the concept, different conceptions of intellect. He might suppose at this first stage, for example, that physical grace of the sort achieved in ballet is one form of intelligence. But he must then test these different conceptions against the rules and practices of the game. That test will rule out any physical conception of intelligence. But it may not discriminate between a conception that includes or a conception that rejects psychological intimidation, because either of these conceptions would provide an account of the rules and practices that is not plainly superior, according to any general canons of explanation, to the account provided by the other. He must then ask himself which of these two accounts offers a deeper or more successful account of what intellect really is. His calculations, so conceived, oscillate between philosophy of mind and the facts of the institution whose character he must elucidate.

This is, of course, only a fanciful reconstruction of a calculation that will never take place; any official's sense of the game will have developed over a career, and he will employ rather than expose that sense in his judgments. But the reconstruction enables us to see how the concept of the game's character is tailored to a special institutional problem. Once an autonomous institution is established, such that participants have institutional rights under distinct rules belonging to that institution, then hard cases may arise that must, in the nature of the case, be supposed to have an answer. If Tal does not have a right that the game be continued, it must be because the forfeiture rule, properly understood, justifies the referee's intervention; if it does, then Fischer has a right to win at once. It is not useful to speak of the referee's "discretion" in such a case. If some weak sense of discretion is meant, then the remark is unhelpful; if some strong sense is meant, such that Tal no longer has a right to win, then this must be, again, because the rule properly understood destroys the right he would otherwise have.[18] Suppose we say that in such a case all the parties have a right to expect is that the referee will use his best judgment. That is, in a sense, perfectly true, because they can have no more, by way of the referee's judgment, than his best judgment. But they are nevertheless entitled to his best judgment about which behavior is, in the circumstances of the game, un-

[18] *See* Dworkin, *The Model of Rules*, 35 U. CHI. L. REV. 14, 32–40 (1967).

reasonable; they are entitled, that is, to his best judgment about what their rights are. The proposition that there is some "right" answer to that question does not mean that the rules of chess are exhaustive and unambiguous; rather it is a complex statement about the responsibilities of its officials and participants.

But if the decision in a hard case must be a decision about the rights of the parties, then an official's reason for that judgment must be the sort of reason that justifies recognizing or denying a right. He must bring to his decision a general theory of why, in the case of his institution, the rules create or destroy any rights at all, and he must show what decision that general theory requires in the hard case. In chess the general ground of institutional rights must be the tacit consent or understanding of the parties. They consent, in entering a chess tournament, to the enforcement of certain and only those rules, and it is hard to imagine any other general ground for supposing that they have any institutional rights. But if that is so, and if the decision in a hard case is a decision about which rights they actually have, then the argument for the decision must apply that general ground to the hard case.

The hard case puts, we might say, a question of political theory. It asks what it is fair to suppose that the players have done in consenting to the forfeiture rule. The concept of a game's character is a conceptual device for framing that question. It is a contested concept that internalizes the general justification of the institution so as to make it available for discriminations within the institution itself. It supposes that a player consents not simply to a set of rules, but to an enterprise that may be said to have a character of its own; so that when the question is put — To what did he consent in consenting to that? — the answer may study the enterprise as a whole and not just the rules.

IV. Legal Rights

A. Legislation

Legal argument, in hard cases, turns on contested concepts whose nature and function are very much like the concept of the character of a game. These include several of the substantive concepts through which the law is stated, like the concepts of a contract and of property. But they also include two concepts of much greater relevance to the present argument. The first is the idea of the "intention" or "purpose" of a particular statute or statutory clause. This concept provides a bridge between the political justification of the general idea that statutes create rights and those hard cases that ask what rights a particular statute has created. The second is the concept of principles that "underlie" or are "embedded in" the positive rules of law. This concept provides a bridge between the political justification of the doctrine that like cases should be decided alike and those hard cases in which it is unclear what that general doctrine requires. These concepts together define legal rights as a function, though a very special function, of political rights. If a judge accepts the settled practices of his legal system — if he accepts, that is, the autonomy provided by its distinct constitutive and regulative rules — then he must, according to the doctrine of political responsibility, accept some general political theory that justifies these practices. The concepts of legislative purpose and common law principles are devices for applying that general political theory to controversial issues about legal rights.

We might therefore do well to consider how a philosophical judge might develop, in appropriate cases, theories of what legislative purpose and legal principles require. We shall find that he would construct these theories in the same manner as a philosophical referee would construct the character of a game. I have invented, for this purpose, a lawyer of superhuman skill, learning, patience and acumen, whom I shall call Hercules. I suppose that Hercules is a judge in some representative American jurisdiction. I assume that he accepts the main uncontroversial constitutive and regulative rules of the law in his jurisdiction. He accepts, that is, that statutes have the general power to create and extinguish legal rights, and that judges have the general duty to follow earlier decisions of their court or higher courts whose rationale, as lawyers say, extends to the case at bar.

1. The Constitution. — Suppose there is a written constitution in Hercules' jurisdiction which provides that no law shall be valid if it establishes a religion. The legislature passes a law purporting to grant free busing to children in parochial schools. Does the grant establish a religion? [19] The words of the constitutional provision might support either view. Hercules must nevertheless decide whether the child who appears before him has a right to her bus ride.

He might begin by asking why the constitution has any power at all to create or destroy rights. If citizens have a background right to salvation through an established church, as many believe they do, then this must be an important right. Why does the fact that a group of men voted otherwise several centuries ago prevent this background right from being made a legal right as well? His answer must take some form such as this. The constitution sets out a general political scheme that is sufficiently just to be taken

[19] *See* Everson v. Board of Educ., 330 U.S. 1 (1947).

as settled for reasons of fairness. Citizens take the benefit of living in a society whose institutions are arranged and governed in accordance with that scheme, and they must take the burdens as well, at least until a new scheme is put into force either by discrete amendment or general revolution. But Hercules must then ask just what scheme of principles has been settled. He must construct, that is, a constitutional theory; since he is Hercules we may suppose that he can develop a full political theory that justifies the constitution as a whole. It must be a scheme that fits the particular rules of this constitution, of course. It cannot include a powerful background right to an established church. But more than one fully specified theory may fit the specific provision about religion sufficiently well. One theory might provide, for example, that it is wrong for the government to enact any legislation that will cause great social tension or disorder; so that, since the establishment of a church will have that effect, it is wrong to empower the legislature to establish one. Another theory will provide a background right to religious liberty, and therefore argue that an established church is wrong, not because it will be socially disruptive, but because it violates that background right. In that case Hercules must turn to the remaining constitutional rules and settled practices under these rules to see which of these two theories provides a smoother fit with the constitutional scheme as a whole.

But the theory that is superior under this test will nevertheless be insufficiently concrete to decide some cases. Suppose Hercules decides that the establishment provision is justified by a right to religious liberty rather than any goal of social order. It remains to ask what, more precisely, religious liberty is. Does a right to religious liberty include the right not to have one's taxes used for any purpose that helps a religion to survive? Or simply not to have one's taxes used to benefit one religion at the expense of another? If the former, then the free transportation legislation violates that right, but if the latter it does not. The institutional structure of rules and practice may not be sufficiently detailed to rule out either of these two conceptions of religious liberty, or to make one a plainly superior justification of that structure. At some point in his career Hercules must therefore consider the question not just as an issue of fit between a theory and the rules of the institution, but as an issue of political philosophy as well. He must decide which conception is a more satisfactory elaboration of the general idea of religious liberty. He must decide that question because he cannot otherwise carry far enough the project he began. He cannot answer in sufficient detail the question of what political scheme the constitution establishes.

So Hercules is driven, by this project, to a process of reasoning that is much like the process of the self-conscious chess referee. He must develop a theory of the constitution, in the shape of a complex set of principles and policies that justify that scheme of government, just as the chess referee is driven to develop a theory about the character of his game. He must develop that theory by referring alternately to political philosophy and institutional detail. He must generate possible theories justifying different aspects of the scheme and test the theories against the broader institution. When the discriminating power of that test is exhausted, he must elaborate the contested concepts that the successful theory employs.

2. *Statutes.* — A statute in Hercules' jurisdiction provides that it is a federal crime for someone knowingly to transport in interstate commerce "any person who shall have been unlawfully seized, confined, inveigled, decoyed, kidnapped, abducted, or carried away by any means whatsoever. . . ." Hercules is asked to decide whether this statute makes a federal criminal of a man who persuaded a young girl that it was her religious duty to run away with him, in violation of a court order, to consummate what he called a celestial marriage.[20] The statute had been passed after a famous kidnapping case, in order to enable federal authorities to join in the pursuit of kidnappers. But its words are sufficiently broad to apply to this case, and there is nothing in the legislative record or accompanying committee reports that says they do not.

Do they apply? Hercules might himself despise celestial marriage, or abhor the corruption of minors, or celebrate the obedience of children to their parents. The groom nevertheless has a right to his liberty, unless the statute properly understood deprives him of that right; it is inconsistent with any plausible theory of the constitution that judges have the power retroactively to make conduct criminal. Does the statute deprive him of that right? Hercules must begin by asking why any statute has the power to alter legal rights. He will find the answer in his constitutional theory: this might provide, for example, that a democratically elected legislature is the appropriate body to make collective decisions about the conduct that shall be criminal. But that same constitutional theory will impose on the legislature certain responsibilities: it will impose not only constraints reflecting individual rights, but also some general duty to pursue collective goals defining the public welfare. That fact provides a useful test for Hercules in this hard case. He might ask which interpretation more satisfactorily ties the language the legislature used to its

[20] *See* Chatwin v. United States, 326 U.S. 455 (1946).

constitutional responsibilities. That is like the referee's question about the character of a game. It calls for the construction, not of some hypotheses about the mental state of particular legislators, but of a special political theory that justifies this statute, in the light of the legislature's more general responsibilities, better than any alternative theory.[21]

Which arguments of principle and policy might properly have persuaded the legislature to enact just that statute? It should not have pursued a policy designed to replace state criminal enforcement by federal enforcement whenever constitutionally possible. That would represent an unnecessary interference with the principle of federalism that must be part of Hercules' constitutional theory. It might, however, responsibly have followed a policy of selecting for federal enforcement all crimes with such an interstate character that state enforcement was hampered. Or it could responsibly have selected just specially dangerous or widespread crimes of that character. Which of these two responsible policies offers a better justification of the statute actually drafted? If the penalties provided by the statute are large, and therefore appropriate to the latter but not the former policy, the latter policy must be preferred. Which of the different interpretations of the statute permitted by the language serves that policy better? Plainly a decision that inveiglement of the sort presented by the case is not made a federal crime by the statute.

I have described a simple and perhaps unrepresentative problem of statutory interpretation, because I cannot now develop a theory of statutory interpretation in any detail. I want only to suggest how the general claim, that calculations judges make about the purposes of statutes are calculations about political rights,

---

[21] One previous example of the use of policy in statutory interpretations illustrates this form of construction. In Charles River Bridge v. Warren Bridge, 24 Mass. (7 Pick.) 344 (1830), *aff'd*, 36 U.S. (11 Pet.) 420 (1837), the court had to decide whether a charter to construct a bridge across the Charles River was to be taken to be exclusive, so that no further charters could be granted. Justice Morton of the Supreme Judicial Court held that the grant was not to be taken as exclusive, and argued, in support of that interpretation, that:

> [I]f consequences so inconsistent with the improvement and prosperity of the state result from the liberal and extended construction of the charters which have been granted, we ought, if the terms used will admit of it, rather to adopt a more limited and restricted one, than to impute such improvidence to the legislature.
>
> . . . .
>
> . . . [Construing the grant as exclusive] would amount substantially to a covenant, that during the plaintiffs' charter an important portion of our commonwealth, as to facilities for travel and transportation, should remain *in statu quo*. I am on the whole irresistibly brought to the conclusion, that this construction is neither consonant with sound reason, with judicial authorities, with the course of legislation, nor with the principles of our free institutions.

Id. at 460.

might be defended. There are, however, two points that must be noticed about even this simple example. It would be inaccurate, first, to say that Hercules supplemented what the legislature did in enacting the statute, or that he tried to determine what it would have done if it had been aware of the problem presented by the case. The act of a legislature is not, as these descriptions suggest, an event whose force we can in some way measure so as to say it has run out at a particular point; it is rather an event whose content is contested in the way in which the content of an agreement to play a game is contested. Hercules constructs his political theory as an argument about what the legislature has, on this occasion, done. The contrary argument, that it did not actually do what he said, is not a realistic piece of common sense, but a competitive claim about the true content of that contested event.

Second, it is important to notice how great a role the canonical terms of the actual statute play in the process described. They provide a limit to what must otherwise be, in the nature of the case, unlimited. The political theory Hercules developed to interpret the statute, which featured a policy of providing federal enforcement for dangerous crimes, would justify a great many decisions that the legislature did not, on any interpretation of the language, actually make. It would justify, for example, a statute making it a federal crime for a murderer to leave the state of his crime. The legislature has no general duty to follow out the lines of any particular policy, and it would plainly be wrong for Hercules to suppose that the legislature had in some sense enacted that further statute. The statutory language they did enact enables this process of interpretation to operate without absurdity; it permits Hercules to say that the legislature pushed some policy to the limits of the language it used, without also supposing that it pushed that policy to some indeterminate further point.

B. *The Common Law*

1. Precedent. — One day lawyers will present a hard case to Hercules that does not turn upon any statute; they will argue whether earlier common law decisions of Hercules' court, properly understood, provide some party with a right to a decision in his favor. *Spartan Steel* was such a case. The plaintiff did not argue that any statute provided it a right to recover its economic damages; it pointed instead to certain earlier judicial decisions that awarded recovery for other sorts of damage, and argued that the principle behind these cases required a decision for it as well.

Hercules must begin by asking why arguments of that form are ever, even in principle, sound. He will find that he has available no quick or obvious answer. When he asked himself the parallel question about legislation he found, in general democratic theory, a ready reply. But the details of the practices of precedent he must now justify resist any comparably simple theory.

He might, however, be tempted by this answer. Judges, when they decide particular cases at common law, lay down general rules that are intended to benefit the community in some way. Other judges, deciding later cases, must therefore enforce these rules so that the benefit may be achieved. If this account of the matter were a sufficient justification of the practices of precedent, then Hercules could decide these hard common law cases as if earlier decisions were statutes, using the techniques he worked out for statutory interpretation. But he will encounter fatal difficulties if he pursues that theory very far. It will repay us to consider why, in some detail, because the errors in the theory will be guides to a more successful theory.

Statutory interpretation, as we just noticed, depends upon the availability of a canonical form of words, however vague or unspecific, that set limits to the political decisions that the statute may be taken to have made. Hercules will discover that many of the opinions that litigants cite as precedents do not contain any special propositions taken to be a canonical form of the rule that the case lays down. It is true that it was part of Anglo-American judicial style, during the last part of the nineteenth century and the first part of this century, to attempt to compose such canonical statements, so that one could thereafter refer, for example, to the rule in *Rylands v. Fletcher*.[22] But even in this period, lawyers and textbook writers disagreed about which parts of famous opinions should be taken to have that character. Today, in any case, even important opinions rarely attempt that legislative sort of draftsmanship. They cite reasons, in the form of precedents and principles, to justify a decision, but it is the decision, not some new and stated rule of law, that these precedents and principles are taken to justify. Sometimes a judge will acknowledge openly that it lies to later cases to determine the full effect of the case he has decided.

Of course, Hercules might well decide that when he does find, in an earlier case, a canonical form of words, he will use his techniques of statutory interpretation to decide whether the rule composed of these words embraces a novel case.[23] He might well

---

[22] L.R. 1 Ex. 265 (1866), *aff'd*, L.R. 3 H.L. 330 (1868).

[23] But since Hercules will be led to accept the rights thesis, *see* pp. 1091–93 *infra*, his "interpretation" of judicial enactments will be different from his interpretation of statutes in one important respect. When he interprets statutes he fixes to some statutory language, as we saw, arguments of principle or policy that

acknowledge what could be called an enactment force of precedent. He will nevertheless find that when a precedent does have enactment force, its influence on later cases is not taken to be limited to that force. Judges and lawyers do not think that the force of precedents is exhausted, as a statute would be, by the linguistic limits of some particular phrase. If *Spartan Steel* were a New York case, counsel for the plaintiff would suppose that Cardozo's earlier decision in *MacPherson v. Buick*,[24] in which a woman recovered damages for injuries from a negligently manufactured automobile, counted in favor of his client's right to recover, in spite of the fact that the earlier decision contained no language that could plausibly be interpreted to enact that right. He would urge that the earlier decision exerts a gravitational force on later decisions even when these later decisions lie outside its particular orbit.

This gravitational force is part of the practice Hercules' general theory of precedent must capture. In this important respect, judicial practice differs from the practice of officials in other institutions. In chess, officials conform to established rules in a way that assumes full institutional autonomy. They exercise originality only to the extent required by the fact that an occasional rule, like the rule about forfeiture, demands that originality. Each decision of a chess referee, therefore, can be said to be directly required and justified by an established rule of chess, even though some of these decisions must be based on an interpretation, rather than on simply the plain and unavoidable meaning, of that rule.

Some legal philosophers write about common law adjudication as if it were in this way like chess, except that legal rules are much more likely than chess rules to require interpretation. That is the spirit, for example, of Professor Hart's argument that hard cases arise only because legal rules have what he calls "open texture."[25] In fact, judges often disagree not simply about how some rule or principle should be interpreted, but whether the rule or principle one judge cites should be acknowledged to be a rule or principle at all. In some cases both the majority and the dissenting opinions recognize the same earlier cases as relevant, but disagree about what rule or principle these precedents should be understood to have established. In adjudication, unlike chess, the argu-

---

provide the best justification of that language in the light of the legislature's responsibilities. His argument remains an argument of principle; he uses policy to determine what rights the legislature has already created. But when he "interprets" judicial enactments he will fix to the relevant language only arguments of principle, because the rights thesis argues that only such arguments acquit the responsibility of the "enacting" court.

[24] MacPherson v. Buick Motor Co., 217 N.Y. 382, 111 N.E. 1050 (1916).

[25] H.L.A. HART, *supra* note 18, at 121–32.

ment *for* a particular rule may be more important than the argument *from* that rule to the particular case; and while the chess referee who decides a case by appeal to a rule no one has ever heard of before is likely to be dismissed or certified, the judge who does so is likely to be celebrated in law school lectures.

Nevertheless, judges seem agreed that earlier decisions do contribute to the formulation of new and controversial rules in some way other than by interpretation; they are agreed that earlier decisions have gravitational force even when they disagree about what that force is. The legislator may very often concern himself only with issues of background morality or policy in deciding how to cast his vote on some issue. He need not show that his vote is consistent with the votes of his colleagues in the legislature, or with those of past legislatures. But the judge very rarely assumes that character of independence. He will always try to connect the justification he provides for an original decision with decisions that other judges or officials have taken in the past.

In fact, when good judges try to explain in some general way how they work, they search for figures of speech to describe the constraints they feel even when they suppose that they are making new law, constraints that would not be appropriate if they were legislators. They say, for example, that they find new rules imminent in the law as a whole, or that they are enforcing an internal logic of the law through some method that belongs more to philosophy than to politics, or that they are the agents through which the law works itself pure, or that the law has some life of its own even though this belongs to experience rather than logic. Hercules must not rest content with these famous metaphors and personifications, but he must also not be content with any description of the judicial process that ignores their appeal to the best lawyers.

The gravitational force of precedent cannot be captured by any theory that takes the full force of precedent to be its enactment force as a piece of legislation. But the inadequacy of that approach suggests a superior theory. The gravitational force of a precedent may be explained by appeal, not to the wisdom of enforcing enactments, but to the fairness of treating like cases alike. A precedent is the report of an earlier political decision; the very fact of that decision, as a piece of political history, provides some reason for deciding other cases in a similar way in the future. This general explanation of the gravitational force of precedent accounts for the feature that defeated the enactment theory, which is that the force of a precedent escapes the language of its opinion. If the government of a community has forced the manufacturer of defective motor cars to pay damages to a woman who was injured because of the defect, then that historical fact must offer some reason, at least, why the same government should require a contractor who has caused economic damage through the defective work of his employees to make good that loss. We may test the weight of that reason, not by asking whether the language of the earlier decision, suitably interpreted, requires the contractor to pay damages, but by asking the different question whether it is fair for the government, having intervened in the way it did in the first case, to refuse its aid in the second.

Hercules will conclude that this doctrine of fairness offers the only adequate account of the full practice of precedent. He will draw certain further conclusions about his own responsibilities when deciding hard cases. The most important of these is that he must limit the gravitational force of earlier decisions to the extension of the arguments of principle necessary to justify those decisions. If an earlier decision were taken to be entirely justified by some argument of policy, it would have no gravitational force. Its value as a precedent would be limited to its enactment force, that is, to further cases captured by some particular words of the opinion. The distributional force of a collective goal, as we noticed earlier, is a matter of contingent fact and general legislative strategy. If the government intervened on behalf of Mrs. MacPherson, not because she had any right to its intervention, but only because wise strategy suggested that means of pursuing some collective goal like economic efficiency, there can be no effective argument of fairness that it therefore ought to intervene for the plaintiff in *Spartan Steel*.

We must remind ourselves, in order to see why this is so, of the slight demands we make upon legislatures in the name of consistency when their decisions are generated by arguments of policy.[26] Suppose the legislature wishes to stimulate the economy and might do so, with roughly the same efficiency, either by sub-

---

[26] In Williamson v. Lee Optical Co., 348 U.S. 483 (1955), Justice Douglas suggested that legislation generated by policy need not be uniform or consistent:

> The problem of legislative classification is a perennial one, admitting of no doctrinaire definition. Evils in the same field may be of different dimensions and proportions, requiring different remedies. Or so the legislature may think. Or the reform may take one step at a time, addressing itself to the phase of the problem which seems most acute to the legislative mind. The legislature may select one phase of one field and apply a remedy there, neglecting the others. The prohibition of the Equal Protection Clause goes no further than the invidious discrimination.

Id. at 489 (citations omitted).

Of course the point of the argument here, that the demands of consistency are different in the cases of principle and policy, is of great importance in understanding the recent history of the equal protection clause. It is the point behind attempts to distinguish "old" from "new" equal protection, or to establish "suspect" classifications, and it provides a more accurate and intelligible distinction than these attempts have furnished.

sidizing housing or by increasing direct government spending for new roads. Road construction companies have no right that the legislature choose road construction; if it does, then home construction firms have no right, on any principle of consistency, that the legislature subsidize housing as well. The legislature may decide that the road construction program has stimulated the economy just enough, and that no further programs are needed. It may decide this even if it now concedes that subsidized housing would have been the more efficient decision in the first place. Or it might concede even that more stimulation of the economy is needed, but decide that it wishes to wait for more evidence — perhaps evidence about the success of the road program — to see whether subsidies provide an effective stimulation. It might even say that it does not now wish to commit more of its time and energy to economic policy. There is, perhaps, some limit to the arbitrariness of the distinctions the legislature may make in its pursuit of collective goals. Even if it is efficient to build all shipyards in southern California, it might be thought unfair, as well as politically unwise, to do so. But these weak requirements, which prohibit grossly unfair distributions, are plainly compatible with providing sizeable incremental benefits to one group that are withheld from others.

There can be, therefore, no general argument of fairness that a government which serves a collective goal in one way on one occasion must serve it that way, or even serve the same goal, whenever a parallel opportunity arises. I do not mean simply that the government may change its mind, and regret either the goal or the means of its earlier decision. I mean that a responsible government may serve different goals in a piecemeal and occasional fashion, so that even though it does not regret, but continues to enforce, one rule designed to serve a particular goal, it may reject other rules that would serve that same goal just as well. It might legislate the rule that manufacturers are responsible for damages flowing from defects in their cars, for example, and yet properly refuse to legislate the same rule for manufacturers of washing machines, let alone contractors who cause economic damage like the damage of *Spartan Steel.* Government must, of course, be rational and fair; it must make decisions that overall serve a justifiable mix of collective goals and nevertheless respect whatever rights citizens have. But that general requirement would not support anything like the gravitational force that the judicial decision in favor of Mrs. MacPherson was in fact taken to have.

So Hercules, when he defines the gravitational force of a particular precedent, must take into account only the arguments of principle that justify that precedent. If the decision in favor of

Mrs. MacPherson supposes that she has a right to damages, and not simply that a rule in her favor supports some collective goal, then the argument of fairness, on which the practice of precedent relies, takes hold. It does not follow, of course, that anyone injured in any way by the negligence of another must have the same concrete right to recover that she has. It may be that competing rights require a compromise in the later case that they did not require in hers. But it might well follow that the plaintiff in the later case has the same abstract right, and if that is so then some special argument citing the competing rights will be required to show that a contrary decision in the later case would be fair.

2. *The Seamless Web.* — Hercules' first conclusion, that the gravitational force of a precedent is defined by the arguments of principle that support the precedent, suggests a second. Since judicial practice in his community assumes that earlier cases have a *general* gravitational force, then he can justify that judicial practice only by supposing that the rights thesis holds in his community. It is never taken to be a satisfactory argument against the gravitational force of some precedent that the goal that precedent served has now been served sufficiently, or that the courts would now be better occupied in serving some other goal that has been relatively neglected, possibly returning to the goal the precedent served on some other occasion. The practices of precedent do not suppose that the *rationales* that recommend judicial decisions can be served piecemeal in that way. If it is acknowledged that a particular precedent is justified for a particular reason; if that reason would also recommend a particular result in the case at bar; if the earlier decision has not been recanted or in some other way taken as a matter of institutional regret; then that decision must be reached in the later case.

Hercules must suppose that it is understood in his community, though perhaps not explicitly recognized, that judicial decisions must be taken to be justified by arguments of principle rather than arguments of policy. He now sees that the familiar concept used by judges to explain their reasoning from precedent, the concept of certain principles that underlie or are embedded in the common law, is itself only a metaphorical statement of the rights thesis. He may henceforth use that concept in his decisions of hard common law cases. It provides a general test for deciding such cases that is like the chess referee's concept of the character of a game, and like his own concept of a legislative purpose. It provides a question — What set of principles best justifies the precedents? — that builds a bridge between the general justification of the practice of precedent, which is fairness, and his own decision about what that general justification requires in some particular hard case.

Hercules must now develop his concept of principles that underlie the common law by assigning to each of the relevant precedents some scheme of principle that justifies the decision of that precedent. He will now discover a further important difference between this concept and the concept of statutory purpose that he used in statutory interpretation. In the case of statutes, he found it necessary to choose some theory about the purpose of the particular statute in question, looking to other acts of the legislature only insofar as these might help to select between theories that fit the statute about equally well. But if the gravitational force of precedent rests on the idea that fairness requires the consistent enforcement of rights, then Hercules must discover principles that fit, not only the particular precedent to which some litigant directs his attention, but all other judicial decisions within his general jurisdiction and, indeed, statutes as well, so far as these must be seen to be generated by principle rather than policy. He does not satisfy his duty to show that his decision is consistent with established principles, and therefore fair, if the principles he cites as established are themselves inconsistent with other decisions that his court also proposes to uphold.

Suppose, for example, that he can justify Cardozo's decision in favor of Mrs. MacPherson by citing some abstract principle of equality, which argues that whenever an accident occurs then the richest of the various persons whose acts might have contributed to the accident must bear the loss. He nevertheless cannot show that that principle has been respected in other accident cases, or, even if he could, that it has been respected in other branches of the law, like contract, in which it would also have great impact if it were recognized at all. If he decides against a future accident plaintiff who is richer than the defendant, by appealing to this alleged right of equality, that plaintiff may properly complain that the decision is just as inconsistent with the government's behavior in other cases as if *MacPherson* itself had been ignored. The law may not be a seamless web; but the plaintiff is entitled to ask Hercules to treat it as if it were.

You will now see why I called our judge Hercules. He must construct a scheme of abstract and concrete principles that provides a coherent justification for all common law precedents and, so far as these are to be justified on principle, constitutional and statutory provisions as well. We may grasp the magnitude of this enterprise by distinguishing, within the vast material of legal decisions that Hercules must justify, a vertical and a horizontal ordering. The vertical ordering is provided by distinguishing layers of authority; that is, layers at which official decisions might be taken to be controlling over decisions made at lower levels. In the United States the rough character of the vertical ordering is apparent. The constitutional structure occupies the highest level, the decisions of the Supreme Court and perhaps other courts interpreting that structure the next, enactments of the various legislatures the next and decisions of the various courts developing the common law different levels below that. Hercules must arrange justification of principle at each of these levels so that the justification is consistent with principles taken to provide the justification of higher levels. The horizontal ordering simply requires that the principles taken to justify a decision at one level must also be consistent with the justification offered for other decisions at that level.

Suppose Hercules, taking advantage of his unusual skills, proposed to work out this entire scheme in advance, so that he would be ready to confront litigants with an entire theory of law should this be necessary to justify any particular decision. He would begin, deferring to vertical ordering, by setting out and refining the constitutional theory he has already used. That constitutional theory would be more or less different from the theory that a different judge would develop, because a constitutional theory requires judgments about complex issues of institutional fit, as well as judgments about political and moral philosophy, and Hercules' judgments will inevitably differ from those other judges would make. These differences at a high level of vertical ordering will exercise considerable force on the scheme each judge would propose at lower levels. Hercules might think, for example, that certain substantive constitutional constraints on legislative power are best justified by postulating an abstract right to privacy against the state, because he believes that such a right is a consequence of the even more abstract right to liberty that the constitution guarantees. If so, he would regard the failure of the law of tort to recognize a parallel abstract right to privacy against fellow citizens, in some concrete form, as an inconsistency. If another judge did not share his beliefs about the connection between privacy and liberty, and so did not accept his constitutional interpretation as persuasive, that judge would also disagree about the proper development of tort.

So the impact of Hercules' own judgments will be pervasive, even though some of these will be controversial. But they will not enter his calculations in such a way that different parts of the theory he constructs can be attributed to his independent convictions rather than to the body of law that he must justify.

He will not follow those classical theories of adjudication I mentioned earlier, which suppose that a judge follows statutes or precedent until the clear direction of these runs out, after which he is free to strike out on his own. His theory is rather a theory about what the statute or the precedent itself requires, and though he will, of course, reflect his own intellectual and philosophical convictions in making that judgment, that is a very different matter from supposing that those convictions have some independent force in his argument just because they are his.[27]

3. Mistakes. — I shall not now try to develop, in further detail, Hercules' theory of law. I shall mention, however, two problems he will face. He must decide, first, how much weight he must give, in constructing a scheme of justification for a set of precedents, to the arguments that the judges who decided these cases attached to their decisions. He will not always find in these opinions any proposition precise enough to serve as a statute he might then interpret. But the opinions will almost always contain argument, in the form of propositions that the judge takes to recommend his decision. Hercules will decide to assign these only an initial or prima facie place in his scheme of justification. The purpose of that scheme is to satisfy the requirement that the government must extend to all the rights it supposes some to have. The fact that one officer of the government offers a certain principle as the ground of his decision may be taken to establish prima facie that the government does rely that far upon that principle.

But the main force of the underlying argument of fairness is forward-looking, not backward-looking. The gravitational force of Mrs. MacPherson's case depends not simply on the fact that she recovered for her Buick, but also on the fact that the government proposes to allow others in just her position to recover in the future. If the courts proposed to overrule the decision, no substantial argument of fairness, fixing on the actual decision in the case, survives in favor of the plaintiff in *Spartan Steel.* If, therefore, a principle other than the principle Cardozo cited can be found to justify *MacPherson*, and if this other principle also justifies a great deal of precedent that Cardozo's does not, or if it provides a smoother fit with arguments taken to justify decisions of a higher rank in vertical order, then this new principle is a more satisfactory basis for further decisions. Of course, this argument for not copying Cardozo's principle is unnecessary if the new principle is more abstract, and if Cardozo's principle can be seen as only a concrete form of that more abstract principle. In that case Hercules incorporates, rather than rejects, Cardozo's account of his decision. Cardozo, in fact, used the opinion in the

[27] *See* pp. 1101–09 *infra.*

earlier case of *Thomas v. Winchester*,[28] on which case he relied, in just that fashion. It may be, however, that the new principle strikes out on a different line, so that it justifies a precedent or a series of precedents on grounds very different from what their opinions propose. Brandeis' and Warren's famous argument about the right to privacy [29] is a dramatic illustration: they argued that this right was not unknown to the law but was, on the contrary, demonstrated by a wide variety of decisions, in spite of the fact that the judges who decided these cases mentioned no such right. It may be that their argument, so conceived, was unsuccessful, and that Hercules in their place, would have reached a different result. Hercules' theory nevertheless shows why their argument, sometimes taken to be a kind of brilliant fraud, was at least sound in its ambition.

Hercules must also face a different and greater problem. If the history of his court is at all complex, he will find, in practice, that the requirement of total consistency he has accepted will prove too strong, unless he develops it further to include the idea that he may, in applying this requirement, disregard some part of institutional history as a mistake. For he will be unable, even with his superb imagination, to find any set of principles that reconciles all standing statutes and precedents. This is hardly surprising: the legislators and judges of the past did not all have Hercules' ability or insight, nor were they men and women who were all of the same mind and opinion. Of course, any set of statutes and decisions can be explained historically, or psychologically, or sociologically, but consistency requires justification, not explanation, and the justification must be plausible and not sham. If the justification he constructs makes distinctions that are arbitrary and deploys principles that are unappealing, then it cannot count as a justification at all.

Suppose the law of negligence and accidents in Hercules' jurisdiction has developed in the following simplified and imaginary way. It begins with specific common law decisions recognizing a right to damages for bodily injury caused by very dangerous instruments that are defectively manufactured. These cases are then reinterpreted in some landmark decision, as they were in *MacPherson*, as justified by the very abstract right of each person to the reasonable care of others whose actions might injure his person or property. This principle is then both broadened and pinched in different ways. The courts, for example, decide that no concrete right lies against an accountant who has been negligent in the preparation of financial statements. They also

---

[28] 6 N.Y. 397 (1852).

[29] Warren & Brandeis, *The Right of Privacy*, 4 HARV. L. REV. 193 (1890).

decide that the right cannot be waived in certain cases; for example, in a standard form contract of automobile purchase. The legislature adds a statute providing that in certain cases of industrial accident, recovery will be allowed unless the defendant affirmatively establishes that the plaintiff was entirely to blame. But it also provides that in other cases, for example, in airplane accidents, recovery will be limited to a stipulated amount, which might be much less than the actual loss; and it later adds that the guest in an automobile cannot sue his host even if the host drives negligently and the guest is injured. Suppose now, against this background, that Hercules is called upon to decide *Spartan Steel.*

Can he find a coherent set of principles that justifies this history in the way that fairness requires? He might try the proposition that individuals have no right to recover for damages unless inflicted intentionally. He would argue that they are allowed to recover damages in negligence only for policy reasons, not in recognition of any abstract right to such damages, and he would cite the statutes limiting liability to protect airlines and insurance companies, and the cases excluding liability against accountants, as evidence that recovery is denied when policy argues the other way. But he must concede that this analysis of institutional history is incompatible with the common law decisions, particularly the landmark decision recognizing a general right to recovery in negligence. He cannot say, compatibly with the rest of his theory, that these decisions may themselves be justified on policy grounds, if he holds, by virtue of the rights thesis, that courts may extend liability only in response to arguments of principle and not policy. So he must set these decisions aside as mistakes.

He might try another strategy. He might propose some principle according to which individuals have rights to damages in just the circumstances of the particular cases that decided they did, but have no general right to such damages. He might concede, for example, a legal principle granting a right to recover for damages incurred within an automobile owned by the plaintiff, but deny a principle that would extend to other damage. But though he could in this way tailor his justification of institutional history to fit that history exactly, he would realize that this justification rests on distinctions that are arbitrary. He can find no room in his political theory for a distinction that concedes an abstract right if someone is injured driving his own automobile but denies it if he is a guest or if he is injured in an airplane. He has provided a set of arguments that cannot stand as a coherent justification of anything.

He might therefore concede that he can make no sense of institutional history except by supposing some general abstract right to recover for negligence: but he might argue that it is a relatively weak right and so will yield to policy considerations of relatively minor force. He will cite the limiting statutes and cases in support of his view that the right is a weak one. But he will then face a difficulty if, though the statute limiting liability in airplane accidents has never been repealed, the airlines have become sufficiently secure, and the mechanisms of insurance available to airlines so efficient and inexpensive, that a failure to repeal the statute can only be justified by taking the abstract right to be so weak that relatively thin arguments of policy are sufficient to defeat it. If Hercules takes the right to be that weak then he cannot justify the various common law decisions that support the right, as a concrete right, against arguments of policy much stronger than the airlines are now able to press. So he must choose either to take the failure to repeal the airline accident limitation statute, or the common law decisions that value the right much higher, as mistakes.

In any case, therefore, Hercules must expand his theory to include the idea that a justification of institutional history may display some part of that history as mistaken. But he cannot make impudent use of this device, because if he were free to take any incompatible piece of institutional history as a mistake, with no further consequences for his general theory, then the requirement of consistency would be no genuine requirement at all. He must develop some theory of institutional mistakes, and this theory of mistakes must have two parts. It must show the consequences for further arguments of taking some institutional event to be mistaken; and it must limit the number and character of the events than can be disposed of in that way.

He will construct the first part of this theory of mistakes by means of two sets of distinctions. He will first distinguish between the specific authority of any institutional event, which is its power as an institutional act to effect just the specific institutional consequences it describes, and its gravitational force. If he classifies some event as a mistake, then he does not deny its specific authority, but he does deny its gravitational force, and he cannot consistently appeal to that force in other arguments. He will also distinguish between embedded and corrigible mistakes; embedded mistakes are those whose specific authority is fixed so that it survives their loss of gravitational force; corrigible mistakes are those whose specific authority depends on gravitational force in such a way that it cannot survive this loss.

The constitutional level of his theory will determine which mistakes are embedded. His theory of legislative supremacy, for example, will insure that any statutes he treats as mistakes will lose their gravitational force but not their specific authority. If he denies the gravitational force of the aircraft liability limitation statute, the statute is not thereby repealed; the mistake is embedded so that the specific authority survives. He must continue to respect the limitations the statute imposes upon liability, but he will not use it to argue in some other case for a weaker right. If he accepts some strict doctrine of precedent, and designates some judicial decision, like the decision denying a right in negligence against an accountant, a mistake, then the strict doctrine may preserve the specific authority of that decision, which might be limited to its enactment force, but the decision will lose its gravitational force; it will become, in Justice Frankfurter's phrase, a piece of legal flotsam or jetsam. It will not be necessary to decide which.

That is fairly straightforward, but Hercules must take more pains with the second part of his theory of mistakes. He is required, by the justification he has fixed to the general practice of precedent, to compose a more detailed justification, in the form of a scheme of principle, for the entire body of statutes and common law decisions. But a justification that designates part of what is to be justified as mistaken is prima facie weaker than one that does not. The second part of his theory of mistakes must show that it is nevertheless a stronger justification than any alternative that does not recognize any mistakes, or that recognizes a different set of mistakes. That demonstration cannot be a deduction from simple rules of theory construction, but if Hercules bears in mind the connection he earlier established between precedent and fairness, this connection will suggest two guidelines for his theory of mistakes. In the first place, fairness fixes on institutional history, not just as history but as a political program that the government proposed to continue into the future; it seizes, that is, on forward-looking, not the backward-looking implications of precedent. If Hercules discovers that some previous decision, whether a statute or a judicial decision, is now widely regretted within the pertinent branch of the profession, that fact in itself distinguishes that decision as vulnerable. He must remember, second, that the argument from fairness that demands consistency is not the only argument from fairness to which government in general, or judges in particular, must respond. If he believes, quite apart from any argument of consistency, that a particular statute or decision was wrong because unfair, within the community's own concept of fairness, then that belief is sufficient to distinguish the decision, and make it vulnerable. Of course, he must apply the guidelines with a sense of the vertical structure of his overall justification, so that decisions at a lower level are more vulnerable than decisions at a higher.

Hercules will therefore apply at least two maxims in the second part of his theory of mistakes. If he can show, by arguments of history or by appeal to some sense of the legal community, that a particular principle, though it once had sufficient appeal to persuade a legislature or court to a legal decision, has now so little force that it is unlikely to generate any further such decisions, then the argument from fairness that supports that principle is undercut. If he can show by arguments of political morality that such a principle, apart from its popularity, is unjust, then the argument from fairness that supports that principle is overridden. Hercules will be delighted to find that these discriminations are familiar in the practice of other judges. The jurisprudential importance of his career does not lie in the novelty, but just in the familiarity, of the theory of hard cases that he has now created.

V. Political Objections

The rights thesis has two aspects. Its descriptive aspect explains the present structure of the institution of adjudication. Its normative aspect offers a political justification for that structure. The story of Hercules shows how familiar judicial practice might have developed from a general acceptance of the thesis. This at once clarifies the thesis by showing its implications in some detail, and offers powerful, if special, argument for its descriptive aspect. But the story also provides a further political argument in favor of its normative aspect. Hercules began his calculations with the intention, not simply to replicate what other judges do, but to enforce the genuine institutional rights of those who came to his court. If he is able to reach decisions that satisfy our sense of justice, then that argues in favor of the political value of the thesis.

It may now be said, however, by way of rebuttal, that certain features of Hercules' story count against the normative aspect of the thesis. In the introductory part of this essay I mentioned a familiar objection to judicial originality: this is the argument from democracy that elected legislators have superior qualifications to make political decisions. I said that this argument is weak in the case of decisions of principle, but Hercules' story may give rise to fresh doubts on that score. The story makes plain that many of Hercules' decisions about legal rights depend upon judgments of political theory that might be made differently by different judges or by the public at large. It does not matter, to this objection, that the decision is one of principle rather than policy. It matters only that the decision is one of political conviction about which reasonable men disagree. If Hercules decides cases on the basis of such judgments, then he decides on the basis of his own convictions and preferences, which seems unfair, contrary to democracy, and offensive to the rule of law.

That is the general form of the objection I shall consider in this final Part. It must first be clarified in one important respect. The objection charges Hercules with relying upon his own convictions in matters of political morality. That charge is ambiguous, because there are two ways in which an official might rely upon his own opinions in making such a decision. One of these, in a judge, is offensive, but the other is inevitable.

Sometimes an official offers, as a reason for his decision, the fact that some person or group holds a particular belief or opinion. A legislator might offer, as a reason for voting for an anti-abortion statute, the fact that his constituents believe that abortion is wrong. That is a form of appeal to authority: the official who makes that appeal does not himself warrant the substance of the belief to which he appeals, nor does he count the soundness of the belief as part of his argument. We might imagine a judge appealing, in just this way, to the fact that he *himself* has a particular political preference. He might be a philosophical skeptic in matters of political morality. He might say that one man's opinion in such matters is worth no more than another's, because neither has any objective standing, but that, since he himself happens to favor abortion, he will hold anti-abortion statutes unconstitutional.

That judge relies upon the naked fact that he holds a particular political view as itself a justification for his decision. But a judge may rely upon his own belief in the different sense of relying upon the truth or soundness of that belief. Suppose he believes, for example, that the due process clause of the Constitution, as a matter of law, makes invalid any constraint of a fundamental liberty, and that anti-abortion statutes constrain a fundamental liberty. He might rely upon the soundness of those convictions, not the fact that he, as opposed to others, happens to hold them. A judge need not rely upon the soundness of any *particular* belief in this way. Suppose the majority of his colleagues, or the editors of a prominent law journal, or the majority of the community voting in some referendum, holds a contrary view about abortion. He may decide that it is his duty to defer to their judgment of what the Constitution requires, in spite of the fact that their view is, as he thinks, unsound. But in that case he relies upon the soundness of his own conviction that his institutional duty is to defer to the judgment of others in this matter. He must, that is, rely upon the substance of his own judgment at some point, in order to make any judgment at all.

Hercules does not rely upon his own convictions in the first of these two ways. He does not count the fact that he himself happens to favor a particular conception of religious liberty, for example, as providing an argument in favor of a decision that advances that conception. If the objection we are considering is pertinent, therefore, it must be an objection to his relying upon his own convictions in the second way. But in that case the objection cannot be a blanket objection to his relying upon any of his convictions, because he must, inevitably, rely on some. It is rather an objection to his relying on the soundness of certain of his own convictions; it argues that he ought to defer to others in certain judgments even though their judgments are, as he thinks, wrong.

It is difficult, however, to see *which* of his judgments the objection supposes he should remand to others. We would not have any such problem if Hercules had accepted, rather than rejected, a familiar theory of adjudication. Classical jurisprudence supposes, as I said earlier, that judges decide cases in two steps: they find the limit of what the explicit law requires, and they then exercise an independent discretion to legislate on issues which the law does not reach. In the recent abortion cases,[30] according to this theory, the Supreme Court justices first determined that the language of the due process clause and of prior Supreme Court decisions did not dictate a decision either way. They then set aside the Constitution and the cases to decide whether, in their opinion, it is fundamentally unfair for a state to outlaw abortion in the first trimester.

Let us imagine another judge, called Herbert, who accepts this theory of adjudication and proposes to follow it in his decisions. Herbert might believe both that women have a background right to abort fetuses they carry, and that the majority of citizens think otherwise. The present objection argues that he must resolve that conflict in favor of democracy, so that, when he exercises his discretion to decide the abortion cases, he must decide in favor of the prohibitive statutes. Herbert might agree, in which case we should say that he has set aside his morality in favor of the people's morality. That is, in fact, a slightly misleading way to put the point. His own morality made the fact that the people held a particular view decisive; it did not withdraw in favor of the substance of that view. On the other hand, Herbert might disagree. He might believe that background rights in general, or this right in particular, must prevail against popular opinion even

[30] Roe v. Wade, 410 U.S. 113 (1973); Doe v. Bolton, 410 U.S. 179 (1973).

in the legislature, so that he has a duty, when exercising a legislative discretion, to declare the statutes unconstitutional. In that case, the present objection argues that he is mistaken, because he insufficiently weighs the principle of democracy in his political theory.

In any case, however, these arguments that seem tailor-made for Herbert are puzzling as arguments against Hercules. Hercules does not first find the limits of law and then deploy his own political convictions to supplement what the law requires. He uses his own judgment to determine what legal rights the parties before him have, and when that judgment is made nothing remains to submit to either his own or the public's convictions. The difference is not simply a difference in ways of describing the same thing: we saw in Part III that a judgment of institutional right, like the chess referee's judgment about the forfeiture rule, is very different from an independent judgment of political morality made in the interstices provided by the open texture of rules.

Herbert did not consider whether to consult popular morality until he had fixed the legal rights of the parties. But when Hercules fixes legal rights he has already taken the community's moral traditions into account, at least as these are captured in the whole institutional record that it is his office to interpret. Suppose two coherent justifications can be given for earlier Supreme Court decisions enforcing the due process clause. One justification contains some principle of extreme liberality that cannot be reconciled with the criminal law of most of the states, but the other contains no such principle. Hercules cannnot seize upon the former justification as license for deciding the abortion cases in favor of abortion, even if he is himself an extreme liberal. His own political convictions, which favor the more liberal justification of the earlier cases, must fall, because they are inconsistent with the popular traditions that have shaped the criminal law that his justification must also explain.

Of course, Hercules' techniques may sometimes require a decision that opposes popular morality on some issue. Suppose no justification of the earlier constitutional cases can be given that does not contain a liberal principle sufficiently strong to require a decision in favor of abortion. Hercules must then reach that decision, no matter how strongly popular morality condemns abortion. He does not, in this case, enforce his own convictions against the community's. He rather judges that the community's morality is inconsistent on this issue: its constitutional morality, which is the justification that must be given for its constitution as interpreted by its judges, condemns its discrete judgment on the particular issue of abortion. Such conflicts are familiar within individual morality; if we wish to use the concept of a community morality in political theory, we must acknowledge conflicts within that morality as well. There is no question, of course, as to how such a conflict must be resolved. Individuals have a right to the consistent enforcement of the principles upon which their institutions rely. It is this institutional right, as defined by the community's constitutional morality, that Hercules must defend against any inconsistent opinion however popular.

These hypothetical cases show that the objection designed for Herbert is poorly cast as an objection against Hercules. Hercules' theory of adjudication at no point provides for any choice between his own political convictions and those he takes to be the political convictions of the community at large. On the contrary, his theory identifies a particular conception of community morality as decisive of legal issues; that conception holds that community morality is the political morality presupposed by the laws and institutions of the community. He must, of course, rely on his own judgment as to what the principles of that morality are, but this form of reliance is the second form we distinguished, which at some level is inevitable.

It is perfectly true that in some cases Hercules' decision about the content of this community morality, and thus his decision about legal rights, will be controversial. This will be so whenever institutional history must be justified by appeal to some contested political concept, like fairness or liberty or equality, but it is not sufficiently detailed so that it can be justified by only one among different conceptions of that concept. I offered, earlier, Hercules' decision of the free busing case as an example of such a decision; we may now take a more topical example. Suppose the earlier due process cases can be justified only by supposing some important right to human dignity, but do not themselves force a decision one way or the other on the issue of whether dignity requires complete control over the use of one's uterus. If Hercules sits in the abortion cases, he must decide that issue and must employ his own understanding of dignity to do so.

It would be silly to deny that this is a political decision, or that different judges, from different subcultures, would make it differently. Even so, it is nevertheless a very different decision from the decision whether women have, all things considered, a background right to abort their fetuses. Hercules might think dignity an unimportant concept; if he were to attend a new constitutional convention he might vote to repeal the due process clause, or at least to amend it so as to remove any idea of dignity from its scope. He is nevertheless able to decide whether that concept, properly understood, embraces the case of abortion. He is in the shoes of the chess referee who hates meritocracy, but is nevertheless able to consider whether intelligence includes psychological intimidation.

It is, of course, necessary that Hercules have some understanding of the concept of dignity, even if he denigrates that concept; and he will gain that understanding by noticing how the concept is used by those to whom it is important. If the concept figures in the justification of a series of constitutional decisions, then it must be a concept that is prominent in the political rhetoric and debates of the time. Hercules will collect his sense of the concept from its life in these contexts. He will do the best he can to understand the appeal of the idea to those to whom it does appeal. He will devise, so far as he can, a conception that explains that appeal to them.

This is a process that can usefully be seen as occupying two stages. Hercules will notice, simply as a matter of understanding his language, which are the clear, settled cases in which the concept holds. He will notice, for example, that if one man is thought to treat another as his servant, though he is not in fact that man's employer, then he will be thought to have invaded his dignity. He will next try to put himself, so far as he can, within the more general scheme of beliefs and attitudes of those who value the concept, to look at these clear cases through their eyes. Suppose, for example, that they believe in some Aristotelian doctrine of the urgency of self-fulfillment, or they take self-reliance to be a very great virtue. Hercules must construct some general theory of the concept that explains why those who hold that belief, or accept that virtue, will also prize dignity; if his theory also explains why he, who does not accept the belief or the virtue, does not prize dignity, then the theory will be all the more successful for that feature.

Hercules will then use his theory of dignity to answer questions that institutional history leaves open. His theory of dignity may connect dignity with independence, so that someone's dignity is compromised whenever he is forced, against his will, to devote an important part of his activity to the concerns of others. In that case, he may well endorse the claim that women have a constitutional liberty of abortion, as an aspect of their conceded constitutional right to dignity.

That is how Hercules might interpret a concept he does not value, to reach a decision that, as a matter of background morality, he would reject. It is very unlikely, however, that Hercules will often find himself in that position; he is likely to value most of the concepts that figure in the justification of the institutions of his own community. In that case his analysis of these concepts will not display the same self-conscious air of sociological inquiry. He will begin within, rather than outside, the scheme of values that approves the concept, and he will be able to put to himself, rather than to some hypothetical self, questions about the deep morality that gives the concept value. The sharp distinction between background and institutional morality will fade, not because institutional morality is displaced by personal convictions, but because personal convictions have become the most reliable guide he has to institutional morality.

It does not follow, of course, that Hercules will even then reach exactly the same conclusions that any other judge would reach about disputed cases of the concept in question. On the contrary, he will then become like any reflective member of the community willing to debate about what fairness or equality or liberty requires on some occasion. But we now see that it is wrong to suppose that reflective citizens, in such debates, are simply setting their personal convictions against the convictions of others. They too are contesting different conceptions of a concept they suppose they hold in common; they are debating which of different theories of that concept best explains the settled or clear cases that fix the concept. That character of their debate is obscured by the fact that they do value the concepts they contest, and therefore reason intuitively or introspectively rather than in the more sociological mode that an outsider might use; but, so long as they put their claims as claims about concepts held in common, these claims will have the same structure as the outsider's. We may summarize these important points this way: the community's morality, on these issues at least, is not some sum or combination or function of the competing claims of its members; it is rather what each of the competing claims claims to be. When Hercules relies upon his own conception of dignity, in the second sense of reliance we distinguished, he is still relying on his own sense of what the community's morality provides.

It is plain, therefore, that the present objection must be recast if it is to be a weapon against Hercules. But it cannot be recast to fit Hercules better without losing its appeal. Suppose we say that Hercules must defer, not to his own judgment of the institutional morality of his community, but to the judgment of most members of that community about what that is. There are two apparent objections to that recommendation. It is unclear, in the first place, how he could discover what that popular judgment is. It does not follow from the fact that the man in the street disapproves of abortion, or supports legislation making it criminal, that he has considered whether the concept of dignity presupposed by the Constitution, consistently applied, supports his political position. That is a sophisticated question requiring some dialectical skill, and though that skill may be displayed by the ordinary man when he self-consciously defends his position, it is not to be taken for granted that his political preferences, expressed casually or in the ballot, have been subjected to that form of examination.

But even if Hercules is satisfied that the ordinary man has decided that dignity does not require the right to abortion, the question remains why Hercules should take the ordinary man's opinion on that issue as decisive. Suppose Hercules thinks that the ordinary man is wrong; that he is wrong, that is, in his philosophical opinions about what the community's concepts require. If Herbert were in that position, he would have good reason to defer to the ordinary man's judgments. Herbert thinks that when the positive rules of law are vague or indeterminate, the litigants have no institutional right at all, so that any decision he might reach is a piece of fresh legislation. Since nothing he decides will cheat the parties of what they have a right to have at his hands, the argument is plausible, at least, that when he legislates he should regard himself as the agent of the majority. But Hercules cannot take that view of the matter. He knows that the question he must decide is the question of the parties' institutional rights. He knows that if he decides wrongly, as he would do if he followed the ordinary man's lead, he cheats the parties of what they are entitled to have. Neither Hercules nor Herbert would submit an ordinary legal question to popular opinion; since Hercules thinks that parties have rights in hard cases as well as in easy ones, he will not submit to popular opinion in hard cases either.

Of course, any judge's judgment about the rights of parties in hard cases may be wrong, and the objection may try, in one final effort, to capitalize on that fact. It might concede, *arguendo,* that Hercules' technique is appropriate to Hercules, who by hypothesis has great moral insight. But it would deny that the same technique is appropriate for judges generally, who do not. We must be careful, however, in assessing this challenge, to consider the alternatives. It is a matter of injustice when judges make mistakes about legal rights, whether these mistakes are in favor of the plaintiff or defendant. The objection points out that they will sometimes make such mistakes, because they are fallible and in any event disagree. But of course, though we, as social critics, know that mistakes will be made, we do not know when because we are not Hercules either. We must commend techniques of adjudication that might be expected to reduce the number of mistakes overall based on some judgment of the relative capacities of men and women who might occupy different roles.

Hercules' technique encourages a judge to make his own judgments about institutional rights. The argument from judicial fallibility might be thought to suggest two alternatives. The first argues that since judges are fallible they should make no effort at all to determine the institutional rights of the parties before them, but should decide hard cases only on grounds of policy, or not at all. But that is perverse; it argues that because judges will often, by misadventure, produce unjust decisions they should make no effort to produce just ones. The second alternative argues that since judges are fallible they should submit questions of institutional right raised by hard cases to someone else. But to whom? There is no reason to credit any other particular group with better facilities of moral argument; or, if there is, then it is the process of selecting judges, not the techniques of judging that they are asked to use, that must be changed. So this form of skepticism does not in itself argue against Hercules' technique of adjudication, though of course it serves as a useful reminder to any judge that he might well be wrong in his political judgments, and that he should therefore decide hard cases with humility.

JOSEPH RAZ

Authority and Justification

This article defends a certain conception of the nature of practical authority, that is, authority with power to require action. The explanation proceeds through normative theses of three kinds. One concerns the type of argument required to justify a claim that a certain authority is legitimate. The second states the general character of the considerations which should guide the actions of authorities. The last concerns the way the existence of a binding authoritative directive affects the reasoning of the subjects of the authority. The explanation and defense of the three theses is preceded by an introductory section defending the general approach to the analysis of authority adopted here, and introducing some of the themes which are explored in greater detail later in the article.

I. Authority and Reason

It is common to regard authority over persons as centrally involving a right to rule, where that is understood as correlated with an obligation to obey on the part of those subject to the authority. Robert Ladenson has recently challenged this common view. He agrees that political authority is a right to rule, but denies that it entails an obligation to obey. That political authority is a right to rule means, according to him, that "strong reasons can be advanced for holding that possession of the governmental power and acceptance by those one presumes to govern of its exercise jointly constitute a justification for coercive acts which would

I am grateful to R. M. Dworkin, J. M. Finnis, K. Kress, D. Miller, and to the Editors of *Philosophy & Public Affairs* for helpful comments on earlier drafts of this article.

otherwise be immoral."[1] Power over a person here is not normative power. It means "the ability to make that person do what one wishes."[2]

It is clear that not every power amounts to an authority. My neighbor can stop me from growing tall trees in my garden by threatening to burn rubbish by my border. He, therefore, has some power over me but no authority. Nor does his power turn into an authority just by the fact that I acquiesce and do not pick a fight with him. An authority, according to Ladenson, has a justification-right to possess and exercise its power. A justification-right is contrasted with a claim-right in not implying any obligations. My neighbor's justification-right to threaten me does not mean that I have a duty to obey him. It merely means that he does no wrong in threatening me and this is compatible with my having a right to resist him.[3]

Let us therefore assume that such threats are in general wrong because they interfere with a person's use of his own property. Let us further assume that my neighbor has nevertheless the right to threaten me either because my growing tall trees will greatly harm his interests, or for whatever other reason seems an acceptable justification, provided it is compatible with our final assumption, that is, that I have the right to resist him (both his and my rights being justification-rights). It seems clear that my neighbor does not have authority over me just because he can affect my behavior and would be justified in doing so. If this is authority, we all have authority over our neighbors. Nor is it clear whether Ladenson would deny that. He adds two further elements to his explanation of political authority. First, it is authority to use coercion. Second, it is justified by the fact that its possessor successfully exercises governmental power with the acquiescence of his subjects. It is tempting to say that these two conditions do not belong to an explanation of authority over persons generally. They simply establish which authorities are political authorities. But perhaps it is wrong to factor out the explanation of political authority into two separate parts, an explanation of authority and

1. R. Ladenson, "In Defense of a Hobbesian Conception of Law," *Philosophy & Public Affairs* 9, no. 2 (Winter 1980): 139.

2. Ibid., p. 137.

3. If I understood his meaning, Ladenson regards "having a justification right to do A" as meaning being justified in doing A. This is to confuse "having a right to do A" with "doing A is alright." But my argument does not depend on rejecting Ladenson's conception of rights.

of what makes it political. Let us therefore examine the two conditions that Ladenson requires.

It seems plain that the justified use of coercive power is one thing and authority is another. I do not exercise authority over people afflicted with dangerous diseases if I knock them out and lock them up to protect the public, even though I am, in the assumed circumstances, justified in doing so. I have no more authority over them than I have over mad dogs. The exercise of coercive or of any other form of power is no exercise of authority unless it includes an appeal to compliance by the person(s) subject to the authority. That is why authority is typically exercised by giving instructions of one kind or another. But appeal to compliance makes sense precisely because it is an invocation of the duty to obey.

Some, particularly those with Hobbesian sympathies, may think that there is an alternative and a better explanation of the fact that authority is usually exercised by issuing directives. These are, they will say, threats or coercive threats. There can indeed be no doubt that threats are another type of what may be loosely called "appeals to compliance." Nor do I doubt that all political authorities must and do resort to extensive use of and reliance on coercive and other threats. Yet all legal authorities do much more. They claim to impose duties and to confer rights. Courts of law find offenders and violators guilty or liable for wrongdoing. None of these or similar claims have much to do with threatening people. To threaten is not to impose a duty, nor is it to claim that one does. None of this shows that legal authorities have a right to rule, which implies an obligation to obey. But it reminds us of the familiar fact that they claim such a right, that is, they are de facto authorities because they claim a right to rule and because they succeed in establishing and maintaining their rule. They have legitimate authority only if and to the extent that their claim is justified and they are owed a duty of obedience. Ladenson's mistake is to think that since there can be political authority which is not owed a duty of obedience, there can also be one which does not claim that it is owed such a duty.

It should be clear by now that Ladenson's last condition—that the authority has a justification-right to use coercion because it regularly exercises governmental power with the acquiescence of its subjects—cannot retrieve the situation. Acquiescence seems relevant to the explanation of de facto authority rather than to that of legitimate authority. To have effective political control requires, in the circumstances of our world, a high degree of acquiescence. Ladenson's conception of authority amounts to a claim that all de facto authorities are legitimate. It is a familiar Hobbesian view which will be challenged in the next section. But can it really be claimed to be faithful to the main features of the notion of political authority prevalent in our culture?

To test it, try to imagine a situation in which the political authorities of a country do not claim that the inhabitants are bound to obey them, but in which the population does acquiesce to their rule. We are to imagine courts imprisoning people without finding them guilty of any offense. Damages are ordered, but no one has a duty to pay them. The legislature never claims to impose duties of care or of contribution to common services. It merely pronounces that people who behave in certain ways will be made to suffer. And it is not merely ordinary people who are not subjected to duties by the legislature; courts, policemen, civil servants, and other public officials are not subjected by it to any duties in the exercise of their official functions either.

Two things stand out when contemplating a political system of this kind. First, it is unlikely that any such society ever existed. Societies we know about invariably are subject to institutions claiming a right to bind their subjects, and when they survive, this is in part because at least some of their subjects accept their claim. Second, if such a society were to exist we would not regard it as being governed by authority. It is too unlike the political institutions we normally regard as authorities.

The two points are related. The second is a conceptual point. But we have the concept of authority that we do because in our world societies are governed by institutions claiming and being acknowledged to have the right to bind their subjects. Ladenson's analysis is not merely not an analysis of the concept of authority which is part of our cultural tradition. It is an analysis of a concept that does not have much use in our world.

To conclude: Ladenson offers an explanation of legitimate authority in terms of de facto authority. It is justified de facto authority. De facto authority is then understood as some form of power over people. The analysis fails because the notion of a de facto authority cannot be understood except by reference to legitimate authority. Having de facto authority is not just having an ability to influence people. It is coupled with a claim that those people are bound to obey.

How is authority to be related to the nebulous notion of a valid requirement for the obedience of one's subjects? As Richard Flathman disapprovingly remarked, "There has been a remarkable coalescence of opinion around the proposition that authority and authority relations involve some species of 'surrender of judgment' on the part of those who accept, submit or subscribe to the authority of persons or a set of rules and offices. From anarchist opponents of authority such as William Godwin and Robert Paul Wolff through moderate supporters such as John Rawls and Joseph Raz and on to enthusiasts such as Hobbes, Hannah Arendt and Michael Oakeshott, a considerable chorus of students have echoed the refrain that the directives . . . of authority are to be obeyed by B irrespective of B's judgments of their merits."[4]

But what is "a surrender of judgment"? H.L.A. Hart, who has recently added his voice in support of this kind of analysis, provides the following explanation. "The commander characteristically intends his hearer to take the commander's will instead of his own as a guide to action and so to take it in place of any deliberation or reasoning of his own: the expression of the commander's will . . . is intended to preclude or cut off any independent deliberation by the hearer of the merits pro and con of doing the act."[5] This explanation is, however, implausible. Surely what counts, from the point of view of the person in authority, is not what the subject thinks but how he acts. I do all that the law requires of me if my actions comply with it. There is nothing wrong with my considering the merits of the law or of action in accord with it. Reflection on the merits of actions required by authority is not automatically prohibited by any authoritative directive, though possibly it could be prohibited by a special directive to that effect.

Richard Friedman offers an explanation aimed at the same target which avoids this objection:

> The idea being conveyed by such notions as the surrender of private judgment . . . is that in obeying, say, a command simply because it comes from someone accorded the right to rule, the subject does not make his obedience *conditional* on his own personal examination and evaluation of the thing he is being asked to do. Rather, he accepts as

4. R. E. Flathman, *The Practice of Political Authority* (Chicago: University of Chicago Press, 1980), p. 90.

5. H.L.A. Hart, *Essays on Bentham* (Oxford: Oxford University Press, 1982), p. 253. I used to hold a similar view. See my comment on Chisholm in *Practical Reasoning*, ed. S. Korner (Oxford: Basil Blackwell, 1974).

> a sufficient reason for following a prescription the fact that it is prescribed by someone acknowledged by him as entitled to rule. The man who accepts authority is thus said to surrender his private or individual judgment because he does not insist that reasons be given that he can grasp and that satisfy him, as a condition of his obedience.[6]

Is this conception of authority correct? One point to remember (it is consistent with Friedman's account) is that a person may have limited authority (for instance, in matters concerning football only, or in military affairs, but not in the conduct of the economy). It should be noted that Friedman's explanation shows how misleading the metaphor of "surrendering one's judgment" can be. Unlike Hart's, Friedman's explanation shifts the emphasis from the subjects' deliberations to their actions. The subjects accept that someone has authority over them only if their willingness to do his bidding is not conditional on their agreement on the merits of performing the actions required by the authority.

This condition is open to two interpretations. The minimalist interpretation maintains that they are willing to obey if they have no judgment of their own on the merits of performing the required action. They will not then defer decision until they form their own judgment. The maximalist interpretation claims that the subjects accept that they should obey even if their personal belief is that the balance of reasons on the merits is against performing the required act.

The minimalist interpretation is too weak since it assumes that people are never bound by authority regarding issues on which they have firm views. The maximalist interpretation is more promising, and the views to be argued for in the rest of this article explore and develop it. Either way no surrender of judgment in the sense of refraining from forming a judgment is involved. For there is no objection to people forming their own judgment on any issue they like. Nor does one surrender one's judgment if that means acting against one's judgment. For an authority is legitimate only if there are sufficient reasons to accept it, that is, sufficient reasons to follow its directives regardless of the balance of reasons on the merits of such action.

There are more ways than one in which a metaphor can mislead. It

6. R. B. Friedman, "On the Concept of Authority in Political Philosophy," in *Concepts in Social and Political Philosophy*, ed. R. E. Flathman (New York: Macmillan, 1973), p. 129.

can sometimes mislead people who perceive clearly the fallacies the metaphor invites and therefore reject it altogether, turning a blind eye to the true insight it encapsulates. This happened to the many theorists who thought they had a simple explanation for the confusion of thought which led to the surrender of judgment metaphor. According to them, to accept the legitimacy of an authority is simply to accept that whatever other reasons there may be for a certain action, its being required by the authority is an additional reason for its performance. Inasmuch as that additional reason may tip the balance, one can perhaps overdramatize the situation by saying that an authoritative requirement is a reason to act against the balance of reasons on the merits of the case. This means no more than that the authoritative requirement is an additional factor. Much the same can be said of any reason for action. The fact that it will rain tomorrow, for example, may mean that I should not go to London, even though the balance of reasons on the merits of my going (that is, all the reasons pro and con but the rain) suggests that I should go.

This description of the relevance of authority to practical reasoning is profoundly misguided. It is wrong not in what it says, but in what it leaves out and implicitly denies. To be sure, if a person accepts the legitimacy of an authority then its instructions are accepted by him as reason for conforming action. But until we understand how and why the instructions are such reasons and how they differ from ordinary reasons, we will not begin to understand the nature of authority. Perhaps the point can be best brought out by considering authority first as it functions in one, not untypical, context.

Consider the case of two people who refer their dispute to an arbitrator. He has authority to settle the dispute for they have agreed to abide by his decision. Two features stand out. First, the arbitrator's decision is for the disputants a reason for action. They ought to do as he says because he says so. But this reason is related to the other reasons which apply to the case. It is not (like the rain in the example of my going to London) just another reason to be added to the others, a reason to stand alongside the others when one reckons which way is better supported by reason. The arbitrator's decision is meant to be based on the other reasons, to sum them up and to reflect their outcome. He has reason to act so that his decision will reflect the reasons which apply to the litigants. I shall call reasons of this character dependent reasons. I shall also refer to his decision as a dependent reason for the litigants. Notice that in this second sense a dependent reason is not one which does in fact reflect the balance of reasons on which it is based. It is one which is meant to do so.

This leads directly to the second distinguishing feature of the example. The arbitrator's decision is also meant to replace the reasons on which it depends. In agreeing to obey his decision they agreed to follow his judgment of the balance of reasons rather than their own. Henceforth, his decision will settle for them what to do. Lawyers say that the original reasons merge into the decision of the arbitrator or the judgment of a court, which, if binding, become *res judicata*. This means that the original cause of action can no longer be relied upon for any purpose. I shall call a reason which displaces others a preemptive reason.[7]

It is not that the arbitrator's word is an absolute reason which has to be obeyed come what may. It can be challenged and justifiably refused in certain circumstances. If, for example, the arbitrator was bribed, or was drunk while considering the case, or if new evidence of great importance unexpectedly turns up, each party may ignore the decision. The point is that reasons that could have been relied upon to justify action before his decision cannot be relied upon once the decision is given. Note that there is no reason for anyone to restrain their thoughts or their reflections on the reasons which apply to the case, nor are they necessarily debarred from criticizing the arbitrator for having ignored certain reasons or for having been mistaken about their significance. It is merely action for some of these reasons which is excluded.

The two features, dependence and preemptiveness, are intimately connected. Because the arbitrator is meant to decide on the basis of certain reasons, the disputants are excluded from later relying on them. They handed over to him the task of evaluating those reasons. If the disputants do not then reject these reasons as possible bases for their own action, they defeat the very point and purpose of the arbitration. The only proper way to acknowledge the arbitrator's authority is to take it to be a reason for action which replaces the reasons on the basis of which he was meant to decide.

7. In the first chapter of *The Authority of Law* (Oxford: Oxford University Press, 1979), I explained some of the formal features of preemptive reasons. My analysis has been criticized by Flathman in *The Practice of Political Authority*, among others. It is not possible to reply to the criticism here.

II. The Dependence Thesis

The crucial question is whether the arbitrator's is a typical authority, or whether the two features picked out above are peculiar to it and perhaps a few others, but are not characteristic of authorities in general. It might be thought, for example, that the arbitrator is typical of adjudicative authorities, and that what might be called legislative authorities differ from them in precisely these respects. Adjudicative authorities, one might say, are precisely those in which the role of the authority is to judge what reasons apply to its subjects and decide accordingly, that is, their decisions are merely meant to declare what ought to be done in any case.

A legislative authority on the other hand is one whose job is to create new reasons for its subjects, reasons which are new not merely in the sense of replacing other reasons on which they depend, but in not purporting to replace any reasons at all. If we understand "legislative" and "adjudicative" broadly, so the objection continues, all practical authorities belong to at least one of these kinds.[8] It will be conceded, of course, that legislative authorities act for reasons. But theirs are reasons which apply to them and which do not depend on, that is, which are not meant to reflect, reasons which apply to their subjects. A military commander should order his troops in the way best calculated to achieve victory at a minimal cost. If he wisely orders his men to occupy a certain hill, it does not follow that they had reason to occupy that hill even before they were ordered to do so. Parliament is to distribute the burden of taxation in an equitable way, but it does not follow that the citizens had any reason to pay tax before the passing of the (just) tax law.

These are telling points. But the argument is by no means over. First, even if not all legislative authorities share the characteristics of dependence and preemptiveness we found in the arbitrator's case, it is plain that some do. Consider, for example, an act of Parliament imposing on parents a duty to maintain their young children. Parents have such a duty independently of this act, and only because they have it is the act justified. Parliament, of course, is not limited to the enactment of laws where there is a prior obligation on the subjects to behave in the required way. But

8. This would be a very wide interpretation indeed. It would, e.g., count my instruction to my son to be back by midnight as legislative, and the policeman's order to move on when a driver stops in a prohibited zone as adjudicative. But this liberality does not affect the argument.

there can be, and perhaps there are authorities which are so limited. Note that the decrees of such a body will be binding even if they in fact err as to what people's obligations are. The arbitrator's decision is binding even if mistaken and so are the decrees of our imagined legislator. Both are meant to decide on the basis of dependent reasons and therefore their decisions are preemptive.

The example shows that the objector's neat distinction between adjudicative and legislative authorities is mistaken. The mark of the adjudicator is simply that he is called upon to decide what parties in dispute should have done or should do in the circumstances of a particular case. Nevertheless, the objector may well remain convinced that many legislative authorities are not meant to act on dependent reasons and that their directives are not preemptive. So let us consider his examples with some care.

One simplifying assumption has to be explained before we proceed. We have been concerned with the authoritative imposition of duties. But authorities, even practical authorities, do much else besides. They can declare that a certain day shall be a national holiday, that a certain organization shall have legal personality, that a person shall be granted citizenship or shall be divorced or excommunicated, that certain land shall be dedicated to the public, or that some people shall have certain rights, and much else.

Concentration on the imposition of duties does not, however, distort our understanding of authority since all the other functions authorities may have are ultimately explained by reference to the imposition of duties. The possession of citizenship, for instance, is important because it confers rights (such as the right to vote in general elections) and duties (such as the duty of loyalty). Rights themselves are grounds for holding others to be duty-bound to protect or promote certain interests of the right-holder. Legal personality is the capacity to have rights and duties. In every case the explanation of the normative effect of the exercise of authority leads back, sometimes through very circuitous routes, to the imposition of duties either by the authority itself or by some other persons. It is therefore possible to explain "authority" by explaining the sense in which authorities can impose duties.

One difficulty is that prising apart the imposition of duties from other effects of the exercise of authority is far from straightforward. Consider a tax law again. It not only imposes a duty to pay, but also sets up (not necessarily in the same statute) the machinery for collecting and distributing the money. When the imagined objector said that there was no reason to pay the money now due as tax before the tax law was passed, he was of course right. But is this because there was then no machinery for collecting and distributing the money or because there was no authority-imposed duty to pay it?

For the first two years of World War I there was no conscription in Britain, but there was machinery to recruit volunteers. So this may be the sort of case we are looking for, a case in which the effect of the duty can be separated from the effect of other aspects of authoritative action. In this case, at any rate, the conclusion is clear. By and large, those who approved of conscription when it came did so because they believed that everyone had a duty to serve in the armed forces in any case, or at least that everyone ought to have done so. They would have denied that the conscription law had imposed a completely new duty. It merely declared what people ought to have done. Because the doubters were bound by the fact that they acknowledged the authority of Parliament to follow Parliament's judgment as to what their duties were, its act is not merely dependent on those duties but also preempts them.

We are to imagine a situation in which the State provides all the services it currently provides, let us say roads and a sewerage system, free education and a free health service, social security and unemployment benefits, and the like. They are provided by raising money from the public for a state-run charity, contributions to which are voluntary, but which publishes guidelines for self-assessment for those who wish to use them. I hope it will be agreed that those who think that the tax law is justified do so partly because they believe that there is in the circumstances imagined a reason to contribute voluntarily a sum which is equivalent to a just tax.

Let us take stock of the argument so far. I am arguing for one main thesis claiming that authoritative reasons are preemptive: *The fact that an authority requires performance of an action is a reason for its performance which is not to be added to all other relevant reasons when assessing what to do, but should exclude and take the place of some of them.* It will be remembered that the thesis is only about legitimate authority. It is relevant for the explanation of de facto authorities because every de facto authority claims or is acknowledged by others to be a legitimate authority. But since not every authority is legitimate, not every authoritative directive is a reason for action.

Furthermore, authoritative directives are not beyond challenge. First, they may be designed not to determine finally what is to be done in certain circumstances but merely to determine what is to be done on the basis of certain considerations. For example, a directive may determine that from the economic point of view a certain action is required. It will then replace economic considerations but no others. Or the authority may direct that the final decision must be based on economic considerations only, thus replacing all but the economic factors. Even where an authoritative decision is meant to settle finally what is to be done, it may be open to challenge on certain grounds, for example, if an emergency occurs, or if the directive violates fundamental human rights, or if the authority acted arbitrarily. The nonexcluded reasons and the grounds of challenging an authority's directives vary from case to case. They determine the conditions of legitimacy of the authority and the limits of its rightful power.

This point is worth emphasizing not only because of its importance in the developing argument to follow, but also because it marks the way in which my use of "the limit of an authority's rightful power" differs from some common uses (though it conforms with others including the legal usage). Sometimes authorities are understood to be limited by the kinds of acts they can or cannot regulate (given some restrictive ways of classifying acts). In this article authorities are said to be limited also by the kinds of reason on which they may or may not rely in making decisions and issuing directives, and by the kinds of reasons their decisions can preempt.

The argument for the preemption thesis proceeds from another, which I shall call the dependence thesis. It says: *All authoritative directives should be based, in the main, on reasons which already independently apply to the subjects of the directives and are relevant to their action in the circumstances covered by the directive.* Such reasons I termed above "dependent reasons." The examples of conscription and taxation were intended to give the dependence thesis some plausibility, and in particular to disprove the suggestion that dependence is the mark of adjudication. But doubts are bound to linger and further clarifications are required to dispel them.

A few preliminary points. The dependence thesis does not claim that authorities always act for dependent reasons, but merely that they should do so. Ours is an attempt to explain the notion of legitimate authority through describing what one might call an ideal exercise of authority. Reality has a way of falling short of the ideal. We saw this regarding de facto authorities which are not legitimate. But naturally not even legitimate authorities always succeed, nor do they always try to live up to the ideal. It is nevertheless through their ideal functioning that they must be understood. For that is how they are supposed to function, that is how they publicly claim that they attempt to function, and, as we shall see below, that is the normal way to justify their authority (that is, not by assuming that they always succeed in acting in the ideal way, but on the ground that they do so often enough to justify their power), and naturally authorities are judged and their performance evaluated by comparing them to the ideal.

Remember also that the thesis is not that authoritative determinations are binding only if they correctly reflect the reasons on which they depend. On the contrary, there is no point in having authorities unless their determinations are binding even if mistaken (though some mistakes may disqualify them). The whole point and purpose of authorities, I shall argue below, is to preempt individual judgment on the merits, and this will not be achieved if in order to establish whether the authoritative determination is binding individuals have to rely on their own judgment of the merits.

Nor does the thesis claim that authorities should always act in the interests of their subjects. Its claim is that they should act for reasons which apply also to their subjects, but these need not be reasons advancing their interests. A military commander, for example, should put the defense of his country above the interests of his soldiers. He may therefore order them to act against their own interests. But then soldiers are supposed to put their country above their personal interests, and only because of this should they obey their commander.

Much of the resistance to the dependence thesis comes from confusing it with a claim about what authorities do in fact, or with the view that requires authorities to act only in the interests of their subjects. But the most common confusion is between the dependence thesis and another which can be called *the no-difference thesis*, which asserts that *the exercise of authority should make no difference to what its subjects ought to do*, for it ought to direct them to do what they ought to do in any event.[9] It may appear that the dependence thesis entails the no-difference thesis. But this is not the case. There are at least four ways in which authority acting correctly may make a difference to what its subjects ought to do, which are all consistent with the dependence thesis.

First, the dependence thesis does not exclude the authority from acting for additional reasons which apply to it alone, and not to its subjects. All it requires is that it shall act primarily for dependent reasons. The force of the qualification and the role other reasons are allowed to have will be explained below. Typical examples of considerations which affect authoritative decisions but do not apply to individuals acting on their own are considerations arising out of the needs and limitations of bureaucracies. They have to be considered alongside substantive considerations which do apply to the individual subjects of the law or any other authority. The intrusion of the bureaucratic considerations is likely to require a solution which differs from the one an individual should have adopted if left to himself. But since the right authoritative solution is also, we assume, based on some dependent reasons, it conforms to the dependence thesis.

Second, many aspects of every action we perform for a reason are not uniquely determined by reasons. I have a reason to buy a loaf of bread but, let us assume, no reason to prefer a sliced loaf to an unsliced one or vice versa. Since I have a reason to buy a loaf of bread, I have a reason to buy a sliced loaf, as well as a reason to buy an unsliced one. But I have no reason to get one rather than the other. Since there is no other kind of bread, inevitably if I do as I have reason to and buy a loaf, I will buy one or the other. That is, in acting for the best reasons I will also inevitably transcend reason and take a deliberate decision (e.g., to buy a sliced loaf) concerning some aspects of which reason is undetermined.

The same general considerations apply to directives issued by authorities. The legislator, for example, has reason to impose a certain tax. There are reasons showing that it is better to require that the tax be paid either in quarterly or in monthly payments. These intervals are superior to all others. But while some reasons favor monthly payments and others favor quarterly ones, neither is sufficient to establish the superiority of doing it one way rather than the other. In this situation the authority

9. The no-difference thesis is about what happens if authorities reach the right decision. Since their directives are binding even when mistaken, they do then make a difference.

may leave the choice to individuals, but sometimes there are decisive reasons against doing so. Then the authority has to decide on one of the two or more acceptable options.[10] When this happens the authoritative directive does make a difference. Without it individuals would have had a choice of which of the acceptable solutions to adopt. The authority quite properly denies them the choice and exercises it itself.

Third, one important function of authoritative directives is to establish and help sustain conventions, Conventions are here understood in a narrow sense in which they are solutions to coordination problems, that is, to situations in which the vast majority have sufficient reason to prefer to take that action which is (likely to be) taken by the vast majority. Where there is a coordination problem the issuing of an authoritative directive can supply the missing link in the argument. It makes it likely that a convention will be established to follow the authoritatively designated act. It is often the proper job of authorities to issue directives for this purpose. Such authoritative directives provide the subjects with reasons which they did not have before. They therefore make a difference to their practical deliberations, and serve to refute the no-difference thesis.

These cases are not only common (though they hardly ever occur in the much oversimplified form we have considered), but are also of some theoretical interest. Once the directive is issued, individuals have reasons to take the action it requires which they did not have before because now there is ground to expect that a convention will be formed. But while this shows that the directive made a difference, it does not refute the dependence thesis. The authority took the action in order to help generate a convention. In so doing it acted for a dependent reason, for the assumption is that individuals have reason to wish for a convention and hence reason to take action to help form one. Every person in the group concerned has, before the directive is issued, a reason both to form a convention and to follow it once formed. This is the reason for which the legislation is adopted and it is, for the legislator, a dependent reason.

Fourth, prisoner's-dilemma type situations are another class of cases where authorities make a difference while conforming with the dependence thesis.[11] In these cases while people have reason to act in a certain

10. It would be a mistake to think of them as exactly tied options. All that is assumed here is that reasons are insufficient to establish the superiority of one option over the others.

11. On the role of authorities in prisoner's-dilemma type situations, see Ullman-Margalit, *The Emergence of Norms* (Oxford: Oxford University Press, 1980).

way given the situation they are in, they also have reason to change the situation. It is this feature, shared by cases where there are coordination problems, which enables authorities to make a difference while acting on dependent reasons. It should be remembered that many moral theories may land their adherents in prisoner's-dilemma type situations. The problem does not arise merely through lack of moral fiber.[12]

The considerations adumbrated above do not prove the dependence thesis. They adduce support for it mainly by removing misunderstanding and a few possible objections. Implicitly the argument appeals to our common understanding of the way authority should be exercised. The argument gains much strength by considering the case of theoretical authority, that is, authority for believing in certain propositions. Nowadays it is not the fashion to talk of authorities in this context. Instead we have experts. But the notions are very similar, at least in all that matters to our concerns.

There is likely to be ready agreement that experts of all varieties are to give advice based on the very same reasons which should sway ordinary people who wish to form their minds independently. The experts' advantage is in their easy access to the evidence and in their better ability to grasp its significance. But the evidence on which they should base their advice to me is the same evidence on which it would have been appropriate for me to form my own judgment. It is possible that practical and theoretical authorities have little in common. But it is more likely that, while they provide reasons for different things, they share the same basic structure. If so, the fact that a dependence thesis is true of theoretical authorities is strong evidence to suppose that it holds for practical authorities as well.

III. The Justification of Authority

The dependence thesis, it will be remembered, is a moral thesis about the way authorities should use their powers. It is closely connected with a second moral thesis about the type of argument which could be used to establish the legitimacy of an authority. I shall call it *the "normal justification thesis."* It claims that *the normal and primary way to establish that a person should be acknowledged to have authority over*

12. For an analysis of the way prisoner's dilemma problems arise within the bounds of various moral theories, see D. Parfit, *Reasons and Persons* (Oxford: Oxford University Press, 1984), chap. 4.

another person involves showing that the alleged subject is likely better to comply with reasons which apply to him (other than the alleged authoritative directives) if he accepts the directives of the alleged authority as authoritatively binding and tries to follow them, rather than by trying to follow the reasons which apply to him directly.

This way of justifying a claim that someone has legitimate authority, that is, that those subject to his authority should acknowledge the authoritative force of his directives, is not the only one. It is, however, the normal and primary one. Consider the case of a person whose reason for accepting his friend's advice is that the friend will be hurt if he does not. This may well be a perfectly good reason for accepting advice, but it is not the normal reason. It is regrettable that the friend will be hurt if his advice is not followed after it was given due consideration, or at least it is regrettable that he will be hurt to a degree which justifies this reaction. The friend himself does not intend his advice to be accepted for that reason, and is likely to be doubly hurt if he finds out that his advice was judged mistaken on the merits but was followed in order not to hurt him. The friend will be hurt because even when this is a good reason to accept advice, it is not a reason to accept it as a piece of advice. It is a reason to accept it as a way of being kind to a friend.

The normal reason for accepting a piece of advice is that it is likely to be sound advice. The normal reason to offer advice is the very same. It will be clear that these judgments of normality are normative. But we can understand the very nature of advice only if we understand in what spirit it is meant to be offered and for what reasons it is meant to be taken. The explanation must leave room for deviant cases, for their existence is undeniable. But it must also draw the distinction between the deviant and the normal, for otherwise the very reason why the "institution" exists and why deviant cases take the special form they do remains inexplicable.

The example of advice is close to the case of authority. Indeed some, though not all, advice is authoritative advice. It is, for example, sometimes justifiable to accept someone's authority in order not to hurt his feelings. Many grown-up people feel obliged by such considerations to continue to acknowledge the authority of their parents over them. But just as in the case of advice, and for the very same reasons, such grounds for recognizing the authority of another, even though sometimes good, are always deviant grounds.

Slightly different considerations show that some reasons for recognizing the authority of another are secondary. To call them secondary means that they are valid reasons which are, in normal cases, sufficient only in combination with the primary reasons (whereas deviant reasons may validly replace the normal reasons). Accepting the authority of a person or an institution is, for example, a way of defining one's own identity as a member of a nation or some other group, though needless to say it is unlikely to be the only way any person will express his identification with such a group. Such a reason can be perfectly valid, but only (according to the normal justification thesis) if the normal and primary justification applies to the same case as well. The secondary justification serves to lower the burden of proof required to establish the primary justification, that is, they may suffice in conjunction in circumstances in which the primary justification will not by itself be enough to establish the legitimacy of an authority. But reasons of identification and self-definition cannot by themselves establish the legitimacy of an authority.

Identification is a common and often proper ground for accepting authority. It is therefore important to establish the reasons why it is no more than a secondary justification dependent on the availability, at least to a certain degree, of another justification. Acceptance of an authority can be an act of identification with a group because it can be naturally regarded as expressing trust in the person or institution in authority and a willingness to share the fortunes of the group which are to a large extent determined by the authority. But trust in an authority is trust that the authority is likely to discharge its duties properly. It therefore presupposes a principle which should govern its activities. Accepting the authority as a way of identifying with a group is justified only if the trust is not altogether misplaced. Otherwise the odd situation may result that a person will quite properly express his identification with a group by supporting an institution which grossly betrays its duties to the group. For the same reasons one cannot properly express one's willingness to share the fortunes of a group by submitting to an authority which grossly betrays the trust it owes to the group. Identification with the group in such circumstances calls for the rejection of that authority.

The dependence and the normal justification theses are mutually reinforcing. If the normal and primary way of justifying the legitimacy of an authority is that it is more likely to act successfully on the reasons which apply to its subjects, then it is hard to resist the dependence thesis. It merely claims that authorities should do that which they were appointed to do. Conversely, if the independence thesis is accepted, then the case for the normal justification thesis becomes very strong. It merely states that the normal and primary justification of any authority has to establish that it is qualified to follow with some degree of success the moral principle which should govern the decisions of all authorities. Together the two theses present a comprehensive view of the nature and role of legitimate authority. They articulate the service conception of the function of authorities, that is, the view that their role and primary normal function is to serve the governed. This, to repeat a point made earlier, does not mean that their only role must be to further the interest of each or of all of their subjects. It is to help them act on reasons which bind them.

The service conception, that is, the two theses taken together, clarifies one point which the dependence thesis itself left vague. As we saw, the thesis requires authorities to act primarily for dependent reasons. But it left unexplained the place and possible importance of the others. The justification thesis, which explains that acting for the dependent reasons is the normal function of authorities, explains the point. Sometimes one has to act for nondependent reasons. Bureaucracies, for example, are almost invariably forced to embrace a *de minimis* rule in order to be able to achieve their tasks where it really matters. The justification thesis, in other words, establishes the subservience of the nondependent reasons which should guide authoritative action to the dependent ones.

It will be noticed that the normal justification thesis identifies the case that must normally be established to show that a person has authority. It is not a matter of showing that he is entitled to have authority, but that he has it, that he is an authority, with all the consequences which follow from this fact. The main objection to this point revolves around the feeling that a person can have authority, be an authority or in authority, only if his authority is recognized by some people whose identity varies with the nature of the authority. The difficulty in assessing this point is that in most cases the normal justification cannot be established unless the putative authority enjoys some measure of recognition and exercises power over its subjects. There is a strong case for holding that no political authority can be legitimate unless it is also a de facto authority. The case for the legitimacy of any political authority rests to a large extent on its ability to solve coordination problems and extricate the population from prisoner's-dilemma type situations.

These considerations explain why to say of someone that he is entitled to have authority means that he should be in a position of real power, for then he will have legitimate authority. They may be sufficient to account for the feeling that as a matter of meaning, recognition is a condition of possessing legitimate authority. If I am right, then this is not a matter of meaning but of normative justification.

The normal justification thesis allows for deviant and secondary reasons. Apart from these it is meant to account for the reasons there can be for accepting authorities. But a complete justification of authority has to do more than provide valid reasons for its acceptance. It also has to establish that there are no reasons against its acceptance which defeat the reasons for the authority. Because the reasons against the acceptance of authority vary, it is not possible to discover in advance how strong the reasons for acceptance of the authority need be to be sufficient.

Some reasons against the acceptance of authority pertain, with varying force, to many situations. One recurring kind of reason against accepting the authority of one person or institution is that there is another person or institution with a better claim to be recognized as an authority. The claim of the second is a reason against accepting the claim of the first only when the two authorities are incompatible, as are the claims of two governments to be legitimate governments of one country. Sometimes there are two compatible authorities whose powers overlap, as is the case with the authority of both parents over their children.

Another cluster of recurring considerations concerns the intrinsic desirability of people conducting their lives by their own lights. This obviously applies to some areas of life more than to others, to choice of friends more than to choice of legal argument in a court case. The case for the validity of a claim to authority must include justificatory considerations sufficient to outweigh such counterreasons. That is one reason why the case is hard to make. But if anarchists are right to think that it can never be made, this is for contingent reasons and not because of any inconsistency in the notion of a rational justification for authority, nor in the notion of authority over moral agents.

IV. The Preemptive Thesis

From the dependence and normal justification theses it is but a short step to the preemption thesis. It turns on the general relation between the justification for a binding directive and its status as a reason for action, and more generally the relation between rules as reasons for action and their justification. Consider the rule that when being with one person and meeting another, one should introduce them to each other. The fact that this is a sound, valid, or sensible rule is a reason for anyone to act in accordance with it. It is a sound rule because it facilitates social contact. But the fact that introducing people to each other in those circumstances facilitates social contacts is itself a reason for doing so. Do we then have two independent reasons for introducing people? Clearly not. When considering the weight or strength of the reasons for an action, the reasons for the rule cannot be added to the rule itself as additional reasons. We must count one or the other, but not both. Authoritative directives are often rules, and even when they are not because they lack the required generality, the same reasoning applies to them. Either the directive or the reasons for holding it to be binding should be counted, but not both. To do otherwise is to be guilty of double-counting.

This fact is a reflection of the role of rules in practical concrete decisions. They provide an intermediate level of reasons to which one appeals in normal cases where a need for a decision arises. Reasons of that level can themselves be justified by reference to the deeper concerns on which they are based. The advantage of normally proceeding through the mediation of rules is enormous. It enables a person to consider and form an opinion on the general aspects of recurrent situations in advance of their occurrence. It enables a person to achieve results which can be attained only through an advance commitment to a whole series of actions, rather than by case-to-case examination.

Most importantly, the practice allows the creation of a pluralistic culture. For it enables people to unite in support of some "low or medium level" generalizations despite profound disagreements concerning their ultimate foundations which some seek in religion, others in Marxism or in Liberalism, and the like. I am not suggesting that the differences in the foundations do not lead to differences in practice. The point is that an orderly community can exist only if it shares many practices and that in all modern pluralistic societies a great measure of toleration of vastly differing outlooks is made possible by the fact that many of them enable the vast majority of the population to accept common standards of conduct.

More directly relevant to our case is the fact that through the acceptance of rules which set up authorities, people can entrust judgment to another person or institution which will then be bound, in accordance with the dependence thesis, to exercise its best judgment primarily on the basis of the dependent reasons appropriate to the case. Thus the mediation of authorities may, where justified, improve people's compliance with practical and moral principles. This often enables them better to achieve the benefits that rules may bring as explained above, and other benefits besides.

These reflections on the mediating role of authoritative directives and of rules generally explain why they are reasons for actions. Ultimately, however, directives and rules derive their force from the considerations which justify them, that is, they do not add further weight to their justifying considerations. In any case in which one penetrates beyond the directives or the rules to their underlying justifications one has to discount the independent weight of the rule or the directive as a reason for action. Whatever force they have is completely exhausted by those underlying considerations. Contrariwise, whenever one takes a rule or a directive as a reason one cannot add to it as additional independent factors the reasons which justify it.

Hence the preemption thesis. Since the justification of the binding force of authoritative directives rests on dependent reasons, the reasons on which they depend are (to the extent that the directives are regarded simply as authoritative) replaced rather than added to by those directives. The service conception leads to the preemption thesis. Because authorities do not have the right to impose completely independent duties on people, because their directives should reflect dependent reasons which are binding on those people in any case, they should have the right to replace people's own judgment on the merits of the case. Their directives preempt the force of at least some of the reasons which otherwise should have guided the actions of those people.[13]

13. A. M. Honoré pointed out that even if an (informal) arbitration concluded in my favor, if I later become convinced that my original claim was mistaken, I should acknowledge the claim of the other litigant rather than rely on the arbitrator's decision. Here it seems as if, contrary to the preemption thesis, the original reasons are not preempted by the arbitrator's decision. Nevertheless one's duty undergoes a complete change in such circumstances. I may rely on the arbitrator. I may say that we both agreed that our relations will be governed by his decision, that I would have gone along with it had he made a mistake which harmed me. I would be rather ungenerous and unfriendly but nevertheless formally correct. The situation is the same as in cases of agreement. I buy a chest from you and a price is agreed. It then transpires that the chest is a valuable antique and the price I paid is ludicrously low. If I ought to pay a fair price for what I buy, then I ought to come back and add to the agreed price.

The preemption thesis will be readily accepted inasmuch as it concerns successful authoritative directives, that is, those which correctly reflect the balance of reasons on which they depend. But, a common objection goes, the thesis cannot justify preempting reasons which the authority was meant to reflect correctly and failed to do so. Successfully reflected reasons are those which show that the directive is valid. They are the justification for its binding force. Therefore, either they or the directive should be relied upon, but not both, that is not if relying on both means adding the weight of the directive to the force of the reasons justifying it when assessing the weight of the case for the directed action. Reasons that should have determined the authority's directive but failed to do so cannot be thought to belong to the justification of the directive. On the contrary they tell against it. They are reasons for holding that it is not binding. The preemption thesis is wrong in claiming that they too are preempted.

So much for the objection. It fails because its premise is false. Reasons which authoritative directives should and fail to reflect are nonetheless among the reasons which justify holding the directives binding. An authority is justified, according to the normal justification thesis, if it is more likely than its subjects to act correctly. That is how the subjects' reasons figure in the justification, both when they are correctly reflected in a particular directive and when they are not. If every time a directive is mistaken, that is, every time it fails to reflect reason correctly, it were open to challenges as mistaken, the advantage gained by accepting the authority as a more reliable and successful guide to right reason would disappear. In trying to establish whether or not the directive correctly reflects right reason the subjects will be relying on their own judgments rather than on that of the authority, which, we are assuming, is more reliable.

These reflections suggest another objection to the preemption thesis. It says[14] that in every case authoritative directives can be overridden or disregarded if they deviate much from the reasons which they are meant to reflect. It would not do, the objection continues, to say that the legitimate power of every authority is limited, and that one of the limitations is that it may not err much. For such a limitation defeats the preemption thesis since it requires every person in every instance to consider the

14. This objection was first put to me by R. M. Dworkin who is not responsible for the way it is treated here.

merits of the case before he can decide to accept an authoritative instruction.

The objection does not formally challenge the preemption thesis. It does not claim that the reasons which are supposed to be displaced by authoritative instructions are not replaced by them but should count as additional independent reasons alongside the instructions. Its effect is to deny that authoritative instructions can serve the mediating role assigned them above. That role is to enable people to act on nonultimate reasons. It is to save them the need to refer to the very foundations of morality and practical reasoning generally in every case. But as the directives are binding only if they do not deviate much from right reason and as we should act on them only if they are binding, we always have to go back to fundamentals. We have to examine the reasons for and against the directive and judge whether it is justified in order to decide whether its mistake, if it is not justified, is large or small. The mediating role is unobtainable.

The failure of this objection stems from its confusion of a great mistake with a clear one. Consider a long addition of, say, some thirty numbers. One can make a very small yet clear mistake as when the sum is an integer whereas one and only one of the added numbers is a fraction. On the other hand, the sum may be off by several thousands without the mistake being detectable except by laboriously going over the addition step by step. Even if legitimate authority is limited by the condition that its directives are not binding if clearly wrong, and I wish to express no opinion on whether it is so limited, it can play its mediating role. Establishing that something is clearly wrong does not require going through the underlying reasoning. It is not the case that the legitimate power of authorities is generally limited by the condition that it is defeated by significant mistakes which are not clear.

The preemption thesis depends on a distinction between jurisdictional and other mistakes. Most, if not all, authorities have limited powers. Mistakes which they make about factors which determine the limits of their jurisdiction render their decisions void. They are not binding as authoritative directives, though the circumstances of the case may require giving them some weight if, for example, others innocently relied on them. Other mistakes do not affect the binding force of the directives. The preemption thesis claims that the factors about which the authority was wrong, and which are not jurisdictional factors, are preempted by the directive. The theses would be pointless if most mistakes were jurisdictional or if in most cases it were particularly controversial and difficult to establish which are and which are not. But if this were so, then most other accounts of authority would come to grief.

V. Objections

I will conclude this article by considering a few objections to the account of authority suggested above which challenge its general orientation.

Three theses were presented as part of an explanation of the concept of authority. They are supposed to advance our understanding of the concept by showing how authoritative action plays a special role in people's practical reasoning. But the theses are also normative ones. They instruct people how to take binding directives. The service conception is a normative doctrine about the conditions under which authority is legitimate and the manner in which authorities should conduct themselves. Is that not a confusion of conceptual analysis and normative argument? The answer is that there is an interdependence between conceptual and normative argument.

The philosophical explanation of authority is not an attempt to state the meaning of a word. It is a discussion of a concept which is deeply embedded in the philosophical and political traditions of our culture. The concept serves as an integral part of a whole mesh of ideas and beliefs, leading from one part of the net to another. There is no, nor has there ever been, complete agreement on all aspects of the concept's place and its connection with other concepts. But there is, as part of our common culture, a good measure of agreement between any two people on many, though frequently not the same, points. Accounts of "authority" attempt a double task. They are part of an attempt to make explicit elements of our common traditions, a highly prized activity in a culture which values self-awareness. At the same time such accounts take a position in the traditional debate about the precise connections between that and other concepts. They are partisan accounts furthering the cause of certain strands in the common tradition, by developing and producing new or newly recast arguments in their favor. The very activity is also an expression of faith in the tradition, of a willingness to understand oneself and the world in its terms and to carry on the argument, which in the area with which we are concerned is inescapably a normative argument, within the general framework defining the tradition. Faithfulness to the shape of common concepts is itself an act of normative significance.

How can the account of authority offered here be thought to represent important strands in Western thought? As John Bell pointed out to me, if there is a common theme to liberal political theorizing on authority it is that the legitimacy of authority rests on the duty to support and uphold just institutions, as, following Rawls, the duty is now usually called. But that duty is of course dependent on a prior understanding of which institutions are just. The account here offered is meant as a beginning of an answer to that question. Or rather it contributes by setting the question in a certain way. One has a duty to uphold and support authorities if they meet the conditions of the service conception as explained above.

To the extent that legitimate authorities have power over us, the preemption thesis governs our right attitude to them. The duty to uphold and support just institutions does not come into play. It is primarily an other-regarding duty. I have a duty to support just governments in foreign countries, even though they have no legitimate power over me and I have reason to support the authority of my neighbors over their children. In other words, the duty to uphold and support just institutions comes into play when the conditions of legitimacy implied by the service conception of authority are satisfied. It then supplements the preemption thesis by showing that we should be concerned not merely to have the proper attitudes to those in authority over us, but also to those in authority over others.

Finally, let us return to our starting point. What is wrong with regarding an authoritative directive as one additional prima facie reason for the action it directs, which supplements, rather than supplants, the other reasons for and against that action? The service conception established that the point of having authorities is that they are better at complying with the dependent reasons. Take a simplified situation. I regularly confront a decision whether or not to sell certain shares of stock in varying circumstances. Suppose that it is known that a financial expert reaches the "right" decision (whatever that may be) in twenty percent more cases than I do when I do not rely on his advice. Should I not, when confronting such decisions, carry on as before but take his advice as a factor counting in favor of the decision he recommends?

Perhaps I should always take the case for his solution as being twenty percent stronger than it would otherwise appear to me to be. Perhaps some other, more complicated formula should be worked out. In any case would not the right course require to give his advice prima facie rather than preemptive force? The answer is that it would not. In cases about which I know only that his performance is better than mine, letting his advice tilt the balance in favor of his solution will sometimes, depending on my rate of mistakes and the formula used, improve my performance. But I will continue to do less well than he does unless I let his judgment preempt mine.

This way of reasoning is unrealistically simple even in the relatively straightforward circumstances of simple stock-selling decisions. But it helps to illustrate the general lesson. If another's reasoning is usually better than mine, then comparing on each occasion our two sets of arguments may help me to detect my mistake and mend my reasoning. It may help me more indirectly by alerting me to the fact that I may be wrong, and forcing me to reason again to double-check my conclusion. But if neither is sufficient to bring my performance up to the level of the other person, then my optimific course is to give his decision preemptive force. So long as this is done where improving the outcome is more important than deciding for oneself, this surrender of judgment and acceptance of authority, far from being either irrational or an abdication of moral responsibility, is in fact the most rational course and the right way to discharge one's responsibilities.

LEGAL FORMALITY*

DUNCAN KENNEDY†

> And in this law of Nature, consisteth the Fountain and Originall of JUSTICE. For where no Covenant hath preceded, there hath no Right been transferred, and every man has right to every thing; and consequently, no action can be Unjust. But when a Covenant is made, then to break it is *Unjust*: And the definition of INIUSTICE, is no other than *the not Performance of Covenant.*[1]

1. My first purpose in this essay is to clarify that version of the liberal theory of justice which asserts that justice consists in the impartial application of rules deriving their legitimacy from the prior consent of those subject to them. I will try to show that we can increase our understanding of this argument by recasting it in the form of what I will call the model of formality.

2. In particular, the model of formality is helpful in dealing with the best known of the specific manifestations of the problem of justice in the liberal state, that of the relations between a democratic legislature, an independent judiciary, and private litigants. Take it as a premise that the state may legitimately coerce an individual only if the state action represents the will of a legitimate legal sovereign. Take it as another premise that legitimate legal sovereignty can reside only in a government that is representative of the fundamentally independent and often conflicting wills of the citizenry, "representative" being used here to include both pure majoritarianism and more complex constitutional systems, but with no suggestion of the precipitation of a "general will." Then the fact that in the liberal state it is judges,

* For Friedrich Kessler. This essay has its roots in conversations with Harry Wellington. Richard Epstein, Charles Fried, Phillip Heymann, Brad Honoroff, Morton Horwitz, Louis Jaffe, Arthur Leff, Frank Michelman, Laurence Tribe, David Trubek, Roberto Unger, and Arthur von Mehren commented helpfully on earlier drafts. Errors are mine alone.

† Assistant Professor of Law, Harvard University.

1 Thomas Hobbes, Leviathan 74 (Rhys ed. 1914).

not legislative bodies or elected executive officers, who are in charge of the application of state force to the citizens presents a problem. The version of liberal theory with which I am concerned in this essay attempts to resolve this problem through the idea that the legitimate legal sovereign, representing the citizenry, should make *rules* applying to the various situations in which state coercion might be used. Judges should then apply those rules, acting as agents of the sovereign. According to the theory, legal coercion will then be legitimate, or at least as legitimate as the political process that defines sovereignty.

3. My approach to this doctrine is through an integrated body of postulates and arguments designed to make the best possible case that judges ought to conceive themselves as rule appliers doing the will of law makers postulated to be legitimate. I mean to use the concept of formality to bring together three main strands in liberal theory. These are the contractarian political doctrine of Hobbes and Locke,[2] the tradition of legal positivism from Bentham and Holmes through H.L.A. Hart,[3] and the welfare economic analysis of writers like J.S. Mill and Coase.[4] My conception of the argument in favor of rule application has also been influenced by recent theories of judicial function and judicial role,[5] and by the attempts of scholars to plumb the

[2] Thomas Hobbes, *supra* note 1; John Locke, The Second Treatise of Civil Government, in Two Treatises of Government (Peter Laslett ed. 1960); The Federalist Papers (Rossiter ed. 1961); C. B. Macpherson, The Political Theory of Possessive Individualism: Hobbes to Locke (1962).

[3] Jeremy Bentham, Theory of Legislation (R. Hildreth, trans. 1864); Oliver Wendell Holmes, Jr., The Common Law (1923), and The Path of the Law, 10 Harv. L. Rev. 457 (1897); 2 Max Weber, Economy and Society: An Outline of Interpretive Sociology 641-900 (Guenther Roth & Claus Wittich eds. 1969); David M. Trubek, Max Weber on Law and the Rise of Capitalism, 1972 Wis. L. Rev. 720; Hans Kelsen, Pure Theory of Law and Analytical Jurisprudence, 55 Harv. L. Rev. 44 (1941); Friedrich Kessler, Natural Law, Justice and Democracy: Some Reflections on Three Types of Thinking about Law and Justice, 19 Tul. L. Rev. 33 (1944); Richard A. Wasserstrom, The Judicial Decision: Toward a Theory of Legal Justification (1961); H. L. A. Hart, The Concept of Law (1961); Charles Fried, Two Concepts of Interests: Some Reflections on the Supreme Court's Balancing Test, 76 Harv. L. Rev. 755 (1963). See also Note, Civil Disabilities and the First Amendment, 78 Yale L.J. 842 (1969).

[4] John Stuart Mill, Principles of Political Economy (Winch ed. 1970); Lionel C. Robbins, An Essay on The Nature and Significance of Economic Science (2d ed. 1935); William J. Baumol, Welfare Economics and the Theory of the State (2d ed. 1965); Johannes de v. Graaff, Theoretical Welfare Economics (1967): R.H. Coase, The Problem of Social Cost, 3 J. Law & Econ. 1 (1960); Mancur Olson, The Logic of Collective Action; Public Goods and the Theory of Groups (1965); Frank I. Michelman, Property, Utility and Fairness: Comments on the Ethical Foundations of "Just Compensation" Law, 80 Harv. L. Rev. 1165 (1967); Guido Calabresi, Transaction Costs, Resource Allocation and Liability Rules—A Comment, 11 J. Law & Econ. 67 (1968); A Mitchell Polinsky, Probabilistic Compensation Criteria, 86 Q.J. Econ. 407 (1972).

[5] Louis L. Jaffe, Judicial Review: Question of Law, 69 Harv. L. Rev. 239 (1955); Henry M. Hart & Albert M. Sacks, The Legal Process: Basic Problems in the Making and Application of Law (Tentative ed. 1958); Herbert Wechsler, Toward Neutral

mystery of formalism in the law of contracts.[6] I have found the critics of liberalism[7] as helpful as the proponents, and have tried to use their insights to make the theory as rigorous and complete as possible.

4. The model of formality is *not* a description in the usual sense: it consists solely of postulated concepts and logical connections between them. Throughout this essay, I label the parts of the model in such a way as to facilitate its use in analyzing the problem of the relations between a legislature postulated to be legitimate because somehow "representative," judges, and litigating private parties. But the same model, with the parts relabeled, is useful in analyzing the other specific manifestations of the underlying dilemma of the liberal theory of justice. For example, the problem of formalism in contract law can be conceived as that of the relations between parties who have unanimously agreed to a set of rules, a judge, and those same parties appearing to challenge or defend the rules as they have worked out in practice. Likewise, one can approach the institution of "procedural formalism" (the writ system, the Roman *formula*) and "formalities" (the seal, the Statute of Wills, recording statutes) as attempts to deal with the same fundamental problem of legal order. Much of the exposition of the model of formality is a generalization of earlier theoretical work provoked by these particular instances.

5. My second purpose in this essay is to contribute to the critique of the

---

Principles of Constitutional Law, 73 Harv. L. Rev. 1 (1959); Jan G. Deutsch, Neutrality, Legitimacy and the Supreme Court: Some Intersections Between Law and Political Science, 20 Stan. L. Rev. 169 (1968); Karl N. Llewellyn, The Common Law Tradition: Deciding Appeals (1960), and On Reading and Using the Newer Jurisprudence, 40 Colum. L. Rev. 581 (1940); Charles E. Clark & David M. Trubek, The Creative Role of the Judge: Restraint and Freedom in the Common Law Tradition, 71 Yale L.J. 255 (1961); Lon L. Fuller, The Morality of Law (1964), and The Anatomy of Law (1968); Ronald M. Dworkin, The Model of Rules, 35 Chi. L. Rev. 14 (1967).

6 Rudolf von Ihering, L'Esprit du Droit Romain §§ 50-55 (Meulenaere trans. 1877); Samuel Williston & George J. Thompson, A Treatise on the Law of Contracts (1936); Karl N. Llewellyn, What Price Contract?—An Essay in Perspective, 40 Yale L.J. 704 (1931); George K. Gardner, An Inquiry into the Principles of the Law of Contracts, 46 Harv. L. Rev. 1 (1932); Lon L. Fuller & William R. Perdue, Jr., The Reliance Interest in Contract Damages, I, 46 Yale L.J. 52 (1936); Lon L. Fuller, Consideration and Form, 41 Colum. L. Rev. 799 (1941); Arthur T. von Mehren, Civil Law Analogues to Consideration: An Exercise in Comparative Analysis, 72 Harv. L. Rev. 1009 (1959); Friedrich Kessler & Edith Fine, *Culpa in Contrahendo*, 77 Harv. L. Rev. 401 (1964); John Calamari & Joseph Perillo, A Plea for a Uniform Parol Evidence Rule, 42 Ind. L. Rev. 333 (1967). See also F. W. Maitland, The Forms of Action at Common Law (1936); S. F. C. Milsom, Historical Foundations of the Common Law 1-85 (1969).

7 John R. Commons, Legal Foundations of Capitalism (1957); Georg Lukacs, Reification and the Consciousness of the Proletariat, in History and Class-Consciousness (Rodney Livingstone trans. 1971); E. B. Pashukanis, The General Theory of Law and Marxism, in Soviet Legal Philosophy (1951); Lon L. Fuller, Positivism and Fidelity to Law—A Reply to Professor Hart, 71 Harv. L. Rev. 630 (1958); Roberto Unger, Knowledge and Politics (unpublished manuscript, Harvard Law School). See also the works of Lon L. Fuller and Ronald M. Dworkin cited *supra* at note 5.

version of the liberal theory of legal justice represented by the model of formality. My argument is that a distinction between rule making and rule applying cannot be made to legitimate the coercive power of judges because a theory based on this distinction cannot deal in a satisfactory way with the contingent in History. In other words, this version of liberal thought has been unsuccessful in the attempt to use a theory of rules to transfer the postulated legitimacy of decision based on consent to the judicial administrators of a body of legal rules. I concede for the sake of the argument that rules are at least sometimes perfectly clearly applicable to particular situations, so that the judge cannot in good faith hesitate as to what the theory requires of him. My assertion is that *even under these most favorable conditions* the judge cannot legitimately conceive of himself as a rule applier. The argument is interesting, if it is valid, because it is quite distinct from and more general than the familiar criticisms of positivism, rule utilitarianism, and judicial restraint.

6. My third purpose is to show that while various familiar criticisms of judicial formalism have led American legal thinkers to restate the theory of the judicial role, none of the reformulations manages to evade the fundamental dilemma set out in the second part of this essay.[8] This I attempt to demonstrate through a brief review of prevalent attitudes toward judicial power, emphasizing the ways in which they transform without salvaging the underlying structure of formality.

I. The Theory of Formality

> The professional philosopher, who has no understanding of the peculiar technical interests and needs of law, can see nothing in formalism but . . . a clear derangement of the relationship between form and content. Precisely because his vision is directed to the core of things, . . . this anguished, pedantic cult of symbols wholly worthless and meaningless in themselves, the poverty and pettiness of the spirit that inspires the whole institution of form and

[8] For example, it is a common position that formality denies the judge his proper role as a *non-legislative rule maker*. The theorist then puts forward a set of rules about what kinds of decision are apt for judicial (as opposed to legislative) law making, and urges upon us that so long as the judge *restricts himself within the limits set down*, he can forget about the dilemmas of the mechanical rule applier. Here the theory of formality is driven from the battlefield of substantive law but appears to survive in the maquis of "institutional competence."

> results therefrom—all this, I say, must make a disagreeable and repugnant impression on him. . . . Yet we are here concerned with a manifestation which, just because it is rooted in the innermost nature of law, repeats itself, and will always repeat itself, in the law of all peoples.[9]

A.

7. As I will use the term here, a formal system is one that takes it as a premise that there are only two processes of decision a theorist need take into account when he sets out to build a theory of social order. These are rule application and decision according to purposes, or substantive rationality. Decision according to rule means, in the ideal typical case, the application of *per se* rules, that is, decision by the selection of one (or very few) easily identifiable aspect of the situation, and the justification of the decision uniquely by appeal to the presence or absence of that element. An example of rule application is the dismissal of a suit on an uncontested oral promise on the ground that the Statute of Frauds required a writing.[10] At the other pole, *ad hoc* or substantively rational decision making involves an identification of purposes and then an assessment or weighing by the decision maker of all those aspects of the situation which he feels have some bearing on the achievement of those purposes. Some cases are those of a regional planner

[9] Rudolf von Ihering, 2 II Der Geist das Romischen Recht 478-79 (1883) (A. von Mehren trans.).

[10] This essay is concerned with the activity of judges deciding lawsuits, and the rules discussed are directives to the judge about how to do this. "If such and such facts are found, then do thus and so." As I use the term, it is part of the definition of a rule that it is "absolute" within its scope: if the judge finds such and such to be the case, he either applies (or follows) the rule by doing thus and so, or the rule is no longer in force. It is likewise a matter of definition that rules can only be administered "mechanically," if by this is meant that the judge, as a rule *applier*, must proceed like a machine to do thus and so once such and such are established. See note 15 *infra*. There is, however, no necessity that the rule the judge applies be in any sense "general." When a judge decides a contract case, he may have to establish whether or not a particular named party did or did not do particular acts with regard to a single transaction in named goods. The contract in this situation operates as the factual predicate of a rule the judge administers, although it is hard to imagine a less general prescription. See Ronald M. Dworkin, *supra* note 5, at 22-29; Hans Kelsen, *supra* note 3, at 54-57; H.L.A. Hart, Positivism and the Separation of Law and Morals, 71 Harv. L. Rev. 593, 614-15, 623-24 (1958) (although Hart's concept seems to require *some* generality); Max Weber, 2 Economy and Society, *supra* note 3, at 653-54 (rule application is "law-finding"); French Civil Code, Art. 1134: "Agreements legally formed have the force of law over those who are makers of them."

On the relationship between rules as thus conceived and principles, policies, equity, standards, presumptions and discretion, see note 11 *infra*.

deciding where to locate a dam, a Congressman deciding how to vote on a tariff proposal, or a court deciding a nuisance case.

8. The cases of substantively rational decision that will concern us here are those in which the purposes (values, ends, goals, interests, desires) of the decision maker are in conflict. When this is the case, rational decision involves a comparison of the possible outcomes in terms of some measure more general than any of the conflicting purposes. The decision making process consists, first, of bringing together these heterogeneous purposes on the same plane, within a common field, and, second, of identifying, by means of an objective standard, the outcome that "maximizes" the more general measure by achieving the best "mix" of purposes.[11]

[11] This footnote deals with the question of the role in the theory I am describing of discretion, principles (*e.g.* no one should profit by his own wrong), policies, equity, standards (*e.g.* due care, good faith), and presumptions (*e.g.* one is presumed to know the normal consequences of one's acts). The theory of legal formality consists of the working out of a model; thus it is based on the notion that we will get further with the enterprise of understanding, designing and justifying legal practices if we begin by making some very powerful "simplifying assumptions." The most important of these is that all decisions in the system consist either of rule application or of a substantively rational weighing of purposes, or of some mixed form. Principles, discretion, policies, equity, standards and presumptions are thus dispensed with as distinct elements in the analysis—either they are assimilable to one of the ideal types of decision (or a mixed type) or the theory is simply *not about them*. Consequently, none of them is mentioned in the exposition of the theory in Part I of this essay.

Of course, theories tend to try to expand their scope to cover as much of reality as possible, and the theory of formality is no exception. A basic strategy of the theory is to identify substantively rational decision with discretion, and then to assert that principles, policies, standards, equity and presumptions are all simply technical terms for grants of discretion by the rule maker to the rule applier. Thus the theory assimilates each of the concepts without any revision of the fundamental postulate.

First, standards, etc., are clearly not rules in the sense of the term used here, since they do not identify small groups of easily determined factual aspects of situations as the triggers for the mechanical application of official sanctions. Principles and standards may be asserted to be a part of the bases of decision although taken as a body they are highly contradictory; while rules either fully determine the situations to which they apply or are "no longer in force," a particular principle may be "in force" in some sense even though the result it suggests is rejected in most of the cases to which it is relevant. Even their strongest advocates claim only that principles and standards "guide" (as opposed to "controlling") decision. See Ronald M. Dworkin, *supra* note 5.

But that principles, etc., are not rules does not mean that they are necessarily merely indicators of grants of discretion—of a power to make substantively rational determinations in terms of the purposes of the decision maker. It is possible that they represent processes of decision whose psychological reality is fundamentally different from that of the maximizer or interest balancer. And if this special decision process (or processes) accounts for most of what is important in the law, then the choice of simplifying assumptions on which it is built may have rendered the theory of formality trivial or irrelevant from the very outset.

I think this the most convincing of the objections to the postulates of formality. In note 65 *infra* I mention some of the rather powerful counterarguments. See also note 41 *infra*. In the text, however, I simply assume that the theory of formality can deal with principles, policies, standards, equity and presumptions, either by assimilating them to discretion or by excluding them altogether.

9. The assertion that substantively rational process is as much a characteristic of social systems as of individual psyches is a vital step in the construction of the theory of formality. The conflicting desires of the individual have their equivalent in the conflicting interests of the group members, and rules like majority vote or money bid take the place of notions like the maximization of utility. Some examples of systems that we commonly conceive as designed to produce substantively rational decision in the sense adopted here are: a market for goods, the "marketplace of ideas," a legislature, interest groups in a pluralist democracy, and two parties negotiating a contract.[12]

10. We are accustomed to think of each of these systems as permitting the reflection (or expression, or representation) of each of a set of conflicting purposes in an outcome that is *controlled* by none of them. Everything depends on the force (power, weight, influence) of the competitors, and this, in turn, is determined by the factual situation within which the system exists. Thus the outcome is neither "natural" in the sense of being altogether beyond anyone's control, nor "deliberate," in the sense of being decided in advance by a manager or dictator. Someone sets up the system (except perhaps in the case of the psyche), and whoever performs this constitutional function is, in one sense at least, responsible for the results. But each decision reflects

[12] See Kenneth J. Arrow, Social Choice and Individual Values (2d ed. 1963) and James M. Buchanan & Gordon Tullock, The Calculus of Consent, Logical Foundations of Constitutional Democracy 11-62 (1962). It is a paradox of some interest that substantively rational decision in the presence of conflicting ends or interests cannot be conceived without reference either to the opposed concept of decision according to rule or to that of a natural harmony of ends or interests. This is the "formal" element in the model of substantive rationality. See *id.* and also H. L. A. Hart, *supra* note 10, at 603; Lon L. Fuller, *supra* note 7, at 638-41. First, unless natural harmony produces unanimity, the interaction of "raw interests" is in itself incapable of generating any resolution or common will. Out of the clash of interests (ends, desires, wants, objectives) can come only the fact of conflict. Cf. C. B. Macpherson, *supra* note 2, at 93-94. In order for the clash to have a larger significance—to represent an "outcome"—an "objective," "external," "dis-interested" rule or standard must intervene to assess or measure or evaluate what has happened. Second, unless some natural harmony spontaneously defines its boundaries, a substantively rational decision process implies some criteria that permit us to decide that it *is* in fact a process, rather than just a conflict of randomly colliding forces. These criteria take the form of rules defining those interests that are to be counted or included at the moment when we apply our objective rule of outcome determination (*e.g.*, if the institution of substantively rational decision is a legislature, rules come in both to indicate what number or combination of votes is required for decision and to decide who can vote). Finally, the notion of a decision *process* implies some stability over time, and therefore either a natural harmony that preserves the process from transforming itself into another process, *or* some rules having that effect, such as those forbidding the competing interests from adopting particular tactics thought to be destructive or destabilizing. The remainder of this essay simply assumes that a legitimate and stable substantively rational legislative process is in existence, sustained by some combination of rules and harmonies. The question addressed is whether such an institution can transfer its postulated legitimacy to its judicial agents. See §§ 1, 2. As to whether the rule applying pole of the dichotomy is not as dependent on substantive rationality as substantively rational decision is on rule applying, see note 14 *infra*.

the natural "surround" that determines the force of the competing values or interests, rather than the specific intention of a particular actor.[13]

11. *Formality* consists in the attempt to accomplish substantively rational results—*i.e.*, to achieve outcomes that "maximize" a set of conflicting purposes—through the substantively rational formulation and mechanical application of rules rather than directly through substantively rational decision processes. *Legal formality* is a characteristic of any legal system that can be described in the following way: (a) the purpose of the system is to serve the

[13] The *internal structure* of the concept of substantively rational process I develop here is that of the neoclassical economist's model of action as rational choice and of the psychological model of the self as the passive locus of appetites and aversions. For economics, see generally Lionel C. Robbins, *supra* note 4; Erich Roll, A History of Economic Thought 368-414 (3d ed. 1954). For psychology, see, *e.g.* Kurt Lewin, The Conceptual Representation and the Measurement of Psychological Forces, 1 Contributions to Psychological Theory, No. 4 (1938); Neale E. Miller, Experimental Studies in Conflict, in 1 Personality and the Behavior Disorders 431 (J. Hunt ed. 1944); Mathilda Holzman, Theories of Choice and Conflict in Psychology and Economics, 2 J. Conflict Resolution 310-20 (1958). This psychological/economic model is intimately related to the ontological postulates of liberal theory concerning facts and values. See §§ 17-20. Something very close to my distinction between substantive rationality and rule application is implicit in Lon Fuller's distinction between the "economics of marginal utility" and the "economics of exchange." See Lon L. Fuller, The Morality of Law, *supra* note 5, at 28. See also the discussion of interest balancing as a technique of judicial decision in §§ 72-78.

The name "substantive rationality" and its place in the theory of formality derive not from the tradition of political economy and behaviorist psychology but from Weber. Throughout *Economy and Society*, Weber emphasizes the opposition between processes he calls "substantively rational" (or "value rational") and those he calls "formally (or instrumentally) rational." Substantive process is associated with direct application of systems of values to particular situations, with concern for the achievement of outcomes rather than with the following of procedures, with the actual distribution of values rather than with efficiency in allocation of resources, and with flexible "administration" as opposed to legalistic "adjudication." Formal rationality, in the domain of law, is associated with the process of formulating and applying rules in the sense of the term used here (see note 10 *supra*). See 1 Max Weber, *supra* note 3, at 85-86; 2 *id.* 645-58, 809-15, 880-95; 3 *id.* 976-80. See also David Trubek, *supra* note 3, at 730, 733-34, 736, 744, 749. In all of these respects, my approach is identical to that of Weber.

Nonetheless, substantive rationality and rule application as I define them *differ radically in their internal structure from Weber's concepts.* Substantively rational process as I define it involves conflicting values whose application to particular circumstances is determined by an objective standard, an "ordering principle," or, in other words, a *rule.* See *supra* note 12 for a full discussion. As a consequence, this process is, *in Weber's terms*, inherently "formal." 1 Economy and Society 26. Weber's concepts of value rationality (*id.* at 24-25) and of substantive rationality in economics (*id.* 85-86) and law (2 *id.* at 657) are not employed in this essay.

Finally, Weber's conception of formal rationality in legal thought (*id.* at 656-57) includes a body of premises about the way in which rules should be developed and related to one another (*e.g.*, gaplessness, logical subsumption) as well as the notion of mechanical rule application I develop here. See *supra* note 10. It is an important aspect of the theory of formality that it excludes all such notions about how rules ought to be developed from the account of why judges should be rule appliers. See §§ 15, 16. Thus Weber's opposition of the substantive to the formal in modern law bears little relation, as far as the *definition of concepts* is concerned, to that of this essay.

conflicting ends of a legitimately representative lawmaker; (b) a substantively rational law-making process produces a body of rules designed to achieve these ends; (c) rule appliers apply the rules to cases presented to them by disputing private parties.

12. The essence of rule application, as I defined it above, is that it is *mechanical.* The decision process is called rule application only if the actor resolutely limits himself to identifying those aspects of the situation which, *per se*, trigger his response. He must *never* ask whether giving this particular response, in light of the total situation including *but not limited* to the *per se* elements, is best. The minute he begins to look over his shoulder at the *consequences* of responding to the presence or absence of the *per se* elements he has moved some distance toward substantively rational decision.[14] So long as he refuses to look over his shoulder, then from the point of view of anyone concerned with the particular consequences, anyone for whom this particular act of adjudication has a purpose, his action will—barring a providential arrangement of the universe not to be considered here—occasionally have effects on the litigants just the opposite of those desired. For example, the Statute of Frauds was intended to prevent the manufacture of evidence, but occasionally works as an escape hatch for a shady operator dealing with a legal neophyte.[15]

[14] Per se rules come to the judge as verbal formulas; it is up to him to fit the mass of facts the case presents into the categories that indicate what action he should take. This "fitting" of facts to categories can only be accomplished, within the framework of liberal psychological premises, through some process of "balancing" or "weighing" of cognitive stimuli some of which suggest one classification and some another. The definitions of the words that are used in per se rules are not "given" by nature, but constructed by man on the basis of experience. The rule applier participates in this social process of definition each time he confronts stimuli that might be characterized in more than one way. Furthermore, the theory of definition dominant within liberal thought is that the rule applier can choose between classifications only by reference to the *purposes* that the distinction in question serves for the community that makes it. This theory asserts that difficulties of definition arise when conflicting purposes suggest different resolutions of a classificatory ambiguity. It is therefore possible to imagine cases in which the rule applier's action in choosing one definition from among a number suggested by the press of conflicting ends or interests differs little from a legislator's decision as to what rule should govern particular facts. See Lon L. Fuller, *supra* note 7, at 661-69. Of course, it is also possible to imagine the problem obviated by the existence of a profound cultural harmony among men concerning the definitions that best serve their ends. It follows that rule application balances precariously between substantive rationality on the one hand and natural harmony on the other, much as rational decision balances between natural harmony and rule application (see note 12 *supra*). Do rule application and rational decision, the two processes whose polar opposition structures the Liberal Theory of Legal Justice, then collapse into one another? It seems best to delay consideration of this problem until the basic dichotomy between the factual-objective and the normative-subjective has been introduced in §§ 17-20, trusting in the meanwhile to the reader's grasp of what is, after all, a commonplace distinction usually made without difficulty.

[15] *Cf.* Bourke v. Callanan, 160 Mass. 195, 197 (1893) (Holmes, J.):
"We are aware that by our construction . . . the statute of frauds may be made an

13. Yet around this "absolutism" of the rule applier, his perverse self-denial, his refusal to have any purposes outside the application itself or to regard the consequences of his action, cluster many of the deepest and most intense emotions associated with legal as opposed to other kinds of process. Witness the passion aroused by legalism, bias, impartiality, fairness.[16] Why, then, do formal systems exist? Why would a person or a group attempt to achieve substantively rational results, accomplish purposes, through the formulation and application of rules?

> One way of interpreting the Hobbesian sovereign is as an agency added to unstable systems of cooperation in such a way that it is no longer to anyone's advantage not to do his part given that others will do theirs. By

---

instrument of fraud. But that always is true, whenever the law prescribes a form for an obligation. The very meaning of such a requirement is that a man relies at his peril on what purports to be such an obligation without that form."

All rules, in the conception employed here, have the characteristics Ihering ascribed to the rules prescribing specific forms for the legally effective expression of intention:

"The law may have many purposes, for example, securing of proof, avoiding rash action, overreaching, and so on. It is irrelevant whether the purpose can actually be achieved through the form, whether it can also be reached in another way, even whether the party has actually reached the purpose in another way: the legislator did not wish to leave the problem of reaching this goal to the insight and free decision of the party [or of the judge charged with administering the form—D. K.]; instead, the legislator took the matter in hand and made exclusive and necessary the way of reaching the result that seemed good to him."

Rudolf von Ihering, *supra* note 9, at 475 (same passage may be found at 3 L'Esprit du Droit Romain, *supra* note 6, at 162). See also 1 *id.* at 51-56.

16 "The function of the judiciary is simply, is it not, to administer justice? . . . The judges and the jury must be impervious to considerations of state or to howls for blood. The accused may be politically noxious; the victim may have been a popular figure. No matter. Every person, however high or low, where life or liberty is concerned, is to be judged by the known law, pursuant to the due observance of the established rules for the law's enforcement. And in the private law—the law of *meum* and *tuum*—the objectives are the same. No person, public or private, if he unlawfully injures my person, or fails to fulfil his obligations, or takes my property, shall escape the disinterested judgment of the law. . . ."

Louis L. Jaffe, English and American Judges as Lawmakers 11-12 (1969).

"Let us listen to the ethical complaint against formalism. What an ignoring of moral feeling on the part of law to declare that the given word does not bind because of the smallest formal defect, to leave the most extreme abuse of confidence not merely unpunished but even without criticism, to create a safe hiding place through form for evil and deceit! What a corrupting influence this daily spectacle must have upon the people's feeling for law. Does not silencing the voice of this feeling amount to destroying it? Does not the treatment of form as alone decisive amount to undermining the basis of intercourse, good faith?"

Rudolf von Ihering, *supra* note 9, at 490-91 (same passage may be found at 3 L'Esprit du Droit Romain, *supra* note 6, at 175).

> keeping watch and enforcing sanctions, the sovereign acts to inhibit violations and to restore the system when violations occur; and the belief in the sovereign's efficacy removes instability of both kinds.[17]

B.

14. Liberal theory intimately links formality with the notion that, given human nature, men living in a world without a state, *and dependent on one another for good and ill*, will find themselves constantly at odds. Men, therefore, band together and create a State, which uses force governed by rules to control conflict. But perhaps the single most important ambiguity in liberal thought is that concerning the process by which rules are supposed to perform this function of control.

15. In very general terms, the two divergent conceptions are as follows:

(a) Much social conflict is illusory, arising from the peculiar structure of unregulated social life as a game of "Prisoner's Dilemma," in which each individual behaves badly (destructively of others' satisfactions) because afraid that if he behaves well the others will take advantage of him. Specific rules of conduct backed by sanctions for misbehavior can transform this perverse structure of social life so that everyone is better off than he would be if left to his own devices. The rationale for the State is that it makes everyone better off (and so is entitled to everyone's obedience) precisely by promulgating and enforcing these specific rules. Rules thus transform much conflict into harmony, the remaining conflict being irreducible but not serious.[18]

[17] John Rawls, The Sense of Justice, 72 Phil. Rev. 281, 290-91 (1963).

[18] On Prisoner's Dilemma, see R. Duncan Luce & Howard Raiffa, Games and Decisions: Introduction and Critical Survey 88-113 (1957). On the notion that the state should be conceived as a device for dealing with the underlying problem of "externalities" or "public goods" (of which Prisoner's Dilemma is a dramatization), see William J. Baumol, *supra* note 4; Mancur Olson, *supra* note 4. In this conception, the paradigm of state action is the enforcement of contract, which permits the cooperative "solution" of the game of Prisoner's Dilemma. See Robert Birmingham, Legal and Moral Duty in Game Theory: Common Law Contract and Chinese Analogies, 18 Buff. L. Rev. 99 (1969).

This conception does *not* treat the state as an alternation of substantively rational decision between conflicting ends and rule application. Rather, it takes the rational working out of the implications of the *shared* end of making everyone better off as the key to state action of all kinds. The sharp opposition of legislative and judicial functions dissolves since both institutions are seen as capable of this kind of rationality. Chief Justice Shaw gave classic expression to this view in Norway Plains Co. v. Boston & Maine R.R., 67 Mass. (1 Gray) 263, 267-268 (1854):

"It is one of the great merits and advantages of the common law, that, instead of a series of detailed practical rules, established by positive provisions, and adapted to the precise circumstances of particular cases, which would become obsolete and fail, when the practice and course of business, to which they apply, should cease or change, the common

(b) Conflict for scarce goods is the fundamental fact of social life, a product of the inherent insatiability of human desires rather than of any perverse structure. The problem of social life is to order the waging of this conflict so that society does not dissolve into a perpetual struggle to the death. The means to this end is the substantively rational arrangement of compromises, always unsatisfactory to all interests represented, but accepted as a lesser evil than the unrestrained struggle that is the only alternative. The rationale for the State is that it is a useful instrument for the negotiation and implementation of such compromises, which will be honored only to the extent that they are enforced. Rules, whose content is contingent on the interplay of the particular interests compromised rather than determined by the application of reason to the structure of the situation, are important on two counts. First, they are a convenient administrative technique for carrying out the underlying compromises. Second, their observance prevents the State apparatus (as opposed to the postulated legitimate legislative body) from becoming an actor with its own interests generating as much conflict with the citizens as it suppresses between them.[19]

16. The notion that we can adequately account for most of the legal order by an appeal to common ends and reason, which together generate a specific body of conflict-eliminating rules, is an important one. I mean in a later essay to examine its late nineteenth century and contemporary expressions. Still, the dominant modern view seems to be that as soon as we get beyond a few elementary legal institutions (some very crude form of property, contract and tort) the body of specific rules represents not reason but the compromise of conflicting interests. Here, I will limit the discussion to this second conception of rules, in order to show that in its strict positivist version[20] formality is incapable of offering a stable solution to the problem of justice in the liberal

law consists of a few broad and comprehensive principles founded on reason, natural justice, and enlightened public policy modified and adapted to the circumstances of all the particular cases which fall within it. . . ."

[19] The first approach (§ 15a) I derive loosely from Locke and the traditions of natural law and welfare economics, while I associate the second with legal positivism and Hobbes. But nothing could be further from my intention than to continue the argument between these two schools. Quite the contrary, as I conceive them the positions sketched in § 15a and § 15b differ only in this: the first urges that common ends, Reason, and plausible empirical assumptions permit us to say a good deal *both* about the form of law and about its content; the second position, with which the rest of this essay is concerned, is that common ends and Reason compel a decision in favor of rules as the form of law but permit no conclusions about questions of content. The rest of this Part is an elaboration of the positivist argument for rules. It is based, exactly like the natural law arguments for, say, freedom of contract, on a combination of postulates, factual assertions, ethical or normative statements, trains of deduction, and what not. The argument *is* positivist, however, in that it insists on postulating a rigid ontological dichotomy of facts and values, as is explained at length in §§ 17-20. See also note 25 *infra*; cf. H. L. A. Hart, *supra* note 10, at 601 n.25, 622-24.

[20] For a discussion of the sense in which what follows is addressed to "positivism," see note 19 *supra* and note 25 *infra*.

state. This will involve a more detailed examination of the rationale of rules in the conception in question, and this examination must begin with a reference back to the fundamental premises of liberal thought.

17. For our purposes, the most important of these underlying premises or postulates is the opposition of facts to values, of the objective to the subjective, of nature to man. Values, wants, purposes, desires, ends constitute the domain of subjective existence, which is what defines the individual man in opposition to nature. Values, wants, purposes, desires, ends *exist*; they are no less real than stones or legs; but (whatever may at first appear) there is no way for one person to participate directly in another person's experience of them. This is crucial because the experience of values not only defines the state of being human, it also motivates all genuinely human action. In other words, it is a postulate of the theory that action is the product of (is powered by; is driven by) the value/desire/purpose dimension of existence. This is the root of the concept of man as a "maximizer," which means simply that behavior is the resultant of the interaction of conflicting values/desires/purposes. It is also the root of the notion of the insatiability of human desire, which is a tautology within the theory since the quest for satisfaction of desire through purposive action to attain values is the very definition of humanity.

18. It is an aspect of the nature of the subjective that because all values are inherently *arbitrary*, there is no possibility of rationally persuading another of the "correctness" or "justness" of any particular value or desire, no matter how much our agreement with others may suggest that we are dealing with something highly determinate. Thus the postulate that action is the product of value/desire/purpose implies that in relation to one another men are *indeterminate*; since we can neither participate in another's experience of values nor control him through reason, we must deal with his ultimate freedom to contradict our expectations, no matter how much we may believe we understand the "laws" of his behavior. Thus the theory postulates true lawfulness only of the opposed realm of nature.

19. According to the theory, everything that exists that is not a part of the domain of the subjective belongs to the domain of nature, or of "fact." Facts are homogeneous and *objective*, in the sense that (whatever may at first appear) people experience them through cognitive faculties that are common to humankind. Facts are "out there," and inherently identical with themselves no matter who is experiencing them. As a result, people tend to reach a consensus, through such techniques as measurement and rational argument, about what is and what is not true of the external world. Moreover, the objective, the world of facts, is inherently *orderly*; we operate on the assumption that everything that happens in it is the result of the operation of determinate physical laws, however much our inability to state those laws might suggest that we were dealing with arbitrariness.

20. Given these premises, the distinction between substantively rational

decision and rule application takes on a new significance. Substantive rationality involves the expression, interaction and measurement of values in conflict, and the assessment of the implications for those conflicting values of infinitely complex factual situations. As a result, theorists of formality consider it to be *inherently uncertain and unpredictable.* Rule application, in sharp contrast, involves the objective or "cognitive" operation of identifying particular factual aspects of situations followed by the execution of unambiguous prescriptions for official action. In short, according to the theory of formality, *it is inherently certain and predictable.*[21] Substantively rational processes are disorderly in that they simply reflect or express the blind force of the various interests or desires represented. Rule application is arbitrary from the point of view of the litigant, but highly orderly *as a process,* since it involves such operations as the measurement of facts and the working out of the logical implications of prescriptive statements.[22] The certainty and orderliness of

[21] The contrast of rule application and substantive rationality as decision techniques rests on the fundamental liberal distinction between facts and values. It should now be clear that to attack this contrast on the ground that rule application and substantive rationality merge into one another (see *supra* notes 12 and 14) is to attack the *premises* of the theory, rather than just a set of definitions. If we can only decide what the facts of the case are by reference to some purpose, then the domain of fact cannot have the ruled character predicated of it. Thus associationism—the doctrine that factual knowledge is built up through an objective, ruled, "scientific" process of unconscious induction from the raw data of the senses—becomes essential to the coherence of liberal theory. Without it, facts are indistinguishable from values. A doctrine like pragmatism—which denies the autonomous reality of both fact and value—therefore has threatening implications for the legitimacy of the liberal legal order, as the American legal realists quite clearly saw. Their opponents saw it as well: "[T]o insist on the distinction [between 'is' and 'ought'] is to emphasize that the hard core of settled meaning is law in some centrally important sense and that even if there are borderlines, there must first be lines. If this were not so the notion of rules controlling courts' decisions would be senseless as some of the 'Realists'—in their most extreme moods, and, I think, on bad grounds—claimed." H. L. A. Hart, *supra* note 10, at 614-615.

Yet the threat is not a serious one. In the absence of a theory of knowledge that establishes the objectivity of facts, liberal theorists turn to the alternative pillar of a natural harmony (see *supra* note 12). They point to the reality of very widespread consensus concerning a large class of non-abstract cognitions. *Some* factual judgments are anchored in the inherent stability of *culture,* of which law is only a part. The judge who is called on only to make choices about the classification of highly concrete aspects of the situation will find himself constrained simply because *no one* will find plausible his redefinition of all dogs as cats. See, *e.g.,* Louis L. Jaffe, *supra* note 5 at 239-46; Henry M. Hart & Albert M. Sacks, *supra* note 5, at 127-28; Ernest Nagel, Fact, Value, and Human Purpose, 4 Natural L. Forum 26, 35-36 (1959). Thus the validity of the fact/value ontology is less important to the theory than the assertion that there exists *some* body of potential predicates for rules that will guarantee certainty in judicial administration. When we recognize this as the crucial issue, the debate about formalism suddenly takes on a new aspect: it is essentially a debate about what sorts of things properly belong in the class of potential predicates for rules. See note 22 *infra.*

[22] Two interpretations of the concept of rule application, based on two interpretations of "the factual," are possible, according to whether or not psychic states (specific intent, malice, carelessness, good faith) are treated as distinguishable, for the purposes of the rule

rule application make it the ideal instrument for a liberal state conceived as a device for the negotiation and implementation of compromises of the conflicting insatiable desires of the citizenry.[23]

> [G]eneral rules are necessary to . . .
> any dispensation, whose object is to

---

applier, from "value judgments" (this house is beautiful, this division is just). In one interpretation, the legislative ideal is a system of rules whose only predicates are *external* facts, determinable without reference to the testimony of any experient about his own subjectivity. Even where the theory of legal obligation or responsibility rests on a notion of intent or fault or some other psychic disposition, this approach requires that the actual rules embodying the theory speak in terms of "objective manifestations" or "external standards." See Oliver Wendell Holmes, Jr., The Common Law, *supra* note 3, at Lectures 2 and 3; Lon L. Fuller, *supra* note 6, at 808; Roscoe Pound, Individual Interests of Substance—Promised Advantages, 59 Har. L. Rev. 1, 25 (1945).

Within this conception, in turn, there are different degrees of rigor. At the extreme, one could insist that all legal rules having to do with the creation of obligation should have as their predicates the performance of acts prescribed by the legal system for that purpose and that purpose alone. The seal, recording statutes, the formalities of early Roman law and the civil law notarial act would then be models for all legal institutions. And the certainty of rule application in contrast to substantively rational processes would then quite clearly derive not from the ontological status of the "factual" predicates of the rules, but from a careful construction of agreed signs for the communication of legal intent. See *supra* note 21. The works cited in note 6 *supra* take this approach to formalities. In § 35 and note 40 *infra* I apply it to the regime of rules in general.

In the alternative view, judgments about particular psychic states are judgments of fact. Psychic states are treated as part of the physical, objective universe, even if particularly difficult to establish with certainty. In this conception, they are quite radically unlike the inherently subjective characteristics of otherwise indisputably objective entities (the beauty of houses, fairness of exchanges). The administration of justice would be compromised by a commission to make the latter kind of "political," "legislative," or simply "non-judicial" determination, but "the state of a man's mind is as much a fact as the state of his digestion." (Edgington v. Fitzmaurice, [1885] L.R. 29 Ch. Div. 459, 483 (C.A.).) This notion is fully consistent with the postulates of the liberal theory: the judge's mental operations are conceived as the cognitive ones of finding facts in order to apply pre-existing rules. It is only when the judge rejects this conception and asserts his own legitimate legislative power, or when he claims the role of mediator, or of Khadi doing justice after the fact without regard to rules, that we can speak of a truly nonformal theory of legal justice.

The best general discussion of this subject is 3 Rudolf von Ihering, *supra* note 6, at § 50, especially 158-164, 185-187, and 1 *id.* at 51-56. See also 2 Max Weber, *supra* note 3 883-85, 656-67; Lon L. Fuller, *supra* note 6; Stewart Macaulay, Justice Traynor and the Law of Contracts, 13 Stan. L. Rev. 812, 813-17 (1961).

[23] The distinctive characteristic of the theory of formality is exactly this linkage of the postulated dichotomies of rule application vs. substantive rationality and objective fact vs. subjective value. My view is that the four elements constitute a single complex, composite premise, rather than four distinct premises, or one or two premises with logical derivations therefrom, but I don't believe that for the purposes of this paper anything hinges on this issue. I certainly don't intend to make any arguments dependent on the logical relationship between the four concepts. It is enough that they "resonate" or reinforce one another, and together make the assertion that there are two radically different kinds of process more credible than it would be without the coincidence of the two dichotomies.

> influence the conduct of reasonable creatures.
>
> For if, of two actions perfectly similar, one be punished, and the other be rewarded or forgiven, which is the consequence of rejecting general rules, the subjects of such a dispensation would no longer know, either what to expect or how to act. Rewards and punishments would cease to be such—would become accidents. Like the stroke of a thunderbolt, or the discovery of a mine, like a blank or benefit ticket in a lottery, they would occasion pain or pleasure when they happened; but following in no known order, from any particular course of action, they could have no previous influence or effect upon the conduct.[24]

C.

21. The liberal state, in the conception we are concerned with here, exists solely for the purpose of preventing a disastrous tailspin into civil war. This objective the liberal state achieves by imposing a compromise on citizens each struggling for a maximum share of scarce satisfactions. Thus the state is conceived as an intervenor in an already established situation, that in which each individual engages in an unrestrained struggle for what he thinks valuable. The only purpose of intervention is the negative one of stabilizing the situation (value is *created* only by the activity of individuals consuming reality), and this purpose is one that *everyone* shares. Indeed, the premise that everyone wants security is as fundamental as (or perhaps it should be seen as an aspect of) the notion that human action is powered by effort to attain values. *No* values can be attained without some means of preventing civil war; there is no point in trying to avoid civil war except to maximize values, since all activity, once peace is established, consists in maximization.

22. But if everyone shares the objective of preventing civil war, why do we need the state to do it for us? The answer of the theory is that the state of nature is a situation in which no one can *trust* anyone else. What defines the individual human is the indeterminacy and arbitrariness of his will in the pursuit of value. No one can ever be sure that another's substantively rational calculation of his conflicting ends will result in a decision to recipro-

[24] William Paley, Principles of Moral and Political Philosophy bk. II, ch. 7 (1788).

cate one's niceness with niceness of his own. And given the fact of interdependence, as soon as you are nice, you make yourself vulnerable to the other's nastiness and create an incentive for him to betray you. The function of the state is to provide him a conscience—to make sure that he is not tempted by the hope of increasing his share to violate the terms of the compromise and so begin the downward spiral of violence.[25]

23. But while it is absolutely necessary that the state *somehow* perform the function of security, there are restraints that rule out a number of institutional possibilities.

(a) The complexity and uncertainty of the universe of fact make it impossible to imagine a complete one-time before-the-fact ordering that would finally assign everyone his share of every pot of values that might be created.

(b) For the state to engage in substantively rational after-the-fact *ad hoc* compromises of disputes as they arise would create intense uncertainty about how the state would intervene in conflicts over distribution; the result would be a flood of conflicts that would eat up all the time of the constituents of the state, so that no one would have a chance to engage in the private maximization that was the point of the enterprise.

(c) Delegating the function of substantively rational after-the-fact *ad hoc* compromise of disputes or of before-the-fact planning to agents would be equally self defeating, since the agents would then engage in maximizing *their* ends, with the result that some social interests would be strengthened (by acquiring access to state force) at the expense of others, and the level of conflict might well increase rather than decline.[26]

24. Formality is supposed to respond to this dilemma as follows.

(a) By a process of negotiation between the various interests represented in the postulated legitimate legislature, substantively rational processes

[25] Thus the conception of the state as a compromiser of conflicting interests has something in common with the state conceived as the promulgator of the natural law of cooperation described in § 15a above. At the root of both notions is the prisoner's dilemma situation in which everyone acts rationally but everyone ends up losing, unless some outside force makes it possible for the players to form binding agreements. See note 18 *supra*. The difference between the two conceptions lies in the degree to which they generalize the prisoner's dilemma idea to explain and justify the whole body of civil law. In the compromise conception, the rules can do no more in the way of eliminating conflict than restrain the slide into civil war. *Any* set of rules that will stabilize the situation takes men out of the prisoner's dilemma of the war of all against all, but *no* set of rules can do more than compromise the competition for values in stabilized civil society. In the natural law conception, the rules can do much more than simply prevent disaster: with the aid of Reason, men can design them in such a way that they will be individually just, fair and good for all men, as well as expedient for purposes of stabilization. The reason for this is that the basic problems that give rise to conflict are seen as essentially illusory; the state can make them disappear by rules that foster (i) trust, which causes (ii) such a large increase in everyone's well-being that (iii) what appeared a struggle to the death is reconceived as a brisk squash match. See note 19 *supra*.

[26] See, *e.g.*, John Locke, *supra* note 2, at § 13.

produce a set of rules for state action. These are based on an estimate by each participant of what the effect of each rule will be on him in the situations in which he expects it to be applied, and then a balancing off of the good results of the rules against the bad ones. The final legislative decision does *not* represent a substantive prescription of how everything should in fact be divided. Rather, the application of the rules to the pre-existing struggle for welfare changes that struggle, and indirectly brings about the agreed distribution. The process of choosing rules is very time consuming and uncertain, but it doesn't have to be done very often.[27]

(b) Rule appliers implement the compromise indirectly by following the rules that distribute goods, or structure the various situations in which the private parties themselves decide on their distribution. The certainty of the process of rule application controls those to whom the legislature delegates the task. They can't become an independent center of power because it is easy to review and correct their action when necessary.[28] The certainty of the process also drastically reduces litigation. The impulse to enlist the state on one's side in the struggle for welfare shifts to lobbying the legislature, where it belongs.[29]

[27] The rules with which this version of positivism is concerned are rules of *official* conduct. Of course, a particular rule, *e.g.* that murderers should be imprisoned, *may* have the effect of creating a rule of *private* conduct, for example refraining from murder. But the ruledness of private conduct is an *indirect* result of the application of rules of official conduct. Given the postulated freedom and indeterminacy of the individual human will, the most the state can *ever* do is to alter the structure of alternatives among which the individual exercises his inherent maximizing power of choice (see §§ 17-19). The significant point about this is that *norms*, meaning regularities of conduct based *both* on social sanctions and on the individual's sense of their intrinsic value or "oughtness," are radically dissociated from law (if, indeed, they can have any place at all in a theory postulating that human action is a mere resultant of desires in conflict). It is easy to slip into the habit of referring the notion of a rule to a maxim like "promises should be kept." But the type of rule I discuss in this paper is better illustrated by the precept: "In a contract lawsuit, the breaching promisor is made to pay the promisee expectation damages."

[28] "It has been frequently remarked with great propriety that a voluminous code of laws is one of the inconveniences necessarily connected with the advantages of a free government. To avoid an arbitrary discretion in the courts, it is indispensable that they should be bound down by strict rules and precedents which serve to define and point out their duty in every particular case that comes before them. . . ."

The Federalist No. 78, at 471 (Rossiter ed. 1961) (Hamilton).

This may be usefully compared with the views of Chief Justice Shaw in Norway Plains Co. v. Boston & Maine R.R., *supra* note 18. H. L. A. Hart has remarked that those "responsible for the conception of the judge as an automaton, are not the Utilitarian thinkers. The responsibility, if it is to be laid at the door of any theorist, is with thinkers like Blackstone and, at an earlier stage, Montesquieu. The root of this evil is preoccupation with the separation of powers and Blackstone's 'childish fiction' (as Austin termed it) that judges only 'find,' never 'make,' law."

H. L. A. Hart, *supra* note 10, at 610.

[29] The most elaborate extant description of how a functioning system of rules works

25. Yet although formality seems to present an ideal response to the problem of the most efficient or convenient mechanism for implementing the legislative compromise, it has a number of characteristics that may surprise:

(a) The rules that emerge from the negotiations do not represent an attempt to determine the "right" or "just" solution to conflicts, but rather each is a piece of a larger puzzle accepted not for its own sake but in exchange for benefits or injuries received through other rules. The rules may include all kinds of things—price supports, restrictions on travel, etc.—besides the classic rules of property, tort and contract with their claims to representing reason rather than mere interest. It is only *as a whole* that they constitute an acceptable compromise. It is only as a whole that the legislature approves them. And it is only as a whole that they acquire whatever legitimacy the legislative action can bestow.[30]

(b) The duty to submit to the rules is, therefore, unrelated to their content. It derives from the legitimacy of the whole compromise rather than from that of the particular command. The proper response if one feels that the rule the judge is applying is unjust cannot be to disobey him; it must

---

to accomplish the purposes of the sovereign is that of Professor Fuller, who employs the hypothetical case of a tyrant obliged by the necessities of government to embrace a "morality of law." The postulated legitimate legislature of the model of formality finds itself in a similar situation, and adopts a similar set of policies. There are two differences: in the theory of formality the legislature acts in a substantively rational fashion, with "morality" excluded altogether as a category, and once the system of rules is established, judges administer it in the "mechanical" and "absolutist" fashion described *supra* at § 12. See Lon L. Fuller, *supra* note 7, at 644-45; and his The Morality of Law, *supra* note 5.

[30] *Cf.* C. B. Macpherson, *supra* note 2, at 57-58.

"The possessive market model requires a compulsive framework of law. At the very least, life and property must be secured, contracts must be defined and enforced. The model also permits state action much beyond this minimum. The state may control land use and labour use, may interfere with the free flow of trade by embargoes and customs duties, may assist one kind of industry and discourage another, may provide free or subsidized services, may relieve the destitute, may require minimum standards of quality or of training, and may by these and other kinds of interference prevent prices (including wages) reaching the levels which an unregulated or less regulated market would produce. What the state does thereby is to alter some of the terms of the equations each man makes when he is calculating his most profitable course of action. But this need not affect the main-spring of the system which is that men do calculate their most profitable courses and do employ their labour, skill, and resources as that calculation dictates. Some of the data for their calculations is changed, but prices are still set by competition between the calculators. The prices are different from what they would be in a less controlled system, but as long as prices still move in response to the decisions of the individual competitors and the prices still elicit the production of goods and determine their allocation, it remains a market system. The state may, so to speak, move the hurdles to the advantage of some kinds of competitors or may change the handicaps, without discouraging racing. The state may, of course, deliberately or otherwise, by the same sort of intervention put racing out of business. But it need not do so."

rather be to go to the legitimate legislative body and pursue one's interest in a different rule to whatever conclusion, postulated to be legitimate, may emerge.[31] Likewise, the judge's duty to behave formally, to look only to rule application, does not derive from the legitimacy of the particular rule in question, but only from that of the body of rules as a whole. There is no basis for the judge to refuse to enforce a rule he thinks unjust because there is no requirement that particular rules *be* just; only that taken together they represent a legitimate compromise. The judge has no function but to execute this compromise as the servant of the legislature.

(c) The process of rule application itself has nothing to do with "justice" or "right." It is not only purely cognitive (fact oriented); it is merely a *cost*, an unfortunate necessity of the perverse structure of the state of nature, and can neither generate nor implement any value except the value of abiding by the results of the substantively rational postulated legitimate legislative compromise.

(d) Since state action via rules is purely instrumental—representing the best possible solution to the administrative problem of enforcing a compromise rather than any independent commitment to any particular rule or body of rules, or to the processes of rule formulation or rule application—there is no reason why the state can't act in a non-ruled manner, by direct legislative determination of disputes or by direct legislative redistribution of values, whenever that appears desirable.

> Freedom of Men under Government,
> is, to have a standing Rule to live by,
> common to every one of that Society, and
> made by the Legislative Power erected
> in it; A Liberty to follow my own
> Will in all things, where the Rule
> prescribes not; and not to be subject to
> the inconstant, uncertain, unknown,
> Arbitrary Will of another Man.[32]

D.

26. Thus far, I have dealt only with the question of the role the state will assign to rules in its program to achieve its objective of preventing civil war.

[31] In this view, the rules simply restructure the alternatives open to the individual private actor (see notes 27 and 30 *supra*). The duty to submit is a duty either to obey or to pay the price. It is *not* a duty to accept the intrinsic rightness of the particular restructuring the legislature has accomplished. In this view, contract law, for example, does no more than create a choice between performance and paying damages. "[T]he immediate legal effect of what the promisor does is, that he takes the risk of the event, within certain defined limits, as between himself and the promisee." Oliver Wendell Holmes, Jr., *supra* note 2, Lecture 8, at 300.

[32] John Locke, *supra* note 2, at § 22.

The analysis proceeded under the constraint that the state could not use techniques that would make it impossible for its individual constituents to achieve their private objective of maximizing their welfare. The conclusion reached was that rules would be important, but that their particular content would not be, nor would there be any reason to use rules when other stabilization devices suggested themselves. But the state perspective—that of predominant concern with preventing civil war—is not identical with the social. Prevention of civil war is adopted by the citizens as a *means*—albeit indispensable—to the end of maximizing their respective welfares. No analysis of the place of rules in the liberal state is complete unless it takes into account this more general objective and asks what role rules play in the private maximization process. In short, it is necessary to reverse the approach of the last section: here we will consider the uses of rules for welfare maximization subject to the constraint of avoiding civil war.[33]

27. *The role of rules in the liberal state is to provide autonomy.* Freedom or liberty in liberal theory refers first to the postulated indeterminacy of the individual will, its arbitrariness in the choice of values to pursue. Second, freedom refers to the extent to which the individual is actually able to achieve the satisfaction of his desires (the realization of his values). In other words, the degree of freedom is identical with the degree of satisfaction or *welfare.* Autonomy, by contrast, does *not* refer to the degree of satisfaction, but to the *character of the circumstances on which satisfaction is dependent.* An individual has complete autonomy when he is dependent for the satisfaction of desire only on events ordered according to rules. So long as the only obstacles to the realization of his values are ruled facts, rather than arbitrary or indeterminate events beyond his control, his autonomy is complete, *even if he has no freedom at all because utterly unable to realize his values.* Conversely, one can have a great degree of freedom (high level of actual satisfaction of desire) without any autonomy at all (where the high level depends on the arbitrary, subjective wills of others).[34]

28. The concept of autonomy is not distinct from the concept of events ordered by rules. Autonomy *means* that the actor contends only with circumstances that are ruled. Thus the unknown in nature, the uncertain, the apparently random or arbitrary phenomena with which everyone must contend,

[33] The reader may find it helpful at this point to refer to notes 19 and 25 *supra* which discuss the relation of my argument to the traditional categories of positivism and natural law.

[34] The concepts of security, freedom and autonomy are very closely allied in liberal thought. I distinguish autonomy from security as more general: it refers to the degree of ruledness in general while security refers more specifically to rules restraining other men from forcibly depriving the actor of life, liberty or property (but see "security of transaction," which is identical to autonomy as I use it). Many liberal writers use the word freedom to denote the concept I call autonomy; my usage is intended only to avoid confusion with other common senses of the word.

reduce autonomy as much as the unknown in society. Objective fact is postulated in liberal theory to be ordered according to rule, but everyone recognizes that we do not have anything like the ability to predict exactly all factual events. Thus there may be only a little difference between the actual disorder of nature in our current state of knowledge and the actual disorder of private action, postulated to be arbitrary, indeterminate and uncertain, but subject to some degree of control by a state anxious to prevent the slide into civil war. And once private individuals have created the state, it too becomes a circumstance relevant to the satisfaction of desire, and the degree to which it acts according to rules becomes an element contributing to the autonomy or lack of it of its constituents. In short, from the point of view of the concept of autonomy there is no difference at all between the laws of natural phenomena, the civil laws controlling private activity, and the rule of law governing state action. All are alike in that to the extent that they are in force, individuals have autonomy, though they may have no freedom. To the extent that they are not in force, individuals have no autonomy, though their freedom be complete.

29. Autonomy is only desirable as a means to the end of welfare (the satisfaction of desire; freedom). As already shown, some degree of this means is necessary if men are to attain *any* of the end: men create the state to provide the minimum of autonomy they need if freedom is to have any meaning. In its absence, when I regularize my action I am vulnerable to your arbitrary and indeterminate response to the temptation offered by my exposure. Since this is true of everyone, no one will supply the good of ruled behavior. Autonomy of the kind necessary to prevent civil war is thus what economists call a public good, meaning that an individual cannot increase the supply of the good ruledness (*i.e.*, by acting according to rule) without conferring on others a benefit that they are not obliged to reciprocate. But when the citizens have created the state to provide the autonomy necessary to prevent civil war, they will have to decide on the *degree* of ruledness that ought to prevail in a stabilized society.[35]

30. For each participant in the negotiation of the compromise that constitutes the body of rules, there is a problem of balancing areas of constraint against areas in which he will be free to pursue his interests to the utmost. Other things being equal, each would like to have everyone else constrained to fixed rules, and then go freely about the maximizing of his satisfactions. In this ideal situation of total autonomy, he would never have to worry about arbitrary or uncertain interferences with his planned level of welfare.

31. But in order to assure himself that others can't destroy him, each participant finds himself obliged to agree to some restraints on himself. The particular complex of rules that emerges from this process of trading off one's

[35] See § 22 and notes 18 and 25 *supra*.

own freedom against that of others is a major element in the environmental structure within which private activity aimed at individual welfare takes place (other elements include the known laws of nature, ad hoc state action, and chance events). Thus the rules do much more than just prevent civil war: how each person ultimately fares in the competition not for survival but for welfare, *i.e.*, the actual freedom each person enjoys, is a direct function of the particular substantive provisions in force.[36]

32. The question of how the citizens will ever manage to create a compromise compact of this type, as well as that of the particular rules they will choose, is beyond the scope of this paper. In short, I ignore the whole problem of legitimate political action. What concerns us here is *not* the content of the rules, but the question whether the state may disregard rules altogether.

33. At first blush, this question appears much less problematic than that of what rules and how many to adopt. The state is different from its individual constituents whose bargaining produces the rules of distribution of scarce values. The *only* purpose of the state is the provision of security, and this can virtually always be achieved by rule making and rule application.[37] Subjection to the processes of rule making and rule application—as opposed to discretionary or ad hoc intervention—deprives those who control the state of an instrument for the pursuit of their private interests; it robs them of the chance to exercise their free will through its mechanisms; but *this loss does not count*. As *citizens*, there is no one who feels this deprivation as a loss to himself. *Indeed, every citizen has an interest, ceteris paribus, in the limitation and constraint of the state to action according to rule in all cases*. For this reason, the change from a discretionary state, or a state acting generally according to rule but with discretionary interludes or even just occasional aberrations, can be said to increase *social welfare*, if we define social welfare as increased when a change is made that makes everyone better off according to his own view of his own better-offness.

34. There are two aspects to this argument that deserve separate consideration. First is the treacherous *ceteris paribus* provision. The notion is that we can deal with the question of whether or not all state action should be according to rule on the assumption that all that matters is the effect of our decision on *the total of satisfactions before distribution*. The introduction of ruledness is compared to an invention that increases the number of shoes that

[36] It is important to keep in mind at this point that we are talking about rules of *official* conduct whose influence on private activity occurs indirectly through a restructuring of the alternatives open to private actors. The "restraints" consist in the adjustment of the network of official sanctions to encourage some kinds of activity and discourage others. See *supra* notes 27, 28, 30, 31.

[37] The whole doctrine of *raison d'état* nestles snugly within the phrase "virtually always."

two men working together can produce during a single day. The argument is that even though it is possible that the invention will somehow upset the balance of power between the two so that one of them will end up worse off than before, we can still say that the invention is desirable because we *could* use it to increase the welfare of each. In this case, the invention consists in the elimination of nonruled state action. Some nonruled action—mistakes—may have been harmful to everyone. But others helped some at the expense of others. The introduction of total ruledness will affect the balance of satisfactions among those who were helped and those who were hurt by the earlier unruled behavior. The argument asserts that at the point of introducing total ruledness we *could* compensate all the losers and still have enough new benefits left over to make at least some better off. For example, at the moment of transition we could arrange to negotiate a new body of rules for the non-discretionary state to enforce, and grant each party a veto to protect him against any new set-up he thought worse than the old mixed rule/discretion situation.[38]

35. But what *are* these advantages of ruled state action that make it possible to benefit everyone? The answer is that the elimination of uncertainty about what the state will do means that by advance planning private parties can adjust their conduct so as to turn favorable intervention to maximum favorable effect, while minimizing the occasions of adverse intervention. Suppose that every conceivable situation affecting *A* and *B* is covered by a rule; whatever *A* may do or wish to do that affects *B* (*i.e.*, that has a relation to his purposes) is either required, permitted, permitted on pain of paying something to someone, or forbidden. If *A* and *B* *plan* their activities (both individual and collective) with the rules in mind, and if they are able to carry out their plans, *they will be able to control precisely and completely the part that the rule appliers and the rules play in their lives.*[39] Indeed, by

[38] There are other possible criteria of a desirable change which could also be used to justify the institution of formality within the context of liberal theory. For example, if one takes the maximization of a social welfare function as the only basis for action, one could argue that we should establish formality because over the long run everyone has a "positive *expected* payoff" from mechanical rule application, even though everyone may be worse off in the short run and some people will certainly be worse off in the long run as well. A contractarian might argue that an idealized legislature or group of contracting parties will choose a "welfare game" with formality as one of its rules because the efficiency of mechanical rule application is such that the total of positive rewards available for distribution among the players of a formal game will always be greater than those available in an otherwise similar informal game. On this general subject, see A. Mitchell Polinsky, *supra* note 4; and note 39 *infra*.

[39] Of course, *A* and *B* must contend with the fact that they may fail to control the non-legal components in the anticipated situations with the possible result that plans will go astray and *A* or *B* (or both) will find himself dragged against his will within the sphere of application of a rule he would rather have avoided. For each, the other and, to some extent, the self are non-legal components (see note 42 *infra*). Thus a party may

announcing which facts will provoke it to particular actions, the state has put itself at the disposal of the parties. They can use the factual predicates of the rules as a sort of language by which to communicate their intentions and command particular action.[40]

36. Now suppose that the rule system contains gaps. Situations arise in

---

exert no control at all over the rule applier. The discussion in the text, however, assumes a perfectly certain universe, or at least one in which all possible future states of the world are knowable in advance, and transaction costs are low enough so that the parties can plan even for the most unlikely among them. In Part II of this essay, I examine the consequences of relaxing the assumption of certainty, the question being whether a judge called on to administer a formal regime under uncertainty can legitimately behave mechanically. In other words, I examine the question of permissible judicial attitudes to welfare games like that described in note 38 *supra.*

[40] A classic statement is that in 2 Theophilus Parsons, The Law of Contracts 1-2 (1855):

"The importance of a just and rational construction of every contract and every instrument, is obvious. But the importance of having this construction regulated by law, guided always by distinct principles, and in this way made uniform in practice, may not be so obvious, although we think it as certain and as great. If any one contract is properly construed, justice is done to the parties directly interested therein. But the rectitude, consistency, and uniformity of all construction enables all parties to do justice to themselves. For then all parties, before they enter into contracts, or make or accept instruments, may know the force and effect of the words they employ, of the precuations they use, and of the provisions which they make in their own behalf, or permit to be made by other parties.

"It is obvious that this consistency and uniformity of construction can exist only so far as construction is governed by fixed principles, or, in other words, is matter of law."

See also the following:

"The thing which characterizes the law of contracts and conveyances is that in this field forms are deliberately used, and are intended to be so used, by the parties whose acts are to be judged by the law. To the business man who wishes to make his own or another's promise binding, the seal was at common law available as a device for the accomplishment of his objective. In this aspect form offers a legal framework into which the party may fit his actions, or, to change the figure, it offers channels for the legally effective expression of intention. It is with this aspect of form in mind that I have described the third function of legal formalities as 'the channeling function.'

"In seeking to understand this channeling function of form, perhaps the most useful analogy is that of language. . . ."

Lon Fuller, *supra* note 6, at 801. This view of the working of a system of formal rules is not limited to the law of contracts and conveyances. Speaking of "wills, gifts, contracts, marriages, and the like," H. L. A. Hart says that through the legal rules "the individual's choice is brought into the legal system and allowed to determine its future operations in various areas thereby giving him a type of indirect coercive control over, and a power to foresee the development of, official life." Punishment and Responsibility; Essays in the Philosophy of Law 45 (1968). In the same essay, Hart argues that rules of criminal law perform the same function. *Id.* at 22-24; 44-49. And Holmes made much of the importance of developing the rules of tort liability in such a way as to facilitate their use in the rational adjustment of private action to regular patterns of official legal response. See Oliver Wendell Holmes, Jr., *supra* note 2, at Lecture 3.

See notes 21 and 22 *supra* for a discussion of some of the problems that arise when the legislator attempts to formulate legal rules in such a way as make them effective in communicating the parties' intention to the judge, rather than simply relying on the postulated certainty of the factual predicates of rules in general.

which two inconsistent rules must be applied, if each is to be enforced according to its own definition of its sphere of application; other situations arise in which *no* rule is available.[41] Parties *may* be able to arrange their affairs so as never to fall within the area of uncertainty, albeit at some undefined cost in restriction of their freedom. But there now exists a class of situations into which they can enter only at the price of licensing someone—either the rule applier himself wearing another hat or some other *ad hoc* intervenor—to shape their relationship according to his arbitrary and inherently indeterminate view of the appropriate outcome. If we suppose that the repertoire of official behavior (*i.e.*, the possible state responses to the situation) does not change when an official acquires discretionary power, the parties become less well off. The situation may be compared to that of a group who live near the mouth of a volcano. So long as they have precise knowledge of when it will erupt and how violently, they may not suffer much, and may even benefit from its proximity. Without the ability to predict, they would have to choose between a drastic restriction of activities now become risky and moving to a less desirable but safer location.[42]

[41] Of course, all conceivable actual systems of rules *do* contain many gaps, inconsistencies, and ambiguities, so that it is inevitable that someone other than the legislature will have to exercise continuing "discretion" (*supra* note 11) in keeping the system in repair. This proposition is sometimes put forward as a criticism of the argument for formality. If all that is meant is that the formal system cannot operate in the absence of pre-established rules, then the objection is valid but uninteresting. The theory is designed to explain why we should strive for the *ideal* of a consistent, gapless and unambiguous system, mechanically operated; it does not assert that we can attain the goal. In a more sophisticated form, however, the argument has more bite. It may be asserted that gaps, inconsistencies, and ambiguities are so prevalent in any real system, and occur with such regularity precisely at the most important moments in a real system's history, that the theory of formality can be accepted as true but dismissed as trivial. This argument is closely connected with that for "principles" as representing a distinct process of decision (see note 11 *supra* and the discussion in Part III of the Third Way, §§ 79-85) and with that for the proposition that "facts" cannot be found without an assessment of "purposes" (see notes 14 and 21 *supra*). This is not the place to argue the merits of this objection to formality. For what it is worth, my feeling is that a vast amount of energy goes into the fabrication of gaps, inconsistencies, and ambiguities where the "real" objection is to the consequences of a formal system we can neither accept nor replace. It is for this reason that it seems important to press on with the critique of formality *on its own terms*. Cf. H. L. A. Hart, *supra* note 10, at 606-11.

[42] In Chapter II of Punishment and Responsibility (*supra* note 40), H. L. A. Hart constructs an argument for excuses in criminal law, and for such defenses as fraud, mistake, incapacity and duress in civil law, that both implicitly assumes and exactly parallels the defense of judicial rule application offered here. Hart argues that the aim of assuring private welfare through a predictable and responsive administration of justice is separate from that of achieving the substantive goals of criminal and civil law, and that the two goals can be conceived as to be maximized each subject to the constraint of the other (see *id.* at 245 (note)). He then shows how excuses and defenses increase the ability of parties to control the legal system because they decrease the chance of inadvertent triggering of an unwanted official response. The whole discussion assumes that judges are attentive *only* to these communications, *i.e.*, that they are rule appliers. See notes 39 and 40 *supra*.

37. To summarize, there are two reasons for a rule applier to steel himself to disregard every aspect of the situation other than that factual aspect he is directed to ascertain. First, if he considers the effects of his decision, whether on the litigants or on society at large, or allows himself to be swayed by considerations of fairness, right, justice or mercy, he has usurped the function of the postulated legitimate legislative body. He is then transforming himself into a private center of power, or putting himself at the disposal of some existing center, and this conduct threatens to destroy the precarious fabric of compromise that is civil order. Second, blind rule application promotes the general welfare. By acting formally, the judge does his part toward the "naturalization" of society, that is, toward increasing the ruledness of the social events the individual must deal with in his maximizing activities.[43]

II. The Critique of Formal Justice

> To the care of the soveraign, belongeth the making of Good Lawes. But what is a good Law? By a Good Law, I mean not a Just Law: for no Law can be unjust. The Law is made by the Soveraign Power, and all that is done by such Power, is warranted and owned by every one of the people; and that which every man will have so, no man can say is unjust. It is in the Lawes of a Commonwealth, as in the Lawes of Gaming; whatsoever the Gamesters all agree on is Injustice to none of them.[44]

A.

38. In this part I present a criticism of the theory of formality.[45] I have cast much of it in the form of an argument by the litigant to the judge for a

[43] "Law is at the same time a form of external authoritarian regulation in one aspect, while in the other it is a form of subjective private autonomy. In the one case, that which is basic and essential is the index of unconditional obligation and coercion from without; in the other the index of freedom, guaranteed and acknowledged within certain boundaries. Law comes forth at one time as a principle of social organization, and at another time as a means for individuals 'to be disunited, being in society.' . . ."

E. B. Pashukanis, The General Theory of Law and Marxism, in Soviet Legal Philosophy 111, 150 (1951).

[44] Thomas Hobbes, *supra* note 1, at 185.

[45] There are many others. See, *e.g.*, the works of Karl Llewellyn, Lon L. Fuller, and Ronald Dworkin cited *supra* note 5, Fuller's The Law in Quest of Itself (1940), and Llewellyn's, A Realistic Jurisprudence—The Next Step, 30 Colum. L. Rev. 431 (1930). Objections other than the one I develop here are discussed *supra* in notes 11, 12, 14, 21 and 41. In Part III, *infra*, I will discuss various formulations of the judicial role designed

reprieve from rigid rule application. The judge offers a series of justifications of his obduracy. It is important to be clear at the outset that the litigant is *not*, at this stage, arguing for victory on the merits of his claim against his opponent. He is only arguing that the judge should *hear* him on the merits. In the case of the Statute of Frauds, he is asking a chance to offer his proof that there *was* a contract, although unwritten. The minute the judge acknowledges that this offer of proof might have an effect on the outcome, the litigant has surmounted the barrier of formality, which consists exactly in refusal to consider such collateral factual aspects once it is established that mechanical rule application dictates a particular result. In other words, formality consists *not* in the activity of *following* rules, but in the process of their rigid application. The judge who reaches his decision by substantively rational processes is not acting formally, even if he follows the rule ninety-nine times in a hundred.

39. *Formality itself represents a compromise of conflicting claims: The heterogeneity of values and the multiplicity of factual situations, in a world of purposive actors, forces the group to admit an element of the arbitrary and irrational into its governance.* Suppose the group could, without sacrifice by each individual of the time he needs to devote to pursuit of his own objectives, and without creation of hopeless uncertainty, use its substantively rational legislative process to resolve all possible disputes in advance or preside over each quarrel as it arose. Litigants would have to accept the results as per se legitimate, since it is a postulate of the theory as I have been developing it that the group has evolved a legislative mechanism whose representativeness is of such a character that its decisions generate political obligation.[46]

40. The institution of formality represents the explicit abandonment of this ideal of adjudication. Under a formal regime, a person involved in a dispute expects to be within the power of an official applying a pre-existing body of rules; by the time the dispute has arisen, it is already too late for resort to the legislature, even were that body organized in such a way as to make it capable of handling more than a small fraction of the flow of contro-

---

either to respond to criticisms like these or to replace formality altogether. I feel uneasy at this fragmented treatment of other objections than the one I present in this part, but have been unable to devise anything better.

[46] There is every reason to suppose that a legislature adjudicating disputes would assess the effects of basing its decisions on rules, and, if it did use rules, the effects of occasional relaxation or revision of rules in particular cases. In other words, the process of collective decision is distinguished from formality by the fact that it is the sovereign itself that decides, and so can adopt any approach that seems desirable, whereas formality means rule application by an official and nothing else.

Of course, in some nonpolitical sense the outcome even of legislative adjudication might be unjust. The losing party might have every reason to feel that malice or cupidity or stupidity or mendacity had clouded the judgment against him. But the postulate of legislative legitimacy means precisely that the citizen feels obliged to obey despite *this* kind of defect in the result.

versies. Formality therefore means that the litigant can gain nothing from a complete consensus of those represented in the political process that the rule in question, if applied according to its terms, will work an undesirable result. Even were he to convince the rule applier that not a single legislator, in a regime of legislative as opposed to formal adjudication, would vote for his opponent's position (*no one* applauds the sharp operator who uses the Statute of Frauds to evade an agreement with a legal neophyte), it would do no good. More: the litigant can gain nothing even though he convinces the rule applier that none of the parties to the compromise of which the rule was originally a part anticipated or desired the result the judge is about to bring about.

41. But if all this is true, why should the rule applier feel obliged to carry out and the litigant feel obliged to obey the formal mandate? The litigant claims that the substantively rational compromise to which he agreed in order to avoid civil war allotted him a greater share of the benefits of group living than he will receive if the rule is applied formally. The response is—silence. To each appeal to the substantive values the community was to achieve through the rules, the answer will be that the formal or processual values of judicial subordination and legal certainty forbid the rule applier even to *listen* to a plea that can be properly addressed only to a legislature everyone knows to be inaccessible.

42. How then, does the theory of formality claim to transfer the postulated legitimacy of legislative decision to the administration of the system of rules? In one version of the argument, the answer is that we should conceive the fractious litigant claiming entitlement to a legislative adjudication as reneging on an earlier agreement to forego such luxuries so that the group could get on with the business of private maximization. We are to suppose that when an individual joins the group he recognizes that he cannot conceivably, given the heterogeneity of values, the multiplicity of facts and the limits of existence in time, expect that disputes in general will receive anything like the "full treatment." We are to suppose that he therefore thinks it to his advantage to "contract" that neither he nor any other member of the community should be entitled to anything more than formal process.[47] It follows that the pathos I attempted to inject into the description of his plight before a stony rule applier and a busy legislature was altogether misplaced.

43. In another version, the social maximizer objects to the improper opposition of "substantive" to "formal or processual" values in adjudication. He points out that the decision to deny the litigant a hearing on the question of how we would decide his case, *if* values were homogeneous, facts uniplex

[47] See John Stuart Mill, *supra* note 4, at bk. II, ch. 1, § 2, for an illustration of this form of argument with reference *not* to formality in general but to a body of rules of property to be formally administered.

and time unlimited, is anything but irrational or arbitrary. Since the social maximum can *only* be achieved by sacrificing some litigants—*i.e.*, since processual costs are just as real as substantive ones—the sacrifice is not arbitrary but rather just. Indeed, a legal system that permitted this one litigant to be an exception to the general rule of denial of a hearing on substantive issues would be quintessentially unjust. And a society in which no one could achieve his objectives because everyone was constantly engaged in collegial resolution of the disputes that sprang up on all sides the minute the group rose from judgment would be quintessentially irrational.[48]

44. The rest of this part is devoted to showing, within the general framework already postulated, one of the limitations of these contractarian and utilitarian justifications of formality. My purpose is a vindication in the language of Reason of the pity and fear aroused in us by the image of a fellow human being at grips with institutions of formal justice.[49]

45. The objection to formality I will propose arises out of the very structure of formal institutions. That objection is that the formal system is already in decay at the moment the litigant protests against its arbitrary disposition of his case. It follows from the definitions of rule making and rule applying that rule making takes place under *uncertainty*. The making is based on a set of hypotheses or probabilistic judgments about how the total situation of the group will look if such and such rules are applied to such and such factual situations. The rules themselves, however, are by definition inflexible rather than probabilistic; once enacted, they must be enforced even if the non-legal components in the situations to which they are applied differ utterly from those the rule makers anticipated.

46. Consider a hypothetical case in which all the participants in the process of rule making, all the representatives of the conflicting interests to be maximized, share a single estimate of the probabilities of future events. On the

[48] See note 38 *supra*. I found the following suggestive as well:

"Both bona fide purchase for value after fraud, etc., and unwillingness to recognize economic duress, seem to me impregnated strongly with recognition that life and transactions must after all go on, upon whatever basis we have at the moment. The one stresses highly legitimate expectations; the other protects what may be conceived as illegitimate expectations; yet a solid common core they have. In less sophisticated law the same common core is again apparent, although coupled this time with the power of word-magic or form-magic. If you have sealed and delivered, you are bound. Unless you plead in words to the indictment, you simply cannot be tried. You can be put to the *peine forte et dure* (life must go on! ours, if not yours) but that produces neither trial nor conviction."

Karl N. Llewellyn, *supra* note 6, at 728, n.49.

[49] Rereading recently Llewellyn's great essay, "What Price Contract?," I came across the following: "One turns from contemplation of the work of contract as from the experience of Greek tragedy. Life struggling against form, or through form to its will—'pity and terror'—. Law means so pitifully little to life. Life is so terrifyingly dependent on law." *Id.* at 751.

basis of this estimate, they argue and negotiate toward agreement on a set of rules. The result is a compromise: the rules dispose of all situations that have a probability of arising, each particular rule being more or less satisfactory to each interest. If the joint estimate is accurate, the rule *appliers* then proceed to implement the compromise merely by carrying out their function of mechanical enforcement. Each interest receives its "due" in the form of an expected number of adjudications in its favor.

47. A first problem arises from the fact that we are unable to predict the future, and worse at prediction the farther we try to reach forward in time. In the beginning, even given uncertainty, the officials apply the rules to situations approximating those they were designed for, and at least approximately implement the compromise the rules represent. But with the cumulative working out of divergences the world comes finally to bear little or no resemblance to that anticipated. The interaction of the old rules with the new situation begins to generate anomalies, patterns of behavior quite different from those the rules were designed to induce, and distributive results that contradict and then transform everyone's expectations.[50]

48. According to the theory of formality, no matter how great the gap that has developed between the planned compromise of claims and the actual distribution the rules are bringing about, the litigant must accept the results mechanically administered him by the rule applier. He is to say to himself: "I gambled: the universe may differ from what I anticipated, and my share turned out smaller than all had thought it would be, but I assumed the risk." Or perhaps he is to say: "I am the egg society must break to make the omelette of welfare; the bad consequences of exceptions to the rules would clearly outweigh, in this case and in every other, any gains we might derive from attempts to preserve the contours of the original compromise."

49. The difficulty with insisting on these responses is that the logic of formality *recognizes no limits*. Extremism is at the very core of rule applica-

[50] There are a number of alternative ways to express the fundamental idea of the cumulative divergence of factual patterns from those anticipated. One formulation opposes the Order of History to the Order of Reason (or of Ideas), and asserts that the Order of History is *never* reducible to the Order of Reason (or of Ideas), so that every reasoned construction ultimately finds itself marooned in its own historical moment. A superficially less metaphysical formulation asserts that each of the expectations of the rule makers was *probabilistic*; over time, the actual unfolding of events shows some of the rule makers' gambles to have been losing ones; events that had been thought unlikely occur frequently, anticipated events fail to occur at all, and the impossible and inconceivable become actual. Each unexpected event has its own consequences reacting back upon the gambles that *did* pay off. There is no reason whatever to suppose that over time the various divergences will cancel each other out; indeed, such a natural balance of fortuity would be a fluke. As time passes, more and more events that were not or could not have been anticipated become possible and then actual. Eventually it comes to be flatly impossible or extremely unlikely, given what we know today, that tomorrow's events will have any resemblance at all to yesterday's predictions.

tion. Formality demands the same passive response of the litigant *no matter how radical the discontinuity of plan and reality*.[51] The litigant's hypothetical contract turns out to be a monstrous affair, a "naturalization" of the rule applier that makes him insensible by agreement to the worst distortions of the compromise he administers.

50. This is particularly clear when the parties to the substantively rational rule making process are capable of acting on distinct hypotheses about the circumstances to which the rules will be applied. The compromise represented by the body of rules may then be a false one, based on inconsistent expectations of those involved. It is then *inevitable* that from the perspective of those whose expectations are disappointed the rules will implement not what they thought they had agreed to, but something they thought had no chance of occurring. Yet given the premise of a formal order, the losers could proceed only on the basis of *some* estimate, so that no matter how great their loathing for risk they *had* to wager on the future. They took the risk without "assuming" it.[52]

> The Court is not unsympathetic to plaintiff's plight but "[s]tability of contract obligations must not be undermined by judicial sympathy."
> It has been the sacredness of contractual

[51] See §§ 12-13, and notes 10, 15 and 16 *supra*.

[52] "When all the people had assembled in the galleries, . . . the king . . . gave a signal, a door beneath him opened, and the accused subject stepped out into the amphitheatre. Directly opposite him, on the other side of the enclosed space, were two doors, exactly alike and side by side. It was the duty and the privilege of the person on trial to walk directly to these doors and open one of them. He could open either door he pleased. He was subject to no guidance or influence but that of the aforementioned impartial and incorruptible chance. If he opened the one, there came out of it a hungry tiger, the fiercest and most cruel that could be procured, which immediately sprang upon him, and tore him to pieces, as a punishment for his guilt. The moment that the case of the criminal was thus decided, . . . great wails went up from the hired mourners . . . .

"But if the accused person opened the other door, there came forth from it a lady, the most suitable to his years and station that his Majesty could select among his fair subjects; and to this lady he was immediately married, as a reward of his innocence. It mattered not that he might already possess a wife and family, or that his affections might be engaged upon an object of his own selection. The king allowed no such subordinate arrangements to interfere with his great scheme of retribution and reward. . . .

"This was the king's semibarbaric method of administering justice. Its perfect fairness is obvious. The criminal could not know out of which door would come the lady. He opened either he pleased, without having the slightest idea whether, in the next instant, he was to be devoured or married. . . .

"The institution was a very popular one. . . . [T]he thinking part of the community could bring no charge of unfairness against this plan; for did not the accused person have the whole matter in his own hands?"

Frank Stockton, The Lady or the Tiger?, in The Lady or the Tiger and Other Stories 4-6 (1908).

> obligations which has prevented courts of equity from imposing justice in many circumstances. Nevertheless, it is anticipated that ameliorative legislation . . . will shortly be a reality and perhaps this very case may provide the stimulus necessary to enactment. Copies of this opinion shall be sent to the appropriate legislative committees. The Court cannot legislate and is constrained to grant defendant's motion and deny plaintiff's motion despite the apparent inequities.[53]

B

51. The judge will be the more reluctant to accept the litigant's anti-formal arguments because they are almost wholly negative: they undermine the legitimacy of rule application without suggesting a valid alternative role for the judge. To begin with, how is he to decide that the actual situation is significantly different from that anticipated? The expectations of the participants are both highly subjective and quite possibly conflicting. Second, supposing that divergence is established or assumed, how is the judge to decide whether or not the actual distribution is, given the changes in circumstances, in harmony with the original agreement? The notion of an appeal to the "spirit" of the original compromise—that is, to its purposes against its manifestation in the form of rules—makes no sense because the rules, in the conception involved here, *have no spirit*. Particular rules have no purposes except as pieces in a larger compromise of interests. It was always contemplated that each rule would work adversely to some actors some of the time; the objective was to balance off these adversities in a whole acceptable to all. The only way to find out how the rules would have differed if they had been expected to apply to different circumstances would be to re-enact the legislative process. The litigant thus appears to be proposing that the judge foresake the secure and stable occupation of rule application for the obviously dangerous job of substantively rational arbiter of disputes about a constantly changing pattern of distributive justice and injustice.

52. The judge will be tempted to respond that it is precisely because things change that we have permanent legislatures. They may not help the individual litigant, but they do keep the overall compromise from disintegration or transformation. As a result, the rule applier should be just that and no more. The

[53] Division of Triple T Service, Inc. v. Mobil Oil Corp., 60 Misc. 2d 720, 733, 304 N.Y.S.2d 191, 204 (1969), aff'd without opinion, 34 A.D.2d 618, 311 N.Y.S.2d 961 (2d Dep't 1970) (citations omitted).

disappointed litigant *can* claim the honors of the sacrificial victim, but so long as the legislature exists he cannot claim he has been sacrificed arbitrarily to a now non-operative compromise. There is nothing "rule utilitarian" about a formal system; it is fully capable of evolving. If change cumulates so that the rules appear irrational, if it turns out that some good faith expectations were radically erroneous, the cure is at hand. The point is that evolution is the work of the legislature, not the rule applier.

53. But unless *some* time is allowed to pass between the establishment of the formal system and adjustments of it to take account of the actual working of the rules, we are not dealing with a formal structure at all. If every application of the rules can lead to a successful appeal for a substantively rational readjustment of the rule system in order to compensate for unanticipated consequences, then the group harvests none of the benefits of formality.

54. During this necessary interval between rule-making and readjustment, the uncertain interplay of actors within the structure of rules changes the community, the legislature, and the distributive functions the rules perform. The particular factual elements that evoke particular official responses still occur, but they occur with unexpected frequency or infrequency, and they appear embedded in larger factual situations no one had anticipated. As a consequence, rigid rule application begins to transform the relationship of the group members to one another. The pattern of production and distribution of valued objects, including production and distribution of power in the rule-making institutions, changes.

55. The process of change does more than prevent the rules from implementing the original compromise. It creates for them a whole new set of functions; they become bulwarks of a whole new set of interests. The formal system becomes an expression of a new constellation of forces it has itself blindly created. Each formal application of the rules takes the litigant and the rest of society farther and farther from the situation within which he thought he had secured, through formality, the position formality is now denying him.[54]

[54] "Law *must* grow fixed, in most of its parts, and relative to most of the ways of society apart from law. And the ancient problem must continue to recur. . . . [*T*]*o the extent of* such divergence between non-legal obligation and the legal obligation officially recognized on the same facts, the legal obligation . . . comes to function also as a *source of risk*. If the other party appeals to law, then to the extent that the obligation is viewed by layman and by law-man differently, I shall either get less, or be held to more, than the customary understanding calls for. And I repeat, such a divergence, such an incursion of risk, is a constant tendency as soon as legal technique becomes specialized, as soon as officials begin looking for their solutions not directly at the life before them, but indirectly at the deposits of their own or their predecessors' prior dealings with similar situations. . . . And surely it is obvious that as the law of contract thus constantly grows rigid upon its own premises and to itself ('certain and reckonable' or 'out

56. But one can grant that the litigant can never appeal to the same legislature twice, that he never gets a chance to redesign the original compromise so that it will work out in practice, and still defend formality. The postulate of legislative legitimacy implies that later legislative acts control earlier ones, so that one is never *entitled* to have a present situation disposed of in accordance with either the letter or the general sense of a previous legislative arrangement. Just as the legislature can legitimately repeal earlier rules and pass new ones, so it can legitimately maintain a body of rules in existence for reasons directly opposed to those that led an earlier legislature to enact them. It follows, according to the theory of formality, that so long as the postulated legitimate legislative process is in existence, there can be no validity to the charge that the actual situation diverges so far from the expectations underlying the rules that their formal application would be unjust. This brings us finally to the heart of the moral objection to formality: *The judge cannot claim that legislative acquiescence legitimizes his action because he himself creates, through his decision of particular cases, the situation from which will emerge an as yet indeterminate constellation of legislative power.*

57. Within the theory of formality there is no distinction between political and economic motives: all action is conceived as driven by the subjective and individual value/desire/purpose dimension of existence. All actors are conceived as bundles of interests in process of maximization, whether through private (*i.e.*, economic) activity within the structure of rules or through public (*i.e.*, political) activity within a legislative structure postulated to be representative. I have already pointed out that the content of the rules formulated in the public legislative sphere heavily conditions the outcome of the struggle in the private sphere. This private outcome in turn automatically reacts back upon the political struggle, in two ways. The private outcome creates interests in the continuation or modification of the rules that produced it, and distributes among those represented in the legislature whatever resources may be necessary to produce results in its substantively rational process. It follows that when the judge influences the private outcome he also influences the public outcome that will reflect it.[55] Granted that the

of date and over-formal'—the phrasing is immaterial) it offers the cautious and canny layman an advantage over his unschooled adversary."

Karl N. Llewellyn, *supra* note 6, at 713-14 (emphasis in original).

[55] This conclusion, which is implied in the premises of the model of formality, is also the starting point for modern liberal political theory. From Locke to the *Federalist*, it is a constant theme that representative institutions are inevitably the locus of factional disputes between groups defined in terms of economic interests. *Cf.* C. B. Macpherson, *supra* note 2; Charles A. Beard, An Economic Interpretation of the Constitution of the United States (1913). One modern equivalent is the theory of "interest groups," or "pluralism," which asserts that through the interplay of legislative bargaining (or "logrolling," which is the exact analytic equivalent of the institution

legislative decision *will be* legitimate, however it may dispose of the litigant's claim that the rules should be revised. The problem is that a judge who has a measure of influence over *what* that postulated legitimate decision will be cannot treat it as an external, objective factor validating whatever he may choose to do. He must justify his contribution to the legitimate response rather than be justified *by* it.[56]

---

of contract in the private sphere) groups and potential groups safeguard their shares of welfare and assure an equitable distribution of new benefits. See, *e.g.*, David B. Truman, The Governmental Process; Political Interests and Public Opinion (1951); Robert A. Dahl, Who Governs? Democracy and Power in an American City (1961); Nelson W. Polsby, Community Power and Political Theory (1963); and the discussion in Mancur Olson, *supra* note 4, at 111-31 and Theodore Lowi, The End of Liberalism: Ideology, Policy and the Crisis of Public Authority 1-97 (1969). A distinct modern development is the attempt at an actual fusion of political and economic theory based on the rigorous application of the postulates described in §§ 17-20 above to political behavior. In this version, the process of logrolling is still the key, but we are offered an economic analysis of the conditions under which it will make everyone better off, at least by reference to his initial endowment of resources (derived from the outcome of private activity), and suggestions concerning the impact of the structure of the political process (*e.g.*, voting rules) on the outcome. See Anthony Downs, An Economic Theory of Democracy (1957); James M. Buchanan & Gordon Tullock, *supra* note 12; and the discussion in William J. Baumol, *supra* note 4, at 1-48. Finally, the most formal of all the approaches is that of "n person game theory," which generalizes to all kinds of bargaining conclusions such as the following:

"Everything that has been said . . . about the useful properties of equilibrium prices is *relative* to the initial commodity distribution. If that is unfair, no amount of economic and social 'efficiency' in the exchange mechanism will do more than make the best of a bad job . . . ."

Peter Newman, The Theory of Exchange 122 (1965) (emphasis in original). See also Michael Leiserson, Game Theory and the Study of Coalition Behavior, in The Study of Coalition Behavior: Theoretical Perspectives and Cases from Four Continents (S. Groenning, E. W. Kelley & M. Leiserson eds. 1970).

In short, I think it fair to say that it is a postulate of liberal political theory in practice, as well as in the model of this essay, that the "natural surround" (see § 10) which conditions the outcome of a substantively rational political process is private economic activity within the structure of rules created by earlier phases of that same political process.

56 My purpose in this section has been to present a logical property of the model of formality, rather than to put forward any particular historical thesis or hypothesis. The dilemma of the judge derives from the *possibility* that his action will have decisive redistributive effects, rather than from certainty about what those effects will be. Given the possibility, he cannot refuse the parties a hearing—and that represents *ipso facto* the abandonment of formality.

Nonetheless, some undocumented illustrations may be helpful. The most familiar and most spectacular is the case of reapportionment, where the mechanical application of an old formula often creates a distribution of political power bearing no resemblance at all to that the rules once reflected. All other examples are less clear because the link between the rules and political power is less direct. On a grand scale, it is often argued that the regime of free contract and free competition of the early 19th century, established by a nation of economic individualists to favor equality and initiative, became in the second half of the 19th century both the creator and the bulwark of a system of bureaucratic enterprise and monopolistic markets. A common interpretation of subsequent develop-

58. This justification can only take the form of a non-formal explanation of why it is that following the rule in question is better or worse than not following it. The judge is sworn to carry out the legislative will, but the legislature is perforce silent on the subject of what its will *should be*. Since he can claim neither that the rules implement the original compromise nor that the legislature will take care of the problem of distributive justice without regard to his action, he must confront his political obligation as a citizen, or his moral duty to his fellow man, or his religious duty, or his conception of his own self-interest, or whatever else it may be that is decisive for him when his duty as a public servant is no longer clear. Nothing could be further from the formal process of mechanical rule application.

59. Having followed the argument step by step to this point, it may be helpful to attempt a more general statement of the flaw in the logic of formality. The particular beauty of the theory as I laid it out in Part I derived from the coincidence of *two* purposes behind the practice of mechanical rule application. The rule applier both implements the compromise by which the community legitimately disposes of the problem of distributive justice, *and* provides a highly certain framework for private maximizing activity. The introduction of uncertainty into the model destroys this coincidence by creating the possibility that the rules will overthrow rather than execute the original compromise. The judge then faces a choice. He can declare his willingness at least to *consider* the possibility that he should disregard the rule and examine the question of distributive justice. In this case, he abandons formal process and overthrows the formal order, even if he ultimately decides to follow the rule in the particular case before him. Litigants

---

ments is that these new interests came to control the legislatures to such a degree that they could shape the new regime of regulation in their favor rather than in that of the smaller enterprisers who raised such a hue and cry against them. See James Willard Hurst, Law and the Conditions of Freedom in the Nineteenth Century United States (1956); Gabriel Kolko, The Triumph of Conservatism (1963); and James Weinstein, The Corporate Ideal in the Liberal State: 1900-1918 (1968). On a much smaller scale, the formal interpretation of the contracts between the automobile manufacturers and their dealers creates a situation in which the manufacturers' economic power, already great, becomes relatively even greater, making it all the more difficult for the dealers to achieve any meaningful impact, either through private bargaining or through the legislature, on those same contracts. See Stewart Macaulay, Law and The Balance of Power: The Automobile Manufacturers and Their Dealers (1966).

Finally, at an absolute minimum, the judge is *always* working some kind of distributive effect between plaintiff and defendant. If the parties are represented in the political process, and if their status in that process is a function of their successes and failures in the private maximization struggle, then their ability to achieve distributive justice for themselves as individuals will be affected. Even if this effect is *de minimis* in each case taken separately, the judge must contend with the fact that *taken together* a multiplicity of such rule applications define the most fundamental characteristics of the political system—*e.g.*, through the protection of private property. See, for example, Robert L. Hale, Force and the State: A Comparison of "Political" and "Economic" Compulsion, 35 Colum. L. Rev. 149 (1935).

will ever after have to contend with his substantively rational decisions as to whether or not they will receive the benefit of the rule.

60. The alternative is for the judge to find some way to dispose of his responsibility to implement a compromise distribution, and return to formal rule application with the single purpose of securing the certainty of the framework for private maximizing. The notion that the continuous existence of the legislature relieves the judge of any responsibility for distribution accomplishes just this result. If we could accept it, the judge could go back to mechanical rule application and simply forget about the question of what has happened to the original compromise. Unfortunately, the judge himself is a political actor in the creation of the legislative constellation of forces that supposedly legitimates his decisions. The litigant is therefore entitled to ask him to justify his decision as a citizen, and this he cannot do without abandoning formal process.

61. At this point in the argument, it is customary to propose that the legislature could relieve the judge of responsibility for distributive justice by *decreeing* that he act formally. Admitting that the judge will be unable to make up his *own* mind to apply the rules mechanically, the argument is that once the legislature makes a decision *for* him, his difficulties disappear. The proposition is complex and deserves a thorough hearing.

62. One of its meanings is that the judge should *presume* that the legislature intended him to go on applying the rule no matter how absurd or unjust its application might become, leaving it to future legislatures to make any necessary corrections. In this branch of the argument, the next question must be, "Why make such a presumption?" One sort of answer is that as a matter of fact legislatures intend that judges act formally, but this is beside the point. We are concerned here with how the state *should* be organized, not with how any particular legislature in fact conceives an ideal allocation of legal functions.

63. Another answer is the assertion that the legislature *ought* to decree that judges act formally. Given the "social maximizing" point of view, the argument must be that everyone will be better off if the legislature so instructs the judge. And this in turn is based on the claim that over the long run *any* judicial discretion is more dangerous than a mechanical procedure. The thesis is that informality cannot be restrained: once a little is introduced into the system, certainty begins to erode. The process of erosion stops only when the situation becomes an intolerable combination of the total denial of private autonomy with explosive litigiousness. Of course, the countervailing danger is that the set of rules mechanically applied to a changing background of private activity will end by working a de facto revolution that will overthrow the original compromise; but here at least there is some hope that the legislature will act in time to save the status quo.

64. The problem is that we cannot say the legislature *ought* to gamble on formality rather than putting its trust in a little judicial tinkering. Certainly it is possible to imagine a legislature deciding, rightly or wrongly, that a particular statutory scheme should be mechanically applied; but this is not an argument that will persuade the judge that the legislature should *always* be presumed to have so decided. In short, there is no basis for the position that the *theory itself* requires the legislature always to decree formality.

65. The other branch of the argument is much more modest. It asserts that if the legislature *has* decreed formality, the judge should obey. He should regard himself as the servant of the rule making body. If it is their desire to gamble on formality, he has no other duty than to roll the dice.

66. Yet the judge must ask exactly the same question about this rule as about any other that comes to him from the legislature. Its enactment represented a compromise of interests based on some set of quite possibly conflicting expectations about how its application would affect the future distribution of satisfactions. The theory behind enforcing it is that through rules the state implements the more general compromise necessary to preserve order while maximizing private autonomy within a stabilized civil society. But this particular rule, like any other, may have utterly lost its sense within the projected compromise and have become a threat to the original settlement. The judge's blind adherence to its command may so alter the balance of power that those who will benefit by its continued application will be able to block its repeal, while those who once favored it will find it threatening their most vital purposes. Where should the judge's loyalty lie? Loyalty to the rule is a decision for a particular political outcome; disregard of the rule threatens the very mechanism of order through compromise.

67. This dilemma is identical, at one remove, with that confronting the judge when the legislature leaves open the issue of formality and abandons him to his perplexities. An explicit enactment leaves him no better off than he was before, and on reflection this should not surprise. In the conception we are discussing, *all* laws are gambling contracts, as Hobbes saw long ago. *All* laws pose for judge and litigant the question whether they should accept a conception of the administration of justice as a mechanism for the collection of the resulting debts. It makes no sense to expect that yet one more gamble—a gamble on gambling—will make that problem go away.

68. Let me now try to state the dilemma of formality in terms of the model of welfare economics to which it owes much of its structure. The argument for mechanical rule application *as an aid to private maximization* is based on the concept of economic efficiency. The complete "naturalization" of the state was supposed desirable because the benefits that would result *could* be used to make everyone better off than they were when judges had a measure of discretion. Such a proposal provokes the question who is going to take care of the

consequences of the change for the *actual* distribution of welfare. The theory of formality proposes to the judge that this is the role of the legislature. Because it took all distributive effects into account in drafting the rules, he can apply them mechanically, thereby increasing the efficiency of private maximization. The objection to formality is that the enforcement process through which the judge achieves these allocative effects cannot be treated in isolation from the legislative mechanism that supposedly legitimates the distribution of welfare existing at any given time. Given the postulated representative character of legitimate political institutions, the analytic separation of allocation from distribution breaks down as soon as we relax the implicit assumption that all activities are either simultaneous or perfectly certain. The judge finds himself confronting the characteristic dilemma of the welfare economist who must choose between putting forward changes whose allocative advantages are legitimate only if unlikely redistributions are actually carried out, and restricting himself to less attractive changes whose actual distributive consequences are more likely to be acceptable to him.[57] The difference is that usually on a small scale, but *in fact,* the judge carries out operations the economist only proposes.

69. The contractarian is wrong to argue that we somehow assume the risks

[57] Calabresi's treatment of this issue in The Costs of Accidents: A Legal and Economic Analysis 31-33 (1970), is worth extended quotation for several reasons. It is an unusually precise and frank statement; it illustrates the *implicit* appeal to the legislature—the supposed proper instrument of redistribution (a "political" question)—as a technique legitimating a virtually exclusive analytical preoccupation with allocation (impliedly "nonpolitical"); yet it concludes that the welfare economist must eschew any formal rule of ignoring distribution, even supposing the existence of a legitimate legislature. The position of the judge differs from that of the Calabresian analyst, but not, I have tried to show, in such a way as to reduce his responsibility for the consequences of his acts.

"[P]eople have sought to use accident law as a means of reducing inequalities in income distribution, or of attacking problems of depression and unemployment. . . .

"Regarding these and similar goals, the fact [*sic*] is that we usually would do far better to attack the particular problem directly rather than through accident law. If subsidies to developing industries seem sensible, it is best to give them openly, with visible decisions as to who should pay, rather than through a system which removes some or all of the costs of accidents from the activities causing them and hides this subsidization by placing these costs on undefined or unrepresented groups.

"I do not mean to say that such "outside" goals can be totally ignored. . . . A system of accident law that exacerbates unequal distribution of income or favors monopolies will violate our moral framework, therefore seeming unjust. To this extent these outside goals remain relevant and will tend to prevent some systems from gaining acceptance. Whether this is a good result in any given case will depend not only on whether there are outside means for redressing the undesirable outside effects of the proposed system of accident law, but also on whether the undesirable effects will in fact be redressed if the system of accident law is adopted. If there are no readily available outside means for redressing the undesirable effects, . . . then it is proper to view these outside effects as costs of accidents and consider them in our analysis of such costs."

See also Guido Calabresi & A. Douglas Melamed, Property Rules, Liability Rules, and Inalienability: One View of the Cathedral, 85 Harv. L. Rev. 1089 (1972).

of formal administration of our social compacts and so cannot demand of the judge that he hear our claims on the merits. The point is that our compromises, our agreements, our commitments, even our triumphs, if they attain concrete expression *only* in the form of rules, always lead us astray. The judge should let us try to explain what has happened and propose a way out before he makes the situation perhaps irreparably worse. In the end he may decide we do not deserve to be excused from rigid application of the rule. But we should reject the idea that he need not even *listen.* Nor should we accept the maximizer's bland assurance that the litigant's sacrifice is on the altar of the common good. It may be true that everyone, or almost everyone, derives some benefit from the initial establishment of a process of formal dispute resolution. But the point is that some grow fat on arrangements designed to promote equality, succeed by tactics thought so surely self-destructive there was no need to condemn them, while good faith and fair dealing bring others to the wall. The rules, once caught up in time, *may* still serve the common good; they *certainly* serve a congeries of private goods. The judge cannot escape his measure of responsibility for the character of social life by the plea that "The rules did it."

70. I conclude that it is always at least *possibly* true of an existing formal system that contingency has unraveled the plan of social order until the litigant denied more than formal justice can say, without a trace of sour grapes, that he has been, not sacrificed, but simply exploited. The judge must take responsibility himself for deciding whether that possibility has become actual in the particular case before him.

III. Making the Problem Go Away

> Let us not be impatient with our forefathers. "Discretion" is not of necessity "the law of tyrants," and yet we may say with the great Romanist of our own day that formalism is the twin-born sister of liberty. As time goes on there is always a larger room for discretion in the law of procedure; but discretionary powers can only be safely entrusted to judges whose impartiality is above suspicion and whose every act is exposed to public and professional criticism. One of the best qualities of our medieval law was that in theory it left little or nothing, at all events within the sphere of procedure, to the discretion of the justices. *They themselves desired*

> *that this should be so and took care that it was or seemed to be so. They would be responsible for nothing beyond an application of iron rules.*[58]

71. We have reached the stage not of solutions to the problem of formality but of what I will call "attitudes of repose," meaning to suggest that what counts is that they terminate a discussion whose perennial character must cause profound disquiet among legal thinkers committed *both* to democracy and to judicial creativity.[59] I will describe and summarily criticize two such attitudes that the reader should find familiar.

72. I will call "neo-positivism" the doctrine that deals with the dilemma of formality by recognizing a measure of legislative power in the judge while maintaining the basic intellectual structure of the earlier theory—the linked dichotomies of rule application vs. substantive rationality and objective fact vs. subjective value.[60] It is easy to state the fundamental difficulty facing all neo-positivist solutions to the problem of formality. Having conceded that judges must and should exercise legislative power, neo-positivists have to decide whether the *limits* of the area of discretion can be defined by rules. If the judge may act legislatively only with regard to subjects or questions or according to techniques delineated by rules, then he is open to the charge that he has reinstated formality as the guardian of the boundaries of discretion. If he concedes the discretionary character of the decision to exercise discretion, he is open to the charge that he has abolished all distinctions of jurisdiction between courts and legislatures, leaving the judge "at large."[61]

[58] 2 Frederick Pollock & Frederic William Maitland, History of English Law ch. 9, § 1, at 561 (1st ed., 1895) (emphasis supplied).

[59] "What then are the functions of the judiciary in a modern democratic state? This smooth-seeming question, a question which I am posing here in the bland terminology of a college text-book, is tearing at the vitals of the law faculties and the bar associations of America." Louis L. Jaffe, *supra* note 16, at 9. See also the remark of H. L. A. Hart quoted *supra* note 28.

[60] Holmes, in So. Pacific Co. v. Jensen, 244 U.S. 205, 221 (1916) (dissenting opinion), gave a classic statement of the neo-positivist stance:

"I recognize without hesitation that judges do and must legislate, but they can do so only interstitially; they are confined from molar to molecular motions. A common law judge could not say I think the doctrine of consideration a bit of historical nonsense and shall not enforce it in my court."

Fuller suggests the response in his discussion of the case of a trial judge who must contend with an appellate court whose "decisions in the field of commercial law simply do not make sense." Fuller's judge needs guidance, but "it may be impossible for him to know whether his supreme court would regard any particular contribution of his as being wide or narrow." Lon L. Fuller, *supra* note 7, at 646-47.

[61] Some good examples of neo-positivism as I use the term here are Roscoe Pound, The Theory of Judicial Decision, 36 Harv. L. Rev. 641, 802, 940 (1923); Paul A. Freund, The Supreme Court of the United States, Its Business, Purposes and Performance (1961);

73. For example, it is common for neo-positivists to argue that there are whole subject matter areas within which social control should be "delegalized," or remitted to "administrative decision," or to the "case by case approach" or simply to discretion. Within these areas, according to the argument, a regime of rules, whether legislatively or judicially created, leads to rigidity and arbitrariness because ***no*** set of rules, no matter how often reformulated, can adequately protect the conflicting and confused social interests particular cases present. Depending on the writer, it follows that family law, rate regulation, sentencing of criminals, licensing, treatment of juvenile offenders, abridgments of the First Amendment in the interest of national security, determinations of negligence, or administration of protections for the criminal accused, should be left to unruled ad hoc decision. Other (or the same) writers argue that property, commercial law, the law of wills, the First and Fourth Amendments, antitrust, taxation, family law, and various other subjects, require a fundamentally different approach designed to protect the interest in "security."

74. But should the judge use *rules* to decide the proper categorization of a particular case or a particular subject matter? If so, how does he deal with the dilemma of formality? For example suppose a categorization of cases involving the formation of contracts as appropriate for formal treatment. Further suppose that sophisticated franchisors take advantage of the enthusiasm of potential franchisees and habitually induce substantial reliance before the parties have put anything in writing. Can the judge, perhaps using a confused version of the doctrine of promissory estoppel, create a new area of ad hoc, unruled, after-the-fact decision for certain types of contracts or contracting parties? If not, why not?

75. When a case falls within the area appropriate for formality, so that

---

Richard A. Wasserstrom, ***supra*** note 3; Frank I. Michelman, Property, Utility and Fairness: Comments on the Ethical Foundations of "Just Compensation" Law, 80 Harv. L. Rev. 1165 (1967).

The debate between "absolutists" and "balancers" in First Amendment law has evoked a number of interesting articles concerned with formality and neo-positivism. See, *e.g.*, Dennis v. United States, 341 U.S. 494, 524-25, 542-43 (1951) (Frankfurter, J., concurring); Laurent B. Frantz, The First Amendment in the Balance, 71 Yale L.J. 1424 (1962); Thomas I. Emerson, Toward a General Theory of the First Amendment, 72 Yale L.J. 1 (1964); Charles A. Reich, Mr. Justice Black and the Living Constitution, 76 Harv. L. Rev. 673, 736-44 (1963); Kenneth L. Karst, Legislative Facts in Constitutional Adjudication, 1960 Sup. Ct. Rev. 75; Wallace Mendelson, On the Meaning of the First Amendment: Absolutes in the Balance, 50 Calif. L. Rev. 821 (1962); Laurent B. Frantz, Is the First Amendment Law?—A Reply to Professor Mendelson, 51 Calif. L. Rev. 729 (1963).

Antitrust law has produced its own far less elaborate version of the same discussion. See Robert H. Bork, The Rule of Reason and the Per Se Concept: Price Fixing and Market Division, 74 Yale L.J. 775 (1965); Derek C. Bok, Section 7 of the Clayton Act and the Merging of Law and Economics, 74 Harv. L. Rev. 226, 295-98 (1960); Thomas E. Kauper, The "Warren Court" and the Antitrust Laws: of Economics, Populism and Cynicism, 67 Mich. L. Rev. 325 (1968).

resort to ad hoc decision is inappropriate, does the judge still have a measure of rule-making power? If he does not, the dilemma of formality applies in full force. If he does have rule-making power, how does he decide when to exercise it? If there are *rules* about when the judge can make law and when he must apply the legislative provision regardless of consequences, are they subject to exceptions? For example, suppose we concede that the area of criminal law should be governed formally. Further suppose that it is an area within which the rule-making power belongs to the legislature. Does it follow that judges should *never* do violence to the language of criminal statutes in order that they may achieve their manifest purpose?

76. Doubtless the reader familiar with modern styles in legal acadamese has noticed a "tension," a "balancing test," and the problem of "judicial attitude" peeking their heads over the horizon. The second attitude of repose in the face of the contradictions of formality consists in bringing those familiar characters into the foreground. The prescription to the judge is that in each case he should weigh the loss of the values of certainty and subordination to the legislature against the gains in the achievement of substantive social goals that will result if he disregards the existing rule.

77. Although processual and substantive values are thus placed in "tension" and must be "balanced," the judge is not conceived as *wholly* at large. If he is conscientious in carrying out this mental operation, carefully tallying all the bad consequences as well as the good, he will find himself constantly confronting *the dilemma of his own political power*. On the one hand, the rewriting of rules and the fashioning of ad hoc exceptions involve denying autonomy to private actors and assuming the power of choice among ends, a process postulated to be subjective, inherently arbitrary, and legitimate only when done democratically. Every act of judicial rule making is therefore in some measure an act of usurpation. On the other hand, the legislature may be corrupt or anaesthetized or simply overworked, and one of the parties may be attempting the legal murder of the other.

78. According to this view, there is nothing in our legal knowledge properly so called to help the judge with the "difficult and delicate task" of deciding whether or not to intervene. If one is a "passivist," the only guarantees of successful judging are the general attitude of humility, the recognition of the limits of reason, and the ability to tolerate uncertainty that go with "emotional maturity" (or perhaps "the tragic view of life"). If one is an "activist," the only guarantee of successful judging is the combination of real insight into social reality with passionate commitment to the ideal of justice. In short, the activist/passivist adopts not an attitude of repose but an expressive gesture: he throws up his hands (ironically, cynically, sentimentally or even sacerdotally) and places his faith in legal education and the political victories of his friends.

79. What I will call the Third Way is a construct of my own intended to show a unity in the work of Lon Fuller, Karl Llewellyn, and Hart and Sacks.[62] The Third Way differs most strikingly from neo-positivism in that it arises from a general critique of the postulates of formality drawn from the natural law tradition on the one hand and from pragmatism on the other. It represents a much more ambitious undertaking than neo-positivism, proposing a radical reconception of the situation of the judge rather than merely our reconciliation with the ruins of earlier intellectual accomplishments.

80. Yet the Third Way maintains a good deal of the structure of formality. Legal rules are still conceived as a backdrop against which, or as a structure within which, "private orderers" pursue their conflicting interests. It is still a postulate that the content of the body of law in force is indeterminate, a product of substantively rational compromises of interests in conflict rather than of reason. It is still a postulate that these substantively rational compromises can be legitimate only if created by a body representative of the conflicting wills of the citizenry, and that such a body is radically unsuited for the detailed administration of the rules it promulgates. The Third Way addresses precisely the central problem of formality: The institution to which the legislature delegates the task of directing the actual application of coercive power over the citizenry must somehow attain legitimacy for its actions. Finally, the solution the Third Way offers for this problem bears a distinct family resemblance to that offered by formality. The coercive power of courts is legitimate because exercised in a way that (a) clearly relates the application of force to the substantively rational compromises of the legislature, and (b) permits private parties to predict in advance how particular disputes will be decided.

82. Yet the Third Way is founded on a *rejection* of the formal solution, a rejection encompassing both the legal ideal of a gapless, fully defined system of rules and the notion that rule application is a desirable conceptualization of the judicial role. Like neo-positivism, the Third Way proposes in the place of formality a solution that accords the judge a measure of law-making power. Unlike neo-positivism, it challenges the notion that there are only two kinds of decision process. And it denies that *all* questions relating to the compromise of conflicting claims that is the legal order are equally resistant to judicial resolution. In short, the Third Way asserts that there is a judicial method distinct both from substantive rationality and from rule application, and that there are judicial questions peculiarly suited to resolution according to this method.[63]

[62] See the works cited *supra* note 5.

[63] The position of Hart and Sacks and of Llewellyn is quite closely connected with that described *supra* at § 15a. See also § 16 and notes 19 and 25. They differ from the classic natural law and welfare economics tradition (*e.g.*, Locke, J. S. Mill, Rawls,

82. Judicial method and judicial question are not really distinct concepts. The Third Way asserts that while a substantively rational legislature alone should make basic decisions defining fundamental social institutions and practices, the result of legislative action is a body of rules imbued with *intelligible purposes*. Judicial questions are those arising "interstitially," within the context of these basic arrangements. The judicial method—sometimes referred to as "reasoned elaboration"—consists in resolving judicial questions by reference to the purposes implicit in the pre-existing structure. Because reasoned elaboration requires the judge both to investigate and to extend creatively the purposes of the legislature, it lacks the mechanical certainty of rule application. On the other hand, the judge is working with legal arrangements that have objectively determinable purposes and practicing a body of known techniques within a highly developed professional tradition rather than attempting to create solutions out of whole cloth. The method should be far *more* certain than substantive rationality.[64]

83. There are two lines of criticism to which the Third Way is particularly open. First, there is the question whether the departure from the assumptions of formality can be justified. Can we distinguish judicial from legislative questions with any degree of certainty at all? Not if all rules are compromises, reflecting a temporary abandonment of the struggle of opposing forces, rather than the achievement of a harmony incompatible with the arbitrary character of human desires, values and purposes. But even supposing that we develop a way to tell the kinds of question apart, are there really two distinct methods of law making, so that the *way* the judges do things can be distinguished from the way legislatures do them? The proponent of formality is likely to respond

Coase) in that they recognize the existence of a set of questions concerning the fundamental legal institutions and rules of the society that are inherently "legislative," or "not amenable to Reason," and therefore beyond judicial competence. Thus they are advocates of "interstitial natural law," an attempted synthesis of the opposed traditions.

[64] It is characteristic of this position that its advocates teach their method of determining and then elaborating these common ends only by example, insisting that they can show how it should be done in particular cases even if they cannot tell us in general terms what it is they are doing. They make it clear only that they are speaking of an art, craft or skill, a prudential discipline that can be assimilated neither to the logic of the formalist nor to the discretion of the activist/passivist. See Karl N. Llewellyn, *supra* note 5; and Henry M. Hart and Albert M. Sacks, *supra* note 5, at 155-68. ("The technique of reasoned elaboration which courts pursue or ought to pursue in the effort to arrive at decisions according to law defies any facile generalization which will convey in itself a working understanding." *Id.* at 164.)

What gives this position strength, in spite of its inarticulateness, is that it appeals to our sense of the legitimacy of judicial gap-filling and contradiction-resolving. We expect and accept as natural, proper and indeed obligatory, although we cannot very adequately explain, that judges will make rules in such cases. We have no sense that by doing so they usurp the law making authority of the legislature. Moreover, we are far from feeling that the results of such judicial activity are inherently irrational, arbitrary or even extremely uncertain. The Third Way asserts that cases involving more obvious judicial initiative are amenable to a similar method.

that the burden of proof is on the Third Way to show that legal theory can produce a more precise model of *any* law making process than that of substantive rationality.[65]

84. But neither of these questions falls within the scope of this essay, which has all along assumed the validity of the basic postulates of formality,

[65] The nature of the criticism of these aspects of the Third Way will vary according to whether the proponent puts most emphasis on the technical aspects of the method—*i.e.* the appeal to purpose—or its existential or psychological aspect—*i.e.* the judge's commitment to finding *the* right answer. I can do no more here than sketch what seems to *me* the main outlines of the criticism.

First, with respect to the argument from purpose, both in the Hart & Sacks Legal Process materials (*supra* note 5) and in Llewellyn's The Common Law Tradition (*supra* note 5) my perhaps over critical eye finds constant equivocation about whether the purposes to be furthered are the very concrete partisan ends of particular constellations of legislative power, or some set of much vaguer purposes thought to be "inherent in the enterprise of social living" (or whatever). Since the choice of purposes to further will often be radically different according to the referent group chosen, the absence of principles of selection is crippling. Second, the notion of a hierarchy of purposes, ranging up from notions like "no man should profit from his own wrong" to "the law should not encourage wrongdoing" to "the law should attempt to maximize valid human satisfactions" fails to deal with the "ideological" character of explanations of legal rules. Most particular arguments about legal questions reflect larger arguments—moral absolutism vs. utilitarianism; the appeal to status vs. the appeal to contract; the ideal of atomistic competition vs. that of regulated bigness; the demand for business statesmanship and fiduciary attitudes vs. a faith in self-interest. If there are *any* decisions that are inherently "legislative," it must be those between these basic orientations. Yet once the decision at this level is made, the particular application is often obvious, so that "reasoned elaboration" is superfluous. *Cf.* Karl Mannheim, Ideology and Utopia, An Introduction to the Sociology of Knowledge (1936).

As for the psychological branch of the notion that there is a peculiarly judicial method, the first difficulty is that the basic tendency of modern legal scholarship seems to be to show that we can make sense of fundamental legal principles, such as "no liability without fault" or "promises should be kept" only by interpreting them as invitations to weigh the social costs and benefits of alternative outcomes. See, for example, Guido Calabresi, *supra* note 57, and Richard A. Posner, A Theory of Negligence, 1 J. Leg. Stud. 29 (1972), in torts, and Robert L. Hale, Bargaining, Duress and Economic Liberty, 43 Colum. L. Rev. 603 (1943), and Louis L. Jaffe, Law Making by Private Groups, 51 Harv. L. Rev. 201 (1937), in contracts. No progress *at all* is visible in the attempt to deal with legal doctrine as a manifestation of particular psychological phenomena or of an obscure practice of moral argumentation quite different from utilitarian calculation.

A second kind of criticism asserts that the opposition of rules and substantive rationality exhausts the fundamental categories of decision processes, and that vague claims that there exists a third mode of decision are both wrong and dangerous. This argument is closely connected with the ontological postulates about facts and values discussed in §§ 17-20 above. The theory of legal formality is based on the notion that all "subjective" decision processes, that is, those based on the weighing of conflicting values as opposed to the identification of "objective" facts, share the essential characteristics of uncertainty and indeterminacy. Outside the realm of "fact," the results of decision can be neither justified nor invalidated otherwise than by an appeal to arbitrary and conflicting "value judgments." Does the advocate of the Third Way propose a different set of postulates? If so, one would like to hear them, and to compare them with earlier attempts, such as those described and criticized in Morton White, Social Thought in America: The Revolt Against Formalism (2d ed. 1957), and H. L. A. Hart, *supra* note 10, at 620-29.

the better to examine the logic of the system of thought those postulates produce. For us, the important thing is that the Third Way is no less dependent on rules, and thus no less vulnerable to the dilemma of formality, than the system it aspires to replace. It is implicit in the proposed justification of judicial power that:

(a) The judge must use *only* the judicial method of reasoning from the predetermined purposes embedded in the body of substantive law that frames a given dispute. If the judge uses substantively rational legislative techniques, his decision cannot be legitimate because it is not representative.

(b) The judge must decide *only* judicial questions, those amenable to solution by appeal to the purposes of the body of law within which they arise. If the judge decides a non-judicial question, he must either do so using a method unsuited to the task, or he must adopt a substantively rational method to which he has no legitimate claim because he is not representative.

85. These are classic examples of those injunctions the judge cannot apply mechanically, and so cannot honor except on the basis of his own investigation of the legal and institutional situation. And such an examination once commenced must cover exactly the range of considerations the legislature itself would canvass. The judge thus finds himself once again in his characteristic dilemma: he cannot avoid engaging in substantively rational decision making, but must do so without a theory that will legitimize his action.

86. If one feels, as I do, that the problems of formality persist in the face of all expedients to salvage it, one comes finally to question not so much rule application or rule making as the notion that the legal process must reduce itself to a staccato alternation between them. In short, the way is open to ask whether there may not be a conception of justice in which we demand of the judge, acting *as* a judge rather than as a legislator or administrator, that he decide the merits of disputes even though he is unable or unwilling to rationalize his action *either* in terms of the application of an existing rule or in terms of the formulation and application of a new one. I mean to explore this possibility in a later essay.

Viewpoint

Feminism, Marxism, Method, and the State: Toward Feminist Jurisprudence

Catharine A. MacKinnon

I

Feminism has no theory of the state. It has a theory of power: sexuality is gendered as gender is sexualized. Male and female are created through the erotization of dominance and submission. The man/woman difference and the dominance/submission dynamic define each other. This is the social meaning of sex and the distinctively feminist account of gender inequality.[1] Sexual objectification, the central process within this

For A. D. and D. K. H. In addition to all those whose help is acknowledged in the first part of this article, "Feminism, Marxism, Method, and the State: An Agenda for Theory," *Signs: Journal of Women in Culture and Society* 7, no. 3 (Spring 1982): 515–44 (hereafter cited as part 1), my students and colleagues at Yale, Harvard, and Stanford contributed profoundly to the larger project of which both articles are parts. Among them, Sonia E. Alvarez, Jeanne M. Barkey, Paul Brest, Ruth Colker, Karen E. Davis, Sharon Dyer, Tom Emerson, Daniel Gunther, Patricia Kliendienst Joplin, Mark Kelman, Duncan Kennedy, John Kaplan, Lyn Lemaire, Mira Marshall, Rebecca Mark, Martha Minow, Helen M. A. Neally, Lisa Rofel, Sharon Silverstein, Dean Spencer, Laurence Tribe, and Mary Whisner stand out vividly in retrospect. None of it would have happened without Lu Ann Carter and David Rayson. And thank you, Meg Baldwin, Annie McCombs, and Janet Spector.

Marxism appears in lower case, Black in upper case, for reasons explained in part 1.

1. Much has been made of the distinction between sex and gender. Sex is thought the more biological, gender the more social. The relation of each to sexuality varies. Since I believe sexuality is fundamental to gender and fundamentally social, and that biology is its social meaning in the system of sex inequality, which is a social and political system that does not rest independently on biological differences in any respect, the sex/gender distinction looks like a nature/culture distinction. I use sex and gender relatively interchangeably.

dynamic, is at once epistemological and political.[2] The feminist theory of knowledge is inextricable from the feminist critique of power because the male point of view forces itself upon the world as its way of apprehending it.

The perspective from the male standpoint[3] enforces woman's definition, encircles her body, circumlocutes her speech, and describes her life. The male perspective is systemic and hegemonic. The content of the signification "woman" is the content of women's lives. Each sex has its role, but their stakes and power are not equal. If the sexes are unequal, and perspective participates in situation, there is no ungendered reality or ungendered perspective. And they are connected. In this context, objectivity—the nonsituated, universal standpoint, whether claimed or aspired to—is a denial of the existence or potency of sex inequality that tacitly participates in constructing reality from the dominant point of view. Objectivity, as the epistemological stance of which objectification is the social process, creates the reality it apprehends by defining as knowledge the reality it creates through its way of apprehending it. Sexual metaphors for knowing are no coincidence.[4] The solipsism of this ap-

2. This analysis is developed in part 1. I assume here your acquaintance with the arguments there.

3. Male is a social and political concept, not a biological attribute. As I use it, it has *nothing whatever* to do with inherency, preexistence, nature, inevitability, or body as such. It is more epistemological than ontological, undercutting the distinction itself, given male power to conform being with perspective. (See part 1, pp. 538–39, n. 56.) The perspective from the male standpoint is not always each man's opinion, although most men adhere to it, nonconsciously and without considering it a point of view, as much because it makes sense of their experience (the male experience) as because it is in their interest. It is rational for them. A few men reject it; they pay. Because it is the dominant point of view and defines rationality, women are pushed to see reality in its terms, although this denies their vantage point as women in that it contradicts (at least some of) their lived experience. Women who adopt the male standpoint are passing, epistemologically speaking. This is not uncommon and is rewarded. The intractability of maleness as a form of dominance suggests that social constructs, although they flow from human agency, can be less plastic than nature has proven to be. If experience trying to do so is any guide, it may be easier to change biology than society.

4. In the Bible, to know a woman is to have sex with her. You acquire carnal knowledge. Many scholarly metaphors elaborate the theme of violating boundaries to appropriate from inside to carry off in usable form: "a penetrating observation," "an incisive analysis," "piercing the veil." Mary Ellman writes, "The male mind . . . is assumed to function primarily like a penis. Its fundamental character is seen to be aggression, and this quality is held essential to the highest or best working of the intellect" (*Thinking about Women* [New York: Harcourt, Brace, Jovanovich, 1968], p. 23). Feminists are beginning to understand that to know has meant to fuck. See Evelyn Fox Keller, "Gender and Science," *Psychoanalysis and Contemporary Thought* 1, no. 3 (1978): 409–33, esp. 413; and Helen Roberts, ed., *Doing Feminist Research* (London: Routledge & Kegan Paul, 1981). The term "to fuck" uniquely captures my meaning because it refers to sexual activity without distinguishing rape from intercourse. At least since Plato's cave, visual metaphors for knowing have been central to Western theories of knowledge, the visual sense prioritized as a mode of verification. The relationship between visual appropriation and objectification is now only begin-

proach does not undercut its sincerity, but it is interest that precedes method.

Feminism criticizes this male totality without an account of our capacity to do so or to imagine or realize a more whole truth. Feminism affirms women's point of view by revealing, criticizing, and explaining its impossibility. This is not a dialectical paradox. It is a methodological expression of women's situation, in which the struggle for consciousness is a struggle for world: for a sexuality, a history, a culture, a community, a form of power, an experience of the sacred. If women had consciousness or world, sex inequality would be harmless, or all women would be feminist. Yet we have something of both, or there would be no such thing as feminism. Why can women know that this—life as we have known it—is not all, not enough, not ours, not just? Now, why don't all women?[5]

---

ning to be explored. "The knowledge gained through still photographs will always be . . . a semblance of knowledge, a semblance of wisdom, as the act of taking pictures is a semblance of wisdom, a semblance of rape. The very muteness of what is, hypothetically, comprehensible in photographs is what constitutes their attraction and provocativeness" (Susan Sontag, *On Photography* [New York: Farrar, Straus & Giroux, 1980], p. 24). See part 1, pp. 539–40, n. 59.

5. Feminism aspires to represent the experience of all women as women see it, yet criticizes antifeminism and misogyny, including when it appears in female form. This tension is compressed in the epistemic term of art "the standpoint of all women." We are barely beginning to unpack it. Not all women agree with the feminist account of women's situation, nor do all feminists agree with any single rendition of feminism. Authority of interpretation—the claim to speak as a woman—thus becomes methodologically complex and politically crucial for the same reasons. Consider the accounts of their own experience given by right-wing women and lesbian sadomasochists. How can patriarchy be diminishing to women when women embrace and defend their place in it? How can dominance and submission be violating to women when women eroticize it? Now what is the point of view of the experience of all women? Most responses in the name of feminism, stated in terms of method, either (1) simply regard some women's views as "false consciousness," or (2) embrace any version of women's experience that a biological female claims as her own. The first approach treats some women's views as unconscious conditioned reflections of their oppression, complicitous in it. Just as science devalues experience in the process of uncovering its roots, this approach criticizes the substance of a view because it can be accounted for by its determinants. But if both feminism and antifeminism are responses to the condition of women, how is feminism exempt from devalidation by the same account? That feminism is critical, and antifeminism is not, is not enough, because the question is the basis on which we know something is one or the other when women, all of whom share the condition of women, disagree. The false consciousness approach begs this question by taking women's self-reflections as evidence of their stake in their own oppression, when the women whose self-reflections are at issue question whether their condition is oppressed at all. The second response proceeds as if women are free. Or, at least, as if we have considerable latitude to make, or to choose, the meanings if not the determinants of our situation. Or, that the least feminism can do, since it claims to see the world through women's eyes, is to validate the interpretations women choose. Both responses arise because of the unwillingness, central to feminism, to dismiss some women as simply deluded while granting other women the ability to see the truth. These two resolutions echo the object/subject split:

The practice of a politics of all women in the face of its theoretical impossibility is creating a new process of theorizing and a new form of theory. Although feminism emerges from women's particular experience, it is not subjective or partial, for no interior ground and few if any aspects of life are free of male power. Nor is feminism objective, abstract, or universal.[6] It claims no external ground or unsexed sphere of generalization or abstraction beyond male power, nor transcendence of the specificity of each of its manifestations. How is it possible to have an engaged truth that does not simply reiterate its determinations? *Dis*-engaged truth only reiterates *its* determinations. Choice of method is choice of determinants—a choice which, for women as such, has been unavailable because of the subordination of women. Feminism does not begin with the premise that it is unpremised. It does not aspire to persuade an unpremised audience because there is no such audience. Its project is to uncover and claim as valid the experience of women, the major content of which is the devalidation of women's experience.

This defines our task not only because male dominance is perhaps the most pervasive and tenacious system of power in history, but because it is metaphysically nearly perfect.[7] Its point of view is the standard for

---

objectivity (my consciousness is true, yours false, never mind why) or subjectivity (I know I am right because it feels right to me, never mind why). Thus is determinism answered with transcendence, traditional marxism with traditional liberalism, dogmatism with tolerance. The first approach claims authority on the basis of its lack of involvement, asserting its view independent of whether the described concurs—sometimes because it does not. It also has no account, other than its alleged lack of involvement, of its own ability to provide such an account. How can some women see the truth and other women not? The second approach claims authority on the basis of its involvement. It has no account for different interpretations of the same experience or any way of choosing among conflicting ones, including those between women and men. It tends to assume that women, as we are, have power and are free in exactly the ways feminism, substantively, has found we are not. Thus, the first approach is one-sidedly outside when there is no outside, the second one-sidedly inside when someone (probably a woman) is inside everything, including every facet of sexism, racism, and so on. So our problem is this: the false consciousness approach cannot explain experience as it is experienced by those who experience it. The alternative can only reiterate the terms of that experience. This is only one way in which the object/subject split is fatal to the feminist enterprise.

6. To stress: the feminist criticism is not that the objective stance fails to be truly objective because it has social content, all the better to exorcise that content in the pursuit of the more truly point-of-viewless viewpoint. The criticism is that objectivity is largely accurate to its/the/a world, which world is criticized; and that it becomes more accurate as the power it represents and extends becomes more total. Analogous criticisms have arisen in the natural sciences, without being seen as threatening to the "science of society" project, or calling into question that project's tacit equation between natural and social objects of knowledge. What if we extend Heisenberg's uncertainty principle to social theory? (Werner Heisenberg, *The Physical Principles of the Quantum Theory* [Chicago: University of Chicago Press, 1930], pp. 4, 20, 62–65). What of the axiomatic method after Gödel's proof? (See Ernest Nagel and James R. Newman, *Gödel's Proof* [New York: New York University Press, 1958].)

7. Andrea Dworkin helped me express this.

point-of-viewlessness, its particularity the meaning of universality. Its force is exercised as consent, its authority as participation, its supremacy as the paradigm of order, its control as the definition of legitimacy. Feminism claims the voice of women's silence, the sexuality of our eroticized desexualization, the fullness of "lack," the centrality of our marginality and exclusion, the public nature of privacy, the presence of our absence. This approach is more complex than transgression, more transformative than transvaluation, deeper than mirror-imaged resistance, more affirmative than the negation of our negativity. It is neither materialist nor idealist; it is feminist. Neither the transcendence of liberalism nor the determination of materialism works for us. Idealism is too unreal; women's inequality is enforced, so it cannot simply be thought out of existence, certainly not by us. Materialism is too real; women's inequality has never not existed, so women's equality never has. That is, the equality of women to men will not be scientifically provable until it is no longer necessary to do so. Women's situation offers no outside to stand on or gaze at, no inside to escape to, too much urgency to wait, no place else to go, and nothing to use but the twisted tools that have been shoved down our throats. If feminism is revolutionary, this is why.

Feminism has been widely thought to contain tendencies of liberal feminism, radical feminism, and socialist feminism. But just as socialist feminism has often amounted to marxism applied to women, liberal feminism has often amounted to liberalism applied to women. Radical feminism is feminism. Radical feminism—after this, feminism unmodified—is methodologically post-marxist.[8] It moves to resolve the

8. I mean to imply that contemporary feminism that is not methodologically post-marxist is not radical, hence not feminist on this level. For example, to the extent Mary Daly's *Gyn/Ecology: The Metaethics of Radical Feminism* (Boston: Beacon Press, 1978) is idealist in method—meaning that the subordination of women is an idea such that to think it differently is to change it—it is formally liberal no matter how extreme or insightful. To the extent Shulamith Firestone's analysis (*The Dialectic of Sex: The Case for Feminist Revolution* [New York: William Morrow & Co., 1972]) rests on a naturalist definition of gender, holding that women are oppressed by our bodies rather than their social meaning, her radicalism, hence her feminism, is qualified. Susan Griffin's *Pornography and Silence: Culture's Revolt against Nature* (San Francisco: Harper & Row Publishers, 1982) is classically liberal in all formal respects including, for instance, the treatment of pornography and eros as a distinction that is fundamentally psychological rather than interested, more deeply a matter of good and bad (morality) than of power and powerlessness (politics). Andrea Dworkin's work, esp. *Pornography: Men Possessing Women* (New York: Perigee Books, 1981), and Adrienne Rich's poetry and essays, exemplify feminism as a methodological departure. This feminism seeks to define and pursue women's interest as the fate of all women bound together. It seeks to extract the truth of women's commonalities out of the lie that all women are the same. If whatever a given society defines as sexual defines gender, and if gender means the subordination of women to men, "woman" means—is not qualified or undercut by—the uniqueness of each woman and the specificity of race, class, time, and place. In this sense, lesbian feminism, the feminism of women of color, and socialist feminism are converging in a feminist politics of sexuality, race, and class, with a left to right spectrum of its own. This politics is struggling for a practice of unity that does

marxist-feminist problematic on the level of method. Because its method emerges from the concrete conditions of all women as a sex, it dissolves the individualist, naturalist, idealist, moralist structure of liberalism, the politics of which science is the epistemology. Where liberal feminism sees sexism primarily as an illusion or myth to be dispelled, an inaccuracy to be corrected, true feminism sees the male point of view as fundamental to the male power to create the world in its own image, the image of its desires, not just as its delusory end product. Feminism distinctively as such comprehends that what counts as truth is produced in the interest of those with power to shape reality, and that this process is as pervasive as it is necessary as it is changeable. Unlike the scientific strain in marxism or the Kantian imperative in liberalism, which in this context share most salient features, feminism neither claims universality nor, failing that, reduces to relativity. It does not seek a generality that subsumes its particulars or an abstract theory or a science of sexism. It rejects the approach of control over nature (including us) analogized to control over society (also including us) which has grounded the "science of society" project as the paradigm for political knowledge since (at least) Descartes. Both liberalism and marxism have been subversive on women's behalf. Neither is enough. To grasp the inadequacies for women of liberalism on one side and marxism on the other is to begin to comprehend the role of the liberal state and liberal legalism[9] within a post-marxist feminism of social transformation.

As feminism has a theory of power but lacks a theory of the state, so marxism has a theory of value which (through the organization of work in production) becomes class analysis, but a problematic theory of the state. Marx did not address the state much more explicitly than he did women. Women were substratum, the state epiphenomenon.[10] Engels,

---

not depend upon sameness without dissolving into empty tolerance, including tolerance of all it exists to change whenever that appears embodied in one of us. A new community begins here. As critique, women's communality describes a fact of male supremacy, of sex "in itself": no woman escapes the meaning of being a woman within a gendered social system, and sex inequality is not only pervasive but may be universal (in the sense of never having not been in some form) although "intelligible only in . . . locally specific forms" (M. Z. Rosaldo, "The Use and Abuse of Anthropology: Reflections on Feminism and Cross-cultural Understanding," *Signs: Journal of Women in Culture and Society* 5, no. 3 [Spring 1980]: 389–417, 417). For women to become a sex "for ourselves" moves community to the level of vision.

9. See Karl Klare, "Law-Making as Praxis," *Telos* 12, no. 2 (Summer 1979): 123–35; Judith Shklar, *Legalism* (Cambridge, Mass.: Harvard University Press, 1964). To examine law as state is not to decide that all relevant state behavior occurs in legal texts. I do think that legal decisions expose power on the level of legitimizing rationale, and that law, as words in power, is central in the social erection of the liberal state.

10. Karl Marx, *Capital, Selected Works*, 3 vols. (Moscow: Progress Publishers, 1969), 2:120, 139–40; *The German Ideology* (New York: International Publishers, 1972), pp. 48–52; *Introduction to Critique of Hegel's Philosophy of Right*, ed. Joseph O'Malley, trans. Annette Jolin (Cambridge: Cambridge University Press, 1970), p. 139; Marx to P. V. Annenkov, 1846, in *The Poverty of Philosophy* (New York: International Publishers, 1963), pp. 179–93, 181.

who frontally analyzed both, and together, presumed the subordination of women in every attempt to reveal its roots, just as he presupposed something like the state, or state-like social conditions, in every attempt to expose its origins.[11] Marx tended to use the term "political" narrowly to refer to the state or its laws, criticizing as exclusively political interpretations of the state's organization or behavior which took them as sui generis. Accordingly, until recently, most marxism has tended to consider political that which occurs between classes, that is, to interpret as "the political" instances of the marxist concept of inequality. In this broad sense, the marxist theory of social inequality has been its theory of politics. This has not so much collapsed the state into society (although it goes far in that direction) as conceived the state as determined by the totality of social relations of which the state is one determined and determining part—without specifying which, or how much, is which.

In this context, recent marxist work has tried to grasp the specificity of the institutional state: how it wields class power, or transforms class society, or responds to approach by a left aspiring to rulership or other changes. While liberal theory has seen the state as emanating power, and traditional marxism has seen the state as expressing power constituted elsewhere, recent marxism, much of it structuralist, has tried to analyze state power as specific to the state as a form, yet integral to a determinate social whole understood in class terms. This state is found "relatively autonomous." This means that the state, expressed through its functionaries, has a definite class character, is definitely capitalist or socialist, but also has its own interests which are to some degree independent of those of the ruling class and even of the class structure.[12] The state as such, in this view, has a specific power and interest, termed "the political," such that class power, class interest expressed by and in the state, and state behavior, although inconceivable in isolation from one another, are nevertheless not linearly or causally linked or strictly coextensive. Such work locates "the specificity of the political" in a

11. I am criticizing Engels's assumptions about sexuality and women's place, and his empiricist method, and suggesting that the two are linked. Friedrich Engels, *Origin of the Family, Private Property and the State* (New York: International Publishers, 1942).

12. Representative works include Fred Block, "The Ruling Class Does Not Rule: Notes on the Marxist Theory of the State," *Socialist Revolution* 33 (May–June 1977): 6–28; Ralph Miliband, *The State in Capitalist Society* (New York: Basic Books, 1969); Nicos Poulantzas, *Classes in Contemporary Capitalism* (London: New Left Books, 1975), and *Political Power and Social Classes* (London: New Left Books, 1975); Goran Therborn, *What Does the Ruling Class Do When It Rules?* (London: New Left Books, 1978); Norberto Bobbio, "Is There a Marxist Theory of the State?" *Telos* 35 (Spring 1978): 5–16. Theda Skocpol, *States and Social Revolution: A Comparative Analysis of France, Russia and China* (Cambridge: Cambridge University Press, 1979), pp. 24–33, ably reviews much of this literature. Applications to law include Isaac Balbus, "Commodity Form and Legal Form: An Essay on the 'Relative Autonomy' of the Law," *Law and Society Review* 11, no. 3 (Winter 1977): 571–88; Mark Tushnet, "A Marxist Analysis of American Law," *Marxist Perspectives* 1, no. 1 (Spring 1978): 96–116; and Klare (n. 9 above).

mediate "region"[13] between the state as its own ground of power (which alone, as in the liberal conception, would set the state above or apart from class) and the state as possessing no special supremacy or priority in terms of power, as in the more orthodox marxist view.

The idea that the state is relatively autonomous, a kind of first among equals of social institutions, has the genius of appearing to take a stand on the issue of reciprocal constitution of state and society while straddling it. Is the state essentially autonomous of class but partly determined by it, or is it essentially determined by class but not exclusively so? Is it relatively constrained within a context of freedom or relatively free within a context of constraint?[14] As to who or what fundamentally moves and shapes the realities and instrumentalities of domination, and where to go to do something about it, what qualifies what is as ambiguous as it is crucial. Whatever it has not accomplished, however, this literature has at least relieved the compulsion to find all law—directly or convolutedly, nakedly or clothed in unconscious or devious rationalia—to be simply bourgeois, without undercutting the notion that it is determinately driven by interest.

A methodologically post-marxist feminism must confront, on our own terms, the issue of the relation between the state and society, within a theory of social determination adequate to the specificity of sex. Lacking even a tacit theory of the state of its own, feminist practice has instead oscillated between a liberal theory of the state on the one hand and a left theory of the state on the other. Both treat law as the mind of society: disembodied reason in liberal theory, reflection of material interest in left theory. In liberal moments the state is accepted on its own terms as a neutral arbiter among conflicting interests. The law is actually or potentially principled, meaning predisposed to no substantive outcome, thus available as a tool that is not fatally twisted. Women implicitly become an interest group within pluralism, with specific problems of mobilization and representation, exit and voice, sustaining incremental gains and losses. In left moments, the state becomes a tool of dominance and repression, the law legitimizing ideology, use of the legal system a form of utopian idealism or gradualist reform, each apparent gain deceptive or cooptive, and each loss inevitable.

Applied to women, liberalism has supported state intervention on behalf of women as abstract persons with abstract rights, without scrutinizing the content of these notions in gendered terms. Marxism

13. Poulantzas's formulation follows Althusser. Louis Althusser and Etienne Balibar, *Reading Capital,* trans. Ben Brewster (London: New Left Books, 1968). For Poulantzas, the "specific autonomy which is characteristic of the function of the state . . . is the basis of the specificity of the political" (*Political Power and Social Classes* [n. 12 above], pp. 14, 46). Whatever that means. On structural causality between class and state, see p. 14.

14. See Ernesto Laclau's similar criticism of Miliband in *Politics and Ideology in Marxist Theory* (London: New Left Books, 1977), p. 65.

applied to women is always on the edge of counseling abdication of the state as an arena altogether—and with it those women whom the state does not ignore or who are, as yet, in no position to ignore it. Feminism has so far accepted these constraints upon its alternatives: either the state, as primary tool of women's betterment and status transformation, without analysis (hence strategy) for it as male; or civil society, which for women has more closely resembled a state of nature. The state, with it the law, has been either omnipotent or impotent: everything or nothing.

The feminist posture toward the state has therefore been schizoid on issues central to women's survival: rape, battery, pornography, prostitution, sexual harassment, sex discrimination, abortion, the Equal Rights Amendment, to name a few. Attempts to reform and enforce rape laws, for example, have tended to build on the model of the deviant perpetrator and the violent act, as if the fact that rape is a crime means that the society is against it, so law enforcement would reduce or delegitimize it. Initiatives are accordingly directed toward making the police more sensitive, prosecutors more responsive, judges more receptive, and the law, in words, less sexist. This may be progressive in the liberal or the left senses, but how is it empowering in the feminist sense? Even if it were effective in jailing men who do little different from what nondeviant men do regularly, how would such an approach alter women's rapability? Unconfronted are *why* women are raped and the role of the state in that. Similarly, applying laws against battery to husbands, although it can mean life itself, has largely failed to address, as part of the strategy for state intervention, the conditions that produce men who systematically express themselves violently toward women, women whose resistance is disabled, and the role of the state in this dynamic. Criminal enforcement in these areas, while suggesting that rape and battery are deviant, punishes men for expressing the images of masculinity that mean their identity, for which they are otherwise trained, elevated, venerated, and paid. These men must be stopped. But how does that change them or reduce the chances that there will be more like them? Liberal strategies entrust women to the state. Left theory abandons us to the rapists and batterers. The question for feminism is not only whether there is a meaningful difference between the two, but whether either is adequate to the feminist critique of rape and battery as systemic and to the role of the state and the law within that system.

Feminism has descriptions of the state's treatment of the gender difference, but no analysis of the state as gender hierarchy. We need to know. What, in gender terms, are the state's norms of accountability, sources of power, real constituency? Is the state to some degree autonomous of the interests of men or an integral expression of them? Does the state embody and serve male interests in its form, dynamics, relation to society, and specific policies? Is the state constructed upon the subordination of women? If so, how does male power become state power?

Can such a state be made to serve the interests of those upon whose powerlessness its power is erected? Would a different relation between state and society, such as may pertain under socialism, make a difference? If not, is masculinity inherent in the state form as such, or is some other form of state, or some other way of governing, distinguishable or imaginable? In the absence of answers to such questions, feminism has been caught between giving more power to the state in each attempt to claim it for women and leaving unchecked power in the society to men. Undisturbed, meanwhile, like the assumption that women generally consent to sex, is the assumption that we consent to this government. The question for feminism, for the first time on its own terms, is: what is this state, from women's point of view?

As a beginning, I propose that the state is male in the feminist sense.[15] The law sees and treats women the way men see and treat women. The liberal state coercively and authoritatively constitutes the social order in the interest of men as a gender, through its legitimizing norms, relation to society, and substantive policies. It achieves this through embodying and ensuring male control over women's sexuality at every level, occasionally cushioning, qualifying, or de jure prohibiting its excesses when necessary to its normalization. Substantively, the way the male point of view frames an experience is the way it is framed by state policy. To the extent possession is the point of sex, rape is sex with a woman who is not yours, unless the act is so as to make her yours. If part of the kick of pornography involves eroticizing the putatively prohibited, obscenity law will putatively prohibit pornography enough to maintain its desirability without ever making it unavailable or truly illegitimate. The same with prostitution. As male is the implicit reference for human, maleness will be the measure of equality in sex discrimination law. To the extent that the point of abortion is to control the reproductive sequelae of intercourse, so as to facilitate male sexual access to women, access to abortion will be controlled by "a man or The Man."[16] Gender, elaborated and sustained by behavioral patterns of application and administration, is maintained as a division of power.

Formally, the state is male in that objectivity is its norm. Objectivity is liberal legalism's conception of itself. It legitimizes itself by reflecting its view of existing society, a society it made and makes by so seeing it,

15. See Susan Rae Peterson, "Coercion and Rape: The State as a Male Protection Racket," in *Feminism and Philosophy,* ed. Mary Vetterling-Braggin, Frederick A. Elliston, and Jane English (Totowa, N.J.: Littlefield, Adams & Co., 1977), pp. 360–71; Janet Rifkin, "Toward a Theory of Law Patriarchy," *Harvard Women's Law Journal* 3 (Spring 1980): 83–92.

16. Johnnie Tillmon, "Welfare Is a Women's Issue," *Liberation News Service* (February 26, 1972), in *America's Working Women: A Documentary History, 1600 to the Present,* ed. Rosalyn Baxandall, Linda Gordon, and Susan Reverby (New York: Vintage Books, 1976), pp. 357–58.

and calling that view, and that relation, practical rationality. If rationality is measured by point-of-viewlessness, what counts as reason will be that which corresponds to the way things are. Practical will mean that which can be done without changing anything. In this framework, the task of legal interpretation becomes "to perfect the state as mirror of the society."[17] Objectivist epistemology is the law of law. It ensures that the law will most reinforce existing distributions of power when it most closely adheres to its own highest ideal of fairness. Like the science it emulates, this epistemological stance can not see the social specificity of reflection as method or its choice to embrace that which it reflects. Such law not only reflects a society in which men rule women; it rules in a male way: "The phallus means everything that sets itself up as a mirror."[18] The rule form, which unites scientific knowledge with state control in its conception of what law is, institutionalizes the objective stance as jurisprudence. A closer look at the substantive law of rape[19] in light of such an argument suggests that the relation between objectification (understood as the primary process of the subordination of women) and the power of the state is the relation between the personal and the political at the level of government. This is not because the state is presumptively the sphere of politics. It is because the state, in part through law, institutionalizes male power. If male power is systemic, it *is* the regime.

17. Laurence Tribe, "Constitution as Point of View" (Harvard Law School, Cambridge, Mass., 1982, mimeographed), p. 13.

18. Madeleine Gagnon, "Body I," in *New French Feminisms,* ed. Elaine Marks and Isabelle de Courtivron (Amherst, Mass.: University of Massachusetts Press, 1980), p. 180. Turns on the mirroring trope, which I see as metaphoric analyses of the epistemological/political dimension of objectification, are ubiquitous in feminist writing: "Into the room of the dressing where the walls are covered with mirrors. Where mirrors are like eyes of men, and the women reflect the judgments of mirrors" (Susan Griffin, *Woman and Nature: The Roaring Inside Her* [New York: Harper & Row Publishers, 1979], p. 155). See also Mary Daly, *Beyond God the Father: Toward a Philosophy of Women's Liberation* (Boston: Beacon Press, 1975), pp. 195, 197; Sheila Rowbotham, *Women's Consciousness, Man's World* (Harmondsworth: Pelican Books, 1973), pp. 26–29. "She did suffer, the witch/ trying to peer round the looking/ glass, she forgot/ someone was in the way" (Michelene, "Reflexion," quoted in Rowbotham, p. 2). Virginia Woolf wrote the figure around ("So I reflected . . ."), noticing "the necessity that women so often are to men" of serving as a looking glass in which a man can "see himself at breakfast and at dinner at least twice the size he really is." Notice the doubled sexual/gender meaning: "Whatever may be their use in civilized societies, mirrors are essential to all violent and heroic action. That is why Napoleon and Mussolini both insist so emphatically upon the inferiority of women, for if they were not inferior, they would cease to enlarge" (*A Room of One's Own* [New York: Harcourt, Brace & World, 1969], p. 36).

19. Space limitations made it necessary to eliminate sections on pornography, sex discrimination, and abortion. For the same reason, most supporting references, including those to case law, have been cut. The final section accordingly states the systemic implications of the analysis more tentatively than I think them, but as strongly as I felt I could, on the basis of the single substantive examination that appears here.

II

Feminists have reconceived rape as central to women's condition in two ways. Some see rape as an act of violence, not sexuality, the threat of which intimidates all women.[20] Others see rape, including its violence, as an expression of male sexuality, the social imperatives of which define all women.[21] The first, formally in the liberal tradition, comprehends rape as a displacement of power based on physical force onto sexuality, a preexisting natural sphere to which domination is alien. Thus, Susan Brownmiller examines rape in riots, wars, pogroms, and revolutions; rape by police, parents, prison guards; and rape motivated by racism—seldom rape in normal circumstances, in everyday life, in ordinary relationships, by men as men.[22] Women are raped by guns, age, white supremacy, the state—only derivatively by the penis. The more feminist view to me, one which derives from victims' experiences, sees sexuality as a social sphere of male power of which forced sex is paradigmatic. Rape is not less sexual for being violent; to the extent that coercion has become integral to male sexuality, rape may be sexual to the degree that, and because, it is violent.

The point of defining rape as "violence not sex" or "violence against women" has been to separate sexuality from gender in order to affirm sex (heterosexuality) while rejecting violence (rape). The problem remains what it has always been: telling the difference. The convergence of sexuality with violence, long used at law to deny the reality of women's violation, is recognized by rape survivors, with a difference: where the legal system has seen the intercourse in rape, victims see the rape in intercourse. The uncoerced context for sexual expression becomes as elusive as the physical acts come to feel indistinguishable.[23] Instead of

20. Susan Brownmiller, *Against Our Will: Men, Women and Rape* (New York: Simon & Schuster, 1976), p. 15.

21. Diana E. H. Russell, *The Politics of Rape: The Victim's Perspective* (New York: Stein & Day, 1977); Andrea Medea and Kathleen Thompson, *Against Rape* (New York: Farrar, Straus & Giroux, 1974); Lorenne M. G. Clark and Debra Lewis, *Rape: The Price of Coercive Sexuality* (Toronto: The Women's Press, 1977); Susan Griffin, "Rape: The All-American Crime," *Ramparts* (September 1971), pp. 26–35; Ti-Grace Atkinson connects rape with "the institution of sexual intercourse" (*Amazon Odyssey: The First Collection of Writings by the Political Pioneer of the Women's Movement* [New York: Links Books, 1974], pp. 13–23). Kalamu ya Salaam, "Rape: A Radical Analysis from the African-American Perspective," in *Our Women Keep Our Skies from Falling* (New Orleans: Nkombo, 1980), pp. 25–40.

22. Racism, clearly, is everyday life. Racism in the United States, by singling out Black men for allegations of rape of white women, has helped obscure the fact that it is men who rape women, disproportionately women of color.

23. "Like other victims, I had problems with sex, after the rape. There was no way that Arthur could touch me that it didn't remind me of having been raped by this guy I never saw" (Carolyn Craven, "No More Victims: Carolyn Craven Talks about Rape, and about What Women and Men Can Do to Stop It," ed. Alison Wells [Berkeley, Calif., 1978, mimeographed]), p. 2.

asking, what is the violation of rape, what if we ask, what is the nonviolation of intercourse? To tell what is wrong with rape, explain what is right about sex. If this, in turn, is difficult, the difficulty is as instructive as the difficulty men have in telling the difference when women see one. Perhaps the wrong of rape has proven so difficult to articulate[24] because the unquestionable starting point has been that rape is definable as distinct from intercourse, when for women it is difficult to distinguish them under conditions of male dominance.[25]

Like heterosexuality, the crime of rape centers on penetration.[26] The law to protect women's sexuality from forcible violation/expropriation defines the protected in male genital terms. Women do resent forced penetration. But penile invasion of the vagina may be less pivotal to women's sexuality, pleasure or violation, than it is to male sexuality. This definitive element of rape centers upon a male-defined loss, not coincidentally also upon the way men define loss of exclusive access. In this light, rape, as legally defined, appears more a crime against female monogamy than against female sexuality. Property concepts fail fully to comprehend this,[27] however, not because women's sexuality is not, finally, a thing, but because it is never ours. The moment we "have" it—"have sex" in the dual sexuality/gender sense—it is lost as ours. This may explain the male incomprehension that, once a woman has had sex, she loses anything when raped. To them we *have nothing* to lose. Dignitary harms, because nonmaterial, are remote to the legal mind. But women's loss through rape is not only less tangible, it is less

24. Pamela Foa, "What's Wrong with Rape?" in Vetterling-Braggin, Elliston, and English, eds. (n. 15 above), pp. 347–59; Michael Davis, "What's So Bad about Rape?" (paper presented at Annual Meeting of the Academy of Criminal Justice Sciences, Louisville, Ky., March 1982).

25. "Since we would not want to say that there is anything morally wrong with sexual intercourse per se, we conclude that the wrongness of rape rests with the matter of the woman's consent" (Carolyn M. Shafer and Marilyn Frye, "Rape and Respect," in Vetterling-Braggin, Elliston, and English, eds. [n. 15 above], p. 334). "Sexual contact is not inherently harmful, insulting or provoking. Indeed, ordinarily it is something of which we are quite fond. The difference between ordinary sexual intercourse and rape is that ordinary sexual intercourse is more or less consented to while rape is not" (Davis [n. 24 above], p. 12).

26. Sec. 213.0 of the *Model Penal Code* (Official Draft and Revised Comments 1980), like most states, defines rape as sexual intercourse with a female who is not the wife of the perpetrator "with some penetration however slight." Impotency is sometimes a defense. Michigan's gender-neutral sexual assault statute includes penetration by objects (sec. 520a[h]; 520[b]). See *Model Penal Code,* annotation to sec. 213.1(d) (Official Draft and Revised Comments 1980).

27. Although it is true that men possess women and that women's bodies are, socially, men's things, I have not analyzed rape as men treating women like property. In the manner of many socialist-feminist adaptations of marxian categories to women's situation, that analysis short-circuits analysis of rape as male sexuality and presumes rather than develops links between sex and class. We need to rethink sexual dimensions of property as well as property dimensions of sexuality.

existent. It is difficult to avoid the conclusion that penetration itself is known to be a violation and that women's sexuality, our gender definition, is itself stigmatic. If this is so, the pressing question for explanation is not why some of us accept rape but why any of us resent it.

The law of rape divides the world of women into spheres of consent according to how much say we are legally presumed to have over sexual access to us by various categories of men. Little girls may not consent; wives must. If rape laws existed to enforce women's control over our own sexuality, as the consent defense implies, marital rape would not be a widespread exception,[28] nor would statutory rape proscribe all sexual intercourse with underage girls regardless of their wishes. The rest of us fall into parallel provinces: good girls, like children, are unconsenting, virginal, rapable; bad girls, like wives, are consenting, whores, unrapable. The age line under which girls are presumed disabled from withholding consent to sex rationalizes a condition of sexual coercion women never outgrow. As with protective labor laws for women only, dividing and protecting the most vulnerable becomes a device for not protecting everyone. Risking loss of even so little cannot be afforded. Yet the protection is denigrating and limiting (girls may not choose to be sexual) as well as perverse (girls are eroticized as untouchable; now reconsider the data on incest).

If the accused knows us, consent is inferred. The exemption for rape in marriage is consistent with the assumption underlying most adjudications of forcible rape: to the extent the parties relate, it was not really rape, it was personal.[29] As the marital exemptions erode, preclusions for cohabitants and voluntary social companions may expand. In this light, the partial erosion of the marital rape exemption looks less like a change in the equation between women's experience of sexual violation and men's experience of intimacy, and more like a legal adjustment to the social fact that acceptable heterosexual sex is increasingly not limited to the legal family. So although the rape law may not now always assume that the woman consented simply because the parties are legally one, indices of closeness, of relationship ranging from nodding acquaintance to living together, still contraindicate rape. Perhaps this reflects men's experience that women they know meaningfully consent to sex with them. That cannot be rape; rape must be by someone else,

28. For an excellent summary of the current state of the marital exemption, see Joanne Schulman, "State-by-State Information on Marital Rape Exemption Laws," in *Rape in Marriage,* Diana E. H. Russell (New York: Macmillan Publishing Co., 1982), pp. 375–81.

29. On "social interaction as an element of consent," in a voluntary social companion context, see *Model Penal Code,* sec. 213.1. "The prior *social* interaction is an indicator of consent in addition to actor's and victim's *behavioral* interaction during the commission of the offense" (Wallace Loh, "Q: What Has Reform of Rape Legislation Wrought? A: Truth in Criminal Labeling," *Journal of Social Issues* 37, no. 4 [1981]: 28–52, 47). Perhaps consent should be an affirmative defense, pleaded and proven by the defendant.

someone unknown. But *women* experience rape most often by men we know.[30] Men believe that it is less awful to be raped by someone one is close to: "The emotional trauma suffered by a person victimized by an individual with whom sexual intimacy is shared as a normal part of an ongoing marital relationship is not nearly as severe as that suffered by a person who is victimized by one with whom that intimacy is not shared."[31] But women feel as much, if not more, traumatized by being raped by someone we have known or trusted, someone we have shared at least an illusion of mutuality with, than by some stranger. In whose interest is it to believe that it is not so bad to be raped by someone who has fucked you before as by someone who has not? Disallowing charges of rape in marriage may also "remove a substantial obstacle to the resumption of normal marital relations."[32] Depending upon your view of normal. Note that the obstacle to normalcy here is not the rape but the law against it. Apparently someone besides feminists finds sexual victimization and sexual intimacy not all that contradictory. Sometimes I think women and men live in different cultures.

Having defined rape in male sexual terms, the law's problem, which becomes the victim's problem, is distinguishing rape from sex in specific cases. The law does this by adjudicating the level of acceptable force starting just above the level set by what is seen as normal male sexual behavior, rather than at the victim's, or women's, point of violation. Rape cases finding insufficient force reveal that acceptable sex, in the legal perspective, can entail a lot of force. This is not only because of the way specific facts are perceived and interpreted, but because of the way the injury itself is defined as illegal. Rape is a sex crime that is not a crime when it looks like sex. To seek to define rape as violent, not sexual, is understandable in this context, and often seems strategic. But assault that is consented to is still assault; rape consented to is intercourse. The substantive reference point implicit in existing legal standards is the sexually normative level of force. Until this norm is confronted as such, no distinction between violence and sexuality will prohibit more in-

30. Pauline Bart found that women were more likely to be raped—that is, less able to stop a rape in progress—when they knew their assailant, particularly when they had a prior or current sexual relationship ("A Study of Women Who Both Were Raped and Avoided Rape," *Journal of Social Issues* 37, no. 4 [1981]: 123–37, 132). See also Linda Belden, "Why Women Do Not Report Sexual Assault" (City of Portland Public Service Employment Program, Portland Women's Crisis Line, Portland, Ore., March 1979, mimeographed); Diana E. H. Russell and Nancy Howell, "The Prevalence of Rape in the United States Revisited," in this issue; and Menachem Amir, *Patterns in Forcible Rape* (Chicago: University of Chicago Press, 1971), pp. 229–52.

31. Answer Brief for Plaintiff-Appellee at 10, People v. Brown, 632 P.2d 1025 (Colo. 1981).

32. Brown, 632 P.2d at 1027 (citing Comment, "Rape and Battery between Husband and Wife," *Stanford Law Review* 6 [1954]: 719–28, 719, 725).

stances of women's experienced violation than does the existing definition. The question is what is *seen as* force, hence as violence, in the sexual arena. Most rapes, as women live them, will not be seen to violate women until sex and violence are confronted as mutually definitive. It is not only men convicted of rape who believe that the only thing they did different from what men do all the time is get caught.

The line between rape and intercourse commonly centers on some measure of the woman's "will." But from what should the law know woman's will? Like much existing law, Brownmiller tends to treat will as a question of consent and consent as a factual issue of the presence of force.[33] Proof problems aside, force and desire are not mutually exclusive. So long as dominance is eroticized, they never will be. Women are socialized to passive receptivity; may have or perceive no alternative to acquiescence; may prefer it to the escalated risk of injury and the humiliation of a lost fight; submit to survive. Some eroticize dominance and submission; it beats feeling forced. Sexual intercourse may be deeply unwanted—the woman would never have initiated it—yet no force may be present. Too, force may be used, yet the woman may want the sex—to avoid more force or because she, too, eroticizes dominance. Women and men know this. Calling rape violence, not sex, thus evades, at the moment it most seems to confront, the issue of who controls women's sexuality and the dominance/submission dynamic that has defined it. When sex is violent, women may have lost control over what is done to us, but absence of force does not ensure the presence of that control. Nor, under conditions of male dominance, does the presence of force make an interaction nonsexual. If sex is normally something men do to women, the issue is less whether there was force and more whether consent is a meaningful concept.[34]

To explain women's gender status as a function of rape, Brownmiller argues that the threat of rape benefits all men.[35] She does not specify in what way. Perhaps it benefits them sexually, hence as a gender: male initiatives toward women carry the fear of rape as support for persuading compliance, the resulting appearance of which has been called consent. Here the victims' perspective grasps what liberalism applied to women denies: that forced sex as sexuality is not exceptional in relations between the sexes but constitutes the social meaning of gender: "Rape is a man's act, whether it is male or a female man and whether it is a man relatively permanently or relatively temporarily; and being raped is a woman's experience, whether it is a female or a male woman and whether it is a woman relatively permanently or relatively

33. Brownmiller (n. 20 above), pp. 8, 196, 400–407, 427–36.

34. See Carol Pateman, "Women and Consent," *Political Theory* 8, no. 2 (May 1980): 149–68.

35. Brownmiller (n. 20 above), p. 5.

temporarily."[36] To be rap*able,* a position which is social, not biological, defines what a woman *is.*

Most women get the message that the law against rape is virtually unenforceable as applied to them. Our own experience is more often delegitimized by this than the law is. Women radically distinguish between rape and experiences of sexual violation, concluding that we have not "really" been raped if we have ever seen or dated or slept with or been married to the man, if we were fashionably dressed or are not provably virgin, if we are prostitutes, if we put up with it or tried to get it over with, if we were force-fucked over a period of years. If we probably couldn't prove it in court, it wasn't rape. The distance between most sexual violations of women and the legally perfect rape measures the imposition of someone else's definition upon women's experiences. Rape, from women's point of view, is not prohibited; it is regulated. Even women who know we have been raped do not believe that the legal system will see it the way we do. We are often not wrong. Rather than deterring or avenging rape, the state, in many victims' experiences, perpetuates it. Women who charge rape say they were raped twice, the second time in court. If the state is male, this is more than a figure of speech.

The law distinguishes rape from intercourse by the woman's lack of consent coupled with a man's (usually) knowing disregard of it. A feminist distinction between rape and intercourse, to hazard a beginning

36. Shafer and Frye (n. 25 above), p. 334. Battery of wives has been legally separated from marital rape not because assault by a man's fist is so different from assault by a penis. Both seem clearly violent. I am suggesting that both are also sexual. Assaults are often precipitated by women's noncompliance with gender requirements. See R. Emerson Dobash and Russell Dobash, *Violence against Wives: A Case against the Patriarchy* (New York: Free Press, 1979), pp. 14–20. Nearly all incidents occur in the home, most in the kitchen or bedroom. Most murdered women are killed by their husbands, most in the bedroom. The battery cycle accords with the rhythm of heterosexual sex (see Leonore Walker, *The Battered Woman* [New York: Harper & Row Publishers, 1979], pp. 19–20). The rhythm of lesbian S/M appears similar (Samois, eds., *Coming to Power* [Palo Alto, Calif.: Up Press, 1981]). Perhaps most interchange between genders, but especially violent ones, make sense in sexual terms. However, the larger issue for the relation between sexuality and gender, hence sexuality and violence generally, including both war and violence against women, is: What *is* heterosexuality? If it is the erotization of dominance and submission, altering the participants' gender is comparatively incidental. If it is males over females, gender matters independently. Since I see heterosexuality as the fusion of the two, but with gender a social outcome (such that the acted upon is feminized, is the "girl" regardless of sex, the actor correspondingly masculinized), battery appears sexual on a deeper level. In baldest terms, sexuality is violent, so violence is sexual, violence against women doubly so. If this is so, wives are beaten, as well as raped, *as women*—as the acted upon, as gender, meaning sexual, objects. It further follows that all acts *by anyone* which treat a woman according to her object label "woman" are *sexual* acts. The extent to which sexual acts are acts of objectification remains a question of our account of our freedom to make our own meanings. It is clear, at least, that it is centering sexuality upon genitality that distinguishes battery from rape at exactly the juncture that both the law, and seeing rape as violence not sex, does.

approach, lies instead in the *meaning* of the act from women's point of view. What is wrong with rape is that it is an act of the subordination of women to men. Seen this way, the issue is not so much what rape "is" as the way its social conception is shaped to interpret particular encounters. Under conditions of sex inequality, with perspective bound up with situation, whether a contested interaction is rape comes down to whose meaning wins. If sexuality is relational, specifically if it is a power relation of gender, consent is a communication under conditions of inequality. It transpires somewhere between what the woman actually wanted and what the man comprehended she wanted. Instead of capturing this dynamic, the law gives us linear statics face to face. Nonconsent in law becomes a question of the man's force or the woman's resistance or both.[37] Rape, like many crimes and torts, requires that the accused possess a criminal mind (mens rea) for his acts to be criminal. The man's mental state refers to what he actually understood at the time or to what a reasonable man should have understood under the circumstances. The problem is this: the injury of rape lies in the meaning of the act to its victims, but the standard for its criminality lies in the meaning of the same act to the assailants. Rape is only an injury from women's point of view. It is only a crime from the male point of view, explicitly including that of the accused.

Thus is the crime of rape defined and adjudicated from the male standpoint, that is, presuming that (what feminists see as) forced sex is sex. Under male supremacy, of course, it is. What this means doctrinally is that the man's perceptions of the woman's desires often determine whether she is deemed violated. This might be like other crimes of subjective intent if rape were like other crimes. But with rape, because sexuality defines gender, the only difference between assault and (what is socially considered) noninjury is the meaning of the encounter to the woman. Interpreted this way, the legal problem has been to determine whose view of that meaning constitutes what really happened, as if what happened objectively exists to be objectively determined, thus as if this task of determination is separable from the gender of the participants and the gendered nature of their exchange. Thus, even though the rape law oscillates between subjective tests and more objective standards invoking social reasonableness, it uniformly presumes a single underlying reality, not a reality split by divergent meanings, such as those inequality produces. Many women are raped by men who know the meaning of their acts to women and proceed anyway.[38] But women are also violated

37. Even when nonconsent is not a legal element of the offense (as in Michigan), juries tend to infer rape from evidence of force or resistance.

38. This is apparently true of undetected as well as convicted rapists. Samuel David Smithyman's sample, composed largely of the former, contained self-selected respondents to his ad, which read: "Are you a rapist? Researchers Interviewing Anonymously by Phone to Protect Your Identity. Call. . . ." Presumably those who chose to call defined their acts as rapes, at least at the time of responding ("The Undetected Rapist" [Ph.D. diss., Claremont Graduate School, 1978], pp. 54–60, 63–76, 80–90, 97–107).

every day by men who have no idea of the meaning of their acts to women. To them, it is sex. Therefore, to the law, it is sex. That is the single reality of what happened. When a rape prosecution is lost on a consent defense, the woman has not only failed to prove lack of consent, she is not considered to have been injured at all. Hermeneutically unpacked, read: because he did not perceive she did not want him, she was not violated. She had sex. Sex itself cannot be an injury. Women consent to sex every day. Sex makes a woman a woman. Sex is what women are *for*.

To a feminist analysis, men set sexual mores ideologically and behaviorally, define rape as they imagine the sexual violation of women through distinguishing it from their image of what they normally do, and sit in judgment in most accusations of sex crimes. So rape comes to mean a strange (read Black) man knowing a woman does not want sex and going ahead anyway. But men are systematically conditioned not even to notice what women want. They may have not a glimmer of women's indifference or revulsion. Rapists typically believe the woman loved it.[39] Women, as a survival strategy, must ignore or devalue or mute our desires (particularly lack of them) to convey the impression that the man will get what he wants regardless of what we want. In this context, consider measuring the genuineness of consent from the individual assailant's (or even the socially reasonable, i.e., objective, man's) point of view.

Men's pervasive belief that women fabricate rape charges after consenting to sex makes sense in this light. To them, the accusations *are* false because, to them, the facts describe sex. To interpret such events as rapes distorts their experience. Since they seldom consider that their experience of the real is anything other than reality, they can only explain the woman's version as maliciously invented. Similarly, the male anxiety that rape is easy to charge and difficult to disprove (also widely believed in the face of overwhelming evidence to the contrary) arises because rape accusations express one thing men cannot seem to control: the meaning to women of sexual encounters.

Thus do legal doctrines, incoherent or puzzling as syllogistic logic, become coherent as ideology. For example, when an accused wrongly but sincerely believes that a woman he sexually forced consented, he may have a defense of mistaken belief or fail to satisfy the mental requirement of knowingly proceeding against her will.[40] One commentator notes, discussing the conceptually similar issue of revocation of prior consent (i.e., on the issue of the conditions under which women are

39. "Probably the single most used cry of rapist to victim is 'You bitch . . . slut . . . you know you want it. You *all* want it' and afterward, 'there now, you really enjoyed it, didn't you?' " (Nancy Gager and Cathleen Schurr, *Sexual Assault: Confronting Rape in America* [New York: Grosset & Dunlap, 1976], p. 244).

40. See Director of Public Prosecutions v. Morgan, 2411 E.R.H.L. 347 (1975); Pappajohn v. The Queen, 11 D.L.R. 3d 1 (1980); People v. Mayberry, 15 Cal. 3d 143, 542 P.2d 1337 (1975).

allowed to control access to their sexuality from one time to the next): "Even where a woman revokes prior consent, such is the male ego that, seized of an exaggerated assessment of his sexual prowess, a man might genuinely believe her still to be consenting; resistance may be misinterpreted as enthusiastic cooperation; protestations of pain or disinclination, a spur to more sophisticated or more ardent love-making; a clear statement to stop, taken as referring to a particular intimacy rather than the entire performance."[41] This equally vividly captures common male readings of women's indications of disinclination under all kinds of circumstances.[42] Now reconsider to what extent the man's perceptions should determine whether a rape occurred. From whose standpoint, and in whose interest, is a law that allows one person's conditioned unconsciousness to contraindicate another's experienced violation? This aspect of the rape law reflects the sex inequality of the society not only in conceiving a cognizable injury from the viewpoint of the reasonable rapist, but in affirmatively rewarding men with acquittals for not comprehending women's point of view on sexual encounters.

Whether the law calls this coerced consent or mistake of fact, the more the sexual violation of women is routine, the more beliefs equating sexuality with violation become reasonable, and the more honestly women can be defined in terms of our fuckability. It would be comparatively simple if the legal problem were limited to avoiding retroactive falsification of the accused's state of mind. Surely there are incentives to lie. But the deeper problem is the rape law's assumption that a single, objective state of affairs existed, one which merely needs to be determined by evidence, when many (maybe even most) rapes involve honest men and violated women. When the reality is split—a woman is raped but not by a rapist?—the law tends to conclude that a rape *did not happen.* To attempt to solve this by adopting the standard of reasonable belief without asking, on a substantive social basis, to whom the belief is reasonable and why—meaning, what conditions make it reasonable—is one-sided: male-sided. What is it reasonable for a man to believe concerning a woman's desire for sex when heterosexuality is compulsory? Whose subjectivity becomes the objectivity of "what happened" is a matter of social meaning, that is, it has been a matter of sexual politics. One-sidedly erasing women's violation or dissolving the presumptions into the subjectivity of either side are alternatives dictated by the terms

41. Richard H. S. Tur, "Rape: Reasonableness and Time," *Oxford Journal of Legal Studies* 3 (Winter 1981): 432–41, 441. Tur, in the context of the Morgan and Pappajohn cases, says the "law ought not to be astute to equate wickedness and wishful, albeit mistaken, thinking" (p. 437). In feminist analysis, a rape is not an isolated or individual or moral transgression but a terrorist act within a systematic context of group subjection, like lynching.

42. See Silke Vogelmann-Sine et al., "Sex Differences in Feelings Attributed to a Woman in Situations Involving Coercion and Sexual Advances," *Journal of Personality* 47, no. 3 (September 1979): 420–31, esp. 429–30.

of the object/subject split, respectively. These are alternatives that will only retrace that split until its terms are confronted as gendered to the ground.

Desirability to men is commonly supposed to be a woman's form of power. This echoes the view that consent is women's form of control over intercourse, different but equal to the custom of male initiative. Look at it: man initiates, woman chooses. Even the ideal is not mutual. Apart from the disparate consequences of refusal, or openness of original options, this model does not envision a situation the woman controls being placed in, or choices she frames, yet the consequences are attributed to her as if the sexes began at arm's length, on equal terrain, as in the contract fiction. Ambiguous cases of consent are often archetypically referred to as "half won arguments in parked cars."[43] Why not half lost? Why isn't half enough? Why is it an argument? Why do men still want "it," feel entitled to "it," when women don't want them? That sexual expression is even framed as a matter of woman's consent, without exposing these presuppositions, is integral to gender inequality. Woman's so-called power presupposes her more fundamental powerlessness.[44]

III

The state's formal norms recapitulate the male point of view on the level of design. In Anglo-American jurisprudence, morals (value judgments) are deemed separable and separated from politics (power contests), and both from adjudication (interpretation). Neutrality, including judicial decision making that is dispassionate, impersonal, disinterested, and precedential, is considered desirable and descriptive. Courts, forums without predisposition among parties and with no interest of their own, reflect society back to itself resolved. Government of laws not men limits partiality with written constraints and tempers force with reasonable rule following. This law aspires to science: to the immanent generalization subsuming the emergent particularity, to prediction and control of social regularities and regulations, preferably codified. The formulaic "tests" of "doctrine" aspire to mechanism, classification to taxonomy. Courts intervene only in properly "factualized" disputes,[45] cognizing social conflicts as if collecting empirical data. But the de-

43. Note, "Forcible and Statutory Rape: An Exploration of the Operation and Objectives of the Consent Standard," *Yale Law Journal* 62 (1952): 55–56.

44. A similar analysis of sexual harassment suggests that women have such "power" only so long as we behave according to male definitions of female desirability, that is, only so long as we accede the definition of our sexuality (hence, ourselves, as gender female) to male terms. We have this power only so long as we remain powerless.

45. Peter Gabel, "Reification in Legal Reasoning" (New College Law School, San Francisco, 1980, mimeographed), p. 3.

marcations between morals and politics, the personality of the judge and the judicial role, bare coercion and the rule of law,[46] tend to merge in women's experience. Relatively seamlessly they promote the dominance of men as a social group through privileging the form of power—the perspective on social life—feminist consciousness reveals as socially male. The separation of form from substance, process from policy, role from theory and practice, echoes and reechoes at each level of the regime its basic norm: objectivity.

Consider a central example. The separation of public from private is as crucial to the liberal state's claim to objectivity as its inseparability is to women's claim to subordination. Legally, it has both formal and substantive dimensions. The state considers formal, not substantive, the allocation of public matters to itself to be treated objectively, of private matters to civil society to be treated subjectively. Substantively, the private is defined as a right to "an inviolable personality,"[47] which is guaranteed by ensuring "autonomy or control over the intimacies of personal identity."[48] It is hermetic. It means that which is inaccessible to, unaccountable to, and unconstructed by anything beyond itself. Intimacy occurs in private; this is supposed to guarantee original symmetry of power. Injuries arise in violating the private sphere, not within and by and because of it. Private means consent can be presumed unless disproven. To contain a systematic inequality contradicts the notion itself. But feminist consciousness has exploded the private. For women, the measure of the intimacy has been the measure of the oppression. To see the personal as political means to see the private as public. On this level, women have no privacy to lose or to guarantee. We are not inviolable. Our sexuality, meaning gender identity, is not only violable, it *is* (hence we are) our violation. Privacy is everything women as women have never been allowed to be or to have; at the same time the private is everything women have been equated with and defined in terms of *men's* ability to

46. Rawls's "original position," for instance, is a version of my objective standpoint (John Rawls, *A Theory of Justice* [Cambridge, Mass.: Harvard University Press, 1971]). Not only apologists for the liberal state, but also some of its most trenchant critics, see a real distinction between the rule of law and absolute arbitrary force. E. P. Thompson, *Whigs and Hunters: The Origin of the Black Act* (New York: Pantheon Books, 1975), pp. 258–69. Douglas Hay argues that making and enforcing certain acts as illegal reinforces a structure of subordination ("Property, Authority, and the Criminal Law," in *Albion's Fatal Tree: Crime and Society in Eighteenth Century England,* D. Hay et al., eds. [New York: Pantheon Books, 1975], pp. 17–31). Michael D. A. Freeman ("Violence against Women: Does the Legal System Provide Solutions or Itself Constitute the Problem?" [Madison, Wis., 1980, mimeographed], p. 12, n. 161) applies this argument to domestic battery of women. Here I extend it to women's situation as a whole, without suggesting that the analysis can *end* there.

47. S. D. Warren and L. D. Brandeis, "The Right to Privacy," *Harvard Law Review* 4 (1890): 193–205.

48. Tom Gerety, "Redefining Privacy," *Harvard Civil Right–Civil Liberties Law Review* 12, no. 2 (Spring 1977): 236.

have. To confront the fact that we have no privacy is to confront our private degradation as the public order. To fail to recognize this place of the private in women's subordination by seeking protection behind a right to that privacy is thus to be cut off from collective verification and state support in the same act.[49] The very place (home, body), relations (sexual), activities (intercourse and reproduction), and feelings (intimacy, selfhood) that feminism finds central to women's subjection form the core of privacy doctrine. But when women are segregated in private, one at a time, a law of privacy will tend to protect the right of men "to be let alone,"[50] to oppress us one at a time. A law of the private, in a state that mirrors such a society, will translate the traditional values of the private sphere into individual women's right to privacy, subordinating women's collective needs to the imperatives of male supremacy.[51] It will keep some men out of the bedrooms of other men.

Liberalism converges with the left at this edge of the feminist critique of male power. Herbert Marcuse speaks of "philosophies which are 'political' in the widest sense—affecting society as a whole, demonstrably transcending the sphere of privacy."[52] This does and does not describe the feminist political: "Women both have and have not had a common world."[53] Isolation in the home and intimate degradation, women share. The private sphere, which confines and separates us, is therefore a political sphere, a common ground of our inequality. In feminist translation, the private is a sphere of battery, marital rape, and women's exploited labor; of the central social institutions whereby women are deprived of (as men are granted) identity, autonomy, control, and self-determination; and of the primary activity through which male supremacy is expressed and enforced. Rather than transcending the private as a predicate to politics, feminism politicizes it. For women, the private necessarily transcends the private. If the most private also most "affects society as a whole," the separation between public and private collapses as anything other than potent ideology. The failure of marxism adequately to address intimacy on the one hand, government on the

49. Harris v. McRae, 448 U.S. 287 (1980), which holds that withholding public funds for abortions does not violate the federal constitutional right to privacy, illustrates. See Zillah Eisenstein, *The Radical Future of Liberal Feminism* (New York: Longman, Inc., 1981), p. 240.

50. Robeson v. Rochester Folding Box Co., 171 NY 538 (1902); Cooley, *Torts*, sec. 135, 4th ed. (Chicago: Callaghan & Co., 1932).

51. This argument learned a lot from Tom Grey's article, "Eros, Civilization and the Burger Court," *Law and Contemporary Problems* 43, no. 3 (Summer 1980): 83–99.

52. Herbert Marcuse, "Repressive Tolerance," in *A Critique of Pure Tolerance*, ed. Robert Paul Wolff, Barrington Moore, Jr., and Herbert Marcuse (Boston: Beacon Press, 1965), pp. 81–117, esp. p. 91.

53. Adrienne Rich, "Conditions for Work: The Common World of Women," in *Working It Out: Twenty-three Women Writers, Artists, Scientists, and Scholars Talk about Their Lives and Work*, ed. Sara Ruddick and Pamela Daniels (New York: Pantheon Books, 1977), pp. xiv–xxiv, esp. p. xiv.

other, is the same failure as the indistinguishability between marxism and liberalism on questions of sexual politics.

Interpreting further areas of law, a feminist theory of the state will reveal that the idealism of liberalism and the materialism of the left have come to much the same for women. Liberal jurisprudence that the law should reflect society and left jurisprudence that all law does or can do is reflect existing social relations will emerge as two guises of objectivist epistemology. If objectivity is the epistemological stance of which women's sexual objectification is the social process, its imposition the paradigm of power in the male form, then the state will appear most relentless in imposing the male point of view when it comes closest to achieving its highest formal criterion of distanced aperspectivity. When it is most ruthlessly neutral, it will be most male; when it is most sex blind, it will be most blind to the sex of the standard being applied. When it most closely conforms to precedent, to "facts," to legislative intent, it will most closely enforce socially male norms and most thoroughly preclude questioning their content as having a point of view at all. Abstract rights will authoritize the male experience of the world. The liberal view that law is society's text, its rational mind, expresses this in a normative mode; the traditional left view that the state, and with it the law, is superstructural or epiphenomenal expresses it in an empirical mode. Both rationalize male power by presuming that it does not exist, that equality between the sexes (room for marginal corrections conceded) is society's basic norm and fundamental description. Only feminism grasps the extent to which the opposite is true: that antifeminism is as normative as it is empirical. Once masculinity appears as a specific position, not just as the way things are, its judgments will be revealed in process and procedure, as well as adjudication and legislation. Perhaps the objectivity of the liberal state has made it appear "autonomous of class." Including, but beyond, the bourgeois in liberal legalism, lies what is male about it. However autonomous of class the liberal state may appear, it is not autonomous of sex. Justice will require change, not reflection—a new jurisprudence, a new relation between life and law.

University of Minnesota Law School

Acknowledgments

Austin, John. "The Province of Jurisprudence Determined." In John Austin, ed., *The Province of Jurisprudence Determined* (New York: Humanities Press, 1965): 9–33,118–91. Courtesy of Yale University Cross Campus Library.

Holmes, O.W. "The Path of the Law." *Harvard Law Review* 10 (1897): 457–78. Courtesy of Yale University Law Library.

Hohfeld, Wesley Newcomb. "Some Fundamental Legal Conceptions as Applied in Judicial Reasoning." *Yale Law Journal* 23 (1913): 16–59. Courtesy of Yale University Law Library.

Pound, Roscoe. "The Scope and Purpose of Sociological Jurisprudence." *Harvard Law Review* 25 (1912): 489–516. Courtesy of Yale University Law Library.

Cohen, Felix S. "Transcendental Nonsense and the Functional Approach." *Columbia Law Review* 35 (1935): 809–49. Courtesy of Fred B. Rothman & Company.

Llewellyn, Karl N. "A Realistic Jurisprudence—The Next Step." *Columbia Law Review* 30 (1930): 431–65. Courtesy of Fred B. Rothman & Company.

Kelsen, Hans. "What Is a Legal Act?" *American Journal of Jurisprudence* 29 (1984): 199–212. Reprinted with the permission of the University of Notre Dame. Courtesy of the *American Journal of Jurisprudence*.

Kelsen, Hans. "On the Theory of Interpretation." *Legal Studies* 10 (1990): 127–35. Reprinted with the permission of Butterworth Legal Publishers. Courtesy of Yale University Law Library.

Hart, H.L.A. "Positivism and the Separation of Law and Morals." *Harvard Law Review* 71 (1958): 593–629. Courtesy of Yale University Law Library.

Fuller, Lon L. "Positivism and Fidelity to Law—A Reply to Professor Hart." *Harvard Law Review* 71 (1958): 630–72. Courtesy of Yale University Law Library.

Dworkin, Ronald M. "The Model of Rules." *University of Chicago Law Review* 35 (1967): 14–46. Reprinted with the permission of the University of Chicago Law School. Courtesy of Yale University Law Library.

Dworkin, Ronald. "Hard Cases." *Harvard Law Review* 88 (1975): 1057–109. Reprinted with the permission of Harvard University. Courtesy of Yale University Law Library.

Raz, Joseph. "Authority and Justification." *Philosophy and Public Affairs* 14 (1985): 3–29. Reprinted with the permission of the Princeton University Press. Courtesy of Yale University Sterling Memorial Library.

Kennedy, Duncan. "Legal Formality." *Legal Studies* 2 (1973): 351–98. Reprinted with the permission of Butterworth Legal Publishers. Courtesy of Yale University Law Library.

MacKinnon, Catharine A. "Feminism, Marxism, Method, and the State: Toward Feminist Jurisprudence." *Signs* 8 (1983): 635–58. Reprinted with the permission of the University of Chicago Press, publisher. Copyright 1983 by the University of Chicago. All rights reserved. Courtesy of *Signs*.